Princeton Theological Monograph Series

Dikran Y. Hadidian

General Editor

31

FEMALE AND MALE
THE CULTIC PERSONNEL
The Bible and the Rest of the Ancient Near East

RICHARD A HENSHAW

FEMALE AND MALE

THE CULTIC PERSONNEL

The Bible and the Rest of the Ancient Near East

PICKWICK PUBLICATIONS
An imprint of *Wipf and Stock Publishers*
199 West 8th Avenue • Eugene OR 97401

Pickwick Publications
An imprint of Wipf and Stock Publishers
199 West 8th Avenue, Suite 3
Eugene, Oregon 97401

Female and Male
The Cultic Personnel: The Bible and the Rest of the Ancient Near East
By Henshaw, Richard A.

ISBN: 1-55635-015-5
Publication date 1/1/1994

TABLE OF CONTENTS

PREFACE

INTRODUCTION

Intro.1. Overall Aspects of this Work 1
.1.1. Context and Purpose
.1.2. How to read a lexical text
.1.3. Titles and functions
Intro.2. A classification of cultic officials in Mesopotamia used throughout this work. 9
.2.1. Paradigm for study
.2.2. Classification of cultic officials
Category No. 1. Chief functionary; chapter 1
Category No. 2. Singer, lamenter, musician, dancer; chapter 2
Category No. 3. Incantation expert, diviner, ecstatic, exorcist, prophet, seer, magician, witch, healer, sorcerer; chapter 3
Category No. 4. Offices related to sexuality; chapter 4 and Appendix 3
Category No. 5. Offices auxiliary to the main cult; Appendix. 5
.2.3 Description of Appendices

Intro.3. Cautions and limitations of this study 11

CHAPTER ONE
Titles of Important Cultic Officials In The Hebrew Bible, Ebla, Emar, Mesopotamia and Ugarit 17

1.1 The Titles of important cultic officials in the Hebrew Bible Mesopotamia, Ugarit, Ebla and Emar
1.2. Continuity and Change -- Mesopotamia
1.3. sanga / *šangû*
1.4. The highest officials in the Hebrew temple rites
1.4.2 *kôhēn*
1.4.3 *gĕbîrā*
1.4.4 queen mother" at Ebla
1.4.5 *kāmār*
1.4.6 "ministering women"
1.4.7 *nĕtînîm*
1.5. Offices auxiliary to the main cult in ancient Hebrew life
1.5.2 *raqqahôt, ṭabbāḥôt, ʾôpôt*
1.5.3 *šômēr hassap*
1.5.4 *sagan, segen*
1.5.5 women as worshippers
1.6. High cultic ranks and their ritual in Mesopotamia
1.7. $gudu_4$ / *pašīšu* and pa_4-šeš / *ahu rabû*
1.8. The various $gudu_4$-x offices
1.9. The $šita_x$ and the various $šita_x$- officials

1.9.2 šita, nam-šita
1.9.3 šita = *ellu* , *ramku*
1.9.4 šita$_x$-abzu
1.9.5 šita$_x$-ki-gal-la
1.9.6 šita$_x$-ab-ba
1.9.7 šita$_x$-UNU
1.9.8 šita$_x$-gal, šita-AB.DI ^{d}Inanna, šita ^{d}Inanna
1.9.9 šita-èš
1.9.10 šita-du$_{11}$-du$_{11}$
1.10. nu-èš (nisag) /*nešakku*
1.11. síg-bar-ra / *luhšû*
1.12. LÚ.KISAL.LUH / *kisalluhhu* and MÍ.KISAL.LUH/ *kisalluhhatu*
1.13. lú-mah / *lumahhu* /*lumakku*
1.14. gudu$_4$-abzu / *gudapsû*
1.15. SUH.BU / *susbû* // associated with *ramku*
1.16. išib / *išippu*
1.17. gada-lá / *gadalallû* // šà-gada-lá
1.18. en (m.) / *enu*
1.19. en (f.) and nin-dingir / *entu* or *ugbabtu* (see also Sec. 4.9)
1.19.12 nin-dingir at Emar
1.19.13 other cultic officials at Emar
1.20 *zirru* (f.)
1.21. lagar / *lagaru* /*lagallu*
1.22. abrig (AB.NUN.ME.DU) / *abriqqu*
1.23. engiz (EN.ME.GI$_4$) / *engisu*
1.24. kišib-gál / *kišibgallu*
1.25. enkum / *enkummu* // ninkum / *ninkummu*
1.26. endub / endib / *endubbu* / *endibbu*
1.27. ennigi / *ennigû*
1.28. a-tu
1.29. a-tu$_5$
1.30. TU
1.31. làl
1.32. *šelutu*
1.33. *pālihtu*
1.34. é-gi$_4$(-a)
1.35. *kumru* and *kumirtu*
1.36. *mukkallu*
1.37. zabar-dab$_5$ (UD.KA.BAR.DAB.BA) / *zabardabbu*
1.38. ŠEŠ.GAL / *šešgallu*
1.39. gal-zu-ukkin-na / *rabi puhri*
1.40. AB.(A).AB.DU$_7$ /DU / *ababdû* or *ešabdû*
1.41. a-ga-am (f.)
1.42. LÚ.MAŠ and MÍ.MAŠ
1.43. PA.KAB.DU /*širku* and *širkatu*
1.44. *kiništu*
1,45. TU.É / *ērib bīti*
1.46. *maqaltānu*
1.47. *ramku* and *murammiku*
1.48. Peg deposits and basket carriers

1.49. The king
1.50. Ugaritic cultic functionaries
1.50.1 *inš, inš ilm*
1.50.2 *inšt*
1.50.3 *khnm*
1.50.4 *rb khnm*
1.50.5 *nqdm*
1.50.6 *ṯnnm*
1.50.7 *rb mrzḥ*
1.50.8 *ytnm*
1.50.9 *tbṣr*
1.50.10 *kumru*, (?)
1.50.11 ^{lú}*ša nāqî*
1.50.12 *klt bt špš,*
1.50.13 miscellaneous

CHAPTER TWO
Singers, Musicians and Dancers 84

2.1. Singers, musicians and dancers.
2.1.2 Names of musical instruments in Mesopotamia
2.2. Instrumentalists
2.3. The main actors: gala (UŠ.KU) / *kalû* // gala-mah / *kalamahu*
2.3.3 possible women gala's
2.4. Main actors: nar / *nāru* and *nārtu* // *zammāru and zammārtu* // *zammeru and zammertu* // *nargalla*
2.5. Other singers and instrumentalists: LÚ.TUR.MEŠ and LÚ.GAL.MEŠ
2.6. Others: sur$_9$ / sur(ru) / *surrû* // *surmahhu*
2.7. Others: alan-zu / *aluzinnu*
2.8. Main actors: balag-di / *ṣārihu* // i-lu-di /*munambû* // NAR.BALAG / tigi/ *tigû* and *tigītu*
2.9. Others: búr-balag
2.10. Main actors: balag / balag-íl / *ša balamgi* // *nāš balamgi* // *ēpiš balamgi*
2.11. Others: šìr-sag / *ša sirhu* // lú-šìr
2.12. Others: še-en-nar
2.13. Main actors: muš-lah$_4$ / *mušlahhu* and *mušlahhatu*
2.14. Others: dam-ab-ba
2.15. Others: lú-ér // mí-ér / *bakkā'u* and *bakkītu* // ér-ra / *ša bakkīti*
2.16. Others: ama-ér(-ra) / *ama'errû*
2.17. Others: èš-ta-lá /*aleštalû* and *aleštalītu*
2.18. Others: ér-sig$_7$
2.19. Others: mí-gù-mur-ak
2.20. Others: *lallāru* and *lallār(i)tu*
2.21. Others: *malīlu* // *ša malīli*
2.22. Others: *mušarrihtu*
2.23. Others: si-dù
2.24. Others: u$_4$-da-tuš
2.25. Dancers in Mesopotamia

2.26. húb/ (*ša*) *huppû* , see also App. 3.15
2.27. Singers and dancers in the Hebrew Bible
  2.27.2. list of Biblical musical instruments
2.28. Miriam
2.29. Jephthah's daughter
2.30. The king in Israel
2.31. *mešorer* and *mešorerāh*
2.32. *nōgēn*
2.33. *šarîm* /*šarôt*
2.34. Other women singers
2.35. (root) *s-p-d*
2.36. *'alamôt*
2.37. *mĕbasseret* // announcers of joy
2.38. Weepers // mourners
2.39. Rejoicing
2.40. Dancing in the Hebrew Bible
2.41. Ugaritic singing titles
  1. *kṯrt* , 2. *mšspdt* , 3. *bkyt* , 4. *šr* *ᶜṯtrt* , 5. *mṣlm*
2.42. Dancers at Ugarit

CHAPTER THREE.
Diviners, Magicians, Ecstatics and Wise Men and Women 135

3.1. Diviners, magicians, ecstatics and wise men and women
  Note on *mušlahhu* and *mušlahhatu*
3.2. máš-šu-gíd-gíd / HAL / *bārû* and *bārītu*
3.3. Dream interpreter: ensi / *šā'ilu* and *šā'iltu* // *edammû* and *edammētu* // *harṭibi* //sag-šè-ná-a //*mupaššer šunāti* // šabra / *šabrû*
3.4. MAŠ.MAŠ / šim-mu$_2$ / mu$_7$-mu$_7$ / *āšipu* and *āšiptu* // AZU / *asû* // *asātu,* 3.4.7 MAŠ.MAŠ = *āšipu* or *mašmaššu* ?
3.5. *mullilu*
3.6. sanga$_2$-mah / *šangammahu*
3.7. Witches : Uš$_{11(12)}$ (KAxBE).ZU / *kaššāpu* and *kaššāptu* // *mušēlû* and *mušēlītu* // *mušēlit eṭimme* // *muppišu* and*muppištu* // *muppišānu* // *multēpišu* and *multēpištu* // *muštēpišu* and *muštēpištu* // *ša eṭimme* // *ēpišu* and *ēpištu* passim // see also Secs. 3.20, 3.21, 3.22, 3.23
3.8. NUN.ME / *apkallu* and *apkallatu* // *luhšû*
3.9. *mukkallu*
3.10. abrig / (AB) NUN.ME.DU) / *abriqqu*
3.11. igi-du$_8$
3.12. Ecstatics: lú-gub-ba and lú-al-è/e$_{11}$-dè / *mahhû* and *muhhû* // *muhhūtu* // *šarbu* // *šēhānu* // *ša šēhi*
3.13. Ecstatics: AN.GUB.BA / *angubbû*
3.14. Ecstatics: ní-su/zu-ub / *zabbu* and *zabbatu*
3.15. Ecstatics: *āpilu* and *āpiltu*
3.16. Ecstatics: *qabbā'u* and *qabbātu*
3.17. *raggimu* and *raggim* / *ntu*
3.18. *hābit mê*
3.19. lú-giš-gi and mí-giš-gi / *naqmu* and *naqimtu*

3.20. Witches: an-ni-ba-tu / *eššeb / pu* and *eššeb / putu*
3.21. Witches: zilulu / *sahhiru* and *sahhirtu*
3.22. Witches: x-e$_{7/11}$-dè / *naršindu* and *naršindatu*
3.23. Witches: *agugilu* and *agugiltu*
3.24. *muššipu* and *muššiptu* // *mussiru*
3.25. ki-sì-ga / *kišpū*
3.26. Lecanomancy (oil omina)
3.27. Observers of birds / *dagil issure*
3.28. Fowler: *(u)sandû*, *mušākil iṣṣurē*
3.29. Libanomancy (smoke divination): *muššakku*
3.30. Aleuromancy (divination by flour)
3.31. Divination by arrows
3.32. Divination in the Hebrew Bible, with a few notes on Ugaritic practices:
  .1. Child sacrifice
  .2. *qôsēm*
  .3. *mĕ ᶜônēn*
  .4. *mĕnaḥēš*
  .5. *mĕkaššep*
  .6. (root) *h-b-r*
  .7. *šōʾēl ʾôb* "asker of an ʾ*ôb*"
  .8. *yiddĕ ᶜōnî*
  .9. *dōrēš' ʾel hammētîm* "seeker of the dead"
  .10. *ṭerapîm* (objects)
  .11. ʾ*iṭṭîm* "spirits of the dead"
  .12. *ḥarṭôm* "magician"
  .13. *ḥôlēm ḥalom,* "dreamer of dreams"
  .14. ʾ*aššapim*
  .15. *mĕlaḥeš*
  .16. *ḥakam ḥărāšîm* "wise one of sorcery"
  .17. Hepatoscopy
  .18. Astrology
  .19. Words
  .20. Sitting under trees
  .21. Prophecy
    .1. Huldah
    .2. Ebla
  .22. Future telling
  .23. Other forms of magic
  .24. Ordeal
3.33. Ugaritic diviners

CHAPTER FOUR

Officiants Who Interpret Sexuality and Fertility. 191

4.1. Fertility and sexuality
4.2. Sexuality, human and divine. The lexical evidence
4.3. lukur (SAL + ME) / *nadītu*
4.4. šu-gi$_4$-(a) / *šugētu*
4.5. [,] lukur / *sahiptu*
4.6. LÚ.SUHUR.LÁ/ *kezru* and MÍ.SUHUR.LÁ / *kezertu*
4.7. ŠEŠ / *sekertu*

4.8. nu-bar / *kulmašītu*
4.9. nin-dingir-(ra) / *ugbabtu* / *gubabtu* or *entu*
4.10. egi-zi / *igiṣītu* and egi-zi-gal / *igiṣīgallatu*
4.11. nu-gig / *qadištu* // nu-gig-gal // nu-gig-tur // LÚ.NU.GIG (once)
4.12. nu-gig / *ištarītu*
4.13. ama-lul / *amalu* and *amalītu*
4.14. kar-kid / *harimtu* "prostitute" as a cultic figure
4.15. PAP.PAP
4.16. kurun (KAŠ.DIN(.NA) and others) / *sābû* and *sabītu*
4.17. *mārat ili /ilāni*
4.18. The Hebrew Bible: *qādēš* and *qĕdēšāh* (see also 4.24.3)
  1 Deuteronomy 23.18 translations throughout the ages
  2 bibliography of studies of "sacred prostitution"
4.19. Ugaritic cognate *qdš*
4.20. Herodotus I, 199
4.21. Influences of Her I, 199 on later literature
4.22. "Sacred prostitition" in Greece, Mesopotamia and the Hebrew Bible
  4.22.1 what "they" said it was: the Greeks
  4.22.2 J.P. Asmussen
  4.22.3 B. Brooks, Mesopotamia
  4.22.4 G. von Rad, Bible
  4.22.5 E. J. Fisher, Bible
  4.22.6 E. Yamauchi, Bible
  4.22.7 W. von Soden, Mesopotamia and the Bible
  4.22.8 W.G. Lambert, Mesopotamia
  4.22.9 W. Kornford, Mesopotamia and the Bible
  4.22.10 J. Plessis, Mesopotamia
  4.22.11 W. Helck, Mesopotamia
  4.22.12 T. Jacobsen, Mesopotamia
  4.22.13 M.D. Arnaud, Mesopotamia
  4.22.14 S. Hooks, Hebrew Union College thesis, ANE and Bible
  4.22.15 Rooms or buildings as part of the temple, in"which"sacred prostitution" or "sacred marriage" could have taken place: *ag(a) runnu*, *ašlukkatu*, *bīt erši*, *gagû*, *gigunû*, *giparu*, *hammutu*, *kiṣṣu*, *kummu*, *nēmedu*, *papāhu*, *parakku*, *paramāhu*, *sāgu* / *sukku*, *simakku*, *šubtu*, *ta'u*.
  4.22.16 Preliminary summary

4.23. Sacred marriage, Mesopotamia
  4.23.1 .1 and .2 the Greeks
  4.23.3 Mesopotamian artifacts depicting sexual intercourse
  4.23.4 "sacred marriage" texts, Enmerkar, Iddin-Dagan
  4.23.5 S.N.Kramer, *The Sacred Marraige Rite*
  4.23.6 sacred marriage texts: Shulgi and Gudea
  4.23.7 Mari
  4.23.8 A. Spycket

4.23.9 Kramer's "sacred marriage texts"
4.23.10 other aspects
4.24. Preliminary studies of cultic titles from the Hebrew Bible.
1 Brooks' studies, .2 *nĕtînîm*, .3-4 *qādēš* and *qădēšā*,
5*yôšebet*, .6 *ṣōʾbôt*, .7 *ᶜalmāh*, .8 *nābî'* and *nĕbîʾāh*,
.9 possible cognate at Emar
4.25. The fertility cult in the Hebrew Bible, with some notes from Ugaritic
4.25. 2 PNs
4.25. 3 J.P. Asmussen
4.25. 4 *hanna ᶜarah*
4.25. 5 Dog
4.25. 6 H.G. May
4.25. 7 Raymond Collins
4.25. 8 Buis and Leclercq

4.26 Commit Apostasy / Join Oneself to Idols / Commit Prostitution
4.26.1 Variety of usage of metaphors
4.26.2 Queen of Heaven

4.27 Homosexuality

APPENDIX ONE
A Middle Assyrian Ritual With qadistu's And A sangû 271

KAR 154, a MA text with *qadištu* 's and a *šangû*

APPENDIX TWO
The Naked Figurines 277

App. 2.1 The naked figurines, especially those in Palestine
App. 2.2 Cylinder and stamp seals

APPENDIX THREE
The assinnu, kurgarrû and Similar Functions 284

App. 3.1 The terms
App. 3.2 LÚ.UR.SAL / *assinnu*
App. 3.3 KUR.GAR.RA / *kurgarrû* // *rab kurgarrû* //
3.3.6 *nāš patri*
App. 3.4 Transvestism
App. 3.5 sag-ur-sag
App. 3.6 *parrû*
App. 3.7 pi-li-pi-li / *pilpilû* // *apillû* and *apillatu* // *pilpilānu*
App. 3.8 *kulu'u*
App. 3.9 *sinnišānu*
App. 3.10 *nāš pilaqqi*
App. 3.11 *aguhhu*
App. 3.12 *ararû* // *šudarāru*
App. 3.13 sag-bur and bur-sag // bur-ra / *burru* // *abru* // *aplu*
App. 3.14 HUB / *huppû*, see also Sec. 2.26
App. 3.15 The Hebrew Bible

App. 3.16 The wider Semitic world
App. 3.17 Conclusions

APPENDIX FOUR
What Happened In The èš-dam/astammu House? 312

App. 4.1 What happened in the *aštammu* -house?
App. 4.2 *anzanīnu* and nimgir-si / *susapinu*
App. 4.3 *napṭaru* and *napṭarṭu*

APPENDIX FIVE
Functionaries Auxiliary to the Mesopotamian Cult 324

BIBLIOGRAPHY AND ABBREVIATIONS 329

INDICES 351

PREFACE

I especially wish to dedicate this book to the memory of A. Leo Oppenheim, who in my early days of study in the Dictionary Room of the Oriental Institute was kind in sharing his wide scholarship and common sense with a fledgling researcher. At the same time, there were others who helped me out a great deal: Erica Reiner, I.J. Gelb, Robert Biggs and Samuel Greengus.

I was assisted in the reading of tablets in the Students' Room of the British Museum by E. Sollberger, Abe Sachs and at the School of Oriental and African Studies by Donald J. Wiseman.

At Hebrew Union College in Cincinnati my feet already had been planted firmly on the ground by the superb methodology of Mat Tsevat and Sheldon Blank. In Sumerology I was brought a long ways from nothing by William W. Hallo, and in Assyriology by Julius Lewy.

At Cambridge University where I did much of the research I was helped by the friendly assistance of J.V. Kinnier Wilson, and in Baghdad by Nicholas Postgate.

The MS was read (at least in part) by Isaac Kikawada of the University of California, John Maier of the State University of New York at Brockport, and Jared Jackson of Pittsburgh Theological Seminary. I apologize to them for errors remaining after receiving their excellent advice.

I owe a debt of gratitude beyond words to Prof. Ed Mineck of the National Technical Institute for the Deaf at the Rochester Institute of Technology, my computer consultant. I could not have done anything on my old Macintosh without his expert advice in innumerable crises.

Finally I want to acknowledge the long hours my wife Marjorie put in checking the indices, ferreting out many errors, and keeping me sane throughout it all. And to my son Richard and my daughter Kathleen for putting up with me during the years while the work was in progress.

Richard A. Henshaw
March 30, 1994

FEMALE AND MALE: THE CULTIC PERSONNEL
The Bible and the Rest of the Ancient Near East

INTRODUCTION

Intro. 1 Overall Aspects of This Work

Intro.1.1 In the actions and words of the religion of **Israel** as presented by prophets, historiographers, psalmists and untitled theologians, which have come down to us within the covers of one canonical set of scriptures of the ancient Hebrew people, **women appear to play a small role.** Yet in those of the religions of **Mesopotamia**, and to a lesser extent of **Ugarit**, in the documents that have come down to us,[1] **women have a vital role to play**, a significant one, and are mentioned often.

This book will present many of the **texts which pertain to women in the cultus** of Old Testament times and the wider ancient Near East, of course bringing in men also, and we will be especially interested in their **titles**. Since there is such a large number of these, some will be treated rather thoroughly, some will be given a smaller space,while others will merely be listed. **Cult** is defined here as widely as possible, including functions pertaining to sacrifice, offering, prayer, divination, singing and dancing, whether within or without a sacred precinct, whether state-related or private.

The Ancient Near East (ANE) for our purposes is defined as ancient Mesopotamia, north and south, as far back as written texts go; ancient Syria, especially Ugarit (though Ugaritic cultic texts are few); and Palestine. We will use Neo-Assyrian times (first half of first millenium B.C.E.) as the datum point for Mesopotamia, but we will have to bring in material from the third millenium to the first[2] with some exceptions, stopping short of the Hellenistic materials, with the exception of a small amount of usage of Thureau-Dangin's magnificent study of Seleucid texts.[3] We will touch upon Ebla from time to time, and bring in some newly translated texts from Emar. Egypt is excluded because it developed its own special religious world and language. Hittite studies are excluded because that is a whole other area and has its own methodology. Ancient Iran and Elam only touch the edges of our field. Hurrian and Urartian texts are not in enough quantity to use, and the languages are imperfectly understood. In general, the dating will be taken from *CAH*^{3}.

Texts after Neo-Assyrian and Neo-Babylonian times tend to show too much Greek, native Anatolian or Egyptian influences to be useful to our subject without expanding it greatly.[4] We will thus in general limit ourselves to the pre-Alexandrian ANE. Material quoted here from Palestine comes mostly from the Hebrew Bible but at times from other texts and archaeological sources.

The strength of this type of study lies in placing a large number of texts together and having them interact with one another. There is no end to the search, so I feel that now is the time to stop and make a kind of synthesis. It may turn out to be inaccurate when the next text in the area shows up. Our conclusion must not be done until the very end.

Some of these functionaries are represented by only a few texts, sometimes only one or two. But these may be given a wider meaning when placed in juxtaposition with other texts with similar officiants. For instance, it is useful to study the *ištarītu* in conjunction with the *qadištu* (see Secs. 4.11 and

4.12) especially when so few entries for the former have been discovered. When this is done we find at times that the several offices are very close, though my conclusion will be that there are no strictly synonymous terms; we know that some have coalesced at later times. To widen this idea, we realize that "a single text has only part of a meaning...texts don't have meanings except in relation to other texts."[5]

I attempt to hold to a unified methodology throughout, but that is difficult because of the many aspects belonging to the subject. Phyllis Bird's studies of women in the ancient world ask questions somewhat differently from ours, but a selection of her methodological warnings is apropos here: 1) the work being studied should be seen in relation to the total religious life, 2) some of the answers to our questions are unavailable and unrecoverable, so our results will be somewhat partial and skewed [this is true of a great deal of ANE studies in general, RAH], 3) Israelite life and other ANE societies may be studied together, there being some similarities among them, 4) we should note the androcentric bias in much of the previous research.[6]

Female religious officiants fill very few named or alluded to offices in the Hebrew cult, and Ugarit yields very few female titles, but in Mesopotamia we find scores of titles in lexical lists, prayers, hymns, legal texts, proverbs, letters, administrative lists and other literature. This profound difference is partially due to the much greater span of history represented by the Mesopotamian texts, partly by their greater geographical spread, but mainly because of the complexity of their practices. Of course, this is somewhat an argument from silence, because despite the details of the Books of Exodus through Deuteronomy, the Psalms, and scattered references to worship elsewhere in the Hebrew Bible, we know virtually nothing about the actual words and ritual of the sacrificial services in Jerusalem in the First Temple.[7] A rare text for the Hebrew Bible is that of the harvest offering of Deut 26.3-11, which gives just enough specifics to imply that much is missing.

Also, alongside the state-sponsored cult in Israel there was the religion of the people, a series of folk practices which reached back hundreds of years and may have pre-dated the official cult, yet continued to remain on the fringes of the official cult. Very few ritual notes for these diverse practices have been preserved, and what we glean about them comes from art, personal names, geographical names and certain excavated artifacts. Every so often we can detect an earlier practice behind the later,as in the Passover rituals in Exodus 12, or an eating taboo as in Gen 32.32. Deut 14.3-21 contains a number of other eating taboos.

The religion of any people is impossible to characterize in anything approaching fullness, because of its rich mixture of the official worship of the high gods and the rest of the pantheon with such aspects as individual piety, family gods, personal gods as shown in proper names, prayers for the sick, dying and the dead, the worship of the city gods with its political overtones, the retelling of ancient myths with their sometimes accompanying ritual, to say nothing of the border areas of magic, witchcraft, ancestor worship and animism.

Especially is this true of ancient religions, because we can only use what the accident of archaeological discovery has brought down to us, a tiny percentage of the whole. The complexity of the texts we do have makes one suspect that only partial information is given even in all of them taken together. Much of the ritual appears piecemeal in other forms, as myths, letters, economic texts, personal names and hymns. Oppenheim's well-known scepticism about "Why a 'Mesopotamian religion' should not be written,"[8] I take seriously, but. I do not share his extreme negativeness.

True, this type of study done in these pages is beyond the scope of one, or even a team of researchers. True, only a little of the total corpus is in, but we can say something, and others may build upon this. Levine and Hallo[9] make a distinction between "descriptive" and "prescriptive" ritual texts, the former including offering lists and the latter prescriptions of ritual acts. I would go further and comment that the prescriptive texts which have come down to us still do not give the detail that would allow us to perform the rite fully, probably because the officiants had memorized the rite over many years, or because it was kept a secret among them, and perhaps never written down, or perhaps it could be done in several ways.

In the case of the dream, the prayer, and the mystic vision, the worshipper meets the god directly,[10] but ordinarily the communication is done through functionaries, men and women who have often devoted their lives to the deity whom they serve. To oversimplify the picture, we could say that when they speak, the deity speaks.[11] Often the text shows a sliding back and forth from deity to officiant, a purposefully metaphoric presentation to bring the two as close together as possible.

One finds that **males filled the majority of cultic roles** in the centuries here studied. I will thus have to spend some time on the male roles, devoting even a majority of the space to them, but whenever possible I am going to emphasize **the roles that women filled**, even adding speculation when appropriate.[12] We will find that in the case of a major offering as the sacrifice of an animal, men were the officiants.[13] But in many cases, as, for instance, the major myth of The Descent of Inanna/Ishtar to the Netherworld, the male is subordinate to the female throughout, and any (presumed) ritual accompanying this would be to a large measure the actions of the female.

Many offices include **male and female counterparts**, and especially was this true in Mesopotamian divination and music. In some Mesopotamian cultic offices of higher significance, however, **women were the sole holders of these ranks**, and this will be commented upon. More and more evidence points towards women having roles in the cult of the countries of the ANE because of the nature of **polytheism**, and when we turn our interest to the Hebrew Bible and **monotheism**, especially ritual at a single shrine, we discover that women were excluded to a large extent.[14] However if we read our biblical texts carefully we will find that there were **many cultic roles filled by women**.

Throughout I will concentrate on presenting **the texts themselves**, so that material for further study will be made readily available. This has been done piecemeal in the past, but here, I believe, is done for the first time to such an extent.

Though biblical texts are juxtaposed with other ANE texts in the present work, I am conscious of the fact that the Hebrew Bible had a purpose quite different in much of its content from that of Mesopotamian literature, and whereas there are perhaps 8000 words[15] in the Hebrew Bible, there are hundreds of thousands of texts from Mesopotamia, many of which have still not been published or even read. I will not attempt a modern assessment of what used to be called the"Bible-Babel question"or"pan-Babylonianism,"but will of necessity touch upon it, yet treading somewhat gingerly in this mine-field.

There are many aspects to this subject, and these too, will be dealt with sometimes rather fully, sometimes less so. First and foremost, a special emphasis will be **the titles of cultic officiants**. These will be given as fully as possible and will result in a checklist of considerable proportions. Many of these appear in connected texts, but some appear only in lexical lists, for the definition of which see Bibliographic Abbreviations, at the end.

Intro.1.2 At this point we interpose a unit for the non-specialist: **how to read a lexical text**, using as an example the one in Sec.4.4. All of our entries of this type are from the MSL (Materials for the Sumerian Lexicon) series, and are "dictionaries" that the Sumerians and their successor Akkadian scribes made to teach their students Sumerian-Akkadian "equivalences." These turn out not to be our definition of dictionary entries but their lists of words, sometimes equivalent but at other times only in the same ambience, almost what we would find in a modern-day thesaurus entry.

(example) 4.4šu-gi$_4$(-a)/*šugetu*

4.4.1 Stepping gingerly into this morass of similar titles, we note the entry *šugētu* next on OB Proto-Lu line 710, Sec 4.2. [This is.an Old Babylonian lexical list called "Proto-Lu" because it was a forerunner of an OB Lu list. This is so called because it leads to the more complex Lu = ša list composed in NA times. (The Old Babylonian period encompassed approximately 1900-1600 B.C.E., and the Neo-Assyrian one the first half of the first millenium B.C.E.) The reference to *sugetu* is found in:

22 ^{d}Inanna	*na-di-tu*
23 [SAL] ME$^{lu\text{-}kur}$	MIN
24 [SAL] ME	*šu-gi-tu*
25 [SAL] ME	*e-li-tu*
26 [SAL] ME-gal	ŠU-*lu*
27 [SAL] ME-^{d}Utu	*en-ti* ^{d}šamaš
28 [SAL] ME-kaskal	*šu-gi-tu*
29 [ama]-lukur	MIN
30 [x] -⌈x⌉-lukur	*sa-hi-ip-tu*

Lu = ša IV MSL XII 129

all lines This MSL text has two columns, with Sumerian on the left and Akkadian on the right. I have chosen lines 22-30 out of the middle of the longer text because this block contains the titles I am interested in at this time.

line 22 Three dots means that something is missing in the original. ^{d} indicates the Sumerian word "dingir" meaning divinity. Inanna is the goddess of love and war that we discuss often in these pages. *na-di-tu* is in italics because it is the practice to put Akkadian terms in italics. It is the normal Akkadian reading of the Sumerian sign lukur, see next line.

line 23 The brackets indicates that SAL is not in the text but can be filled in because we know from other texts that is the missing sign. SAL.ME is in caps because those are the names we give to these signs, not their readings; the actual way they are read is lu-kur, which the scribes tell us in small superscript. MIN is their word for "ditto."

lines 23,24,25 all read SAL.ME, i.e., lukur, in the Sumerian column, but different readings in the Akkadian column, indicating that this word has three Akkadian "equivalences":*nadītu, šugītu,* and *tēlitu.*

lines 26,27,28 The scribe now lists three different qualifications to the basic word lukur, which translate into three different offices in Akkadian.

line 26 When -gal is added to SAL.ME (=lukur) it is read *lukurgallu,* as indicated by the ŠU (= the latter,i.e.,lukur+gal) plus a phonetic indicator *-lu.*

line 27 When ^{d}Utu (the Sumerian name for the sun-god) is added to lukur the reading is *enti* ^{d}Samas,i.e., *entu* of Shamash (the Akkadian name of the sun-god). This shows the strong relationship between lukur, normally understood as *nadītu,* and *entu* one of the highest woman officiants we discuss in these pages, see Sec.1.19.

line 28 When kaskal "journey" or "road" is added to lukur we learn to our surprise that this is also read *šugītu*, cf.line 24. This problem is discussed in Secs.4.3.1 and 4.4.1

line 29 The problem of the use of ama "mother" is a complex one, and is discussed in Sec.4.8.2.

line 30 x indicates that the original shows a sign there but it is broken so much that it cannot be read. In the Akkadian column, the meaning of the word *sahiptu* is unknown, and, in fact, this is the only entry so far found for it.

reference to Lu = ša IV MSL XII 129. This is the fourth tablet of the series Lu = sa, and is found in the MSL series volume XII p.129.

Intro.1.3 Since we will find that the number of offices filled is high and more nuanced than our society, we hesitate using the more simplified terms from our Euro-American vocabulary as "priest," "priestess," "bishop," "minister," "acolyte," and so forth, lest one read back into this quite different world too many of the connotations of our own.[16] There are a few ranks which are analagous to present-day thought-forms and practices but not many. We will present our own five-fold classification.

We naturally want to know what these officiants do in the cult, but here we will be greatly hampered by the nature of the texts. Very seldom do we find a full ritual[17] described, with complete prayers, rubrics listing actions, and a description of the furnishings of the cultic places. We suspect that full liturgies were never written down, and that the few we have are merely ritual notes to remind the officiant of what he has already memorized. Indeed, the secret of the complete ceremony must be kept[18] Thus it is that we have to turn to the literary texts and the lexical texts, which by comparing contiguous entries can give more information than a mere single listing would indicate.

Our most important questions are simple ones: who presented the offerings to the deities? Who were present and who assisted the chief liturgical officer? Did the people participate and in what measure? What liturgical actions were used in the purification, anointing, processing, pouring, burning, and other actions? Indeed, why is the concept of purification so prevalent in our texts? Does this cover a multitude of ideas? And, the most important question of all: how this material relates to the whole concept of fertility. Our texts provide only a small amount of the answer to these most basic of questions.[19]

Sometimes the title of the official is given as"x of a divine name." The supreme example of this is in the cult of Inanna/Ishtar[20] and her circle, going back to the earliest times in Mesopotamia, at least to the so-called Early Dynastic I Period, perhaps 3000 B.C.E[21] A goddess Annunitum from this circle is found in Ur III, OB and Mari texts, with officiants who remind us of Ishtar's. Gödecken[22] lists these, with references only, as šabra of Annunitum (Ur III), *šangû* (OB), *muhhutum* (Mari), *assinnu* (Mari), KAL.MAH(OB), *kulmašītum* (?OB), *qadištum* (? OB). She calls Annunitum"eine kriegerische aggressive Ishtar."(p. 154). Here as with some other myths of the Inanna/Ishtar cycle war and sex are put together.

It is Inanna's/Ishtar's cult from which many of the titles of woman officiants come. She of course has her home in Mesopotamia, and the western ANE world had its own indigenous culture, but the latter's goddesses and some of their characteristics can be explained as roughly (but only roughly) similar to hers. When we meet Anat, Astarte, Asherah and Qudshu, we must try to take them on their own merits and, indeed, much of what we learn about them and related deities from archaeology is in the form of folk religion, never appearing in the classical literary texts. We will be cautious in going back and forth between east and west on the subject of these goddesses, some of whose aspects relate to fertility, a primary study here. The counterparts to these are also found in most other ANE cultures, such as Hittite, Hurrian, South Arabic, Aramean, Phoenician, and others, but not necessarily with all the same aspects.

The aspects of Inanna/Ishtar are too many even to be summarized here, and they depend upon what century one is speaking of, and what cult center is represented, so I give just a few that I hope are universal. She is a warlike creature, but we are going to emphasize here her character as a sexual creature. Her dress in OB texts includes silver *urû*'s "vulvas."[23] It includes the *aguhhu,* an unknown element which produces sexual attractiveness.[24] In the Descent of Inanna she wears a pectoral named "Man-come!" In NA times she is *belet inbi u aguhhi* "lady of fruitfulness and sexuality" on a ritual tablet.[25] She is described in an OB document as:*šāt mēleṣim ru'āmam labšat za'nat inbi miqiam* (word?) "wrapped in charm and lovliness, adorned with attractiveness and sexual appeal."[26] Her temple is decorated with *kuzbu* "(sexual?)beauty."[27] Her ziggurat is *bīt laleia* "the temple/house of my pleasure,"i.e, sexual pleasure? She is androgynous. She dances around gods and kings in her *zikrūtu* "manliness."[28] As for western parallels, Thureau-Dangin[29] points out two west Semitic PNs: ʾṯtr ab and ʾṯtr um,"ʾṯtr is father" and "ʾṯtr is mother, "thus androgyny. R.Harris provides a powerful characterization of Inanna/Ishtar in a new article: "Inanna-Ishtar as paradox and a coincidence of opposites, *HR* 30 (1990-91) 261-278.

Art represents a powerful check on our textual material, and the relatively small amount of art discovered from ancient Palestine includes mosaics, building layouts, pottery, figurines of men, women, animals, fabulous creatures and deities, stamp seals[30] and a few cylinder seals.[31] Many of the latter two contain fertility motifs. In contrast, a large number of cylinder seals, monumental slab sculpture, and frescoes show up in Mesopotamia. Since art in the ANE seldom appears with accompanying text, we usually have to make an educated guess as to the subject matter. Despite the large number of studies, there are very few on Mesopotamian art by those who specialize in this world, and fewer still about the figures as such in the art, and fewer still about what offices those figures fill.

A new study by Julia M. Asher-Greve of Basle[32] uses art, mostly glyptic but some sculpture also, from the Uruk IV period (3100) to the end of the Early Dynastic period (approx.2700-2400),[33] to show the place and function of women in that society, and these turn out to be mostly cultic examples. The limited data available may make these results unrepresentative of the period, but it is an important study.

She deals with art and texts, but the texts she mentions treat only three functionaries: nin-dingir, lukur and nu-gig.[34](See chap. 4 for a discussion of these offices.) She finds nin-dingir's of the deities Baba, Gatumdu, Hendursag, Ninazu and Pabilsag. There are many in the cultic personnel of Lagash (Girsu). The lukur's are sometimes called nin-ensí-ka" the lady of the ensi-ruler." A lower ration is given to the nu-gig's. They could be married, sometimes to men in high positions.

In these early exemplars women bring offerings and pray. Seals[35] show a motif of "squatting women" with both arms raised in prayer, sometimes before an emblem, and shown in a row. There are processional scenes, and one (tablet 20) shows a woman with a pigtail standing before a temple (as it is stylized in cylinder seals), holding one end of a four-or five-foot object, a stole-shaped piece of cloth. The temple seems to have on its extremities the Inanna pole and ring emblem. A wavey flag-like emblem is also held down by her, and extends from a pole on the top of the temple. Two men in cultic nakedness process towards her with vessels of some type in their hands. Between the men and the woman offered are two goats eating from bushes. The woman is an important cultic functionary--her proximity to the temple indicates her high rank--and the men are secondary functionaries. The goats are perhaps the animals of the sacrifice. Other seals of this type come from the British Museum and appear in the book by Wiseman.[36]

Many scholars use the term "sacred" or "cultic prostitute" for some of the woman officiants, and describe their alleged actions rather imaginatively. This whole concept must be redefined, re-entitled, or perhaps not used at all. These ideas are often based tenuously on an important text in Herodotus I, 199 that will be dealt with rather fully in Sec. 4.20. This term has even found its way into the translated text of the Hebrew Bible (Sec. 4.18.1) from the earliest times and this continues today. We will argue that there is little basis for the concept "sacred prostitution," even though aspects of the Inanna/Ishtar cult do portray sexuality. We will find that women were the ones often called upon in the cult to symbolize the sexuality of the human race. But even here we understand that the wider subject is that of **fertility**, the need for humans, animals and plants to continue through the next generation. This basic need, as with others, is put into a story, acted out and prayed for in the cult. This ongoingness of life is the most basic need of living creatures.[37]

Thus there are fertility cults. These are emphasized in the Hebrew Bible as, e.g., in Deut 7.13 with the Lord's promises of blessing the fruit of the human body, the fruit of the ground, and the animals. This also appears in myth, i.e. "story," as in Gen 1.28, where the man and the woman are told to be fruitful and multiply, in Gen 6.19 where those entering the ark are to be male and female, and especially in Gen 8.22 where the Lord promises that fertility will go on. This same emphasis is given in Mesopotamia.

Indeed the mysterious forces of life and fertility are related. This has been made a part of all of the world's religions, in one way or another. Israel's cult prayed for fertility but did not have fertility rites as such. Mesopotamian cults had the rites but where, how often, and by whom they were performed can be gleaned only from somewhat ambiguous texts. **Women were especially called upon** to act in the role of officiant here, perhaps on analogy with human birth.

Ugaritic texts reflect an all-pervasive fertility myth.[38] Baal's fertility aspects are not directly stated, but when Baal is risen (49:III:12-13) "the heavens rain oil, the wadies run with honey, "and bring fertility. The window in Baal's house is that through which rain from heaven comes (with the same kind of statement in Mal 3.10). El roams the mountain mourning Baal's death like Jephthah's daughter does her own virginity's death, Jud 11.37. The Israelites cut themselves, perhaps for the dead Baal, Deut 14.1,as El did for dead Baal (67, VI.15).

Van Zijl goes into more aspects of Ugaritic fertility motifs.[39] He understands the Baal-Yamm myth to be an expression of fertility, because Baal cannot defeat Yamm until the rainy season starts (p.323). And when Baal wins the battle, there is renewed fertility over the earth. The Baal-Mot motif is an agricultural cycle which indicates that fertility will return to the earth when Baal returns from the underworld (p.324).[40]

De Moor, on the other hand, is cautious in interpreting Ugaritic texts as seasonal. He summarizes the objections of Cassuto, who thinks that the whole epic is no more than an allegory of a single natural phenomenon of the drying up of the vegetation in the summer and the renewal in the rainy season(p.24). Gordon[41] thinks that the texts tell us nothing of any annual death and revival of Baal. Baal is a fertility but not a seasonal god.

Keeping in mind, then, that the ultimate subject is **fertility**, we will find that a major aspect of our subject is **sexuality**, in all of its variations. Sexuality is the milieu in which fertility is carried out, the social/ psychological/physiological construct that ensures it. The new sexology manuals describe sexuality as a "social construct mixing sensuality, reproductive life, eroticism and gender-role performance, diffused throughout all social and personal life in activities, feelings and attitudes."[42] Some of its aspects in the ANE are what we today would call "abnormal sexuality." There we will find officiants in roles related to nakedness, prostitution, fornication, homosexuality (but not lesbianism), pederasty, bestiality, incest, transvestism, bisexuality, hermaphroditism/androgyny,[43] adultery and virginity, as well as the common words for the several kinds of sexual intercourse. Love will come into the picture but,again,that is a vast subject. We will see that many of these aspects are under the purview of Inanna/Ishtar.[44] These may be criticized in the lawcodes of the Hebrew Bible and in its stories but are treated in their own way in Mesopotamia.

This subject is close to another called, "sacred marriage," on analogy with Greek practices. (Secs.4.23.1,4.23.2) We are a little uneasy about borrowing the Greek term *hieros gamos* to entitle this. This is yet another subject about which there is quite a bit of disagreement about what actually took place in "the ceremony," and there was probably not one ceremony. Here the texts--and there are several types of them--are mostly from Mesopotamia, and are in poetical, mythological or metaphoric language. They are ambiguous on purpose, in our opinion. The question "what really happened?" is the wrong one to ask of this material. We are pursuing a will-o'-the-wisp if we think that we ever can find this out. The texts were not meant to answer this modern question, but to give the action and story ,i.e., the symbols, the emotions, the theology with its technical and numinous terms, and only to allow the participant and viewer to see a small piece of the mystery. We must allow the texts to speak in their own language, to give the picture as they wished to describe it.

Much of this material is presented in the form of myth (story). When this appears it is often presumed that some kind of ritual lay behind it. Without going through all the ramifications of the old so-called "myth and ritual school"[45] many scholars even today use some form of this kind of thinking.

A subject which is often brought up in studies of this type is that of the so-called "mother goddess" or"earth-mother." She appears in our area especially in Anatolia, at Çatal Hüyük and Hacilar and in other material 7000-3000B.C.[46] We have not yet found any clues as to whether the figures appearing there are goddesses or their functionaries or votaries; probably they are both. Aspects of this, if they appear at all, are hidden in more sophisticated texts of later ages. Goddesses in Mesopotamia are called "mother," especially prevalent in PNs.[47] In Israel we have fewer examples, but note Eve as*ʾēm kāl ḥāy* "the mother of all living" (Gen 3.21) and Deborah called *'ēm bĕyisrāʾēl* "a mother in Israel" (Jud 5.7). In birth texts there are birth goddesses, as in Atrahasis who are usually minor figures. In later times Inanna/Ishtar watches over the birth to protect it.

Finally, each of the various aspects of the cultic treated in these pages has a history. In any field it is instructive to discover how some of the modern positions were arrived at. It gives us a perspective, because we ourselves are in the middle of a movement, and our knowledge will be superseded by that of the next age. Furthermore, giving the history of research is a way of acknowledging some great scholars of the past who are often downplayed merely because they lived in times when they did not have as many tools and as much textual material as we now have. If we read them without being critical of the technical details they are often found to have profound insights. We want to pay tribute to some of these. We thus bring to this study a bibliography of books and articles going back to the late 19th century, see Bibliographic Abbreviations.

Intro.2 A Classification of Cultic Officials in Mesopotamia

Intro. 2.1 Since Mesopotamian worship life is more complex than Hebrew, I am going to use the former as our paradigm. The richest study of this is that of J. Renger[48] who presents a triparte classification of the "Priestertum" for Old-Babylonian times: 1) cult priests (Kultpriester), 2) speakers of wisdom (Wahrsager) and 3) incantation priests (Beschwörungspriester).[49]

We have several comments to make on this very neat list, especially in view of our interest in finding as many female officiants as possible:

1) The word "priest" is too limited and too definite. In European languages it refers only to the cultic officiant who is in charge of the sacrifice; in the Hebrew Bible it is customary to translate *kohen* as "priest," though his offices go beyond that of the sacrifice, as we shall see. The European word represents the Latin *sacerdos* and the Greek *hieros*, each carrying with it practices from its own culture. The spread of meaning of the word "priest" is brought out in the *Oxford English Dictionary*, s.v.

With respect to the third sub-classification, Oppenheim[50] explains that "the Mesopotamian diviner is not a priest, but an expert technician and, first of all, a scholar," categories which do not seem "cultic" to us in our western world. We will see in chapter 3, however, that this office has some characteristics which we today would call "priestly." Since we are planning to fling our net onto as wide a spread of religious practices as possible, we fall back on the term "cultic officiant," though admittedly this is an awkward term.

2) The priest in our biblical and western understanding performs the actions in a sacred place, a temple or consecrated space, but in the ANE the text often does not say where the cultic words were said, whether in a "temple"[51] or another sacred structure, and whether indoors or outdoors. We detect worship in the art, but much of this is symbolic, as cylinder seals, with one figure in a presentation scene raising a forearm in prayer before a deity, or a costumed figure anointing a "tree of life" with a cone, or a number of figures facing a central crowned figure, who is a deity. In Assyrian slab sculpture, in an army camp, we see two cultic officials preparing a rite before a small portable altar.[52] Scenes of musicians abound, but no temple surroundings are shown.[53] In Palestine there is archaeological and textual evidence that the courtyard of the temple was the venue for some forms of divination, and sometimes animal sacrifice.[54] The service inside the temple was for priests only.

3) Sometimes there is an overlap between two or more of our categories, especially between titles in incantation texts and those using priest-singers. Sometimes persons are found with more than one title.

4) Accurate, satisfying translations of the titles of many of these officiants are beyond our knowledge, so we sometimes must translate according to the root meaning of the word, as far as modern lexicography can tell us, but by this we do not mean to imply that this fully describes the function.[55]

Intro. 2.2 We attempt, therefore, a new classification of all who were in any way connected with the cult:

Category **No. l.** The chief functionary who uses the liturgical words and actions related to sacrifice or other offering, in our chapter 1.

Category **No. 2.** Singer, lamenter, musician, dancer, in our chapter 2.

Category **No. 3.** Incantation expert, diviner, ecstatic, exorcist, prophet, seer, magician, witch, healer of diseases, sorcerer, in our chap. 3.

Category **No. 4.** Officiant relating to sexuality, fertility, in our chapter 4, and Appendix 3.

Category **No. 5.** Officiants auxiliary to the main worship, either assisting in the cultic actions themselves, or supplying appurtenances therefore, which will not be discussed in any extensive way, because there are so many of them, but will appear throughout, in Appendix 5.

Intro., 2.3..Appendix No.1 will present an important text *KAR* 154 showing the cultic actions of one of our more significant woman officiants, the *qadištu* ; **Appendix No.2** will discuss the naked figurines; **Appendix No.3** will put together in a way not found elsewhere the important bisexual or hermaphroditic officiants *assinnu, kurgarrû* and such like; **Appendix No.4** will discuss what little we know of a special room, temple or house called the *bīt aštamme*, where drinking and sex and the cult took place;**Appendix No.5** will list a few of the many officiants auxiliary to the ritual actions, not cultic as such, but necessary that the cult might go on.

Intro.3 Cautions and Limitations

Necessary parentheses and cautions on this new classification are: 1) These actions are usually done at a temple or other shrine. The chief figure is often the king, especially in Mesopotamia, and the king is found bearing some cultic titles. The presumed ceremony is usually pictured as a drama, a cultic drama, with the functionaries as actors. 2) These are only sometimes associated with a temple, but singers take part in a wide variety of rites, and to entitle them merely"singers" does not show how significant they were in the rite, and does not describe their main function. They also could be called actors, taking part in the sacred drama. 3) These are not associated with a temple, and are often done one-on-one. There are a great number of titles and much overlap in them. Maybe some of these are merely descriptive terms for the main offices. 4) We will spend a good deal of time dealing with these officiants, because this goes to the heart of what this book is all about. 5) These ranks are usually those of the non-cultic world, but show up as associated with the temple because they were used in many ways to assist in the extensive cultic life.

In the survey to follow, we are forced to go through the millenia in broad sweeps, corresponding to our broad questions, but keeping NA times as much as possible as a datum point. Many of our lexical texts come from the NA period, though in large part they represent earlier traditions. It would have made a neater study if only this one period had been discussed, as we have said, but that would have been difficult without bringing in the background, the vast history of the subject, by which these later times are to be understood, and later terminology and indeed practice was sometimes conservative in the ANE, and is only explained by earlier practices. We know that on the one hand some religious practices changed over the millenia, while on the other hand some remained surprisingly constant.

As we go back and forth from Mesopotamia to the western Semitic world, we will try to avoid what S. Sandmel used to call "parallelomania."[56] What are apparently similar practices in Mesopotamia and Israel are found to grow farther and farther apart the more we study them. But these two poles are being enriched by yet other discoveries in the western semitic world. Ugarit is now an older study, yet texts are being constantly studied anew. Alalakh provides a small yet significant lightly-studied archive. Ebla studies are yet in their infancy, but growing fast. The texts from Emar will show west semitic, Anatolian and Mesopotamian aspects, due to its geographical location. Yet, in general, we will find that there was to some extent a cultural unity in the ANE.

George W. Ahlström brings up another aspect in his characteristically original and pungent way.[57] He discusses the problem of Canaanite elements in the religion of Israel. In an overall picture, the scene is one of gods, with no hint of monotheism, as urged by most Old Testament texts. But there was movement. He paraphrases R. de Vaux's way of putting this: "Yahweh replaced the old divinity and took over his (El's) titles."[58] Ahlström disagrees, because he says that Yahweh and El were the same god under different names. There was no polemic against El or El- deities (p. 13). We do not follow up on this provocative idea, yet following our principle: as the deity does, so his or her cultic officials do. We must be aware of the various interpretations.

In general, we would cautiously say that of course there was borrowing by one civilization of another's practices, especially when the giver was Mesopotamia. Yet there were also indigenous practices in other ANE civilizations. There was resistance to the borrowing, yet when it was imposed by military or political force it took hold. There was much conservatism throughout.

There was continuity through the ages: 1) Inanna and her Akkadian counterpart Ishtar were worshipped in the same sacred spot in Uruk for perhaps 2600 years, from the time of the Baghdad Museum vase from Warka to Seleucid times when she was synthesized with Artemis of Ephesus.[59] 2) The offering material remained fairly constant throughout the centuries and countries. In Ur III times sheep and goats, of carefully specified classes, and oxen were used[60] and we note that in NA times, about 1300 years later, we find roughly the same offerings: sheep, oxen, bread, parts of the animal.[61] 3) Titles of chief officiants remained remarkably constant throughout the years, with each country, of course, using its own variants. We will attempt to find out if or to what extent their functions changed. 4) Actions, such as pouring water, beer or wine, burning the animal, singing, playing musical instruments and dancing, entering the door, processing, using a "hole," preparing food, bowing, putting on garments, acting out a ritual drama--all these continued throughout. 5) Certain forms of prayer continued, and indeed were prevalent throughout the region.[62]

Yet there were areas in which the cultures of the eastern and western ANE differ significantly from one another. 1) Palestine had nothing like the Mesopotamian *kurgarrû* and *assinnu*, hermaphroditic actors who belong to the Inanna/Ishtar cult (see Appendix 3). 2) There was nothing in Palestine like the large numbers of gods found in Mesopotamia, each with a special aspect, or geographical area. 3) The Hebrew Bible has a much more limited range of types of texts than does Mesopotamia, having no economic texts, royal annals, few stylized lamentations, omen texts, no mathematical texts, schoolboy copy texts, lengthy myths, astrological, divination, and other categories. Of course, the range of years of Hebrew literature is much narrower than that of the 2500+ of Mesopotamia.

All of the above comments will be followed through with textual material in the pages below. In our examples, we give as much transliteration as is feasible, but this is for the specialist. Those who know no Akkadian or Sumerian will pick up something of the literary qualities, however, and if a Semitic language is known one can see a little of what is meant.

On every page the reader will see my dependence upon the work of others. Especially are we all beholden to the great dictionaries: The *Chicago Assyrian Dictionary*, the *Akkadisches Handwörterbuch*, and the beginnings of the *Pennsylvania Sumerian Dictionary.* The great *Materialen zum Sumerische Lexikon /Materials for the Sumerian Lexicon*, a lifetime study by Benno Landsberger, continued by Miguel Civil, Erica Reiner, Robert Biggs and others, provides the very basis for much of my work. It is an irony of history that the lists the scribes made up so many thousands of years ago to teach their students are used today by students for somewhat the same purpose. My only claim to originality is to have put this mass of material together in one place, and to reclassify and reorganize it. I have brought previously disparate pieces side-by-side so that a relationship may either be seen or decided against. Because of the inter-relatedness of many of these titles, I felt that I could not omit any, but that makes for a mass of data which is initially unwieldy, hence the classifications. These are partly from the ancients themselves, and partly of our modern doing. In any case, I hope that this book will serve as a kind of a source book and reference, and be a reasonably complete listing, by category, of both female and male cultic officiants.

Notes

1 The archaeologists have recovered their material because of chance discoveries but this is a tiny percentage of the scribes' total output."[The] picture is...spotty...[with] immense gaps in time and space," Oppenheim *Mesop* 11.

2 We will be criticized for jumping around the various centuries and the various cities, for a major center such as Sippar or Ur or Asshur had its own traditions. We would best pause and speak of each of these by itself. More carefully still, we should study one of these over one period, such as the OB one, but if we did this, we would have to wait for another fifty years for enough material for the several periods and places we want to emphasize, so I decided to go ahead with what we have.

3 F. Thureau-Dangin, *Rituels accadiens,* Paris, 1921.

4 We must not, for instance, consider Lucian of Samosata in the 2nd c. A.D. as reflecting "the *locus classicus* of Ishtar worship," as Segal (n. 14, p. 124, below, does).

5 H. Blomm, *Kabbalah and Criticism* 1975, 166, as quoted by Charpin *Clergé* 20 cited after Michalowski *JAOS* 103 (1983) 239 n. 15.

6 Phyllis Bird,"The place of women in the Israelite cultus," in P.D.Miller et al (eds.) *Ancient Israelite Religion*, Philadelphia 1987, pp. 397-419, especially p.399.

7 A few examples of this would be: in Rowley,"The forms and meaning of sacrifice,"*Worship in Ancient Israel*, chap 4, the author is reluctant to give a description of the ritual itself. Kraus comes closer to a description in *Worship in Israel*, 208-218, when he chooses key verses from the Psalms, and pieces them together to make somewhat of a continuity, with much of the result concerning the entrance and exit rites. Some scattered details given in R. deVaux, "The ritual of sacrifice," in *Ancient Israel*, 415ff. Even more detail, indicating how complex the actual cult must have been, is given by M. Haran, "The complex of ritual acts inside the tabernacle," in C. Rabin (ed.), *cripta Hierosolymitana* VIII (Jerusalem, 1961), 272-302. More detail is given by Shmuel Safrai in."Temple Ritual," *Encyclopedia Judaica* 15 (Jerusalem, 1971) 970-8, based on the rich Tannaitic and Amoraic sources, many hundreds of years after the last performance of the actions they are describing, but from strongly conservative sources.

8 Oppenheim *Mesop* 172-182.

9 B.A. Levine and W.W.Hallo, *HUCA* 38 (1967) 17, a comment upon Oppenheim's remarks in the above n. 8.

10 H. Vorlander, *Mein Gott. Die Vorstellungen vom personlichen Gott im Alten Orient und in Alten Testament.* Neukirchen-Vluyn, 1975, *AOAT* 23.

11 A ritual text RS 24.258, *Ugaritica* V545-551, describes a rite in which the gods act like priests: Il offers a sacrifice in his house (I.1) and Ashtart and Anat arrive and offer part of the body of an animal.

12 The Mesopotamians themselves were conscious of their women officials, because they sometimes listed them in separate sections of the lexical lists, as Lu=ša.III ii *MSL* XII 123ff, the whole of col.ii being female officials.

---

13 In the late first millenium, in lands outside of Palestine and Mesopotamia, the female *khnt* "priestess" is found, but these are not within our area of interest. There was a *khnt* at Deir 'Alla (Sec.3.32.2), and at Carthage (Phoenician influence), see Lidzbarski *Ephemeris* III 285 E.*lw'* and *lw't* appear in Minean, see Pedersen *Israel* III-IV 128, but each of these societies had its own way of doing things, and there is no pan-semitic way of enacting the cult, although some titles of officials remained in cognate Semitic languages with functions relative to their own civilization.

14 J.B.Segal,"Jewish Attitudes towards Women,"*JJS* 30(1979) pp.129, 131. To put it in an oversimplified way: we can postulate that in Israel the cultic participation of the female, as goddess or priestess, was curtailed because of the possibility of contamination by cults of Canaanite goddesses.

15 About 8700 words and names in the OT, according to John Gates, *Lexicographical Sources Used by Biblical Scholars.* Society of Biblical Literature, Dissertation Series No.8, 1972, p.12; E. Ullendorff, *Is Biblical Hebrew a Language?* Wiesbaden, 1977, p.5, estimates 7500-8000 "separate words--not roots but individual non-predictable vocabulary entries."

16 Except, of course, for Israel and surrounding countries the word *khn* is normally and appropriately translated "priest."

17 The words for "ritual" are many and varied: *nepestu, dullu, alkaktu, kitkittu, epistu, kididu, parsu,* garza. The Hebrew words are few, the main one being ^{c}*abodah*, usually translated "service," but basically meaning"work," a work done before the Lord. This is the same semantic development as the Greek *leitourgia*, originally a public service, but coming to mean the Divine Service, the Liturgy in Christianity.

18 Oppenheim, *History of Religions* 5 (1966) 252 notes a MA text which warns the worshipper not to divulge (*šutešu*) the teachings of Ishtar.

19 H. Sauren, *XVIIe Rencontre*, Belgium, 1970, 12.

20 The Sumerian reading of INANNA is not agreed upon, and inconsistently with the rest of the designations in the book, it will be read Inanna. Gelb presents a valuable list of syllabic spellings of a group of different goddesses thought to relate to Inanna, concluding that a number of forms of the name of several perhaps independent deities appears, which may later have been conflated. He prefers to read ^{d}Innin and is opposed to understanding it as "lady of heaven,"I.J. Gelb, *JNES* 19 (1960) 72ff; see also Jacobsen *PAPS* 107 (1963) 475 n. 6.

21 *CAH*^{3}1/2 242 (M.E.L.Mallowan).

22 Karen B.Godecken, in a section "Priester der Annunitum," in an overall article on this goddess in *UF* 5 (1973) 148.

23 LB 1090, 2.26, Leemans *Ishtar.*

24 CAD A/1 159f.

25 *KAR* 357.28.

26 CAD I/J 146bf.

27 Livingstone *Poetry* No.8 r.21 (Ass.Photo 6553, K.173/4b), *LKA* 32.

28 OB, *VAS* 10 214 ii l, CAD G 58a, Z 117a.

---

29 Thureau-Dangin, *RA* 31(1934) 139; see also Gröndahl *Ugaritic PNs* 86, 99.

30 Keel *Stempelsiegeln.*

31 L. Gorelick and E.Williams-Forte, *Ancient Seals and the Bible*, Malibu, 1983; Ben-Tor, *Cylinder Seals.*

32 J.M.Asher-Greve *Frauen in altsumerische Zeit*, Malibu, 1985 (Bibliotheca Mesopotamica,18).

33 For the Early Dynastic Period, see Jean Bottero et al, *The Near East: The Early Civilizations,* New York and London, 1967, from German, Frankfurt am Main, 1965, chap.2.

34 Asher-Greve, op.cit.157f. For more details, see Secs.4.9,4.3 and 4.11 respectively.

35 Asher-Greve, op.cit.pls IV and V.Depictions of "Priesterinnen" listed p47.

36 D.Wiseman, *Catalogue of the Western Asiatic Seals in the British Museum.* I. *Cylinder Seals, Uruk-Early Dynastic Periods,* London, 1962, passim.

37 "Religion did not exist for the saving of souls, but for the preservation and welfare of society," W.Robertson Smith, *Religion of the Semites*, pb ed. (1956, originally 1889) p.29. This was quoted with approval by J.W.Rogerson. *ET* 90 (1978-79) 232b.

38 T.Worden, "The literary influence of the Ugaritic fertility myth on the Old Testament,"*VT* 3 (1953) 273-297, giving credit for an expression of this idea by H.G. May in 1932.

39 Pieter J.van Zijl, *Baal, A Study of texts in connection with Baal in the Ugaritic Epics,* Neukirchen-Vluyn, 1972.

40 J.C.deMoor, *The Seasonal Pattern in the Ugaritic Myth of Ba'lu, according to the version of Ilimilku,* Neukirchen-Vluyn, 1971.

41 C.H.Gordon,*Ugaritic Literature,* Rome, 1949.

42 Leonore Tiefer, in Helen Tierney (ed.),*Women's Studies Encyclopedia* I, 346, Westport, 1989; John Money and Herman Mosaph (eds.), *Handbook of Sexology*, Amsterdam, 1977.

43 Researchers usually use the terms bisexuality and hermaphoditism/ androgyny synonymously, though there is the tendency to separate them in some cases. Robert Jean Campbell, *Psychiatric Dictionary* [5], New York and Oxford, 1981, pp.36, 83.

44 But E.D. vanBuren, "Representation of fertility deities in glyptic art, "*Or* NS 24 (1955) p.346 finds that the bestower of fertility was not originally a single deity, but that the principal deity in every locality could provide it. In later times most of the great gods were believed to possess fertility aspects in addition to their more characteristic aspects. See also Frankfort, *Seals,* 110-113, emphasizing the early periods, and saying that "the essential unity of the gods of fertility [are hidden] in various divergent shapes."

45 Or, better, "schools. "The modern history of this, and its later offshoots, are given in Robert Ackerman, *The Myth and Ritual School. J.G. Frazer and the Cambridge Ritualists*, New York and London, 1991. For our purposes, see especially the notes on S.H.Hooke and I.Engnell in op.cit. pp. 192-3. We are not so much interested in this book for the patterns this school discovers, as for the theory that the ritual is often understood to be incorporated into the myth, sometimes without that being stated.

46 Melaart, *Çatal Huyuk* and idem, *Hacilar.*

47 For Sumerian PNs note the many names with ama 'mother' in Limet, *Anthroponomie* 197ff; also, Stamm 83, 209.

48 J.Renger, "Untersuchungen zum Priestertum in den Alt-Babylonische Zeit,"*A* 58 NF 24 (1967), pp.110ff. A valuable further study of some of these titles is given by Dominique Charpin, *LeClergéd'Urau siècle D'Hammurabi (xixe-xviiie sièclesav. JC.).*

49 Renger now (private communication) would entitle the last two categories: "experts in magical practices," and "experts in divinitory practices."

50 A.L.Oppenheim, *La Divination in Mésopotamie Ancienne.*XIVe Rencontre 1965, Paris, 1966, p.40.

51 In Sumerian é, in Akkadian *bītu*, in Hebrew *bayit*, in each case meaning simply "house." In those languages there was no special term for "house of the deity."

52 See chap.2 n. 179.

53 See chap.2 n. 22, and the many illustrations in Hartmann *Musik.*

54 M. Ottoson, *Temples and Cult Places in Palestine,* Uppsala, 1980; e.g. in a temple at Shechem there was a court in front of the temple containing an altar and masseboth, p. 57.

55 As I brought out in *JAOS* 100 (1980) p. 284a, this is a problem in the translation of all of the Mesopotamian titles.

56 S.Sandmel,"Parallelomania,"*JBL* 81(1962)1-13, writing especially about a recent study by NT scholars of the Qumran scrolls. H. Ringgren, *VT Sup* 23 (1972), 1-8 describes some comparative research in the biblical field as a kind of "parallel-hunting." Once it has been established that a certain biblical expression has an apparent parallel outside the Bible, the whole problem is regarded as solved, [without asking] whether or not the extra-biblical element has the same place in life, and the same function in the context of its own culture (p.1).

57 G.W.Ahlström, "Aspects of Syncretism in Israelite Religion," in *Horae Soederblomianae.* V. Lund, 963. BM 170 A7.

58 de Vaux. *AnIs,* 294.

59 R.North, *Or* 26 (1957) 250, passim, in a study of the Warka excavation over the years.

60 So the overwhelming majority of the material. This, however, must be balanced by the specificity of such items as the ubi-bird and gazelle, as shown by the month-names iti u_5-bi mušen-kú "the month:eating the ubi-bird" (third month at Drehem) and iti mas-da kú "the month:eating the gazelle" (first month at Drehem).

61 Menzel *Tempel* IIT 8ff.

62 M.-J.Seux *Hymneset Priersaux Dieux de Babylonieet d' Assyrie*, Paris, 1976. The content, theology and even phraseology of the prayers from east and west semitic areas could be compared and remarkable similarities would be found.

CHAPTER ONE

Titles of Important Cultic Officials In The Hebrew Bible, Ebla, Emar, Mesopotamia And Ugarit

The study of women cultic officials compels us to look at ancient Near Eastern worship life in a new way, from a new direction. It makes us ask questions that perhaps would not have arisen otherwise, and forces us into modes of thinking that are not the standard ones. One of my main interests is in the titles, and what people holding these are described as doing, and I will attempt to provide as extensive a list of these titles as possible. Many of these one can find in the lexical lists, as already noted at the end of the Introduction. Unless shown otherwise I am going to assume that the titles on these lists are "real" titles.

1.2 Continuity and Change -- Mesopotamia

1.2.1 I usually start the study of each word using the MSL texts. I may disappoint some readers in not translating all of the words given on these, but it will be seen below that some of them need more than one-word translations to explain them satisfactorily, and in others of them we simply do not know the technical meaning of the words listed. In some of the earliest texts in Mesopotamian history, in the Sumerian of the Early Dynastic Period (usually considered 2900-2400 B.C.E., although the ED texts may have only appeared in the last part of this period), we find lexical lists which include, among other "secular" ranks, those which we understand from later texts to be cultic; we choose the fullest ED list as an example:

Early Dynastic List E, MSL XII, 17ff,	Later Akkadian "equivalences"
sanga (, m., line 2)	*šangû*
azu (m., f. 47)	*asû*, *asātu*
lukur (f., 51)	*naditu*
šita (m., 52)	*ellu*, *ramku*
gudu$_4$ (m., 64)	*pašīšu*
nu-èš (m., 70)	*nešakku*
nin-dingir (f., 72a)	*entu* or *ugbabtu*
dam-dingir (f., 73)	(none yet discovered)
"wife of the god" or	"wife who is divine"
AMA-^{d}Inanna (f., 74)	*amalūtu/amalītu*
	"mother who is (?) Inanna."
išib (m., 79)	*išippu*
balag-di (m., 98)	*ṣārihu*
lú-šìr (m., 107)	
maš-maš (m., 117)	*mašmaššu*, *āšipu*, *āšiputu*
lú-máš-šu-gíd (m., 130)	*bārû*
nu-gig (f., 135)	*qadištu* and *ištarītu*

On the right are the translations, i.e., the explanations, of the Akkadian scribes themselves, from OB times on, of the Sumerian word. We bring them out at the beginning and hope to show that some of these titles continued throughout Mesopotamian history, almost 2500 years, although undoubtedly in most cases with evolved or different functions. We especially note the number of female officiants on this early list.

1.2.2 Hallo[1] calls attention to the fact that the Sumerian King List (perhaps 3100-2900 in the early entries) listed no women as actors, but the last of the antediluvians, in Shuruppak, in the later Akkadian story only, under the name of Ut-napishtim who had a wife, but no name was given to her. (24)

The famous beautiful female head from Uruk[2] was perhaps a high priestess, perhaps a goddess, perhaps a king's wife, "roles which were to some extent interchangeable." (25) Queen Pu-abi of Ur had a harp[3] indicating that she probably sang, and that probably cultically. Queen Nin-tur (or Nin-banda) in a later stratum from the royal graves of Ur was the wife of the founder (according to the Sumerian King List) of the First Dynasty of Ur. Her titles are given in Hallo *Royal Titles*, with 8 charts of PNs, 30-32.(27)

The wives of the rulers of Lagash, at the end of the Dynastic Age (2500-2300) administered the temples of the chief goddess of the city (28).

1.2.3 Rivkah Harris comments on the *nadītu* of OB times in one of the most detailed studies of any of these officials.[4] Her conclusion is that the lukur of the pre-OB period seems to have been in a different position from the *naditu* of the OB period.[5] In our study of the texts containing the lukur in early periods in Sec. 4.3 we will come to the same conclusion.

1.2.4 Under ideal conditions, as has been stated, the offices should be studied for each city and for each era. Renger has shown how difficult this would be, in a listing of gods with associated GNs and offices for OB times.[6] Reading backwards from Renger's lists, the female offices of nin-dingir was associated with 10 cities and 11 gods, the en (m. or f.) with 5 cities and 4 gods, and the lukur with 4 cities and 4 gods.

1.2.5 And, in turn, something seems to have happened in NA times, for the presumably high-level *nadītu* is found in a list of witches in an incantation text[7] apparently putting this once-high rank in a derogatory category. In another example of this, a NA lexical list has:

I 131 *šá-muk-tum* *na-di-tum* Malku-šarru Explicit

which makes a *nadītu* be a *šamuktu* = *šamhatu* "prostitute,"[8] but this list has its own anomalous raison d'être.

At this early stage in our presentation, we are merely going to note the change in aspect of this title over the years, but we stress that the general area of sexuality seems to have continued, although sometimes we conclude this only from the officiants surrounding her, Sec. 4.3.

1.2.6 The important pre-Sargonic Mes-ane-pada, king of Kish (ca. 2600-2550 B.C.) calls himself dam-nu-gig "husband of a nu-gig."[9] His wife was a nin whose function is not described in this text. Several goddesses are called nu-gig, or by an alternate orthography nu-u$_8$-gig.[10]

1.2.7 The title nu-gig also has had a varied life under its own title and that of one of its "equivalents," *qadištu.* Much has been written on the latter root *q-d-š*, being found in Ugaritic and the Hebrew Bible as well as in Mesopotamia, and we will study it in some detail in Sec. 4.11. Our interest here is in noting its change in usage over the ages. There is a possibility of an ambiguity, because the root *q-d-š* means "holy" and the term *qadištu* in some cases may not be a formal title, but simply mean "holy woman," without referring to any regular cultic rank.

1.2.8 Much later, in NA times, the *qadištu* appears on that same list of witches as the *nadītu*, Sec. 3.20.5. And her relationship to some sort of sexuality is shown by her appearance in a legal text in which she appears in the role of a common street prostitute.[11] But this aspect is not found anywhere else of this title. See Sec. 4.11.

1.2.9 A large number of the offices in MA/NA times dominated by the *šangû* come together in a list of *ginû* "regular" offerings to the goddess Sharrat-nipha, with some ceremonial, in Kar-Tukulti-Ninurta.[12] Bread, meat, honey, salt, oil, beer, hides and wine are given to the *šangû*'s of Sharrat-nipha and the Bit-eqî as well as to officials.

Giving only the titles, omitting lú and mí:

7 *šatammu*
8 *šangû* 's, *kezretu* 's
11 *šangû ša* ^{d}*šarrat-nipha, šangû ša bit eqî*
13 *šatammu, sirāšû*
14 *māru*'s (of the?) *kezretu*'s
19 *šatammu*
20 *nargallum* (sic, with the older *-m*)
22 *šangû*
23 *šangû* ^{d}*šarrat-nipha, nargallu, rab kurgarrû*
25 *šangû ša* ^{d}*šarrat-nipha*
27 *šangû, sirāšû*
29 *šangû ša* ^{d}*šarrat-nipha*
30 *šatammu* (?)
33 *nargallu*
35 *šatammu, sirāšû, šangû* ^{d}*šarrat-nipha*
36 *šangû ša* [*bīt e*]*qî*
39 *bēl pāhete*
r. 2 *šatammu, sirāšû*
r. 4 *šangû* ^{d}*šarrat-nipha* , *šangû ša bīt eqî*
r. 5 *nargallum* (*sic*, with -m)
r. 8 *šangu ša* ^{d}*šarrat-nipha, šangû ša bīt eqi*
r. 9 HAR [ ]
r. 10 *šatammu, sirāšû*
r. 11 *bēl pāhete*
r. 22 *naphar anniu ginû ša* ^{d}*šarrat-nipha* "these are the total of the *ginû*-offerings of Sharrat-nipha"

This will be referred to again at the proper place Sec. 4.6.6; now it suffices to note the wide variety of offices at this temple:

- ø the *šangû*, the *šangû* of Sharrat-nipha,[13] the *šangû* of the Bit-eqî (*RLA* II 40);
- ø the *šatammu* administrator, presumably of the temple;
- ø the *sirāšû* "beer brewer;"
- ø the *bēl pāhete* "governor/Statthalter;"

ø the cultic singing rank: *nargallum*, the only office here with the older -m ending;

ø our Category No. 4 offices of *kezretu,* sons of(?)/apprentice (?) *kezretu*'s and *rab kurgarrî*.

ø The LU.HAR [ ] could be the ÀRA / *ararru* "miller," an office which shows up in some cultic texts, as we understand it a Category No. 5 office, together with *sirašû*.

This variety shows the personnel of the Sharrat-nipha temple, listing in no discernable order a large variety of *šangû*'s, high state officials as well as high temple officials, craftsmen presumably attached to the temple, and the *nargallu*, the only one in this category. The *kezretu* and *rab kurgarrî* are in what we consider a special Category No. 4, officiants who are discussed in chap. 4 and App. 3, respectively.

1.3 sanga / *šangû*

1.3.1 The extensive time range of some of the titles is exemplified by a well-known rank appearing in the earliest Sumerian texts as sanga, and continuing on down to Seleucid texts[14] as *šangû*. He is variously understood as "temple administrator" or "priest," but his function is unsure for the early texts.

In ED lexical lists the readings of which are uncertain the sign appears:

31 SANGA:DÉ
41 SANGA:GÁ x GAR:ME
42 SANGA:GÁ x SAL:ME
43 SANGA:GÁx UD:ME
66 SANGA:SUHUR
70 SANGA:BU:NUN or BU:NUN:SANGA
71 SANGA:NUN or NUN:SANGA
97 SANGA:KURUŠDA
99 SANGA:ÁB:UDU or SANGA.ÁB.KU
100 LAGAR.AB.UDU or LAGAR:AB:KU
114 GAL:SANGA
115 GAL:SANGA:GÁN or GÁNA:SANGA

ED Lu A, MSL XII 10
corrected by Arcari ED List A

The colon indicates that the meaningful order of the signs is unknown.

1 [sa] nga
2 [na] gar
56 sanga:munus:sag:nu:nita

ED Lu B, MSL XII 13

50 sanga-gal
51 sanga-gal:KAŠ

ED Lu C, MSL XII 15

1 [PA.TE.S]I (MSL) / dub-sar (Ebla)
2 sanga
3 QA.ŠU.DU$_8$ = sagi (⌈ì⌉-du$_8$, Biggs)

4 PA.AL = šabra
5 ensi (MSL) / ([x]-si, Biggs)

ED Lu E, MSL XII 17;
Biggs, *Abu Salabikh* 82;
CAD S/1 12a; Pettinato, *OrAn* 15
(1976) 170, from Ebla

A later long list of officials, charcteristics of a person, family terms, musical terminology and so forth shows:

237 SAL + LAGAR$^{\textit{pi-in-qú}}$
238 SAL + LAGAR$^{\textit{qí-in-na-tum}}$
239 SAL + LAGAR$^{\textit{hu-ur-da-tum}}$
240 SAL + LAGAR$^{\textit{šu-úh-hu}}$
241 engiz
242 ensi
242a SAL ensi
243 kišib-gál
244 kišib-lá
245 enkum
246 ninkum
247 abgal
248 ^{áb}abrig

OB Proto-Lu MSL XII 41ff

and the standard NA list shows:

135a	[ensi$_2$]	*iš-ša-ak-ku*
135b	sanga	ŠU
135c	en	*e-nu*
135f	[um-mi]-a	*um-ma-nu*

Lu = ša I MSL XII 97

appearing also on several other NA lists: STT 383 vi 7, MSL XII 236; K.3495v 1, MSL XII 239

In ED Lu A 99 the SANGA deals with (the sacrifice or the administration of) large and small cattle, as does the LAGAR in line 100. The SANGA appears near the beginning in ED Lu B and ED Lu E, and elsewhere there is some indication that the lists begin with the most important ranks. OB Proto-Lu has lugal on line 2, and ED Lu A has ŠITA on line 1. For the SANGA as scribe, see Biggs.[15]

1.3.2 In a Rim-Sin (early OB) slave-sale[16] a number of witnesses appear, with titles, most of which we discuss in these pages. It is significant that they are all in one document, thus perhaps all together in one place. They are, in order, sanga, kišib-gál, ab-a-ab-du$_7$, abrig$_2$, išib, gudu$_4$-abzu, en-nam, nam-šita$_4$, lú-bappir (or, read lùnga, with Borger *Zeichenliste* No. 225), gudu$_4$-Inanna, šu-i, rá-gab, nar-sa ^{d}Enki. These are mostly cultic, and those that are not are apparently auxiliaries, our Category No. 5.

In a Mari ritual, the *šangû* and the *pašīšu* act together at the end of the rite, Sec. 1.6.2. At Mari the *šangû*'s relations with the cult are shown in one letter[17] in which the *šangû* is concerned with the building of the "seat of the goddess," in this case Annunitum, appearing often at Mari as a form of Ishtar. In another[18] the *šangû ša Ištar-pišrā* stands at the door (of the temple) of Bēlet-ekallim. In another the *šangû* reports on his dream about the goddess Bēlet-biri.[19]

1.3.3 In a MA rite[20] the king is crowned (probably) by the *šangû*, and obeisance is made to him by many officials. The *šangû* of Asshur plays on a (name broken) musical instrument and says "Asshur is king! Asshur is king!" until he reaches the door of ^{d}Azu'u, when the king enters. He prostrates himself and rolls over.[21] He stands on the *parakku* dais; he lays down silver and gold, costly bowls and garments at the feet of the god. These were offerings given earlier to the *šangû*.

While the king prepares a dish for Asshur, the *šangû* prepares a dish for "the gods." Animals and stones, first for Asshur and Sherua, then for other high gods, then for minor gods, were given "as a gift." The *birsu* garment (or, "blanket" CAD B 261) is brought, and probably (it is broken here) the special headdress with which the king is crowned, and the *šangû* lays it on the head of the king. Then he prays that Asshur and Ninlil will see to it that it remains for 100 years, that his *šangû*-office and that of his son will be well, and that Asshur will give him *kitta u šalima* "justice and peace." / "truth and health," etc.

After this the noblemen and the *ša rēši šarrānu* bow and kiss the feet of the king. He sits on the throne. The musicians (broken title) make music. Gifts are brought to the king and then brought before Asshur; these are the income of the *šangû rabu*. The *sukkallu rabû* and the *sukkallu šaniu* lay the scepter before the king. The *rab zammaru*'s play their *sammû*-harps and each takes his place before the king. The service ends with a broken list of stones and animals for various gods. In this rite, the king is the chief *šangû* [22] and the named *šangû* is an assistant.

1.3.4 In a rite using symbolic language in which the king acts together with the *šangû*, the *nāru* and the *kurgarrû*'s, the king takes the part of Marduk Nabu.[23] The action of the king and the *šangû* together is NINDA.*ka-ma-nu...u šarqadu* translated by Livingstone as "tossing the cake," but it seems to be some sort of a dance with the "cake."

1.3.5 In a complex 6-column rite[24] from the time of Ashurbanipal, dated 650 B.C.E. by the limmu name, in which the chief actors are the king and a *šangû*, with the king doing most of the cultic acts, the ceremonies last for about 24 days. Only a few notes from this somewhat broken ceremony ("the top half or perhaps slightly more," van Driel) are given. The *šangû* comes into the *bit labbūni*, a part of the temple of Asshur. He binds the *sasuppu* (elsewhere *susippu* and other orthographies) towel or kerchief on the king's waist. The gods Sherua, Kippat-māti and Tashmētu are allowed into the Anu temple. The *šangû* of Anu holds a torch in his hand, goes to the *mušlālu* (staircase or gate) before the king and says, *li-mir* URU KI.MIN BAD "may one see (?) the city and also the wall." Menzel: "hell werden möge die Stadt..." van Driel: "may the town shine..."

Offerings are brought before Asshur and Mullissu (NIN.LIL). The *kalû* comes onto the scene, unfortunately in a broken part. The minor gods Bēl-Agu and Kutatāte take part, as does also Sharrat-nipha. *Hammurtu* beer is served with *akussu* soup. Salt is used by the king several times. The *nargallatu*'s say: Sherua *ta-ta-lad* "Sherua has been born." Most of the aforementioned acts are not done right after one another, but scattered throughout the rite.

1.3.6 Another Istanbul tablet[25] is part of the same tablet as the above, says Menzel, because both use similar grammar and style. The king enters to take care of the gods. The gods use oil, honey and lard. The king (supposedly) heaps up wine. The *kalû*'s take part. Sheep for the gods Ninurta and Nusku are brought out. The *nuhatimmu* "(temple) cook" is present in a broken line, followed by the *šangû* without a verb. The king does much of the action, including causing the gods Sherua and Kippat-māti to stand up.[26]

1.3.7 *KAR* 146 (*VAT* 10112) is a NA *parṣu* "rite" of the king and is one of a number of texts describing a meal, here the *naptanu* meal. It is part of the rite of *mīš pî* /KA.LUH.U.DA "washing of the mouth."[27] There are three participants: the king, the *šangû* and the *nāru* (or, read *zammeru*). Ishtar (i.e., her cultic officiant) leads the king into the temple. There are grain and animal offerings and the burning of honey and oil. He goes before the Sibitti. The *nāru* sings *isinni isinni* "my festival! my festival!" The people then....[28]

The king goes on to make animal sacrifices before Asshur and Ishtar. Spices, honey, oil, beer and wine are offered. The *nāru* sings "let them eat." He places the meal in a hole, pours honey, oil, beer and wine into it also, and fills the hole.[29] He sings i-lu-ri e i-lu-ri.

At the end of the king's meal, the *šangû* "gives water for Ishtar to the king." The people are sent away, and the doors shut. The final portion of the ritual is done with presumably only a few officials present. At the end the king puts his foot on the hole and kisses it.

1.3.8 The next few examples present only selected actions; the liturgies are complex and not completely preserved. *KAR* 215 (*VAT* 8882) is an offering ceremony in the *bīt akīti* "the New Year's temple" of the king, with a small part for the queen, who carries "the weapons."[30] No cultic officials such as the *šangû* appear in the unbroken parts, but perhaps there are some in the broken parts. Blood, fish, oil, honey and wine are offered. There is cleansing.

1.3.9 In *VAT* 13717[31] the king offers food, drink, sheep and salt for dBelat-šadê, Asshur and the Sibitti on the *tamlû* "terrace." The *šangû* gives (?) "hand water." A MÍ.NAR "female musician" appears on the mostly broken reverse.

1.3.10 *VAT* 13596,[32] a fuller text than the others but poorly preserved, takes place partly in the *bīt akīti*. After a long list of deities, meat is brought before Asshur in the *tarbaṣu* "court." The *mukīl appāte* "rein-holder" comes in and holds out a *māhītu* "whip" to the god Asshur. He goes to the *bīt akīti*. The (broken) sing. Near the end the *kalû*'s play the *lilissu* -drums. Asshur sits on the *parakku* "throne dais."

1.3.11 Photo 4123i and 4132f[33] probably takes place in the *bit akiti* "New Years Temple." There is a *parakku* dais. The *šangû* of Asshur lays a bowl on the mouth (?) of the king and sprinkles "hand-water" on him, and does other actions for a cleansing ceremony. He handles the dishes. In the partially destroyed reverse, several incantations are mentioned:"The gods," "The crown whose splendor," "The weapon clothed with splendid light." Who recited them is not preserved. *Kalû*'s and the *šangû* have to do with the *parak šīmāte* "dais of fate" in the partially broken second photo.

1.3.12 In an excerpt from the series *Shumma ālu*[34] a single line tells of the role of the *šangû*. "Then he went to Isin...to be healed. Amel-Bau, a man of Isin, a *šangû* of dMeme, met him, spoke a *šiptu* (EN) "incantation" to him, and healed him.

1.3.13 Menzel[35] has a listing of the many aspects of the *šangû*, a valuable picture of NA times. It would not be useful to summarize and simplify this very full list. She finds, besides *šangû* by itself as a title, also *šangû* (*ša*) DN, *šangû* (*ša*) *bīt* DN, *šangû* (*ša*) GN-city, *šangû rabiu, šangû šaniu, mār šangî*, *šangû ša bīt nuhatimmi*, *šangû karkadinnu* (once?)

1.3.14 Some scholars have attempted to find a female equivalent for this title. In a Mari text,[36] Römer reads one of the broken signs as míSAN[GA] (??), but here Dossin the editor of *ARM* 10 reads míA[l-xxx] -ka. The start of the broken sign as copied could allow it to be completed as SANGA or míSI[D] = *ṭupšarratu* "female scribe." In another place, Bottéro mentions a **šaggitu* (supposedly a female *šangû*)[37] but with no reference and no discussion. Meissner[38] had referred to a list of Aramean, Hittite, Tyrian and Kassite female musicians, in a broken line r.10' of which there are 4 míKID/RID/SANGA (?). Because of the context it is highly doubtful that the sign is to be read míSANGA = *šangitu* or *šagitu* (as he read it). This is example of a mistake perpetuated throughout the years.

Sometimes the goddess acts as sanga, as a Sumerian text which speaks of various rites being carried out: dnin-gal sanga-den-líl-lá-ke4 gišapin-kù mu-un-lá "Ningal the sanga of Enlil has yoked the holy plow."[39] I do not think this indicates that there is a female sanga, but only that Ningal is acting in this male role. Goddesses sometimes take a hermaphroditic role. For completeness, we note the untranslatable entry sanga:munus:sag:nu:nita in ED Lu B 56, Sec. 1.3.1.

1.4 The Highest Officials in the Hebrew Temple Rites

1.4.1 In the western world the practice is usually to have only one person leading the liturgical rites, entitled preost in Anglo-Saxon, prest/preost in Middle English, priest in modern English; in other modern tongues: Priester in German, prêtre in French, sacerdote in Spanish, prete and sacerdote in Italian, svyashchennik in Russian, and so forth. The modern Western European terms come from either the Latin *sacerdus* "one who handles the *sacer* or sacred," or the Greek *presbuteros* "elder." The worship was performed by the one on behalf of the many, common in all religions, because liturgical practice is social not individual.

The word "priest" is used today for the title of the principal functionary at divine services, especially in Christian rites, and specifically in the Roman Catholic, Eastern Orthodox and Anglican Churches. In the aforementioned church worlds only a priest can celebrate the Eucharist (Lord's Supper), give absolution and give the blessing. Our understanding of these practices helps set our mind when we hear the word translated "priest" from the titles of quite different A.N.E. offices.

The anthropologist, in describing primitive cultures, would use the term priest for one who performs a sacrifice, usually an animal sacrifice, although it is also used in this field for the one who was in charge of temples or shrines. In general the priest (as westerners translate it) alone can lead the ritual drama.

Today's usage stems from the earliest Christian church. The word *presbuteros* in the New Testament was used only of church leaders,[40] but in the second century[41] this office was found in the Latin-speaking church in the priestly term *sacerdos,* on analogy to the Hebrew Bible's term *kōhēn*, in charge of the liturgical rites. Much of the early understanding of this term was related to the rather full description in the Hebrew Bible of the priesthood.

1.4.2 It is surprising that in the Hebrew Bible no description of the duties of the priest is to be found in any detail. His functions are performed mainly in the temple. The only word used in the O.T. for this office is *kohen*, with the feminine *khnt* not appearing except in cognate languages in countries outside Israel. The priests are sometimes referred to as *mešartim* "ministers" (not referring to a female! -- Isa 61.6, Jer 33.21, Joel 1.9.13, 2.17), although this may not be a title as such.

The functions of the *kōhēn* are to be servants of God, not at all representatives of the community,[42] embodying traditional knowledge handed on down from past generations (Kraus, 100)[43] These can be classified as:

1) cultic: offering of sacrifices on the altar (Lev 9.12f, of Aaron the archetypical priest), blessing the people (Deut 21.5, Josh 8.33), cursing the one who does not conform to the words of the torah (Deut 27.13-26), probable recitation of liturgical texts accompanying ritual acts (Rowley, 135), waving the offering (Lev 23.20), blowing the *šofar* on the day of atonement (Lev 25.9) and at other times (Num 10.10), carrying the ark (Deut 10.8, 31.9.25), burning the incense (Ex 30.7, 1 Sam 2.28), caring for the lamps (Ex 27.20f), placing the bread on the table (Lev 24.5f), pouring the libation (Ex 25.29, 37.16), distinguishing between the holy and the profane (Lev 10.10, Ezek 22.26, 44.23) as a guardian of the holiness of the community (Kraus, 100);

2) divination, as consulting the *ʾûrîm* and *tumîm* (Deut 33.8, Num 27.21), casting the lots in the scapegoat ceremony (Lev 16.8-10), carrying out the ordeal (Num 5.11-31);

3) taking care of diseases and impurities (Lev 14.48, Deut 24.8, Ezek 44.23), not as a physician, but as a guardian of the ritual purity of the community (Rowley *Worship* 103);

4) judging, with judges (Deut 17.9, 19.17); settling disputes (Deut 21.5);

5) teaching torah (Deut 33.10), in which the sacral and the ethical are integrated (Hos 4.1ff, Zeph 3.4), and giving the word of God, the "oracle" and the prayer (Krau, 100).

Once in the Pentateuch there is *hakkōhēn haggādōl* "the high priest" Num 35.25.28, but he appears in Josh 20.6 in a position which indicates administrative leadership, Sometimes this rank appears as *kōhēn hārōʾš* "first priest" 2 Kings 25.18. The *ziknē hakkōhănîm* "elder priests" may simply be an honorable title, 2 Kings 19.2 (repeated Isa 37.2), Jer 19.1. There were *kōhănē hammišneh* "second priests" 2 Kings 23.4, 25.18 (repeated in Jer 52.24). Sometimes the priestly rank was designated by the wearing of a linen ephod 1 Sam 2.18, 22.18. The priest is *hakkōhēn hammāšiaḥ* "the anointed priest" Lev 4.3 and passim. Many functions similar to these will show up again below, as we study the cultic life of Mesopotamia.

If we use Mesopotamia as a point of comparison we suspect that many of the rites in Israel were also presided over by the king. We have an example of David dancing before the ark, 2 Sam 6.16. We see the king acting in some of the psalms, as Ps 2.11, 45 passim, 68. 29. But in the main rites as described in Exodus, Leviticus and Deuteronomy, the priest is the cultic actor.

The *kōhēn*[44] "priest" of the Hebrew Bible, kept this title over the course of the first millenium and beyond, with the only major change in function being that the office became more political at the time of the Maccabees and beyond. This title occurs in the Bible only in the m., but outside that in cognate Semitic languages as m. and f. At Deir 'Alla we find a woman *rqḥt mr.wkhnt* "*rqḥt* - perfumer and priestess." [45]

There is a woman called *rb khnm* in the Punic from Carthage.[46]

1.4.3 Less known is the office of *gĕbîrā* "queen mother." Her position is often described as equal to that of the king. He bowed to her, 1 Kings 2.19. She received subjects in audience, 1 Kings 2.13f. She sat at the right hand of the king, 1 Kings 2.19. She wore a crown, Jer 13.18. She crowned "King Solomon" as the figure is called on his wedding day, Song of Songs 3.11. The names of the queen mothers are often mentioned; the names of the queen seldom. Only one text concerning her has cultic associations. In 1 Kings 15.13, among other suppressions of foreign cult practices, Asa removed his mother from the dignity of the *gĕbîrā* -ship because she had had an abominable image made for Asherah.[47]

1.4.4 There is someone whom Pettinato understands as "queen mother" at Ebla: ama-gal-en "honored mother of the king" according to his translation. No cultic role has as yet surfaced, but only a political one, that it was she who decided to whom the succession was to be given.[48]

1.4.5 The *kāmār*, appearing only in the plural, is only a priest of foreign gods in the Hebrew Bible, and is to be compared to the *kumru* and *kumirtu* in Akkadian texts, Sec. 1.35. In 2 Kings 23.5 these officials were deposed by Josiah; earlier kings of Israel had ordained them to burn incense in the high places. Their practices are only mentioned tangentially: they exult over the calves of Beth-aven in Hos 10.5, a criticism. In Zeph 1.4 their names shall be cut off, along with the remnant of Baal, although the MT has *kāmār*'s with the *kōhēn*'s.

A new study of *kāmār* by Görg[49] shows that earlier studies related it to ecstatic rituals, especially dances. Analysis of a possible Egyptian etymology shows the same kind of association.

1.4.6 It is seen, then, there there were no women inside the temple as personnel, but immediately outside the temple, and, indeed, in a special area, we find the "ministering women,"[50] Ex 38.8, and we recall that during the wilderness wanderings, some rites were carried out at the door Ex 40.6.12.

1.4.7 *Nĕtînîm*[51] appearing only in Ezra-Nehemiah-Chronicles was at first thought to be from a root *n-t-n* "give" but then the form would be anomalous. In Ezr 7.24 they, together with priests, Levites and other temple servants, were not to be taxed, so they were treated as temple personnel. 1 Chron 9.2 also lists them with priests and Levites. They may have been housed together, Neh 3.31, as many officiants in Mesopotamia were. There were overseers over them, Neh 11.21, as there were over the Levites. Post-biblical Jewish tradition claims that they were of non-Jewish origin. There is nothing to indicate any relationship to sexuality, and no females show up in our texts. Families and individuals are listed under this title.

1.5 Offices Auxiliary to the Main Cult in Ancient Hebrew Life

1.5.1 One of our classifications in The Introduction was Offices Auxiliary to the Main Cult, consisting of an array of personnel to uphold the temple services, provide food, clothing, cleaning, animal husbandry, and the like. These are so numerous that we mention only a few of them as they arise, and as we know their titles.

1.5.2 The *raqqāḥôt* "perfumers," *ṭabbāḥôt* "cooks," and *ʾōpôt* "bakers," 1 Sam 8.13, will be the offices the king will summon your daughters to fulfill. These seem to be for the court, but the *mirqaḥat* "perfumer" of Ex 30.25.35 and 37.29 (*rōqēaḥ*, masc.) makes a sacred anointing oil of the finest spices for the tent of meeting and the ark of the testimony.

1.5.3 *šōmēr hassap* "keeper of the threshhold" 2 Kings 25.18 = Jer 52.24. The same term in 2 Chron 34.9 may be a different office (de Vaux). These are only m.

1.5.4 *Sāgān* or *segen* is not found in Biblical Hebrew as a priestly figure, but in Talmudic Hebrew the word is used for "chief" (of the *kōhănîm*).[52] This term is borrowed from the construct form of Akkadian *šaknu"* governor, prefect."[53] These are only m.

1.5.5 Women were worshippers,[54] although no titles appear, unless we have missed some in the verbs used. Women sang songs of praise, 1 Sam 2.1-10. They presented prayers of petition, 1 Sam 1.10-16. They performed vows, 1 Sam 2.ll, 24-28, Num 30.3-15. They sought oracles, 2 Kings 4.21ff. Women as mothers played a role more basic and related to the life-giving role of the Hebrew God than any of the others. New mothers went through cleansing rituals, Lev 12.1-8, 15.29f. They could communicate directly with the deity, Jud 13.2-7.

In Ex 4.24-26 Zipporah performed circumcision on her son. Manoah and his wife (Jud 13.15-23) seem to have participated together in a sacrifice. Women had access to the holy place, according to Kraus' understanding of 1Sam 1.[55]

The fullest study of this subject is Vos *Women*. He points out that women were less likely than men to have theophoric names, but that does not indicate that they were excluded from the cult (36). Most of the terminology used to refer to the Hebrew God is masculine in gender, but this is due to the nature of Hebrew grammar,[56] the masculine gender often including women. We must not take this masculinity narrowly because, for instance, God is also described by theriomorphisms (Lam 3.10, Hos 5.12.14, 11.10, 13.7) but we are not thereby allowed to think of God as an animal.

Males appeared before the Lord three times a year (Ex 23.17, 34.23, Deut 16.16) but their offering was not only for males but included females. The male was there in her interest as well as his. That was his role. The role of the woman was as mother, although the description of Deborah as a "mother in Israel" (Jud 5.7) still remains to be explained, but it is a hapax in this usage. It is in a very old stratum. The woman came to the cult as circumstances permitted, 1 Sam 1.7.(50). The passage concerning *ʾim nepeš* "if a person" in Lev 4.27ff, on comparison with other such passages shows that this includes male and female; however, a woman would not have been in a position to commit some of the sins mentioned in the first few chapters of Leviticus. Either a man or a woman may make the vow of a Nazirite, Num 6.2.

As we bring out in our chapter 2, women engaged in cultic singing and dancing (Ex 15.20, 1 Sam 18.6, 21.11). Vos feels that women played an important but by no means exclusive role in dancing (158, but his examples do not conclusively show the actions of women). Several scholars say that women had a chief role in mourning.[57]

Vos stresses (174-192) the role of women as prophetesses. He favorably quotes Pedersen[58] in explaining the role of Miriam at the side of Aaron in the controversy text of Numbers 12, that this indicates that there was a female element in the cult, because Aaron was the eponymous priest.

To whatever extent women were excluded from the temple, it may have been the product of a gradual development, as Segal interprets it.[59] Women participate in the sacrifice with their husband, Jud 13.15-23. Women had access to the holy place, according to Kraus.[60]

Women had roles in foreign and forbidden cultic practices. They sat at the gate of the temple weeping for Tammuz, Ezek 8.14. They made cakes for the Queen of Heaven, Jer 7.18, and burned incense and poured out libations to her, Jer 44.17.

1.6 High Cultic Ranks and their Ritual in Mesopotamia

1.6.1 In Mesopotamia, there was no one highest cultic rank, as there is in the Hebrew Bible, and in our own culture today. Those in our Category No. 1 in Chapter 1 come the closest to this. Though many more are given below, this category's most important titles, many of which are related to one another in the documents and the lexical lists are:

gudu$_4$ (UH + ME)/*pašīšum*,
sanga/*šangû*
lú-mah/*lumahhu*
udu$_4$-abzu/*gudapsûm*
išib/*išippum*
nu-èš/*nešakkum*
šita$_x$
en/*enu* and *entu*

from OB or earlier

Above we gave some examples of the king and *šangû* in action in the ritual. We add a few more here to show what varieties we have.[61] Those with the most details come from late Assyrian times, Sec. 1.3.4. We will find them much more complex than a simple "offering" of "sacrifice." Much of them will be understandable only in parts, but as we go on with our examples, a pattern of types will begin to be formed.

1.6.2 We mention first a rare example of one from Mari in the Ishtar temple.[62] The king is present, the *kalûm*'s sing and the *muhhûm*'s "go into a trance." (broken line ii 21-4). The songs of the *kalûm*'s, with chant titles given,[63] are accompanied by *halhallatum*-drums. The *ākilum*[64] eats, the *mubabbilum*-acrobat performs, and the *humūšum* "wrestlers" come forward. The *huppûm* do their dance (or tumbling). The *kāpištu* -women perform their act. The *kisalluhatum* "courtyard purifiers" do something (verb broken). The *luhšûm* brings water in a *banduddû*-bucket from the temple and pours the water three times before the goddess. When they come to a certain song the *šangûm's*[65] and the *pašīšum*'s approach, and one of the *šangûm's* and one of the *pašīšum's* offer the water before the goddess. One of the *pašīšum's* offers "before the veil."[66] Along the edge of col. I, almost as an afterthought, there are instructions to hold the water and food for the needs (or, desires) of the *muhhûm's*.

Despite the detail, the text seems to be merely cue-lines to the officiants, and the detailed description of the rite is not given, nor the interaction of the various parts commented upon. The liturgy seems to be neatly divided into two parts: the opening activities and chants, and the closing offering by the special officiants. We notice here that the *pašīšum* and the *šangûm* act together in a rite, so the latter cannot be explained merely as a temple administrator. The king's part in the rite is not clear, as it is in other rites. The female *kisalluhatu*'s liturgical actions, though not preserved, certainly do not fit the translation usually given (Sec. 1.12) The various acrobats and jugglers may be types of dancers.

1.6.3 The following texts show only male ritual personnel present. In the MA/MB period, in a fragment of a part of the *akitu* (New Year's) festival[67] held in the temple of Ishtar, the king and the *šangû* seem to alternate ritual acts throughout the rite, although the king is the leading actor. The *šangû* and the king stand before "the gods." The king and the *šangû* install Marduk, apparently his image, on the *parak šīmāte* "dais of the fates." A lamb is placed on the sacrificial fire. The king scatters flour over the lamb "instead of the *šangû*." He pours out wine and beer on the ground. The *šangû* offers Marduk "hand-water." The *šangû* and the king stand before Marduk. In the broken parts remaining, the king does the rest of the rite. There is a strange broken line (r. 11) in which the *šangû's* (plural) do something, these not appearing before in the plural.

Here also we have but rubrics to a ceremony, without the words or anything near the full actions being given. There is a sacrifice, which we are used to looking for, but the action of pouring seems to be the most important ritual action.

1.6.4 Another MA text[68] has only two actors, a suppliant and a *šangû* of Ishtar. It is held in the room of the temple called *bīt eqî*,[69] in Kar-Tukulti-Ninurta. The suppliant brings a sacrificial animal, enters the *bīt eqî*, and does some ritual acts of offering of incense, food and drink offering, and prostration. The *sangû's* place is one of blessing, assurance to the suppliant of happiness and health from Ishtar. Oppenheim remarks that it is unusual not to have the *šangû* in more of a ritual role.

1.7 gudu$_4$/*pašīšu* and pa$_4$-šeš / *ahu rabû*

1.7.1 We now turn to the highest officials by title. The Akkadian root of the term gudu$_4$ (UH.ME)/*pašīšu* means "to anoint.[70] The title appears in the earliest Sumerian lists, ED Lu E, Sec. 1.2.1. The gudu ^{d}gú-lá appears on a "contract" from Shuruppak,[71] in a list of witnesses others of which are a-zu$_5$, bappir-èš, sagi, dub-sar, and the gudu^4 appears in an OB list:

205 en
206 lagar
207 nu-èš-a
208 gudu$_4$
209 gudu$_4$-abzu
(and 7 more gudu$_4$- offices)

OB Proto-Lu MSL XII 40

In the canonical NA list Lu =ša, there is a long section on the *pašīšu* himself (IV 51-60, MSL XII p. 130f), and further sections on gudu$_4$-abzu ranks (IV 61-68, mostly broken) and further gudu$_4$-ranks (IV 69-75), both much broken. The section on the *pašīšu* himself is unfortunately mostly broken in the Sumerian column but contains individual signs which could give us some information.

1.7.2 The gudu$_4$ section in Lu = ša is followed by a pa$_4$-šeš section:

76	[pa$_4$] -šeš	*ra-bi a-hi*
77	[pa$_4$] -šeš	*a-ša-ri-du*
78	[nu] -^{eš}èš	*ni-šak-ku*
79	[šidim] -mah	*ši-ti-im-ma-hu*

Lu = ša IV MSL XII 131

indicating a different office, or an alternate reading. On an ED 3 text[72] pa$_4$-šeš ^{d}sú-en is the father of a *šangû* of ^{d}sú-en. One usually distinguishes between pa$_4$-šeš = *ašarēdu* or *ahu rabû* and gúda = pa$_4$-šiš = *pašīšu*. The pa$_4$-šeš appears in:

345	šeš
345a	šeš-[bar]
346	šeš-gal
347	šeš-banda$_3$^{da}
348	pa$_4$-šeš
349	nin$_9$

OB Proto-Lu MSL XII 45

which appear to be kinship terms, yet the Lu = ša IV list above puts it near the cultic title *nešakku*.

In the OB Proto-Lu text, perhaps the scribe put all the ses titles together, whatever the meaning. But if pa$_4$-šeš = *ašarēdu* is different from pa$_4$-šeš = gudu$_4$ = *pašīšu*, the former is also associated closely with the nu-èš, as seen in Lu = sa IV.

The number and nature of occurrences of pa$_4$-šeš collected by A. Sjöberg[73] add more evidence to its being a separate office. It appears first as a title at Fara.[74] A bilingual[75] entitles an officer of the temple: nu-èš pa$_4$-šeš ù šu-gi-na / *né-šak-ku a-hu ra-bu-ú ù šu-gi-na-ku*. In the myth Lahar and Ashnan line 110 has: gudu$_4$ pa$_4$-šeš lú-a-tu$_5$-àm. These three dress Lahar's "ewe's" for šu-luh "purification."[76] There is a pa$_4$-šeš of An: pa$_4$-šeš-an-na.[77]

We conclude that pa$_4$-šeš is a separate office, but mysteriously it is the same category as the gudu$_4$, and even appears like it in association with the *nešakku*. The Akkadian equivalent *ahu rabû* is a simple translation from the Sumerian signs, but its sense eludes us. Lu =ša IV.76 even puts the syllables *rabî ahi* in the same order as the older signs. Sollberger concludes that pa$_4$-šeš (=*ašarēdu* and *rabî ahi*) should be kept apart from *pašīšum* = gudá.[78]

1.7.3 A nam-gudu$_4$-é-^{d}mar-du$_2$ has a bala "term of duty" of 5 days a year. A nam-gudu$_4$-é-lugal-ab-a has a bala of 15 days a year.[79] The nam-gudu$_4$-^{d}nin-urta has a bala of 2 months a year.[80]

1.7.4 Royalty often held the titles of high offices. This was probably more than honorary, because of the significant position of the king in many of these rituals. For OAkk kings as PAP.ŠEŠ.AN, see n. 78.

In a Gudea text (Cyl A 29.6) the stone reservoir of the temple was like the é-gudu4-kù "the pure/holy gudu-house" with a never-failing supply of water. This ties in the gudu4 with ritual cleansing, as is the case with many other offices. Perhaps the water was for purification purposes, and the é-gudu4 was a temple or a part thereof.[81]

1.7.5 In a lawsuit about provisions in a field and a bala in the temple of Baba, the parties in the suit are a gudu4-dba-ba6, his brother and father.[82] The gudu4 appears with other significant offices. In a mu-túm "delivery" text of oxen and lambs for various gods and goddesses, the mu-túm's were: PN_1 no rank, PN_2 sanga, PN_3 no rank, PN_4 gudu4 dnin-ur4-ra.[83] A mu-túm Enki text, a list of garments, has PNs who are aga_x-uš "constable" and dam-gàr "merchant" as well as the same PN_4 gudu4 above.[84] A zi-ga "taken" text has PN gudu4 dna-na-a, Shulgi 41.[85] A mu-túm text concerned with animals, has a PN gudu4 dInanna, Amar-Sin 9. In a text concerning grain, PN g[ud]u4 is described as šu-ba-ti-éš "received," Shulgi 44.[86] A lú-SAR,[87] a gala (Sec. 2.3) and a gudu4 receive rations in a large tablet, no date.[88] In a text from Umma a gudu4-dnin-hur-sag pays the gú-na tax, Ibbi-Sin 1.[89]

1.7.6 In OB Larsa, the gudu4-meš had a šu-ti-a "receipt," and they did the níg-gi6 "night vigil."[90]

1.7.7 In the Mari rite summarized above Sec. 1.6.2, the *šangû* and the *pašīšu* together offer water before the goddess.

1.7.8 In a NA richly endowed partially bilingual text recovered by R. Borger[91] there are a series of incantations. A *nešakku* or a *pašīšu*[92] of Enlil and Ninlil enters the temple of Enlil and Ninlil for the first time. The *ummanu* -scholars, the other *nešakku's*, the pa4-šeš "great brother" and the *šuginakku* -barbers lead him into a place called ki-a-tu5-a / *ašar ramku* (sic) "place of cleansing"(I.5). They purify him and put fear and humility (*ašaru*) into him (I.8).

Then a list of sins which would deny admittance to the temple, as not washing with water, touching something filthy, not putting the angry tongue to one side, reminding us of some "sins" in *Shurpu* Tabl II. Then a list of incantations for the bronze shearing knife, perhaps used by the barber, each unit from here on ended by a standard line: eme-hul-gál bar-šè hé-em-ta-gub "may the angry/evil tongue go aside."

Towards the end (IV.6) there is the incantation:"I am a *pašišu*, a *ramku* of Enlil.[93] My insides are the *apsû*. My face is called...."Towards the end the text prays that mouth, hand, foot, body (or, skin) be clean, ending with the above standard line.

So the text describes the cleansing of officials with the body and the tongue, and especially the latter, but what is the nature of the "evil tongue" is not discernable. Borger (163b) compares Exodus 29, Leviticus 8 and 21 and Numbers 6 and 8. This is a very rich text, and we are just skimming over the surface of it. The sita appearing in I.1 and the pa4-šeš "great brother" in I.5 are unexpected, but cf. nam-šita = *ikribu* "blessing, prayer."[94]

1.7.9 Because the *pašīšu* appears in NA texts, we would look for it on one of the "practical vocabularies":

200 [dub-sar-zà] -ga *za - [za]k-ku*
201 [dub-sar-à-šà] -ga *šá-as - [su]k-ku*

202 [LÚ.UH + M] E   *pa - [ši] -šu*
203 [LÚ.NU.Eš]   *[ni-š]ak-ku*

Igituh

We note that the pair *pašīšu -nešakku* has continued throughout the ages, starting as nu-èš-a - gudu$_4$ lines 207-8 in OB Proto-Lu. Sec. 1.7.1.

1.7.10 gudu's take a large part in the ershemma's, as given in detail by Cohen.[95] A gudu$_4$ speaks in a obscure line in a lament, a word-play, over the wounded Nergal by her mother: gudu$_4$-e gù-dé--de "the gudu$_4$ cries out."[96]

1.7.11. gudu$_4$ / *pašīšu* so far discovered appears as male only.

1.7.12 Male *pašīšu*'s appear at Ebla, but there seems also to have been a female *pašīšu* there: pa$_4$-šeš sal ^{d}Be SAL "female *pašišu* of Bēlatu."[97] The editor finds further officials at Ebla which interest us:[98]

ensi	(written)	EN.LI	"seer, dream interpreter"
pa$_4$-šeš (1764 iv 2)			*pašīšu* "the anointed, the anointer"
šeš-eb-2			translation?

1.8 gudu$_4$-x offices

These will turn out to be only lexical entries. Perhaps some of these are descriptive terms rather than separate offices. The gudu$_4$-bal-lá = SU-*u* (*guduballû*) is a gudu$_4$ official who has a bal "turn" of office, Lu = ša IV 72, MSL XII 130. CAD G 120a describes it as "alternating in office." It also occurs among other gudu$_4$ entries as gudu$_4$-bal-a, OB Proto-Lu 212, MSL XII 40.

The gudu$_4$-bal-lá-tur-ra =ŠU-*u* (*guduballaturru*), Lu = ša IV 73, MSL XII 130 is an apprentice, or minor gudu$_4$ officiant who has a bal "turn" of office.

The similar gudu$_4$-bal-tuš-a, OB Proto-Lu 212c, MSL XII 40, is an apprentice gudu$_4$ who has a turn of office.

The gudu$_4$-bal-(lá)-ta-è-⌈a⌉, OB Proto-Lu 212a, MSL XII 40; Lu = ša IV 74, MSL XII 131 is a gudu$_4$ official who has gone out of his turn of office.

The gudu$_4$-bal-(lá)-gub-ba-(a) = *ša manzalti*, Lu = ša IV 75, MSL XII 131; OB Proto-Lu 212b, MSL XII 40 is a gudu$_4$ who is established in his turn of office.

The gudu$_4$-su$_6$-lá OB Proto-Lu 210, MSL XII 40, is a gudu$_4$ who wears a beard (?)

The gudu$_4$-zi-ni-šè-ku$_4$-ra OB Proto-Lu 211, MSL XII 40 is a gudu$_4$ who enters into the zi-ni.

The gudu$_4$-sag-luh-ha Lu = ša IV 69, MSL XII 130 is the gudu$_4$ with purified head (?), or is a chief purifier.

1.9 The various šita$_x$ officials

1.9.1 There seems to be a hierarchy of position in the lexical lists:

1 ŠITA.GIŠ.NAM (i$_9$)
2 NAM:HUB
----

14 GAL:ŠITA$_x$

ED Lu A MSL XII 10

as noted in Sec. 1.3.1.

1.9.2 To look further for the šita in lexical lists:

51 lukur
52 šita
53 geme$_2$

ED Lu E MSL XII 17

254 ÙH-^{d}INANNA
255 ŠITA-^{d}INANNA
256 GIŠ.BU-ud

OB Proto-Lu MSL XII 42

95a	[lú] garza	EN *pár-ṣi*
95b	[nam] -šita	*šu-u*
96	nam-šita	*ka-ri-bu*
97	lú-šu$_{12}$-dè	KI.MIN
98	gada-lá	ŠU-*lu*
99	šà-gada-lá	*la-biš ki-te-e*

Lu =ša IV MSL XII p. 131

112 ši-ta ŠITA *ik-ri- [bu]* S^b I 112, read as
CAD I/J 32a and Ea II.33a,
MSL XIV 248

Nam-šita in the above list is treated as an office, not an abstract "šita-ship," or the like. Charpin[99] finds nam-šita$_4$ (or nam-šita$_x$, *REC* 316) to be a title carried by several clergy of the Ekishnugal and the Ningal temples in OB times. This term does not appear in the OB lexical lists because it is "une formation artificielle recénte." (p. 259).

A *kāribu* is one who does a religious act described by *karābu* "blessing and several other acts." He is a kind of "pray-er." *ikribu* is the noun associated with this (S^b above, and A II/iv Sec. 1.9.3). This may be the Akkadian reading of šita, or the Akkadian reading of siskur, references in AHw s.v.

R. Borger[100] on the other hand reads nam-šita$_4$ as *pašīšūtu*, an expected form. But nam-išib is a title, a similar formation.[101] There is a vessel called šita$_x$-kù "pure šita."[102] This is held by the išib[103] and the nu-èš,[104] two officials often mentioned with the šita$_x$.

1.9.3 There are equivalences of šita to *ellu* "clean, holy," and *ramku* "washed," "purified."

6'	[ši-ta	ŠITA	]
7'			*[i]k-ri-bi*
8'			*[ka]-ri-bi*
9'			*[el] -lu*
9a'			*ra-am-ku*

A II/iv MSL XIV 267

Renger feels that the two terms *ellu* and *ramku* are not to be taken as equivalences to šita, but do give us the general area of the work.[105] šita$_x$^{ki} [106] is a type of place-name which uses professions, ranks or officers.

1.9.4 The šita$_x$-abzu may describe the šita's duties, or stand for another office.[107] In an epithet of the goddess Nusku, there is a call : "oh šita$_x$ (*REC* 316)-abzu, you sprinkle the temple court."[108] J.J.A. van Dijk concludes[109] that this is an official closely related to the gudu$_4$.

The abzu / *apsû* could be the large container of water in temples.[110] Strangely, and coincidentally or as a continuation of an ancient practice, the courtyard of the Hebrew temple also contained a large water basin, 1 Kings 7.44.[111] This could also relate to the mythology of the abzu.[112] Certain deities had names N-abzu: Dumuzi-abzu (84), Nin-abzu (508), Ensi-gal-abzu (526),and many more.[113] Other titles with abzu are: gudu$_4$-abzu, šita$_x$-abzu and gada-lá-abzu.

1.9.5 A similar title is šita$_x$-ki-gal-la[114] "šita$_x$ of the underworld."

1.9.6 The šita$_x$-ab-ba[115] serves a bala-term. Van Dijk[116] quotes a year-name šita$_x$-ab-ba maš-e mu-na-pà "year: the šita$_x$-ab-ba was called by oracle-kid." This calling procedure was used by the highest of offices: lú-mah, en and nin-dingir.[117]

1.9.7 The šita$_x$-UNU takes part in a seven-day rite at Larsa.[118] šita-UNU is found on a seal[119] along with PN gudá-abzu of King Lipit-Estar of Ur. He serves a bala-term.[120] Renger understands this as šita$_x$-eša$_x$.[121]

1.9.8 We also find šita$_x$-gal,[122] šita$_x$(REC 316) -AB.DI ^{d}inanna,[123] as well as simply šita$_x$-^{d}inanna.[124]

1.9.9 The šita-èš "šita of the èš-sanctuary" appears on the ration list *YOS* V 163, Sec. 1.37.1. The šita-èš ^{d}Ningal appears on a seal.[125] Renger (ibid.) thinks of this rank as a purifier, and that the closeness to the title agrig shows that one is his administrative title and the other his religious one in the Ningal temple. Charpin (p. 215) finds that the religious title is *gudapsûm* of Nanna and the administrative title is šita-èš. Finally there is an OB (Samsu-ditana) seal of a šita-èš.[126]

1.9.10 The šita-du$_{11}$-du$_{11}$ speaks in some way to the king in a broken portion of the myth Inanna and Bilulu.[127] In conclusion, it is not clear just what the various šita officials did, but the rank was among the highest. His action of "purifier," if we can relate it closely to *ellu* or one who is "washed," i.e., purified himself (?), puts it beside other offices. The *ramku*, *kisalluhhu*, *atû, luhšû, abriqqu* and many other offices have "purification" at least as one of their duties.

1.10 nu-èš/nisag/*nešakku*

1.10.1 This office is so intertwined with the gudu$_4$, išib, and šita, being next to them or one removed from them, on the lexical lists[128] that it should be considered with them. It is also in a group *nešakku, enu, edammû, pašīšu, gudapsû* in *Erimhuš* V 14, MSL XVII 67. D.O. Edzard lists syntactical usages.[129] For Ur III references, see Hallo[130] who shows that the office could be passed on from father to son, and belong to "one of the most prestigous families." He could at the same time be šabra of Inanna (p. 91).

From OAkk to NA times he was associated with Enlil, see CAD N/2 190f. **In** a NA Ishtar hymn[131] the title nu-èš-mah ^{d}en-líl-lá-ke$_4$...appears in a single ruled line, perhaps not "chief *nešakku* but a "great *nešakku of Enlil."*

1.10.2 A text perhaps from OAkk[132] mentions the wife of a nu-èš.

1.10.3 In an OB hymn to the temple at Kesh[133] associated with Ninhursag primarily, but later with Nintu, Ninmah and other associated goddesses[134] there is a listing of functionaries each doing one thing. The list contains entries that could be compared to a section of the OB Proto-Lu list:

OB Proto-Lu MSL XII 40f (with gaps)		Kesh Temple Hymn 174	
205	en	108	en
207	nu-èš-a	106	nu-èš
208	gudu$_4$, followed by 8 more gudu$_4$ ranks		
226	a-tu	109	a-tu
227	a-tu	110	tu
228	làl-e-šà-ga	111	làl
245	enkum	112	enkum
		107	lugal-bur-ra
		113	pa$_4$-šeš

Many of those in the lines in OB Proto-Lu between these offices are the ones discussed in these pages. The pairing gudu$_4$-nu-èš is discussed in Sec. 1.7.2. The lugal-bur-ra reminds us of the sag-bur-ra, App. 3.13. For pa$_4$-šeš see Sec. 1.7.2.

1.10.4 In a bilingual NA text brought together by Borger[135] and discussed above under Sec. 1.7.8, the nu-èš / *ni-šak-ku* is treated in the same way as the nam-šita (here read *pa-ši-šu*) as he is brought into the temple of Enlil or Ninlil for the first time.

1.10.5 A unilingual text praising Enlil in his Ekur-temple at Nippur, described in successive lines the gudu$_4$-abzu (*gudapsû*) and the nu-èš / *nešakku*):

58 abzu gudu$_4$-bi šu-luh-ha túm-ma-me-eš
59 nu-èš-bi šita$_x$ (REC 316)-kù-ge du$_7$-a-me-eš
Falkenstein *Götterlieder* 13f

"the gudu$_4$-abzu's are fit for the šuluhha-rites
the nu-èš's are filling up the pure šita$_x$"

The šuluhha rites are purifying ones, like the *ramku* rites immediately above. The šita$_x$ is a vessel or a prayer.[136] If a prayer, the line may be translated "complete the šita$_x$ prayer."

1.10.6 Various cultic officiants are brought together in the NA *Examentext A.*[137] A scribe is examining his son, and asks if he knows:

[eme-n] u-èš eme-išib eme-gudu$_4$
[l] išan nešakku lišan [išippi lišan pašīši ...]

"the (technical) language of the *nešakku*, the language of the *išippu* the language of the *pašīšu*," indicating that cultic texts would require a specialized vocabulary, apparently different for each type of officiant.

In NA times a mythological text might describe a *barû* as the offspring of a LÚ.NU.Eš *šá za-ru-su ellu* "a *nešakku* of pure descent." [138] A *nešakku* could be *ākil bārê* "chief of the *bārû* diviners."[139] Here we note something not mentioned above, that he could play the role of diviner. In a NA royal annal of Sargon's, the *nešakku's*, the *ramku's* and the *surmahhu's* (Sec. 2.6) are placed in the gods' service.[140]

1.10.7 The *nešakku* could mix his cultic office with political office; in NB times he could be the *guennakku* "governor of Nippur."[141] In NB times he could be the *ērib bīti* of Nabû and the *šākin ṭēmi* "governor" of Borsippa.[142] He could be the *gudapsû* of Nusku and *hazannu* "mayor" of Nippur.[143] The same person is also found as *laputtû* "mayor" of Der.[144]

1.11 síg-bar-ra /*luhšû*

AHw puts *luhšû* and *lukšû* together; CAD separates them.[145] Late lexical lists have:

37	[gu-du]	UH-ME (sign)	[*pa-ši-šu*]	
38	[lu-u]h-šá	UH-ME (sign)	[*lu-uh-šu-ú*]	S^b I
				MSL III p. 98
101	síg-bar-ra	ŠU-*ú*		
102	síg-bar-ra	*luh-šu-ú*		
103	UH.ME.U$^{\text{lu-uh-sá}}$	MIN		
				Lu = ša IV MSL XII 132
155	[ú-lu	HIxNUN.ME.U	*me-he-e šu-u-t*] i	
156	[luh-šá	HIxNUN.ME.U	*luh-šu*] *-u*	
157	[ú-ru	HIxÁŠ *e-r*]*u-u*		
				Aa V/2 MSL XIV p. 418
114	gu-du	HIxNUN.[ME	*pa*] *-ši-šu*	

117	luh-šá	HIxNUN.ME.U	*luh-šu-ú*	
				Ea V MSL XIV 400
10'	[gu-t] u	HIxNUN.ME	*pa-ši-šu*	
11'	[luh] -šá	HIxNUN.ME.U	*uh-šu-ú*	
12'	[ú-r] u	HIxÁŠ *e-ru-ú*		
				A MA excerpt of Ea V MSL XIV 404

The surrounding entries in Aa: "storm wind from the south" (line 155) and "copper" (?, line 157) do not fit into the category, so the scribe may have been putting all the HIx-entries together; however, the pair *luhšû* - *erû* also appears in the MA excerpt.

We conclude that the ancients considered *luhšû* close to gudu$_4$/*pašišu*. The Mari Ishtar rite described in Sec. 1.6.2, shows the *luhšû* bringing water from the *bīt iltim* "temple of the goddess" -- Ishtar? in a bucket. The equivalence to síg-bar-ra "with loose hair" shows that this profession also, as with some others, wears the hair loose as a cultic act.

1.12 LÚ.KISAL.LUH / *kisalluhhu* // MÍ.KISAL.LUH / *kisalluhhatu*

1.12.1 The title, from kisal "courtyard" and luh "to clean," is usually translated "courtyard sweeper" or "courtyard purifier," the latter making more sense. This is one of the many offices described as purifiers. It occurs often at Mari, especially the *TEM* 4 collection,[146] though as early as OB, and the lexical entries are:

316a	sag-ús
317	kisal-luh
318	SAL kisal-luh
319	ama

OB Proto-Lu MSL XII 44

and so on to many ama-forms, some of which are cultic functions. The NA counterpart:

1	[PA].ŠA$_6$	*ki-sal-lu-hu*
2	[kisal] -luh	*ki-sal-lu-hu*
3	[SAL kisa] l-luh	*ki-sal-lu-ha-tu*
4	[ugula-ki] sal-luh	*a-kil ki-sal-lu-hi*
5	kak-ì-lá	*na-du-ú* GIŠ.KAK

Lu = ša II i MSL XII 116

continues the tradition to NA times.

Dossin[147] describes the kisal as a room off the courtyard. In a distribution list of sheep and *malāku*-cuts of meat[148] the *kisalluhhatu* appears together with the female ranks of *kezretum, sekretum*(?), *ṭupšarratu* and SAL.NAR.TUR.TUR.

1.12.2 In the Mari rite described in Sec. 1.6.2, the *kisalluhhatu*'s do something for which the verb is broken off, but the action is followed by the *luhšû*, also a cleansing office, bringing water. The *kisalluhhatu* appears also at Nuzi, OB and Chagar Bazar.[149]

A *nadītum* gave her slave girl *ana ki-sa-lu-hi*.[150] The *kisalluhhu* appears with the Ì.DU$_8$ /*atû* several times.[151] See App. 5 for the *atû*.

Is this office mainly in the fringe provinces, and not in central Babylonia, after OB times?

1.13 lú-mah / *lumahhu* / *lumakku*

1.13.1 In OAkk times[152] a *lumahhu* of Inanna of Girsu is found. The lu-mah/*lumahhu* is found in Ur in a room or building called the *gigunû,* Sec. 4.22.15.2, perhaps the sanctuary on top of the ziggurat. In the Lamentation Over the Destruction of Ur[153] lú-mah-zu gi-gun$_4$-na-kù-za šà gada la-ba-an-lá "your lu-mah in your holy gigun is not clothed with linen." This lack of the sign of his authority is a result of the destruction of Ur.

Anu and Ishtar together are on the *parakku* "throne dais" in the *gigunû* of Ishtar.[154] In Aratta, a foreign country somewhere in southern Persia, the išib, lú-mah and gudu$_4$ lived in the gi$_6$-par$_x$-ra,[155] a building or a building unit. The scribe may have described this on analogy with Mesopotamian practice.

1.13.2 As with several of the officials, the lú-mah was "chosen by kid," i.e., by divinitory rites, in Sumerian times. In an incantation to Utu, the sun god, it says that if Utu does not come out, the lu-mah and the nin-dingir will not be chosen by kid.[156]

In the standard Gilgamesh epic[157] the cultic officials found in the netherworld are *enu*, *lagarru*, *išippu*, *lumahhu* and *gudapsû* of the great gods. A similar list in the so-called "Death of Gilgamesh," is: *enu*, *lagarru*, [*išippu*] *lumahhu*, NIN.DINGIR (*ugbabtu* or *entu*), *pašišu*, *gadalallû* (? reading of šà-gada-lá).[158] In a hymn to Inanna/Ninegalla, the goddess of war, in the netherworld there are found the en, lu-mah and nin-dingir.[159] In an Ur III composition, the "Death of Urnammu,"[160] the classes found in the netherworld are: išib, lu-mah, [gu] -tuku (read $gudu_4$-kù) and, in the next line, nin-dingir, chosen by sheep-omen.

In a section listing male and female officials in a list of me's in a myth of Inanna and Enki[161] we find an order: nam-egí-zi, nam-sipa "shepherdship," nam-lugal "kingship," nam-nin-dingir, nam-išib, nam-lú-mah, nam-$gudu_4$, females and males together.

1.13.3 In NA lists:

4	*ú-mah-hu*	*pa-ši-šu*	
5	*šá-an-gam-ma-hu*	*pa-ši-šu*	
			Malku-šarru IV (CAD L 244c)

200	$gudu_4$-tur-ra	*lu-ma-ak-ku*	
201	nu-^{es}èš	*né-šak-ku*	
202	susbu^{bu}	*r̆a-am-ku*	
203	$sanga_2$-mah	ŠU-*hu*	
			Lu = ša I, Excerpt I MSL XII 102

202	[gud] u_4	*pa* - [*ši*] -*šu*	
203	[LÚ.NU.ÈŠ]	[*ni-š*] *ak-ku*	
204	[LÚ]	x-y-*k u*	
205	LÚ.$GUDU_4$-tur-ra	[*x-x*] -*k u*	
			Igituh

Igituh 204, comparing Lu = ša I 200-203, could be *LÚ.SUH.BU ⸢*ra-am*⸣-*ku*

2	lú uz-ga	x [ ]	
3	lú $gudu_4$-zi-ni-šè-ku_4-ra	*lu-um-m* [*a -ak-ku*]	
			OB Lu C_5 MSL XII 195

For a further *susbû* entry related to *ramku* see Sec.1.15.2.

So again we see that in NA times the offices tend to become interrelated. The Malku = šarru list again shows not equivalences but offices in the general area of one another. The *lumahhu* is described as a (type of?) *pašīšu* once, and then in a more reliable list as a junior or apprentice gudu$_4$-tur-ra, perhaps read **pašīšu ṣihru*.

The variant orthography *lumakku* with k for h is found also in *šamahtu* / *šamaktu* and *luhšû* / *lukšû*.[162] Finally, the lú-mah = *lumahhu* might get confused with the ^{lú}*mahhû* ecstatic, as in the OAkk entry: ^{lú}*mah-im ša* ^{d}Inanna *ša* Gír-su^{ki}.[163]

1.13.4 CAD s.v. *lumahhu* puts the following entry alone in a lower category. The LÚ.MAH lights a *gizillû rabû*, in a late text.[164] This light was used by *mašmaššu*'s for healing in NA texts, by the *ērib-bīti* to indicate an eclipse in a NB and Hellenistic text, and by the *bārû* in a MB text.[165] This could be a *lumahhu* in a lower level duty rather than a different office. We do not know his duties well enough in earlier times, so we cannot say this is a different office.

1.14 gudu$_4$-abzu/*gudapsû*

1.14.1 In the rather mysterious gudu$_4$-abzu/*gudapsû* we understand the term gudu$_4$ as qualified by the term abzu (Akkadian *apsû*), a mythological designation of the primal waters which existed before the creation of the great gods,[166] and a large container of water in temples,[167] perhaps showing up as a model or symbol.

1.14.2 The term gudu$_4$-abzu goes back to OB, see the OB Proto-Lu list Sec. 1.7.1. It continues to appear in lexical lists down to the canonical NA Lu = ša in a way that adds another dimension because of the surrounding offices:

194	nin-dingir-ra	*en-* [*tum*]
195	nin-dingir-ra	*ug-bab-tum*
196	nu-gig	*qa-diš-tum*
197	nu-bar	*kul-ma-ši-tum*
198	gudu$_4$-abzu	ŠU-u
199	gu] du$_4$-síg-bar-ra	*šu-' -ú-ru*
200	gudu$_4$-tur-ra	*lu-ma-ak-ku*
201	nu-^{eš}èš	*né-šak-ku*
202	susbu^{bu}	*ra-am-ku*
203	sanga$_2$-mah	ŠU-*hu*

Lu = ša I MSL XII p. 102

A broken section of gudu$_4$-abzu officials also appears later in Lu = ša IV 61-68 (MSL XII 130) with only a few signs remaining. Erimhuš V, Sec. 1.15.2, has a pair gudu$_4$ - gudu$_4$-abzu. Some of the entries on the list immediately above have the older ending-*um*, perhaps showing that they were taken from older lists, while some have the later ending-*u*. The group just before the gudu$_4$-abzu contains a series of important female cultic officiants on which see chapter 4. The scribes seemed to consider the gudu$_4$-abzu a type of gudu$_4$-office. But there is always the possibility that they were merely putting all those offices with similar signs together, with no comment about their function.

The ešda vessel was held by the išib-mah, gudu-abzu, nu-èš and susbû.[168]

We saw above that the $gudu_4$ and nu-èš were paired. In NB times the *nešakku* could be the *gudapsû* of Nusku and the *hazannu* "mayor" of Nippur.[169]

1.14.3 The *gudapsû* was one of the cultic officials in the netherworld, Sec. 1.13.2. In an OB letter[170] the *gudapsû* acts together with the *šatammu*, *qabbā'u* "speaker," $di\text{-}ku_5$ "judge," ú-túl-meš "Oberhirten," *šangû* and *ērib bīti* in opening the "house of the daughter of Shulgi."

1.15 SUH.BU/*susbû* // associated with *ramku*

1.15.1 The *susbû* appears in Lu =ša I Sec. 1.13.3 as a *ramku* "purification official." Another association with this office appears with several other entries:

82 [x]-gal-u_4-da	ŠU-**ku*	
83 [MUŠ] $^{su\text{-}úš}$-bu	ŠU-*ú*	(= *susbû*)
84 [MÚŠ] -bu	*ra-am-ku*	

Lu = ša IV MSL XII 131

and also with another:

7 *su-us-bu-ú*
8 *gu-kal-lum* (variant *mu* -)

Malku = šarru IV,
K.11773 CT 18, 14

A parallel LTBA 2, 11 adds = *ra-am-ku* to Malku IV, 7. *Gukallu* = gukkal "fat-tailed sheep" would make no sense, but *mukkallum* is a "priest" Sec. 1.36.

1.15.2 An important lexical list has:

7 NUN$^{ab\text{-}gal}$ME	*ap-kal-lum*	
8 $^{i\text{-}ši\text{-}ib}$ME	*a-ši-pu*	
9 ME^{MIN}-gal	*i-šib-gal-lum*	
10 SUH$^{su\text{-}us\text{-}bi}$BU	*su-us-bu-ú*	
11 $^{i\text{-}ši\text{-}ib}$ME	*i-šip-pu*	
12 NAGA$^{na\text{-}ga\text{-}tu\text{-}ub}$DÚB	*ra-am-ku*	
13 en	*e-nu-um*	
14 nu-èš	*ne-šak-ku*	
15 e-da-mú-ra	*e-dam-mu-ú*	mú per CAD E 22b
16 $gudu_4$	*pa-ši-šu*	
17 $gudu_4$-abzu	*gu-da-ABZU-ú*	

Erimhuš V
MSL XVII 67

Again the *susbû* is in a group with the *ramku*, the latter listed as an office.

1.15.3 *susbûtam epšeku* "I exercise the *susbû* office" is a single entry in a connected text.[171] The susbu / *ramku* does the ŠU.LUH *ša a-nim* "cleansing of An(?)."[172] He also appears associated with the *apkallu*.

In The Nanshe Hymn the goddess's servants appear.[173] The ensi brings her "first fruits" (line 47). Offerings come from the bur-sag (64, a place -- Heimpel). The kuš-lá (102) and the gada-lá (103) are servants of Nanshe. The šita$_x$(*REC* 316)-ab-a serves a bala-term, for Nanshe (117). A susbû serves a bala with food (šuku, 119). A sanga is in the house (temple, 120). There is cleansing (zalag). The enkum and ninkum cleanse (šu-luh,133).

The text is greatly concerned with Nanshe's role, but I am interested in the cultic officials surrounding her. Those with familiar titles I have picked out to note, but others are hidden. The city is ABxHA^{ki} She protects the widow and orphan, paradigmatic words for the powerless in society. There are rites. Some officiants have failed in their duties -- is this mythological language for historical events? -- and have to be removed. Nanshe is enthroned before the gods of Lagash.

1.16 išib / *išippu*

Renger[174] puts this in the category "Beschwörungspriester." This may be shown in ED Lu E:

76 ensi
77 AN-[igi?]-du$_8$
78 ⌈x⌉-šeš
79 išib
80 ì-rá-rá

ED Lu E MSL XII 18

where igi-du$_8$ and ensi are both in our diviner category, see Secs. 3.11 and 3.3; ED Lu E sometimes puts its offices in order in small groups.

Yet in the several cases enumerated below, the išib is alongside high cultic officials as the gudu$_4$. Ningizzida, called išib-mah "chief išib," holds the holy éš-da vessel (see n. 168) which could be of gold.[175]

Enki/Ea is especially the god of the išib-craft.[176] Other deities to whom išib is related are Ninduba, Ninšubur, dingir-ig-gal-la.[177]

In a composition which may have been written not long after the death of Ur-Nammu,[178] there are found in the netherworld the išib, lú-mah, [gú] -tuku (gudu$_4$), nin-dingir-ug$_5$-ga ("of the dead"), and we have put the lú-mah and gudu$_4$ in our Category No. 1. Does this indicate a funerary cult? Examentext A, Sec.1.10.6, also tends to put the išib in Category No. 1, and indicates that cultic texts containing these titles require a specialized vocabulary.

As is true with many offices, this one also is described as a "purifier," which we may perhaps understand as one who sanctifies, or makes things holy, or makes areas into a sacred space:

1	[i] -šib	ME	*mi-mu-ú*	*i-šip-pu*
2				a-si-pu
3				el-lu

4 ra-am-ku
5 šip-tum

A I/5 MSL XIV 223

Unexpectedly, this list has an *ašipu*, a physician/diviner, see Sec. 3.4. Erimhuš V also has this strange relationship, Sec. 1.15.2.

In the canonical list Lu =ša there is an isib section:

42	i-ši-ib^{ME}	*i-ši-ip-pu*
43	[iš] ib-an-na	*i-ši-ip* ^{d}*a-ni*
44	[M] E.^{d}NIDABA	*i-ši-ip* ^{d}Nidaba
45	išib-gal	ŠU
46	išib-ki-gal	ŠU
47	išib-maš-šu-gál	ŠU
48	maš-šu-gál	ŠU
49	l á l-bi-gál	ŠU
50	l á l-bi-gál	*qa-ab-bi-ru*

Lu = ša IV MSL XII p. 130

This shows that there is an *išippu* of Anu and of Nidaba, and that there was a chief *išippu.* The *qabbiru* has to do with *qebĕru* "burial of the dead." The last two entries of the Sumerian column appear also in:

251 sanga$_2$
252 sanga$_2$-mah
253 a-bi-gal [179]
254 ÙH-^{d}INANNA
255 ŠITA ^{d}INANNA

OB Proto-Lu MSL XII 42

Other lu-lists have

2 lú išib (ME) = *a-ši-* [*pu*]
3 lú ME.ME = MIN

Kish Fragment II
MSL XII p. 231

which again seems to be a confusion between lú ME = išib = *išippu* according to Lu =ša IV above, and lú-ME or lú-ME.ME = *ašipu*. But instead of criticizing the scribes for possible errors, let us try to explain it: he was probably listing similar signs or words together. See Sec. 3.4.

1.17 gada-lá / šà-gada-lá / *gadalallû*

The Sumerian "linen-carrying" indicates "linen-clad."[180] An older lexical list has

8 gada-lá
9 šà-gada-lá
10 šà-túg-lá

SLT 240 vii

leading to an OB listing

553c	si-min-lá
554	gada-lá
555	šà-gada-lá
556	šà-tu_9-ba_{13}-lá
557	bur$^{ú r}$
(and 5 more bur-offices)	

OB Proto Lu MSL XII 53

and later to a NA list

96	nam-šita	*ka-ri-bu*	
97	lú-$šu_{12}$-dè	ḲI.MIN	
98	gada-lá	ŠU-*lu*	
99	šà-gada-lá	*la-biš ki-te-e*	"one clothed in linen"
100	šà-túg-TUG-lá	MIN *na-al-ba- ši*	"clothed with a *nalbašu* cloak"

Lu = ša IV MSL XII 131

205	še-bi-da	*e-gu-ú*
206	gada-lá	KI.MIN
207	bur-ra	KI.MIN
208	bur-ra	*bur-ru-ú*

Lu =ša IV MSL XII 135

The gada-lá has been found, as well as above in OB Proto Lu, several times in the literature near the bur. For a commentary on the bur-offices, see App 3.13.

Gudea Cylinder B has Ningirsu assign places in Eninnu's courtyard to kuš-lá "skin-clad" and gada-lá "linen-clad."[181] The "skin-clad" and the "linen-clad" are juxtaposed also in The Nanshe Hymn.[182] The šà-gada-lá appears in a Bīt-Rimki text among purification ranks, Sec. 1.25.3, and in a Song to Ninurta.[183]

A NA bilingual text has:

[lú].gada.lá abzu.ke_x
lābiš kitî ša ap-si-[i]

4 R Add. p. 4 to pl. 18* No. 3 r.7f (CAD A/2 p. 196a)

"the **gadalallû* of the *apsû,*" would be the expected Akkadian reading of the Sumerian line, but instead there appears what seems to be a descriptive term, *labiš kitê* "the one clothed with linen of the *apsû*," as in Lu = ša IV 99 above. Line 98 would indicate **gadalallû*, though that orthography has not yet been found for an official, though it has for a linen garment.[184]

Nin-šubur is described as dingir-gada-lá-abzu "the linen-clad god of the abzu," the sanga-gal, the ba-an-gi_4-$šag_5$ "kindly ba-an-gi_4" in a letter.[185] Here the god is clothed in the vestments of the office studied here.

In *šumma alu* Tabl 88[186] there are a series of lines 51-54 reading DIŠ AŠ GADA.LÁ É.DINGIR..."if on a *gadalallû* (if correct reading) of the temple" such-and-such appears, then so-and-so will happen. What might happen has to do with an image, an animal or a bird.

Thus it appears that the cultic officiant was named for the linen garment. There were several officiants clothed in linen: the lú-mah (see n. 159 above), the $gudu_4$,[187] and we are reminded of David clothed in a linen ephod in 1 Sam 2.18. There remains the possibility that this is a descriptive term rather than the name of an office.

The Akkadian ^{túg}*gadalû* also could be a linen wrap, so context would have to decide whether the text refers to a garment or an office. The cultic figures of the netherworld are described in a broken section in the "Death of Gilgamesh," and these include a $gudu_4$ described as šà gada-lá, Sec. 1.21.4, so here it may simply be a $gudu_4$ clad in linen, rather than a double rank.

The šà-gada-lá appears in Sec. 1.17 in the OB Proto-Lu list, and several times in the literature.[188]

1.18 en (m.) / *enu*

One of the highest ranks, the en, is depicted by a sign which is perhaps the picture of a ceremonial boat or a festive hat.[189] This has two aspects, that of *enum*, *entum* a cultic one, and that of *belum* a leadership one,[190] but perhaps we should not separate the two categories.

En refers basically to a successful business manager, and he has the power to make things thrive and produce prosperity (102, Weadock). Thus the marriage of the entu provided the power to produce abundance. The entu also prayed for the life of the king (103 -- this is another genre completely from that of a business manager!).[191]

It shows up as early as ED times:

13 EN.IB/EB
14 GAL.ŠITA$_x$
15 NUN.ME (abgal)

ED Lu A MSL XII, 10,
with Arcari ED List

which may be our en because it is followed by the high cultic office SITA$_x$. Early kings as En-Shakushanna king of Uruk en ki-en-gi,[192] Lugal-kineshedudu of Uruk, and Lugal-zaggisi of Uruk ('Third Dynasty" of Uruk) had en as one of their titles.

The office can be filled by either males or females, and the Sumerian practice of graphic signs does not allow us to determine which, unless context helps. The general practice was that the en (m.) served when the main deity was f., and the en (f.) when the main deity was m (see n. 190). In Akkadian texts, of course, the *enu* is male and the *entu* is female, though rarely *enu* is female. The en and lagar perform me-offices for the temple of Gudea.[193] In Ur III times we see the en (male) in years a and b of Ur-Nammu which tell of the en of Inanna of Uruk chosen by kid (i.e., by extispacy).[194] In an OB hymn to the temple at Kesh[195] similar functions are done by the nu-èš, lugal-bur-ra, en, a-tu, tu, làl, enkum, pa_4-šeš. The sign en appears among the by-now-familiar high ranks in an OB list:

205 en
206 lagar
207 nu-èš-a
208 gudu

209 $gudu_4$-abzu

OB Proto-Lu MSL XII p. 40

It continues to show up on the Erimhuš list above, Sec. 1.15.2, found amidst the highest of offices, *nešakku, pašīšu* and *gudapsû*.

The *enu* and others are listed as of the *ramku ekišnugal ù bītāte ilāni* "*ramku*-office of Ekishnugal (temple of Ur) and the houses of the gods."[196] This could either be a multiple office -- the others holding their own main office and the *ramku* - office--or simply a purification role described by *ramku*. An entry in OB Proto-Lu indicates that the *ramku* in his office wore a leather garment.[197] The goddess Nisaba appoints an en (IV.25) in the composition nin-mul-an-gim "lady like the stars of heaven"[198] which the editor names "The Blessing of Nidaba by Enki." The en will return by blessing Nisaba.[199] The en is associated with the mùš or múš (VI.39), as this office is in other places.[200] Inanna gave to Ishme-Dagan nita dam ki-ág-a-ni-šè "to her beloved spouse" nam-en "the office of en" and nam-lugala "the office of king." 201 Later the king seems to abandon his title of en to the cultic officiants who specifically hold that title. The title en of Uruk was held by kings in Ur III times, Isin-Larsa, OB with a few others in Kassite and MB, Seux *Epithètes* 396f.

1.19 en (f.) and nin-dingir/entu or *ugbabtu* (see also Sec. 4.9)

1.19.1 The en (female) is one of the most important woman officials in cultic life, and commentators are fond of translating her name as "high priestess." This is misleading because, first, even though of high office, she is not presented as chief over any other officials, and second, her functions are not those we usually associate with the priestly one (Intro p. 3).

She starts showing up early, perhaps ED III and Agade with en ^{d}Utu and nin-dingir ^{d}Pa-bil-sag appearances.

Her study is a complex subject, and worthy of a lengthy monograph in itself. We will bring out only some of the high points here. The en and nin-dingir are difficult to distinguish, see remarks by CAD E 173. The nin-dingir is read in Akkadian as either *entu* or *ugbabtu*. In Sumerian, en is either m. or f. The following deities have either en's (e.), nin-dingir's (n.d.), i.e., *entu*'s or *ugbabtu*'s in their cult; references are from various sources:[202]

Ur III

^{d}Amar-Suen
Bau n.d.
Enki or Eridu e
Gatumdu n.d.
Hendursag n.d.
Inanna e.
Ishkur n.d.
Lugal-amar-da (marda) n.d.
Meslamtaea n.d.
Nindar n.d.
Nin-gili n.d
Nin-nigin n.d

Old Akkadian

Enlil e.
IM n.d.
Nin-shubur n.d.

Old Babylonian

IM n.d.
Lugal-erra n.d.
Lugal-Gudua n.d.
Lugal-marad n.d.

mA-nA

Ninurta e
Sin n.d.

nB

Nanna e.

Nin-gilim n.d.
Nin-shubur n.d.
Ninurta e
Shu-zi-an-na n.d.
Utu n.d.

In Ur III times, however, the overwhelming number of the en's are of Inanna.

1.19.2 The en (f.) dwelt in the gipar (gi$_6$-par).[203] This was in the kisal-bar-ra "outer courtyard."[204] However in Sippar her cloister was the *gagû*. Sec. 4.22.15.4, but in late Babylonian texts there was an *entu*-house.[205] They may have been buried together, because Enanedu set up a shrine over the resting places of the former en's.[206]

1.19.3 There are several equivalents for en (f.). A term SAL.NUNUZ.ZI ^{d}Inanna, describing Enheduanna, is explained[207] by nunuz (emesal) = munus "woman", zi "true", so, with a leap, (en) SAL.NUNUZ.ZI = (en) true woman (of Inanna). This ideogram combination appears in a lexical list among male and female cultic ranks:

230 egi-zi
231 egi-zi-an-na
232 nin-dingir
232a [nin-dingir-^{d}nin]-urta
233 en-zirru
234 en-(nu)nuzzi
235 en-ukurrim

OB Proto-Lu MSL XII p. 41

For en-zirru$_x$ (EN.MÍ.ME.NUNUZ.ZI.^{d}NANNA) see Sec. 1.20; and for some of the others on this list, see chapter 4.

Another lexical list confirms some of the above considerations:

[en.nunuz.zi] ^{d}[Utu] [MIN (=*enu*) *ša* ^{d}Utu]

Antagal G 14 MSL XVII 221

1.19.4 When we come to Akkadian times, the high rank *entu* often translates the ideogram nin-dingir. This is also the ideogram for *ugbabtu,* and this problem is further discussed in Sec 4.9. Here we want to emphasize the high office of *entu* so despite the irregular division of the nin-dingir between this chapter and chapter 4, we emphasize the *entu* here. In early lists the nin-dingir shows up among other high ranks (note gaps):

51 lukur
52 šita
64 gudu$_4$
70 nu-èš
72a nin-dingir
73 dam-dingir

74	AMA.^{d}INANNA
79	išib

ED Lu E, MSL XII 17f

There are gaps between these similar ranks, but they seem to form a pattern. Some of these high ranks appear together in the Erimhuš V list, Sec. 1.15.2.

Nin-dingir is understood by CAD E 173 as "lady (who is) a deity." Both nin-dingir and nin-dingir-ra (normally "lady of a deity) appear on NA lists:

4	[SAL + K] U$^{e\text{-}ri\text{-}i\check{s}}$	MIN (= *bēltu*)
5	[ni] n	*en-tu*
6	[nin] -dingir	MIN
7	[nin] -dingir	*gu-bab-tu*
8	[nin-^{d}] nin-urta	*en-ti* ^{d}Nin-urta

Lu = ša IV MSL XII 128

194	nin-dingir-ra	*en-* [*tum*]
195	nin-dingir-ra	*ug-bab-tum*
196	nu-gig	*qa-diš-tum*
197	nu-bar	*kul-ma-ši-tum*

Lú = ša I MSL XII , 102

The latter entries show that these scribes had two separate understandings of nin-dingir-(ra), *entu* and *ugbabtu* (sometimes *gubabtu*), and we today find difficulty in deciding which is which on some texts, as will be seen.

1.19.5 Names of actual en's (female) start showing up with the famous en-he-du$_7$-an-na, the en of Nanna at Ur, the daughter of Sharrum-ken (Sargon) the first king of the Old Akkadian dynasty.[208] The story that he was the product of an *entu* shows that they could have children, as does the text that Ur-Nammu's son Shulgi (of the Ur III dynasty) was born of an *entu* at Nippur. The frontispiece of Hallo and van Dijk show Enheduanna's image, a rare portrait of a female cultic officiant.[209] One hand is raised in prayer. She wears a tall conical hat and a full-sleeved dress. There are attendants before and behind her. A sacrificial stand is in front of the lead figure. The text tells of her being a warrior (lines 11ff). She sings an i-lu "dirge" with a balag-a-nir "harp of dirge" (line 33). She recites Inanna's šìr-kù "sacred song" (line 63). She carries the ritual basket (line 68).

1.19.6 Another statue of an en (f.), this time also of Nanna of Ur, was excavated at Ur.[210] It is quite mutilated, showing only the clasped hands, some folds of the robe, and a foot. She is seated. It is diorite, of fine workmanship. The dedicatory inscription,[211] in the style of a ruler, is to Ningal. Her name is En-an-na-tum-ma, and she is the daughter (dumu!) of Ishme-Dagan king of Sumer and Akkad in the 20th c. B.C.E. She proclaims her activity in authoritative words. She calls herself ki-ág "beloved" of the deity, as the kings of old Sumer used to. She dedicated this statue of herself "for her life," again a term used by the kings of old.

1.19.7 In Ur III times she was chosen by extispicy, and was installed into office as shown by year-names.[212]

The en continues to appear on OB Proto-Lu, Sec. 1.7.1.[213] The *entu* as an historical figure, all of Nanna / Suen has been studied by Böhl.[214] Thirteen of them are known, all daughters or sisters of the king, from Sargonic to OB times, then a leap to NB times under Nabonidus (Nabu-na'id).[215] A special story is attached to the latter. The text says that Nanna requested an *entu*, as shown by an eclipse of the moon, and the extispicy gave a favorable omen. Thus astrology and extispicy were brought together.[216] The é-gipar was renovated, and the one chosen, the daughter of the king was installed. Then the king, in a magnanimous display befitting this great occasion, remitted the *ilku* tax and established the freedom of several cultic ranks, among them the *enu*, the *išippu*, and the *lagaru*.[217] We saw in Sec. 1.13.2 that these were also found in a Gilgamesh text as dwellers in the netherworld.

In the Codex Lipit-Ishtar[218] the female ranks of nin-dingir, lukur and nu-gig are mentioned together as living in their father's house like heirs. This was presumably during the time they exercised their respective offices. Codex Hammurapi §§178-179 has a more complicated case of the disposal of the dowry of three sisters: the *entum* or *ugbabtum* (nin-dingir), the *nadītum* (lukur) and the *sekretum*. For these latter two ranks, see Secs. 4.3 and 4.6.

Nisi-inisu is a nin-dingir of ^{d}Lugal-banda, and the daughter of Sin-Kashid.[219]

1.19.8 In an OB liver omen, the *entum* will die and an *ugbabtum* will be installed[220] We would like to argue that the two ranks filled somewhat the same role, but the evidence is sparse. CAD E 173b says that this text shows that the *ugbabtu* was a lower rank than the *entu*. Why does it show this?

1.19.9 In the OB Atrahasis, among the created beings are to be the *ugbabtum*, the *entum*, and the *igiṣītum*, who are to be tabooed or cursed so that they not bear children. Again a relationship between the offices is noted.[221]

1.19.10 In early OB times, a remarkable text shows up on the base of a clay cone.[222]It is a first-person account of an en-^{d}Nanna whose name was en-an-e-du$_7$ ("en agreeable to An"), one meaning of du$_7$.[223] There is no hint in the text that she was a woman. She calls herself dumu Kudur-Mabug (line 30, dumu usually "son") and calls Rim-Sin, king of Larsa, šeš-mu "my brother." (22). She herself is the nun-ní-tuk "reverent prince(cess)." (9)

She giš-hur šu-luh nam-dingir-šè...pà-da (8) "proclaims the ordinances and the šu-luh rites for the divinity." She is an en igi-du$_8$-a ^{d}Nanna ^{d}Nin-gal-bi "an en looked upon (or, "presented to"--Charpin) by Nanna and Ningalbi" (10-11). She prayed for the life of Rim-Sin (21). Her administrative role shows in that she reinforced the bricks of the holy gipar, made the wall and created the buildings anew (31-33), as well as the walls of the cemetery of the en-en-e-ne-libi-ra-me-eš "old en's." (34-5). Here are distinct cultic roles.

In the time of Gungunum and Rim-Sin of Larsa, the en's (f.) made sá-dug$_4$ offerings.[224] This was done in the Nin-gal temple at Ur.

Penelope Weadock presents a thorough study of the gipar, normally the home of the en,[225] yet in the Lipit-Ishtar Lawcode (see n. 218) she may live in her father's house. She does lustrations,[226] manages the estates belonging to the gipar, prays for the life of the king, and participates in the sacred marriage. This last is a complex story, and is best discussed in a unit by itself, Sec 4.23.

There was a *giparu* for Ningal in Haran[227] and one for Sin in Ur.[228] The é-gi$_6$-pàr "gipar- temple/house" sometimes gi$_6$-pàr-kù "pure, holy gipar" was the residence of an *entu* of Nanna at Ur.[229] CAD G 84b calls the gipar "the place of the fertility rite of the 'sacred marriage'." That is the direction our thinking is going, but we cannot yet say there was one "fertility rite," or if there was it was solely for fertility, or that there was an institution we may accurately entitle "the sacred marriage." See Sec. 4.20.

1.19.11 In OB times some of the instances arise which show the possible sexual perversions of the en, all on omen texts. In an omen protasis[230] the *enu* (m.) will repeatedly have sexual intercourse with the *enu* (f.). And again, one who frequents the temple will repeatedly have sexual intercourse with an *enu* (f.) or an *ugbabtu*.[231] An *entu* frequented by a *pašīšu* is not agreeable to the god.[232] We cannot tell from the nature of the texts whether this happens seldom or often.

An unusual liver omen states: *entu aššum la erēša qinnassa ušnâk* [233] "the *entu* will permit anal intercourse in order not to become pregnant," showing her possible promiscuity. A liver omen gives a dire report on a possible action of an *entu* [234] related to the presence of holes in various parts of the liver: "if the head of the 'station' is perforated and the perforation goes through: the *entu* will keep stealing the consecrated property, (but) they will seize her and burn her." And closer to our field of interest: "if the middle of the 'station' is perforated and the perforation goes through: the wife of the *šangû* will keep stealing from the consecrated property or a *sangu* will keep having sexual intercourse (*itanayak*) with the *entu*."

Another standard one contains the line *entu in-nak* "the *entu* will have illicit sexual intercourse."(see n. 232)

1.19.12 Straddling the east and west Semitic worlds, the ancient city of Emar has yielded a cache of ritual texts, written in Akkadian, but with west Semitic elements. We comment here on one of them, Emar 369, first published by Arnaud[235] and now studied thoroughly by Fleming,[236] from whom come many of the following notes.

Emar (present-day Meskene/Maskanah) was a site in northern Syria, some 50 miles west and a little south of Aleppo, just about where the Euphrates has come out of its northern flow and turned eastwards. It was on one of the ancient itineraries, as shown by Hallo.[237] The texts are of the 13th century B.C.E. and seem to draw from the spheres of Mesopotamia and west Semitic / Ugarit (Fleming 2) with also some Hurrian and Hittite elements. Eblaite and Ugaritic texts are also mixed in this regard.

Emar 369 text A line 1 has: *ṭup-pu pár-ṣi* NIN.DINGIR ^{d}IM *ša* ^{uru}[*E-m*]*ar* "tablet of the rites of the NIN.DINGIR of the god IM of the city of Emar."

NIN.DINGIR is read in Mesopotamia as *entu* or *ugbabtu*, but there is no reason, as Fleming points out, to read it that way at Emar. Dietrich, however, reads *entu*. Fleming gives other possible readings, based on one of the texts at Emar (81f). Likewise no syllabic spelling of the god ^{d}IM appears at Emar; it is probably the storm god, read Teššub/p by the Hurrians, Ba^{c}lu or Haddu or Hadad by the west Semites, and Adad by the Mesopotamians, but in this in-between culture, since the name has not yet been found in syllabic form, we cannot guess the pronunciation.[238]

He is the main god of the ritual. His consort is Hebat, a Hurrian goddess of the Ishtar type.

Emar 369 concerns a 9-day (63) ritual (Dietrich, 7-day), called "prescriptive" (70) because of the lack of detail, containing mostly what I have called rubrics. The text is for the administrators and has no flowing liturgy, but that is the way most ancient ritual texts were, according to my research. The NIN.DINGIR to be installed is never given a personal name, and our text may be one which could be used by any called to this office. *Puru* "lots(?)" are used to choose her (line 2). She comes from a "son of Emar" (line 3). She starts the ceremony from the house of her father. There are offerings of animals, wine, there is a *qaddišu* "remembering as sacred" ceremony for all the gods of Emar, in the midst of shaving (*gallubu*, line 9).[239]

Oil is poured on the NIN.DINGIR's head by the ^{lú}HAL[240](line 20). Four tables are set up before the gods: one for ^{d}IM, one for ^{d}[ ],[241] and two for the "gods below" (DINGIR.MEŠ.KI.TA), translated by Fleming as "underworld gods." (pp. 74ff)

The *mallaku* "installation" itself starts with a procession, in which $^{\text{lú.meš}}$*za-ma-ru* "singers" take part. The NIN.DINGIR carries a ^{gis}TUKUL.DINGIR.MEŠ "divine weapon," and they go in and out of various "houses," five processions in all. In a wine and beer ceremony, the men of the *qidašu* (and?) the *hussu* -men take part (line 38).[242] The NIN.DINGIR is seated on her throne and before her is set a new table of her father's house (line 40). The $^{\text{lú.meš}}$*ši-bu-ut* URU.KI "city elders" fall at her feet (line 44) and she is given gifts by her brothers (line 45). There are many offerings for several people. On the third day the *nugagtu* gives forth her cry (line 48).[243] "Seven and seven" of the *hamša'u* [244] men feast at the house of the NIN.DINGIR

She leaves the house and her head is covered as a bride (line 62). She goes to the temple of ^{d}NIN.KUR[245] then to that of ^{d}IM. Here the elders (presumably the city elders of line 44) again take part. She goes up to her bed and lies down (line 75).[246] The share of the meats is carefully set down. Later the NIN.DINGIR sits down to her banquet (line 84). The text ends with a note that when she "goes to her fate," there will be the listed offerings (line 91) but this section is short.

1.19.13 Other Emar texts have other cultic officials. Emar 275[247] has a ^{lú}*zābihu* "sacrificer" of ^{d}Ninurta, a ^{lú}*wābil i-la-i* "porteur d'idoles" (Arnaud) or "bearer of gods" (Fleming 85 n. 56), these together with the NIN.DINGIR *ša* ^{d}IM and the ^{lú}HAL being summed up as ^{lú}*ellūtu* "pure/holy men."

Other miscellaneous apparent officials from Emar 446[248] are the $^{\text{lú.meš}}$*ga-ma-ru* (?), the ^{lú}*za-bi-hi* , the $^{\text{lú(meš)}}$*nu-Bu-ha-an-ni*, the $^{\text{lú.mes}}$*mar-za-hu ša mi-Ki*. The last is to be compared with Hebrew *marzeaḥ*, Ugaritic *mrzḥ* and Ugaritic syllabic *marzi 'u* "a professional or religious group" (CAD), "ein Priester (?)" (AHw, sub *marza'u*. See O. Eissfeldt, *Ugaritica* 6 187ff.)

Tsukimoto[249] finds two terms *anabi'atu* and *munabi' atu* which seem to be related to the Hebrew *nābî'* "prophet." These would remind us the feminine prophetic-like activity at Mari, going backwards in time, and to the Hebrew prophetess, going forward. This may be compared to *munabbû* / *munambû* OB Lu D 250ff, which may be from the root *nabû*. A more detailed discussion is in Sec. 4.24.9.

1.19.14 In general, that sexuality was an aspect of the practices and the symbolism of the en is shown in the common, but not absolute, practice of the sex of the en being the opposite of the sex of the deity served.[250]

1.19.15 In NA/NB times, an incantation text[251] shows that the *qadištu*'s carry the *terinnu* "fir/pine cones" (for anointing) in conjunction with the *entu*'s carrying the *terhu*-vessels for libation. Atrahasis[252] in a late Assyrian version (following up the OB version, see above) decrees that there will be women who bear children and women who don't (i.e., who are destined not to?). There will be Pašittu-demons who snatch children. There will be *ugbabtu*'s (*uk /g-ba-ak-ka-ti*), *entu*'s (*e-ne-ti*) and *igiṣītu*'s who are *ikkibu* [253] and[254]....

We have already commented on the anomalous character of this lexical list:

131	šá-muk-tum	*na-di-tum*
132	up-pu-uš-tum	"
133	šá-mu-uh-tum	*qa-diš-tum*
134	ug-bab-tum	*en-tum*
135	ug-bab-tum	*as-sin-na-tum*

Malku = šarru I (explicit)

We take it as a derogatory statement to say that the *nadītum* is a *šamuktum* (=*šamuhtum*) "prostitute," or is it simply a description? Does this hearken back to the type of illicit sex mentioned directly above? The *qadištu* as a cultic figure will be studied extensively in Sec. 4.11. The *entu* is indeed in a cultic category like the *ugbabtum*; as we have seen, they share the same ideograms, but these have not been equivalent ranks as they have come down through the ages. Because the *ugbabtu* seems to be an interpreter of sexuality, we have put her in Sec. 4.9, but this shows the somewhat arbitrary nature of our classification system. The highly unusual nature of line 135 is discussed in App. 3.2.8.

A relationship of the *entu* with two other offices is shown in another Lu = ša entry:

26 [SAL.M] E - gal	=	ŠU-*lu*
27 [SAL.M] E -^{d}utu	=	*en-ti* ^{d}šá-maš
28 [SAL.M] E-kaskal	=	*šu-gi-tu*

Lu = ša IV MSL XII p. 129

These two high ranks, the *lukurgallu* (line 26) and the *šugētu* (line 28) will be discussed in Secs. 4.3 and 4.4 respectively. If this entry represents actual texts it would seem to indicate that the cultic activity of the *entu* continued into NA times.

1.20 zirru / *zirru* (f.)

The orthography is shown by:

zi-ir-ru EN.NUNUZ.ZI ^{d}ŠEŠ.KI = *e-nu šá* ^{d}Sin

Diri IV 55, Proto-Diri 386,
CAD E 178a, 2 a 1'

CAD calls her: "a high-priestess of Sin," AHw: "Bezeichnung der *entu* des Sin." This may be reflected in a lexical entry:

233 en-zirru (EN.MÍ.ME.NUNUZ.ZI)
234 en-(nu)nuzzi
235 en-ukurrim
236 en-šennu

OB Proto-Lu, MSL XII 41

En-zirru is the title of En-ana-tuma of Ur on a brick.[255] Several entries appear in emesal lamentations: zirru dam-^{d}Nanna-ke$_4$ / *zi-ir al-ti* ^{d}*Sin.*[256] These are among many who go to the temple in prayer (šùd / *ikribu*). She is spoken of as the wife of Nanna/Sin.

1.21 lagar/*lagaru* /*lagallu*

1.21.1 We have already seen the lagar acting along with other high offices. As long ago as Early Dynastic times, the sign LAGAR whether different or the same as our later lagar appeared on the lexical lists:

99 SANGA:ÁB.UDU or ÁB.KU
100 LAGAR:ÁB.UDU or ÁB.KU
101 GAL:PA:DU$_6$:ÁB.UDU

ED LU A MSL XII 11,
with Arcari

These cultic officials had to do with both cows and sheep, if the readings are áb udu. Later entries show this office in several different roles, one associated with the *kalû* and another next to the en. In a long section showing "equivalences" to the *kalû*:

242	$^{zu-ur}$sur$_9$	MIN (i.e., *kalû*). EME.SAL
243	lagar	MIN.EME.SAL
244	la-bar	MIN.EME.SAL

Nabnitu IX (= X)
MSL XVI 122

and as a high official treated with the en and nu-èš:

205 en
206 lagar
207 nu-èš-a
208 gudu$_4$
209 gudu$_4$-abzu
(and so on to many other high cultic ranks)

OB Proto-Lu MSL XII 40

The Nabnitu list indicates strangely that lagar was the eme-sal form of *kalû*. In this list, labar is the eme-sal form of lagar. The relationship to *kalû* may be shown in the Malku IV 15 entry: [*la*]-*ga-r*]*u* = [*k*]*a-lu-u,*[257] as well as the entry la-bar = *ka-lu-ú* in Lu = ša Excerpt I, Sec. 2.13.2, Nabnitu IX, Sec. 2.6 and Lu = ša IV, Sec. 2.3.14. La-bar appears as a lamentation singer.[258]

As in the OB Proto-Lu list, the order en-lagar-nu-èš appears also in the Hymn to Enlil.[259]

1.21.2 The order en-lagar appears in OB Proto-Lu above and often.[260] In a hymn to Enlil quoted by Alster[261] Nintu gives birth to the en, the lagar and the king on the holy bara$_2$.[262]

In the long hymn to Enlil, in his temple the Ekur, there were the en, lagar, gudá abzu, and nu-èš in that order.[263] In the establishment of the temple by Gudea, é-e en ba-gub la-gal ba-gub "there stood in the temple the en, there stood in the temple the lagal (performing the me's)." [264]

1.21.3. There was an en and a lagar in the Ekur, Enlil's temple at Nippur. A year-name of Enlil-bani (of Isin, 1861-1838) is: mu ^{d}en-líl-ba-ni lugal lagar-^{d}en-líl-lá ba-hun-gá "year: Enlil-bani the king was installed as lagar of Enlil or: the year of Enlil-bani's reign when the lagar of Enlil was installed."[265]

1.21.4 In the "Death of Gilgamesh"[266] a broken section listing the cultic officials of the underworld has:

23 [en u] g_5-ga-ra lagar u[g_5-ga-ra
24 [l] ú-mah nin-dingir [ ]
25 $gudu_4$ šà-gada-lá

with the en ug_5 and lagar ug_5 "dead en and dead lagar" side-by-side, then the lú-mah, nin-dingir and the linen-clad $gudu_4$ official. In the standard Gilgamesh epic[267] those cultic officials in the underworld are *enu, lagaru, išippu, lumahhu, gudapsû* of the great gods, somewhat the same order

1.21.5 In an incantation to Utu[268] two lines have:

45 ^{d}utu za-da-nu-è la-ga-ar nu-gil-l[e xx]
46 ^{d}utu za-da-nu-è lú-mah nin-dingir maš-(e)-nu-dib

"Utu, without you coming out, the lagar will not circle (?)/dance(?), Utu without you coming out the lú-mah and nin-dingir will not be chosen by kid." Whether circle or dance we will see in Sec. 2.25 that cultic officials do this often.

1.21.6 In the myth of Inanna and Enki the first me's to be mentioned are the nam-en and nam-lagal, the two high offices.[269] Farber-Flügge discusses on p. 102 the possibility that the lagar/lagal was either masculine or feminine, and repeats Alster's idea that the en and the lagal represent the male and female principles, but notes the lack of evidence for this.

1.21.7 In a long hymn to Enlil we find:

6 é-a en-bi é*-da† ⌜mú-a⌝•
7 lagar^{+}-bi šu-silim-ma hé-du_7-àm

(Text B) TMHNF III No. 18,
Transliterated and translated with notes
by Falkenstein *Götterlieder* 13, 56-57.

*Other texts have e
†da seems to have an extra vertical wedge
•mú-a read by Alster(see n. 263) from variants; not enough to read in Text B
$^{+}$TMHNF's text read by Falkenstein as túl "fountain, well," but by Alster as lagar.

"in the temple its en has increased with it/its lagar is suited for a peaceful hand." (translation not certain)

The "hand" may be the authority or the ability. The en and lagar are on contiguous lines. The next lines have the activities of the gudu-abzu and the nu-èš (cf. the OB Proto-Lu list, Sec. 1.21.1). Falkenstein's understanding would be quite different. Brent Alster gives a full discussion in *JCS* 23, 116f.

Thus there seems to be a hierarchy: en-lagar. Jacobsen[270] says that lagar is the second in the Sumerian priestly hierarchy.

1.21.8 In the study of *UET* VI 69 (Sec.1.22.2) [en] kum ninkum abgal abrig SAL.LAGAR.BE SAL.LAGAR.ME EN [ ] (lines 31-32) appear in a praise of Asalluhi. Following Green[271] the LAGAR.BE and LAGAR.ME are read, respectively, usuh and emeš. They are thus placed with others in a kind of a purification rite. OB Proto-Lu (Sec. 1.3.1) also shows that SAL + LAGAR is associated with those same offices.

In his article Alster, following van Dijk with a line of reasoning that has some leaps in it, suggests that the lagar could be a woman. A standard NA list has:

160	$^{su-ra}$sur$_9$	*su-ur-ru-ú*
161	sur$_9$	*ka-lu-ú*
---	---	---
162	$^{mu-ru-ub}$SAL+LAGAR	KI.MIN
163	la-bar	KI.MIN
164	AN.NU^{su-uk}NUNUZ-$^{pa-da}$pà-da	KI.MIN

Lu = ša IV MSL XII 133f

Referring to the above entry from Nabnitu IX, Sec. 1.21.1, we see again that the lagar is associated with the *kalû* and that it is preceded by the sur$_9$ and followed by the la-bar. This indicates that it is our lagar that is being listed here, not some other office. I don't know what SAL+LAGAR would be, other than a feminine of lagar, which the editors were hesitant to put in probably because it seemed so bizarre. Charpin (263) considers her a "grande prêtresse."

1.21.9 The mention of the *lagaru* continues until late Assyrian and Babylonian times. In the Nabonidus text commented upon by E. Reiner, Sec. 1.19.7, among the *ramkut* ("consecrated personnel"--Reiner) of temples, was the *enu, išippu, lagaru,* and others, not in an order *enu-lagaru* this time. And in a NA collophon (not in Hunger *Kolophone*), we find PN LU *la-gar* ^{d}KUR.GAL.[272] KUR.GAL could be read as either Amurru as in Gilgamesh XI.94 in a PN or Enlil (Deimel *Pantheon* No. 1715), but here because of previous associations, probably as Enlil.

In the same royal annals of Nabonidus[273] he told how he raised his daughter to the *entu*-ship, purified her, and then in a magnanimous display befitting this great occasion, remitted the *ilku* tax and established the freedom of some *kiništu* - personnel of the Ekishnugal and other temples, including ^{lú}*tir-biti* ^{lú}*lagaru*, and they *šākinu taqribti* "set up the wailing." This *taqribu* was done elsewhere by *kalû*'s.[274] The *lallaru*'s laments are also called *qubbu*.[275]

Because of the several contiguities to *kalû* we conclude that one of the functions of lagar/*lagaru* was that of a kind of lamentation singer.

1.22 abrig (AB.NUN.ME.DU) / *abriqqu*

1.22.1 Using OB Proto-Lu line 248, Sec.1.3.1, Charpin[276] puts this office among purifiers, and refers to the lexical lists:

73 ab-ri-ig NUN. ME.DU *ab-ri-qu*
Diri IV

344 NUN.ME.DU *a-ba-ri-[ik]-ku*
Proto-Diri, CAD A/1 62a

1"	[engiz]	*[en] -gi-ṣu*
2"	[endub]	*[e] n-du-bu*
3"	[enkum]	*en-ku-um-mu*
4"	[nin] kum	*nin-ku-um-mu*
5"	kiš[ib] -gal	*ki-ši-ib-gal-lum*
6"	NUN-gal	*ap-kál-lum*
7"	abrig	*ag-ri-qu*
8"	gašam (NUN.ME.TAG)	*em-qu*

Lu = ša II iv MSL XII 121

We would expect kišib-gál. We would expect *ab-ri-qu*, but apparently there was some confusion with *abarakku* (noted in Charpin *Clergé* 392, cf. Proto-Diri, above). Note the order abgal - agrig in Proto-Lu 247-8, Sec. 1.3.1, and Lu = ša above. *emqu* "wise" starts a new section.

1.22.2 As already noted in Sec. 1.21.8, in a long hymn of praise to Asalluhi, a form of Marduk,[277] he is called (line 30) ^{d}Asal-lú-hi nir-gál [en]kum ninkum (line 32) abgal *abrig$_2$ SAL.LAGAR.BE SAL.LAGAR.ME EN.xxx "Asalluhi en qui on met sa confiance, les prêtres enkum, ninkum, abgal, abrig, usuh, emeš, EN..."(Charpin). The order enkum-ninkum-abgal-abrig is the same as that in OB Proto-Lu, above, with the SAL.LAGAR coming after this group in the hymn, instead of before it as in the lexical list, apparently the same SAL.LAGAR. The hymn continues with various lines about purification, and the šu-luh purification rites (line 35).

1.22.3 In a NA bilingual copy of the *miš pî* "opening of the mouth" ceremony, Tablet IV 13-15 [278] the *išippu*, *pašīšu*, *apkallu*, *abriqqu* of Eridu use honey, ghee, cedar and cyprus. In CT 16 37:34[279] the *apkallu* and *abriqqu* prepare a pure ritual.

The purification that has been seen here reminds Charpin (392) of the use of ì "oil" in the šu-luh "purification" rites of UET VI 67, which she transliterates and translates on pp. 366ff, so the engiz, kišib-gál, enkum and abrig (Charpin 381-393) could have been among the purifiers of the Ekishnugal temple.

1.23 EN.ME.GI(4) / engiz / *engiṣu*

We have seen that engiz appears with ensi, kišib-gál, enkum, abrig and others in OB Proto-Lu and Lu = ša II iv (Sec 1.22.1), among purification officiants. But in other lists:

en-gi-iz EN.ME.GI SU *nu-ha-t [im-mu]*
Diri IV 63 CAD E 167b

EN.ME.GI$_4$ *en-gu-ú, [n] u-ha-tim-mu*
Proto-Diri 380 CAD E 167b

it appears as the (temple) cook, and so CAD translates.

He appears in cultic actions, as in a hymn to Nanshe[280] in which (47) the ensi carries a libation (ne-sag-gá) and (49) the engiz AB [ ] "dispose pour elle des plats chauds et froids" (Charpin 382).

In the Lamentation over Sumer and Ur: engiz ensi kišib-gál-bi eš-dašu li-bí-in-du$_7$-us "the engiz, the ensi, the kišib-gál do not take in their hand the ešda-vase."[281] In the Nabonidus text referred to above Sec. 1.19.7, releasing various ranks from duties, there are the *enu, išippu, zabardabbû, sirāšû, arirû* and the *engisu.* Charpin (381f) concludes that this office also has to do with purification.

1.24 kišib-gál / *kišibgallu*

This office appears with engiz, ensi, kišib-lá,[282] enkum and others in OB Proto-Lu (Sec. 1.3.1), and Lu = ša II iv (Sec. 1.22.1), and so one looks for it to be a purification office like them. Its translation "the one having the seal" thus does not explain all his duties.[283] It appears with the aforementioned offices in the Lamentation over Sumer and Ur (Sec.1.23), where the engiz, ensi and kišib-gál are mentioned in connection with an ešda-vase. It is a title carried by several divinities: Enki, Enlil, Nissaba, Haya, and Nin-imma$_3$.[284] Charpin notes that these gods appear in the pantheon of Eridu. Finally the kišib-gál appears on a witness list with šita-èš and gudu$_4$-abzu, ibid.

A strange phrase appears in an OB certificate of loss. Among rations appear some given to gudu$_4$-*ut* kisib-gál (*pašīšūt kišibgallim*), as if the receiver were the *pašišu* - office of the *kišibgallum.*[285] This relationship is heretofore unknown.

1.25 enkum / *enkummu* // ninkum / *ninkummu*

1.25.1 As well as the "purification" type offices mentioned in Secs. 1.21-1.24 others appear in ED lexical lists:

60 ME.EN.GI (engiz)
61 ME.EN.MU (endub)
64 SIG$_7$.NUN.EN. EZENxKASKAL.ME (enkum)
or, in Arcari's reading: SIG$_7$.EN.NUN.ME.EZENxKASKAL
65 SIG$_7$.NUN.NIN.EZENxKASKAL.ME (ninkum)
or, in Arcari's reading: NIN.SIG$_7$.NUN.ME.EZENxKASKAL

ED LU A MSL XII 10
as corrected by Arcari ED List A

Enkum and ninkum appear with the engiz, ensi, kišib-gál and others in OB Proto-Lu 245-6, and Lu = ša II iv 3"-4," Sec. 1.22.1. The reading *enkummu* is from *Diri* IV 67 (unpublished, CAD E 168b) and Lu = ša II iv.

Showing the conservatism of these lists, more than 1000 years later the same titles appear in somewhat the same order in the standard NA list Lu = ša II iv, see Sec. 1.22.1.

1.25.2 Charpin[286] wants to do away with the translations of the dictionaries: "Tempelschatzmeister (?) of AHw 218b and "treasurer (of the temple)" of CAD E 168b.

In the Hymn to Nanshe (see n. 282) line 133:[287] enkum ninkum su-luh im-da-pà-dè "enkum and ninkum call/name/call for the šu-luh-purification rites."

Charpin 389 quotes *VAS* 17 13,5ff, an incantation to purify oil:

abgal^{gal} kù síg-bar-ra ba-an-du
enkum ninkum
im-ta è-ta engur-ta bal-bal-e
dumu-abzu-imin-àm-ne-ne

"the pure abgal with flowing hair
the enkum the ninkum
coming out of clay bal-bal-e from the engur
those seven sons of the abzu"

See Sec. 3.8.5 for the síg-bar-ra "flowing hair." The word engur sometimes appears where the word abzu is expected.[288]

UET VI 69 31-33 quoted above Sec. 1.22.2 shows the enkum ninkum abgal abrig$_2$ SAL.LAGAR.BE SAL.LAGAR.ME EN [.....] together in a hymn of praise to Asalluhi in a purification context. In Inanna and Enki[289] the enkum's take away the má-an-na "boat of heaven," appearing in several different contexts in this myth.

1.25.3 A religious act in a text of Ur-nammu the first king of the Ur III dynasty[290] says that enkum ninkum-e me-téš àm-i-i-ne "the enkum and ninkum give praise" in the context of the power of Urnammu. This again would not fit in with the idea of "treasurer."

Some of these same offices appear in the "Third House" of the series Bit Rimki:

abgal-kù-ga-eridu^{ki}-g[a-k]e$_4$
^{d}enkum-sikil-la-eridu^{ki}-[ga-ke$_4$]
^{d}ninkum-sikil-la-eridu^{ki}-[ga-ke$_4$]
ka-kù-gál-abzu-a [gal] le-eš
šà-gada-lá-eridu^{ki}-ga-k[e$_4$

M.-J. Seux, *Hymnes et Prières* 241,
Charpin 391; *JCS* 21 (1967) 11, 25-29

The same syntax is thus used for: "the holy abgal of Eridu, the pure divine enkum of Eridu, the pure divine ninkum of Eridu, (the three great diviners of the abzu,) the ka-kù-gál of the abzu, the šà-gada-lá of Eridu." The dingir is perhaps a sign of honor, as it is in the bilingual:

^{d}enkum-mah du$_6$-kù-ga ub-ba al-gub-ga
^{d}MIN *ṣīru šubt [u elletu ša ina t]ubqi izzazzu*
Charpin 390

"the divine great enkum of the holy dwelling which stands in the corner" understood as the emblem of the enkum.

1.25.4 As well as purificators, perhaps acting in a different role, Charpin (ibid.) suggests that the enkum and ninkum may be "des sortes de créatures mythologiques," and she especially refers to Inanna und Enki, 11-12; there Farber-Flügge calls them "Dämonen."

1.26 endub/endib */endubbu / endibbu*

The earliest appearance is in ED Lu A (Sec. 1.25.1), following engiz. As several other offices are given equivalences to *nuhatimmu* "cook," so is the endib: en-di-ib EN.ME.ME =ŠU, *nu-ha-* [*tim-mu*] (*Diri* IV 65f, CAD E 162B), and the list in Lu = ša II iv (Sec. 1.22.1) has *en-du-bu,* also following *engiṣu.*

CAD E 162b has "temple cook," and Ahw: "Tempelkuch." Because, however, it is listed with the engiz and enkum in ED Lu A and Lu = ša II iv, which have turned out to be purificators, one looks for the endub to be one, also.

1.27 ennigi / *ennigû*

This appears in a list of clergy en-ni-gi EN.NUNUZ.DÍM = ŠU *Diri* IV 54 (CAD E 169b). It also appears as a place name of the type that expresses a profesional name: IM^{ki} = ennigi, van Dijk*Götterlieder* 78.

1.28 a-tu

An early appearance is:

65 muhaldim
66 TU
67 a-tu
68 gud-[(x)] -SI.A
69 si-DU

ED List C MSL XII 15

Tu as well as a-tu appears with other titles on the Kesh temple list, Sec. 1.10.3. It is surrounded on OB Proto-Lu by women officiants, or those who take women's roles:

225 nin-dingir-^{d}nin-urta
226 a-tu
227 a-tu
228 làl-e-šà-ga
229 šibir-šu-du$_7$
230 egi-zi
231 egi-zi-an-na
232 nin-dingir

OB Proto-Lu MSL XII 41

For line 228, Sjöberg *Temple Hymns* 186a reads làl-zu-šà-ga, with a note to compare làl on the list in OB Proto-Lu, immediately above, which I compare with officials in the Kesh Temple Hymn, Sec. 1.10.3. He does not explain the -zu- for -e-.

The two a-tu's may indicate that there are two Akkadian "equivalences," or maybe, comparing the order on other lists, TU on ED List C = a-tu. There are other possibilities. Since on the Kesh Temple list above,[291] Sec. 1.10.3, the order is a-tu, tu, (gap) làl, and the order in OB Proto-Lu is a-tu, a-tu, làl-e-šà-ga, perhaps the TU in ED List C is the tu in the Kesh list. Or, if TU is read ku_4[292] = *erēbu* "to enter," it may stand for a shortened TU.É = *ērib bīti* (see n. 293), "the one who may enter the temple," Sec. 1.45.

The other lines are explained as: (line 193) ^{giš}šibir-šu-du_7 = KI.MIN (= *assinnu*) Lu =ša IV 103, MSL XII 135; 198 ^{giš}šibir-šu-du_7 = *na-áš ši-bir-ri* "holder of the scepter" Ibid.; egi-zi = *igiṣītu*, Sec. 4.10; nin-dingir = *entu* or *ugbabtu*, Sec. 1.19

Sjöberg op. cit. 186, 109 suggests another possibility: that a-tu may be a graphic variant for a-tu_5, see Sec. 1.2.9, one of the "equivalences" of which is *ramku* :

29	lú a-tu_5-a	*ra-am-kum*
30	lú susbu^{bu}	*ra-am-kum*

OB Lu C_5 MSL XII 195

The *ramku* is ubiquitous so one concludes that the term is used in several different ways. The root meaning of "purification" is itself ambiguous, and pertains to many offices discussed here in these pages. It certainly is treated in the lexical lists as a title in itself.

Finally a-tu is a PN found in many Ur III collections of texts.[293]

1.29 a-tu_5

A form a-tu_5 goes back to OB Lu C_5, Sec. 1.28. Sjöberg takes a-tu_5 as the normal form, and a-tu as a possible variant, ibid.

$Gudu_4$, pa_4-šeš, a-tu_5, appear in order in the myth Lahar and Ashan line 100 in which they dress Lahar's "ewe's" for purification, n. 72. OB Lu, Sec. 1.28 has an "equivalence" ^{lú} a-tu_5-a = *ramku*, one of the purification functionaries. This equivalence also shows up in a NA bilingual in which ki-a-tu_5-a = *ašar ramku* "place of cleansing," Sec. 1.7.8.

1.30 TU

A reference to TU in ED Lu C is found under Sec. 1.28, contiguous to a-tu in ED List C and in the Kesh Temple text, Sec. 1.10.3.

1.31 làl

On the Kesh Temple list Sec. 1.10.3 there is a làl, in an order enkum, lugal-bur-ra, làl, pa_4-šeš. On OB Proto-Lu Sec. 1.28 there is a làl-e-šà-ga; see notes there. Jacobsen *Harps*...384 n.33 reads this as làle and calls it a shortened form for a term for "midwife."

1.32 *šēlūtu*

This office which lacks the mí "female" determinative, and thus may be a mere description, is found related to the gods in NA times. $^{f}PN_1$ *amtu ša šarri* "slave-girl of the king" is dedicated *a-na še-lu-te ša* ^{d}Nin-líl "for a *šēlūtu* of Ninlil" and PN_2 ^{lú}*išparu e-tah-ši* "the weaver married her."[294] PN_1 is sold to

PN_2 the *alahhinatu* of PN_3...the *šakintu* of the *ekallu labiru* "the old palace" as a *še-lu-u-ti sa* dNin-⌈ lil ⌉.[295]

Among gardeners is listed 1 *še-lu-tú*[296] In a text which includes GAL.NINDA, GAL.SIMxA, those who watch the Asshur temple, *lahhinu* of Asshur, doorkeeper of the *parakku*, "the one over the temple of Asshur," each having "responsibility," the *šelutu* plays a role: NINDA.MES KAS.MES *ka-a-a-ma-nu* / *a-ma-ru še-lu-a-ti* / *šá* DINGIR.MES *gab-bu ma-ha-ru* / LU.A.BA E AN.SAR / *pu-tu-hu na-ši*[297] "bread, 'regular' beer, to be seen, the *šelutu*'s of all the gods received, the scribes of the Asshur temple took the responsibility."

Menzel I 24 calls them "Tempelweihen." She explains this title as one covering many kinds of "Tempelweihen" as LÚ/MÍ.MAŠ·MEŠ, LÚ/MÍ.SUHUR.LAL.MEŠ, LÚ.TUR.MEŠ, LÚ.GAL.MEŠ·[298] I explain LÚ.SUHUR.LAL / *kezertu* differently, Sec. 4.6. For LÚ/MÍ.MAŠ see Sec. 1.42. For LÚ.TUR and LÚ.GAL, singers, see Sec. 2.5.

1.33 *pālihtu*

In late NB times, another rank shows up, and we wonder why we haven't heard of it before. In a remarkable poem in the first person by Adda-gupti (reading?), the mother of Nabonidus who had a high cultic office in Haran, she is entitled *pa-li-ih-tu* dXXX dnin-gal dNusku *ù* dsa-dàr-nun-na.[299] She was especially the votary of the god Sin (XXX), so the other deities are add-ons. Since there is no mí determinative, this may be an adjective, not a title. It seems to be a feminine active participle from the root *p-l-h* "fear, honor."

Kings are given the title *pālih* "fearer" of the god or of the word of the god, used from Hammurapi to Neo-Babylonian times.[300] The Sippar exemplar of the Weidner Chronicle[301] has a colophon by Marduk-etir, son of Etir [ ] *pa-líh* dNabû. Note again no lú sign.

1.34 é-gi4-(a)

é-gi4-a is normally *kallātum* "bride, daughter-in-law," as in Proto-Kagal.[302] It is used for é-gi4-a as the daughter-in-law of the god[303] but at Sippar the *nadītum* is daughter-in-law of the goddess.[304]

In a balag composition, the é-gi4 gal, which the editor translates "prioress" laments the loss of her gipar, her companions and her many shrines.[305]

Much information about the Sumerian é-gi4-a in a royal household is given by P. Michaelowski.[306] No cultic connections show. He notes that three other titles of women in the household are dam "wife," nin "queen," and lukur "priestly wife."

There are no cultic terms in an Eshnunna letter[307] addressed by an individual to the É.GI4.A and to the ga-li É.GEME "the whole women's establishment." (Gelb) The term É.GI4.A is also in other letters.[308] Gelb considers this a cloister, since no children are ever mentioned, an argument from silence. In another study he considers the é-gi4 as a female head of a religious establishment called é-geme.[309] as immediately above. The term is also found in OB texts.[310]

1.35 *kumru // kumirtu*

1.35.1 *kmr* is a standard Semitic root, appearing in Phoenician, Imperial Aramaic, Nabatean, Palmyrene and Hatrian, the latter with both *kmr* and *kmrt.* [311] Outside of these Aramaic-type languages, occurences start in OAkk[312] but there it appears as a type of gudu$_4$, as indicated by parallel passages. It appears at Mari in two tablets as witnesses.[313] The root *kmr* is found in Amorite.[314] Gelb lists the forms in PNs: KIMR, KUMR, KUMAR, any of which could be our term.

In a land document in MA [315] PN *ku-um-ru* appears as a witness.

1.35.2 There is one interesting reference to the female ^{mí}*kumirtu* of ^{d}Dil-bat in the context of King Haza-ilu of the land A-ri-bi[316] discussed by Eph'al.[317] Aribi is the word "Arab" in one of several orthographies (Eph'al, 6, but these do not include Urbi 7 n. 23), referring to a special group or nation but also the common name for the nomads, desert dwellers, on the fringe of the Assyrian empire.

These texts seem to indicate (though there is a difference of opinion over this) that the *kumirtu* was the official of Queen Te'elhunu, and Eph'al (n. 400) takes it that she was the "former priestess" of ^{d}Dil-bat.

Because the word in a similar meaning is not found in the dictionaries of classical Arabic, Old South Arabic, or pre-Islamic Arabic[318] (though this is an argument from silence) it is probable that the Assyrians were calling the office by their own term. Von Soden finds it to be a loan-word from Aramaic[319]-- see the references in Jean-Hoftijzer above.

One can do no more than suggest that the office is one whose title is borrowed from Aramaic, and that it is a minor one. More references will be awaited to add to the one female exemplar.

1.36 *mukkallu*

It was noted in Sec. 1.15.1, in a discussion of Malku IV, that following *susbû* a variant of *gu-kal-lum* was *mu-kal-lum*. The only other lexical entry is:

17 LÚ *ap-kal-lu*
18 LÚ *mu* - ⌈*kal* !⌉-*lu*
19 LÚ. | X.X |

STT 382, 383, 384, 385
MSL XII 233

The *mukallu* is clad in *hullānu* and *lubāru* garments, and his head is covered with *tapsû*.[320] *Hullānu* was used for clothing statues of deities, and was sometimes of linen or wool, and was the garment of the *ramku*, near to which the *susbû* is placed on the lists.[321] *Lubāru* also clothes statues, and was worn by the *kalû* [322] and *mušarkisu*, but was also a general word for clothing. The *tapsû* (NA *tapšû*) was used in a mouth-washing ceremony.[323] It was for images of deities.

In a hymn to Nabû, the god is called *b* [*e-lum*] *pal-ku-ú muk-kal-li e-še-eš-tum* [324] "lord, full of knowledge, *mukkallu*.

His proximity to the *apkallu* would cause us to put him with the diviners, but his vestments indicate a cultic official of some sort.

1.37 UD.KA.BAR.DAB.BA / zabar-dab$_5$ / *zabardabbû*

1.37.1 This is a loan-word from Sumerian, meaning "holder of bronze (objects)." A helpful modern-day article by Limet (*RA* 47, 1953, 175-80) concludes that the *zabardabbû* was a cup-bearer, serving palace and temple. Ebeling found a priest who carried wine in a vase.[325] See also Oppenheim *Catalogue*.[326]

There is an important ration list for personnel of the Ekishnugal, the temple of the moon-god Nanna / Sin at Ur, which is helpful in placing several of these offices in categories.[327] Omitting the first four lines:

5 ninda-bi 1,1.3.6 sìla gur
6 0,1.0 gal-zu ukkin-na
7 0,1.0 [za] bar-dab$_5$
8 0,0.1.2 s[ìla ša$_{13}$] -dub-ba
9 0,0.3 sanga
10 0,0.1.2 sì[la AB].A.AB.DU
11 0,0.1.2 sìla šita-èš
12 0,0.1.2 sìla agrig
13 0,0.1.2 sìla ka-zì-da
14 [ ] šà-tam
15 0,0.1.2 sìla KA-ninda
16 (r.) 0,0.1.2 sìla nar-gal
17 0,0.1.2 sìla nar-sa
18 0,0.1.2 sìla gala-mah
19 18 erìn nam-šita$_4$ ù lú-bappir
20 ninda-bi 0,1.4.8 sìla
21 18 nar a-ù-a
22 ninda-bi 0,1.4.8 sìla
23 6 ì-dug$_8$ ninda-bi 0,0.3.6 sìla
24 3 šu-i ninda-bi 0,0.1.8 sìla

The year is called: mu bàd gal urí^{ki}-ma ba-dù "the year: the great wall of Ur was built" and is the 35th year of King Shulgi of the Ur III dynasty. Note that the zabar-dab$_5$ and the gal-zu ukkin-na get the highest of rations. These first few listings remind us of the order:

13 zabar-dab
14 gal-ukkin-na
15 gal-zu-ukkin-na

OB Proto-Lu MSL XII 33

as noted by Charpin 236. CAD s.v. suggests that this is a "high military rank," as well as a "high administrative position," and also indicated as a "priestly official, "whose duties include the carrying of arms for the king." Charpin feels that the zabar "bronze" has to do with a "gobelet" rather than a weapon, and she refers to "presentation scenes" on cylinder seals. She finds zabar-dab$_5$'s of the gods Enki and Nanna. She thinks of a cup-bearer, and the usual title for this, sagi, she understands as a lower-level functionary with the zabar-dab$_5$ being the higher level one.

1.37.2 An Ur III text from the time of Shulgi[328] for Lama (protection goddess), describes PN$_1$ zabar-dab$_5$ of PN$_2$ the en of Nanshe fashioning a headdress, which is the hi-li "sexual attractiveness" of Nanshe's nam-mí-ka-ni "femininity." The inscription itself was found on a headdress.[329] A letter of Mari[330] tells of the *zabardabbû* of Atamrum, perhaps an important person, delivering wine. 2 dusú-nitá's, a type of donkey, probably a valuable ration, was given to PN ^{lú}zabar-dab$_5$.[331] The PN zabar-díb appears nine times among the Ur III Drehem texts from Birmingham.[332]

1.37.3 Among those ranks for whom taxes were remitted upon the occasion of Nabonidus' installation of his daughter as *entu*, Sec. 1.19.7, was the *zabardabbû*. This list has some high ranks, as *enu, išippu, lagarru*, and some craft ranks, as *engiṣu* "temple cook," *itinnu* "architect," and the *āriru* "miller." The order may indicate the significance of his work in the temple: *enu, išippu, zabardabbû,* KUL.LUM (*bārû*).

1.37.4 A *zabardabbû* of Ešarra, the main temple of Asshur, is the father of a MAŠ.MAŠ of the temple of Asshur.[333]

In a long list of *ginû* "regular" offerings for Ishtar and Nanna of the Eanna temple in Uruk,[334] there are internal hierarchies, showing the high place of the *zabardabbû*. Choosing three sections:

12 LÚ	*kalû* (UŠ.KU)
13 LÚ	*nāru* (NAR)
14 LÚ	*zabardabbû* (UD.KA.BAR.DAB.BU)
15 LÚ	*sirāšû*
34 LÚ	*zabardabbû* (KA.BAR.DAB.BA)
35 LÚ	*kalû* (UŠ.KU)
36 LÚ	*nāru* (NAR)
61 LÚ	*kalû* (UŠ.KU)
62 LÚ	*nāru* (NAR)
63 LÚ	*zabardabbû* (UD.KA.BAR.DAB.BA)
64 LÚ	*sirāšû* (?)

At the beginning of the text are found the *šešgallu* (line 3), *šatammu* (7), *šangû narkabti* ("*šangû* of the battlewagon," 10), and at the end:

94 LÚ	*šešgallu* (ŠEŠ.GAL)
95 LÚ	*mahhû* (GUB.BA) "ecstatic"
96 LÚ	*kurgarrû* (KUR.GAR)
97 LÚ	*ṭābihu* (GÍR.LÁ) "daggerman"

The distribution is mostly to cultic officials and food-related offices. At the head of each section are the king, *šešgallu*, *ērib bīti's*, *šatammu*. The *zabardabbû* seems to be as important as the *kalû* and the *naru*.

1.38 ŠEŠ.GAL / *šešgallu*

1.38.1 In OB Proto-Lu Sec.1.7.2, the šeš-gal appears, but the surrounding words do not help, because the scribe simply collected all the signs containing šeš. AHw s.v. indicates two meanings, one the expected one: "grosser Bruder" (older brother?) and the other: "ein Oberpriester." On lexical lists:

115 *šeš-gal-lum*
118 *ú-ri-gal-lum*

Aa Tablet I/6 = 6 (Ea I 260-97)
MSL XIV 228

AHw lists these under the first category, that of "grosser Bruder." AHw s.v. *šešgallu* reads the signs this way, not **urigallu*, a word for their standard or emblem. (See CAD G 8a, s.v. *gadalu*, 2.)

1.38.2 In the list of ranks given *ginû* "regular" offerings for Ishtar and Nanna of the Eanna temple at Uruk in Sec. 1.37.4, there seems to be a kind of internal hierarchy, and the *šešgallu* is found just below the king.

1.38.3 LU ŠEŠ.GAL-*tú* (*šešgallūtu*) is bestowed as an office before Sin who dwells in Harran in a NA royal annal note.[335] In a NB kudurru, a number of temple personnel with typical NB titles are listed: *šarru* "king," *mār šarri* "crown prince," *rubû* "prince," *aklu* "leader," *šāpiru* "commander," *dayanu* "judge," *šatammu* (see App. 5), *šākin ṭēmi* "one in charge of the instruction or understanding," usually "governor," *šešgallu*, *ērib bīti's*.[336]

1.38.4 A functionary who appears often at Ebla is the šeš-2-eb.[337]

1.39 gal-zu-ukkin-na / *rabi puhri*

In Sec. 1.37.1, we saw a high rank gal-zu-ukkin-na (*YOS* V 163.6) receiving as much ration as the *zabardabbû*. In NA times[338] this office is given an equivalent of *rab (i) puhri* "master of the assembly," although the Sumerian indicates "the great wise one of the assembly". Charpin *Clergé* 236 finds only one other occurrence[339] dated in the 10th year of Rim-Sin of Larsa. There he speaks in conjunction with some judges over a land dispute. No direct cultic elements have been found as yet.

The gal-ukkin-na (above 1.37.1 from OB Proto Lu) is not related, being *muwirrum / mu'irrum* "commander," despite the two together on the same list.

1.40 AB.(A).AB.DU_7/DU / *ababdû* or *ešabdû*

Its reading (it may be EŠ.(A).AB.DU(7)) and its etymology are uncertain. In an OB legal document,[340] the AB.AB.DU is the first witness, others being *ša nindabû*, *rab banî*, *purkullu* "seal cutter," and *šumēlu* (LÚ.Á.GÙB.BU). On other witness lists with *ababdû* from OB times others were cultic officials, as *šangû* and *kišibgallu* (CAD A/1 2b).

On the ration list *YOS* V 163 (Sec. 1.37.1) the *ababdûm* appears surrounded by cultic figures.[341] There could have been three *ababdûm*'s in the Ekishnugal at the same time in the reign of Rim-Sin, and perhaps two at the same time in the same sanctuary.[342] The AB.AB.DU_7 *ša* ^{d}Nergal was the addressee of a letter.[343] CAD A/1 2a calls the *ababdû* an "administrative temple official."

1.41 a-ga-am (f.)

There is a women's office a-ga-am about which we know very little. It appears with muš-lah$_4$, nar, sagi "cupbearer," ì-dug$_8$, šu-ku$_6$ "fisherman," mušen-dù[344] in the temple of ^{d}Shulgi in Guabba. She appears with bur-sag, ga-íl "carrier of cheese (?)," gemé-kikken "flour miller," nar, má-lah$_4$, kisal-luh and mušen-dù.[345] She appears in a long text from Lagash as a-ga-am ^{d}nin-dar-a ki-ès-sá^{ki} "the agam of Nindara of (the place) Kiessa.[346]

1.42 LÚ.MAŠ and MÍ.MAŠ

This apparently simple but actually mysterious term appears in several NA lexical lists:

11 ⌜LÚ.X.X⌝
12 LÚ.MAŠ$^{ma-\ ⌜šu-ú⌝}$
13 SAL.MAŠ
14 LÚ.⌜PA$_4$.BIL⌝.[GA$^?$]

Sultantepe VIII MSL XII 236

The reading is thus given as *mašû* (CAD M/1, 401a, but not as a title).

12 LÚ.NINDA.KU$_7$.KU$_7$
13 LÚ.BAR/MAŠ // LÚ.NU.GIG
14 LÚ (erasure)

Kouyunjik List K. 4395 iv
MSL XII 239

There are several female officials who appear on the Sultantepe list, but only male offices appear on the Kouyunjik list, some of which are cultic in nature. There are two other examples in K. 4395 of two entries on one line, and in both of these cases they are variant spellings. There are instances in that list of two orthographies written on contiguous lines. But LU.MAŠ is difficult to explain as a variant of LÚ.NU.GIG.

It is found on the curse formula in a NA contract:[347] LÚ.MAŠ and MI.MAS to Adad, along with *kezru*'s and *kezertu*'s to Ishtar. Menzel[348] puts them under a category called *šeluāte* "Tempelweihen."

1.43 PA.KAB.DU / *širku* and *širkatu*

The *širkutu* was an order of men and women related to various deities, as Shamash, Nabû, Marduk, Ishtar.[349] They could be workmen or women, deal in money affairs, and have seals (p. 28). They were marked with a star (*kakkabtu*) upon the hand, and could be handed over to Ishtar while in slave status. One religious act described rather cryptically by Dougherty (68) is unfortunately brief: PN the *širku* (PA.KAB.DU) of the goddess Bēlit of Uruk entered the gate *ina eli ta-bi-e ša* ^{d}Askayaitum...*šal-la-tum* GAL- *tum* "in connection with the rising / resurrection of Askayaitum, the great booty." Was the *širku* himself the "great booty" of the service of "rising of the god?"

The word appears rarely in Assyrian, and in Babylonian especially in the late periods. A few appearances are female.

1.44 *kiništu*

This word appears in various orthographies: *kiništu, kinaštu, kinartu, kinaltu.* It is defined as: "a class of priests of low status (concerned with the preparation of food offerings)." (CAD s.v.) It appears to be from the Aramaic root *k-n-š*.[350] In one case the word-sign appears as lúUKKIN, usually *puhru* "assembly," but here AHw reads *kiništu*.[351] It appears mostly in NB contexts, and is rare in NA.

This term summarizes a list of cultic officials who had their taxes and other duties remitted upon the consecration to the *entu* - ship of Nanna of the daughter of Nabonidus, Sec. 1.19.7. Line 70 calls them lú*ki-ni-iš-tum* "the collegium of priests."[352] Since some of these are on a high level, the word in this case could not mean those of low status.

They had the authority to speak together with the *ērib bīti*'s to the *puhur* lú*māre Babili u Uruk* "the assembly of the citizens of Babylon and Uruk" concerning food to be given for the *makkūru* "property" of Eanna.[353] They seems to appear often with the *ērib bīti's* (see references in CAD K and AHw, s.v.), and both of these generalized offices may be related in some way.

In a Neriglissar text[354] there are the *ramkūti kiništi* é-sag-ila, "the purification collegium and *kiništu's* of (the temple) Esagila." The "and" is indicated because the *ramkūt* and *kiništu* appear as separate listings on a Nebuchadnezzar text.[355]

1.45 TU.É / *ērib bīti*

In an OB letter, the *gudapsû* acts together with the *qabbā'u* "speaker" the *šangû* and the *ērib bīti* in opening the "house of the daughter of Shulgi."[356] In NB times, the high rank *nešakku* could be *erib biti* of Nabû, Sec. 1.10.7. In a *ginû* offering, the *ērib bīti's* are together with the king, the *šangû, šatammu and šešgallu*, Sec. 1.37.4. The *kiništu*'s appear together with the *erib biti*'s often, Sec. 1.44.

This rather vague-sounding office starts appearing in OB times, but it has not yet been found in lexical lists. It can appear in the singular or the plural. It can appear as *ērib bīti* of a god-name. It appears most often in NB and Seleucid times, although a few entries in NA are also found. In NB the office could be held jointly with other offices: *šatammu*, *šākin ṭēmi*, *nešakku*, *šangû*, *ṭupšarru*, *kalû* (Sec. 2.3.18).

CAD lists several examples of the *ērib bīti* engaging in ritual acts, but the most details are found in Seleucid texts, when things had changed from earlier times. CAD calls him a "person admitted to all parts of the temple," but I don't know what that means in practice. Despite the relatively large number of occurrences, none of them describe what this person does, before Seleucid times.

1.46 *maqaltanu*

There is one reference in the dictionaries to this word, ABL 633 r.(!)6, s.v. It corrects Waterman's reading. A LÚ.SAG *ma-qa-al-ta-a-nu* of the god

Ba'al Rakkab of Sam'al is in a broken context at the beginning of the letter.[357] If it is from a West Semitic root, it could be from *m-q-l* "to burn." A burnt-offering is called *maq (a)lutu*, CAD M/1 252.

1.47 *ramku // murammiku*

1.47.1 At times the term *ramku* seems to be an adjective "washed, purified" and at times to be the name of an office. When the latter, it is difficult to decide whether it is an office in itself, or a generalized term for a type of officiant, as *ērib bīti* or *kiništu*. It is listed along with other ranks in:

201	nu-^{eš}èš	*né-šak-ku*
202	susbu^{bu}	*ra-am-ku*
203	sanga$_2$-mah	ŠU-*hu*

Lu = ša I MSL XII 102

There is a *ramku* among other leather-clad offices:

550	kuš$^{[a\text{-}gu\text{-}úh\text{-}hu\text{-}um\ ]}$ lá
551	kuš [ ]-*ni* - [ ] lá
552	kuš ⌈*na-ah* ⌉-*la-ap-tum* lá
553	kuš$^{ra\text{-}am\text{-}kum}$ lá
553a	kuš[*š*]*a si-bi-ir-ri* lá

OB Proto-Lu MSL XII 52f

A *pašīšu* in a NA incantation text (n. 89 and Sec. 1.7.8) calls himself a *ramku*.

1.47.2 *ramku* is a word used in a similar way to other terms for "clean, pure": *ellu, ebbu* and *šuluhhu,* the latter literally having to do with the washing of the hands, but it came to mean washing in general. Washing hands and mouth were ritual acts. AHw s.v. *šuluhhu* notes a possible priestly office ^{lú}ŠU.LUH/*šuluhhu*.[358]

1.47.3 Laessøe[359] noted the profession *murammiku*, some kind of cleaner, from the same root.

1.48 Peg-deposits and basket-carriers

The peg-deposits probably depict only men.[360] Some kanephoroi/ai "basket-carriers" were women, as seen in the statuary. There is mention of basket-carrying in The Exaltation of Inanna, line 68. See also Iraq 10 (1948) 97, and Hallo, HUCA 33, 11 n.79.

1.49 The king

In Mesopotamia and in Israel, the king is often the chief cultic actor, as seen in many of the above references. The titles of and offices held by the king do not necessarily describe his actions -- they may be honorary. We find[361] the king entitled *išippu* (NA), *pašīšu* (OAkk), *šabrû* (NA), *šangû* (NA), en (Ur III, OB), išib (Ur III, OB).

In most of the MA and NA rites summarized on 6ff above the king is the main actor, often with the *šangû*. He plays a musical instrument in Secs. 2.3.9, 2.4.5, and 2.4.10, thus taking a musician role.

1.50 Ugaritic Cultic Functionaries

1.50.1 *inš, inš ilm*: Many Ugaritic officiants can, with a greater or lesser measure of surety, be related to a Hebrew or a Mesopotamian office. Not so with the *inš* and the *inš ilm.* Tarragon[362] after giving evidence that it is not a name of a deity, shows the difficulty in being precise about its function. The *inš ilm* appears mostly in rituals of "purification et de désacralisation du roi," as well as in a "ritual de transfert des divinités." (133). One text[363] is a mixture of Ugaritic and Hurrian, and what is offered is Hurrian, *athlm,* but some animals in Ugaritic are also offered.

1.50.2 *inšt*: A substantive *inšt* is found in texts outside of ritual ones, in lists of professions or guilds:

qd (?) [*šm*	]	
mr'u *s* [*kn*	]	
mr'u *'ib* [*rn*	]	
mdm	1	
'inšt	[ ]	
nsk.ksp	2	"silversmith"
yṣḥm	1	
ḥrš mrkbt	1	"wagonmaker"
ḥrš qṭn	1	"maker of *qṭn*"
ḥrš bhtm	2	"maker of houses"

UT 114, CTA 73

Dietrich and Loretz[364] note that Aistleitner, J.C. de Moor, Whitaker, van Zijl, and C.H. Gordon take *minšt* from *a-n-š*, I "be weak," II "be a companion, intimate friend." Dietrich and Loretz refer to *'nš* "man." In the phrase *inš.ilm* the translation could be "belonging to the gods." The appearance of *'inš* in several lists shows perhaps a profession or a place in society. Many more references are needed to say anything more definite. However, there may be no relationship between the *inšt* and the *inš,* and there is no indication that the former is the feminine of the latter.

1.50.3 *khnm* "priests" cognate with Hebrew *kōhānîm* are found on lists side-by-side with the *qdšm*, Sec. 4.19. The *khnm* are not mentioned in connection with any ritual, although it is an argument from silence to make such a statement when new texts are still being discovered. The feminine is not attested. The king of Ugarit, as in the Hebrew Bible, acts the role of priest at times.

1.50.4 *rb khnm* are found associated with rituals, but we do not know the liturgical role they played, and if we should understand them analagously with their Hebrew cognates.[365]

1.50.5 *nqdm* are usually translated "shepherds," but the title may not concern the shepherd of the fields but be symbolic, rather than agricultural, and we compare the use of sipa "shepherd" as the title of the leader in ancient Sumer. In the Hebrew Bible, the prophet Amos, in Amos 1.1 and Mesha king of Moab 2 Kings 3.4 are designated *nōqĕdîm*, in two quite different social roles.

Dietrich and Loretz [366] suggest that they are some sort of animal commissioners in the palace. Despite the closeness to *khnm* on some lists, nothing yet discovered indicates that the *nqdm* are personnel of the cult. The *rb nqdm* and *rb khnm* sometimes appear together.[367]

1.50.6 *ṯnnm*: A term associated with the *khnm, nqdm and qdšm* is the *ṯnnm*. On the lists the order is always *ṯnnm, nqdm, khnm, qdšm*. Rainey [368] suggests "archers." B. Cutler and J. Macdonald picked this up, but later suggested they were merchants of herds,[369] associated with *nqdm*, as Rainey had said. The *ṯnnm* are present, without association with *khnm,* in other texts and the suggestions run from "gardes" to "sacristains."[370]

1.50.7 *rb mrzḥ*: The name of a feast-institution of some sort, societal but with religious dimensions.[371] Pope relates the feast to the departed ancestors. Other scholars emphasize its drinking aspect. It occurs among Akkadian texts from Ugarit.[372] Eissfeldt[373] gives the etymology. Lewis[374] gives a run-down of present-day research, taken from his longer study.[375]

1.50.8 *ytnm* are translated by T. Yamashita[376] as "votary members of a temple guild," but this is too much under Biblical influence, according to Tarragon.[377]

1.50.9 *tbṣr* Rainey [378] finds a *tbṣr klt.bt špš* "*tbṣr* - bride of the temple of Shapash, the sun-goddess." Whether this is a title and will turn out to be a priestess or not must await further references. The Akkadian cognate *kallātu* "bride" is used as an epithet of certain goddesses in OB, NA and NB times, some related to Shamash the sun-god, CAD K 81bf.

1.50.10 *kumru*(?). Rainey finds[379] a possible reference to Hebrew *kōmēr* and Akkadian *kumru* : *bītum*^{tum} ^{d}*ba'al huršan* [*ha-zi*] *ú* ^{lú} $^{(?)I}$*kug-um-*[*ra-šu* (??)] *a-na* ^{I}*KAR* ^{I}*kusuh la-a ú-te-bu-ú* "the temple of Ba'al of Mount [Hazi] and its (?) *kumru* (?) against KAR kušuh are not erected." See Sec. 1.35.

1.50.11 ^{lú}*ša nāqî* "libation pourers," Rainey ibid., RS 16.257:B, III, 56, *MRS* III, among a list of PNs, designated as ^{lú}*aširuma* "instructors," priests, ^{lú}UN.TU, ^{lú}mur'u *usriyanni*, and ^{lú}*ša* KU[ ] , cooks.

1.50.12 *klt bt špš* "bride of the sun temple." See Sec. 1.50.9.

1.50.13 Other miscellaneous positions are listed by Dietrich and Loretz: *barû* as *hupše* and *name* classes; *nāru* as *haniahhe* and *eku* classes; *nāru* as *ehele* and *šūzubu* classes. [380]

Notes

1 W. W. Hallo, "Women of Sumer," in B. Schmandt-Besseret (ed.), *The Legacy of Sumer*, Malibu, 1976, from lectures given in 1975, 23-40.

2 A. Parrot, *Sumer* 87; H. Lentzen, *ZA* 45 (1939) 85-7.

3 L. Woolley, *The Royal Cemetery, UE* II (1934) pl. 110 and passim.

4 Harris *Sippar*, Index p. 392; "Hierodulen," *RLA* IV 391-3; "The naditu woman," in *Studies Oppenheim* 106-135. Her studies especially deal with the texts from Sippar.

5 Harris *Sippar* 305.

6 J. Renger, "Gotternamen in der altbabylonischen Zeit," in Falkenstein AV.

7 *Maqlû* III 40ff. There are problems in understanding this combination of ranks, however. Some do not fit into the category of witch. See Sec. 3.20.5.

---

8 There are two regular words for "prostitute": *harimtu*, the usual one, and *šamhatu*, in several orthographries. We do not know the nuances of meanings of the two words.

9 Sollberger and Kupper *Inscriptions* IB4a.

10 dNin-in-si-na, Gurney, *OECT* V No. 8.22; Inanna in Iddin-Dagan's "sacred marriage hymn," *JCS* 25 (1973); Chiera *SRT* 1.

11 Ana ittišu 7, III, 1-21, MSL 1 99-101.

12 Assur Photo 4128, Ebeling Stiftungen IV. Postgate *Royal Grants*, 120, considers it a NA copy of a MA text. Corrections of Ebeling's transcription by R. Frankena, *OLZ* 51 (1956) cols. 134ff with notes by Postgate *Royal Grants*, 118ff. Transliteration in Menzel *Tempel* II T8-11. Copy of selected lines in *Or* 17 pls. 32-34

13 The orthography shown by dGAŠAN-*at-ni-ip-ha ABL* 1221.r.6. CAD E 253b: Bēlat-natha. CAD N/2 s.vv., *nathi, niphu* A p.243b; Schramm *Einleitung* II 90f: 2 (Shalmaneser III) shows that there are two temples, of dBēlat-natha and dBēlat-nipha. It is difficult to decide in any one case between Sharrat- and Bēlat-.

14 Hunger *Kolophone* No. 152.

15 R.D. Biggs, *Or* NS 36 (1967) 59.

16 *UET* V 191 (U.7836 gamma), in Charpin *Clergé* 85.

17 *ARM* 10 52.7.

18 *ARM* 10 50.14ff.

19 *ARM*10 51.9.

20 K. Fr. Muller, *Das Assyrische Ritual* , *I MVAG* 41/3 (1937) pp.4-58.

21 Root *garāru*, "touches his forehead to the ground" Muller ibid. 20; "rolls over" CAD; "creeps along the ground," AHw 902b, in any case an expression of humility.

22 A title found with many NA kings, Seux *Epithètes* 287.

23 Livingstone *Poetry* No. 37.19' = K.3476 = CT 15 43f.

24 A. 125, transliterated and translated with notes in Menzel *Tempel* II No. 24, editio princeps van Driel *Cult of Assur* 122-131.

25 A. 181, transliterated and translated with notes by Menzel *Tempel* II No. 26, editio princeps van Driel *Cult of Assur* 196-7.

26 Note closeness of this portion with Speleers *Recueil* 308:5; see CAD L 25b.

27 Translated by E. Ebeling, *Or* 21 (1952) 142ff, the whole series being given by G. Meier, *AfO* 12 (1937-49) 40-45.

28 Ebeling: "withdraw," but he filled in this broken word from another line. This brings up the difficult question of whether or not there were people outside of cultic officials present at a ritual of this kind. This shows that there were, at least at the first part, as does *RA*cc 91.20 and r. 4 when "the people" are sprinkled by the *Kalamahu* (CAD N/2 285b). These still could refer to minor cultic officials rather than ordinary citizens. In the Bīt Rimki ritual (Laessøe Bīt Rimki 26 ii 7 p. 102) NITA u SAL "men and women" participate in the early stages. In a nB (?) ceremony, the *lilissu*-kettledrum was played at the great gate of E-Babbar and all the people of Uruk saw it and (presumably) heard the *kalû*'s saying, "There is an eclipse" *RA* 23:19 and 21.

29 Note the case of a *nāru* performing ritual acts.

30 E. Ebeling, *Or* 20 (1951) 401-5.

31 E. Ebeling, *Or* 22 (1953) 25-27.

32 E. Ebeling, *Or* 22 (1953) 27-32.

33 E. Ebeling, *Or* 22 (1953) 36-40.

34 A Cavigneau *Bagh Mitt* 10 (1979), copy p. 112, transliterated p. 115, translated p. 116, first year of Marduk-balassu-iqbi, i.e., about 818 B.C.E.

35 Menzel *Tempel* I 130ff.

36 *AOAT* 12p. 35, to *ARM* 10, 34.3'.

37 J. Bottéro, in P. Grimal (ed.), *Histoire Mondiale de la Femme* I 218.

38 Meissner *BuA* II 69, commenting on *ADD* 827 r.10. I have collated this, and it is a difficult sign to read. This list has been collated by F.R. Kraus, and commented upon by B. Landsberger, Baumgartner AV 202ff, see App.3.3.1. In 1911 C. Frank, *Studien zur babylonische Religion* I Strassburg, 1911, p. 50 had taken up Johns' original reading in *ADD* and listed it as SALŠID, the female *šangû*.

39 *STVC* 75, A. Falkenstein, *ZA* NF 13 (1947), 215, as quoted in H. Sauren, *XVII Rencontre 18.*

40 In the Book of Acts 14.23 and 20.17 this office has oversight of the congregation. In 1 Pet 5.1, it seems to be an office-bearer. In Titus 1.5 they take part in ordinations. In Rev 4 and elsewhere in the book they take a liturgical role. The interpretation of the usage in 2 and 3 John, as the writer, is not agreed upon, G. Bornkamm, *TDNT* VI 1968 (1959), 670.

41 Tertullian, *De Baptismo,* xvii; *De exhortatione castitatis*, vii.

42 M. Haran in Fox *Temple* 18.

43 There are hundreds of books on this topic, but only a few take up seriously the subject of function: Kraus *Worship*; Rowley *Worship*; M. Haran "Priests and Priesthood. Cultic Functions, *EncJud* 13 1076-1080; L. Sabourin, chap 4, "Israelite Priesthood," in *Priesthood. A Comparative Study*. Leiden, 1972; H. Ringgren, *Israelite Religion*, Philadelphia, 1966 (German, Stuttgart, 1963) 209-212.

44 *k-h-n*, the standard root in West Semitic languages. Ranging back and forth among Semitic languages can be misleading, but we merely note here that in some Ugaritic texts, *khn* is explained as *šangû*. PRU II No. 26 and PRU VI No. 93.

45 I.41 A Palestinian site dated perhaps in the first part of the first millenium B.C.E. A.Caquot and A. Lemaire, *Syria* 54 (1977) 200, line 11. the editors say that the word *khnt* could be analyzed differently.

46 Lidzbarski *Ephermeris* III 57D, in *KAI* 95.1.

47 Zafrira Ben-Barak, "The status and right of the gebira,"*JBL* 110 (1991) 25. See especially G.W. Ahlström, *Aspects of Syncretism in Israelite Religion* (Lund: Gleerup, 1963), p. 61; he would emphasize the religious nature of the office, pp.57-88, especially p. 75. Redactional information, including a list of PNs, is found in Baruch Halpern and David S. Vanderhooft, *HUCA* 62 (1991), 197-9; n. 44 suggests a cultic position for her.

---

48 G. Pettinato, *Ebla. A New Look at History*, Baltimore and London, 1991 (Italian original, Milano, 1986), an up-date of an earlier work: *The Archives of Ebla*, Garden City, 1981, p. 76.

49 Manfred Görg, *BN* 30 (1985) 7-14.

50 Should we take this as a title, as some do? Mirrors would have something to do with the enhancement of beauty. But this is not enough information to make a decision about the sexual life of these women. Many imaginative explanations of them have been given, and the root *ṣ-b-'*, usually meaning "work," has been noted often, relating them to the ones of 1 Sam 2.22. The fullest discussion seems to be that of John I. Durham. *Word Biblical Commentary. Vol. 3. Exodus.* Waco, 1987, 487f.

51 B.A. Levine, "The Netinim,"*JBL* 82 (1963) 207-12; J.P. Weinberg, *ZAW* 87 (1975) 355-71; B.A. Brooks, *JBL* 60 (1941) 233f; J. Gray, *Legacy of Canaan VT* Supp 5 (1957) 158 relates them to the Ugaritic *ytnm* (Gordon *UT* 1169, under *ytn*) "temple servitors."

52 Jastrow *Dictionary* 955b.

53 R. Henshaw, *JAOS* 88 (1968) 467.

54 Bird (chap. 1 p. 10 n.1), p. 409. Mayer I. Gruber, "Women in the cult according to the Priestly Code," in J. Neusner et al (eds.), *Judaic Perspectives in Ancient Israel.* Philadelphia, 1987, 35-48, points out that women participated in the cult by attendance, vows and slaughtering. He stresses the instruction in Deut 31.10-12 that "all Israel...men, women and little children" shall gather before the Lord at the Feast of Booths. He tries to show that the P document presents a more positive view of women in the cult than other strata. This is a valuable article, correcting the views of some previous ones. In an early study, I. J. Peritz,"Women in the Early Hebrew Cult."*JBL* 17 (1898) 111-148 shows that even though women may have had a minor role in the later cult, that was not true for the early periods.

55 Kraus *Worship* 174. The so-called Court of the Women was the product of a later age, and not part of the first temple, see *JE* xii 88, 90. Athaliah the mother of Ahaziah the king of Judah entered the temple, 2 Kings 12.13, but this was an unusual time of high emotion.

56 *GKC* §122g (1910 edition)

57 E. Jacob, *IDB* III p. 453; L. Kohler, *Hebrew Man* 35; Y. Kauffman, *Religion of Israel* (abridged by M. Greenberg), Chicago, 1960, 312; de Vaux *AnIs* 60.

58 Pedersen *Israel* III/IV 166f; Winter *Frau u Gottin* 57. For Miriam as prophetess see Sec. 4.24.8

59 Segal, *JJS* 30 (1977) 128.

60 Kraus *Worship* 174, citing 1 Sam 1.

61 Baruch Levine finds two categories: "descriptive ritual texts" and "prescriptive ritual texts," *JCS* 17 (1963) 105-111; in C.L. Meyers and M. O'Connor (eds.), *The Word of the Lord Shall Go Forth*, Winona Lake, Indiana, 1983 467 and n. 1. There are relatively few descriptive ritual texts (in his terminology) that have come down to us, and those which have show only a small part of the total action, and use few words. This may be due to a secrecy controlled by the high cultic officiants, as in the Greek Eleusinian mysteries. One text has it: "The worshipper

must not divulge the teachings of Ishtar": quoted by A.L. Oppenheim, *HR* 5 (1965) 252a, to *KAR* 139.

62 G. Dossin, *RA* 35 (1938) 1-13.

63 One of which (iii 14) is an ershemma, Krecher *Kultlyrik* 34.

64 The name means "eater." Various guesses about what this means are "sword-swallower," or and "fire-eater."

65 Spelled *šagû* (pl.) here, as often at Mari, J. Renger *ZA* 59 105 n. 561.

66 *šitru* "veil," rather than *šiṭru* "writing," in i.ll, iv 9.27, *ARMT* 13 (1964) 162, notes to Lettre 22.41.

67 F. Kocher, *ZA* 50 (1952) 192-202.

68 *KAR* 139, translated and discussed, especially with respect to the term *pû lišānu* (KA.EME "mouth and tongue") by A.L. Oppenheim, *HR* 5 (1966) 250-65.

69 An inner room of a temple, so far found only of a goddess.

70 Renger, *ZA* 59, 143 n.722 gudu4 was formerly read šudug2. Sollberger *Correspondence* 124 no. 259 gives a "possible alternative reading" of šutug. See 114 gu-du HIxNUN.[ME *pa*]-*ši-šu* 115 šu-tug HIxNUN.[ME] *šu-tuk-ku*, Ea V, MSL XIV 400.

71 M. Lambert, in Unger AV No. 1 V 7.

72 T. Jacobsen, *OIP* 58, p. 293f, Nos. 4 and 6.

73 Falkenstein AV 216; see also Borger *BiOr* 30 (1973) 174bf; M. - J. Seux argues for the existence of the title *pašīš* Anim, *RA* 63 (1969) 94.

74 A. Deimel, *Fara* 2 61 No. 70 II 9.

75 K. 2856 I 5f, *AJSL* 35, 136.

76 B. Alster and H. Vanstiphout, *ASJ* 9 (1987) 22, 110.

77 *BE* 29, 1 II 34.

78 *JEOL* 20 (1968) 66, discussing the epithet pa-šiš for Manishtusu. Sharru-ken holds the title PAP.ŠEŠ.AN of An "*pašīšu* of An," *AfO* 20 (1963) 41, 47, as did Manishtusu and Naram-Sin; Seux *Epithètes* 222.

79 *BE* 6/2 7:1-10, *PSD* 74a.

80 *PBS* 8/2, 131; *BE* 6/2,37 (case); *OECT* 8,16; *PSD* 74b.

81 Jacobsen *Harps*...424.

82 Falkenstein *Gerichtsurkunden* 112:8-11.

83 Kang *Drehem* No. 177, year partially destroyed.

84 Kang *Umma* No. 289, no year.

85 Keiser *Drehem* No. 493.

86 Grégoire *Archives* No. 183.

87 For the various possibilities, see note II' 12, 250.

88 Grégoire *Archives* No. 200.

89 Oppenheim, *Catalogue* E4, with many other gudu4 references. Most collections of Ur III economic texts contain several gudu4 references of many different deities: Enki, Nanna, Ninhursag, Ninurta, Baba.

90 E. Kingsbury, *HUCA* 34 (1963) 6 lines 42f.

91 R. Borger, *BiOr* 30 (1973) 163-176, with 7 plates of photographs of tablets.

92 The Sumerian line has nam-sita, which in OB times and before was a separate office from the *pašīšu* / gudu4, but in these late times and

especially in the"pseudo-learned" Sumerian of our text (Borger p. 163b) perhaps some titles have become conflated, as god-names have.

93 gá-e-me-en gúda šu-luh-ha [d]En-lil-la-me?- [en] IV 16. *Ramku* may be a rank by itself, or simply an indication, as the root says, of a purification official.

94 *MSL* 4, 206, 84 with note.

95 Cohen *Lamentations* 104, 112, a + 217; 133, 140, d + 186; and passim.

96 Cohen *Ershemma* No. 164.30, 94.

97 TM.75.G.525, G. Pettinato *Archives* 252.

98 G. Pettinato, "Culto ufficiale ad Ebla," *OrAn* 18 (1979) 85-215, with indices, photos of TM.75.G.1764 and 2238, and transliterations and translations of 1764, 2075, 2238, 11010+.

99 Charpin *Clergé* 133, 178, 200, 235, 257, 259, 363 and Sec. 1.3.2.

100 R. Borger *Zeichenliste* No. 442.

101 CAD I 243b.

102 van Dijk *Götterlieder* 127f. There is also an eš-da vessel closely related to the $\check{s}ita_x$-vessel, Ibid., 130. Note that both of these terms consist of a sibbilant followed by a dental.

103 TCL XV 25,6, quoted in van Dijk *Götterlieder* 128.

104 Op. cit. 129.

105 Renger *Priestertum ZA* 59.

106 In the Dumuzi ershemma CT XV 19.9, as a place where lamentation is to be said: see Cohen *Eršemma* No. 165.9.

107 Falkenstein *Gerichtsurkunden* I 65 and n. 6.

108 *JCS* 4, 238f:22, from Renger, *ZA* 59, 129, n. 667. This indicates a role for this rank also as a purification priest (ibid. 131).

109 van Dijk *Götterlieder* 130.

110 CAD A/2 197a.

111 P. Reymond relates it to the *apsû. L'Eau, sa vie, et sa signification des l'Ancien Testament* (SVT 6) Leiden(1958), 226; Burrows *Or* NS 1 (1932) 239; S. Terrien *VT* 20 (1970) 323 n. 2.

112 There is a "rite of the *apsû*" mentioned in *PBS* 12/1 No. 6b.11f.

113 Schneider *Götternamen* s.vv. Burrows op. cit. 235 finds 26 names in Deimel *Pantheon*.

114 *SLTN* 88, 27, from van Dijk *Götterlieder* 127.

115 Hymn to Nanshe 117-118, *PSD* 75a, see note 280.

116 van Dijk Götterlieder 126, from *RT* 210 I 6.

117 Schneider *Zeitbestimmung*.

118 E. Kingsbury, *HUCA* 34 (1963) 10, 93.

119 *UET* I 107, van Dijk *Götterlieder* 126.

120 Unpublished, van Dijk *Götterlieder* 127.

121 *ZA* 59, 130.

122 van Dijk *Götterlieder* 126.

123 D.O. Edzard, *AfO* 22 (1968-9) 15, 41.

124 OB Proto-Lu 255, Sec. 1.9.2.

125 *ZA* 59, 130 n. 669, in Charpin *Clergé* 214.

126 *VAS* 22,18, Charpin *Clergé* 489 n. 2.

127 T. Jacobsen, *JNES* 12 (1953) 178, 157: nam-šita du_{11}-du_{11} lugal-la [ ]

128 ED Lu E and OB Proto-Lu in Secs. 1.2.1, 1.7.1.

129 *ZA* 55 (1963) 94. He suggests "man of the èš-shrine," the nu- as used in nu-gig and nu-bar.

130 W.W. Hallo *JNES* 31 (1972) 87ff.

131 *KAR* 306.32.

132 G.G. Hackman, *BIN* 8 157.7f.

133 Gene B. Gragg, "The Kesh Temple Hymn," in Sjöberg *Temple Hymns* 174.

134 Ibid. 161.

135 *BiOr* 30 (1973) 164ff.

136 van Dijk *Götterlieder* 127f.

137 A. Sjöberg, *ZA* 64 (1975) 142, 21.

138 W.G. Lambert, *JCS* 21 (1967) 132, 27.

139 *AS* 17 No. 56.2, in CAD N/2 191.

140 Winckler *Sar* pl. 36 No. 76, 157.

141 *PBS* 13 64.11, *BBSt* No. 3 i 46, CAD N/2 191a.

142 *JAOS* 88 (1968) 126 I b:11.

143 Hinke *Kudurru* iii 11, CAD N/2 191a Nebuchadrezzar I.

144 Hinke, op. cit., ii 12f, CAD N/2 191a.

145 Note this shift also in lumahhu-lumakku, 1.13.3.

146 M. Birot, *RA* 50 57ff.

147 Dossin in Birot *RA* 50 58 n. 8.

148 *ARM* 7 206.9.

149 At Nuzi: HSS 14 140.17; at Chagar Bazar: *Iraq* 7 56A 982 et al.

150 *VAS* 8 55.13 (OB).

151 *PBS* 1/2 135.11, *UET* 5 868.17, *JCS* 102.2, all from CAD K 419.

152 *MAD* 3 171.

153 M. Witzel *Or* NF 14 (1945) 196ff, 15 (1946) 468ff; translated by Kramer *ANET* 462.

154 CAD G 69b.

155 CAD G 83.

156 máš-(e)-nu-dib. G. Castellino, *OrAn* 8 (1969) 10.47. And again together: lú-mah nin-dingir máš-e nu-mu-an-da-[pà], *Belleten* XVI 360, per G. Castellino, *ZA* 52 (1957) 38. Again in a long hymn to Enlil, the order lú-mah nin-dingir appears. These will not be chosen by kid without Enlil. Falkenstein, *Götterlieder* 17,112.

157 *Gilg* VII iv 46-8.

158 In a broken section UM 29-16-86, copy by S.N.Kramer, *BASOR* 94 p.5. My readings follow B. Alster, *JCS* 23 (1971) 116f. See also below under išib, for another occurrence of the lú-mah in the netherworld, with some other ranks. Both lists are compared in C1. Wilcke, XVIIth Recontre, 84n.

159 B. Alster, *ASJ* 5 (1983) 12.

160 S.N.Kramer, *JCS* 21 (1967) 118,77-78.

161 Inanna and Enki 54, lines 11-15. The me is one of the elements of civilization that is under the control of the great gods.

162 AHw s.v. *lumahhu* puts this and lumakku together. CAD s.v. separates them because they find the latter spelled once *lummakku*. CAD separates luhšu and lukšu also, Sec. 1.11.

163 Gelb Old Akkadian 171.

164 *RAcc* 119.28 This could not be a ^{lú}MAH = ṣīru "chief" because of context.

165 References in CAD s.v. *gizillû*.

166 Enuma elish line 3, E.A. Speiser, *ANET* 61, text in W.G. Lambert, *The Babylonian Epic of Creation. The Cuneiform Text,* Oxford, 1966. There is a "rite of the *apsû*" mentioned in *PBS* 12/1 6. 11f. Certain deities had names DN-abzu, Sec. 1.9.4.

167 CAD A/2 p. 197.

168 van Dijk *Götterlieder* II 81. 6 (*TCL* XV 25) with notes pp. 128ff.

169 Hinke *Kururru* iii ll.

170 *LIH* 83 r.31, R Frankena *AbB* II No. 65, 15 (BM 26959).

171 *PBS* 1/2 135.23f, van Dijk, *Sagesse* 128, 24.

172 J.J.A. Van Dijk, *Falkenstein AV* 246f.

173 W. Heimpel, *JCS* 33 (1981) 65-139 with text copies, transliteration, translation and notes. Jacobsen *Harps*...126-142 gives his own translation.

174 Renger *Priestertum*, *ZA* 59 124.

175 Ibid. 130.

176 ^{d}Ea bēl *iššipu* [*t i*], 5 R 51 iii 71, from Sjöberg, *Temple Hymns* 61b

177 Sjöberg, *Temple Hymns* 61b.

178 I.e., after 2096 B.C.E., S.N. Kramer, *JCS* 21 (1967) 104 n.1.

179 Notes on *MSL* XII 70 give a variant orthography of á and gál. This allows us to look for funerary relationships.

180 H. Waetzoldt, *RLA* 6 (1980) 27.

181 Gudea Cyl B vi 19; F. Thureau-Dangin, *TCL* VIII p. xxxvi *SAKI* 126 vi 19 transliterates but incorrectly in places; Jacobsen *Harps*...430 understands these as, respectively, field hands and house servants. See also Kuk Won Chang, *Schicksalbestimmung*, 26.

182 Jacobsen *Harps*...133.

183 Falkenstein *Götterlieder* 99 commentary to line 5.

184 144 túg [gad] a-lá *ga-da-la-lu-u Erimhuš* V *MSL* XVII 73.

185 C.B.F Walker and S.N.Kramer, *Iraq* 44 (1982) 81, 5; Igituh App. A i 40, in CAD G 8a. The editor finds (?) the ba-an-gi$_4$ also in the Inanna hymn in-nin-šà-gur$_4$-ra, A Sjöberg, *ZA* 65 (1975) 237 n. to line 158.

186 CT 39, 33, 51/4 = K. 3811, studied in F. Nötscher, *Or* (OS) 31 (1928), 64 (but with unacceptible readings). Moren *ShummaAlu* 223 discuses this section only in general.

187 gudu$_4$ šà-gada-là, n. 107b, 45, or is this a separate official, as in Lu = ša IV 99, above?

188 *STVC* 34 iii7, *PSD* 138a; Michaelowski, *Lamentation Sumer and Ur* 447.

189 Jacobsen *Harps*...107 n.18.

190 D.O. Edzard, *RLA* IV (1975) 336. Enmerkar and Gilgamesh were en's. Urnanshe was the en of Lagash, *PSD* B, 139b, Nanshe Hymn 35. Their cultic duties are not mentioned, but these were undoubtedly part of the

position as "economic manager," see T. Jacobsen, *JNES* 12 (1953) 180f and A. Falkenstein, *Cahiers d'Histoire Mondiale* I (1954) 784-814, especially 795ff.

191 Penelope Weadock, *Iraq* 37 (1975) 101-28.

192 Second Uruk, C.J. Gadd, *CAH*[3] 1/2 114.

193 Jacobsen *Harps*...413a + Gudea Cylinder A.

194 *RLA* 2 (1938) 140, Schneider, *Zeitbestimmungen* 46.

195 Gene B. Gragg, "The Kesh Temple Hymn," in Sjöberg *Temple Hymns* 1174, 106 and notes.

196 A.T. Clay, *YOS* 1, No. 45, 71, 26ff (transliteration) and pl. xxxv (copy), the NB dedication of Nabonidus' daughter.

197 kuš $^{\text{ra-am-kum}}$ - lá OB Proto-Lu 553, MSL XII 53; Lu = ša IV 88 MSL XII 131.

198 W. W. Hallo, XVII. *Rencontre*, 123ff.

199 šud$_x$ (KAxSU)-dè mu-un-rá.

200 Falkenstein *Götterlieder* 96f; J. Renger, *ZA* 58 (1967) 127, these references from Hallo, op. cit. 132.

201 Spycket *Statues* 102.

202 *AAS, SL,* CAD E 172, M. Sigrist, *Neo-Asyrian Account Texts in the Horn Archaeological Museum.* Berrien Springs, 1984; N. Schneider, *Or* 45-46 (1930); AHw 230.

203 Jacobsen *Harps*...63 n. 4. In NB times at Ur it is called the É.GI$_6$.PAR *kummi ellu* "pure/holy *kummu*" *YOS* 1 45 i 39.

204 *IAK* 108 n. 2.

205 CH §110.37 has an *entu* or *ugbabtu* in the *gagû*. An astronomical text has an entry ga-gi-e = É en-ti, CAD E 172b, lexical section.

206 C.J. Gadd, *Iraq* 13 (1951) 27-39, line 34ff.

207 *UET* I 104,105, Charpin *Clergé* 195.

208 Hallo *Exaltation*, with further notes by W.H. Ph. Römer, *UF* 4 (1972) 173-206. Her further works, showing that she was a great creator of literature, are listed ibid., 173f. Sargon himself was the product of a union between an en and an unknown father, according to a late story (CT 13, 42, 1f. See E.A. Speiser's translation in *ANET* 119, where *enitum* should not be "changeling" but simply is one of the forms for *entum*.), Maybe she prostituted herself, maybe she adopted children because she could not have them. This could be considered a boast of the king, because the *entu* was an important person, usually the daughter of a king or the like.

209 Shown as U.6612 in L. Woolley, *UE* IV, Philadelphia, 1956, pl. 41(d).

210 *Antiquaries Journal* 6 (1916), pl. LII, facing 375.

211 C.J. Gadd and L. Legrain, *UET* I, No. 103, corrected by Spycket *Statues* 77.

212 mu en ^{d}inanna unu^{ki} máš-e ì-pà "year: the en of Inanna of Uruk was chosen by kid," the 2nd year of Ibbi-Sin at Drehem; mu en-unu$_6$-gal ^{d}inanna ba-hun "year: the en of the great festival hall of Inanna was installed," the 5th year of Amar-Sin at Drehem. Others mention the en of Nanna of Ga-eš$_5$, 9th year of Amar-Sin; the en of Eridu, the 8th year of Amar-Sin; for others see Schneider *Zeitbestimmungen* 46-48, but it is difficult to tell if these are m. or f.

213 Hammurapi may have put an end to the place of the en. W. von Soden, "Sumer..." *Propylaen Weltgeschichte* I 599.

214 *Symbolae Koschaker* 151-178, with additions and corrections by E. Sollberger, *AfO* 17 (1954-6) 23ff.

215 There were a few others entitled en in between these times, and some consider them artificial and ephemeral, E. Sollberger, *AfO* 17 (1954-6) 26. A daughter of king Ninurta-apil-ekurra (1192-1180) was a NIN.DINGIR.RA (*VAS* NF 53:8f), Menzel *Tempel* I, 249. And an *entu* appears in a NA text as having anal intercourse, see n. 233.

216 The omen texts are commented upon by C.J. Gadd, *Divination* 33.

217 Editorial history in Berger *Neubab*. See there for transliteration and translation.

218 §22. F.R. Steele, *AJA* 52 (1948) 425, translated *ANET* 160.

219 *StOr* 49 (1980) 180a, Sollberger et Kupper *Inscriptions* IV Dlf.

220 Goetze *Omen* No. 38 r. 11ff, translated CAD E 173a; J. Nougayrol, *JNES* 9 (1950) 52.

221 Atrahasis 102, 6.

222 C.J. Gadd, *Iraq* 13 (1951) 27-39; BM 130729; Translated Sollberger et Kupper *Inscriptions* IVB 14h; Karki *StOr* 49 151-2; Charpin *Clergé* 200-201.

223 En-ane-du "prêtresse parée par le ciel" Sollberger *Inscriptions* 300.

224 H.H. Figulla, *Iraq* 15 (1953). They are probably en's, as determined by their names.

225 Penelope N. Weadock, *Iraq* 37 (1975) 102-5.

226 The en as well as the *gudapsû* does the šu-luh rites (or carries the šu-luh vessel), van Dijk, *JCS* 19 (1965) 199f. Also *TMF* NF 4, line 117, and Hallo *Exaltation* 57 n.47.

227 Streck *Asb* 288, 10f.

228 *UET* 1 187, 3 (Nabonidus), CAD G 84a.

229 CAD G 84 "Amar-Suena, beloved of Nanna, built the holy gipar and made his en to enter it." Sollberger *Inscriptions* IIIA3d = Hallo *HUCA* 33, 8. The plan of the more than 80-room building is shown in Leonard Woolley and Max Mallowan, *UE* VII (1976) pl. 118, reproduced by Charpin *Clergé* 193, and *Iraq* 37 (1975) pl. XXVI.

230 CT 44.18; H. Hunger, von Soden AV 136 B 14 (BM 92685 = DT 78), in an astrological omen, with the same term; and cf. an OB liver model, in CT 6 2 case 42.

231 *uštahha*, II/2 of *šuhhu* "to impregnate," J. Nougayrol, *RA* 44 (1950) 27,41; 30,49.

232 J. Nougayrol, "Textes hepatoscopiques d' époque ancienne," *RA* 44 (1950) 28, *RA* 62, 172.

233 Biggs *ŠÀ.ZI.GA* 41, CT 31 44 i 10 (K. 8325), quoted CAD E 325b. The broken portions from CT 31 are restored from similar texts. The many appearances of this text show its popularity.

234 Nougayrol, *RA* 38 77, Starr Diviner 100.

235 Daniel Arnaud, *Recherches au pays d'Astata: les textes sumériens et accadiens.* VI.3, Paris, 1986.

236 Daniel Fleming, *The Installation of Baal's High Priestess at Emar,* Scholars Press, Atlanta, 1992. See also M. Dietrich, "Das Einsetzungsritual der Entu von Emar (Emar VI, 369)"; *UF* 21 (1989) 47-100.

237 W.W. Hallo,"The Road to Emar," *JCS* 18 (1964) 57-88.

238 F.M. Fales shows the reading as Adad in the forthcoming *Mélanges P. Garelli,* and Fleming argues for the reading Ba[c]al, Fleming 214ff.

239 A tonsure or head shaving (?) are followed by tables being set for the former NIN.DINGIR, the NIN.DINGIR of Dagan, the EN "lord" of Su-ú-mi, the *maš'artu,* the king of Emar, and the king of Shatappi. The *maš'artu,* a previously-unknown Akkadian word (98f), does not have an obvious Akkadian root, though the author (99) refers to *ša'āru* "to be victorious; to vanquish," concerning battle (CAD). Cf. also the south Semitic root: ta'aru (Arabic) "take vengence." Text Emar 370 is the installation of a *maš'artu,* Fleming 209ff. Shatappi (102) is only in Text A, location unknown.

240 Usually *bārû* in Mesopotamia, and a diviner there, but there is no indication of that activity at Emar. Instead he has temple administrative functions of a high order (87-92).

241 Fleming guesses this is Hebat.

242 Perhaps *qidašu* is an offering (95), and *hussu* perhaps those who recall the departed (Fleming 97) or are "Ritualmeister" (Dietrich).

243 Fleming refers to *nagāgu* "to bray" (CAD) but also a sound coming from human beings.

244 The root meaning is "five," but with a west semitic aleph ending.

245 A deity second only to the [d]IM in the ceremony. Among things given her are a [giš]NÁ "bed," a chair and a footstool (line 70). The bed is in the *bīt urši* "bedroom" supposedly, although the corresponding Akkadian term is *bīt erši*, the term *uršu* being found at Amarna and Ugarit.

246 There is no evidence of any sexual activity, but it is implied here because of the above marriage element in the rite. Fleming (192) does not agree, but thinks only of the personal domain of the princess.

247 Fleming 84f transliterates lines 1-14.

248 Fleming 269.

249 A Tsukimoto, *AJBI* 15 (1989) 3ff.

250 T. Jacobsen, *ZA* 52 (1957) 107 n. 32. Often there is no evidence to determine this. In the Hymn to Enlil, Nippur seemed to have a male en for a male god, *Harps*...105 n. 13.

251 *Maqlû* VI.40.

252 Lambert-Millard *Atra-hasis* 102.

253 "taboo" (Lambert and Millard, though criticized by CAD I/J 57b); "sacred" but doesn't fit the context; perhaps something like "abhorrent," or "evil."

254 If *pursi,* as Lambert and Millard,"cutting off childbirth (?)"165n.

255 *UET* I 104, 105, Charpin *Clergé* 105.

256 Cohen *Lamentations* 304, c + 142; 235, c + 268.

257 CAD L 37a.

---

258 *StOr* 1, 32: 1, *PSD* 177a. Here the la-bar, a lamentation singer, is described as "a dragon without rival." Labar as a variant of lagar is given by: Jacobsen *Harps*...105 n. 14.

259 Jacobsen *Harps*...105.

260 B. Alster *JCS* 23 (1971) 116f discusses this contiguity.

261 Ibid. 117.

262 *PSD* B 134a, Hymn to Nintu.

263 Falkenstein *Götterlieder* 13 lines 56-59, translated 21; and by Jacobsen *Harps*...105; Alster, op. cit., 116 note to 12-13, reads lagar for Falkenstein's túl, as does Jacobsen, reasonable, given the regular order of these four officials. The Nabnitu reference that la-bar is emesal for lagar is also noted in Krecher *Kultlyrik* n. `105.

264 Gudea A XX.21, translated Jacobsen *Harps*...413. The variant lagar/lagal is shown on the sign-list called Proto-Ea by CAD L 37a, but A VIII in MSL II 133, 50: la-gal LAGAR *la-gal-l* [um]. For this variation, probably to be explained by the shift from one liquid to another, see Renger *Priestertum ZA* 59 122 n.614b. Very early the variant lagal appears in Gudea. The Akkadian form also varies between *lagaru* and *lagallu*, CAD L s.v.

265 Alster, op. cit. 117.

266 UM 29-16-86, copy S.N. Kramer, *BASOR* 94, 5, transliteration p. 8 and Alster op. cit. 117. My readings follow Alster, except for more careful indication of gaps,. n. 263.

267 Gilgamesh VII iv 47f.

268 G. Castellino, *OrAn* 8 (1969) 10.

269 Inanna and Enki I, 26, discussion 101f.

270 Jacobsen *Harps*...105.

271 M.W. Green, *Eridu in Sumerian Literature,* Ph.D. dissertation, University of Chicago, 1975, quoted by Charpin *Clergé* 363.

272 3 R 52, 2,63 = *ACh Ishtar* XXIII.

273 *YOS* 1 45 ii, 28 transliterated and translated F.M.T. Bohl in *Symbolae Koschaker*.

274 *TuL* No. 27, lines 6f, 14, 16; *RA* cc 16, 28; 44,4.

275 W.G. Lambert, *AfO* 19 (1959-60) 58, 133, in a NB *unninu* - prayer to Marduk.

276 Charpin *Clergé* 392.

277 *UET* VI 69, U.7758, transliterated and translated, after collation, by Charpin *Clergé* 358ff. Hallo remarks on the identification of Asalluhi and Marduk in the Larsa era in *AOAT* 25 216.

278 K.2946 i 14f, unpublished, Charpin *Clergé* 366.

279 Charpin *Clergé* 392, CAD A/1 62b.

280 W. Heimpel, *JCS* 33 (1981) 84, new translation by Charpin *Clergé* 382f and Jacobsen *Harps*...126ff.

281 Charpin 388a; Michalowski *Lamentation Sumer Ur* line 445: "did not prepare the ceremony." *UET* VI/2 133,39 = 134, 7.

282 gál and lá seem to alternate at times, Charpin 388.

283 In an OB text a *kišibgallum* has seals with him, Pinches Berens 102 r.20 CAD K. 451a.

284 Quoted by Charpin *Clergé* 388; see also her n. 1.

285 *UET* V 586, U. 7795h, Charpin *Clergé* 114.

286 Charpin *Clergé* 390.

287 Quoted by Charpin *Clergé* 389.

288 Equivalent in MSL 2 128 ii 25; new edition MSL XIV 180, 70 (Ea I); Jacobsen *JNES* 5 139 n. 21, Bilingual texts use *apsû* for engur, CAD A/2 194af.

289 *Inanna and Enki* II i 7, 32, Charpin 390.

290 *SRT* 11, G. Castellino *ZA* 53 (1959) 106.18 as quoted Sjöberg *Temple Hymns* 186.

291 A. Sjöberg has examples of TU = ku_4 = *erēbu*, *Or* 33, 108; Hallo *HUCA* 33 (1962) 16 and n. 134; many lexical examples, CAD E 259; but J. Krecher *Kultlyrik* 180 argues against the equivalence. He understands TU as a variant of túm.

292 As Borger, *AOAT* 33 No 58.

293 Oppenheim *Catalogue* 180, Fish *Catalogue* 8, Jones-Snyder 360, Gregoire *Archives* 265, and many more. This is a class of PNs which denote professions and titles.

294 ND 2316.1-5. *Iraq* 16 (1954) 40.

295 ND 2309.9 *Iraq* 16 (1954) pl. VII.

296 Fales *Censimenti* No 21 (ADB 5) VIII, 13.

297 Ebeling *Stiftungen* VII; newly edited Menzel *Tempel* T26,9'-13'.

298 Menzel *Tempel* 300.

299 *AnSt* 8, 46 i 3.

300 Seux *Epithètes* 212ff.

301 IM 124470, F.N.H. Al-Rawi, *Iraq* 52 (1990) 8.

302 Proto-Kagal D 10, MSL XIII p.86, OB Proto-Lu 303, 304, MSL XII 43; Lu = ša III 76, MSL XII 126.

303 Romer *Königshymnen* 248.

304 Harris *Sippar* 307.

305 J.A. Black, *ASJ* 7 (1985) 22, 149. There are several other references to this office in this composition.

306 P. Michaelowski *JAOS* 95 (1957) 718.

307 I.J. Gelb, *MAD* I 290.

308 I.J. Gelb, *MAD* I 282.3, 315.10.

309 I.J. GElb, *RA* 66 (1972) 3f.

310 *VAS* VII 185-187 = KU 1289-1291 (Dilbat) and *YOS* II 45 (Larsa?).

311 Jean-Hoftijzer s.v.

312 Hirsch *Untersuchungen* 55f.

313 *ARM* VIII, 1, 37, 38, 39, 44, an adoption contract. Other witnesses are *malāhum* "boatman," and *ṭupšarrum* "scribe."

314 Gelb, *Amorite* 306.

315 *KAJ* 179.24, limmu before 911 = C. Saporetti, *Cybernetica Mesopotamica* Data Sets: Cuneiform Texts. Vol. 1 (DSC 1), Malibu, 1979, 57.

316 Streck *Asb* 216, 15.1, 218, 15.12, 222, 19.12 in a broken context.

317 Israel Eph'al, *The Ancient Arabs,* Jerusalem, 1982, 118 n. 400.

318 It is not found in a similar meaning in Wehr, Lane, Dozy nor in the *Wörterbuch der klassischen Arabische Sprache*, Wiesbaden; it is not found in Jaon C. Biella, *Dictionary of Old South Arabic, Sabaean*

Dialect. Harvard Semitic Series, 25, Scholars Press, 1982. It is not found in G. Lancaster Harding, *An Index and Concordance of Pre-Islamic Arabian Names and Inscriptions,* Toronto, 1971. The reference to *kamir* in R. Dozy, *Supplement aux Dictionnaires Arabes,* Paris, 1967[3], s.v., is to a dictionary of Hebrew roots.

319 Von Soden has only the bare notes in *OR* 35, 13, 70 and *OR* 46, 189, 70.

320 *UVB* 15 40:5.

321 423 [túg.A.SU] *šá ra-am-ku húl-la-nu* HAR-gud D to Tabl. III, MSL X 141 = B V i 20, MSL X 138.

322 Uruanna III 544, uruanna: *maštakal* pharmaceutical series, unpublished, see CAD L 228b.

323 *TuL* 103, 13.

324 R.E. Brunnow *ZA* 4 (1889) 252 I 9, updated by W. von Soden, *ZA* 61 (1971) 50, 41, K. 2361.

325 E. Ebeling, *MAOG* 15 1/2 (1942) 128.

326 Oppenheim *Catalogue* 208 n.93.

327 *YOS* V 163, transliterated and extensively discussed by Charpin *Clergé* 234.

328 W.W. Hallo, *HUCA* 33, (1962) 32, listed in Sollberger and Kupper, *Inscriptions* IIIA2u, the copy in CT 5 pl. 2, BM 12218, older *SAKI* 194x.

329 Photo in D.J. Wiseman, *Iraq* 22 (1960) pl. xxiib.

330 *ARM* 13 126 Kibri-Dagan to Zimri-Lim.

331 Fish *Catalogue* 34 No. 228.

332 Watson Birmingham, index p. 47.

333 Livingston *Poetry* No. 39, colophon. = VAT 8917 = *KAR* 307.

334 *Ash* 1922.256, *OECT* 1, pl. 20f, *Iraq* 45 (1983) 188.

335 Streck *Asb* 250, 17 (he read *urigallutu*).

336 *VAS* 1 36 ii 17-20, *CAD* E 291a.

337 *MEE* 2, index Nomi di Professioni e Funzioni 235; *MEE* 4 403.

338 Lu = ša I. 117, MSL XII 96.

339 *UET* V 247.

340 Sjöberg AV 352, 12 (*PBS* 5 100).

341 Charpin *Clergé* 241.

342 Charpin *Clergé* 242f.

343 *YOS* II, 129.1, CAD A/1 2b.

344 CT 7, 13 (BM 12939), in Limet, *XX Rencontre* 84.

345 *RTC* 399 XII 7-9, in Gregoire, *Archives* 219.

346 TU 157 0205, Pettinato *Waetzoldt Vocabulario* 1/1 220, from Reisner *Telloh.*

347 Postgate *Palace Archive* No. 17.30 ND 496.

348 Menzel, *Tempel* 300.

349 R.P. Dougherty, "The Shirkutu of Babylonian Deities" New Haven, 1923 (*YOR* 5/2) is an early study.

350 W. von Soden, *Or* 46 (1977) 189, 69.

351 CT 49p. see AHw 877a.

352 As translated by E. Reiner, *Thwarts* 4.

353 G. Contenau, *TCL* 13 (Paris, 1929), transliterated and translated by Moore *Neo-Babylonian* No. 182.

---

354 S. Langdon, *Neubab* 216, 9 Leipzig, 1912 (VAB 4).

355 *YOS* 1 45 ii 30, CAD K 386ab.

356 Kraus *AbB* II No. 65,15.3.

357 See note in B. Landsberger, *Sam'al* 45, Ankara, 1948 (not available to me), CAD M/1 240a.

358 PN ^{lú}SU.LUH *YOS* 13.30,4.

359 Laessøe *Bit Rimki* 23 n. 41, see CAD M/2 217b.

360 R. Ellis, *Foundation Deposits in Ancient Mesopotamia.,* New Haven, 1968, 73.

361 Seux *Epithètes* passim, s.vv.

362 Tarragon *Culte* 131-4.

363 *Ugaritica.* VII RS 24.291 = KTU 1.132.

364 M. Dietrich and O. Loretz, *UF* 9 (1977) 47-50, See also Fisher *Ras Shamra* II s.v.

365 Tarragon *Culte* 134f.

366 M. Dietrich and O. Loretz, *UF* 9 (1977) 336-337.

367 Tarragon *Culte* 135-136.

368 A.F. Rainey, *JNES* 24 (1965) 23.

369 B. Cutler and J. Macdonald, *UF* 8 33, and later *UF* 9 26-27.

370 Tarragon *Culte* 137.

371 M. Pope in G.D. Young (ed.), *Ugarit in Retrospect* 159-79.

372 CAD M/1 321a s.v. *marzi'u.*

373 *Ugaritica* 6 187ff.

374 Theodore J. Lewis, *ABD* I 581f.

375 T.J. Lewis, *Cults of the Dead in Ancient Israel and Ugarit,* Atlanta, 1989.

376 T. Yamashita, Fisher *Ras Shamra* II 53. See B. Levine *JBL* 82 (1963) 207-12.

377 Tarragon *Culte* 144-147.

378 A.F. Rainey, *BiAr* 28 (1965) 124, *UT* 1175.2 = *PRU* 2 No. 175.

379 Op. Cit., RS 16.276 = *PRU* 3, 72.

380 M. Dietrich and O. Loretz *WO* 5 (1969) 87-9.

CHAPTER TWO

Singers, Musicians And Dancers

2.1.1 Category No. 2 (Intro. 2) consists of cultic singers, musicians and dancers, with the actions most often being those of lamenting and weeping. Sometimes they were in fixed forms as the ershemma, the shuilla and the ershahunga.[1]

These actions might at first be considered as auxiliary to those we usually call cultic, yet one of the highest and most oft-appearing of ranks is in this group, the gala/*kalû*. In Mesopotamia officiants in this category fill an important role. They sing the great canonical lamentations, sometimes in emesal.[2] (See Other Abbreviations). Musicians often appear in the art, so we can get a rare glimpse of what a cultic officiant looked like, albeit undoubtedly stylized. There are few overall books on the subject.[3]

2.1.2 There are many musical instruments used in Mesopotamia, with their names appearing in the texts as well as in the lexical lists; we give here a partial but representative list of those related to the officiants we are interested in. Please note that each of these have several orthographies and we give only a few. Furthermore, in a technical field such as this, the translations can only be in the general area, rather than represent scientific accuracy.

1 adab / a-da-ba / *adapu* Pre-Sargonic. *HSS* III 25 r. ii 10 = Or 34 54; HAR-gud II 193, MSL VII 153.

2 algar "drum." M. Duchesne-Guillemin *JNES* 29 (1970) 200f, especially discussing its origins; Jacobsen *Harps*...123; giš-al-gar "drumstick" CAD A/1 378b. Sec. 2.6.1.

3 *algarsurrû* "lyre." Jacobsen *Harps*...362b (The Cursing of Akkadê); "plectrum or drumstick," CAD A/2 338a.

4 *alû* / giš/kuš-á-lá "kettledrum." Livingstone *Poetry* No. 28 r.15; the player *ša alê* OB Lu A 247, MSL XII 165; kuš-á-lá *Lamentation Over Sumer and Ur* 436; lú-á-lá *ED* Lu E 101, MSL XII 18; *Shurpu* IV.90

5 *arkatu* / *ariktu* /giš-gíd-da "long pipe." Livingstone *Poetry* No. 4.9' Played by *naru* Sec. 2.4.7

6 balag/*balamgu* "lyre" and/or "harp." *PSD* B 75a; Michalowski, *Lamentation over the Destruction of Sumer and Ur*, 441. The player is *ša balamgi* for balag-a-nir, Secs. 1.19.5, 2.10.4.

7 balag-di(-da)/*timbuttu* and other equivalents "harp," "lyre." *Examentext A* 28, *PSD* 79d. The player is *ša timbutti*, OB Lu A 250, MSL XII 165.

8 *baṣillatu*. CAD B 134b, AHw 110b.

9 *dubdubbu*. Livingstone *Poetry* No. 8. r.16'.

10 *embubbu* /*enbubbu* /*ebubbu* /gi-gíd "flute." The description is given as ér-gi-di-da *takribti ebubbim* "wailing of the *ebubbu*, with ér "lament," and gíd "be long, make a long (-sounding noise," *OBGT* XIII, MSL IV 120. See also gi-SUD MSL VII 49 beta, 69. The player is *ša embubbi* CAD E138a.

11 gi-gíd and gi-SUD. See *malilu*, *embubu*, *nišhu*, *šulpu*.

12 giš-har-har. See har-har.

13 GIŠ.ZÀ.MÍ. See *sammû*.

14 gi-zi-gíd-gíd. See *sassanu*.
15 *halhallatu*. See šem.
16 har-har/giš-har-har. *Examentext A* 28; *ZA* 64 144.28; *PSD* 79c.
17 *harhadû* /*hurhadû* "lyre." lexical only, *Diri* III 46; CAD H 100a.
18 *harru* "lyre." MSL VI, 142, 162.
19 *inu*. A.D. Kilmer, Landsberger AV 263, CAD I/J 151b.
20 *išartu*. HAR-gud to HAR-ra VII B, MSL VI 142, 162.
21 *kanzabu* "clapper." Livingstone *Poetry* No. 4.8'. Played by *naru* Sec.2.4.7.
22 *kiš* /*skilatu* "clappers." Pallis *Akitu* pl. 8 (CT 15, 44.29), used by *kurgarrû*'s, App. 3.3.3.
23 *kisurratu* "a flute." *Hh* IX, MSL VII 49, with a group *embubu* and *ša balangi*.
24 ^{kuš}ub. See n. 55 below.
25 *kušgugalû* (reading?)/KUS.GU$_4$.GAL "a drum." CAD K 598.
26 lilis/*lilissu* "kettledrum." Inanna and Iddindagan, 41, *PSD* 76d. Sec. 1.3.10. Used by *kalû*, Ebeling *Parfümrez* pl. 15 IV 12; *Shurpu* III 88.
27 *malgatu*. CAD: "a type of literary composition;" AHw: "Malgu-Pauke."
28 *malīlu* = GI.GÍD. *ED* Lu E 102, MSL XII 18; OB Lu A 242, MSL XII 165; *ša malīli* "flutist" Livingstone *Poetry* No. 4.9'. Played by *nāru* Sec. 2.4.7. Confusion with *embubbu*.
29 *manzû* /me-zé "a bronze drum." *KAR* 360.5, translated Borger *Esarh* 91; Cohen *Lamentations* 422, a + 41, *PSD* B 76b; *Shurpu* III 88.
30 meze. See *manzu*.
31 *mindiu*. CAD M/2 85b, *Diri* III 53; MSL 6 p. 119.
32 *mirītu* /*zamirītu*. *OECT* I pl. 2 ii 29; see Castellino *Two Shulgi Hymns* B, 165. From Meri = Mari?
33 NAR.BALAG. See tigi.
34 *nigkalagû* /URUDU.NÍG.KALA.GA. "a drum." CAD N/2 215.
35 *nišhu* /gi-SUD "a reed instrument," lexical only. *Hg* A ii 36f, MSL VII 69
36 *ni'u*. *Maqlû* VII 163, played by *kaššāpu* "sorcerer" and *kaššāptu* "sorceress."
37 *pagû* / SA.LI. AHw 809b; *SBH* No. 56 r. 72; A.D. Kilmer, *Or* 29 (1960) 275, 7. Played by *naru* Sec. 2.4.5.
38 *pigû*. Livingstone *Poetry* No. 8 r.12'.
39 *pi* /*alaggu* "lyre." Livingstone *Poetry* No. 8 r.13'; Photo 6553, *LKA* 32. Played by *assinnu* (?); *Shurpu* III 90.
40 *pitnu* /sa or na$_5$. Salonen *Möbel* 207ff; A.D. Kilmer, Landsberger AV 263. Played by *nāru ṣehru* Sec. 2.4.5.
41 *qanû* "reed pipe." CAD Q 89 4c.
42 *sabītu*, from the country Sabu. *OECT* I pl. II ii 29, Eridu Hymn, Ur III. Played by gala, *JCS* 10 30 No. 9.11.
43 SA.LI. See *pagû*.
44 *sammû* / GIŠ.ZÀ.MÍ "lyre," came to be a word for "praise." Thureau-Dangin *HCS* 159; Livingstone *Poetry* No. 4.8'; *Examentext A* 28; *PSD* 79a. See *nāš* ^{giš}*sammî* in the MB text AfO 18 46, 82 (a title?) Played by *nāru* Sec. 2.4.5. Can be of gold, in a NB list of instruments for the temple, R.P. Dougherty, *YOS* 6 62.28; *Shurpu* III 91.

45 *samsammu*. See *zamzammu*.
46 *sassannu* "a reed flute," [gi-z] i.gíd.gíd = *sa-as-sa-an-nu*. Listed with other reed flutes in MSL VII 40; MSL IX 183, 237 (*Hh* IX, with 6 equivalents, mostly broken). Played by *ša sassanni* / *zanzanni*, OB *Lu* D 245, MSL XII 208; *z/samz/sammu*, *Iraq*, Spring 1981 p. 82b; *JAOS* 103(1983) 276, 27.
47 si-in "drum." Gudea Cyl B xv 20-22.
48 *ṣibattu* "pipe." *Šhurpu* III 91.
49 *ṣinna* /*etu* / GIŠ.PA(.PA), a wind or percussion instrument. Livingstone *Poetry* No. 4.9'; played by the *nāru* Sec. 2.4.7.
50 *šebītu* "small harp." Livingstone *Poetry* No. 4.8'. Played by the *naru* Sec. 2.4.7. MSL VI, 119, 51; 123, [75]. *šut...še-bi-ti* "the player on the *šebītu*. *BA* 5, 564, 8. Cf. še-bi-da = *e-gu-ú*, Lu = ša IV 205, MSL XII 135, perhaps a manner of plucking the strings.
51 šèm/*halhallatu* "tambourine-like drum." *Lamentation over Sumer and Ur* l. 436. Accompanies ersemma Cohen *Ershemma* 36f. and gave the name to it. *Shurpu* III 89.
52 *šulpu* /gi-di "a musical instrument (?)." Played by lú-gi-di, OB Lu A, MSL XII 165, 244; MSL VII 69,37, 49 beta.
53 *tab* /*palu* of wood, perhaps a percussion instrument. Thureau-Dangin *HCS* 159; MSL VI 125, 116. Played by the *nāru* Sec. 2.4.5; *Shurpu* III 89.
54 *telītu*. Played by lú balag-balag-di in OB Lu A 251, MSL XII 165; lexical only; *ša telītum* Sec. 2.8.1.
55 *tibulû* "lute" (?). AHw 1356a, MSL VI, 119, 54/6, *Diri*.
56 *tigû* /tigi (NAR.BALAG) "a harp used in the Inanna cult." Jacobsen *Harps*...12a; "Trommel," AHw 1356b. Played by *kalû* and *tigû*.
57 *tim/bbuttu* "a harp." *ZA* 64 144.25; *Examentext A*; *Shurpu* III 37.90.
58 *tindu* "lyre"(?). AHw 1360a; corresponds to the *zannaru* in MSL VI, 142, 170.
59 ub /*uppu* "drum." Inanna and Ebeh *Or* 40/1 (1971) 18 line 52 (174). A lú-ub$_x$-kug-ga plays it, Sec. 3.3.2. A *kalû* plays it, *RAcc* 20,3. In UrIII Inanna gave the ^{kuš}ub and lilis to the gala, Sec. 2.3.12.
60 *urza(ba)bītu* "lyre" (?). MSL VI 157, 222; AHw 1437a.
61 *ušnaru* "lyre." MSL VI 119, 44; AHw 1441b.
62 (giš) zà-mí. see *sammû*.
63 *zamzammu Hg* A II 191; MSL VII 153; corrected MSL VIII/2 141; lament in OB Uruk, M.W. Green, *JAOS* 104 (1984) 276, 12.17. Sec. 2.4.5.
64 *zannaru* "lyre." CAD Z 46b; AHw 1510b.

2.2 Instrumentalists

2.2.1 The above list shows that several instrumentalists were entitled by the name of their instrument, either metonymically, or *ša* (the instrument). Though we have too few examples, I suspect that all instrumentalists were entitled as the latter, in at least one of their titles.

2.2.2 Much of the singing is in the form of weeping, and both officiants and goddesses do this, although it is doubtful if we should separate the two in mythological texts. S.N. Kramer describes the Sumerian prototypes of the weeping goddess.[4]

2.2.3 To study the types and titles of songs is outside our field, but one, the *inhu,* stands out as mentioned frequently. In *KAR* 154 (studied in some detail in Appendix 1) the *qadištu* sings the *inhu* before Adad (lines 4,8,9). If this is from the root *n-w-h* "to be at rest," the songs could be explained as done to soothe the heart of the deity. If the root is *a-n-h* "to sigh, etc." this would indicate a mood of lament, distress, being sorry, groaning, etc. The *naru* sings an *inhu* in the Akitu festival in Seleucid times, 2.3.18. The *assinnu* sings an *inhu*, chap 4, (see n. 156); App. 3.2.2. The *kulmašītu* sings it, Sec. 4.8.4, towards the end.

2.2.4 Some of the earliest officiants who appear in musical roles are nar, balag, balag-di:

76 SIG_7.PAP.NUN.ME (isimud)
77 AL:NAR (LAK 243)
78 GAL:BALAG
79 GAL: SU_{12}

ED Lu A MSL XII 11, with Arcari ED List A

7 ad-KID
8 balag-di
9 gu_4-di
10 nar
11 šidim

ED Lu B MSL XII 13

20 téš-tuku
21 lú-nar
22 lú-šìr
23 lú-BÚR:balag
24 lú-RI:x

ED Lu C MSL XII 14

26 simug
27 nar
28 $muš-lah_4$
29 PAP.PAP

ED Lu E MSL XII 17

94 lú-NAR
95 ur-húb
96 lú-DI
97 lú-^{gis}úr
98 balag-di
99 [za?] -⌈am⌉
100 ⌈x:x⌉
101 lú-á-lá
102 lú-gi-di
103 lú-g[i] -|x|

104 lú-BÚR:balag
105 lú-X
106 [ ]
107 lú-šìr
108 lú-ad

ED Lu E MSL XII 18

lú-á-lá and lú-gi-di (not discovered elsewhere) are the ones who play the instruments of these names, see Sec. 2.1.2. For lú-šìr see Sec. 2.11, below.

Gala also shows up early.[5] An ED Queen Pu-abi (formerly read Shub-ad) had a harp[6] showing that she probably sang, and that probably in the cult.

The lukur (Sec. 4.3.1) Kubatum was the author of love songs, one of which is to the king.[7] According to Hallo[8] she appears to have a genuine romantic attachment to Shu-Sin, the fourth king of the Ur III dynasty. Her fame shows up in that her name and title are inscribed on beads.[9]

2.3. The main actors: gala (UŠ.KU) / *kalû* // gala-mah./.*kalamahu*

2.3.1 The gala-mah goes back at least to the Lagash I period, as one of the witnesses to a real estate transaction, along with a bur-sag, a sanga and some secular offices.[10] The gala-mah plays the ub, šem and lilis in A. Falkenstein, "Fluche über Akkade."[11] In Ur III times, the gala-mah appears on a ration list for the Ekishnugal temple (Sec. 1.37.1). In OB times, one finds the gala-mah AN-^{d}INANNA[12] and the gala-mah ^{d}Nanna.[13]

2.3.2 In archaic Lagash, a gala followed by eme-sal appears[14] an indication that he recites in the emesal dialect, see below Sec. 2.6, Nabnitu IX.242 (MSL XVI 122). In the 5th year of UruKAgina (now read Uruinimgina) many gala from various cities show up, as well as TAR.LUH (not in Deimel SL) and NAR on the rev. All are summed up as UŠ.KU/gala.[15]

In the Gudea literature, one finds the gala and ama-ér described as playing the balag in the graveyard and singing an ír "lament."[16] Even though at later times the gala and the nar perform two different functions, in this early period we find difficulty separating them. In one of the "sacred marriage" texts, Inanna's song to her vulva, and thus a fertility motif, is sung by both the gala and nar in parallel lines,[17] showing that the two offices work together.

2.3.3 More interesting for our purposes, some of the early gala's may have been women[18] and the office of nar in these early texts may have been held by women.[19] Though without titles associated with them, a number of sculptures are of female musicians and singers.[20] Gelb found in an Ur III text some um-ma-ír "wailing (old) women" listed among the gala, the whole summed up by géme-dumu-dingir-ne-ne "women and children of the gods" (i.e., temples)[21] He goes on to argue that the gala may have been "pederast, homosexual, transvestite, eunuch or the like"(74). I have found that the abnormal sexual categories that older scholars impute to some of these offices have no basis, and I argue against them several times in this study.[22]

There is a line in an Ur III text listing a woman gala: 2 gala mí gil-sa (line 26), among other gala's, and nar's including a nar mí gil-sa (line 11).[23] There is a possibility of other female gala's, this time gala-mah's of Lagash, Girsu, Siraran and ^{d}Nin-marki listed as dam "wives" of other men,[24] but there are internal arguments against it, because of the way the texts are set up. A daughter of Sargon held the title balag-di ^{d}Sin.[25] We have given enough examples to show that some, maybe only a few, of the gala's were women, but this is enough to show their part in the activity of this office. None of the later *kalû's* have so far been found to be female.

2.3.4.1 Some texts illustrate or symbolize the irregular sexual nature of the gala. The galatura "apprentice gala (?)"/"assistant gala (?)" in the Descent of Inanna is found together with the kurgara [26] as the latter is found among wailing offices in Lu = ša IV 180, Sec. 2.3.14 They are able to circumvent the doorkeeper, bypassing the elaborate procedure Inanna had to go through, I suggest that this was because of their irregular sexuality. The two are significant actors in the denoument of the plot, which belies the supposed junior position of the galatura.[27]

Another association of the gala/*kalû* with sexuality is shown in a Sippar text, in which 11 *harimtu's* "prostitutes" are under the *Kalamāhu*.[28] Did they serve as singers?

2.3.4.2 I.M. Diakonoff[29] thinks that they were eunuchs and because they were not real men had to use emesal. There is much argument against this, though I would retain the concept of "irregular sexuality."

2.3.5 Other terms for a minor *kalû* official are found. The title after a PN is ŠAMAN$_2$.LÁ UŠ.KU[30] which may be read *šamallû kalê* "assistant to the *kalû.*" *Kalû agašgû* "young *kalû* " seems to use the modifier in the title in the same way as *šamallû.* [31] A form which appears only once, and that on a lexical list, is the UŠ.KU.ÚS.SA =ŠU-*ú* = *galaussû*,[32] literally "the one following the *kalû*,"apparently a *kalû* of secondary rank. The gala-hal-tuš-a = ŠU-*ú* is an apprentice *kalû,* and is read *hallatuššu* or *galahallatuššu*.[33] The *hallatuššu* are OB apprentice singers of a *sipittu* lament.[34] See Lu =ša IV Sec. 2.4.7 for similar appearences of the nar.

2.3.6 In Ur III texts we have a few precious examples of men from other professions entering upon the office of gala. Gelb[35] gives some of these, with the standard phrase: u$_4$ nam-gala-šè ì-in-ku$_4$-ra "when he entered the gala-office." He points out the offices held previous to his new (and higher) office: mu "baker," rá-gaba "courier," lú-giš-ban "archer," mar-tu "Amorite." The gala's offer animals to the temple upon their entrance into this office.[36] Another text has: u$_4$-nam-gala-šè-ni-in-ku$_4$-ra "(animals given for Akbani the Mari-man) on the day when he entered the office of gala."[37]

2.3.7 That there were large numbers of nar's and gala's in the Ur III dynasty is shown by a text listing 180 nar and 62 gala from temples in seven localities in the Lagash province.[38]

2.3.9 The ub and lilis instruments appear in a myth of the fashioning of the gala by Enki[39] in an OB balag-composition. The instruments are to utter *ahulap* "oh!, ah!, would that it were...!," indicating a groan or a sigh or a deep suplication by the worshipper, asking for pardon or mercy or calling that it is enough. The gala/*kalû* is to play these to soothe the angry heart of Inanna. The song done by *enenu*-praying is described as ír-šà-ne-ša$_4$ "whining lament," CAD E 164a. See further Sec. 2.3.16.

A regular duty of the gala/*kalû* was to recite the balag composition, done to assuage divine anger. The OB compositions, the oldest, were in emesal, a dialect of Sumerian used especially by the *kalû*.[40] The latest balag's were in Seleucid times. The content is close to that of the lamentations over the destruction of a city: the land has been overrun, the wrath of the god has come down upon us, the temple and people have been destroyed, the goddess wails.

Another composition recited by the *kalû* in emesal was the ersemma, discussed in detail by Cohen.[41] This was often appended to the balag in the first millenium, but originally was a different genre (8) A few examples are found in the 2nd millenium, but almost all we know about the *kalû's* recitations is from the lst millenium. (4f). One reference from Mari has the *kalû* reciting an eršemma to the accompaniment of the *halhallatu*.[42] This is done by the king, the *kalû* and several others (see further 10 below.) Cohen concludes that the *kalû* composed as well as sang the ershemma's (37).

The *kalû* also does the lamentation chant type ersahunga in the first millenium. This is done on the *halhallatu*.[43] The Seleucid exemplars of (perhaps) earlier complex rituals[44] are recited by the *kalû*, but with interaction by other officials, the balag chant being but one element in the total. One is a ritual when a temple foundation is laid.[45] Again, rubrics only are given, with many of the details missing, but enough so that we can see there a great amount of work, but we do not know how many assistants were present, nor the length of time involved.

In an ershemma of Ninisina[46] the negative opening lines complain of:

> 23 gala-e šà-mu nu-šed$_7$-dè-mu
> 24 gudu$_4$-mu sil$_6$-lá nu-mu-ni-ib-bé-un-du$_{11}$-ga-mu
>
> "the gala who does not calm my heart, my gudu$_4$ who does not speak joyfully."

This is a rare case of a gala and a gudu$_4$/*pašišu* brought together. Here the gudu$_4$ seems to be doing a work similar to that of the gala, but speaking sil$_6$ "joyfully." A gudu$_4$ is also mentioned in another eršemma as one who speaks[47] using a clever play on words: gudu$_4$-e gù^{gu}-dé^{de} "the gudu$_4$ calls out."

A namburbi, with ritual more elaborate than the usual, incorporates an eršemma and eršahunga, "that headache, plague, pestilence may not approach the king's ho[rses and] troops[48] the incipit being known from a catalogue of *kalû* -texts, the officiants being perhaps a *kalû* (though not mentioned) and the king.

The first two kirugu's "sections" of the "Lamentation over the Destruction of Ur"[49] lists all the gods and goddesses who abandoned temples in the city, with goddesses greatly predominating (kirugu l) and the city setting up a lament (kirugu 2), both of these being in emesal. The prevalent deities are Ningal and Nanna. The pleas are to Nanna, but the house, the city and the land are Ningal's (lines 295, 95 and 107, 102 respectively). The remaining sections are in emegir but with a number of emesal orthographies, so perhaps were authoried by individuals who were used to emesal, i.e., *kalû*'s. It was probably recited by a *kalû*.

2.3.10 In contrast to the significant role mentioned above, and reminding us of the way other officiants (mostly those in our Category No. 4) were disparaged, the gala is the butt of several, sometimes obscure, proverbs:[50] gala-pe-el-lá ú-gi-gíd-a-kam "a disgraced gala becomes a flutist," No. 2.54, in which several professionals take a calling on a lower level. He is not trusted near a house (?) 2.97. (The gala sign is not sure here, according to T. Jacobsen, 535). His twisted mentality causes him to throw his son into the water because he didn't fulfill impossible tasks 2.99. (A translation by T. Jacobsen, p.482, refers to the gala building cities and giving life to the nation, which he does if his chants are efficacious.). He alludes in emesal to some parts of his anatomy (anus? so Gordon) belonging to Inanna and thus for love and sex, 2.100. An obscure proverb relates to the gala who comes upon a lion in the steppe (and perhaps lacked courage) and then goes to the "gate of Inanna." 2. 101. A gala's boat has sunk, and he acknowledges in emesal the help of Enki, 2.103 (Or, in Jacobsen's translation (484) he criticizes Enki while praising him perfunctorily.)

An obscure proverb refers to the eating habits of the gala, 2.104. The slave of a gala complains about his food rations, 2.105 (Or, is bragging about them, according to T. Jacobsen's translation, 484). A short proverb could tell us the manner of the gala's singing the incantations (tu_6-tu_6) if we could understand the use of the sign bàd, 2.106.

2.3.11 To show their place in the economic, social and political spheres we note the appearance of gala's in Sumerian contracts. From a collection by A. Falkenstein:[51] A gala was maškim in the sale of a slave of a $guda_2$ No. 135.7. A gala buys a slave No. 81. A gala claims a piece of property No. 199 III. A gala has a question about the gravesites which the galamah's of the city had founded No. 101.10. In an economic document in the context of measurements of orchards, the garden of a gala-mah, the é-mí "woman's house," and $guda_2$ appear.[52] He appears as a witness on a Larsa contract.[53]

Turning to Akkadian times, outside of the ritual another life of the *kalû* is found in several references in *ADD* texts. *ADD* 851 lists PNs with titles, from the time of Asshurbanipal, with totals of something (not indicated): MAŠ.MAŠ.MEŠ (I.18) "exorcists,"*bārû* II.6 "diviners," A.BA [ ] II.16 "scribes"...*kalê* III.7 "singers," *dāgil iṣṣurē* II.11 "bird diviners," *harṭibi* IV.2 "dream interpreters," A.BA.MEŠ *musuraya* IV.6f "scribes of Egyptian." This is a miscellany of incantation officials, *kalû*'s and scribes. Their PNs could be found in no other NA text, neither in *ADD*, nor *ABL*, nor SAA nor Nimrud tablets, nor *CTN* nor other miscellaneous NA sources, so we could not track down further information about them. Driel 55 finds Ishtar-shum-erish the *rab ṭupšarri* a well-known name, appearing in *ADD* 851 without title.

What were all these officiants doing together? In *ABL* 33, many of these same offices (*ṭupšarrē*, *bārû*, *mašmaššu*, *dāgil iṣṣurē*) and others take an oath of loyalty on the 16th Nisanu. *ADD* 851 is dated 16 Tebetu, with 10 months between them. *ADD* 874.7 has *kalû* among broken PNs and titles, with]NAR[on line 9. The *kalû* and the MAŠ.MAŠ work together *ABL* 361 r.10, Luckenbill *AnnSen* 81, 27. For their purposes, the Assyrian government does not classify its officials as we do in this study!

2.3.12 In later times the *kalû* is the master of several instruments: the *manzû* [54] the *lilissu*,[55] the ub/*uppu* (see n. 55), the balag (see n. 16), the *halhallatu*,[56] the ^{kuš}ub, (see n. 55), the *tigû*.[57]

2.3.13 After a long section of names of laments, OB Proto-Lu lists singers and musicians, showing the large number of titles:

641 nar
642 nar-gal
643 NAR.BALAG / tigi
644 nar-sa
645 blank
646 nar-igi-suhur-lá

647 nar-igi-lugal
648 nar-KA-silim-ma
648a [na]r-inim-bal-bal
648b nar-[KAxX]-dùg-ga
648c nar-[KAxX]-nu-dùg-ga
648d nar-zé-za
649 nar-hal-la-tuš-a
649a [na] r-èš-a
649b [nar h]a-lam-x-x
650 nar-kéš-da
651 muš-lah$_4$
652 muš-lah$_4$-gal
653 gala
654 gala-mah
655 gala-mah-lugal
656 gala-lugal
657 gala-lugal-ra-ús-sa
658 gala-ma-da-ab-ús
659 [am]a-ér-ra
660 balag
661 b[al]ag-gá
662 [ba]lag-íl

OB Proto-Lu MSL XII pp. 56f

and in a list of various kinds of šìr "music,":

587 šìr
588 šìr-kù
589 šìr-ha-mum
590 šìr-nam-nar
591 šìr-nam-gala
592 šìr-nam-šub
OB Proto-Lu MSL XII p. 54

showing the prevalence of the many nar- and gala- offices.

The two offices NAR.BALAG/tigi "singer on the balag" and nar-sa "singer on a gut-instrument" beside one another in lines 643-644 indicate that nar is the term for instrumentalist, as well as singer, and, in fact, the two probably were thought of as together, for there was no singer who could not play a certain instrument.[58]

In OB times, in a seven-day cult at Larsa, many officials took part, including those in our....

Category No. 1: gudú (lines 43, 114, 115, 117, 121, 152)
en (line 82)
NU.EŠ/nisag (line 88)
šita$_x$-UNU (lines 93, 120)
egir šita$_x$-UNU (line 94)

Category No. 2: singers: nar (lines 30, 84, 87, 113)
nar-gal (line 86)
mí-nar-lukur (lines 97, 101)
gala (lines 51, 85)

Category No. 3: diviners: gub-ba (line 89)

Category No.,5, functions auxiliary to the temple:

šu-i	"barber" (lines 38,98,102,104)
KAŠ.LUL	"cupbearer" (line 81)
lú-bappir	"brewer" (lines 83,90)
rá-gaba	"constable" (line 91, of the en of Shamash)
dím	"builder" (line 92)
kisal-luh	"courtyard purifier" (line 99)
ì-dug$_8$	"doorman" (line 103)
húb-bi	"dancers" (line 96)
ararru	"miller" (line 105)
mí-kisal-luh	"courtyard purifier, f. (100)
mí-àra	"miller, f." (lines124, 152)
gala-mah	(line 125)

This shows better than any of our other examples of two or three acting together, that a great number of different officials, with quite different functions, were used together for some purpose, so a liturgy such as this one had not only one aspect, but many. [59] As Kingsbury says, "the exact event eludes us" (p. 23), but the text seems to be a ration or inventory list, rather than a prescriptive ritual (RAH).

An obscure, broken, ritual involves the sukkal "vizier" of Enlil, and beer which in lines 25ff he (the gala?, line 71) pours out for Enlil. Later in the text Inanna's sexual ability, or lack thereof, is the topic (lines 137ff).[60]

2.3.14 As seen by the above OB lexical lists, there are many types of gala's. The NA lists show these grouped with balag-x on Lu = ša and with nar on igituh:

160	$^{\text{su-ra}}$sur$_9$	*su-ur-ru-ú*
161	sur$_9$	*ka-lu-ú*
162	$^{\text{mu-ru-ub}}$SAL+LAGAR	KI.MIN
163	la-bar	KI.MIN
164	AN.NU$^{\text{su-uk}}$NUNUZ-$^{\text{pa-da}}$pà-da	KI.MIN
165	lú-ér-ra	KI.MIN
166	lú-ér-pà	KI.MIN
167	$^{\text{ga-la}}$ARAD.KU	KI.MIN
168	^{MIN} UŠ.KU	KI.MIN
169	gala-mah	SU-*hu*
170	gala-ús-sa	SU-*ú*
171	gala-hal-tuš-a	SU-*ú*
172	gala-zé-è	*a-su-ú*
173	gala-kéš-da	MIN *ki-is-ri*
174	balag-íl	*na-áš ba-lam-gi*
175	balag-di	*sa-ri-ru* (phonetic variant of *sa-ri-hu* ?) (CAD S 112B)
176	balag-i-lu-di	*mu-nam-bu-u*

177	hul-a-li	*lal-la-ru*
178	SAL hul-a-li	*lal-la-ar-ti*
179	ka-kù-gal	ŠU-*lu*
180	kur-gar-ra	ŠU-*u*
181	ama-ér-ra	ŠU-*u*

Lú-ša Tabl IV
MSL XII 133f

20	[L]Ú.UŠ[KU]	[*ka-lu-ú*]
21	[L]Ú.UŠ.KU-m[ah]	[ŠU-*hu*]
22	[L]Ú.NAR	[*na-a-ru*]

Igituh

gala-ma /*galamahhu* would be a chief gala. For gala-ús-sa /*galaussu* and gala-hal-tuš-a see Sec. 2.3.5. A gala-zé-è /*aṣû* might be one who has an outgoing song or tone or place in the procession. Could zé be a phonetic indicator? CAD A/2 385a: "solo singer." The gala-kéš-da / MIN (i.e. *aṣû*) *kiṣri*, may be the outgoing *kalû* of the group, indicating that they sang together in some way. CAD A/2 385a: "chorus." A *munambû* is a balag-di who sings the i-lu, perhaps a wail, and so far has shown up only in a lexical list. There is a male *lallaru* and a female *lallārtu*, "wailer," see Sec. 2.20. The kurgara/*kurgarrû* is an office which will be discussed in App. 3.3. Here we learn that part of his function was musical. ama-ér-ra /*ama'irru* Sec.2.16 is one of a number of officiants whose title begins with ama-[61] perhaps to be understood as "mother of mourning," or "mother who is mourning." This is a female rank, appearing among other cultic wailers. On that utopian day when there would be no troubles, the gala would not bring the harp and the ama-ér-ke$_4$ (with -k and -e) would sing no lament.[62]

2.3.15 There is a NA series *[iškaru] kalûtu: nēmeq* ^{d}Ea *kalûtu niṣirti apkalli ša ana nūh libbi ilāni rabūti suluku* "the wisdom of Ea the *kalûtu* (-series) secrets of the *apkallu*'s, which to give rest to the hearts of the great gods is fitting,"[63]

This is the key to what the *kalû* does. A valuable catalogue of incipits several columns long[64] has been studied many times, especially in earlier days by F. Thureau-Dangin and S. Langdon.[65] Under *iškar kalûti* "series *kalûtu"* there appears a list of ér.šèm.ma.mes ki.du.du "ershemma's *kidudû*-rites." Other columns list balag's and šu-ila's.

There are two OB ershemma catalogues from the British Museum published by S.N. Kramer in the Salonen Festschrift.

2.3.16 We now refer to some rituals, and find examples of the *kalû* operating in conjunction with some other office. In a NA letter[66] in a context about *dullu* "rites," the author has made a burnt-offering (*maqalūtu*), and the cleansing rite (*takpirtu*) has been done, and the matter has been entrusted to a *kalû* and a MAŠ.MAŠ. In conjunction with the opening of a canal, and perhaps the rites in connection with this, Sennacherib sent a MAŠ.MAŠ and a *kalû*.[67]

A NA copy of a probably earlier ritual text[68] shows the *kalû* killing the slave-girl who slept with Dumuzi with his *manzû,* paralleled with three others who kill her. This idea of killing in the midst of the ritual will be discussed in App. 3.3.5, in connection with the *kurgarrû* (lines 16f here) The *kalû* sings praises with the *manzû* and *halhallatu* in a hymn. [69] We will see there that cultic officials carry weapons as well as musical instruments.

A NA (?) rite[70] takes place partly in the *bīt akīti*. "Their meat" is brought before Asshur. The *mukīl appāte* "rein holder" comes in and holds a whip (*mahītu*) towards the god Asshur (28, 16), and goes on to the *bīt akīti*. The (broken) sing. Near the end the *kalû*'s (29, left side, 12) play the *lilissu* -drums.

The *nēpišu* "ritual" of the *kalû* is found in its greatest detail in Seleucid times. After the pouring of beer, wine and milk, the reciting of a ér-šem$_4$-šà-hun-gá the MAŠ.MAŠ and the *kalû* "purify the city."[71] Again we have an entry which seems to be a rubric only, with no description of the probably complex rites with which this was to be accomplished. In Seleucid times also we find the *kalamāhu* performing functions that are usually found as part of the *šangû*'s ritual, as making an animal sacrifice.[72] He has water poured (?) over his hands by (?) a *mahhû* in an akītu "New Year's" rite in the Anu-temple at Uruk,[73] and he goes on to lift up his (?) hands to Anu. In late Babylonian texts the *kalamahu* is often "the scribe of Anu."[74]

The *kalû* plays the bronze *lilissu* and *uppu* - drum. These two instruments, with their Sumerian equivalent names of lilis and ub, are shown to be provided for the gala, after his fashioning by Enki, in the OB balag-composition noted Sec. 2.3.9. The ritual continues by bringing a bull without blemish, inspected by an expert, into the *bīt mummi*.[75] Incense and the pouring of beer follow. Food offerings are laid out. (See n. 61) F. Thureau-Dangin, *RA* 17 (1920) 53-111 (*RAcc* 1-59). 12 garments for the 12 gods are set down, with 12 tables of food and a brick for ^{d}Lum-ha[76] is put down. Incantations (*šiptu*) are sung, to the accompaniment of the *halhallatu*-drum. The animal is slain, the fire is kindled, and parts of it are burned "before the *lilissu*."[77] This part ends by the pouring of beer, wine and milk. A rite then brings out the *lilissu* before the gods. Hymns are recited. Censer and torch purify the *lilissu* A lamentation is sung. Then an interesting note that the uninitiated are not allowed to see the rites.[78]

In another text having to do with *kalû*'s and incantation[79] the sacrificial animal is purified with censer and torch, and a *zisurrû* "(magic) circle of flour" is drawn about him. An incantation is whispered into the right and left ears of the animal, then he is burned before ^{d}Lumha (see above n. 76). The *kalû* says an incantation three times, after each saying: *epšeti annati* DIM.ME.ER *kili* (*b*) *-ba i-tip-pu -uš a-na-ku ul e-pu-uš* "these actions are the totality of the gods who have made them; it is not I who have done it." This is done on a favorable month and a favorable day. Finally, a note that the *kalamahu* shall not eat the meat of the animal.

In another *nēpeši ša qāt* ^{lú}*kalê* "ritual in the jurisdiction of the *kalû* " rite[80] when the walls of the temple of Anu fall down (perhaps necessitating a reconstruction) on a favorable month and day, at night sacrifice is made to the god of the temple and to the goddess (^{d}Ishtar) of the temple and the spirit (^{d}lamassi) of the temple. A sacrifice for Ea and Marduk is made. A lamentation and an ershemma are recited. In the morning food is offered to Ea, Shamash and Marduk and chants are done on the *halhallatu*. (The text goes on) on an auspicious day the king purifies himself and says in a loud voice his confession to Anu, Enlil and Ea. Then there is an ershemma for the king. Then: If you do this, *lemuttu* "misfortune/danger" will not come near to the king."(38,13). This last idea seems to be the purpose of this part of the rite.

Related to this is the tablet of ^{lú}*kalû ṣihru* of Uruk "apprentice *kalû*."[81] When the walls of the temple fall, in view of demolition, then to refound the temple, food, beer, wine, milk, fire are brought, the rites including the eršemma SAL ù-li-l[82] the *kalû* chants. The *itinnu*, usually "builder," of the temple puts on a clean/pure garment, puts a tin bracelet on his hand, takes a lead axe and removes the first brick (CAD I 297b), and puts it in a special house (or temple). The *kalû* pours out the honey, ghee, milk, beer, wine and fine quality oil, then chants before the brick "when Anu created heaven..." This shows as well as any example that, for Seleucid times, the *kalû* does sacrificial functions as well as musical ones.

The Seleucid rites described in *RAcc* are complex, and one is suspicious that in Seleucid times things changed somewhat from earlier periods, but we give them as examples of the most detailed that we have from any period, and we may be justified in studying them because they probably go back in part to earlier times. In the *šuluhhu* "hand-washing" rites, the actors are MAŠ.MAŠ's *kalû*'s and *nāru*'s.[83]

Another action of the *kalû* in Seleucid times happens when a temple foundation is laid.[84] Again, rubrics only are given, with many of the details missing.

As is the *kalû*[85] the *kalamahu* is often a scribe, indeed in texts which describe the *kalu*'s own rite.[86]

2.3.17 In Seleucid times astronomical aspects begin showing up: ^{lú}*ṭupšar* Enuma ^{d}Anu ^{d}Enlila ^{lú}*kalî* ^{d}Anu u An-tu$_4$ Uruk-ú "the scribe of (the important astronomical series) Enuma ^{d}Anu ^{d}Enlil of the *kalû*'s of Anu and Antu in Uruk.[87] This is a vast subject, for which we do not give a bibliography.

2.3.18 The *kalû* and the *nāru* often act together, as shown above in texts as well as lexical lists. They seem to complement each other. When rebuilding a temple, at the sacrifices the *kalû* sings the *taqribtu*-rite and the *nāru* sings the *inhu*-song.[88] In the *akītu* rite, in the Anu-temple at Uruk in Seleucid times, on the 7th day, amidst many offerings, a mere group of listings appear without verbs: *zimri ša nāri u kalî* "*zimru*-songs of the *nāru* and *kalû*."[89] NA annals list the *nāru*'s and *kalû*'s together.[90]

As was true of many offices in post-OB times, the *kalû* often held multiple offices. In MB and NB times, he could be a scribe (see n. 85), a *šangû*,[91] or an *ērib bīti* (see n. 91).

2.4 The main actors: nar/*nāru* and *nārtu* // *zammāru and zammārtu // zammeru and zammertu // nargallu*

2.4.1 Nar appears in the earliest lists Sec. 2.2.4: ED Lu B, near balag-di; ED Lu C near lú-šìr and ED Lu E, near muš-lah$_4$, titles which show up later as types of singers. In List OB Proto-Lu, 15 different types are given, Sec. 2.3.13.

We have seen how difficult it is to separate the nar and the gala. There is one main difference between them, however. In later times, the *kalû* appears only in the masculine (although a few female gala's are found in Sumerian times), whereas there are many *nārtu*'s, the *nāru* (m.) and *nārtu* (f.) seem often to be paired and it is usually difficult to separate the role of the *nāru* from that of the *nārtu*.

2.4.2 There is some uncertainty regarding the reading of the sign NAR in Akkadian. The NA lexical lists read *na-a-ru*,[92] and in other texts, Nuzi and NA, *nu-'a-ru*[93] but CAD N/l p.379a suggests that NAR is to be read as *zammāru*, with the standard Semitic root for singing *z-m-r*, while AHw divides the NAR between *nāru*, *zammāru* and *zammeru*. At Nuzi and NA, as well as the orthography *na-a-ru*, one finds *nu-a-ru* and, showing that an aleph sound is probably understood here, in the form *nu-'a-ru*,[94] perhaps the same word but under foreign language influence. The lexical entries listed below, however, indicate that there are three ranks: *nāru/nārtu*, *zammāru/zammārtu and zammeru/zammertu*.

2.4.3 The oldest orthography of the second is a place-name fromš supposedly OB Chagar Bazar, URU za-am-ma-ra-nim^{ki} [95]. CAD's only entry for *zammaru* is MA, of a ^{lú}⌜*za-ma*⌝*-ru* receiving sheep.[96]

Other examples of this orthography are: ^{lú}*rab za-ma-ri ADD* 537.5 (Kwasman No. 296), ^{lú}*rab za-am-ma-re-e ADD* 284 r.6 (Kwasman No. 295), with the same witnesses as *ADD* 537 and in the same order. A ^{lú}*rab za-ma-re* plays a *sammû* in a MA ritual, MVAeG 41/3 14, 10, Leipzig, 1937 8-19 and then takes his place before the king. In a list of high officials of Nebuchadnezzar, there is a *rab za-am-ma-ri*. Others on the list are heads of provinces or cities, and a scribe, a chief boatman, a chief merchant, several *qīpu*'s, and a group of *šangû*'s (^{lú} É.MAŠ).[97]

2.4.4 As we saw above in Sec. 2.2.4, the nar and GAL:NAR (LAK 243) appear on the earliest lists: ED List B (Fara), ED List C (Fara), ED List E (Abu Salabikh). All of these appear to be males, but the office of nar in these early times may have been held by women, according to Hartmann Sec. 2.3.3. As was seen above in the OB Proto-lu list relating to the gala, there are 15 different types of nar on it,[98] and one of them, the NAR.BALAG (read *tigû*) indicates by the signs that a balag is played.[99]

2.4.5 The *nāru* is found playing a variety of musical instruments. In Ur III times, we find nar's singing to Shulgi with tigi-drums, Klein *Shulgi* p. 199 A.81. This appears to be a scene in the palace, and may not have cultic elements. They used the *ni'u*, Maqlu VII 163. In NA times, the *nāru ṣehru* "assistant *naru*" (?) plays the *pitnu*, a stringed instrument, probably with a resonant box as a part of it.[100] In a rare mention, the *nāru* is associated with the *pagû*-instrument.[101] In NA royal inscriptions, they are found playing the *sammû* and *tāb/palu*.[102] There is a *nāš* ^{giš}*sammû* in a MB text[103] but we do not have enough information to decide whether this is another name of the *naru* who carries the *sammû*.

The nar probably recited myths and epics.[104]

In an Ur III economic text, 2 silver rings 10 shekels each for the nar-mí (f.), as well as for the daughter of the king show the high social level of this office.[105]

Another large Ur III text[106] lists without other comment a number of nar's, gala's and other musical ranks including a gala (f.), a nar (f.), and a muš-lah$_4$ in temples, with several of them from é ^{d}Shulgi, which Gelb translates "household of Shulgi" and Limet translates "temple of Shulgi." This may refer to the king himself, and so be from the royal household, or to a temple of the divinized Shulgi, in which case the singers are a part of the temple staff. The latter is more of a possibility when we see that the term é ^{d}Shulgi appears with é-^{d}Dumu-zi, é-^{d}Gatumdu, é-^{d}Nanshe and others.

In this text nar seems to include muš-lah$_4$'s (Sec. 2.13.1) as well as u$_4$-da-tuš's (Sec. 2.24). This would indicate that there were two general words for singers/instrumentalists: nar's and gala's.

In OB times of Abi-eshuh rations were given through PN *nārtum*.[107] Nothing here hints at a cultic use, but we may note that this is an important enough person to be referred to by name. The nar's get a šu-ti-a "receipt" in the previously noted Larsa cult tablet[108] and rations are given to the mí-nar-lukur-meš.[109] Are these the nar's of the lukur's, or another office in which a lukur has some of the functions of a nar?

In line 646 of OB Proto-lu, Sec. 2.3.13, among types of nar's appears the nar-igi-suhur-lá "the nar (who is) before the *kezertu.*" As we will see in Sec. 4.6, the *kezertu* is one of those offices whose function is to interpret sexuality, so here the nar is tied into this Category IV aspect also.

Most of the occurrences of the nar in OB times are found in economic texts, with no information about activities. Once the *nāru hallatuššu* "apprentice *nāru* " sings a lament called *sipittu*.[110] The reading is uncertain.[111]

In an Uruk lament, composed under Ishme-Dagan, after the king himself has played the tigi and the zamzam, and brought a lament (ér), then:[112]

nar-gal-zu šìr-ra hu-mu-ni-ib-túm-túm
"let your nar-gal ('s?) perform songs there."

i.e., at the gipar in Uruk. For the cultic use of the gipar, see Secs. 1.18.2, 1.18.10.

2.4.6 The *kalû* and *nāru* do not appear on the standard OB Lu list, Sec. 2.8.1, though it has a long broken section, MSL XII 208, 254ff, but on the OB Proto-Lu, Sec. 3.3.13. The female *nārtu* starts showing up in OB times, but nothing is known about how her activity differed from that of the *nāru*, if it did.

Two Assyrian *nārtu*'s appear as early as the Mari tablets.[113] Economic texts list several *nārtu*'s. In a large tablet, in which all the listed names are of females receiving rations, there is MÍ.NAR.MEŠ GAL "female chief musicians,"[114] MÍ.NAR.TUR.MEŠ[115] "female youthful musicians" or "female musicians of minor rank," MÍ.NAR.MEŠ.TUR.TUR "very young musicians" (in training?).[116] Though these seem to be ranks from the palace, the presence of cultic functionaries among them, as the *ugbabtu* (NIN.DINGIR) *ša* Addu[117] and the *kisalluhhatum* "female courtyard purifier" gives an indication that these musician ranks are cultic, also. Once 90 are counted on one tablet, with other female officiants[118] as [*k*]*izretum*, [*se*] *kretum*, *kisaluhhatum*, ^{mí}DUB.SAR, [^{mí}N]AR.TUR.TUR, *mahisatum* "weavers," Ì.DU$_8$, *mušahhitum* The first two ranks will be dealt with in Secs. 4.6 and 4.7 respectively, as female ranks which have something to do with sexuality and fertility.

As well as these, the usual LÚ.NAR.MEŠ appear in groups [119] or individually.[120]

2.4.7 The *nāru* in NA times is shown by the two entries on Lu = ša:

210	NAB	*na-a-ru*	
211	nar	KI.MIN	
212	nar-nar	*šá-ak-ki-nu*	
213	NAB-gal	*nár-gal-lu*	nàr: CAD N/l 352a
214	nar-gal	KI.MIN	

215	nar-tur	*hal-la-tu-šu-u*
216	nar-gal-tus-a	KI.MIN
217	nar-pà-da	*am-ru*
218	nar- [ ]	[ ]*-lu*

Lu =ša Tabl IV MSL XII 135

7	[nar]	*na-a-ru*
8	[nar-ga] l	LÚ.NAR-*gal-lu*
9	[nar-tu]r	LÚ.NAR *ṣe-* [*eh-ru*]
10	[nar]	LÚ.NAR [ ]

Proto-Lu Fragment III MSL XII 83

The *nārtu* appears in her own right in a long section of Lu = ša of ranks with the SAL "woman" sign, in the midst of which there appears:

16 SAL ù-li-li	*za-am-me-er-tu*
17 SAL ù-šè-lá	*za-am-me-er-tu*
18 SAL $^{na-ar}$nar	*na-ar-* [*tu*]
19 SAL $^{na-[ar]}$[na] r-r`a	*na* - [*ar-tu*]
20 [SAL NAR] BALAG	*te-g* [*i-tu*]

Lu = ša III ii MSL XII 124

to be compared to:

226	[NAR]$^{te-gi}$BALAG	*i-g* [*u-ú*]
227	BALAG.NÁR	MIN
228	BÁLAG.LÍL	MIN
229	LÍL.BALAG	MIN

Lu = ša IV MSL XII 136

KAR 146 is another *naptanu* "meal" rite, with three cultic actors: the king, the *šangû* and the *nāru,* described in Sec. 1.3.7.

In another rite (*parṣu*) for the *nāru* [121] concerning *arnu* "sin, wrongdoing," *kamānu*-cakes are used, leading to dancing and singing (r.8) related to many gods: Shamash, Ishtar, Enlil, Asshur, Ea and Anu.

VAT 10464 [122] belongs to the *akītu* festival. At the end of r. II, a *nāru*, then broken. A message comes to Asshur, and is put around the neck or box (*g/qúb-ba-ni*) of the *rab šibirte*. There are offerings and a seal brought for the standard (*urigallu*).

A large collection of NAR's is found in Kinnier Wilson *Wine Lists*, discussed on his pp. 76-8.[123] They are described as ^{kur}Aramayu, ^{kur}Arpadayu (f.), ^{kur}Aššurayu, ^{kur}Hattayu, ^{kur}Kaššayu. The *zammāre / nāre labbašūte* Kinnier Wilson takes as "musicians of the royal cloth"(76). But the word simply means "clothed, vested." It may refer to an unknown ceremony, or refer simply to them being especially clothed, equipped for the office. How would they differ from others not so designated? *ADD* 696 uses *lab-ba-šú-te* several times in its 14 short lines. Added to these are the *ša ūme* "day laborers," totalled as LÚ.ERIN.MEŠ "workers." For a similar term, see šà-gada-lá = *lābiš kitê* "clothed with linen," following gada-lá = ŠU-*lu* in Lu = ša IV 98f, MSL XII 131.

Kinnier Wilson (77) refers to Kassite texts which have ^{lú}*nāru* ^{lú}*Elamu* "Elamite" and ^{lú}*nāru* ^{lú}*Subaru* "Subarean," from Dur-Kurigalzu, O.R. Gurney, *Iraq* 11 137 No. 7. Add to this ^{mí}*Ṣurraya* (Tyrian) *ADD* 827 + 914 r.8 (collated by me) so we have *nāru*'s from many countries, or in the styles of these countries, or both.

As mentioned above in n. 83 under the *kalû*, in Seleucid times *mašmāšu*'s, *kalû*'s and *nāru*'s take part in the *šuluhhu* "cleansing" rites.

In Ashurnasirpal's annals[124] *nārtu*'s by themselves are taken as tribute. Sennacherib's annals tell of him capturing from Hezekiah among others *nāru*'s and *nārtu*'s.[125] Women singers appear with various titles in the Hebrew Bible, Sec. 2.33, 34, and it would be a rare insight into the Hebrew cult from an outside source if this historical note could be trusted, but this may be standard terminology, because he tells of this same thing elsewhere,[126] applying Akkadian terms to foreign countries. We wonder whether the *nartu*'s are pictured on an obelisk.[127] Eight MÍ.NAR.GAL's are listed among other female cultic officials in a list on the aforementioned tablet *ADD* 827 + 914:

r.5 10 8 MÍ.NAR.GAL
r.6 11 3 MÍ *ár-ma-a-a-te*
r.7 12(?)/ 13(?)MÍ *hat-ta-a-* [*a-te*]
r.8 13 13 MÍ *ṣur-ra-* [*a-a-te*]
r.9 14 13 MÍ.ḲUR.GAR.[RA(?)]
r.10 15 4 (?)/SANGA (?) [ ]
left edge 1 9 MÍ *kaš-šá-* [*a-a-te*]
left edge 2 61 *naphar* MI.NAR.[MEŠ?]

See B. Landsberger in Baumgartner AV, collated by F.R. Kraus and independently by me

where 61 is probably a total of all of these types. These are either nartu's from the countries of Aram, Hatti, Tyre, Kaššu, or are *nartu*'s of the styles called Aramean, Hattian, Tyrian, Kassite, somewhat the same as the male *naru*'s (see n. 123). The appearance of the *kurgarrû* among singers was noted Sec. 2.3.14, but the feminine is inexplicable, see App 3.3.7. The tablet shows the large numbers of different types of *nārtu*'s. We saw above Sec. 2.4.6 that MÍ.NAR.MEŠ.GAL could be contrasted with NAR.TUR and MÍ.NAR.TUR.TUR.

Another tablet, unfortunately broken at the top, perhaps lists unnamed rations to female officiants, the PNs of some being given:

(number omitted) *šaqītu*'s
(lines 3 and 4 are too broken to read confidently)
7 *abarakkatu*'s "steward (f.)," but a traditional translation
1 *hu-ma* ?/*la* ?-*ta-a-te*
10 (?) *nārtu*'s

ADD 828 (82-3-23,9),unpublished

As discussed above in Secs. 1.19.7, 1.21.9, 1.37.3, 1.44, in the royal annals of Nabonidus, the king tells of establishing his daughter as an *entu* of Sin, purifying her, and then as a magnanimous display befitting the great occasion, remitted the *ilku*-tax and established the freedom of the following *ramkut* "consecrated personnel" (so Reiner) of the temples.[128] As given in Reiner's translation the officials are:

enu	"high priest"
išippu	"purification priest"
zabardabbû (UD.KA.BAR.DAB.BA)	
bārû (LÚ.KUL.LUM)	"diviner"
engiṣu	"cook"
āriru	"miller"
rab bānî (GAL.DU)[129]	"master builder"
itinnu (ŠITIM)	"builder"
kisaluhhu	"courtyard purifier"
nidugallum (or, *atugallum*)	"chief doorkeeper"
tīr bīti	"court attendant (?)"
lagaru šakinu taqribti	"the *lagaru* priest who performs rites of homage"
nāru's	"singers"

The text, which lists all the ranks in the singular except the singers, does not describe what they do, but they are probably the notable ranks in the Ekishnugal temple.

Above we saw that the *kurgarrû* appeared in conjunction with the *kalû* in the Descent of Ishtar. Now we find that he appeared with the *nāru*'s also.[130] In this late Assyrian ritual, the *nāru*'s kneel before Ishtar, carrying the *sammû*-harp, the *šebītu*-lyre, the *kanzabu*-clapper, the *malīli*-flute, the *ṣinnetu*-instruments and the *arkati* "long" instruments, while the *kurgarrû* carries female symbols.

2.4.8 The nar-gal/*nargallu* occurs as early as Ur III times, Sec. 1.37.1. We have seen the *nargallu* in NA times [131]in the Lu = ša lists, and the female MÍ.NAR.GAL in the *ADD* 827 + 914 tablet of female officiants, Sec. 2.4.7. There are several more. In an offering text as part of a building inscription in the time of Esharhaddon, one finds, in a broken context: [ ]NAR.GAL.MEŠ ^{lú}GALA.MEŠ ....[132] In a legal tablet [133] found in the Nabû temple at Nimrud, among witnesses are a LÚ.NAR.GAL *ša* ^{d}[Nabû (?)]. The others are a *kalû,* a group of *šangû*'s, several [ ] *bīt ili ša* ^{d}Nabû, and a group of miscellaneous secular offices.

A MA or NA text lists a *ginû*-offering which Tukulti-Ninurta I gives for the goddess Sharrat-nipha in Kar-Tukulti-Ninurta, discussed in Sec. 1.2.6. In this miscellaneous grouping of officials we find the only singing rank, the *nargallum.* These were military people, a "chief of the gate," a *ša husīnišu* merchant, quite miscellaneous, but no other possible cultic offices.

2.4.9.1 There is another term which seems separate from the above, *zammeru* and *zammertu. Zammeru* is found at Mari,[134] with one reference, and on lexical lists, with two equivalents, followed by *nārtu* with two equivalants, see Lú = ša III ii, Sec. 2.4.7.

The protasis *šumma ina āli za-am-mi-ri MIN* (= *na'du*) "if there are many singers in a city"[135] is preceded by *mēlultu* "play," but there is a ritual *mēlultu.*[136]

2.4.9.2 Finally, there is a god-name ^{d}za-me-ru.[137]

2.4.10 In the Assyrian rite edited by Müller, Sec. 1.3.3, the king himself plays on a musical instrument (the name of which is broken) and says "Asshur is king! Asshur is king!" apparently in procession. Here the king plays the role of musician.

2.4.11 Pulling the other nar-ranks together in one place, we have seen that the nar-hal-tuš-a is read *hallatuššu* and is designated NAR.TUR, perhaps apprentice or young NAR. These are found on Lu = ša Tabl IV Sec. 2.4.7, as well as on an OB text singing a *sipittu* -lament.[138] This is to be compared to the gala-hal-tuš-a (Lu =ša Tabl IV, Sec. 2.3.14). The NAR.TUR [139] is read *nāru ṣehru*, and has been found at Mari also, Sec. 2.4.6.

The OB Proto-Lu entries in Sec. 2.3.13: nar-igi-suhur-lá (646) and nar-kéš-da (650), have so far been found only on lexical lists. The nar-sa appears on an OB ration list for the Ekishnugal temple in Ur III times (1.23). The latter could have been the *nāru* who plays the SA "gut," read as *pitnu*, Sec. 2.4.5 and see n. 100. The NAR.BALAG is read *tigû* on Lu = ša, above, a type of drummer, which position can also be held by women as *tigītu*, Lu = ša III ii, Sec. 2.4.7.

Lu = ša IV 217, Sec. 2.4.7 gives nar-pà-da an equivalence to *amru* in Lu = ša IV, above. One could guess that this is a variant of *abru*, App. 3.13, and see this as a variant of *abnu*, App. 3.13.1(see n. 115 there). The nar-nar = *šakkinu* has so far been found only on Lu = ša IV 212, Sec. 2.4.7.

In trying to put this tangled web together somewhat, we note that *kalû* and *nāru* are mentioned together often, that both are associated with the balag, and there are indications that the *nāru* and *kalû* act together, complementing each other especially in the NA annals, mostly in travels, battle scenes or building activites. The *nartu* is quite active, but no f. of *kalû* can be found.

2.5 Other singers and instrumentalists LÚ.TUR.MEŠ // LÚ.GAL.MEŠ

Menzel[140] has discovered an entry TUR.MEŠ in *KAR* 154 r. 11.14, following NAR$_x$.GAL, NU.GIG.MEŠ, but see notes in App. 1. LÚ.TUR.MEŠ and LÚ.GAL.MEŠ are together in a MA Tell Billa tablet.[141] LÚ.GAL.MEŠ appears in a line before LU.NAR in *KAR* 146.[142] This may be shorthand for some other offices, for instance, for NAR.TUR and NAR.GAL.

Menzel puts LÚ.TUR.MEŠ and LÚ.GAL.MEŠ with other "Tempelweihen," Sec. 1.32. LÚ.GAL appears in Lu = ša IV 186, App. 3.13.7, following sag-bur-ra, and with "equivalent" of *assinnu*.

2.6 Others: sur9/sur(ru) /*surrû* // *surmahhu*

The lexical texts relate these offices to the *kalû*:

242 $^{zu-ur}$sur9	MIN (i.e., *kalû*) EME.SAL
243 lagar	MIN.EME.SAL
244 la-bar	MIN.EME.SAL
	Nabnitu IX (=X)
	MSL XVI 122

----

160 $^{su-ra}$sur9	*su-ur-ru-ú*
161 sur9	*ka-lu-ú*

Lu = ša IV MSL XII 133

285	sur-ru	(sign)	*sur-ru-u*
286	"	"	*ka-lu-u*

S_b II MSL III 147

247	[su-ur-ru	x	*ka-lu-u* :	*sur-r*]*u-u*
249	[MIN	ÙZ.SIG_7	[MIN]	MIN

Ea VIII MSL XIV 483

155	ba-⸢x⸣-[		]
156	su-ur-ru	[x	*ka-lu-u*]
157			[*sur-ru-u*]
158	MIN	⸢x⸣ [	MIN]
159			[MIN]
160	su-ur-ru	ÙZ.[SIG_7	*ka-lu-u*]
161			[*su-ru-u*]

Tabl VIII/4 = 42
MSL XIV 512

Thus several lexical texts attest to the closeness of *surrû* and *kalû*.

In a description of the building of Dur-Sarruken, Sargon lists those officials who are: *ithuzi nindanšun lamid pirišti* "related to their order (and) learned in secret(s)." These are: *nešakku*'s, *ramku*'s, and *surmahhu*'s, whom he established.[143]

The *algarsurrû* indicates an algar played by a *surrû*, CAD A/1 s.v.

The paucity of entries of *surrû* and *surmahhu* do not necessarily testify to the lack of importance of this office. In fact, the spread among the lexical texts shows that there are other examples somewhere though so far not found in the texts.

2.7 Others: alan-zu / *aluzinnu*

2.7.1 On OB lexical lists:

580	KU.KU.KU
581	alan-zu
582	u_4-da-tuš
583	húb-bé
584	a-ù-a
585	[è] š-ta-lá
586	[S] AL èš-ta-lá

OB Proto-Lu MSL XII 54

7	lú UD-⸢ak⸣-kéš		*mu-um-mi-du*
8	lú u_4-da-tuš		*a-lu-zi-in-nu*
9	[lú	]-dù	*a-lu-zi-in-nu*
10	[lú	d] ug_4	*e-pi-iš na-mu-tim*
11	[lú	l] a	*me-lu-lu-ú-um**
12	[lú	]	[*m*]*u-ṣi-ih-hu-um*

OB Lu, Fragment II, 12

MSL XII 202,
*corrected per CAD M/2 17a

Continuing to NA lists:

245	alan-zu	*a-lu-zi-n* [*u*]
245a	[u_4-da]-tuš	MIN
246	u_4-da-tuš-ša *	MIN
247	gu-za-tuš-a	MIN
248	hal-la-tuš-a	MIN
249	KU-tar-ra	MIN
249a	[x]-tu-ra	MIN

Lu = ša IV MSL XII 136f

*Corrected to -a according to Gelb, Salonen *Festschrift* 61 in an Ur III text. These are listed among nar's in the text studied, perhaps indicating that they use music as a part of their performance.

272	LÚ še-ì-ág-a	*man-di-du*
273	LÚ alan-zu	*a-lu-zi-nu*
274	LÚ kaš-sa_{10}-sa_{10}	*sab-bi-'u*

Igituh

Aluzinnu "etwa 'Spassmacher, Clown'" (AHw), but also a cultic dancer, acrobat or the like, has equivalents in the Lu = ša lists above. u_4-da-tuš is "bear ward" according to I.J. Gelb, Sec. 2.24, with many examples, noting that they receive bears, and are singers. Maybe they are part of the performance. Peking Opera has acrobatics as part of its performance, something usually surprising to westerners. The hal-la-tuš-a = *hallatuššu* is probably the apprentice *aluzinnu*, on analogy to other ways this word is used.

On OB Proto-Lu a-ù-a means "woe" [144] and though it may be the "Kultperson" listed by AHw s.v. *a'u*, with the functionary known by the words he utters. *e laštalu* and *e laštalitu* are types of singers, Sec. 2.17. So OB Proto Lu here has its own list of cultic singers and musicians. On the OB Lu fragment, *mummidu* (meaning unknown, CAD M/2 196b, AHw 671b), *ēpiš namūtim* "maker of a joke," *mēlulum* "player," *muṣihhum* "clown," shows the *aluzinnu* with other players and actors.

2.7.2 On the other hand, this office has some of the aspects of divination. A question asked him is: *aluzinnu mina teli'i ašipūta* "*aluzinnu*, how is your *ašipu*-craft?"[145]

2.7.3 Foster[146] continues his long-studied self-disclosure of the *aluzinnu*. He concludes that the *aluzinnu* is a clown, a trickster (as defined by anthropologists, especially those who study Native American culture), who ridicules the cultic professions. At times he even acts the part of a woman (75, line 18), reminding us of the *assinnu* and *kurgarrû* of App. 3.

2.7.4 Finally, ^{lú}*a-lu-zi-nu* is a witness in a MA document in which no other witnesses are given titles.[147] This indicates that it is not an ad hoc rank. No feminine form has as yet been discovered.

<u>2.8 Main actors: balag-di/*ṣarihu* // i-lu-di/*munambû* // NAR.BALAG/tigi/ *tigû* and *tigitu*</u>

2.8.1 The balag-di appears as early as ED Lists B and E, Sec. 2.2.4, and on a list of "métiers et emplois" in pre-Sargonic times.[148] It is given in *PSD* s.v., as "lamentation singer, mourner." There may be a female balag-di[149] in Ur III. The reading is such instead of ^{d}DUB.DI or GU$_{x}$.DI, see MSL 3, 191f, MSL 7 136 n. to line 266. Comparing several OB Lu lists for related offices:

	OB Lu A, MSL XII 165		OB Lu D, MSL XII 208
245	lú i-lu-di	*mu-na-[bu-ú]*	line 250
246	lú i-lu-di	*ša ṣi-[ir-hi-im]*	
247	lú^{kuš}á-la	*ša a-li-[e]*	248
248	lú al-gar-su-ra	*mu-ki-il [a-li-e]*	
249	lú balag	*[ša ba-la-an-gi]*	246
250	lú balag-di-da	*ša t[i-im-bu-ut-tim]*	
251	lú balag-balag-di	*ša [te-li-tim]*	247
252	lú balag$^{?}$-di	*ṣa-r[i-hum]*	
253	lú balag-di	*mu-n[a-bu-ú]*	251
254	lú húb	*ša hu-[up-pi-im]*	
255	lú šìr -sag	*š [a]še-er- [š] a-n [i-im]*	

	OB Lu D, MSL XII 208		OB Lu A, MSL XII1 165
246	lú ^{kuš}balag	*ša ba-la- (gi)-i*	line 249
247	lú ^{kuš}balag-balag-di		251
248	lú ^{kuš}á-lá		247
249	lú i-lu	*ša nu-bi-e*	
250	lú i-lu-di	*mu-na-bu*	245
251	lú balag-di		253
252	lú pe-el-lá		

5 lú i-lu-di
6 lú balag-di
7 išib
8 lú mah

OB Lu F', MSL XII 212f

The late Assyrian counterpart reads:

174	balag-íl	*na-áš ba-lam-gi*
175	balag-di	*ṣa-ri-hu* (as corrected)
176	balag-i-lu-di	*mu-nam-bu-u*

Lu = ša IV MSL XII 134

Comparing OB Lu A, line 251, *ša telītim* to a list of some Category IV people in Lu = ša IV, Sec. 4.4.1, we find there that the lukur is given an "equivalent" of *telitu*, usually "the highly capable one" an adjective applied to Ishtar. May we say that *ša telītu* and *telītu* are forms of the same office? The *telītu* instrument could be the element which binds them together. We find the *tim/bbutu*, a harp of some kind, in an analagous usage, see AHw 1354b.

Referring to the Lu =ša IV entries, *PSD* s.v. lists balag-i-lu-di "wailer" as a separate single-entry. This example repeated on the Lu = ša IV entry is yet another combination of lú i-lu-di OB Lu F' above and balag, somewhat redundant, or may it be explained as a description?

In an emesal composition[150] which Römer calls a dialogue between Inanna and a balag-di, the latter appears in a line at the beginning: 2 balag-di u4-ba gel-le-èg gin-na-mu u4-ba me-e-li-e-a "oh balag-di at the time destruction came to me, at that time, ah!" (translation not sure in all aspects) The balag-di is called upon to lament on the balag in a large emesal text.[151] In an emesal dialogue about the storm, the balag-di is spoken to, then, in turn, the god šerida (dšè-ri5-DI).[152]

2.8.2 As seen so far only in OB Lu A and OB Lu D, both the *munam lbbu* and the *sarihu* [153] are types of or equivalents to the balag-di. The sign balag appears in several titles. The NAR.BALAG appears in OB Proto-Lu among other nar titles, and is to be read *tigium*, or *tigû* in NA, according to Lu = ša III, immediately below. The tigi is a harp or drum used in the Inanna cult,[154] and appearing in the Gudea cylinders. There is a female *tigītu* in OB times,[155] and a listing among other female officiants in Lu = ša III, Sec. 2.4.7.

There is a PN *wakil* "overseer" of *tigītu*'s in OB times (see n. 155). Two drums for the *tigītu*'s for the temple are in a text by an OB king of Malgium.[156]

2.8.3 Balag as the name of a rank by itself appears often, see Sec. 2.10. The lists separate the balag from the balag-di. In OB Lu D, Sec. 2.8.1, lú-kuš-balag = *ša ba-la-(gi) - i.* Cohen[157] understands the kuš-balag (= *ša ba-la -(gi)-i* OB Lu D 246, MSL XII 208) as equivalent to the balag of later texts. If this is the case, it would neatly separate the lú-balag = *ša balaggi* and the lú-balag-di = *munabbû*, although the functions of the two we still know little about.

2.9 Others: búr-balag

In the earliest lists:

21 lú-nar
22 lú-šìr
23 lú-BÚR:balag
24 lú-RI:x

ED List C MSL XII 14

101 lú-á-lá
102 lú-gi-di
103 lú-g[i]-⌈ x ⌉
104 lú-BÚR-balag
105 lú-X

ED List E MSL XII 18

A pre-Sargonic/Sargonic lyre player is called búr-balag of denlil in lexical texts.[158]

The lexical list Aa has many Akkadian "equivalents" of BUR.[159] The present office may refer to búr = *pašāru* "to release, loosen."[160] It may refer to the soothing, emotional release and creation of an ease brought about by the music of this instrument.[161] The en(f.) serves Nanna with loosed hands: mus$_2$-bur$_2$-bur$_2$-^{d}Nanna.[162] Perhaps these are hands that loosely go over the strings of the instrument, referring to a style or mode of playing.

The mode is shown also in the lexical list Kagal:

9:7' numdun-búr-re-balag-gá = *na-sà-a-súm*

Kagal, MSL XIII 248

where *nasāsu* ="sing, weep, complain," and numdun=*šaptu* "lip," either of the person or the instrument. In a NA cultic text, [*ša*] *bikīti ibakki* [*ša*] *nissati inassus* "the mourner weeps, the wailer sings a lament."[163]

2.10 Main actors: balag/balag-íl/*ša balamgi* // *nāš balamgi* // *epiš balamgi*

2.10.1 (See also 2.8, balag-di). The balag is played by the gala/*kalû* (Gudea), and the balag-di, Sec. 2.8. It is played in the é-ná-da kù ^{d}nanna-ke "the sacred bedchamber of Nanna."[164] It is also the name of a composition that is sung on this instrument.[165] It is also the name of an office, the lú-balag; PSD lists one occurrence of lú-balag,[166] but we have seen several possible occurrences of this term, Sec. 2.8.3.

2.10.2 A second way the name of this office is used appears in two Lu = ša entries:

26'	[l] ú-ma	*ša-il-tu*
27'	lú-balag-gá	*mu-še-lu-ú* [*e-dim-me*]
28'	lú-sag-šè-ná-a	*mu-pa-šir* [*šu-na-ti*]
29'	x.GAN.RAB.ME.KU	*iš-* [ ]

Lu = ša II iii MSL XII 120

182	[ensi]	*šá-'-i-li*
183	[lú-balag-gá]	[*mu-še-lu-u*] *e-dim-me*
184	(broken)	

Lu =ša I MSL XII 102

The *mušēlû eṭimme* "raiser of a ghost" is one of the names for necromancer. Here we may refer to a characteristic of these lexical lists, that of description. We may understand these lines not as equivalents, but as a note that the necromancer uses the technique of the lú-balag.

2.10.3 We have seen the GAL.BALAG in Sec. 2.2.4. The balag-íl "balag bearer" is probably a different office from the balag-di, Sec. 2.3.14. He appears from Old Sumerian[167] to NA.[168] He appears here among the Förtsch texts in the phrase balag-íl e-ta-ru-a in an inserted clause that is not related to the mu-túm document it accompanies. ru "distance oneself, remove" could describe the mood of the balag.

2.10.4 Perhaps the *ša balamgi* (OB Lu A 249, OB Lu D 246), *nāš balamgi* (MAOG 13/2 46.28) and *ēpiš balamgi* are three terms for the same rank. *ēpiš balaggi/ṣirhi* appears as one reference in the lexical list Alu,[169] but I could not find it in Moren *Shumma Ālu.*

2.11 Others: šìr-sag/*ša ṣirhi* // lú-šìr

2.11.1 The Sumerian šìr/*zamāru* "to sing" appears in several words. šìr-sag/*ša ṣirhi* is a "dirge singer," CAD S 206b, with several lexical and bilingual references.[170] There is a šìr-sag = *ša šeršānum,* MSL XII 165, 255: "singer of *šeršānum*. OB Lu A 246 (Sec. 2.8.1) provides yet another sign: lú i-lu-di = *ša ṣi-ir-hi-im,* i-lu being a lamentation. The šìr-sag appears with a balag-di, the former singing šìr-mah?[171]

2.11.2 So far the lú-šìr has been found only in lexical lists, ED Lu C, Sec. 2.9, and in a list of various kinds of music, in OB Proto-Lu 587, Sec. 2.3.13.

2.12 Others: še-en-nar

A unique occurrence so far is: še-en-nar-e balag-balag ha-ra-sìg-ge "the s. singers will pluck the lyre for you."[172]

2.13 Main actors: muš-lah$_4$/*mušlahhu* // *mušlahhatu*

2.13.1 This office occurs in the earliest lists, as ED Lu E, Sec. 2.2.4., and M. Lambert finds several Pre-Sargonic entries.[173]

In OB it appears in the midst of nar and gala singers:

(lines 641-650, various kinds of nar's)
651 muš-lah$_4$
652 muš-lah$_4$-gal
653 gala
(followed by six more kinds of gala's) OB Proto Lu MSL XII 56

2.13.2 He appears among diviners in NA:

261	LÚ muš-lah$_4$	*muš-la-ha*
262	LÚ EN.ME.LI	*ša-'-i-lu*
263	LÚ gub-ba	*mah-hu-u*
264	LÚ [ní]-su-ub	*zab-bu*

Igituh

and among exorcists and singers in NA:

205	nar-balag	*a-ši-pu*
206	ka-pirig	MIN
207	muš-DU$^{la-la-ah}$DU	*muš-la-la-ah-hu*
208	lú-^{giš}gàm-šu-du$_7$	*muš-ši-pu*
209	la-bar	*ka-lu-ú*

Lu = ša Excerpt I
MSL XII 102

The *mušlalahhu* seems to be a variant of the *mušlahhu*. The latter office seems to have two aspects, that of incantation and that of singing and playing a musical instrument. The name indicates that he is a snake handler, snake charmer, snake conjurer or the like. The usual English translation "snake charmer" and the German one "Schlangenbeschwörer" have different connotations. These actions show up in one text in a proverb having to do with a snake.[174]

2.13.3 In two Ur III letters [175] from the divinized Shulgi, there were singers in the territory of Lagash: gala, muš-lah$_4$ and u$_4$-da-KU (= u$_4$-da-tuš), see Sec. 2.24. In another place a muš-lah$_4$ is a servant of Shulgi.[176] This office appears on Ur III economic texts, CAD s.v. *mušlahhu.*

2.13.4 In NA script, a document says that the *mušlahhu* purified Esagil in an Agum II kakrime text.[177]

A relationship to Marduk is shown by a late NA incantation text:

> *ina balika* lú*āšipu eššepu* MUŠ.LAH$_4$ *ul iba'u sūqa*
> "without you (Marduk) the *āšipu* the *eššepu* (and) the *mušlahhu* do not walk about the street." *KAR* 26.25.

Presumably this means that without Marduk being what he is, or without Marduk's help, these incantation functionaries would not be able to ply their trade, showing again the necessity of the high level god to the presemably lower level action of incantation.

An Esarhaddon inscription[178] lists officials and professionals, perhaps deported from Egypt on his campaign there. These include (all in the plural) the *tašlīšu* "third men (on the battlewagon)," *narkabtu* "battlewagon (drivers)," *mukīl appāti* "rein holders," these three being standard NA designations of army ranks, bowmen, dream interpreters, veterinarians, scribes, *mušlahhu*, *kāṣiru* "textile craftsmen," *nāru,* LÚ.NINDA.MEŠ, *sirāšû*, carpenter for wagons, carpenter for boats. These are mostly military and specialist positions, but include incongruously the two musical offices of *nāru* and *mušlahhu*. These could have been attached to the army, to take care of the cultic acts that we see performed in the slab sculpture.[179]

In the NA incantation text Maqlû [180] among other witches (all female) whose exploits were criticized, was the *mušlahhatum*, the female muš-lah$_4$.

2.14 Others: dam-ab-ba

Though the elements in the word do not imply this, the dam-ab-ba is listed with gala's and women of the temples of Ningirsu and Bau in a pre-Sargonic text from Lagash and described as ír-sig$_7$-me "wailers."[181]

2.15 Others: lú-ér/mí-ér/*bakkā'u* and *bakkītu* // ér-ra / *ša bikīti*

2.15.1 The sign ér and the Akkadian root *b-k-u* are often used for "weeping" offices:

128	lú	[a-nir-ra]	*ša ta-ni-hi-im*
129	lú	ér-[dug$_4$]-dug$_4$	*ba-ka-a-a-ú*
130	lú	ti-rí-da-nu-um	*ša mu-ús-ku la ṭè-hu-šu*

OB Lu A MSL XII 161

The root of *bakka'u* is *bakû* "to weep" and the form indicates "the always weeping one." lú-ír u mí-ír accompany Tammuz when he rises up from the Netherworld.[182] In a NA cultic commentary: the goddess dSakkukutu circumambulates the city, and is a weeping woman for him (*ba-ki-šu ši-i*)[183] in form an abstract word, but apparently an epithet for the goddess. The goddess Belili is called *bakkitu* "the always weeping woman."[184]

2.15.2 The rare *ša bikīti* also appears in a lexical text associated with ér:

126	[lú] ⌈tu⌉-ra	*ma-ar-sum*
127	lú [ér-ra]	*ša* ⌈*bi-i-ki*⌉-[*tim*]
128	lú [a-nir-ra]	*ša ta-ni-hi-im*
129	lú ér-[dug_4]-dug_4	*ba-ka-a-a-ú*

OB Lu A MSL XII 161

A bilingual provides the only other reference to this office as such:

21	mu-lu-ír-ra-ke_x	ír mu-un-šéš-šéš
22	[*ša*] *bi-ki-ti*	*i-bak-ki*

K. 4613, 4R 11.22,
CAD B 225b

"the [*ša*] *bikīti* weeps."

The *balaggu* and the *halhallatu* are used for *bikītu* "weeping." [185]

2.15.3 Many other offices did weeping. The *kizretu* and *harimtu* set up a weeping in the cities.[186] The crown prince and his men wept at the time of Nabonidus.[187] The NB priests' heads were covered with rent garments while they sang *ṣirihtu*, *nissati* and *bikīti* for Sin during the eclipse.[188] The mention of hair sometimes has to do with the disheveled hair worn by mourners in the ancient world.[189] An Izbu commentary relates this to weeping:

ma-la-a *bi-ki-tú*

Izbu Commentary V.170,
Leichty *Izbu* 217

malû being "unkempt hair."

2.15.4 The weeper is often not given a title. The NA letter *ABL* 437, corrected by *LAS* I 280, has a valuable description of rites upon the death of a son of a *šatammu* "administrator" and his wife. They were prepared and wept over (*ibakia*), by whom it is not stated. Burnt offerings, numerous namburbi, *bīt rimki*, *bīt sala' mê*, *nēpeše*-rites of the *āšipūtu*, ershahunga-wails and scribal recitations take place in this letter (lines 15-20), all listed together, which must have taken considerable time. We have discussed many of these here, see Index.

2.16 Others: ama-ér-(ra)/*ama'errû*

The ama-ér appears lamenting with the gala in the Gudea literature, Sec. 2.3.2 (see n. 12). She appears between gala and balag in OB Proto-Lu 659, Sec. 2.3.13. She appears in Lu = ša IV 181, Sec. 2.3.14, between the *kurgarrû* and the pi-il-pi-li, indicating the types discussed in App. 3. In this latter section other ama- ranks are noted, indicating the semantic significance of the term ama "mother."

2.17 Others: èš-ta-lá *e/aštalu* and *e/aštalitu*

The feminine and masculine appear in the lexical lists:

584 a-ù-a
585 [è] š-ta-lá
586 [S]AL èš-ta-lá
587 šìr

OB Proto-Lu MSL XII 54

21 [SA] L èš-ta-lú *eš-ta-l [i-tu]*
22 [SA] L šà-zu *šab-su - [tu]*

Lu = ša Tabl III MSL XII 124

For a-ù-a, cf. the "lullaby" edited by Kramer, with a first line u_5-a a-ù-a.[190] In the OB list, the *eštalû* appear among singers, but in the Lu = ša list the entry occurs before the *šabsūtu* "midwife," but following a division line before which is a section of singers.[191] In OB Mari, this appears as a kind of singer. The *aštalītu*'s (SAL èš-ta-lá in OB Proto-Lu) wear veils (*šitrī*).[192] The Mari rite with acrobats and performers ends with the *pašišu* offering "before the veil" (*šitru*), see Sec. 1.6.2 n. 66.

2.18 Others: ér-sig_7

The ér-sig_7 "wailers" appear in a funerary text in pre-Sargonic times.[193]

2.19 Others: mí-gù-mur-ak

The SAL-KA-HAR-ak, usually "professional mourner" is read mí-gù-mur-ak by B. Alster[194] in a text in which she holds a ring and a spindle, symbol of the feminine. This fits into Alster's translation:

230 munus.gù-mur-ak KAxLI gi_4-gi_4-dam
"the gumurak (f.) shouts again and again"

231 ^{gis}bala har-ra su-na na-mu-un-gál
"she holds a ring and a spindle in her hand"

232 é é-a i-ni-in-ku_4-ku_4-ku_4
"she enters all houses"

233 e.sír e.sír.ra gú mu-un-gíd-gíd-dè
"she stretches her neck in all streets"

The last line hints at a sexual role; the women in Isaiah 4.16 walk with outstretched necks. This functionary is found with others who will appear in chapter 4, having to do with sexuality:

708d SAL suh[ur-lá]

708e SAL ki-zé-er-ak
709 SAL KA-HAR-ak
710 SAL šu-gi$_4$

OB Proto-Lu MSL XII 58

The suhur-lá = *kezertu*, with a variant semi-ideogram ki-zé-er-ak, is one of the foremost interpreters of sexuality, Sec. 4.6. Her hair is a sexual attraction, so AHw 903b s.v. *qardu* suggests "mit schütterem Haar. (?) The šu-gi$_4$ = *šugētu* appears not as often as the former, but is an important member of this group, also, Sec. 4.4.1.

The lexical lists have the present word in two semantic groupings:

341	lú numdun-pi-el-lá	*ša ša-ba-šu qá-al-la*
342	lú KA-HAR-ak	*qar-du-um*
343	lú kiri$_4$-ga-an-lah	*hu-un-nu-nu-ú*

OB Lu MSL XII 168

having to do with the *qardu* "hero," and the other group:

6'	[g]ù-húl-la	*ri-gi$_4$-im hi-e-du-ú-tim*
7'	[g]ù-mur-ak	*qar-du-um*
8'	[gù]-dé-dé	*gú-di-id-du-ú*
9'	[gù-d]é-a	*na-bu-ú*

Kagal D MSL XIII 246

among terms for speaking, calling: *rigim hidūtim* is a "cry of joy," *nabû* is "to name, to call." These do not fit in well with the idea of "hero;" furthermore there are other words nearby both in the OB Lu and Kagal entries which relate to speaking.

So, her role is speaking. The spindle she holds is that typically associated with the female. She is like some sexually-oriented officials, as the *kezertu* and *šugētu*, perhaps with an especially attractive hair-do. She is found on the streets, hinting at the role of streetwalker, stretching her neck in a provocative manner.

2.20 Others: *lallāru* and *lallār(i)tu*

The *lallāru* is a wailer, and appears after balag ranks on Lu = ša IV, 177f, Sec. 2.3.14, and another Lu = ša text:

211	i-lu-di	*mu-nam-bu-ú*
212	1-lu-a-li	*lal-la-ru*
213	lú-gub-ba	*mah-hu-ú*

Lu =ša I, Excerpt I
MSL XII 102

Di in i-lu-di is something like "speak, make a noise," when one compares line 211 to igituh 278, below: LU i-lu-dug$_4$-ga "one who says an i-lu" = *munambû* in both cases.

He wails like a wild bull, and the term is also given to a bird, a bee and a cricket, CAD L 48. Gilgamesh howls at the death of his friend Enkidu like a female *lallāritu*, bitterly.[195]

And in a NA "practical vocabulary" there is found:

276 LÚ e-piš ip-ši — *pa-qa-a-a*
277 LÚ ⌈ hul ⌉-a-lá-bi — *lal-la-ru*
278 LÚ i-lu-dug$_4$-ga — *mu-nam-bu-u*

Igituh

A *dābibtum* "talkative woman" is placed next to *lallartum* again showing the speaking function:

22 [x-li]-li *la-la-ar-tum*
23 [x-di-d]i ⌈*da* ⌉-*bi* -⌈*ib* ⌉-*tum*

Proto-Kagal MSL XIII 86

In a NA prayer to Marduk, a supplicant cries *ki-i lal-la-ri* "like a *lallāru*[196] and in a prayer to Ishtar, the supplicant speaks of his *làl-la-ru*, probably his professional *lallāru*.[197]

Nowhere in these references is there any indication of how the *lallāru* or *lallārtu* cries or acts. They could be part of the cult, because they are among other cultic officials.

2.21 Others: *malīlu // ša malīli*

2.21.1 The lexical lists show:

101 lú-á-lá
102 lú-gi-di
103 lú-g[i] - | x |
104 lú-BÚR:balag

ED Lu E MSL XII 18

166 lú-⌈ e-ne ⌉-[dug$_4$-dug$_4$] — [*mu-um-mi-lum*]
167 lú-má-lal — [*ša ma-la-li-im*]
168 lú-má-da-lá — [*ša ti-la-tim*]

OB Lu A MSL XII 163

242 lú-gi-⌈ di-da ⌉ — *ša ma* - [*li-lim*]
243 lú gi-gíd — *ša en*- [*bu-bi-im*]
244 lú gi-di — *ša su* - [*ul-pi-im*]
245 lú i-lu-di — *mu-na*- [*bu-ú*]

OB Lu MSL XII 165

with *ša malalim* probable, because lú-má-lal seems to be a pseudo-ideogram.

2.21.2 In App. 3.2.4 the *assinnu* and the *kurgarrû* engage in a kind of a dance in the Ishtar cult with the *malīlu*, if correct reading.

2.22 Others: *musarrihtu*

This could be translated "lamenting woman." In *RA* 70 (1976) 112.16, CAD M/2 24ld, the one OB reference uses [*mu*] -*ṣa-ri-ih-tim*, a II/1 f. participle of *ṣarāhu*, but it may be a description, rather than the title of an office.

2.23 Others: si-dù

This appears as a PN in a Sargonic /pre-Sargonic text.[198]

2.24 Others: u$_4$-da-tuš

This office shows up on both early and late lexical lists:

581	alan-zu
582	u$_4$-da-tuš
583	húb-bé

OB Proto Lu MSL XII 54

245	alan-zu	*a-lu-zi-n* [*u*]
245a	[u$_4$-da]-tuš	MIN
246	u$_4$-da-tuš-sa	MIN
247	gu-za-tuš-a	MIN

Lu = ša IV MSL XII 136

For line 246, Gelb, Salonen *Festschrift* 6l, reads u$_4$-da-tuš-a. The u$_4$-da-tuš is a type of singer in Ur III, p. 93f, which appears in a list of gala's, nar's and u$_4$-da-tuš's in a document.[199] I.J. Gelb Sec. 2.7.1 notes that the u$_4$-da-tuš receive bears, so he translates "bear ward." He suggests that they play and the bear performs.

2.25 Dancers in Mesopotamia

2.25.1 Words for dancer are few, although some form of dancing may have accompanied most playing of musical instruments. A dance vocabulary overlaps with words for "play:" *lawû* "to go around;" *gâšu* "to dance;" *melulu* "play, dance;" gil is found in a term nar-sal-gil, a singer-dancer in an Ur III text.[200] A sùh-sùh / *raqqidu* shows up in a text in which a possible drug use is discerned.[201] Perhaps sùh = *ešû* "be tangled, confused" is a way of describing the dancing. The root *r-q-d* is one of the common Semitic roots for dancing.

Raqqidu and *mummillu* appear together as two words for dancer:

235	KA$^{i\text{-}\ulcorner x\urcorner}$-du$_{11}$-du$_{11}$	*za-am-mi-rum*
236	e-ne-du$_{11}$-du$_{11}$	*mu-um-mi-*lum* (text: *rum*)
237	sùh-sùh	*raq-qí-du*
238	gu$_4$-ud-da	MIN
239	kud-da	MIN

Lú =ša IV MSL XII l36

So the terms for dancer are found near the *zammirum* "singer," as is expected. Another *raqqidu* entry justifies our placing the dancer in a category including singers:

220	nab	*na-a-ru*
221	[nar-gal]	[ŠU]-*lum*
222	[gu$_4$-ud-da]	[*ra-a*]*q-qí-du*
223	[ ]	[x-x] -*di-lu*
224	[èš-ta-lú]	[*eš*] -*ta*-[*lu*] -*ú*

Lu = ša I MSL XII 103

nāru and *eštalû* are both types of singers, and surround the word for dancer. *Raqqidu* appears also in a Silbenvocabular:

118	[ab-b] a-ni	a-bu-šu	*lu-ša-nu*
119	[a] b-[b] a-a	a-ba-bi-im	*ra-qí-du-um*
120	[a] b-[b] a-ur	a-bi a-li-im	*am-za-li-lum*

Silbenvocabular A
E. Sollberger, Landsberger AV 24

with *amzalilum* probably being a variant of *anzaninu*, see App. 4.2.

And another early Silbenvocabular, now corrected:

133 gu-ud KU MIN (*tu-kul-tum*) *ša* KU.UD.DU *raq-qí-du*

Yale Syllabary, *YOS* 1, 87,114,
corrected by J. Nougayrol
Landsberger AV p. 33.

2.25.2 The second common word for dancer is *mummillu*:

165	[lú inim-sag$_5$-ga]	[*mu-uš-te-mi-qum*
166	lú ⌈ e-ne ⌉-[dug$_4$-dug$_4$]	[*mu-um-mi-lum*]
167	lú má-lal	[*ša ma-la-li-im*]

OB Lu A MSL XII 162f

and appears also in the Lu = ša IV entry, Sec. 2.25.1.

Among other epithets and descriptions of Ishtar, she is *mu-um-mil-tum* ^{d}iš-tar who gathers the assembly.[202]

In what seems to be a MB lamentation over Babylon (line 1), a scene is described: *ittabiši ina libbišu e-li-lum mu-mi-il-lum* "there is in it *elilum* song and *mumillum* dance.[203]

2.25.3 Another type of dancer has the root *š-h-t*:

9	[nin-dingir]-^{d}nin-urta	*gu-bab-ti* MIN (= ^{d}Nin-urta)
10	[nin-dingir]-^{d}ba-ú	*šá-hi-it-tu*
11	[SAL ma-a] z-za	MIN
12	[ ]-⌈ x ⌉-ta-è	MIN
13	[ ]-⌈ x ⌉-nun-ta-è	MIN
14	[x$^{(x)-r]a}$-peš$_5$$^{pi-iš}$	MIN
15	[x$^{(x)-d]im}$-igi^{i-gi}	MIN
16	[x] -[x]-igi	MIN

Lú =ša IV MSL XII 128f

That *šahittu* has a cultic function is shown by the "equivalence": *ugbabtu*, often given as *gubabtu* in NA, of the goddess Bau. AHw has *šahittu* as "eine (Tanz-) Priesterin?" One compares *šahāṭu* A "to jump, leap; move jerkily" (CAD) but no examples of dancing are given by CAD, except the Erimhuš II entry in the lexical section, in which *šitahhutu*, a I/3 form of *šahātu* appears with *sâru* and *mēlulu*, two terms for dancing. There are three NB PNs: *šá-hi-tum* /*tú-ti* .[204]

Though these above types have so far only been found on lexical texts and PNs, it is just a matter of time before they will be discovered in connected texts, if past experience is any indication.

2.25.4 Much of the cultic dancing is done as a group. A group dance is done in a circle, but only by women, as No. 413 from Nuzi.[205] In a Hellenistic text, the *kurgarrû* and *assinnu ...ultu šu* [*mēli*] [*a-n*]*a imni ilammušunutu* "from left to right they circle around them (i.e., "all the deities"). Here we have a kind of a circle dance, done counterclockwise, about the cult statues of the deities, done in front of Ishtar while she is seated on her *parakku* in the court of the *akītu*.[206]

When the deity is described as engaged in a cultic action, we may understand the cultic functionary in that action; Ishtar dances (root *gâšu*) like a man.[207]

2.25.5 Dance texts are few and far between. In a list of what different groups in society did with the help of Inanna, The Curse of Akkade lists gifts to old women, old men, maidens, young men, children, and then nursing mothers who are dancing to the music of the *algarsurrû* and tigi.[208]

2.26 Others: húb/(*ša*)*huppû* (See further App. 3.14)

The *huppû* appears among acrobats in a cultic text of Ishtar at Mari, as described in Sec. 1.6.2 and Proto-Lu Sec. 2.7.1. Some lexical texts are pertinent here:

(4 balag-related offices), then:

253 lú balag-di	*mu-n* [*a-bu-ú*]
254 lú húb	*ša hu-* [*up-pi-im*]
255 lú šìr-sag	*š* [*a*] *še-er-*[*š*]*a-n* [*i-im*]

OB Lu A MSL XII 165

appearing among singers and instrumentalists. The lú-húb = *ša huppû* is an acrobat of some sort (see Mari text) but because of his placement here, probably a singer/musician also.

Singers also appear with *huppû*:

226 [NAR] $^{te\text{-}gi}$BALAG	*ti-g* [*u-ú*]
-------	
230 a-u$_5$	*a-ú-* ⌈*ú*⌉
231 addir	MIN
232 ugula-nam-tag-ga	*a-kil ár-ni*
233 húb-bé	*hu-ub-bu-u*
234 lú-an-ti-bal	*šá ṣa-ad-di*
---------	
235 KA$^{i\text{-}⌈x⌉}$-du$_{11}$-du$_{11}$	*za-am-mi-rum*

Lu = ša IV MSL XII 136

a-ù-a is a singer in OB Proto-Lu Sec. 2.7.1, and *zammirum* is a singer, but I cannot explain the positioning on this list of *akil arni* "overseer of wrong" nor *ša ṣaddi* "the one of the sign, omen."

2.27 Singers and Dancers in the Hebrew Bible

2.27.1 The number of books and articles on music in the Ancient Near East, see n. 3, and especially that of biblical times is enormous. Most of them concern terms for and descriptions of singing, or a listing of musical instruments, many of which are difficult to find modern equivalents for. Some books are rich in post-biblical rabbinic interpretation, and the extent to which it is proper to extrapolate these back to biblical times depends upon the case.[209]

In a search for titles of professions related to music, these two books provide little. Weisberg[210] points out that there is no word for "guild" in Akkadian, with the exception of one narrow usage after 500 B.C. in Nippur, and this lack holds for the Hebrew Bible also.

2.27.2 Texts and archaeology, two different genres describing the same society, presumably should converge. Musical instruments discovered in archaeological digs include[211] cymbals, drum (?), bells, rattle. Instruments mentioned by the various texts, often used in both sacred and secular contexts, include:

ᶜāśôr.	"a type of *nebel*" Ps 92.9
gittît	Ps 8.1, passim
ḥālîl	"double-pipe wind instrument" 1 Sam 10.5, Jer 48.36
ḥăṣōṣrāh	"trumpet," Num 10.10. Ps 98.6
kinnôr	"a stringed instrument of the lyre family" 1 Sam 10.5, Gen 4.21
mašrôqîtāʾ	"a whistling or piping instrument," Dan 3.5.7
menaᶜanᶜim	only in 2 Sam 6.5, "rattle" (?)
mĕṣiltayim	"cymbals" (?), 1 Chron 13.8 and passim
mĕṣilôt	"bells on horses," Zech 14.20
minnîm	"stringed instrument, lute" (?), Ps 150.4
nēbel	"lyre," 1 Sam 10.5, Ps 57.9
nĕhîlôt	"pipe, flute," Ps 5.1
neqeb	"pipe," Ezek 28.13
paᶜămôn	Ex 28.33.34, 39.25-26, "metal platelets, bells"
pĕsantĕrîn	from Greek *psalterion*, "harp," Dan 3.5.7
qaitrôs	from *kithara* (Gr.), Dan 3.5.7
qeren	"horn," Dan. 3.5.7; *qeren yôbel*, "ram's horn," Josh 6.5
sabbĕkāʾ	from Greek *sambuke*, "lyre" in Dan 3.5.7 and passim
ṣelṣĕlîm	"cymbals," (?), Ps 150.5
šālišîm	"cymbals or struck metal bowls," (?), "sistrum," only 1 Sam 18.6
šôpār	"ram's horn," the only biblical instrument to have survived in Jewish usage, Ex 19.16 and often.
sûmpōnyāh	"all sounding together." Dan 3.5.7
tōp	hand-drum; "tambourine" (SDB) BDB; seemingly the only mention of a drum, Ex 15.20 and often
ᶜûgāb	"harp"(?), "flute"(?, BDB), or a pipe of some sort, Ps 150.4
yubel	"horn," Sendrey (see n. 209), *qeren yôbel* "ram's horn," Josh 6.5

2.27.3 That music and song were part of the temple ritual receives only offhand mention in the Hebrew Bible, with almost no details given. Offerings are given along with the melody of the *nēbel* in Am 5.22f. The *ḥăṣōṣrāh* was blown by the priests over the burnt offerings and peace offerings, Num 10.10, the same instrument that calls them to war. The *šôpār* blast indicates that the Lord is there Ex 19.19. Aaron's ephod had a *paᶜămôn*-bell upon it Ex 28.34.

The psalms provide the best examples of the importance of music in the cult of Ancient Israel.[212] The number of allusions to singing are many, with roots *š-w-r*, *z-m-r*. These psalms are not poems, for there is no word in ancient Hebrew for "poem, poet," so were meant to be chanted. We can detect some of the mood through the words, but the melody and rhythm are mostly lost to us at this late date. Of course, each psalm has come down from our medieval texts with a cantilation which is indicated by the massoretic marks, and these represent a rich tradition, and a type of exegesis of the text. This cannot be used to describe pre-rabbinic biblical music.[213]

The psalms themselves tell in a simple way of the liturgical aspects under which they are sung. Whether the titles were original or added later, they provide information as of the time of later editing. Psalms 120-134 called "a song of *ma ᶜălôt* " usually translated "ascents"[214] have within them much movement-language (121.8, 122.1, 132.7.8) as well as much standing-and-waiting language (125.2, 126.6, 130.5.6, 132.14, 134.1 even by night). One finds processions rather fully described in Ps 68.24-27 and Ps 24.9 in which the Lord himself comes in. In Ezek 44.1-2 the Lord enters the east gate of the temple. Using our imagination a little, Ps 47 describes the people clapping their hands, shouting and singing to the Lord who is remembered for his victories on behalf of his people (vs. 3), giving them the land (vs.4), processing in, if that is the meaning of "gone up"(vs. 4), and sitting on his throne (vs. 5) which we may conjecture as the altar (vs. 8, Ex 25.22).

The Psalms mention several different types of musical instruments, the translations of which are not agreed upon.[215] It will be seen that these are somewhat the same instruments as those used in Mesopotamia, with the exception of the drum, which does not show up in Israel. The singers were undoubtedly always accompanied by music. No mention is made of a guild of singers, but Mowinckel postulates it.[216]In Israel, we find titles of singers, musicians and dancers, but apparently appearing only in minor roles,[217] although we do not have the thorough data we have in Mesopotamia. However, the writings in the Hebrew Bible are tendentious in places, and describe only sparsely the actions of the cult, even the approved ones. Those criticized by the writer are given a word or two, but we expect that they occupied more of a place than that given in the pages of our text. To discover these, we must go to place-names (Sec. 2.38.2 and n. 95) and personal names, though the former often represent the practices of the earlier inhabitants of the land. These, however, often came to be taken over by the Israelites.

2.27.4 A group of primitive prophets, who had just worshippped at the *bāmāh*, are found with *tōp*, *ḥālîl* and *kinnôr*, prophesying, 1 Sam 10.5. With this musical array, they were undoubtedly singing and probably dancing, but the text says that they were "prophesying." Perhaps they were extending the worship they did at the *bāmāh*. There was an ecstatic nature about this, as indicated by verse 6. H.-J. Kraus[218] speaks of the free and roaming nature of such groups, but this is saying too much.

2.27.5 The old idea that singers as cult personnel must have been Levites is argued against by Haran.[219]

2.27.6 The number of musical instruments mentioned in the Hebrew Bible is limited, and not much is made of the characteristics of the various instruments. Extra-biblical material is hard to come by. In Appendix 2 we will study the naked figurines, found in rather standard types. One of these types holds a round object, variously considered the sun disk or a tambourine.[220] If it is a tambourine, what is the word for this tambourine in our texts, and how was it used? It is not in this case carried in the manner of a tambourine, at least a modern day one. If it is a tambourine, the figurine is a cultic functionary, or a goddess portrayed by the role of her cultic functionary.

2.28 Miriam

As in the Ancient Near East in general, singing and dancing in the cult appear to be done by lesser officials in the Hebrew Bible also, although there are exceptions. Miriam, the sister of Moses, is given the anachronistic title *nĕbîʾāh* "prophetess" in Ex 15.20. This is either an anachronistic usage of the term, or a usage more akin to the root meaning of the word. She is described there as "sister of Aaron," which may indicate a liturgical context, because the name Aaron stands for the prototype early priesthood. The Lord spoke through Aaron and Miriam in Num 12.2. Here Miriam seems more closely associated with Aaron than with Moses.

Miriam's first words are described: *watta ᶜan lĕhem* "and she answered them." The answering must be antiphonal, and was probably not to the men of 15.1 as A Dillmann.[221] The object is m. pl., but this is one of the many examples in which the m. especially in the plural is used for the singular.[222]

She played on a *tōp*, usually "timbrel," the same instrument that Jephthah's daughter used, Sec. 2.29, leading women with these instruments in their hands, who were dancing (root *h-w-l*). She was the leader in a dance that is not described as cultic, but she also sings the psalm Ex 15.21 (= Ex 15.1, except for the first word), which praises the Lord's actions in history, so it was a kind of worship. LXX, TargJ and Vulg differ slightly.[223] Miriam was part of a trio: Moses, Aaron and Miriam in Mic 6.4, indicating perhaps an early hierarchy.

2.29 Jephthah's daughter

In a rather obscure tale with folkloristic elements, an oath is taken by a Gileadite Jephthah, the son of a *zônāh* "prostitute," with the result that he has to kill his daughter, whose name is never given (Jud 11.34-40). The first verse of the pericope, vs. 34, reminds us of the action of Miriam, Sec. 3.28. She and her companions went out upon the mountains to bewail root *y-b-l* her virginity before her death. This may also include dance, because earlier she meets her father in 11.34 with timbrels (*tōp*, which may have included song) and dance, root *h-w-l*. This reminds one of the women in the Dionysian cult.[224] This bewailing period has affinities to that which a foreign captive woman shall go through for a month, in which she "bewails" (root *b-k-h* in both contexts) her father and mother, before she becomes the concubine of the captor, Deut 21.13.

Without attempting comparative folklore, it is to be noted that the vow (Lev 27.2-8) and the resultant festival of lamentation are two of the foci around which the story turns. Since the Middle Ages commentators have understood the heroine as dedicated to a life-long virginity. The yearly feast, which is not given a name, died out, perhaps early. Further careful remarks using folklore, Greek literature and rabbinic sources are given by Marcus.[225]

2.30 The king in Israel

As in Mesopotamia, one of the significant cult actors was the king.[226] David dances a cultic dance before the ark, dressed in the priestly ephod 2 Sam 6.14. The word for this action is *mĕkarkēr* in 2 Sam, but *mĕraqqēd* in 1 Chr 15.29. Solomon authorized the building of the temple 1 Kings 5.3ff, and when it was completed he blessed the people 1 Kings 8.14, a prerogative of the priest, and by tradition read a magnificent prayer before the altar in a priestly stance 1 Kings 6.22. The king was installed in his office by the Lord himself Psalm 2.6. This connection continues to be described throughout the books of Kings, culminating with the king reading from the "book of the covenant" in the temple in 2 Kings 23.2, a preface to his reform, which was in large part religious.

2.31 *mĕšôrēr* and *mĕšôrērāh*

These "singers" are found among those, according to a late tradition in 1 Chr 6.18 (EVV 6.33), who performed in the temple in Jerusalem. These two, males and females, were among those who returned to Jerusalem from exile in Ezr 2.65 (// Neh 7.67), and were not necessarily cultic. The text notes that out of 42,360 people there were 7,337 servants, male and female, and 200 singers, male and female (245 Neh 7.67). Maybe the Asaph *mĕšôrēr*'s of Ezra 2.41 and Neh 7.44 were a different type, because of the special place of the Asaphites in the late cult. Because of their number we cannot consider them a high rank.

2.32 *nōgēn*

This player of a stringed instrument appears in what is apparently a procession: first *šārîm* "singers," then *nōgēn*'s, then *ᶜălāmôt* the last two playing the *tōp,* in Ps 68.26 (EVV 25). This root appears as a verb *mĕnaggēn* to describe the instrument on which David played, in 1 Sam 16.16.

2.33 *šārîm* / *šārôt*

These are cultic singers, in procession with *nōgēn*'s, in Ps 68.26 (EV 25). It is not sure that *šārim* and *ḥōllîm* "dancers" in Ps 87.7 are cultic, but what they say could be a praise of God, thus from the cult. *šārîm* were usually men in Chronicles - Ezra - Nehemiah, but *šārîm* (m.) and *šārôt* (f.) appear in Eccles 2.8, 2 Sam 19.36 (EV. 35), 2 Chr 35.25 and Neh 7.67.

2.34 Other women singers

Sirach 9.4 warns against associating with a woman singer, *psallousēs*, lest you get caught in her intrigues. This has hints of prostitution in it, but is this the case in other passages? Women, or at least their leader, sang in Ex 15.20-21. Deborah sang the magnificent psalm/hymn in Jud 5.1ff, which may have been used in the cult, in the way that the psalms with historical content were used. Hannah prayed (*hitpallel*) 1 Sam 1.12, but the poetry came out a song, because there probably was no such thing as verse without song in those days. Women met King Saul 1 Sam 18.6, and the passage does not mention any cultic aspects.

2.35 (root) *s-p-d*

The daughters of Rabbah the city of Ammon cry, root *ṣ-ᶜ-q*, and lament, root *s-p-d*, for their god who is going into exile, Jer 49.3 This is a theme close to Sumerian Lamentation over the destruction of a city.

2.36 *ᶜălāmôt*

Ps 68.26 (EV. 25) must refer to maidens who play the *top*. In Song of Songs 1.3 they love you (i.e., the king), and in 6.8 there are 60 queens, 80 *pilagšîm* (RSV: concubines) and *ᶜălāmôt* without number. In the title of Ps 46, *ᶜal ᶜălāmôt* seems to refer to a musical instrument.

2.37 *mĕbaśśeret* //anouncers of joy

It was women who announced good tidings (root *b-ś-r*), as victory in battle Ps 68.12 (EV 11). Women met King Saul as he came back with singing and dancing, with *tōp,* with joy and with *šālīš* 1 Sam 18.6. Zion, her part taken by a woman, heralds good tidings, Isa 40.9. Maybe in all of these cases, the female Zion is represented by the female cultic officiant.

2.38 Weepers // mourners (Hebrew)

2.38.1 Under this general term, we note that much of the actions of women, and of men sometimes but seemingly in lesser numbers, consists of cultic weeping and wailing, usually with the root *b-k-h*. This is done for much the same reasons as in Mesopotamia.[227]

The form of the typical composition is essentially an intercessory prayer of confession and lamentation, sometimes funerary Deut 34.8. We speak here not of the weeping that is a priestly supplication for sins, as in Joel 2.17, but one that is more universal. In what is perhaps an old poem, the daughters of Israel are told to weep over Saul, 2 Sam 1.24. There may have been a traditional place of weeping to alleviate a plague, for the people did so at the door of the Tent of Meeting, Num 25.6. The daughters of Dibon in Moab have gone up to the high places to weep over their gods, Isa 15.2. Thus it is that the single weeper of Isa 16.9 may very well be a woman. A woman is told in Jer 9.20 to teach her daughter a lament, a *qînāh*.

Women are called upon to do weeping over the destruction of Jerusalem, Jer 9.17-21 and the words seem to indicate that they were professionals. Maybe they lacerated themselves, Jer 16.6, Jer 41.5, Jer 47.5, Deut 14.1, as the Canaanite priests did on Mount Carmel, 1 King 18.28. They offered their hair, Mic 1.16, Deut 14.1, Isa 3.24. They sat upon the ground, Isa 3.26. All these actions seem to have accompanied the weeping.

Women in Ezek 8.14 weeping for Tammuz performed a foreign cult practice, yet done at the gate of the temple. It occurred after Josiah's reform, and is criticized as a *tô ᶜēb* "abomination," yet context indicates that it was a regular practice. Theirs is a description only, with no title. They are in a context with other (male) practicioners, so they would seem to be official.[228]

Am 5.16 uses many of the root words to express wailing, lamentation and mourning, including *mispēd* (see note on Ugaritic women, Sec. 2.41.2). *TDOT* II 229f has a classification: lament over distress, individual lament in the psalms. collective popular laments, Num 25.6.

2.38.2 We turn to place-names which reflect this practice. These appear in Hebrew, or a pre-Hebrew "Canaanite" language, or a folk-etymologized form of Hebrew. The etiologies given in the text are often after the fact, to fit the story. Jud 2.5 tells of a place near Gilgal called Bokim "weepers(m.)." Rebekah's nurse in Gen 35.8 was buried under an oak called 'Allôn bākūt "oak of weeping," perhaps a place-name. These could have been old cultic sacred locations.

2.38.3 The Book of Lamentations, especially chapter 1, with its mention of weeping in 1.2 and 1.16 using feminine imagery, is an echo of the powerful Sumerian lamentations over the destruction of a city, Sec. 2.3.9.

2.39 Rejoicing

It is possible, because of the poetic nature of the vocabulary, we have missed some terms which refer to a type or mood of song. Such an idea is "rejoice," appearing in Hebrew with several terms. *śimḥu* "rejoice in the Lord," Ps 32.11, probably means to sing a psalm which shows joy. When the daughters of Judah rejoice (root gyl) in Ps 97.8, the women probably sing the psalm of rejoicing. The "daughter of Zion"/"daughter of Jerusalem" is told to rejoice (root *g-y-l*) because her king comes in Zech 9.9, probably indicating the singing of particular psalms.

2.40 Dancing in the Hebrew Bible

2.40.1 Music and dancing go together, whether a mere clapping of hands, a movement of only one part of the body, a formal procession, or a free expression of the muscles. The rhythm is often determined by the music, whether regular or irregular or a combination of both. The music can bring on religious exultation and influence the activities of the muscles. This can be planned ahead of time in the carefully trained movements accompanying cultic themes.

Because dancing was so prevalent in the ancient world, the words we find for "dance" are many and varied. Frequently in a circle or a gentle curve, dancing can use little or violent movement of feet, legs, arms, fingers, or the whole body. Sometimes animals, birds or insects are imitated stylistically, sometimes the battle, the hunt, or sexual activities of humans themselves are interpreted. The dance is often meant to influence the activitity represented. It often occurs at key points of life, "rites of passage," as birth, puberty, marriage, a funeral.[229] It is often done at crisis periods, or high points in the liturgical year.

Dance is an ever-changing symbolic movement, sometimes to the rhythm of music, which is itself symbolic, and sometimes not. It can accompany prayer, or, indeed, itself be a prayer.

Dances were an expression in the fertility cult going back to the earliest time of recorded art, according to van der Leeuw.[230] We might quote Havelock Ellis: dance is "the supreme symbol of the spiritual life."[231] From the Upper Palaeolithic Period in Europe, women in dancing scenes along with animals are found in Spain.[232] Evidence of dancing in other Upper Palaeolithic sites in Europe leads Aubrey Burl to suggest that it would be natural to have it happen at the British stone circles.[233]

Dances around the world, from ancient times to the present, are photographed and commented upon briefly in Wosien's book[234] in somewhat the style of the periodical *Parabola*. Dancing in the Ancient Near East fits somewhere among her pictures, but aside from a few examples from Egypt, no dances specifically from the A.N.E. are shown. She indicates that in many if not most of the ancient and primitive dancing, the sexes were separate in group dancing.

2.40.2 The earliest seals found in Palestine show dance scenes, albeit crudely done.[235] These seals show Mesopotamian and Egyptian influence, and are even imports (p. 107). In more detail, they come from Elam via Syria, from Elam via Egypt, from Northern Mesopotamia via Syria, from Southern Mesopotamia (?) via Egypt (p. 108). Yet they have an originality of their own (109).

Several of the images show a row of people holding hands (fig. 18, IIIB-1,2,3; pl. 11, S-5) or holding raised hands (fig. 22, 1), or with one arm raised and one arm lowered (fig. 22, 6,7), or with one leg raised and bent (fig. 22, 8). These seem to depict a dance to the editor (pp. 82,60,) in which analysis he follows C. Epstein.[236]

2.40.3 There are further singing and dancing pictures.[237] W.O.E. Oesterley, a wide-ranging scholar with a sensitivity to ancient Hebrew religion, devotes two chapters of his book on sacred dance to the ancient Israelites.[238] The types of dance are:

1. the processional dance, 2 Sam 6.5, David and the people going before the ark.
2. the dance around a sacred object, as around the Ka'abah at Mecca. No specific examples from the Hebrew Bible are given, but note the march around Jericho in Josh 6.1.
3. the ecstatic dance, 1 Sam 10.12ff, the Canaanite prophets.
4. the dance at festivals, Jud 21.19ff, the daughters of Shiloh.
5. the dance in celebration of victory, Jud 11.34, Jephthah's daughter.
6. the dance at a marriage rite, Song of Songs 6.13.
7. the dance by mourners at a burial rite: see later Jewish literature.

The methodology is that of J.G. Frazer, and the references are wide-ranging. H. Eaton[239] lists somewhat the same situations in which dancing is present:

1. the nubile girls dancing to celebrate a military victory.
2. dancing of the king in a priestly role.
3. group dancing expressing joy in a festival.
4. expressing thanksgiving either of the individual or the people as a whole.
5. dancing by the prophet to accompany his ecstatic behavior.

Specifically in the Hebrew Bible, the Lord's name was to be praised in dancing (*māhôl*) of the sons of Israel in Ps 149.3 with the *tōp*, showing that this is not exclusively a female instrument. He is called to be praised with *tōp* and *māḥôl* "dance" in Ps 150.3, indicating that both men and women do this. Virgins dance *mĕḥôl* in Jer 31.4 and 31.13. Morgenstern mentions dances in the vineyards on the Day of Atonement.[240]

For David's dance, see Sec. 2.30. The *hălîkôt* "processions" of Ps 6.26 into the sanctuary could be considered a kind of dance. The virgin Israel dances with the root *ḥ-w-l* [241] with *tōp* in Jer 31.4.13 probably reflecting a cultic dance done by women. The story of the daughters of Shiloh, who come out to dance in the vineyards in Jud 21.19-23, is told as if it were a mating dance, but could be considered a praise of the God who gave them the vine.[242] But elsewhere the fertility of women and the fertility of the crops are considered together. The daughter of Zion is like a booth in a vineyard in Isa 1.8. Singers *šārîm* and dancers *ḥollîm* praise the Lord together in Ps 87.1. For Miriam's and Jephthah's daughter's dancing, see Secs. 2.28 and 2.29 respectively.

The golden calf, which represented the gods who brought the Israelites out of Egypt, was the object of sacrifice (Ex 32.8) and elicited singing and dancing (Ex 32.18f).

The procession around the city of Jericho in Josh 6 consisted of seven priests who blew *šôpār*'s, with warriors and the numinous ark in the entourage, a kind of a circle dance. Religious images appear throughout the story, for the captured goods were pronounced *ḥerem* to the Lord, sacred vessels in it being placed in the "house of the Lord," whatever that was at the time.

1 Chr 25.6 tells of Heman's 14 sons and 3 daughters under the direction of their father with *mĕṣiltayim*, *nĕbel*'s and *kinnôr*'s in the temple.

2.41 Ugaritic singing titles

2.41.1 kṯrt is translated "songstresses" by many.[243] A. van Selms [244] in an article on the many meanings of this root, rejects "female jubilantes," "fettered women," and something like Hebrew *kāšēr*, and concludes that they operate together as "(divine) handmaids." In Aqhat, in Dan'el's case they are related to conception (KTU 1.17 II 26 and passim).

2.41.2 *mšspdt* "wailing women" 1 Aq 172.183. This root *s-p-d* is also in Hebrew.[245]

2.41.3 *bkyt* "weeping women"[246] may have been professional weepers, probably similar to those found in Israel.

2.41.4 *šr ᶜṯtrt* "singers of Astarte" (see n. 246).

2.41.5 *mṣlm* "cymbalists," Rainey,[247] UT 168 r.13, among professional or guild names.

2.42 Dancers at Ugarit

mrqd "dancer"[248] is a male dancer, using the same root as the Hebrew dancer Sec. 2.29, a common Semitic one, Sec. 2.25.1. In this "Neujahrspsalm" J.C. de Moor [249] in an earlier study of RS 24.252, thinks that the dancers rubbed themselves with oil or fat. There is singing, playing of musical instruments, along with the dancing. Dietrich et al understand *dšn* as "geschmückten," in the sense of makeup.

In a school text, a PN Rapi'u sings and plays the *knr* "lyre," the *tlb* "flute" the *btp* "drum or tambourine," the *mṣltm* "cymbals" with the *dšn* dancers.

When Anat mourns for Aqhat, there are weeping and lamentation, loud cries and lacerations, similar to the weeping women in the cult in Israelite times. We could say that Anat was the model for the Hebrew practice.[250]

De Vaux finds a *b ᶜl mrqd* "Baal of the dance," as reported by J. Gray [251] from *Bulletin du Musée de Beyrouth*, 5 (1941), not available to me.

Notes

1 There are a number of words for types of lament with the first element being ér/ir = *bakû* "to weep," ér/ir is made up of A + IGI, water and eye. The rarer terms show up mostly in lexical texts; there is a 16-item list in *Kagal* A, MSL XIII 232, 7-22.

2 These occur in the post-Sumerian period (Krecher *Kultlyrik* 27). Emesal is discussed in A. Falkenstein, *Das Sumerische,* Leiden, 1959, 18c, and Marie-Louise Thomsen, *The Sumerian Language* (Mesopotamia 10), Copenhagen, 1984, §§559-66. It was used in the literature by women and goddesses, as well as the *kalû*. The emesal literature is given an up-to-date discussion by Cohen *Lamentations I* 11-15. The so-called "Emesal Vocabulary" dimmir-dingir-*ilum,* is a useful, albeit short, list of words in MSL IV 3-44, and Thomsen 288-90. The Akkadian reading of emesal is *ummisallu*, AHw 1416a, and rarely appears.

3 H. Hartmann, *Die Musik der sumerischen Kultur*, Frankfurt-am Main, 1960, is the basic book on the subject. W. Stauder, "Mesopotamia" in *New Grove Dictionary of Music and Musicians* vol. 12, Washington, D.C., 1980, 196-200 is a short article on instruments, with a few further notes on practice, giving only a few terms, but no references to these, making the article quite limited in usefulness. There is however, a good short bibliography. His larger work on which the above was based, W. Stauder "Die Musik der Sumerer, Babylonier u. Assyrer" in Hickman-Stauder *Musik* 171-243 has a long section on instruments with both archaeological and lexical data from CAD, AHw and MSL. He relies heavily on Hartmann *Musik*. A section on names of instruments by types is followed by notes on *gala /kalû* and nar, and a short section on music theory. Henry George Farmer, "The Music of Ancient Mesopotamia" in Egon Wellesz (ed.), *Ancient and Oriental Music*, vol. 1 of *The New Oxford History of Music*, London, 1957, is full of inaccuracies, vague references, less-than-careful translations of Akkadian words, with only a few Sumerian terms, and a mostly out-of-date bibliography. For an attempt to replicate ancient Mesopotamian music, see Anne D. Kilmer, Richard L. Crocker and Robert R. Brown, *Sounds from Silence* (Stereo phonograph record, with booklet), Berkeley, 1976.

4 S.N. Kramer, *BiAr* 46 (1983) 69-80.

5 M. Lambert *Sumer* 10 (1954) lists gala's among other pre-Sargonic métiers, 153.

6 L.Woolley, *The Royal Cemetery* , *UE* II, 1934, pl. 128. See W.W. Hallo, "Women of Sumer," in Schmandt-Besserat 27.

7 S.N. Kramer, *ANET* 496.

8 W.W. Hallo, "Women of Sumer" in Schmandt-Besserat 32.

9 *UVB* 8 (1937) pls. 38f, Sollberger and Kupper *Inscriptions* III A 4m. See also Jacobsen, *JCS* 7 46.

10 W.W. Hallo, *Or* 42 (1973) 238, 28ff.

11 *ZA* 57 NF 23 (1965) 60, 200-203.

12 Of Ishtar of Uruk, Charpin *Clergé* 405.

13 Charpin 250.

14 Allotte de la Fuye, *RA* 18 (1921) 101-121 based on K. 110=CT XI 14-18, lines 37-43 (103), and later in Nabnitu IX 242, MSL XVI 122, Sec. 2.6.

15 *MDP* 159

16 Gudea St. B V 1ff, quoted by J. Renger, *ZA* 59,189, *PSD* 76c.

17 S.N. Kramer, *PAPS* No. 107/6, ii 6f (copy fig. 3, 519, transliteration 505, translation 506)Sec. 4.23.9 No. 7.

18 Hartmann *Musik* 132, 165, with feminine PNs.

19 Hartmann, 149, 151f. In later times, the NAR (f.)/*nartu* often occurs.

20 Hartmann, *Musik* fig. 39 (with drum, from Ur III Lagash), fig. 44 (without instrument, from Ur I Mari).

21 Salonen, Festschrift 70ff. Cf. [am] a-ér-ra, OB Proto Lu 659, Sec. 2.3.13 and Lu = ša IV 181. Sec. 2.3.14.

22 Gordon *Sumerian Proverbs* 248 n. 9 assumes that the gala /*kalû* was a eunuch, as did Allotte de la Fuye, *RA* 18 (1921) 121, Oppenheim *Or* NS 19 (1950) 135 and n.1. This is rightly criticized as based on no evidence by CAD K 94a, by J. Renger *ZA* 59 (1969) 192f, and by Krecher *Kultlyrik* 36. It is true that the NA slab sculpture shows that <u>some</u> singers were eunuchs, but these were from the much later NA civilization. (See A.H.Layard. *Monuments of Nineveh* I pl. 73; II, pl. 49: R. Barnet, *Assyrian Palace Reliefs* pls. 54, 98, 107: L. W. Kings, *Bronze Reliefs from the gates of Shalmaneser,* Band I, 2, upper; Band 1,2, upper.) They are all shown playing harps or lyres, and could be *kalû*'s, *nāru*'s or simply singers *zammeru's*. (word?) They seems to be outside of a cultic setting, but we cannot be sure about this.

23 BM 14618 (96-4-7,7) in Limet *Le Temple et le Culte* 93; see Sec. 2.4.5 for discussion.

24 A. Deimel, *AnOr II* 40-49 (Nos. 3-7), as reported by Gelb, Salonen, Festschrift 72f.

25 M. Lambert, *Sumer* 10 (1954) 162n and *SAKI* 166e; Sollberger and Kupper *Inscriptions* IIA4k.

26 Descent of Inanna, 220ff. See App.3 for details of the *kurgarru*.

27 The reading of the Akkadian is not sure. CAD K 93b, 94a reads UŠ.KU TUR.RU as *kalû ṣihru* or *galaturru*, suggesting that the former is the more likely, but AHw 274b reads *galaturru*. Yet an analagous rank is read *kalamāhu* by CAD K 66a from OB PNs ka-la-ma-hu/hi-im. There will be more of this discussion in App 3.

28 Harris *Sippar* 332 "presumably of the Shamash temple" (ibid.). We might therefore cautiously call them "temple prostitutes," without defining the implications of saying this.

29 *AS* 20 (1976) 115.

30 CT 46 52 r. 6' Hunger *Kolophone* No. 433.4 also: *lú šamalli kalî,* Babylon, unknown origin.

31 *UET* 6 204.46, CAD K 93b.

32 Lu = ša IV 170, Sec. 2.3.14.

33 Lu = ša IV 171, MSL XII 134.

34 *PBS* I/I 11 iv 82 = iii 50, from CAD H 45a.

35 Salonen, Festschrift 67.

36 Other examples of this are in Oppenheim *Catalogue* L20 n.a, Goetze, *JCS* 17 25b, Fish *Catalogue* Drehem No. 189.

37 Watson *Birmingham* I No. 77.8.

38 I. J. Gelb, "Homo Ludens in Early Mesopotamia," Salonen, 43-76. "They are listed as if representing a` related type of pesonnel." 60.

39 S.N. Kramer, *ASJ* 3 (1981) 3, 23.

40 Krecher *Kultlyrik* 29.

41 Cohen *Eršemma* 18ff.

42 G. Dossin, *RA* 35,lff, analyzed by Krecher *Kultlyrik* 34, discussed Sec. 1.6.2

43 Cohen *Eršemma* 32ff.

44 *ANET* 334-38.

45 *RAcc* 42-44, partially translated Cohen *Eršemma* 48.

46 Cohen *Eršemma* No. 159, 23f, 104.

47 Cohen *Eršemma* No. 164.30, 94.

48 R. Caplice, *Or* NS 39 (1970) 121.

49 *ANET* 455ff, text in *AS* No. 12, 1940, with additions and corrections in Borger *HKL* I 245, II 136.

50 All taken from Gordon, *Sumerian Proverbs*.

51 Falkenstein *Gerichtsurkunden*.

52 Bauer *Lagasch* l.

53 Jean *Contrats* No. 34.47.

54 The MA text *KAR* 360.4f, translated by Borger *Esarh* 91 duplicated in Ebeling *Parfumrez* pl. 25.5, of copper.

55 Ebeling *Parfumrez* pl. 15 iv 12, *Or* N.S. 22, 29. A line in the myth Inanna and Ebeh has: gala-ra ^{kuš}ub li-li-is mu-na-sum"to the gala I (Inanna?) have given the ub and lilis," H. Limet, *Or* 40/1 (1970) 18. The *kalû* plays the *lilissu siparru* "of copper" (*RA* 15, 19.21: 23, 14.18) in the temple precincts in a ritual to avert the effect of a lunar eclipse, see CAD K. 93a, L 187a.

56 From Mari, G. Dossin, *RA* 35, 1 ff, analyzed by Krecher *Kultlyrik* 34. Also Weissbach *Misc* 12.12 (=van Dijk, *Sumer* 11 pl. 10).

57 *SBH* 109.79f, Hellenistic times, CAD A/164b, associated with the bur/*abru*-office: na-ám-gala na-ám-bur-ra nar-balag-ta mu-ra-an-gub glossed by Akkadian *kalû abrūtu ina tigî izzazzuni-[kum]* "the *kalû*-office (and) the *abru*-office stand with the *tigû* for you."

58 As indicated by Gelb in Salonen, Festschrift 57, 59.

59 E.C. Kingsbury, *HUCA* 34 (1963) lff.

60 S.N. Kramer, *Or* 54 (1985) 126.

61 OB Proto-Lu lines 319-343, MSL XII 44f lists 28 of them, all not necessarily to be understood as "mother of something," and many familial terms. See Sec. 4.8.2.

62 Gudea St. B V 3f.

63 Streck *Asb* 366.13.
64 4 R 53 (K. 2529).
65 S.L. Langdon, *RA* 18 157ff. For others see Borger *HKL* I 404 t53.
66 *ABL* 361 r.9.
67 Luckenbill *AnnSen* 81, 27.
68 C. Frank, *ZA* 29 (1915) copy 198f, S. Langdon *BL*194, r. 17ff, *ASKT* No. 17.
69 *KAR* 360.4f, dupl. Ebeling *Parfumrez* pl. 25.5 CAD H 41b.
70 *VAT* 13596, E. Ebeling, *Or* 22 (1953) 27-32.
71 *RAcc* 38.10-12, a form of ér-šà-hun-gá, AHw 246a. For the ershahunga and the ershemma, Cohen *Eršemma* 32.
72 *RAcc* 91.20, r.3.
73 *RAcc* 96.3 ends of lines broken, but this is the probable understanding.
74 CAD K.93b.
75 Usually "repair shop" but that doesn't fit here.
76 Lumha is the god of the balag. Thureau-Dangin, op. cit., p. 101 n.13. He is also called Ea *ša kalê* An=Anum (CT 24, 43, 120), see *RLA* 7/3-4 (1968) 168b.
77 Perhaps because it is sacred: ^{d}Lilissu is mentioned among other gods in this rite iii 17.
78 iii 30, p. 69 (*RAcc* 16f line 32).
79 *VAT* 8022 (= *RAcc* 12,13; 20,8, copy *KAR* 60).
80 *AO* 6472, (= *RAcc* 36 ff).
81 RAcc 44 r.16.
82 SAL ù-li-li = *zammertu*, Sec. 2.4.7.
83 *RAcc* 79,45 In 100.17. 23. 24 one (there was no longer any king at that time) makes the libation and in 102.15 the *enu* appears.
84 *RAcc* 42-44, partially translated by M.E. Cohen, *Eršemma* 48.
85 CAD K.93b, c, 1', a'b', multiple offices.
86 *RAcc* 20. 37, n. 66a.
87 Hunger *Kolophone* No. 92, 1.
88 *RAcc* 44.4f. For others singing the *inhu*, Sec. 2.2.3. The *taqribtu* is followed by an erhsemma in 34.6 and 40.7.
89 *RAcc* 89.12.
90 Borger Esarh 24, Ep. 33, 24ff: *išippi āšipi kalê nāre*; Streck *Asb* 270 iv 17f: [^{lú}*k*] *alê* [lú] *nāre*; in a broken context, 271, 17f.
91 *AS* i 36 iv 9, *šangü* of ^{d}Sutitu but *kalû* of ^{d}Nabû. Maybe this indicates a relationship between the rare Sutitu and Nabu. The *ērib bīti* is of Nana, the *šangû* is of ^{d}Usuramassa, a rare name with which deity Nana is related. The *kalû* of Ishtar of Uruk and the *šangû* of ^{d}Nusku appear, *AnOr* 93: 63 (Kandalanu).
92 Sec. 2.4.7, Proto-Lu Fragment III.7.
93 E. Eberling, *Or* NS 17 (1948) 420.
94 ^{lú}nu-'a-ri *LKA* 35 r.5 and r.1 (? with broken signs) in a NA desire for blessing; ^{lú}nu-'a-ri Ebeling *Parfumrez* pl. 49, 19; CAD

N/378b (many at Nuzi); ar-ru = *nu-a-ru* *STT* 402. r.4' in a commentary in Babylonian script. AHw 748bf places all the orthographies under one *nāru* entry, as does CAD N/1, 378, but the latter, 379a, suggests that *nuaru* was a musician different from the *nāru*. One notes, however, that Nuzi orthography differs sometimes from that of standard Akkadian, probably because of the Hurrian language influence.

95 Transcription only, O. Loretz, *AOAT* 1, No. 39.8, 216. This is a place-name of the type which expresses a title or professional name. These are often of craft professions: *gt ngr* "wine vat of the carpenter" *MRS* VII 40,3; [I uru I]na-gar "carpenter" ND 2622.8, *Iraq* 23 (1961) pl. xx in a NA list of cities; [uru]paharani "potter" *KAV* 75.6 in a NA letter. But they also include cultic officials: IM^{ki} = ennigi (a type of priest or priestess) van Dijk *Götterlieder* 78 (Sumerian); *ērib bīti's* (reading of plural unknown); *ARU* 10. 30, ki-abrig "place of the abrig-priest" CAD A/1 62b.

96 *KAJ* 221.3 (Ebeling *MAOG* 7-1/2 48).

97 Unger Babylon 285, 14.

98 M. Lambert, *Sumer* 10 (1954) 178f also list these offices. See Lu = ša IV 226. p.20.

99 See below CAD N/1 378a for other nar-balag references, Ur III and OB.

100 The equivalent ideograms (AHw 869bf) are sa "gut, string" or na_5 "box," Salonen *Mobel* 207ff. It may be 3-stringed, and then would be equated with the inu-instrument: A. D. Kilmer, Landsberger AV 263 gives many characteristics of the *pitnu*.

101 *SBH* No. 56 r. 71f, Hellenistic period: *pa-ge-e ana pit-*[*ni* (?] which may, (according to CAD N/1 377a, lexical section) pick up the name of the *pitnu*, see above. The *pagû* is paralleled in the Sumerian line by SA.LI, an instrument also listed in a miscellaneous list of coefficients (IGI. GUB), A.D. Kilmer *Or* 29 (1960) 275,7.

102 Thureau-Dangin *HCS* 159, as Sargon enters the camp, which may seem like a secular context, but immediately afterwards the king offers a sacrifice. Also in Borger *Esarh* 89 iii 7 in a broken cultic context, and Borger *Esarh* 91, Para 61.2.

103 *AFO* 18, 46, 32.

104 Jacobsen *Harps*...xiii.

105 Limit, *Textes sumeriennes* 37.2.

106 BM 14618 = 96-4-7,7, transliterated in Gelb, Salonen, Festschrift 43-76, and in H. Limet, *Le Temple et le Culte* 93f.

107 Goetze, *JCS* 2, 90, No. 18 (Crozer No. 156). Probably she is from Sippar (Goetze).

108 Kingsbury *HUCA* 34 (1963) 6,30.

109 Ibid. 10, 97. 101.

110 PBS 1/1 11 iv 82 = iii 50, cited in CAD N/1 377a.

111 From Lu = ša IV 215 nar-tur = *hal-la-tu-šu-u*, 216 nar-hal-tuš-a = KI.MIN (*hallatušu*). Yet a bilingual NA text reads nar-tur as *nāra ṣehra*, CAD N/1 376b.

112 M.W.Green, *JAOS* 104 (1984) 276, 12.27.

113 *ARM* 1 119 r.3.

114 *TEM* 4, M. Birot, *RA* 50 (1956) 69 ii 6.

115 *TEM* 4, M. Birot, *RA* 50 (1956) 69 ii 24; nar-tur is read *hallatušu* in a Lu = ša IV list, Sec. 2.4.7.

116 *TEM* r. iii 27.

117 *TEM* 4 i 5.

118 *ARM* 7 206 r.3.

119 *ARM* 9 24 i 49ff.

120 *ARM* 1 12.5, *ša ṣabîm* "of the soldiers," also described as *mār bīt* A. [BA] "member of the house of scribes," line 8. The same name appears in II 4.4.

121 *TuL* No. 22 = *KAR* 141. The term *kamānu* also appears in the clause: *kamānu u-šar-qa-ad* "the *kamānu* brings on dancing" van Driel *Cult of Assur* 88.28. Corrections are from AHw p. 957b. See also *TuL* 90.8.

122 E. Ebeling, *Or* 22 (1953) 32-36. Menzel *Tempel* T80-83.

123 For an index to the Wine List texts, see R. Henshaw, *JAOS* 100 (1980) 303.

124 *AKA* 369 iii 76.

125 Luckenbill *AnnSen* 34.46f.

126 Luckenbill *AnnSen* 52.32, Tiglath-pileser III in *Iraq* 18 125 r.8.

127 MÍ.NAR.MEŠ LÚ.TUR [x x], J.E. Reade, "The Rassam Obelisk," Iraq 52 (1980) 17 lines 3c, notes 18 A 1-3.

128 *YOS* 1 No. 45 ii 65-70. Newly translated by Reiner *Thwarts* 2-5.

129 For the reading, see J. A. Brinkman, Oppenheim AV 26 n. 148. See also the notes of D. Cocquerillat, *WO* 7 (1973) 96, 126ff.

130 K. 3600 + DT 75, K.D. Macmillan, *BA* 5 626 and 564f, Craig *ABRT* No. 55, 6ff.

131 CAD Z 40a says that a later *rab zammāri* replaced the earlier *nargallu*.

132 Borger *Esarh* 93 §64.12.

133 ND5463 B. Parker, *Iraq* 19/2 (1957) pl. 32.

134 CAD Z s.v.

135 CT 38, 5: 105 (*Shumma ālu*).

136 CAD M/2 16a.

137 Brünnow 13787, quoted in Deimel Pantheon No. 1313; 3 R 66 xi 34; SL IV/1, 957, 41; R. Frankena *Tākultu* 119, 243.

138 *PBS* 1/1 11 iv 82 = iii 50, see CAD H 45a. The entries here show that the *hallatussu* has correspondences to both the *nāru* and the *kalû*. The nar-hal-la-tuš-a entry in OB Lu (see above) shows that it goes back to OB times.

139 S.A. Smith, *Miscellaneous Assyrian Texts* 24, 28f, in which nar-tur is translated by *nāra ṣehra*, CAD N/1 376b.

140 Menzel *Tempel* I 286. She calls them "Tempelweihen," 300.

141 J.J. Finkelstein, *JCS* 7 (1953) 140, 20 No. TB 85.

142 *VAT* 10112, *KAR* 146 II 4,5, Menzel *Tempel* II T99.

143 Winckler Sargon "The Display Inscription" No. 76: 157 = Lie *Sargon*. I was unable to consult further discussion in P. Leander, *Uber die Sumerische Lehnsworter im Assyrischen* p.16.

144 S.N. Kramer, *ANET* 652a and AHw 89a (*a' u* "eine Kultperson").

145 *TuL*17.17,variant *a-lu-zi-in ki-i a-ši-pu-ut-ka* (Foster, n. 140a, 71, 9, see next note.).

146 B. Foster, *JANES* 6 (1974) 74-79, referred to by R. Harris in Moran AV 221 n.10.

147 *KAJ* 51.16.

148 M. Lambert, *Sumer* 10 (1954) 162.

149 *JCS* 7 (1953) 46a: Abi-simti was a queen (45) whose sister was balag?-di?, *UET* 111 1504 viii and 1505 ix.

150 W.H. Ph Romer, *BiOr* 40 (1983) 569ff.

151 Krecher *Kultlyrik* III 15, 17, 25, with notes p. 162.

152 C. Wilcke, *AFO* 24 (1973) 15. 2.

153 *Ṣāriru* in Lu = ša IV 175, Sec. 3.3.14, but probably a phonetic variant of *ṣarihu*, CAD S 112a; root *ṣarāra* "sing a lamentation" CAD S 99b, cf. *ša ṣirhi,* Sec. 3.11.

154 Jacobsen *Harps*...12.

155 CT 8, 21 c 10.

156 R. Kutscher and C. Wilcke, *ZA* 68 (1978) 115, 52.

157 Cohen *Lamentations* 28 n. 73.

158 MBI 2 ii 1-2, *PSD* 198b, may be understood as a soother (búr) by means of the balag.

159 MSL XIV 501 f.

160 búr E 3.5 "to loose, to soothe" *PSD* 193a The balag-di does this.

161 I could find no use in AHw s.v. *pašāru* of this word meaning to play an instrument of music.

162 Sulgi O., Klein, *AOAT* 25, 271 ff.

163 4 R 11 23f, CAD N/2 23b. Perhaps *ša nissati* is a description rather than the title of an official.

164 *Lamentation over Sumer and Ur*, 441.

165 Cohen *Balag*, passim.

166 *PSD* s.v. balag B: 1) "lyre player," 2) necromancer.

167 W. Fortsch, texts transliterated and translated in Bauer *Lagasch*, index 583.

168 *VAS* 14, 118 ii 3-4; 14, xii 3. *PSD* 81a. See also *MAOG* 13/2 46, 28.

169 CAD E 238a.

170 See also Zimmern *ZA* 31 120 n. 2.

171 Krecher *Kultlyrik* 56 iii 14-17 = Genouillac Kich 2, C 100:12-15, with notes in Krecher 161ff, *PSD* 80a.

172 Lullaby 45, *PSD* 76d.

173 M. Lambert, *Sumer* 10 (1954) 174.

174 Lambert *BWL* 216, 19f: A mongoose enters the hole of a snake and says:"Greetings. The *mušlahhu* sent me." Is this meant to be humorous?

175 BM 14618, H. Limet, *Le Temple et le Culte* 85 n. 27, E. Sollberger, *Correspondence* Nos. 340 and 339. The former concerns the debt of the gir-sè-ga "servants" of the temple of the divinized Shulgi.

176 CT 7 (pl 13) 24, No.12939.

177 5 R 33 v. 15, from CAD M/2 277a, A 17th c. B.C. Kassite king.

178 H. Winckler, *AoF* II 21ff = *Borger Esarh* 114 §80 (91-51-9, 218), translated A.L.Oppenheim, *ANET* 293 col. A.

179 Barnett *Reliefs* pls 50, 54, 90 98, for the lion hunt; R.D. Barnett, *Sculptures from the North Palace of Ashurbanipal,* London, 1976, pl. LXVIII (Triumphal dance); R.D. Barnett and M. Falkner, *The Sculpture of Ashur-nasir-apli II*, London, 1962, pl. LX, 110 (sacrificing in the camp).

180 *Maqlü* III 43; somewhat the same group in IV, 126, and VII.99, but in the latter a male *mušlahhu* appears.

181 de Genouillac *TSA* 9 = Deimel *AnOr* II 29f, and 38a quoted in Gelb Salonen, Festschrift 65, and SL557, 31. See also Bauer *Lagasch* 66 II.7, following the entry gala-mah-gir-su^{ki}. Bauer prefers to understand ab-ba = *šību* "old man," so literally "spouse of the old man, Klageweiber." Other contexts indicate "eine Art von Klagenpriestern"(Deimel).

182 Descent of Ishtar, CT 15: 47, 37.

183 *ZA* 51 138.67. She is a divine personification of deafness or stupidity but CAD S 363b has its doubts about this.

184 *Shurpu* III.76.

185 *BA* 5 (1903) 667 (4 R 11:22, K. 4613).

186 *KAR* 115 + v 11', See Frankena in Garelli *Gilgamesh.*

187 Klauber *Beamtentum* 22.

188 A.T. Clay, *BRM* 46,44.

189 *AfO* 19 52.159.

190 S. N. Kramer, *ANET* 651-2.

191 *ARM* I 83, 7.9.

192 *ARM* 13 22, 40.44.

193 Genouillac *TSA* 9 = Deimel *AnOr* II 29f.

194 Alster Suruppak 47.

195 In a fragment from Sultantepe, *Gilg* VIII ii 3, O.R. Gurney, *JCS* 8 (1954) 93 r.3 and 94.

196 W. G. Lambert, *AfO* 19 (1959-63) 58 lines 133.

197 W. G. Lambert, *AfO* 19 (1959-63) 52, 146.

198 Alberti Pompaonio Text 2 III 2. Elsewhere, ibid, p. 29, as a professional "lamenter" from Ebla.

199 H. Limet *Le Temple et le Culte* 93f, lines 5.18.63.

200 Oppenheim *Catalogue* Bab 19 (Hussey 9 r.l).

201 W.von Soden, Salonen, Festschrift 328f.

202 E. Reiner and H. Guterbock, "The Great Prayer to Ishtar," *JCS* 21 (1967) 261 NB 38. King *Seven Tablets* II pl. 78, 38, has a su-ila prayer to Ishtar.

---

203 *RT* 29 (1897), 59.2 transliteration only, choosing the syllable spacing.

204 *UET* 4, references in CAD S/1 98a.

205 E. Porada., *Seal Impresions of Nuzi, AASOR* XXIV, New Haven, 1947, 118.

206 *RAcc* 115 r.7.

207 CAD Z 117a.

208 Jacobsen *Harps*...362.

209 Alfred Sendrey, *Music in Ancient Israel,* New York. and London, 1969. A rabbinic emphasis is used throughout, with no attempt to bring in Semitic philology other than Hebrew. It is valuable in its immense amount of references to the Church Fathers and other early texts. Eric Werner, *The Sacred Bridge. The Interpretation of Liturgy in Synagogue and Church during the First Millenium,* New York. and London, 1955 (MS finished 1950), is a superb study and a classic in its own right. However, to consider our interest in titles of functionaries, no leaders seem to be mentioned in the work outside of the "rabbis," "the readers," a "singer." Almost nothing appears on the Hebrew Bible, except for lectionary passages.

210 Weisberg *Guild Structure* 101-3.

211 Bathja Bayer, *Enc Jud.* 12 562.

212 Summarized in Mowinckel *PIW* I 8-12.

213 Werner.

214 Or, "degrees' (Pedersen *Israel* III-IV 424).

215 Examples of which (see list in Sec. 3.27.2) are the *šôpăr* "trumpet, ram's horn" Ps. 150.3; *kinnôr* "lyre, zither," 150.3; *tōp* "timbrel, tambourine" 150.4; *ᶜûgăb* "pipe, flute" 150.4; *ṣelṣĕlîm* "cymbals" 150.5; *nĕbel* "harp" 57.9, (EVV 8); *ᶜāśôr* "lute, lyre" 92.4 (EVV 3); *ḥăṣōṣrāh* "trumpet" 98.6; the *ḥālîl* "shawm, pipe" I Sam 10.5, not mentioned in the psalms.

216 Mowinckel *PIW*, chapter 14. This is to be compared with Weisberg's comment n. 210.

217 Phyllis Bird also finds that female singers, dancers and musicians participate in the cult only as a "lower echelon of the clergy." P.D. Miller et al (eds) *Ancient Israelite Religion,* Philadelphia, 1987, 405.

218 Kraus *Worship* 102.

219 Haran *Temples* 124, n. 21, yet they appear as Levites in post-exilic literature, as 2 Chr 29. 25-30. The nouns *lwy* and *khn* appear only in the masculine in Hebrew, deVaux, *An Is* II, 369.

220 A tambourine, according to George F. Dales, *RA* 57 (1963) 25f, from his Ph.D. thesis: "Mesopotamian and Related Female Figurines," U. of Pennsylvania, 1960.

221 A. Dillmann, *Exodus u. Leviticus*, Leipzig, 1880[2], 160.

222 GKC § 1350.

223 LXX: *aȉsōnmen* "let us sing," Vulg: *cantemos* "let us sing."

224 As vividly portrayed in Euripides' "The Bacchae."

225 D. Marcus, *Jephthah and his Vow,* Lubbock, Texas, 1986.
226 Pedersen, *Israel* III-IV 429.
227 S.N. Kramer, "The weeping goddess," *BiAr* 46 (1983) 69-80.
228 de Vaux, *AnIs II* 383.
229 William Charles Smith and Alexander Bell Filson Young, Encyclopaedia Brittanica 11th ed.1910-11, vii, 794-7.
230 G. van der Leeuw, *Religion in Essence and Manifestation*, 1938, 374.
231 Havelock Ellis, *The Dance of Life* 1923, 65-66.
232 H. Breuil and R. Lantier, *The Men of the Old Stone Age,* New.York., 1965 (Paris, 1959), 194.
233 Aubrey Burl, *The Stone Circles of the British Isles*, New Haven and London, 1976, 85f.
234 Wosien *Dance*.
235 Ben-Tor *Cylinder Seals*, passim.
236 C. Epstein, *IEJ* 22 (1972) 209-17.
237 *ANEP* 63-66, 111, 346; I. Seibert, *Women in ANE* pls. 10, 34, 99; O. Keel, *Symbolism of the Biblical World,* 336-39.
238 Oesterley *Dance* chaps 3-4.
239 Eaton *Dancing* 4-15.
240 J. Morgenstern, *JR* I 249, Mishnah Ta'aniyyot IV 8 and its Gemara. Not mentioned in the Hebrew Bible.
241 J.M. Sasson, "The worship of the golden calf," Gordon AV 151-59, suggests that *maḥôl/mĕḥolāʾ* and verbal forms of the root *ḥ-w-l* may not refer to cultic dancing but to antiphonal singing. Also, Winter *Frau u Göttin* 32-33.
242 Haran *Temples* 299 thinks that because it does not say this explicitly, this was not done in the vineyards, but "presumably in the temple's environs, or in the outskirts of the city." It was not a vintage festival.
243 Fisher *Ras Shamra* Par. II 191.
244 *UF* 11 743f.
245 Discussed within the context of the Ancient Near East by B. Margalit, *the Ugaritic Poem of Aqhat,* Berlin, New York, 1989, Fisher *Ras Shamra* Par.II 191.
246 root *b-k-y-t*.
247 A.F. Rainey, *BiAr* 28 (1965) 124, *UT* 1107.4.
248 *UF* 7 (1975) 115, 211. Here he is further described as *dšn* "fatted, anointed, adorned," or less likely "greased" (Rainey, *JAOS* 94 (1974) 187. See also M. Dietrich et al, *UF* 7 (1975) 117, perhaps related to the New Year's Festival, with singing, playing of musical instruments and dancing.
249 *UF* 1 (1969) 175.
250 As described by Kapelrud *Goddess* 83.
251 J. Gray, *I and II* Kings, London, 1970^2 397.

CHAPTER THREE

Diviners, Magicians, Ecstatics and Wise Men and Women

Note: For *mušlahhu* and *mušlahhatu*, having characteristics of both singer and diviner, see Sec. 2.13, and 3.20.3, 3.20.4, 3.20.5 below.

3.1.1 This branch of study spreads its net far and wide, referring to the manipulation of an unexplained force for the amelioration of lives, personally or in the wider sphere of economics, politics or social movements, that force having a grip on these lives which can only be broken by esoteric methods. In western society we think of magic, horoscopes, sorcery, astrology as a-theistic. In Mesopotamian and Hebrew societies these were not: the gods were called upon and somehow influenced. This was done by scholar-experts, who had studied for many years to learn the formulas, and drew from a number of manuals, and who operated either in parallel to or apart from the temple ceremonies, the latter we understand as state- or royal-controlled. In the *baru*-section below, we see that the king used these diviners almost continually, so in this case there was the utmost cooperation between divination and court.

Our argument for putting this study among that of cultic officials is that there was a relationship between divination and the temple. Starr quotes a text from a liver model of Sin-iddinam, a 19th c. king of Larsa: *annitum amutum ša šarrim Sin-iddinam ša ina bīt* ^{d}*šamaš ina elūni* [*m*] *iqquma* "this is the (appearance of the) liver of king Sin-iddinam who sacrificed in the temple of Shamash at the *elūnu* festival."[1] In the western Semitic world this relationship also occurred. Ottosson[2] notes the finding of a clay model of a liver in the courtyard of a temple, showing that divination was performed in association with the temple. The services inside were for priests only.

The gods prayed to in divination texts of the *bārûtu* type were Shamash and Adad, with Shamash probably the senior of the two.[3] Sin and Ishhara also appear, as do also Nergal and the "great gods."[4]

3.1.2 A. Leo Oppenheim has pointed out the large number of texts coming down to us from ancient Mesopotamia in the area of divination.[5] Some of these are parts of series that are vast in scope, and some of the latter have only been published partially. An overall study of extispicy, with technical terms and a few texts, had been made by Ivan Starr; see n. 18. Much of the large astrological series Enuma Anu Enlil was published by Ch. Virolleaud in *Astrologie chaldéenne* (1909-1912) in transliteration, and organized by E.F. Weidner, *AfO* 14 (1941-44), 17 (1954-56), 22 (1968-69), and a completely new study has been begun by Erica Reiner and David Pingree, *Babylonian Planetary Omens I. Enuma Anu Enlil Tablet 63*, Malibu, 1975, and *II. Tablets 50-51,* Malibu, 1981. A large series is Shumma Alu "If a city (is set on a hill)," dealing with incidents in houses, behavior of animals and other fauna and of humans -- a vast miscellany. It is studied by Sally Moren, in her thesis (see Bibliography). Its 107+ tablets are summarized in that book, along with a full publication, insofar as the texts are known, of tablets 30-34, concerning the antics of lizards, geckos, mongooses, dormice and mice.

The series Shumma Izbu "If an irregular birth" deals with what is to be done with freakish births of humans and animals.[6] R. Caplice has published the series "Namburbi."[7] Hemerologies are part of this subject: lists of auspicious and inauspicious days that ordered the lives of those following them.[8] The *tamītu* texts have been provisionally described by Lambert.[9]

3.1.3 When the pertinent event occurred, a *bārû* was consulted, who through years of study knew where to go in the omen texts to deal with the problem. He would then prepare a report, several of which have been preserved.[10] In the series that have come down to us, the incantation officiant is seldom listed with a title, but only ordered to do or say the ritual, with much of the syntax in the form of "You (the officiant) are to ..." Several of these titles slide into one another. Charpin[11] points out some pairs who work together: *bārû-šā'ilu* and *asû-āšipu*. Falkenstein shows that a-zu (= *asû* "physician") or uzu (NINDA x NUN) was equivalent to *bārû*.[12]

There is a loose relationship among members of this category, in that they were concerned either with healing, or seeing into the future. The rites were done by individuals who may have been self-appointed, if modern-day "primitive cults" can be used by way of analogy, or were of a family which had done this for generations. The Siberian shaman[13] or the Native American "medicine man"[14] are types who were simply there, and every village had to have one. They "saw" things that the rest of us cannot, and for that reason are often called, in the various languages, simply "see-er." The exorcist in the Ancient Near East would attempt to affect the future directly. The witch affects the future or sees things for malevolent, not benevolent purposes. Mourning and lamenting bring past and future together, and uses singing and poetical skills, and the ancients put them in a special category (see our chapter 2). Our reason for listing divination officials in a study among others with which they are usually sharply contrasted is that they also engage in ritual acts, call upon the gods, and sometimes operate in conjunction with the others who are described in our chapters. In contrast to these others, however, the ones studied here often work alone, with rare mention of a temple or holy place.

The rationale of divination then is that there is a mysterious relationship between events in history or countries or individuals and the phenomena observed in the divination material. An observed phenomenon at one time in history would be referred to later on as indicating the same result in history.[15] Oppenheim[16] gives some perspectives which help us understand this phenomenon better. In Mesopotamia it occurs on two levels simultaneously, the popular or folklore level, and the scholarly level, and in the latter the practitioners have to be learned. Divination presents a generalized divine power which is concerned about humans. Though Shamash and Adad are often called upon, they represent but a "superficial mythologization" of a much deeper and earlier religious phenomenon. I (RAH) would relate this to shamanism.

3.2 máš-šu-gíd-gíd /HAL/*bārû* and *barītu*

3.2.1 In our Category III, the *bārû* "diviner" is the profession most often met. This is such a vast subject that only a few notes can be given. The *bārû* using *bīru* "divination" is sometimes put together with the *šā'ilu* "dream interpreter" using *muššakku* "incense."[17] His texts, and some of his rituals, especially those of late NA times, are described by I. Starr and A.L. Oppenheim.[18] This office appeared first in ED times with the Sumerian title máš-šu-gíd-gíd "(towards) the (sacrificial) animal the hand was made long," i.e., stretched out.[19] Shulgi, the second king of the Ur III dynasty, called himself a máš-šu-gíd-gíd.[20] Even though we note that the practice extended down to NA times, it seems to have remained remarkably the same, and even the ritual material, as, e.g., type of flour used, remained the same.[21] There are some exemplars in Ur III times from administrative and commercial documents.[22] Several high cultic officials ask questions of the máš-šu-gíd-gíd. The en and nin-dingir,[23] lú-mah,[24] šita$_x$ (*REC* 316)-ab-ba[25] and išib[26] all use him.

3.2.2 In the earliest lists:

62	lú-gú-šu-du$_8$	
63	lú-máš-šu-gíd	
64	dím$^!$-lá	
		ED List C MSL XII 15

129	TAK$_4$:SAG$_x$:TAK$_4$	
130	lú-máš-šu-gíd	
131	KAK:du$_6$	
		ED List E MSL XII 19

and in the latest lists:

13'	erin$_2$-ka-kéš	ERIN$_2$.MEŠ [*ki*] -*iṣ-ri*
14'	azu	*ba-ru-ú*
15'	[a]-zu	*ba-ru-ú*
16'	ì-zu	MIN
17'	[m] e-zu	MIN
18'	kul-lum	[MIN]
19'	máš-šu-gíd-gíd	MIN
20'	ugula-máš-šu-gíd-gíd	*a-kil ba-ri-i*
21'	ì-gíd-gíd	*ba-ru-tu*
		Lu = ša II MSL XII 119f

and the texts multiply greatly when we come to the late Assyrian times of Esarhaddon and Ashurbanipal.

3.2.3 Lu =ša II above shows that the scribes considered the *bārû* a kind of a physician (a-zu) who knows (zu) (how to use) oil (ì).[27] In the same list line 18', KUL-LUM is one term, not the usual one, for the *sirāšû* "brewer."[28]

3.2.4 In the Lu = ša II iii list, Sec. 3.3.4, a *bārû ša qutrinni* entry shows that the *bārû* uses *qutrinnu* smoke in some way, incense being one of the standard appurtenances of the cult. He had to use subtle understanding of human nature, for he or she had to interpret the many and varied everyday occurrences of life, often using extispicy (inspection of the entrails) and sometimes a knowledge of astrology.[29] This is often accompanied by prayer, used at the appropriate time in the ritual.[30] This is the reason why we put diviners in our cultic categories.

3.2.5 The *bārû* worked at the palace[31] or the temple.[32] Further cultic aspects are shown by a text quoted by A. Falkenstein.[33]

máš-šu-gíd-gíd-e a ^{d}utu-šè mu-un-zi-x

gudá-šu-sikil-gim máš-gíd-gíd-e ^{giš}eren ^{d}utu-šè mu-un-zi-zi-i
"the diviner lifts water to Utu
like a guda with pure hands the diviner lifts cedar to Utu."

The guda is one of the highest offices among cultic ranks, Sec. 1.7. Water is often used in the cult, pouring it or carrying it, and here the diviner is doing a cultic act, and is compared to a high cultic official in the doing of it. The cedar, says Falkenstein, is used for incense.

3.2.6 The Queries (see n. 18) show that a question was given, asking for instance, whether an invasion would happen or would be successful, should such-and-such a plan of action be carried through,[34] whether a princess should be given in marriage to a foreign king, whether tribute should be collected at this time, whether a peace gesture is sincere, whether there shall be a rebellion against the king, whether the king should appoint so-and-so to an office, whether an illness will pass, and even whether the prince should go to the holy places of the gods and offer a gift. The *bārû's* goal was *šulmu* "well-being" for the client.[35] He was the person's advocate.

The *bārû* then knows the formulaic way to express the question, he knows how to look at the exta of the animals, and provide an answer to the king, although the details of the last two items are little known. Sometimes the exta have to be examined by the *ummānu*-scholars rather than the *bārû*,[36] or maybe a *bārû* was called an *ummānu* at this point.

The result of the inspection is checked against standard lists of protases (If an animal looks like this or that...,p. xxxv) and apodoses (...then such-and-such will happen), coming down from Old Babylonian times (Starr *Diviner* 5f). As an example, a NA text[37] reads in part: BE HAR 15 *ta-li-il ri-ṣu-ut* ERIM NUN DINGIR GIN-*ak* "if the lung is 'suspended' on the right, the god will come to the aid of my army." An OB text[38] has: BE ZAG.LU BI.RI *ta-ri-ik qa* [*r* ?-*r*]*a* -*ad* LÚ GA[L? *a-n*]*a* ? LÚ KUR *iš-ta-di-ih* -[*x*] "if the right side of the spleen is dark: the warriors of the king will march on the enemy."

3.2.7 We also find the *bārû* with a private person. He seems to have gone to the person and asked about his concerns. The resulting ritual was religious, i.e., not a-theistic, for Shamash and Adad were called upon, and sometimes other gods were involved.[39] We know little of the actual technique. A *mākaltu*-bowl was used for oil omens in an anointing rite.[40] Lambs were used.[41] The *bārû's* station and importance are shown in the mention of a rite in which he sprinkles a princess.[42] At Mari he was at the same time a scholar and a technician.[43] He examines 4 lambs and gives an omen report (*tērtum*).[44] He makes a report to the king on an eclipse of the moon.[45] He opposes a campaign because the *tērtu*'s were not favorable.[46] Sometimes the *bārû* marches "before the troops."[47] He was a powerful individual. As far as our knowledge goes, only males could fill this office at Mari.

3.2.8 The female *bāriatum* together with the female *ša'ilatum* are found in an Old Assyrian text.[48] A reference in a NA text,[49] in which Gula is referred to: *ba-ra-at* "she is *bārû*," *muššipat* "she is *muššipu* "[50] does not necessarily indicate that there are corresponding female offices.

3.3 Dream interpreter: ensi/*šā'ilu* and *šā'iltu* //*edammû* and *edammētu* // *hartibi* // sag-šè-ná-a / *mupaššer šunāti* // šabra/*šabrû*

3.3.1 A single occurrence with no context appears in OB Lu E:

75 nu-dingir
76 ensi
77 AN-[igi?]-dug

OB Lu E MSL XII 18

Other older lexical lists puts dream interpreters among witches and "prophets":

4	lú sag-[bulug-ga]	*mu-še-li e-ti-m [i]*
5	lú sag-šè-ná-a	*mu-pa-še-er šu-na-tim*
6	lú gissu-è-dè	*mu-še-li si-el-li*
7	lú inim-ma	*ša a-wa-tim*
8	lú inim-dug$_4$-dug$_4$	*mu-ta-wu-ú*

OB Lu C4 MSL XII 194,
duplicated in OB Lu A 357-60
MSL XII 168

mušēli eṭimmi "rouser of a ghost," i.e., "necromancer" and *mupaššer šunātim* "interpreter of dreams" are near in meaning to *ša awatim* "the one of the word." lú inim-dug$_4$-dug$_4$ = *mutawû* means "talkative," and we note again that since OB Lu mixes up genuine offices with mere descriptions of states, *ša awātim* may or may not refer to an office, but cf. *ša awātim* (See n. 207)

The dream interpreter appears often in other lists:

en-si EN.ME.LI ŠU
šá-['i-lu]

Diri IV 61f CAD E 170b

EN.ME.LI *en-su-ú*
ša-i-lum

Proto-Diri 381f CAD E 170b

These seem to indicate that the ensi is the reading of the signs EN.ME.LI and can be read *ensû*, unless this is merely a "learned" interpretation of the scribes.

This is, however, also found among purification offices, Secs. 1.23, 1.24.

241 engiz
242 ensi
242a SAL ensi
243 kišib-gál
244 kišib-lá
245 enkum
246 ninkum
247 abgal

OB Proto-Lu MSL XII 41

499 ensi
500 SAL ensi
501 mur-ra-aš
----

507 máš-šu-gíd-gíd

OB Proto-Lu MSL XII 50

showing that there is a female office of ensi.

3.3.2 An Old Sumerian ration list has a miscellany of cultic officials on it.[51] These are ensi, engiz, $abgal_x$, nin-dingir DN, lú-dingir, lú-dub-alal-urudu, ab-ba-é-gal, lú-níg-ág, lú-ub_x-kug-ga, agrig-ezem, igi-du_8, ì-du_8-èš, ugula. SUMAS.ME-ne (read ugula-luhša-ne), gala-mah, gala, gal-nar, $bahar_2$. The engiz "cook" (but see Sec. 1.23), the lú-dub-alal-urudu "copper tablet scribe (?), the lú-níg-ág "measurer of things (?)," the ugula-luhša (a food administrative rank), and the $bahar_2$ "potter" are the temple personnel who provide auxiliary services for the cult. The nin-dingir's are the high women cultic officials, see Sec. 4.9. The gala's and nar are singers, the lú-ub_x-kug-ga is the one who plays the holy *uppu*-drum. Here are a number of temple personnel of varying types together on one tablet, some we would refer to as "auxiliary" (App. 5), a valuable occurrence.

We note that the ensi-engiz pair occurred in the OB Lu list above, and the Lamentation Over the Destruction of Sumer and Ur,[52] with several others of the same offices. Those who did not prepare the ceremony are the: engiz, ensi, kišib-gál "seal keeper," somewhat the order of the OB Proto-Lu, above. This does not seem to relate to the ensi's "dream interpretation" aspect as do the below examples.

3.3.3 For a man who has fallen under the sway of angry demons, a song has: lú-bé ensi-ra mu-un-pà-dè eger-ra mu-un-zu-zu "this man calls to an ensi, who makes known the future."[53]

3.3.4 The *šā'ilu* /ensi is lit., "asker"[54] and is sometimes associated with the *barû*-diviner:

22'	níg-na-ri-⸢šà?⸣-igi-bar-ra	*ba-ru-ú sá qut-rin-ni*
23'	e[ns] i	*ša-i-lu*
24'	[SAL en] si	*ša-il-tu*
25'	[m]ur-ra-aš	*ša-il-tu*
26'	[l]ú-ma	*ša-il-tu*
27'	lú-balag-gá	*mu-še-lu-ú [e-dim-me]*
28'	lú-sag-šè-ná-a	*mu-pa-šìr [šu-na-ti]*
29'	x.GAN.RAB.ME.KU	*iš* -[ ]

Lu = ša II iii MSL XII 120

Shulgi calls himself "ensi of the land."[55] Gudea calls Nanshe "ensi of the gods."[56] In NA times, the god or goddess of dreams is the son or daughter of Shamash.[57]

The *šā'ilu,* the *bārû* and the *āšipu* are in parallel lines,[58] the *bārû* doing *bīru* "extispicy," the *šā'ilu* doing *muššakku* "libanomancy" and the *āšipu* doing *šiptu* "divination," in a large catalogue. The *šā'ilu* is described as the one who interprets (root *pašāru*) dreams in a hymn to Shamash.[59] With the *makaltu* bowl in front (? Oppenheim) of the *riksu* of cedar, Shamash instructs the *šā'ilu*. He is called *pāširu* "the interpreter" of dreams, indeed, he is the one who sends dreams to humans.

Charpin thus concludes (*Clergé* 384) that the ensi/*šā'ilu* appears in two different contexts: that of dream interpreter, acting with the *barû*, and that of purificator, acting with the engiz / *engiṣu*. His activity in libanomancy is shown in CAD s.v. *muššakku*. In fact, Oppenheim (p. 223) shows that his activities included oneiromancy, libanomancy, lecanomancy and necromancy.

The activity with the engiz indicates that the *šā'ilu* offers the libation, and the *engiṣu* has prepared it as food, "rôles complémentaires" (Charpin). She finds that in some contexts the ensi is the equivalent of lúBAPPIR "brewer" in one place and lúŠIM.SAR/*raqqû* "perfumer" in another.

3.3.5 One of the above terms for dream interpreter may tell a little about how it was done. The term lú-sag-šè-ná-a used by Gudea, the OB Lu C4 (Sec. 3.3.1) and the Lu = ša II iii 28' (above) lists means literally "the one who is at the head (of another) on a bed," i.e., sleeping. The understanding was perhaps gained by sleeping next to the one who wanted his dream interpreted.[60]

A Gudea text plays on the name of the office: gù-dé-a sag-šè-ná mu-ná / inim mu-na-ta-è "Gudea lets the sag-šè-ná lie down, bring out the word for him."[61] The term ná "lie down" is picked up from part of the title of the office "the one who lies at the head," resulting in the "word," i.e., explanation of the dream interpreter.

The Akkadian term *mupaššir šunāti* means simply "interpreter of dreams." The Lu = ša II iii 22' entry shows that the *bārû* uses *qutrinnu*-smoke. The Sumerian part means: "the man who observes the censer."[62]

Other notes showing how they all work together are brought out by Charpin.[63] The Proto-Lu entry Sec. 3.3.1, relating ensi to engiz "temple cook" is like the Lu = ša entry Sec. 3.4.1 relating *āšipu* to ŠIM.SAR = *raqqû* "person dealing in aromatics." These may each be substances with which the diviners work, operated by the experts in their handling. This is one of the reasons why I have provided a Category V in "cultic" officials; they are involved in the cult along with the others.

3.3.6 The female *šā'iltu* was not relegated to female circles alone. In OB times one was used by a woman who also used a male *bārû*.[64] The *bārû* sometimes appears with a female *šā'iltu*,[65] sometimes with a male *šā'ilu*.[66] The *šā'iltu* seems to show up in texts more often than the *baritu*.

3.3.7 The *edammû* "Traumdeuter" (so AHw), "a priest" (CAD) appears on some lexical lists, among the highest of cultic officials:

13	en	*e-nu-um*
14	nu-èš	*ni-šak-ku*
15	e-da-mú-ra	*e-dam-mu-ú*
16	$gudu_4$	*pa-ši-šu*
17	$gudu_4$-abzu	*gu-da-* ABZU-*ú*

Erimhuš V MSL XVII 67

Here surrounded the en, the nu-èš/*nešakku* and the $gudu_4$/*pašišu*, the *edammû* must be more than a mere "dream interpreter," and must perform some duties related to those of these ranks. We also find this office listed among others of our Category No. 1 in an OB list: *pašīšu edammû* lú*nišakku u* AN.GUB.BA.MEŠ [*ša mā*]*hāzi māt* Akkad "of the sanctuaries of the land of

Akkad."[67] An OB letter indicates this, also: *e-da-ma-am ina bīt* Sin "the *edammû* in the temple of Sin."[68] What he does has not yet been discovered.

In the MA-NA god-list An-Anum, this office is part of the Ishtar cult (comparing across the columns):

from the fragments of An = Anum KAV 73

in K. 4349, CT 24, 33	VAT 13034
18 ᵈIštar *šu-* [*ti-tu*]	10]*šu-ti-tu*
19 ᵈIštar x x	
20 ᵈIštar é-dam	11] ⌈*e*⌉-*dam-me-tu*

So Ishtar *šutitu* "the šutean Ishtar" is followed by Ishtar of the é-dam, the house/temple where she lives as dam "spouse," which may be compared to the house/temple èš-dam/*aštammu* where she lives in a way interpreted in App. 4. This is perhaps read here as *edammētu*, the only time *edammû* appears in the feminine, but explainable because Ishtar is a female. So with Ishtar known as a functionary of this type, the *edammû* could be considered part of the Ishtar cult.

And in the canonical series:

93 šà-é-gal *e-kal-lu-ú*
94 šà-é-gal *ša* DUMU É.GAL
95 e-da-mu ŠU-*u*

Lu = ša IV MSL XII 131

he appears among palace residents, showing yet another aspect of this office not indicated in the above two lexical lists.

He appears in a Larsa text in the temple of Sin.[69]

The broken entry *a-da-mu-u* = *š* [*á*] -⌈*'i*⌉-*l* [*u*] [70] is the only connection yet found of *edammû* with a dream interpreter.

3.3.8 Another type of dream interpreter is the *harṭibi*, an Egyptian word on a NA administrative tablet[71] and an Esarhaddon historical fragment.[72] This term is probably the same one as that appearing in the Hebrew Bible in the form *ḥarṭōm* in the plural in Genesis, Exodus and Daniel, and in the singular in the Hebrew and Aramaic portions of Daniel. The Genesis entries in chapter 41, and the Exodus entries in chapters 7-9 treat this office as a magician of Egypt. The Daniel Aramaic entries list him among *'āšap* (Dan. 2.10, cf. Akk. *āšipu*) and Chaldeans. In fact, Daniel himself was *rab ḥarṭumayya* "chief of the *ḥarṭōm*'s" in Dan 4.6 (EV 9).

3.3.9 Whether the *mupaššer šunātim* of the OB Lu Sec. 3.3.1 and the Lu = ša lists Sec.3.3.4 above is another type of dream interpreter or a scribal explanation for lú-sag-šè-ná-a will be seen when more entries in context are found.

3.3.10 The šabra(PA-AL)/*šabrû* begins appearing in OAkk times.[73] The *šabrû* as a dream interpreter is separated by CAD from the *šabrû* as a temple administrator. Compare:

100 sukkal-ensi$_2$ MIN (i.e., *sukkal*) *iš-ša-ku*
101 sukkal é-bar MIN *ša-an-gi-e*

102 sukkal-šabra	MIN *šab-ri-e*	
103 sukkal-mar-tu	MIN *a-mur-ri-e*	

Lu = ša I MSL XII 96
continued from MSL XI 88ff

in which the *šabrû* appears with the $ensi_2$ = *iššakku*, the name for the head of state and the *šangû* one of the head administrators and cultic officials. But in a different context:

134 lúl šabra	ŠU	*rag-gi-* [*mu*]
135 lú-gub-ba	*a-* [*p*]*il-lu-ú*	*aš-šá-* [ ]
136 lú ú-bíl-lá	ŠU	*kut-tim-* [*mu*]

HAR-gud B VI MSL XII 226

In the latter the ŠU = *šabrû* appears in some role as speaker (*raggimu*), close to the ecstatic office lú-gub-ba, a divination office.

The *šabrû* in a context of dreams is found in a dream report of Ashurbanipal.[74]

3.3.11 We sometimes discover no title of dream interpreter in the text, but Oppenheim[75] shows that the supplicant often did the prayer or the ritual act himself, with no intermediary necessary. But he must have been told what prayers to say by the *šā'iltu*/*šā'ilu* or some sort of expert, or maybe when the text says that "the man" says the prayers, in actuality the *šā'iltu*/*šā'ilu* or someone says them on his behalf. In any case, in the dream book and in the rituals there is usually no mention of a divination expert by title, and this is usually the case with other divination texts, also.

3.4 MAŠ.MAŠ / šim-mu_2 /mu_7-mu_7 /*āšipu* and *āšiptu* //AZU/*asû* and *asātu*

3.4.1 We will find the ideographic equivalents for the first of these office many and confusing; as is usually the case they proliferate still more in the lexical lists of the NA/NB period.[76] As long ago as Early Dynastic times we find a mas-mas:

116 šu-lá
117 maš-maš
118 guruš

ED Lu E MSL XII 18

and an OB entry:

418 lú mu_7-dug_4	*ša ši-íp-tim*	
419 lú mu_7-mu_7-gál	*wa-*ši-pu-ú*	* tablet has -PI-
420 lú siskur-re	*ša ni-qi_4-im*	

OB Lu A MSL XII 170

One Nin-ezen of Ki-abrig was termed maš-maš, and he spoke in eme-ha-mun "harmonious, contrasting speech." [77]

There are several NA entries:

146 [NAR.BALAG] *a-š [i-p]u*
147 [l]ú-mu$_7$-[gá] l KI.MIN
148 ka^{ka}-mu$_7$-gál KI.MIN

---

149 ka-kù-gál KI.MIN
150 ka$^{ka\text{-}ap\text{-}ri\text{-}ig}$pirig KI.MIN
151 ŠIM-^{mu}SAR KI.MIN
152 ka-kù-gál KI.MIN (note second entry of this same term)
153 $^{ni\text{-}ig\text{-}ru}$KA x AD.KU KI.MIN

Lu = ša IV MSL XII 133

203 sanga$_2$-mah ŠU-*hu*
204 [maš]-maš *maš-ma-šu*
205 nar-balag *a-ši-pu*
206 ka-pirig MIN

Lu = ša Short Recension = Excerpt I MSL XII 102

207 LÚ.HAL *ba-ru-u*
208 LÚ.maš-maš *a-ši-pu*
209 LÚ.ka-pirig *a-ši-pu*

Igituh, short version

ii 7 LÚ.GUB.BA
8 LÚ.HAL.MEŠ
9 LÚ.MAŠ.MAŠ
10 LÚ.ME.ME
11 LÚ.MAH.MEŠ
12 LÚ.EN.ME.LI

K. 4395 MSL XII 238

and an entry in the Sultantepe list

---

7 LÚ.MAŠ.MAŠ
8 [LÚ].ME.ME
9 [LÚ.ME *a-ši*]-*pi*

STT I MSL XII 233

Another apparently NA list of professions:
1 lú SAG x
2. *a-ši-pu*
3. lú SAG.KAL
4 *a* -⌈*ši-pu* ⌉
5. lú ...
6. *na-* ⌈*a-ru* ⌉
7. lú NAR
8 *na-a-ru*

T.G. Pinches, Abu Habba 83-1-18, 1866, *PSBA* 18 (1 Dec. 1896) pl. 3, col. I

and a list with poorly copied signs:

r.2	]ME	*a-š* (!)-*p* [*u*]
r.3	L]Ú ME.ME	ditto
r.4	L]Ú MAŠ	ditto
r.5	L]Ú MAŠ.MAŠ	ditto

Iraq 6 (1939) 157, No. 17

r.1	LÚ.KA.PIRIG	ditto
r.2	LÚ.KA.LUH.HA	ditto
r.3	LÚ.KA.KU.GA	ditto
r.4	LÚ.INIM.INIM.MA	ditto
r.5	LÚ.UD.KA.BAR	*a-ši-pu*

Iraq 6 (1939) 156, No. 15
corrected by CAD A/2 431a,
lexical section

The LU.ME.ME, next to the LÚ.MAŠ.MAŠ in several of the above NA entries, would seem to indicate *āšipu,* but there is a problem in that LÚ.ME is put opposite *āšipu* on the *Iraq* 6 entry, yet in several other entries ME = išib, see *išippu* lexical section, CAD I/J 242b. Either there is confusion on the scribe's part between *išippu* and *āšipu*, which I doubt, or the scribe was placing two similar-sounding words together, though the offices are not similar. CAD I/J 243a concludes that the reading of LÚ.ME and LÚ.ME.ME in the NB period is *āšipu.*

The ka-kù-gál = *āšipu* entry in Lu = ša IV 152, above, indicates a reading *kakugallu* and Lu = ša IV179 has ka-kù-gál = ŠU-*lu* (*kakugallu*) following the *lallārti* and preceding *kurgarrû* (see App. 3.3):

177	hul-a-li	*lal-la-ru*
178	SAL hul-a-li	*lal-la-ar-ti*
179	ka-kù-gál	ŠU-*lu*
180	kur-gar-ra	ŠU-*u*
181	ama-ér-ra	ŠU-*u*

Lu =ša IV MSL XII 134

The office *āšipu*[78] is well attested. There is a medical series "Enuma ana bit marṣi āšipu illiku "when an *āšipu* (KA.PIRIG) goes into the house of a sick man," published by Labat.[79] Much of his work is with sick people, or those wishing to ward off illness. His technique is multiform, and too complex to summarize, but Ritter helpfully breaks it down: the use of incantations, drugs, figurines, amulets, magic circles made with flour, libations, anointings and some more.[80]

One type of Sumerian text is interpreted by a study of A. Falkenstein: (A MAŠ.MAŠ is speaking): "When I draw near to the sick man, enter his house, put my hand on his head, learn the sinews of his limbs, recite the 'incantation of Eridu' over him, recite the incantation over the sick man..."[81] So the ceremony here is done in a house, there is touching, and there is diagnosis.[82] Elsewhere (Ritter, passim) there is sometimes rubbing, anointing, use of figurines, bandaging, and drugs.

3.4.2 The occurrences of the female *āšiptu* are only as epithets of goddesses, and this is not necessarily an indication that the female office existed in practice.[83] Mari occurrences are discussed by Lebeau.[84]

3.4.3 In a letter to Esarhaddon[85] a MAŠ.MAŠ and a MAŠ.MAŠ *šaniu* "apprentice or assistant" have to do with driving out an evil spirit, using objects like that used the world over by shamans: hanging animals and birds on door posts, putting on a special garment, using incense, circumambulation of the bed of the patient.

A collection of divination texts showing the *mašmaššu* / *āšipu* in action (although the title seldom appears) was published by Ebeling.[86] They concern the relieving of a pregnant woman nearing her time (p. 5, *KAR* 223), making a child rest (pp. 8ff, *KAR*114), relieving a troubled father and a crying mother (p. 13, Thompson *AMT* 96 No. 2), reconciling an angry man (pp. 16ff, *KAR* 63, 43, 62), for a man following an enemy (*KAR* 62), for an entrance into the palace (pp. 30ff, *KAR* 71), an anointing with oil (*VAT* 8230, pp. 37ff), over a *kapasu*-stone that the king may be friendly towards you (pp. 41ff, *VAT* 8014), and a namburbi (pp. 47ff, *KAR* 38). In these *kitkittû* and *parṣu* (both) "ritual" (p. 5.2), certain objects are used: wood and stone, bread, oil, spittle, a ring, a piece of clay, a band of red wool, and many more. Gods called upon include Shamash, Lahmu, Anu and Antu, Gula, Ea, Sin, Ninkarrak, Ishtar, Ninegal, the trio of "great gods" Anu Enlil Ea, the Igigi and Anunnaki. Many more elements appear in this rich collection of materials.

3.4.4 The above is to be compared to the areas in which the *āšipu* was expected to be an expert, listed in *KAR* 44.[87] Many of its lines are untranslatable, others contain technical terms that are as yet inexplicable; several of these are discussed elsewhere in this study, see index. Below we give a representative rather than a complete set of excerpts. It is headed: *rēšē iškari mašmaššūti* / *āšipūti ana ihzi u tāmarti* "headings of the series m./a. for *ihzu* "instruction" and *tāmartu* "observation":

2. ^{d}Libittu "brick-god," *mīš pî* "mouth washing," oil
3. "word of the *apsû*," šuluh "sprinkling" of the gods
4. the place of Shamash; šu-íla "lifting of the hands"
5. rites of the months Du'uzu, Ishtar (?), Abu, Ululu, Tashrītu
6. *sakikkû* - illness, *alamdimmû* - series, *nigdimdimmû* - series, *kataduggû* - series
7. clean water, angry demons
8. *di'u* - head-sickness, *takpertu* -cleansing rite, *maruṣtu* -sickness, sick Asakku-demons
9. head-sickness, neck-sickness
10. Lilu, Lilitu
11. *bīt rimki*, *bīt mēsiri*, mouth washing
12. angry magic, angry curse, releasing magic, releasing a spell
13. "where the sun sets," releasing magic, releasing a spell, seizing Lamashtu
14. *Maqlû*, *Shurpu*, anger of all kinds, to make angry demons good, lifting of the heart (sexual health)
15. for a pregnant woman who is bound, for a woman oppressed by a Lamashtu-demon
16. eye sickness, tooth sickness
17. "heart" sickness, lung sickness, incantation against sickness of any kind
18. cutting off "body-mouth,"*tuganu*-sickness "stomach ulcer- AHw," blockage of a birthing mother
19. to heal snakebite, to heal scorpion bite, *samānu*-disease

20. hurt foot
21. rites for city, house, field, orchard, river, and...for Nisaba
22. locust plague on the steppe
r.1 yard for bovines and sheep, purifying/cleansing horses
r.2 *purussû* "oracles" by stars, birds and cattle, animals of the steppe, *egirrû*-omen of the...stone of all the gods
r.3 "tablets concerning plants for bandage and phylacteries(?)" (CAD s.v. *malālu*)
r.5 *kitkittû* "rituals" of the purifying incantation
r.6 namburbi, rites for every portent of heaven and earth
r.7 to grasp "the total sum of wisdom of the secret of the *kakugallūtu* craft"
r.8 "the sealing of the design of heaven and earth"; the mystery of honey (in the ritual)
r.9 lameness and paralysis, sinew sickness, muscle sickness
r.10 prescription for an-ta-sub-ba / *miqit šamê* "something fallen from the sky," (the disease named for) ^{d}Lugal-urra, "hand of the god," "hand of the goddess," "hand of the demon"
r.11 evil Alu-demon, Lillu, "hand of mankind"
r.12 prescriptions for all kinds (of diseases)
r.13 "until you seize the binding of the *išippūtu*-craft"
r.14 after the animals of the field, eme-sal's
r.15 *kidudû*-rites in the Sumerian language, in the Akkadian language, "you will learn to do research" (CAD)
r.16 "like your worship places," as Anu, Enlil, "when a city is set on a hill"

A sheaf of notes could be appended to this. Many of the other incantation lists have similar lines. Some of these are instructions to the exorcist/physician, others are names of series or names of illnesses; some are immediately recognizable, as *mīš pî, Maqlû, Shurpu, namburbi, bīt rimki, šu-íla*, "When a city is set on a hill."

This list shows that the extent of knowlege required of this office was vast, especially as the officials had to learn the values and technical usages of the ideograms, as well as act as physician. Much of this work was in healing, some in astronomical/astrological subjects; the high gods enter in but they share the stage with demons. It reminds us of 4 R 53, a catalogue (in part) of the rites of the *kalû*, Sec. 2.3.15. It indicates that the place of the *āšipu* is difficult to define, and, indeed, we learn of other actors who take care of these same items, so maybe the *āšipu* has added to his repertory in ever-widening circles as he took on more tasks. To translate simply as "magician"[88] is too simple.

3.4.5 A NA rite for Bēlit-ṣēri uses meat, flour, bread, wine, beer, salt, oil, figs and special vessels.[89] In the left column in a continuation of this or another ritual for the *Mārat nāri* "daughter of the river,"[90] the MAŠ.MAŠ does something broken off with "hand water," and the ^{mí}*qadištu* is removed. Another ritual[91] uses some of the same material, including salt for Bēlit-ṣēri and ^{d}A-ki-si, and neck-meat before Kalluh[92] with no titles.

3.4.6 In the *Bīt rimki* series[93] the officiant is a MAŠ.MAŠ; at times it is spelled out as *a-ši-pu*, Laessøe 36, bottom of page: "When the king enters the "First House" the *mašmaššu* will recite the incantation...and the king will say the incantation...(p. 29). In the ritual for the "Second House" the king tells Shamash that *kišpu* "sorcery" has been used against him, an *ēpištu* "witch" has bewitched him, a *sahhirtu* "sorceress" has "turned" him, playing on the root meaning of this word (p. 38, 9-10A), followed by a vivid description of what a witch could do. It ends in the prayer: "Oh Shamash, may my sorceress (*kaššāptu*) fall, but may I stand," line 44, p. 40, 46a.

The *mašmaššu* brings offerings and performs sacrifices before the king (ibid. p. 84 § 29) thus doing a priestly role, and here, as elsewhere, he shows his subordination to the king by prostrating before him (p. 85, top).

3.4.7 Now to give some evidence for an orthography *mašmaššu* and evidence that it may be a separate office. We saw in Lu = ša Excerpt I, Sec. 3.4.1, that *maš-ma-šu* and *a-ši-pu* were listed as separate entries, but there is always the possibility that there may be a scribal collection of variants. As long ago as Proto-izi, ultimately OB, there was:

29 [maš-maš] *[ma-áš]-ma-šu m*
30 [maš-maš-gal *[ma-áš] -ma-áš-ga-lu-um*

Proto-izi I D iv (bilingual)
MSL XIII 39

the Sumerian side duplicated by the Proto-izi I (unilingual)

523 maš-maš
524 maš-maš-gal

Proto-izi I (unilingual)
MSL XIII 33f

240 *[m]a-aš-ma-šu m*

Proto á = A MSL IX 128

These seem to indicate that, in the scribal vocabulary of the older lexical lists, the two offices *mašmaššu* and *āšipu* are separate. A NA "practical vocabulary" K. 4395 from Kouyunjik, Sec. 3.4.1, makes us wonder if ME.ME is a variant of MAŠ.MAŠ or if MAŠ.MAŠ = *mašmaššu* and ME.ME = *āšipu*. There are a few other entries on this list showing variant orthographies.

A NA ritual text has: *lid-din-ki maš-maš a-ši-pu* ^{d}Asalluhi ^{giš}ga-ZUM ^{giš}du-di-it-tú ^{giš}*pilakku šiddu u kirissu.* "Let Asaluhhi the *mašmaššu* the *āšipu* give you (Lamashtu) a comb, a pectoral, a spindle, a comb and a hair clasp.[94] These are characteristics of a woman. Chapter 4 and App. 3.3.7 goes into this in detail. Asalluhi then has two titles: *mašmaššu* and *āšipu.* Were they synonyms or two separate offices? The principle I follow is that in ANE titles there are no synonyms, using the term as one does in modern linguistics.

In Ludlul bel nemeqi, a composition "almost certainly of the Cassite period," (Lambert), although our earliest copies are from late NA times, neither the *bārû* the *šā'ilu* nor the MAŠ.MAŠ could relieve the sufferer.[95] This prompts us to note that it often seems that the names of the offices, which we carefully try to separate out, are actually interchangeable in certain cases.

The actions of the MAŠ.MAŠ are what one would expect for an *āšipu.* The MAŠ.MAŠ takes the hand of the sick person, and says an incantation before Nusku.[96] The MAŠ.MAŠ does not go into the house of the sick person until sunset.[97] An incantation to ensure business success for the *sābû* "tavern keeper" uses the ritual of a *bārû* (HAL), an *asû*, and a ⌈*maš-ma*⌉-[*šu*].[98] A NA ritual [99] is put in mythic terms:

maš.maš.e.ne an mu-un-azag-ge-e-ne ⌈K⌉ mu-un-sikil-e-ne
maš-maš-šu šá-me-e ul-la-lu ir-ṣi-tim ub-ba-bu
"*mašmaššu* who purifies heaven, who washes earth"

Ishtar is told: the *maš-maš-ši* has *uktappiranni* "wiped me" with a censer (?), the hide of a goat, a cake baked in ashes.[100]

These syllabically written *mašmaššu*'s would indicate that the scribe meant that word and not *āšipu* in these cases. The decision still is not certain. It may very well be that the two are what some people call synonymous, or better stated, that they were two offices earlier that coalesced into one in later times.

3.4.8 Several officials "purify" using the term *ullulu*, the II/1 from *elēlu* "to be pure," including the *mašmaššu*, *mār bārê, išippu, āšipu* [101] and *šangammahu* [102] from NA and NB texts; or šu-luh a Sumerian term. Certain other high officials, our Category No. 1, also "purify." The rites vary, and we list those referred to earlier as related to this activity:

kisalluhu (Sec. 1.12.1)
gudu4 (1.7.4)
the several šita's (1.9.2ff)
gudu4-abzu (1.14)
susbû (1.15.1)
išib (1.16)
gada-lá (1.17)
en (m.) (1.18.1)
en (f.) (1.19.6)
lagar (1.21.8)
abrig (1.22.1)
engiz (1.23)
kišib-gal (1.24)
enkum and ninkum (1.25.1.2)
endub (1.26)
a-tu (1.28)
a-tu5 (1.29)
ramku (1.47)

3.4.9 To turn now to the AZU / *asû*: a text with PN lu-lu a-zu was excavated at Ur by Woolley [103] and this office appears on the earliest lexical lists, ED Lu E, line 47, MSL XII 17, in which similar groups are not together, and one in which similar officials are sometimes together in small groups (note gaps):

1	[sa]nga
8	balag-di
10	nar
17	pa4-šeš
18	gudu4
21	ᵃazu

ED Lu B MSL XII 13

It was common practice however to treat similar offices together in texts. In NA times oaths of loyalty are taken by LÚ.A.BA.MEŠ, [LÚ] *bārû*, [LÚ] MAŠ.MAŠ.MEŠ, [LÚ] A.ZU.MEŠ [LÚ] *dāgil iṣṣurē, manzaz ekalli*" scribe, diviner, exorcist, physician, bird watcher, palace administrator"[104] In a medical text: LÚ.A.ZU, LÚ.MAŠ, LÚ.HAL. LÚ.EN.ME.LI "physician, exorcist (for MAŠ.MAŠ?, but see Sec. 1.42), diviner, dream interpreter."[105] In a hymn of Gula she says *asaku, baraku, ašipak* [106] "I am a physician, I am a diviner, I am an exorcist." And in the Erimhuš list diviners are together:

137	ì-zu	*a-su-ú*	
138	me-zu	*ba-ru-ú*	
139	me-a-zu	*mu-de-e ter-tú*	"one who knows the signs"

Erimhus V MSL XVII 73

collecting together the -zu offices.

3.4.10 We have a problem when we regularly translate a-zu /*asû* as "physician," for then we find it difficult to separate the *āšipu* and *asû*. Ritter attempts to distinguish between *āšipu* "incantation expert" and *asû* "physician" but only succeeds, in my opinion, in showing how close the two are. Both cure the patient, both use incantation, both use the same healing devices, both titles "*āšipu* of the land" and "*asû* of the land" describe Ninisina "the lady of Isin."[107] Biggs[108] says that the medical (*asûtu*) and the magical (*āšipūtu*) are two traditions which the medical texts frequently combine.

3.4.11 The female office is rare. Gula the goddess of healing is not surprisingly called an *asātu*: A PN is: Gula-a-sa-at.[109] She describes herself as *asû, bārû, āšipu*, Sec. 3.4.9. Gula as Ninkarrak is *a-zu-gal-la-tu* [110] An *asâtu* appears at the palace at Larsa in the OB period.[111]

O. Pedersen[112] finds the division between *āšipu* and *asû* questionable. The *asû* and the MAŠ.MAŠ perform the *dulli* "rites" together.[113] In Hellenistic times the MAŠ.MAŠ purifies with the carcass of a sheep.[114]

3.4.12 The Asshur archives at Berlin[115] indicate that some officiants tended to come from certain families of exorcists. Pedersen finds (p. 45) an example of a person who started as *šamallû* "student," then *šamallû* MAŠ.MAŠ *ṣehru* "student, young exorcist," then MAŠ.MAŠ *ṣehru* "young exorcist," then MAŠ.MAŠ "exorcist," then MAŠ.MAŠ *bīt* Asshur "exorcist of the Asshur temple." This appears to be a "rising through the ranks."

Multiple office is shown by a hymn of PN lú maš-maš lú u[m-me-a] tin-tir^{ki} "the mašmaš the sch[olar] of Babylon," who has Gula speaking: (in the words of n. 106, and then): *hi-pu inbu* (160) "sex appeal," *kuzbu* (165) "sexuality" rains down. Inanna/Ishtar claims the same attributes, CAD K 615f).

A NA text *ADD* 953 (unpublished) lists, among other rations, large amounts from the *kitû akiltu* "linen account" for various officials and places, 274 talents in all (iii 4-5). These include the *kiṣir ešši* "new troop" (ii 4), *bīt* SAL.É.GAL "household of the queen" (ii 5), *ka-ṣir* x-craftsman" (ii 13), *rab narkabāte* "wagon drivers" (ii 14), *abarakku* "steward of the temple" (ii 15), then a section about wool, including 2 talents LÚ.MAŠ.MAŠ (r. iv 2) *ša kal šatti* "for the whole year." So here the MAŠ.MAŠ is among tradesmen, military men, the queen's household -- quite a miscellany.

A NA list of functionaries *ADD* 851 lists PNs of 17 MAŠ.MAŠ.MEŠ, with other cultic positions (See n. 71)

3.5 *mullilu*

3.5.1 This seems to be an office in its own right, despite Goetze.[116] The *mullilu* was understood by the scribes to be related to the *mašmaššu*:

109 ma-áš-ma-á[š] [MAŠ·M]AŠ *mul-lil-lum* Aa A= naqu I/6
MSL XIV 227

and to the sanga$_2$ (ÍL.MÁ.DÚB), (note that this is not the sanga = *šangû*):
108 hi-bi-iz TUR.DIŠ *mul-lil-[lu]* Aa A = naqu VI/l
MSL XIV 438

93 sa-an-ga* ÍL.MÁ!.DÚB *mul-li-lu* S^b I
*a variant has sa-an-gu
MSL III 104

124 sanga2 *mul [li-lu]*
Lu = ša IV MSL XII 132

abgal sanga$_2$.ma.da *apkallum mu-ul-li-lum* *ša* [ ]
PBS l/l 11 iv 96 CAD M/2 189a.

We need more references to relate the *mullilu* to the *apkallu* The sanga$_2$ is related somehow to the *šangammahu* and the *šangagallu* (sp.?):

127 [sanga$_2$-gal] (presumed reading) ŠU-*lu*
128 [sanga$_2$-mah] ŠU-*hu*
Lu= ša IV MSL XII 132

3.5.2 *mullilu* may be the II/1 participle of *elēlu* "to be pure," so again we have a "purifying office." Perhaps the *mullilu* (cultic official) carries the *mullilu* (sprinkler)

3.6 SANGA$_2$.MAH /*šangammahu*

This office, not the expected sanga "priest" + mah "high, chief" (*šangû* is always sanga) but an exorcist, appears with various orthographies: *šangammahhu*, *šaggammahu*, *šangammahu*. In a hymn of Sargon[117] he is guided by Ishtar. The next parallel line speaks of guidance to the *asû*, so the two are in the same category.

The title appears among those discussed in this chapter:

202 susbu^{bu} *ra-am-ku*
203 sanga$_2$-mah ŠU-*hu*
204 [maš]-maš *maš-ma-šu*
205 nar-balag *a-ši-pu*
Lu = ša Excerpt I MSL XII 102

and he is described as an *āšipu*: ga!-e lú-mu$_7$-mu$_7$ LÚ.ÍL.MA.DUB.mah me-kù-ga eridu-ki-ga me-en/*a-ši-pu ša-an-gam-ma-hu mu-ul-lil par-ṣi ša eridu a-na-ku* [118] "I am the *āšipu* the *šangammahu* who purifies the *parṣu*-rites of Eridu." Parpola finds further texts in Kinnier Wilson's Wine Lists.[119]

In a lipsur litany, the *šangammahu* kindles the fire, sets up the brazier, and burns the *piširta* "magic ingredients."[120]

A similar or the same rank under a different name is the *šangagalu*. see Sec. 3.5.

3.7 Witches: UŠ$_{11}$($_{12}$)(KAxBE).ZU/*kaššāpu* and *kaššāptu* // *mušēlû* and *mušēlītu* // *mušēlit eṭimme* // *muppišu* and *muppištu* // *muppišānu* //*multēpišu* and *multēpištu* // *mušēpišu* //*muštēpišu* and *muštēpištu* //*ša eṭimme* //*ēpišu* and *ēpišu* passim, and see Secs. 3.20, 3.21

3.7.1 Information is not available to separate the large number of titles of witches. Perhaps many of them are equivalent in function. The witch or sorcerer, by definition, controls much of the same milieu as that of the incantation expert, but there is dread associated with the former, mixed with a desire that he or she be done away with or hurt. The standard complaint of the "righteous sufferer" is that he has been hurt by a witch.[121]

3.7.2 Both the male *kaššāpu* and the female *kaššāptu*, some basic terms for such practices, seem to be described in much the same way. They appear in the lexical lists among some miscellaneous entries:

18	SAL úh-zu	*kaš-šap-tum*
19	SAL IGI.ŠID-e$_{11}$-e-dè	*mu-še* -⌊*li*⌋-*tum*

Lu = ša I, Excerpt II
MSL XII 104

The latter entry is usually given as *mušēlit eṭimme* "raiser of a ghost,"[122] a witch specializing in necromancy. The *kaššāptu* may be from Elam, Qutu, Suta, Lullubu, Hanigalbat,[123] or more likely these refer to styles using names derived from these countries. It furthermore indicates that one conjures up a ghost by playing on the balag.

Witches use common materials in a secret and mysterious way: dust from a house,[124] a stone (see n. 127), flour (Shurpu I 10), onion (I.13), water (I.13), dates (I.13), wool (I.14), goats' hair (I.14), spittle (V-VI.129), thread (V-VI.144f), special plants (VIII.87), incense (IX.96ff). A sickness could be described in terms of this office: SAL.UŠ$_{11}$($_{12}$).ZU *hīrassu* "a sorceress has selected him."[125]

The MÍ.UŠ$_{12}$.ZU / *kaššāptu* would make a man tight for sexual intercourse.[126] Her craft could be dispelled by the ittamir-stone.[127] In other words, sorcery could only be stopped by other sorcery. This is much the same reasoning as used by Moses in confronting the magicians of Egypt, Exodus 7.8-12.

3.7.3 From the lexical lists we find *muppištu*

1'	[SAL]	[x] - [x] - ' -*tu*
2'	[SAL]-⌈x⌉	*la a-ma-lu-uk-tu*
3'	[SAL sa] g-a	*la ka-si-tu*
4'	[SAL] -SAR	*mu-piš-tu*
5'	[SAL] -⌈x⌉	*mu-na-mir-tu*

Lu = ša III ii MSL XII 124

6	[SAL]	*mu* -[*š*]*é-biš-tu*
7	[SAL (šu)-su-ub] -ak	*ma-ši-iš-tu*
8	[SAL]	*mu-pi-iš* -[*tu*]
9	[SAL -du] n?-na	*ša il pa* -⌈ x ⌉-[x]
10	[SAL] -gíd	*ša a-bu-ša* - [*te*]

ibid. p. 123

3.7.4 Compare *muppištu*[128] with *muppišānu* "practitioner of sorcery."[129] In a ritual of the Ishtar/Tammuz cult against magic: *ṣalam muppiši u muppi* [*šti* ZI ...K]U$_5$.RU.DA.HUL.GIG *ipušuni"* statue of the *muppišu* and *muppištu* who practiced *zikurudû* magic against me."[130] Earlier in the text this is linked to *kišpu* magic for the dead, and *zīru* magic related to hatred.

3.7.5 The *multēpišu* is a wizard or witch who uses a *gišhuru* "magic circle."[131]

In a summary statement, *Maqlû* I says that those who have bewitched the subject are: ^{lú}*kaššāpu* (126), ^{mí}*kaššāptu* (127), *ēpišu* (128), *ēpištu* (129), *mul-te-piš-tu* (130), and passim. Because of the s/l shift in late Assyrian, this is probably equivalent to *muštēpisu*, Sec.3.7.7; however is listed separately in *Maqlû* I 16.

3.7.6 *mušēpišu* has been discovered once so far.[132] If the root is *epēšu* "do, perform," we may understand it as a III/1 participle "liturgist" (Caplice)

3.7.7 The witch *muštēpišu* and *muštēpištu* seems to be treated like the *kaššāpu*, *kaššāptu*, *ēpišu*, *ēpištu* in preceding lines in *Maqlû* I 130. The form is a III/2 participle of *epēšu*, also used as a verb in the meaning "to practice witchcraft." [133]

3.7.8 The necromancer *mušēlû eṭimme* "raiser of a ghost" appears only in lexical texts so far. The Lu = ša entry, Sec. 3.3.4, shows that the *šā'ilu* and *šā'iltu* is contiguous with the "raiser of a ghost" and this may relate the two offices. The female *mušēlītu* is found in Sec. 3.7.2, Lu = ša I, Excerpt II. Further entries show up:

356 lú gidim-l ma l	*ša* ⌜*e-te$_4$*⌝*-mi*
357 lú sag-bulug-[g]a	*mu-še-l* [*i*] ⌜*e*⌝-[*te$_4$*]-⌜*mi*⌝

OB Lu A MSL XII 168
(closely duplicated by HAR-gud B VI 148-149, MSL XII 226)

3.7.9 The terms *mušēlû* and *mušēlītu* sometimes appear alone on lexical lists, Sec. 3.7.2.

3.7.10 The *ša eṭimme* "the one of a ghost" is a related office, or another term for the same office, OB Lu A, Sec. 3.7.8.

The verb *elēlu* in the II/l is an action done by the *mašmaššu*, *mār bārê*, *išippu*, *āšipu* in later texts.[134]

3.8 NUN.ME/*apkallu* and *apkallatu* //

3.8.1 The *apkallu* (NUN.ME), usually understood as a wise man, or a sage from the old myths,[135] is also found as a cultic official; CAD s.v.: "a priest or exorcist". Jacobsen describes him as a "wise counsellor" and a high official at court. He said it died out as an office after UruKAgina, but remained in myth.[136]

3.8.2 *Apkallu* appears on the earliest lexical lists:

14 GAL.ŠITA$_x$

15 NUN.ME (abgal)
16 GAL.UNKEN

ED Lu A, MSL XII p. 10,
as corrected by Arcari ED List A

and at Fara.[137] It is found in the later standard lu-lists, sometimes among cultic officiants, sometimes not:

17 á-gál	*le -' -u*	"skilled, powerful"
18 NUN.ME	*ap-kal-lu*	
19 [a]ma-tu	*a-lit-tum*	"parent, begetter, etc."

Igituh, short version

5" kiš[ib]-gal	*ki-ši-ib-gal-lum*	
6" NUN-gal	*ap-kál-lum*	
7" abrig	*ag-ri-qu*	(a variant of *abriqqu*)

Lu = ša II iv MSL XII 121

but it appears among diviners in Erimhuš:

7	NUN^{ab-gal}ME	*ap-kal-lum*
8	$^{i-ši-ib}$M E	*a-ši-pu*
9	ME^{MIN}-gal	*i-šib-gal-lum*

Erimhuš V MSL XVII 67

and by itself in Diri and Proto-Diri.[138] It is also found on the Sultantepe List:

I 15 LÚ ŠIM.⸢SAR⸣
16 LÚ ŠIM.SAR.MEŠ
17 LÚ *ap-kal-lu*
18 LÚ *mu-⸢kal* !⸣-*lu*

Sultantepe List MSL XII 233

in a section beginning with MAŠ.MAŠ (*āšipu* or *mašmaššu*) and ME.ME (probably *āšipu*, despite ME being read IŠIB = *išippu*.) *Apkallu* is also associated with *mukkallu* and *āšipu* in Malku.[139] For the *mukkallu* see Sec. 3.9.

3.8.3 The *apkallu* appears among other cultic officials of our Category No. 1: išib guda NUN.ME NUN.ME.DU Eridu-ga-ke$_4$ = *išippu pašīšu apkallu abriqqu ša Eridu* [140] This is supposedly NA.

The *apkallu* as sage and as official come together. See Sec. 2.3.15 for the secrets of the *apkallu* associated with the wisdom of Ea. A praise of Nabû from the time of Ashurbanipal has: *nēmeqi Ea kalûtu niṣirti apkallum* "the wisdom of Ea, the craft of the *kalû*, the secrets of the *apkallu*.[141]

The *apkallu* used oil in ancient times. The *apkal šamnî* "*apkallu* of the oil" is according to tradition the descendant of Enmeduranki, king of Sippar, found on the Sumerian King List, as well as a subject of myth[142] and later, as found in the statement: *mār barî* NUN.ME Ì.GIŠ.[143]

"The *bārû* is an *apkallu* using oil." Ashurbanipal speaks about a liver omen with the *apkal šamnî's* "the *apkallu*'s using oil."[144]

3.8.4 It is notoriously difficult to discover in the art the actual officials whose texts we are studying, but the similarity between the wisdom-aspect of this official and what we know of the *apkallu* as figurines, would lead us to suggest tentatively that the officials are representatives of the *apkallu*-sages and are shown as figurines and in the slab sculpture.[145]

3.8.5 There is a female *apkallatu*, at least in grammatical form. Gula is described in a NA hymn as *ap-kal-lat ba-ra-at muš-ši-pat mu-us$^!$-sa-at ka-la-ma* "*apkallatu*, *bārītu*, *muššiptu* purifier of all."[146]

A reference to an *apkallatu*'s hair, an item also important in the appearance of the *kezertu*, Sec. 4.6, is found on an ershemma describing various classes in the land:[147] ki-sikil abgal nu-me-a síg-bar-ra bí-in-du$_8$ "the young girl, not an *apkallatu*,[148] lets her hair hang loosely." An abgal with hair hanging loosely down her back is also found in Enki's Journey to Nippur, 48[149] and in a bilingual: nun-me síg-bàr-ra du$_8$-a-ni / *ap-kal-lum pi-ri-it-sú ana warkišu ina wuššurim*,[150] "the *apkallu* lets his hair loose."

Another NA description of the *apkallu* referring to the hair is:

abgal.e síg-bar-ra
ap-kal-lu ša síg-bar /ba-ra-a
"the *apkallu* whose hair is loosed"

K. 8212.12, K. 6462+
W. G. Lambert, *JCS* 21 133

Lambert discusses a NA copy of an earlier ritual text, with a: *ka* (?) *-rib šarri sigbarê* (síg-bar)^e ^{d}šamaš "a *kāribu* (?) of the king, a *sigbarû*"hair-loosened one" of Shamash."[151] The *karibu* appears on lexical lists:

95b	[nam]-sita	SU-*u*
96	nam-šita	*ka-ri-bu*
97	lú-šu$_{12}$-dè	KI.MIN
98	gada-lá	ŠU-*lu*

Lu = ša IV MSL XII 131

as well as connected texts among cultic officials. There is a female *kāribtu* in OB, Mari and NB periods (CAD K. 216). The sometime lack of the LÚ or SAL sign before the word may show that it is a designation, a description of an action, rather than an office in itself (CAD, loc. cit.). The action is *karābu*, blessing, praising, praying, etc.

3.9 *mukkallu*

There is one lexical entry from Sultantepe, Sec. 3.8.2, not very enlightening. There are two textual references, each of which brings its problems. In a NB text, the *mukkallu* was clad in *hullānu* and *lubāru* garments, his head covered with a *tapsû*.[152] *hullānu*, which had a secular use also, was used for clothing statues of the deity, and was sometimes of linen or wool. The *lubāru* was also used for clothing statues, and was worn by the *kalû* and *mušarkisu*. It could also be a general word for clothing. The *tapsû* (NA *tapšû*) was put on in a mouth-washing ceremony.[153]

In a hymn[154] describing Nabû: *b [e-lum] palkû muk-kal-li e-še-eš-tum* "lord, rich (in knowledge),...*e-še-eš-tum* is a puzzle. The èš-èš festival is written with *eš/èš* - in Akkadian and never spelled with beginning syllabic sign e-; CAD s.vv. *išištu* and *ešeštu* compares *ašāšu*. This has several homonymns: "to grieve" or "to catch." The latter has forms beginning with e-; and i-, so this could be the root of our word. Another possibility is *išištum*, meaning unknown, appearing as [*i*]-*ši* (MSL has gig_8)-*iš-tu-um*, on a lexical list.[155] There are two examples of a PN be-el-ti-e-ši-iš-ti in OB letters.[156]

3.10 (AB).NUN.ME.DU/abrig/*abriqqu*

This term appears in OB several times as listed by Charpin.[157] The *abriqqu* is related somehow to the *apkallu*:

245 enkum
246 ninkum
247 abgal
248 ^{áb}abrig

OB Proto-Lu MSL XII 41

3"	[enkum]	*en-ku-um-mu*
4"	[nin]kum	*nin-ku-um-mu*
5"	kiš[ib]-gal	*ki-š-ib-gal-lum*
6"	NUN-gal	*ap-kál-lum*
7"	abrig	*ag -ri- qu*
8"	gaša m	*em-qu*

Lu = ša II iv MSL XII 121

The *ab-ri-qu ša* Eridu was one of those who could perform the *pîka ip-*[*tu-ú*] "opening of the ('your') mouth" ceremony. Others who did this were the *išippu*, *pašīšu* and *apkallu*.[158]

There is a place called ki-abrig[159] one of a classification of place-names with titles.

3.11 igi-du_8

The words simply mean "see-er" or "seer," yet Pettinato Waetzoldt has "seer, surveyor, controller."[160] Gregoire *Archives*[161] has collected many references to one who offers a sacrifice called $sizkur_x$ whose gìr "responsibility" is termed DU.Ú.KA igi-du_8. Gregoire gives the arguments for and against DU.Ú.KA being a personal name, one whose title is igi-du_8. It is found in many collections of Ur III texts as a title.

3.12 Ecstatics: lú-gub-ba and lú-al-è/e_{11}-dè//*muhhû* and *mahhû*//*muhhūtu*//*šarbu*//*šēhānu*//*ša šēhi*

3.12.1 The *mahhû* and *muhhû*, which the dictionaries list together, from the root *mahû* "to become frenzied, go into a trance," leads us into another area related to prophet and shaman. It appears as lú-gub-ba and lú-al-e_{11}/è-dè in lexical texts:

21	lú ^{kaš}kurun$_2$-na	*sà-bu-ú*
22	SAL lú ^{kaš}kurun$_2$-na [162]	*sà-bi-i-tum*
23	lú gub-ba	*mu-úh-hu-um*
24	SAL lú gub-ba	*mu-hu -t* [*um*]
25	lú tilla$_2$	*wa-ṣú-* ⌈*ú*⌉
26	[S]AL lú tilla$_2$(see n. 162)	*wa-ṣi-i-*⌈*tum*⌉
27	lú giš-gi-sag-kéš	*na-aq* -⌈m⌉
28	SAL lú giš-gi-sag-kéš	*na-qi$_4$-im-tu* [*m*]
29	lú ní-su-ub-ba	*za-ab-bu-ú*
30	[SA]L lú ní-su-ub-ba	*za-ba-a-tum*
31	lú ur-e	*za-ab-bu-ú*
32	lú al-e$_{11}$-dè	*ma-hu-ú*

OB Lu A, MSL XII 158
with small variants in B,
MSL XII 177 and Rec D,
MSL XII 204, 207

212	i-lu-a-li	*lal-la-ru*
213	lú-gub-ba	*mah-hu-ú*
214	lú-ni-zu-ub	*za-ab-bu*
215	kur-gar-ra	ŠU-*u*

Lu = ša I, Short Recension,
Excerpt I MSL XII 102f

116	lú ní-su-ub	*mah-hu-u*
117	lú-gub-ba	MIN
118	lú-al-è-dè	MIN
119	SAL al-è-dè	*mah-hu-tu*
120	lú-ní-su-ub	*za-ab-b* [*u*]
121	SAL ní-su-ub	*za-ab-ba-*[*tu*]
122	lú-al-è-dè	*el* -[x]
123	lú-zag-gír-lá	*ša kak-k* [*a*]

Lu = ša IV MSL XII 132

and HAR-gud B VI, Sec. 3.3.10.

3.12.2 An OAkk order of the king says to give grain to the *mahhûm* of Inanna of Girsu[163] so he may be under the aegis of the king. The office here is seen as part of the Inanna cult. A female was placed *ana muhhûtim* "for an ecstatic" by the *ir'emu* "beloved ones" in an obscure context in an unpublished text from Kish.[164]

The gub-ba appears with many other categories of officials (Sec. 2.3.13) in a seven-day ritual at Larsa. He appears as a witness in a Larsa contract.[165]

3.12.3 A female mí-lú-gub-ba occurs in a distribution of grain.[166] A female *muhhutûm* is a prophet at Mari in the Annunitum temple, Sec. 3.15.2. A *šangû* brings the writer of a letter the hair and fringe of the garment of the female *muhhutum*.[167]

3.12.4 In the first part of a rather unusual text from Mari, a full rite with acrobatics[168] described above in Sec. 1.6.2, the *muhhûm*'s go in to a trance.

3.12.5 Several ecstatics tend to be mentioned together (NA), another indication that they all were together in the same place: *kurummatu* rations to the *zabbu*, *zabbatu*, *mahhû* and *mahhûti* you shall set out.[169]

3.12.6 It seems then that the lú-al-è-dè/*mahhû* is a member of the circle of Inanna. He sings a lament with the pilipili, kurgara and sag-ur-sag,[170] officiants we will meet often in App. 3. A possible derogatory remark is that the lú-e_{11}-dè is spoken of as "a good seed of a dog." This must be for lú-al-e_{11}-dè.[171]

Virolleaud[172] finds a NA rite from the K. collection for the first day of Kislimu: *ana* ^{d}šakkan/Sumuqan GIR *liš-ken* ^{lú}GUB.BA *liš-ši-iq*, "let him establish (CAD: do obeisance to) šakkan; let him kiss the *muhhû*. It goes on to offer him water, etc.

As far as our sparse knowledge goes, the male and female varieties of these ecstatics act in the same way.

3.12.7 *šarb /pu* seems to be another type of ecstatic, so far only appearing on lexical lists, close to *mahhû*:

12	lú na-gá-ah	*be-ri-ú-um*	
13	lú sar-da	*šar-bu-um*	
14	lú sar-da	*ma-hu-ú-um*	
15	lú kár-ga	*ta-ap-lum*	
			OB Lu C3 MSL XII 194

238	lú na-gá-⌈ah⌉	(missing)	
239	lú sar-da	*sa-ar-bu*	
240	lú kár-ak	*ṭa-ap-*lum*	
			OB Lu D MSL XII 208

It is also noted in A. Sjøberg, *ZA* 65 (1975) 227 to line 88.

3.12.8 Another ecstatic appears in *mah-hu-ú* = *še-ha-a-nu* Izbu Commentary W 365e, see CAD M/l 90a. This also appears on the Sultantepe list:

VIII 3 LÚ.KA.TAR$^{ši-ha}$ -[*nu*]
4 LÚ.KAK.GIŠ.HI.A

Sultantepe List MSL XII 236

AHw lists *šēhānu* and *šihānu* s eparately. This may be related to *ša sēhi*. In a rite using mythic language,[173] standing with Ninurta, a *ša šēhi* struggles with Anzu.

3.12.9 The ecstatic condition is sometimes described. At Mari: *mahhû ittalk*[*am*] *ana mahe* [*m*] "the *mahhû* comes...a trance."[174] In a standard myth, Tiamat became *mahhûtiš* "like a *mahhû*-state."[175]

3.13 Ecstatics: AN.GUB.BA/*angubbû*

3.13.1 Whether AN.GUB.GA = *angubbû* [176] is an ecstatic office or a divine being or both, this remains to be studied further.[177] In a list of cultic officials:...*pašīšu* AN.GUB.BA.MEŠ [178] and in another list: "the holy *parṣu*'s "rites" of Esagila...(the offerings) I established, *ramki pašiši* AN$^{!}$.GUB.BA.MEŠ

$^{l\acute{u}(?)}$*ba* ??*-ru-te naṣir pirište* "guarding(?) the secrets of the *ramku*'s, *pašīšu*'s and *angubbû*'s,"[179] with the *angubbû* besides the *pašīšu*.

3.13.2 The term appears in mythological contexts: In a hymn to Baba, Baba says she is the sa-pàr!-kala-ga ^{d}nu-nam-nir-ra "the mighty snare-net of Nunamnirra," and an ?-gub-ba é-kur-ra { ka } kurum$_6$ sum-mu "the *angubbû* who sent food to the Ekur."[180] Among suppliant deities before the ka-gal-mah "great gate," there is the an-gub-ba, which Gadd translates "standing god" from gub = *i luzuzzu* "to stand;"[181] they may be gate attendants, as ì-du$_8$ "gatekeeper" of Gadd line 9.

The *angubbû* could be a statue in an Ashurbanipal text, in a broken context: [*pa*] *-ši-šu* $^{l\acute{u}}$AN.GUB.BA.MEŠ *maharšu ul-ziz* "the *pašīšu* and the *angubbû*'s I placed before him (i.e., Marduk?).[182] Or, "the *pašīšu* placed the *angubbû* before him," but the nearby sentences use "I," so the former is the more probable.

In a NA text a line describes (the priests who) *lamed pirišti* AN.GUB.BA.MEŠ" who learn the secrets of the *angubbû*'s.[183] What are the "secrets?" Is this the meaning of the rite, that is never written down?

In a context concerning who may enter the temple, R. Borger has made a study of "Die Weihe eines Enlil-Priesters."[184] One line (I.21f) has: *ana liqūtum la mār* AN.GUB.BA.MEŠ *mudû ša eni ereb bīti iduma la iqabbû* "in the matter of a *liqūtum* who does not come from the *angubbû*'s, a wise one..."A *liqūtum* is an adoptive child, who probably would come from humans.

Again a list of officials, from the Old Sumerian period, but copies mostly from OB: *pašīšu edammû* $^{l\acute{u}}$*nišakku u* AN.GUB.BA.MEŠ ⌊*ša mā*]*hazi māt* Akkadi "of the sanctuary of the land of Akkad,"[185] so there were again many of the *angubbû*'s together with the *pašīšu* and the *nešakku* in cultic surroundings, the latter a high official in our Cat. No. 1.

3.14 ecstatics: ní-su/zu-ub/*zabbu* and *zabbatu*

One of the presumed roots of these words is *zabābu* "be in a frenzy," a rare one, and not yet found referring to a human being. AHw relates *zabbu* to *sabābu* "spreizen, (um)flattern" of a bird, or "aufgeregt wird (?)" of a horse.

The male *zabbu* and the female *zabbatu* appear on the OB lexical lists (Sec. 3.12.1). A hymn to Inanna in OB times has, in a section describing her cultic personnel, a line listing lú-al-è-dè, pi-li-pi-li, kur-gar-ra and sag-ur-sag, the first the *mahhû* ecstatic studied in Sec. 3.12, the others hermaphroditic cultic actors studied in App. 3. This is preceded by a line with less well-known personnel:[186]

lú-giš-gi-sag-kéš ní-su-ub mí-giš-g[i]
šul-a-lum ù-mu-ni-in-AK še-ša$_4$ UD [ ]
"... punishment, moaning ..."
(Sjöberg)

For the giš-gi see Sjöberg,[187] and Sec. 3.19. The ní-su-ub / *zabbu* appears in mixed contexts in OB and NA lists

52	ama-$^{lu-lu}$-lul-la	[ŠU-*tu*]
53	ama-lul-la	*za-ab-ba* -[*tu*]

54 ama-lul-la *mu-ut-til-tu*

Lu = ša III MSL XII 127

and continuing with several other offices beginning with ama-, as well as Lu = ša IV and OB Lu both Sec. 3.12.1, and these are surrounded by *kurgarrû* in Lu = ša I Short Recension, *assinnu* in Lu = ša I Short Recension and Igituh, *kulu'u* in Igituh, indicating perhaps that these cultic actors used ecstasy in their rites.

The males and females of both types appear together. An Ishtar-Tammuz ritual describes *kurummatu*-food for the *zabbu* and *zabbatu*, the *muhhû*'s and *muhhûtu*'s, water, beer and other foodstuffs for the *kaparru*'s "shepherds" of Dumuzi using the divination officials as cultic actors.[188] The ní-su-ub is not a pleasant person to be around, as shown by a text (see n. 187): lú-ní-su-ub-ba-gin$_x$ igi-zu-ta ab-ta-kar-re-dè-eš "like a nisub they flee from your presence."

In a difficult context, a proverb has[189] ní-su-ub mu-lú-e$_{11}$-dè...inim-kúr igi-bal "nisub...you change the face of a strange word."[190] This is not completely understandable, but perhaps it means that his charismatic power changes the meaning of things, or the course of action.

The role of the ecstatic reminds us of the Old Testament prophet and Saul in 1 Samuel chapter 10, especially vs.6, and the Egyptian story of Wenamun.[191]

3.15 Ecstatics: *āpilu* and *āpiltu*

3.15.1 There is no ideogram. A. Malamat suggests that it may be a loan-translation from Hebrew *ʿnh.*[192] The *āpilu*"answerer"is found predominantly at Mari.[193] but at Nuzi a ^{lú}*a-pí-lì* or *a-pì-lì* appears.[194] PN an *āpiltum* comes up with a divine order for the king.[195]

3.15.2 This office appears among the "prophetic" texts from Mari, studied by Noort.[196] Much has been written on this subject since the pioneering article by A. Lods,[197] especially relating this type of text to Old Testament prophecy. Among the thousands of letters from Mari, in 28 of these a figure is reported as quoting the word of the deity. This report is usually quoted by an outside party, whose relationship to this "prophet" is not explained.

The "prophets" have the following titles:

cult persons	laity
āpilum	*awīlum* "a man"
āpiltum	*sinništum* "a woman"
assinnu	*ṣuharum* "a young person, servant"
bārûm	
muhhûm	
muhhûtum	
qabbātum	
šangûm	

Noort Mari p. 70

Others appear as PNs without titles. The *āpilum* appears by far the most often. The speakers either had religious titles, or were untitled, at times even unnamed. Despite (presumed !) diference in function among all of these, each acted as a prophet.[198] The list has both females and males. One outside the list Iṣi-ahu is an *āpilum* of dHišamītum (*ARM* X 53,6), a rare god.[199] Several of the speakers were untitled women, whom we know because the *ARM* X collection[200] contains many letters about women, and in them some of these prophetic texts occur.

Only two of the letters[201] tell of the speakers becoming ecstatic, root *mahû*, but we assume that those telling of the *muhhûm* and *muhhûtum* were referring to this method also, and judging from the emotion with which some of the other speeches were apparently delivered, some of the others were also.

This prophetic kind of activity was done with three somewhat related officials, *muhhûm/muhhûtum*, *āpilum/āpiltum* and *qabbātum*, and the other two, *assinnu* and *šangû* do not historically have this function, and the appearance of 9 non-religious or, at least, non-titled persons, allows us to speculate that the "prophecy" was not done as a function of their offices, but because of some other features now lost to us.

3.16 Ecstatics: *qabbā'u* and *qabbātu*

3.16.1 This is probably from the root *qabû*, and one could relate this to the *qabbā'u* by postulating that the latter has a West Semitic *aleph* at the end. Whether or not the *qabbā'u* "speaker" is an ecstatic could not be determined from the contexts of the OB letters in which he appears. In one case he acts with high cultic officials, as *šangû*, *ērib bīti* and *gudapsû* in opening the "house of the daughter of Shulgi."[202] In another he corresponds with Abi-ešuh about an escaped slave girl of a *nadītu*.[203] The clear *qá-ab-ba -hu-ú* of an OB text translated by A. Goetze[204] and read by him that way, is in a context with a *sābû* "publican" and a *nuhatimmu* "cook." Goetze concludes that *qabbahû* is a police officer.

3.16.2 Only one entry could be found for the *qabbātu* (formerly read *qamātu*): 1 mí*qabā* [*t*]*um ša* dDagan *ša* Terqaki.[205]

The verb is used of those who recite prayers and incantations, CAD Q 30a. Here she gave the message to PN, to be forwarded to the king. There are no circumstances described. A bibliography of discussion of this so-far single occurrence is given by Noort.[206]

3.17 *raggimu* and *raggim/ntu*

3.17.1 A NA three-column HAR-gud text is reproduced in Sec. 3.3.10, and in App. 3.2.7, both with *raggimu*. In the former he is close to ecstatics, in the latter his proximity indicates perhaps that the scribe either considered the *raggimu* to be a hermaphroditic creature like the *assinnu* and *sinnišānu* (see App. 3.9) or was indicating that these latter used techniques like or were a type of a *raggimu*.

The *raggimu* and *raggim /ntu* appear in NB and NA. A vassal-treaty postulated words from "the mouth of a *raggimu* or a *mahhû* or a *māru ša amāt ili*."[207] The latter phrase cannot be found as an office, but perhaps is a catchall term: "son of the word of a god", i.e., one whose calling is to proclaim the word of the deity, as a prophet from the Hebrew Bible. [208] An oracle to Ashurbanipal from Ninlil entitles a *raggintu*.[209]

Towards the end of a long letter of miscellaneous content to the king, in a broken context there is a *raggimu*. No ritual connotations could be found, but earlier in the letter a MAŠ.MAŠ appears.[210]

ADD 860 (unpublished) is a long administrative text in a scheme with several lines PN lú x, then totalled as x *mu-še-bi* (for *mušabi* "dwelling places, seats.") This may be an allocation to various ranks for service performed. III.21 has "total 4 *mušebi* GN, and the previous lines include *bel narkabti* "chariot driver," *rab kiṣir* "soldier," *qurrubūtu* "guard" of the*ummi šarri* "mother of the king," *raggimu.* This is too varied to analyze easily, but it shows that perhaps the *raggimu* was associated with the military on this text.

3.17.2 The female PN *raggintu* brought some garments of the king to GN.[211] A *raggintu* is found prophesying (*tartugumu*) the future.[212] Earlier in this letter rituals are mentioned: the *namburbu*, *bīt rimki*, *bīt sala' mê*, *eršahunga nīpešē ša āšipūtu* "the rituals of the *āšipu*-craft." A letter with a broken context[213] has: *rēš* ^{lú}*raggimānu* ^{mí}*raggimātu*...MAŠ.MAŠ "the head of the r. and r. (with my mouth I [the writer of the letter] bless.)"

The ^{lú}*raggimu* and ^{mí}*raggintu* belong in some way to the temple personnel of Ishtar of Arba'il.[214]

3.18 *hābit mê* (f.)

A *hābit mê* "drawer of water" appears at Mari just before the *nadītum* in a ration list. 13 of them received a distribution of oil by the palace.[215] CAD H s.v. *habû* A gives examples of drawing water for incantation purposes, so perhaps this office is a divinatory one.

3.19 lú-giš-gi and mí-giš-gi / *naqmu* and *naqimtu*

In the OB Lu list Sec. 3.12.1 giš-gi sag-kéš = *naqmu* and SAL.LÚ giš-gi-sag-kéš = *naqimtum* are offices surrounded by *muhhûm* and *zabbum naqmu* is a disease or a bodily defect (CAD s.v.), or (*nak /qmu*)" "Personenbezeichnung" (AHw s.v.), or a person suffering from a disease (*BWL* 299b). But this does not fit into the context of the other words on the OB lexical list, all of them cultic officials.

Referring to the OB Lu list, what sag-kéš adds to the bare form lú-giš-gi is not immediately apparent. sag-kéš...ak = *it'udu* "pay attention to, watch, guard"[216] does not relate to the dictionaries' definition of *naqmu.* If it were taken as giš-kéš-da = *riksu* "binding," as in the Erimhuš text Sec. 3.20.1, it could refer to something that the ecstatic did to the victim.

In the OB hymn to Inanna given in Sec. 3.14, there is a line with her *šul-a-lum* = *ennittu* "(divine) punishment." This is found in bilingual and other texts.[217] še-ša$_4$ = (root) *damāmu* "mourn, moan" follows later in the line so the lú-giš-gi-sag-kéš and the ní-su-ub and the mí-gis-gi might have something to do with the gods' punishment, either seeing that it is done, supervising it, or doing it themselves, and this results in mourning among the recipients and those near them.

3.20 Witches: an-ni-ba-tu /*eššeb/pû* and *eššeb/ûtu*

3.20.1 We start with the many entries on the lexical lists:

r.5	*eš-še-pu* -[*ú*]	
r.6	*pa-ru* -[*ú*]	
r.7	*muš -šu-r* [*u*]	(LTBA has a variant: *uš-šu-ru*)
r.8	*zab-bu*	
r.9	*i-sin-nu-u*	
r. 10	*a-pi-lu-u*	
r. 11	*kur-gar-ru-u*	

CT 18, 5 (K. 4193),
a duplicate of LTBA 2 1 vi

289	lú-an-ni/né-ba-tu	*eš-še-bu-u*
290	giš-kéš-da	*rik-su*
291	^d^dam nun-gal-e-ne	^d^*na-ru-du*

Erimhuš I 289 MSL XVII 20

147	lú-an-né-ba-TU	*eš-še-b /pu-ú*	*mah-hu-ú*
148	lú-gidim-ma	*ša e-ṭim-mu*	*man-za* -[*zu*]-*ú*
149	lú sag-bulug-ga	*mu-še-lu-u e-ṭim-mu*	ÍD ⌜x-x-x⌝

ḪAR-gud
B VI MSL XII 226

263	lú-gub-ba	*mah-hu-u*
264	lú [ní}-su-ub	*zab-bu*
265	lú [ur-mí]	*ku-lu-'u*
266	lú ur-mí	*as-sin-nu*
267	LÚ.PA.GIŠGAL	*sah-hi-ru*
268	lú-an-ni-ba-tu/tú	*eš-še-b /pu-u*
269	lú-x-e_7-dè	*nár-ši-du*
270	lú-kuš-tag-ga	*e-piš ip-ši*

Igituh, short version

4	x	*eš-še-b /pu*	*ip-hur*

CT 18, 2 K. 4214

3.20.2 The Sumerian equivalents in these late lists preserve an ecstatic condition, if we understand them correctly. an-ni-ba-tu is explained by tu = *erēbu* "enter" and ba the locative, so "entered into." an = a god or the god An, ni = "his," so it is his personal or especially worshipped deity who entered into him? Putting it into a participial mode: "he who has been entered into by his god." The HAR-gud transliteration né would indicate an -e[218] postposition.

The Igituh list again juxtaposes several offices which we have (carefully, but theoretically) kept in separate categories: ecstatics, as *mahhû, zabbu*, witches, as *sahhiru, naršindu* and hermaphroditic (App. 3) types as *kulu'u, assinnu*, and *kurgarrû* added also in CT 18,5. This again shows the complexity of the actions of these which we have purposely oversimplified in these pages for the purposes of classification.

The combination of elements an-ni-ba-tu in Igituh 268 has been found two times among personal names in Sumerian texts.[219] Falkenstein thinks that it is a phonetic variant of the common PN an-né-ba-(ab)-du_7,[220] but on several unrelated lexical lists it is in a position of a tribe. For the present, I would rather keep the two PNs separate, and look upon an-né-ba-tu as a PN of the type which shows a title or profession.[221] On several unrelated lexical lists it is in the position of a title.

3.20.3 A relationship of this kind of witch to Marduk is shown by a late incantation text:

24 *ina balīka* lú*bārû ul uš-te-eš-še-er qātsu*
ditto lú*āšipu ana marṣi ul i-tab-bal qāt-su*
25 *ina balīka* lú*a-ši-pu eš-še-b /pu muš-lah*$_4$ *ul i-ba -' ú su-*⌜*qa*⌝

24 "Without you (i.e., Marduk) the *bārû* does not perform well,
ditto, the *āšipu* on the sick man will not lay his hand
25 without you the *āšipu* the *eššep /bu* (and) the *mušlahhu* do not walk about the street

KAR 26, CAD E 371a

presumably meaning: without you heading the cult, without your help.

Thus the *eššeb /pu* is found among witches (in the present section, passim) and incantation experts. In Erimhuš Sec. 3.20.1 it comes before giš-kéš-da = *rik-su* "binding," a term often used of the effect of sickness or witchcraft in *Maqlû*.[222]

3.20.4 The *eššeb /pu* has a special hairdo. A text restored according to CAD E 371b has: *šumma* SÍG *èš-ši-bi-e* (var. *eš-še-bi-e*, CT 28, 10. 17) GAR, i.e., *šumma šārat eššeb /pu šakin* "if the hair (-do) of an *eššeb /pu* is there" (i.e., on a person). This reminds us of other officials, but from Category IV, who have special coiffures, as the *kezertu*.

Being duly cautious that the late Assyrian witchcraft texts may refer to a practice shifted considerably from that of the earlier texts, we refer to yet another *Maqlû* text.[223] A series of lines has: "(if) the (then a list of cultic officials) should bewitch you, (then) I shall break your binding" (i.e., your being bound to the bewitchment). The cultic officials who may bewitch you are listed as *kaššāpe*, *kaššāpāte*, *kurgarrê* (pl.), lú*eššeb /pu*, *naršindu* (pl.), *mušlahhu* (pl.),[224] *agugillu* (pl.), all being what we would usually term witches, except the *kurgarrû* and *mušlahhu*.

In line 92 preceding those, using a root common to Maqlû *bu' û* "seek out," we find *ú-ba-'-kim-ma* lúKUR.GAR.MES lú*eš-še-b /i-e* "I let you (the *kaššāptu*, line 85) seek out the *kurgarrû*'s (and) the *eššeb /pu*'s" perhaps to use them for her purposes.

This proximity of the *eššeb /pu* and *kurgarrû* in the *Maqlû* text could be explained either as a shifting of the earlier function of the *kurgarrû* towards witchcraft, or a shifting or explanation of the witch-like function of the *eššeb /pu* towards the earlier function of the *kurgarrû*. The latter is indicated by the special hairdo of the *eššeb /pu,* but expecially by the proximity of the *eššeb /pu* to the, in order, *kulu'u*, *assinnu*, *sahhiru*, *eššeb /pu* on Igituh, Sec. 3.20.1.

We conclude that the *eššeb /pu* has a function as an ecstatic, a witch and a fertility cult official, the relative emphases of these yet to be determined.

3.20.5 The dark side of divination is shown by this same incantation series *Maqlû*. In III 44ff there is a long section warning against various kinds of female witches and magicians named as follows: *kaššāptu* "witch," *nērtānītu* "murderess,"[225] *elēnītu* "sorceress," *naršindatu* "witch," *āšiptu* "exorcist," *eššeb /putu* "witch," *mušlahhatu* "snake handler, "*agugiltu* "sorceress," *qadištu*, *nadītu*, *ištarītu*, *kulmašītu*, who capture by night, roam about (or, hunt) all day, dirty heaven, touch earth[226] bind the mouths of the gods, bind the knees of the goddesses, killing men, not sparing women, destroyer[227] sneering one (?),[228] against whom evil deeds and magic do not bring on anything..."

This list, which tells us what they thought of witches, also has other categories that we will discuss in chapter 4, under *qadištu*, *nadītu*, *ištarītu* and *kulmašītu*.[229] A similar list has *agugiltu*, *naršindatu* (*nar-šin-na-at*), *mušlahhatu*, *eššeb / putu*, *qurqurratu* "metal worker," and even *mārat āliya* "female citizen of my city" (*Maqlû* IV 124-8), and there is a similar list including *kuttimatu* "goldsmith" and *qumqummatu*[230] with *eššeb /putu* (*Maqlû* VI.19-21). The syntax indicates that *kaššāptu* is the overall term designating these.

3.21 Witches: zilulu/*sahhiru* and *sahhirtu*

3.21.1 The *sahhiru* would be an office similar to those discussed above, as indicated by the lexical lists:

131	[lú] umuš-nu-tu[ku]	[*dun-na*] -mu-ú	*sa* -[*ak-lu*]
132	[lú] zilulu		*sah*-[*hi-ru*]
133	[lú] ur-sal	[*a*] *s-sin-nu*	*sin-niš* -*la* /-[*nu*]
134	lúl šabra	ŠU	*rag-gi*-[*mu*]
135	lú gub-ba	*a*-[*p*]*il-lu-ú* *	*aš-šá* -[ ]

*in place of MSL's -[*b*] *il* - . See App. 3.2.7.

HAR-gud B to "Hh XXV"
MSL XII 225f,
continues MSL XI 88ff

177	[ugula-1-l] im]	*a- kil li-me*
178	[zilu] lu	*sah-hi-rum*
179	[ugni] m	*um-ma-nu*
180	$erin_2$	MIN
181	[$erin_2$-hi] -a	*um-ma-na-a-tú*
182	[ensi]	ša-'-i-*li*

Lu =ša I, short recension
MSL XII 10lf

116	ni-gìn	NIGIN	*pa-ši-rum*
			sa-hi-rum

Aa A = *naqu* Tabl I/2 = 2
MSL XIV 211

A number of witches including the *sahhiru* are brought together in the NA "practical vocabulary" Igituh, Sec. 3.20.1.

The above lists show that the ancients related the *sahhiru* to witches, dream determiners and ecstatics, as well as to the Category IV offices of *kulu'u*, *assinnu* and *harimtu* (SAL.KAR.KID, Sec. 3.21.2) whose sexual activities will be discussed in Appendix 3.

3.21.2 There is a female *sahhirtu*

54 SAL.KAR.KID
55 LÚ.PA.GIŠGAL/ZILULU
56 SAL.PA.GIŠGAL/ZILULU

Sultantepe B VIII MSL XII 237

iii 16	b ad-nigin	*sah-hi-rat*	du-ri
17	uru$_2$-nigin	*sah-hi-rat*	*āli*
18	a-⌈gàr⌉-nigin	*sah-hi-rat*	*u-ga-ri*

SIG$_7$.AL= *nabnitu*
MSL XVI 121

These types of *sahhirtu*: of the fortress, of the city, of the arable land, would seem to be pedlars, "those who go around," rather than cultic figures. But were there women peddlars in that society, solitary figures with no protection? One doubts it. We must consider the possibility that these are cultic figures with a relationship unknown to us. The witch type could be understood as going about for troublesome purposes, or, with CAD, "encircling, ensnaring."

3.21.3 Though the root indicates a going around, going about, and this is picked up in the standard translation "peddler," (AHw 1009a, CAD S 60f), *zilulu* also being "peddler," the lists indicate that it was also thought of in conjunction with, or near, that of *assinnu* (Igituh and HAR-gud) and even in Lu = ša it is followed, though several entries further on, by offices in our Category III, then by those in our Category IV. The Lu = ša entry for *sahhiru* is next to the *ummānu* "expert" entry and may indicate a type of the latter, perhaps in the realm of omens, as indicated by the *šā'ilu* entry following it.

An incantation text broken at the end is designed to combat the sorcery of the *kaššāpu, kaššāptu, zikaru* "man," *sinništu* "woman,"...[*hab*] *lu* "evil doer (m.), *habiltu* "evildoer(f.)," *kurgarru, sah-hi-ru,...naršindu, agugillu*.[231]

In a typical sentence *Maqlû* orders the *ēpištu*: *ipšima iqbû* "make a magic spell, he said," and to the *sahhirtu*: *suhrima iqbû* "bewitch, he said."[232] These are called *kaššāptu* in line 44, indicating that many of these terms for witch are interchangeable.

3.22 Witches: x-e$_{7/11}$-dè /*naršindu* and *naršindatu*

e$_7$ is the reading given DU$_6$-DU by Landsberger and Gurney AS 16; Labat *Manuel*, Borger *Zeichenliste*, AHw and von Soden *Syllabar* read e$_{11}$.

We cannot separate out this office from other types of witches. Its broken ideogram is only found in Igituh, short version 269, Sec. 3.20.1, as *nár-ši-du* with variant *nar-šin-du*. Its occurrences are mostly from *Maqlû*.[233] This witch uses IM/*ṭidu, ṭiṭu* "clay" from the river.[234]

3.23 Witches: *agugillu* and *agugiltu*

In Sec. 3.20.5 the *agugiltu* was listed among other sorceresses. The *agugillu*'s are bewitched in *Maqlû* VII.100. AHw takes this as "Fadenkreuzer (??), etwa Zauberer," from gu "thread" and gil/*egēru* "cross." A similar action shows up in a magical text[235] in which Ishtar supervises the spinning of thread, which is then used to tie up a man, so that Marduk could rip it off, indicating healing.

The only other example of a male is a broken portion in *Maqlû* IV.85: the *a-g[u]-g [i-lu-u]* is beside one of *lišan nukurtum* "foreign speech." Perhaps he uses a special vocabulary, or speaks in a special way.

3.24 *muššipu* and *muššiptu // mussiru*

Only lexical entries could be found:

207	muš-DU^la-la-ah^DU	*muš-la-la-ah-hu*
208	lú-^giš^gàm-šu-du$_7$	*muš-ši-pu*
209	la-bar	*ka-lu-ú*

Lu = ša Excerpt I MSL XII 102

158	lú-gàm-šu-du$_7$	*mu-us-si-ru*
159	lú-nam-tag-ga-du$_8$	KI.MIN

Lu = ša IV MSL XII 133

The gàm / *gamlu* is a curved stick or staff used by the incantation god in *Shurpu* VIII.1. The *mussiru*, a single occurrence so far, is associated with the *muššipu*.

3.25 ki-sì-ga / *kišpu*

CAD lists one entry only as an official: LÚ *ki-iš-pu*.[236] The word is usually used of an offering for the dead. A thorough study of this word is given by Tsukimoto *Totenpflege*.

J.J.A. van Dijk finds a ki-sì-ga edin-na,[237] and finds several examples when ki-sì-ga is not Totenopfer, relating this to ritual cleansing and sickness.

3.26 Lecanomancy (oil omina)

Texts for the practice of lecanomancy have been edited by Pettinato *Ölwahrsagung*. A text mentions observing oil on water.[238] Many officiants used oil. The *mar bari* "member of the guild of diviners," was called *apkal šamnî "apkallu* - expert in oil," Sec. 3.8.3, so the *apkallu* himself uses oil.

3.27 Observer of birds: *dāgil iṣṣurē*

3.27.1 Observation of the flights of birds is attested in Sargonic times,[239] but an indication of this practice does not appear on the lexical lists.

The practice is related to other incantation professions by a NA letter:[240] On the 16th of Nisan the scribes, *bārû*'s, MAŠ.MAŠ.MEŠ, *asû*'s, *dagil issure*'s, and a *manzaz ekalli* will take an oath. It seems that all of these were together in one place. A Hamathite appears in a broken letter regarding a *dāgil iṣṣurē* [ ] Hamataya.[241] If there is nothing or nothing significant in the gap, this is an example of a foreign person in this office. On line 8 the term *mu-du itta* "knowing the sign" would seem to relate to this office, *ittu* "sign" often being used in omen contexts (CAD I s.v. § 2).

Another administrative document *ADD* 851 lists the *dāgil iṣṣurē* among many others, Sec. 3.3.8n.

Selected contracts among the *ADD* tablets were edited early on in *ARU*. Kwasman has now updated these. In No. 236[242] the sealer of a tablet is read by him as a LU *ḍa-gíl a* [ ], and Köhler and Ungnad also read *a*. This could be a distorted MUŠEN "bird" sign, though Kwasman thinks this "unlikely," and he draws the sign.

On a Nimrud tablet a *dāgil iṣṣurē* Kummuhaya "from Commagene" appears in a broken context of horses delivered (?) to a *kallābu*-soldier and others.[243] On another Nimrud tablet, there are rations to a *dāgil iṣṣurē*, as well as the gods Ninurta, Ishtar and Nabû.[244]

Another *dāgil iṣṣurē* [kur*ku*]*mmuhaya* (iv 5) appears in the Nimrud Wine Lists.[245] The text lists a *ginû* offering to, in order after the *dagil issure*, who is first, the queen, military ranks, weavers, *nāṛu*'s of four GNs or types labelled by their GNs including Kummuhaya, and LÚ.NINDA.MEŠ. Because some recipients are in the plural, comparative rank could not be analyzed by quantity. Another wine list [246] perhaps a *ginû* text (the key line is broken) lists lú ⌜da⌝!-[gíl] ⌜ MUSEN!⌝ MEŠ as well as the queen, military ranks, and at the end of the obverse *asû*'s, *bārû*'s, MAŠ.MAŠ.MEŠ, and on the reverse *nārtu*'s, then GNs with a large geographical spread. In another wine list[247] a list of *ginû* to ⌜lú⌝ d⌜a-gíl⌝ ⌜MUSEN!⌝ MEŠ (Kinnier Wilson read L[Ú] G[AL] ⌜SAG.MEŠ⌝), as well as to the queen, military ranks and scribes.

A further wine list[248] is a *ginû* list (probably, broken) to *dāgil iṣṣurē* (so Parpola), the queen, military ranks and, at the end as in No. 8, *nāru*'s, *bārû*'s, MAŠ.MAŠ.MEŠ and *asû*'s. The last example[249] is a fragment, a *ginû* listing [lú*d*]*a-gíl* MUŠEN [MEŠ], the queen and a *rab ša rēši*. The wine lists are so regularly laid out that they allow us to compare them. They show that the *dāgil iṣṣurē* is often mentioned first, before the queen, and separately from the other offices, giving an apparent significance to this office that does not show up in other texts.

Unfortunately, how the *dāgil iṣṣurē* operates, where and with what equipment is unknown. No females are known in the office. It would not be good practice to compare cultures simplistically, so we merely note that the Etruscans used birds in divination,[250] as did the Romans[251] and the Greeks[252]

3.27.2 There are several offices or functionaries at Ebla with -MUSEN in their titles.[253]

3.28 Fowler: MUŠEN.DÙ /(u)sandû , mušākil iṣṣurē

3.28.1 This office appears in several orthographies: *usandû*, *ušandû* and *sandû* probably all stemming from mušen-dù (AHw). It appears in secular groupings:

245	su-ha	*ba-'-i-ru*	"fisherman"
246	mušen-dù	*ú-šá-an-du-ú*	
247	[lú] gišpan-tag-ga	*ma-hi-ṣu*	"hunter"
			Lu = ša I MSL XII 103f
252	LÚ.ŠU.HA	*ba ' -i-ru*	

253 LÚ.mušen-dù *sa-an-du-u*
254 LÚ.ì-šur *ṣa-hi-tu*

Igituh, short version

16 LÚ.UŠ.BAR
17 LÚ.MUŠEN!.DÙ
18 LÚ.ŠU.HA

K. 4395 IV MSL XII 239

11A.1 ⌈LÚ.X.X⌉. [ ]
2 LÚ.MUŠEN.DÙ*sa-an-du-u*
3 LÚ.MUŠEN.DÙ.MUŠEN
4 LÚ.ŠU.HA*ba-'-i-ru*

Sultantepe List IIA MSL XII 233

and in a possibly cultic one:

352	šu-KAŠ$_4$-KAŠ$_4$	*ba-ru-u*
353	šu-e-dè	MIN
353	mušen-dù	*ú-šá-an-du-ú*
354	gu-lá	*ha-bi-lu*

Lu = ša IV MSL XII 139

LÚ.MUŠEN.DÙ appears in MA and Nuzi texts, as well as three of the wine lists[254] in *ginû* texts with the queen, military ranks, palace ranks and craftsmen. One Asshur text has as witnesses four PNs LÚ.MUŠEN.DÙ É Asshur.[255] It is thus possible to understand this rank as a sometime cultic one, in my Category V.

3.28.2 A similar office *mušākil iṣṣurē*[256] "bird feeder" is a witness on a slave sale, followed by a LÚ.MUŠEN.DÙ. This has not yet been found in a cultic context.

3.29 Libanomancy (divination by smoke) /*muššakku*

This is done by the *ša'ilu*, Sec. 3.3.4, and further references to this and the *šā'iltu* are given in CAD M/2, s.v. *muššakku*. It is tied to dream determination.

3.30 Aleuromancy/Divination by flour/zì/*qemu*

See J. Nougayrol, *Or* 32 (1963) 381-6, an OB Louvre tablet AO 3112 dealing with illness.

3.31 Divination by arrows

Arrows were used either by shaking or shooting them in F.R. Kraus, *AfO* Bei 3 (1939) No. 62, cf. 65; Weidner, *AfO* 15 (1951) 102. Cf. the examples in the Hebrew Bible under Sec. 3.32 2.

3.32 Divination in the Hebrew Bible, with a few notes on Ugaritic practices

Among the Mesopotamian there were criticisms here and there of divination, and especially of witches, but in general this practice was a way of life among them, used by kings and higher officers to a great extent, but by the little man, also. Not so among the Hebrews; at least the theologians who gave us our biblical writings were basically opposed to divination in any way. Their paradigmatic statements come out in the lawcodes. The Covenant Code says: you shall not permit a sorceress (*mĕkaššēpāh*) to live (Ex 22.17 EV 18). Similarly using two other words, the Holiness Code has it: you shall not practice augury (root *n-ḥ-š*) or witchcraft (root *ᶜ-n-n*) (Lev 19.26). We note that the translators do not agree on what to do with these technical terms for types of divination. We will discuss them below.

The biblical writers are fond of making lists of these offices. It is characteristic of this literature that often when lists of titles are given, no explanation of meaning or function accompanies them. Maybe the biblical authors were wary of descriptions, in case someone might be attracted to the practices. Prohibited in these lists are:

Deut 18.10-11

(Numbers are of paragraphs referred to below):

1	one who makes his son or daughter pass through the fire, usually considered as child sacrifice.	
2	*qōsēm qĕsāmîm*	"one who practices divination"
3	*mĕᶜônēn*	"soothsayer."
4	*mĕnahēš*	"diviner"
5	*mĕkaššēp*	"sorcerer"
6	*ḥōbēr ḥāber*	"(un)tier of (magic) knots"
7	*šōʾel ʾôb*	"asker of an *'ôb*"
8	*yiddĕᶜônî*	"(divining by a familiar spirit)"
9	*dōrēš ʾel hammētîm*	"one who seeks the dead"

2 Kings 21.6

1	The one who makes his son pass through the fire	
3	*ᶜonēn*	"soothsayer"
4.	*niḥēš*	"diviner"
7.	*ᶜāsāh ʾôb*	"practicing (with) an *ʾôb*
8.	*yiddĕᶜōnîm*	"(divining by) a familiar spirit"

Jer 27.9

21.	*nĕbî'im*	"prophets"
2.	*qōsmîm*	"diviners"
13	*ḥălōmôt*	"dreamers"
3.	*ᶜōnnîm*	"soothsayers"
5.	*kaššāpîm*	"sorcerers"

Isa 3.3

	yô ᶜēs	"counselor"
16	*ḥăkam ḥărāsîm*	"wise one of sorcery"
15	*nĕbôn lāḥaš*	"wise one who whispers"

Lev 19.26.31

4. *niḥaš*	"diviner"
3. *ᶜônēn*	"soothsayer"
7. *'ôbôt*	"by *'ôb's*"
8. *yiddĕᶜōnîm*	"(divining by a) familiar spirit"

The context of the deuteronomic list is that of the deuteronomic torah-code, which urges one not to follow the practices of the dwellers in the land, and these verses are followed by a prophet, whom you shall heed.

Divination is seldom taken seriously by Biblical scholars. One who did so was Alfred Guillaume.[257] Unfortunately his book is seriously flawed, in that its Assyriology is second-hand and out-of-date, and his emphasis on Arabic and Persian practice uses a methodology which we do not use any more, and shouldn't have used in the first place.

Notes given below on these offices have been collected by me for many years, instigated first by a mimeographed sheet by Harry Orlinsky, then two articles by him.[258] We are struck by the fact that even though most of these practices are rejected out of hand, they seemed to be prevalent throughout Hebrew history, and one suspects that, despite the paucity of occurrences in the text, this was due to the biblical traditionalist's careful choice of material, not congruous with the fact that the practice was used everywhere and at every period. We will also note the congruity with similar practices done in Mesopotamia. In fact, if we knew more about the Hebrew practices, they would probably be found even closer.

Notes on these offices must begin by admitting our inability to translate them in a way that shows their function clearly. Many of the translations given above are traditional ones.

1. The question of child sacrifice is not strictly a part of the subject of divination, but we will make a few remarks. Because of its repulsive and primitive nature it is downplayed by many studies of biblical practices, but the listing of it among other divination practices in the torah-codes, and its being put first in the hierarchy of some of them, cause us to take it seriously. The subject is immensely complicated, as brought out by Green.[259] He gives a thorough study of the field and then, in shorter compass, the biblical evidence in chapter ix. It is not strictly to be listed as divination, unless it is a kind of ordeal.

2. *q-s-m* is one of the two major roots used in the Hebrew Bible for divining, the other being *k-š-p*. In Ezek 21.26 (EV 21) the king of Babylon does (root) *q-s-m*, shakes the arrows, inquires of the *tĕrāpîm* and looks at the liver. And anything the king of Babylon does is evil. Indeed these actions turn out to be false divinations (vs. 28, EV 23). Ezekiel criticizes false prophets by saying "They have seen (root) *ḥ-z-h* "a prophetic-type vision" falsely and have divined (root) *q-s-m* a lie," Ezek 13.7. Philistine *qōsēm* work together with their priests, 1 Sam 6.2.

Surprisingly neutral statements. however, appear about the *qōsēm*, even admiration. The tale in Num 22-24 tells of the great Balaam ben Be'or, who was called upon by the Moabites to curse Israel, and who placed himself in the forefront of salvific folklore by refusing to do so, and who was a *qōsēm*, Josh 13.22. He is described as one who could "curse" or "bless" (Num 22.6) He could tell of *naḥaš* and *qesem* (both "incantation," Num 23.23, see our No. 4.) His method was to use a *māšāl* "proverb, parable," Num 23.7. Some have interpreted the *qĕsāmîm* (22.7) that the Moabites brought in their hands when they came to him as some sort of appurtenances for divination. But many commentators[260] now think that they were merchandise to pay for divination.

Typical of the Hebrew Bible, the manner in which the *qōsēm* would proceed as a diviner is not described, but Num 24.1 states that he did not look for *nĕḥāšîm* (see No., 4) but said, in the manner of a later prophet, *nĕ'um* Bil^{c}am "the word of Balaam." (24.3). The commentators seek for words to describe him: He is a kind of a *bārû*, a kind of a *kāhin*.[261]

The Deir 'Alla texts[262] give a *sipr* [bl^{c}m] "account of Bil^{c}am" who was a *ḥzh* "seer" of the gods, and who receives a vision from El, in which his city was to be destroyed by the gods. The entry *khnh* "priestess" in line 11 is broken immediately afterwards, so does not provide a context.

The *qōsēm* is often spoken of positively. In Mic 3.11 the prophets do (root) *qsm* for money, a clever play on words, and it seems that the money is the butt of the criticism rather than the practice of *qōsēm* itself. When Jer 14.14 criticizes the false prophets for prophesying lies, he calls their words "worthless *qesem*," and he did not criticize them for this abomnable foreign practice abhorred elsewhere, but for prophesying something out of their own minds. Isa 3.2f has an astonishing list, those ranks whom the Lord will take away from Judah to punish them: soldiers, the judge, the prophet, the captain of fifty, the nobleman, the counselor, the *qōsēm*, the elder, the one wise in skills and the expert in whispering (root *l-ḥ-s*, see No. 15). Some of these have been spoken well of elsewhere by the prophet, some have been disparaged, but here they are all together, as if saying that these are the ingredients of their society. Ezek 13.9 and 22.28 uses the same terminology, juxtaposing the words "lies" and *qōsmîm*." *Qesem* is on the lips of the king in Prov 16.10, the context showing that this is not wrong.

In later days the term *qesem* came to be divination by lot or sign. Lamentations Rabbah, introduction, describes divination by throwing arrows.[263] The strange scene in 2 Kings 13.15-19 in which Elisha has the king shoot arrows out the window and, in a separate act, strike the ground with a bunch of arrows, would seem to be different from Iwry's description of arrows falling to the ground in a pattern, or arrows on which a name is written, but maybe it is a variant of that.

Qōsēm are found as male only.

3. *mĕ^{c}ônēn* "soothsayer" The word in theory could be either polel from the root *^{c}ayin* "eye" or, more probably, po'el from ^{c}*anan* "cloud." Isa 2.6 says this was a Philistine practice, therefore wrong. Manasseh, the epitome of evil for the deuteronomistic editor, burned his son in the fire, and practiced *^{c}onen*, did *niḥēš*, made an *'ôb*, and had *yiddĕ^{c}ōnîm,* 2 Kings 21.6, all of these on the Deut 18 list.

Lev 19.26-28 has its own list of prohibited practices: no partaking of blood, no (root) *n-ḥ-š* or *ᶜōnēn,* and no cutting of hair or flesh for the dead. This necromantic practice is found in many societies. These practices seem to be of different types, so we cannot explain any one of them by noting what words it is near. *Meᶜônēn* must have been an old practice, because we find a geographical name 'Elon mĕᶜōnnîm "oak of soothsaying" in Jud 9.37. This could have been a newly coined name of the Israelities, but place names of this sort are often conservative, and this may have been a Canaanite place where similar practices were done. The practice is parallel to *kešāpîm* in Mic 5.11.

In Jean-Hoftijzer the root *ᶜ-n-n* I pa is defined as "to augur from clouds," and that seems to be the most satisfactory explanation of the root. No description of the practice is given in biblical texts, so we have to go by the root meaning alone, not a completely satisfactory practice, but a good start.[264]

This office is filled by males only.

4.1. *mĕnaḥēš* "diviner." The Semitic root has several homonymous meanings, but for our purposes two stand out: "serpent" and "bronze." In Num 21.9 Moses made a bronze serpent and set it upon a pole, and if any one had been bitten by a snake, he could look upon it, and be healed. This is an Aesculapian type of healing by sympathetic magic. Joines discusses its probable authenticity, pointing out that in its second mention in another stratum of literature, Hezekiah broke it, 2 Kings 18.4[265] I point out the strange fact that the *nĕḥāš nĕḥōšet* "bronze serpent" brings the two homonymous roots together. Did the ancients see a mysterious relationship between the two? This is interpreted with a different theology in John 3.14f.

Joines (pp. 64-7) points out the many exemplars of a serpent found in Palestine of the second and first millenium, with some of them having fertility aspects.

Manasseh's sins are listed as, among others: *niḥēš* "divining by snakes," 2 Kings 21.6. When Paul was bitten by a snake in Acts 28.4, the natives thought that he must have been a wicked man.

This office was held by males only.

4.2. A further and for us more important aspect of snakes relates to the ancients' practice of relating them to creation and fertility. This is brought out by Gorelick and Williams-Forte.[266] There were snake objects coiling on the outsides of cult cups, bowls and incense burners in the 14-12 c. B.C.E.[267] There is a close connection of the storm-god Baal/Hadad with the serpent and the tree in the MB age in Syria. Among the features that characterize the weather-god is that of brandishing a weapon against a snake, sometimes shown as under the control of this god, as a conquered foe (Gorelick, p. 25), the motif being "Baal au foudre." The weapon is a conflation of the lightning which is under his power and the tree, his earthly resultant.

Later the bull, the usual pedestal of the storm god, is replaced by a snake (Pl. I-2 and p. 29). He gestures towards a nude goddess holding her breasts, as the Palestinian naked figurines (see App. 2) under an arch of vegetal substance, the whole symbolizing fertility. In all of these scenes there is an incense stand, showing that the scene is a cultic one as well as a mythic one.

They summarize (p. 31f): the images show "the weather god's struggle with the serpent, his subsequent victory over it, his worship while holding an emblem of his victory, the tree-weapon or standard, and the worship of the victorious tree-standard."

4.3. Three popular equations of the snake with Prince Yamm, Ugaritic god of the sea, Lotan (*ltn*) the Ugaritic counterpart of the biblical Leviathan, and the dragon *tnn*, cognate with the biblical *tannîn*,[268] gets us into an intertwined network of motifs, with little relationship to the limp snake of the seals, or the snake in Gen 3.

Gorelick notes that the serpent ultimately comes from the realm of Mot, the god of death, underneath the ground, between two mountains (p. 37) and may be Mot himself (p. 38). Thus the battle is against the forces of infertility. The "tree of life," the central motif of many seals, was the weapon used to "slay" death, thus bringing about life, fertility of crops and man, ongoing life and happiness. This is a strong affirmation of an important motif I am trying to bring out in these pages.

5. *mĕkaššēp* together with (root) *q-s-m* provides two of the standard roots in the Hebrew Bible for sorcery or divination. It is the same root as one of the standard words for "witch" in Akkadian, *kaššāp (t)u*, Sec. 3.7. There is no compromise with this kind of sorcery. You must not allow a female *mĕkaššēpāh* to live Ex 22.17 (EV 18) according to the Covenant Code, and in the Deuteronomic Code it is an abomination, Deut 18.12. As was Manasseh, Jezebel was another epitome of evil. Her harlotries and *kĕšāpîm* were many, 2 Kings 9.22. The prophet warns the people about listening to prophets, *qōsmîm*, *ḥălōmôt* "dreamers," *ᶜōnnîm* and *kaššāpîm*, Jer 27.9. We have met all these before, except the dream interpreter, which will be discussed below, No. 13. Note again that we have here a mere listing, with no details of practice. Mic 5.11ff (EV 12ff) prophesies that the Lord will cut off the *kĕšāpîm's* and *meᶜonnîm,* as well as images, *maṣṣēbāh*'s and *ʾăšērîm* "in that day." Mal 3.5 at the end of the prophetic period calls the *mĕkaššpîm* adulterers. No good words here.

6. (root) *ḥ-b-r* "(un)tier of (magic) knots. "Knots are used in divination the world over, as testified by Frazer, *Golden Bough* i, 392. One Assyrian practice is to tie seven pairs of knots on a black and white thread and apply them to a diseased eye.[269] This conflates the ability to solve problems inherent in knots with the need for healing. In *Shurpu* v-vi 160ff several kinds of threads are spun, Ishtar ties the head, hands and feet of a man who needed purifying, so that Marduk may rip them off, thus literally untying them, and metaphorically purifying him. Daniel knew how to interpret dreams, understand riddles, and loose knots, Dan 5.12; i.e., he was a diviner and a wise man together, understood as a solver of problems. Porteous[270] on Dan 5.12 explains it as loosing of spells, lit., loosing of knots. In this he follows Jeffrey *IB* VI.428 who in turn follows Bevan and Charles. Charles' *qtryn* "magic knots," is from E. Bevan, *Commentary on the Book of Daniel.* 1892.

Males only fill this office.

7. *šōʾēl ʾôb*"asker of an *ʾôb.*" This is the first example we list of those many types who communed with the dead. Necromancy was a practice one finds in all primitive religions and just below the surface of modern ones. It has aspects of ancestor worship, and the cult of dead heroes.[271]Much has been written on this mysterious *ʾôb*, but agreement on its meaning seems to have settled down in the last few years. The text of 1 Sam 28.7 describes the witch (text: *ba ᶜalat ʾôb* "mistress of an *ʾôb* ") of En-Dor who divines (root) *q-s-m* by an *ʾôb* She then called up the ghost (word not given) of Samuel to speak with Saul.

Kohler-Baumgartner defines *ʾôbôt* (plural) as "weissagenden Totengeist." They are not instruments of the Totenbefragung. In Talmudic Hebrew and Aramaic the word is used for "ghost," but this may be simply following the Hebrew Bible. In Isa 19.3 the Egyptians "seek the *ʾôbôt,*" along with other words for divination: *'iṭṭîm* "spirits of the dead," probably an Akkadian loan-word, and *yiddĕ ᶜōnîm,* No. 8 below.

H. Hoffner[272] once again called attention, following M.Vieyra[273] to the Hittite-Hurrian *a-a-p /bi* AŠRU "place," "a ritual pit."[274] Hoffner extended this to understand the spirits which came from that pit. J. Lust[275] in a fine article extends the discussion. If the *'ôb* is a ghost, how can one "make" a ghost (2 Kings 21.6) or "destroy" it (1 Sam 28.9) or "burn" it (2 Kings 23.24), he asks. One could explain that *'ôb* also stood for the image of the ghost. He doubts that the word is from Hebrew *'ab* "father." He points out that *tĕrāpîm* is syntactically parallel with *'ôb* in 2 Kings 23.24. The similar term *yiddĕ ᶜōnîm* "those who know" might refer to those who have information only the spirits would know.

Why was divination with *'ôb* forbidden, indeed prescribing the extreme penalty of death, both for men and women, for its use, while divination with *'ēpôd,'ûrîm* and *tummîm*[276] are allowed, and, it might be added, divination with the *tĕrāpîm*? Perhaps it was because the *'ôb* was foreign, with the constant danger of syncretism.

There were place-names apparently from this word: *'ôbôt* Num 21.10f, 33.43f. If this is the same word, these may have been places where people especially went to call up the spirits. A full article[277]exegetes every biblical occurrence of the word. The authors call it an object, a means of divination with the netherworld.

8. *yiddĕ ᶜōni* "those who know," or the like, from the root *y-d-ᶜ* "know," is an office that could be held by either men or women, Lev 20.27. They often occur with the *'ôbôt*, Isa 8.19, 19.3. What is told of the *'ôbôt* is told of the *yiddĕ'ōni* also, and the death penalty for both is prescribed, Lev 20.27. In Isa 8.19 these diviners make strange sounds: "chirp and mutter" (RSV), "squeak and gibber" (REB). It may also be a foreign practice, because in Isa 19.3 the Egyptians do it; or it may be an Israelite interpretation of a foreign practice. J. Lust in the reference given under *'ôbôt*, No. 7 above, discusses these also.

9. *dōrēš 'el hammētîm* "one who seeks the dead" may be a general descriptive term for a practice which would cover several of those above, not a technical term for a practice in itself. They are not to honor/remember the dead by cuttings on their flesh, Lev. 19.28. They may not offer food to the dead, Deut 26.14. Sacrifices to the dead are not allowed, Ps 106.28.

To go beyond our passage in Deuteronomy, we add to the list:

10. *tĕrāpîm,* not an official, but objects used by laypeople, small or life-size, a part of the household. In a pioneering article, Anne E. Draffkorn relates them to the *ilāni* "gods" at Nuzi, and describes them as household gods, the possession of which determined ownership.[278] This got the argument started, and M. Greenberg and M.J. Selman argued against this inheritance claim, and described them as protective.[279] They are associated with the ephod and a shrine (*bēt 'elohîm*) in Jud 17.5. 1 Sam 15.23 has them in parallel with *qesem* "divination," and so criticized by the prophet Samuel. Zech 10.2 has them in parallel with *qôsēm* in this late period. They were purged in Josiah's reform, 2 Kings 23.24, along with *'ôbôt* and *yiddĕᶜōnîm.* Yet Hos 3.4 depicts them as a part of the priestly cult that was taken away in punishment, hence it was something approved.

11. *iṭṭîm* "spirits of the dead" is a loan-word from Akkadian *eṭemmu* "spirit, ghost," (CAD s.v.),[280] and see Sec. 3.7.2 above. It occurs once in Isa 19.3, with the Egyptians seeking them, along with *'ôbôt* and *yidde'onîm*. This is presented as an Egyptian practice, but the word is distinctly Akkadian.

12. *ḥarṭōm*. "magician." As a word used for Egyptian magicians, it appears in Gen 41.24 in the Joseph story, and in Ex 8.14 (EV 18) for the magicians whom Moses encountered. At the other end of biblical history, we find this office as Babylonian officials in Dan 1.20, along with *'aššāpîm*. The word may be a loan from the Egyptian hr.tp or "several other variants."[281] On the other hand, there is the closely-sounding Akkadian word *harṭibi* "interpreter of dreams" although it itself is probably a loan from this same word (svv. AHw, CAD). No description of how dreams were interpreted is given, but we may use Mesopotamian practices for a guideline. For that we can turn to Oppenheim's fine *Dream Book.*

Joseph could interpret (root *p-t-r*) dreams, Gen 41.12, and Daniel had extraordinary powers to interpret dreams (Dan 5.12, root *p-š-r* in Aramaic), explain riddles and loose knots. These do not seem to be terms which represent a nomen professionis.

No female rank shows up.

13. *ḥōlēm ḥălôm* "dreamer of dreams" Deut 13.2 (EV 1). This is found in parallel with the word for prophet, indicating that the prophecy came from the dream. They must not be listened to. Jer 23.23-32 indicates that some who dream may use their dreams to manipulate others, or may even lie about their dreams. Usually the dream is listened to and taken seriously in the Hebrew Bible.

There is no female counterpart.

14. *'aššāpîm*.. Dan 1.20, 2.2 are used as a comparison of Daniel's ability. This is probably a loan-word from Akkadian *āšipu*. Of course, the usage in the Hebrew Bible could have been different from Mesopotamian practice.

Unlike Mesopotamia, however, no female rank shows up.

15. *mĕlaḥēš* "whisperer." After a verse mentioning serpents, a text speaks of the voice of the *mĕlahĕšîm*, and the *ḥôbēr ḥābēr* (see No. 6), Ps 58.6 (EV 5). Serpents are spoken to with (root) *l-ḥ-s* in Jer 8.17, and it is something done to a serpent in Eccles 10.11. Though limited to serpents in the Hebrew Bible, it may have had wider usage. The form in Isa 3.3: *nĕbôn lāheš* "one knowlegeable in whispering" is unusual. The Akkadian *lahāšu* "whisper" leads to *lihšu* "whisper-prayer," used of incantations (CAD, s.v.)

There is no female rank.

We have so few liturgical texts in Ugaritic that we like to bring them in whenever possible. There is an action in one[282] by a *mlḥš* from this same root, translated by the editor as "to murmur." This same word, however, appears in a text:[283] *mnt.nṯk.nḥš* "an incantation for snakebite." A *mlḥš* drives out the poison (line 5)

16. *ḥăkam ḥărāšîm* "wise one of sorcery." This is a single occurrence in the Hebrew Bible, Isa 3.3. The homonomous root *ḥ-r-š* has a number of meanings in Semitic languages, as "laborer, artisan, plow, deaf," as well as its later Hebrew meaning of "sorcerer" (Jastrow) It is also found in Ugaritic (UT No. 668), Arabic, Ethiopic and Syriac.

Though there are "wise women,"[284] there is no female counterpart of this title.

17. Hepatoscopy. In Ezek 21.26 (EV 21) the king of Babylon acts as a diviner by, among other divinitory practices, looking at the liver. This was such a widespread practice in Mesopotamia and elsewhere in the ancient Near East, that we would be surprised not to find it in the Hebrew Bible, yet this is the only occurrence, as far as we can find out. M. Bic,[285] pushing exegesis beyond its legitimate limits, tried to argue that Amos was a liver-diviner, but this has been criticized by almost all commentators.

18. Astrology was prevalent in Mesopotamia, but seldom mentioned in the Hebrew Bible. Isa 47.12 criticizes Babylon for her *ḥĕbārîm* "knots" and her *kĕšāpîm* "sorceries" and then a verse mentioning those who "divide the heavens," and look at the stars, who "let people know from the new moons" what will happen to them (vs. 13). [286] These are among other unusual words of this chapter[287] The text attempts to describe Babylonian astrological and astronomical practices. They divide the heavens into sections, pre-Zodiacal divisions. Can those astrologers save you, the text asks sarcastically. Then a general principle may be called upon here: if the prophets criticize a practice in others, it was probably done in Israel also.

The *gāzrîn* of Dan 2.27 and passim were "dividers, determiners (by looking at the heavens)," thus often "astrologers" by extension.

19. Words used in divination language are often used in other situations, showing perhaps its influence. King Josiah in 2 Kings 22.13 told his priest and his followers to "inquire of the Lord for me," standard divination language.

20. Sitting under trees to hear the word of the Lord was a common practice in Israel. Deborah did it in Jud 4.5. The angel sat under the oak at Ophrah, Jud 6.11. Saul stayed under the pommegranate tree at Migron, 1 Sam 14.2, and under a tamarisk tree at Gibeah, 1 Sam 22.6. In fact, Saul was buried under the tamarisk tree at Jabesh-gilead, 1 Sam 31.13. Offerings made under trees are criticized, Hos 4.13. The rustling of the leaves in the top of a balsam tree became an oracle from the Lord to go out to battle, 2 Sam 5.24. The oak of Moreh "teaching, oracle" was used as a datum point, Gen 12.6, Deut 11.30, Josh 24.26 (under it was set a stone symbolic of the covenant, in the *miqdas* "holy place, sanctuary" of Yhwh). The Lord called to Moses from a thorn-bush, Ex 3.4. One of the places in Israel's war against the Benjaminites is Ba'al-tamar, Jud 20.33, a place named after the *tāmār* "palm-tree". At the tamarisk tree in Beersheba Abraham called upon the name of Yhwh, Gen 21.33.

Manfred Lurker discusses oracles from trees in the Western Semitic world.[288]

21. Prophecy. One hesitates to state, without much qualification, that the prophets were or in what way they were, ecstatics, but the tendency in several of their writings indicates this, and it has spawned a large literature.[289]

In the vivid tale in 1 Sam 10.1-13, Saul, though not usually considered among the ranks of the prophets, acted as one. Immediately after being anointed, itself a powerful sign, he met a band of prophets "prophesying" with musical instruments, vs. 5. These were used to instill the ecstatic state. He also felt the spirit (*ruaḥ*) come upon him, and he prophesied with them (ecstatically), and was turned into another man, vs. 6, one of the definitions of ecstasy. In a variant of this story, he stripped off his clothes and lay naked on the ground all day and all night, 1 Sam 19.24, and those who saw him called him a prophet.

21.1 There were *nĕbîʾāh* 's "prophetesses." One of the most significant of these was Huldah of 2 Kings 22.15-20. She was called upon to interpret the "scroll of the torah," recently found while repairing the temple, and she did so by using a prophetic formula "*kō ʾāmar* Yhwh" "thus says the Lord." (vs. 15) Her prophecy was mainly in cultic terms, prophesying against the people because they had turned to other gods. In the language of the prophetic "I," she says to the king through the messenger: "I will gather you to your fathers," because you "rent your clothes and wept before me." The fact that Josiah was slain in battle (2 Kings 23.29) does not take away the deuteronomic force of the prophecy, given because he was good like no other (2 Kings 23.25). The Hebrew Bible lists six prophetesses, but only Huldah appears in the classical prophetic role.[290] No'adyah the *nĕbîʾāh* put fear into people (Neh 6.14), as did the prophesying women who sewed (Ezek 13.22), but they were false.

21.2 There was a group of women at Ebla, yet to be studied, called *na-bí-ú-tum*, from the same root *nbʾ* from which the Hebrew word for "prophet" came, who were from Mari.[291]

22. A representative of a type of person who predicts the future is found in the *môdîᶜim lĕḥadāšîm* "monthly predictor," literally "the ones who make (things) known for the months" in Isa 47.13.

23. Other forms of magic show up from time to time. Stories were told of Moses using such common practices as striking a rod (Ex 7.8-24), throwing dust into the air (Ex 9.10), spreading his hands towards heaven (Ex 9.22).

From the earliest times until the latest, the *ʾûrîm* and *tummîm*, perhaps sacred lots, sticks or dice, were handled in a way not described, and could come up with a yes or no answer to a question. (See note 276) Ezr 2.63 is an example of its use even in a late date, but the best-known entries are such passages as the pentateuchal ones of Ex 28.30 and Lev 8.8, in which they were in the pockets in the high priestly robe. Though we know little about their use, it may be compared to throwing dice, flipping a coin or "asking" a Ouija board in our own age.

24. Ordeal. In a vivid and apparently lifelike account of the ordeal of a woman suspected of adultery in Num 5.16-28, some of the classic appurtenances of divination were used: holy dust, loosened hair, repeated words, drinking a potion, all the time under heavy psychological pressure from the priest's words and presence. This report shows something we have noticed for Mesopotamia, that the high god and the low practice of divination went hand-in-hand. The ordeal was used in many ways in Mesopotamia, also.

Water was often used in the ordeal in the Hebrew Bible [292] though not plunging the victim into it as in Mesopotamia.[293] The water with powder made of the golden calf in it (Ex 32.20) was forced upon the people by Moses, presumably to bring out the guilty ones by sickness or death.

In the ordeal, the deity is the judge, although that is based on human interpretation. Its result is direct, and the punishment is part of the procedure. The story of Daniel's friends in the fiery furnace (Dan 3) is an ordeal with legendary overtones, the result showing the truth, as in many ordeal trials, but in this case the truth of God and of Daniel and his friends.

In the torah-code Ex 22.6-8 (EV 7-9) the suspected party is to come before or draw near to God, implying some kind of ordeal, the procedure probably left up to the judges.

As an integral part of the early part of some ordeals[294] the oath appears. The form of the oath is often: "If I have (done this or that) .... then (may thus and so happen to me)." The most profound of these is in Job 31.

It is probable that despite the picture one gets by noting the rare usages of the technical terms for magicians and diviners given above, incantation was a normal and oft-used practice in this society as in others around them, and that the Hebrew Bible does not want to give us the balanced picture because its purpose is to present the high theology, not to give "equal time."

Yet the commentators sometimes make the mistake of counting the occurrences and drawing their conclusions from that. The extent of divinatory practices is shown by Haldar.[295]

3.33 Ugaritic Diviners

These have been mentioned passim above. The *mlḥš* drives out the poison of snakebite, Sec. 3.32.15. A standard word for sorcerer is *ḥrš*, Sec. 3.32.16. A word for one who looks at the stars is *ḥbr*, Sec. 3.32.18.

Notes

1 Starr *Diviner* 13, from Goetze Omen No. 1, *YOS* 10 1. Cad A/2 96b translates "this is the liver concerning King Sin-iddinam, on whom in the Shamash temple, in the month Elunu, (the wall) buckled and fell." CAD E 1 36a translates: "this is the (appearance of the) liver which fell to the lot of King Sin-iddinam when he sacrificed (a sheep) in the temple of Shamash at the Elunu festival." Goetze *JCS* 1 265: "upon whom in the temple of Shamash in the month of Elunum the stairs fell."

2 M. Ottosson, *Temples and Cult Places in Palestine*, Uppsala, 1980 29, who is careful about criteria for labeling finds as "cultic objects."

3 Starr *Diviner* 44.

4 Starr *Diviner* 51-2.

5 A.L. Oppenheim, *Ancient Mesopotamia* 15ff.

6 E. Leichty, *The Omen Series Shumma Izbu*, Locust Valley, N. Y., 1970 (TCS 4)

7 R. Caplice, *Or* 34 (1965) I; 36 (1967) II, III; 39 (1970) IV; 40 (1971) V. The name means "its dispelling" *Or* 34, 105.

8 R. Labat, *Hemerologies et Menologies d'Assur*, Paris, 1939.

9 W. G. Lambert, *Divination* 119-123.

10 Moren 22f.

11 Charpin *Clergé* 385.

12 A. Falkenstein, in *Divination* 51. There are other significant "equivalences" to *bārû* here: a-zu or uzú (NINDA.NUN), ì-zu "leconomancer," me-zu, šim-mú.

13 M. Eliade, *Shamanism*. Princeton, 1964[2], Chap 1, 1951[1] French.

14 Ake Hultkrantz, *The Religions of the American Indians*. Berkeley, 1979. (Stockholm 1967), especially Chap 6.

15 A modern study is given in a series of papers published in *La Divination* .J. Nougayrol gives a good general bibliography as of that date in *Ibid.* pp. 16-19.

16 *Ancient Mesopotamia*, 206-227.

17 Lambert *BWL* 38.7

18 Starr *Diviner*. One specialized category of the texts themselves is given in Starr *Queries*, with the *bārû* discussed on pp. xxx-xxxv. This completely updates two pioneering books: J. A. Knudtzon, *Asyrische Gebete an den Sonnengott*. Leipzig, 1893; and E. Klauber, *Politische-Religiose Texte aus der Sargonidenzeit*. Leipzig, 1913, which has the published material. See also A.L. Oppenheim, *Centaurus* 14 (1969) 97-135.

19 A. Falkenstein, *Divination* 46 and Renger *ZA* 59 (1969) 203 n. 939.

20 Starr *Diviner* 105, 234.

21 Friedrich Blome, *Die Opfermaterie in Bablonien und Israel, I*, Rome, 1934. An original piece of work, with many references.

22 Delivery of beer, más-šu-gi$_4$-gi$_4$-d[a], Umma, Oppenheim *Catalogue* D22; máš-šu-gíd-gíd, ba-zi, Drehem, Sigrist *Horn* Nos. 54 and 265; mas-šu-gíd-gíd, Kang Umma No. 310; maš-šu-gíd-gíd and šu-máš-gíd-gíd, Snell *Ledgers*, index 260.

23 Falkenstein *Götterlieder* 16f, 111f.

24 *SAKI* 227, 11c; Falkenstein *Götterlieder I* 17, 112.

25 *SAKI* 227, 11b; *YBT* 1 29 II 5'-8'.

26 *RTC* 208 r.4 et passim. These listed by A. Falkenstein, in *Divination* 51. I obtained much in this section from Falkenstein's richly endowed article, but only selections could be used.

27 The overall sweep of the concept and usage of oil omens in OB times is given by G. Pettinato in *Divination* 95-107, and his book Pettinato *Olwahrsagung*.

28 See also *YOS* 1 45 ii 26, Nabonidus' dedication of his daughter.

29 C.J. Gadd, in *Divination* 21-34.

30 The *bārû* turns to his *ikribu* "prayer, blessing." CT 30 15, 11, in CAD I/J 63a. "The god was not present at the *nīš qāti* "lifting of the hands" prayer of the *mār bārî* CT 31 48 in CAD N/2 295a.

31 CAD B 124a.

32 CAD B 12lb (Genouillac, Kich 1B 295. 5').

33 Falkenstein *Divination* 46, n. 2 continued from his previous page. From UMBS 5 76, VI 3-8.

34 This kind of query is very close to that reported in 2 Kings 22 in which the king asks his court prophets whether his planned attack will be successful.

35 Starr *Diviner* 38. 21: "I perform this extispacy for the *šulmu* of so-and-so," in an OB "prayer of the diviner."

36 *ABL* 975 r.14.

37 *KAR* 422 r.17 (restored from unpublished duplicate K. 4121), see Star *Diviner* 112. The extensive use of specialized ideograms used for this literature make the omens difficult to translate.

38 *RA* 67 45:49, from Starr 21f.

39 Renger *ZA* 59 (1969) 210a.

40 CAD M/1 123.

41 Goetze *JCS* 2 (1948) 74, 2. Crozer, No. 169.

42 Goetze *JCS* 2 (1948) 77, No. 6. 6ff, Crozer No. 172.

43 A. Finet, "La Place du Devin dans la Societe de Mari," in *Divination* 87-93.

44 *ARM* 2 139. 8-10.

45 G. Dossin, *I11RAI*, Paris, 1951 46-48. Cf. Finet, op. cit. , 92 n. 4.

46 *ARM* 2 134. 4f, though the word *bārû* does not appear.

47 *ARM* 2 22. 23f.

48 *TCL* 2. 5, translated by Oppenheim, *Dreams* 221d, H. Hirsch, *AFO* Beih 13/14, 14f.

49 Craig *ABRT* 2 18, 27, K. 232.

50 C.J. Mullo-Weir, *JRAS* 1929, 15. 29, H. Zimmern *ZA* 29 69.

51 Bauer *Lagasch*. Text 126.

52 *Lamentation Over the Destruction of Sumer and Ur*, 445.

53 Chiera *SRT* 6 II 14, from A. Falkenstein *Divination* 54.

54 We are fortunate in having a full study of dream interpretation in ancient Mesopotamia with emphasis on Neo-Assyrian times, done by A.L. Oppenheim *Dream Book*.

55 *STVC* 50, 18-21 = 51, 3-34, in A. Falkenstein *Divination* 53. Also in G.R. Castellino, *Two Shulgi Hymns*. Rome, 1972, 256, 101 (Shulgi C).

56 Falkenstein, Ibid. 54, translated in *Dream Book* 245. A collection of these early texts is given by Charpin *Clergé* 382-4. Charpin 382b: Ningirsu is ensi of the gods, Gudea Cyl A II 17, A IV 12.

57 Oppenheim, *op.cit.* 232b.

58 4 R 22 No. 2.9.11. Quoted by Oppenheim, *op. cit.*, 222b, paralleled by a line from Ludlul II. 6-9, Lambert *BWL* 288f, loc. cit., lines 8-15 transliterated and translated by Charpin 384. See *RA* 38 (1941) 67 n. 2. Technically, *muššakku* is "incense."

59 K. 3182 I 53-4, quoted in Oppenheim, *op. cit.*, 222a, text in Lambert *BWL* 128, 54.

60 Oppenheim *Dream Book* 224; Falkenstein *Divination* 55.

61 Cyl A XX 7-12. This is Falkenstein's interpretation in *Divination* 55f, and Oppenheim's interpretation in his *Dream Book* 224a.

62 Oppenheim 223b.

63 Charpin *Clergé* 385.

64 Harris *Sippar* 188.

65 CAD B 121b, *VAS* 16 22.7: n. 64 above.

66 CAD B 122b, (Lambert *BWL* 38.6), where smoke or incense was used.

67 *UET* 7 155 r.v 10, CAD N/2 191a.

68 *YOS* 2 1:29.

69 *YOS* 2 1:29 (J. Renger, *ZA* 59 (1969) 217 and n. 1031).

70 *Malku IV* 3, CAD E 22a.

71 *naphar* 3 *ḫar-ṭi-bi* , *ADD* 851 iv 2, in a unit summing up three Egyptian (so CAD Ḫ 116a) names. Units on the tablet are 17 MAŠ.MAŠ. MEŠ, 5 *bārû*'s, 9 A.BA [ ] "scribes of ...., 6 *kalu*'s, 6 *dāgil iṣṣurī*'s "bird watchers," 3 *ḫarṭibi*'s, Egyptian scribes, all cultic offices and perhaps part of the temple staff. See also Sec.2.3.11. See van Driel *Cult of Assur* 55, n. 18. As in other *ADD* texts, many of which are the same layout, we can consider these personnel all together in one place to receive a tax release, or rations or some kind of recognition from the king.

72 *ḫar-ṭi-*[ ] (Bu 91-5-9, 218), Borger *Esarh* §80, from Winckler *AOF* II 21ff, translated by A. Oppenheim, *ANET* 293.

73 At Nuzi (Gasur), T.J. Meek, *HSS* 10 71,4; 72 ii 12; šabra-é (Naram-Sin) H. Hirsch, *AfO* 20 (1963) 21b.

74 K. 2652, Streck *Ashurbanipal* II 190, 25ff, restored by CAD S/1 15a.

75 Oppenheim *Dreams* 300-307.

76 CAD A/2 431.

77 Sjöberg *Mondgott* 140.7 and p. 144.

78 Later lexical lists relate the *āšipu* with the MAŠ.MAŠ and CAD A/1 435a concludes that LÚ.MAŠ.MAŠ represents the same person as the *āšipu* and is "most likely to be read as *āšipu*, except in a few literary texts where *mašmaššu* occurs as a learned word." Pedersen *Archives* 44, n. 19 wisely notes that the Americans tend to read *āšipu* and Germans *mašmaššu*.

79 Labat *TDP* 2.1.

80 E. Ritter, "Magical expert (*āšipu*) and physician (*asû*) notes on two complimentary professions in Babylonian medicine." Landsberger AV 299-321.

81 Falkenstein *Haupttypen* 29.

82 Ritter, Landsberger AV 307ff.

83 sim-mu$_2$ kalam-ma "*ašiptu* of the land" and a-zu-gal "chief physician" are epithets of the goddess Nininsina, time of Sin-kashid of Uruk, D.O. Edzard, *Sumer* 13 (1957) p. 186; I Kärki, *StOr* 49 (1980) 183f. Later an epithet of Gula was *azugallatu* "female great physician," Tallqvist *Götterpitheta* 317. A PN is Gula-a-sa-at "Gula (is) an *asâtu* "*BE* 15 200 iii 13, CAD A/2 347a.

84 Marc Lebeau, "Les Institutions Sacerdotales de Mari," *AIPHOS* 24 (1980) 53-82, Bruxelles.

85 *ABL* 24 = Parpola *LAS* I 172.

86 E. Ebeling, "Aus dem Tagewerk eines assyrischen Zauberpriesters," *MAOG* 5/3, Leipzig, 1931, 3-52. *VAT* 8240 = *KAR* 1 38, Ebeling p. 49, a namburbi, colophon, has MAŠ.MAŠ bīt ^{d}[Asshur].

87 *KAR* 44 (*VAT* 8275); transliteration and translation as of this early date by H. Zimmern *ZA* 30 (1915-16) 206ff; see 79-7-8, 250, 11 + lines out of the middle of a text (Bezold), close but with no duplicated lines. This is as yet unpublished, as noted in Reiner *Shurpu* 3, and Bezold *Catalogue* gives no readings. Discussed in J. Bottéro, "Magie A" §45, *RLA* 7 3/4, 1988. It is "evidemment plus ancienne que la copie qu'il nous en reste." He reads *āšipu*.

88 J. Bottéro, *RLA* 7/3-4. "Magie. A" 226ff.

89 *VAT* 10568a, E. Ebeling, *Or* 22 (1953) 42-45, copy in *Or* 17 (1948) pl. 17.

90 Offerings are given to DUMU.! SAL.ID / *marat nari* "daughter of the river" (*ABL* 977 r. 11, Parpola *LAS* I 218), with rituals against various sicknesses.For this demon, see also *KAR* 141 (partially broken) and Ebeling *Parfumrez* 17.

91 *VAT* 10448 Ebeling, op.cit. 45f. Several more ritual texts are in this collection, with the king, *šangû*, NAR, *rab šibirti* as ritual actors.

92 *KAV* 42 II 40.

93 Laessøe *Bīt Rimki* 29, 2.

94 4 R 50 iii 49-50, duplicated *KAR* 239 ii 21ff, in the Lamashtu cycle.

95 *BWL* 38f II 6-9. One variant (notes) has ma⌈š-m⌉aš-šu, for MAŠ.MAŠ line 9, and maš-maš-šu for MAŠ. MAŠ line 108.

96 *KAR* 58ff, a šu-ila CAD A/2 434ab: *āšipu*.
97 *KAR* 92.29.
98 *KAR* 144. 1, *ZA* 32 (1918-19) 164 or 174.
99 K. 11173 K.D. Macmillan, *BA* V (1906) 638, r. 7f, transliterated 576.
100 E. Ebeling, *MVAG* 23/2, 22. 45 (*KAR* 42).
101 CAD E 81b, 82a.
102 CAD E 80b, lexical section.
103 Kramer, *The Sumerians* 99, dated by him at 2700 B.C.E. The PN also appears at Fara III 33.
104 *ABL* 33.8.
105 Labat *TDP* 170. 14, CAD A/2 347a.
106 *Or* 36 (1967) 128: 183.
107 Ritter ashipu /asû 299-321.
108 R. Biggs, *RLA* 7 624a.
109 BE 25 200 iii 13, and Clay PN 159.
110 *Shurpu* IV, 107.
111 *Musée du Louvre -- Départment des antiquites orientales: textes cuneiformes*. Paris, 1926, 10 107:27. This reference from R. Harris, in John G. Gammie and Leo G. Perdue (eds.), *The Sage in Israel and the Ancient Near East,* Winona Lake, 1990, 11.
112 Pedersen *Archives* 58 n. 36.
113 *ABL* 1133 r. 11, CAD A/2 346a.
114 *RAcc* 141. 354, CAD K 179d.
115 Pedersen *Archives*.
116 A. Goetze, *JCS* 9, 15, 53, who refers to a cultic vessel (CAD: "sprinkler") only, as did B. Landsberger, quoted by A. Falkenstein *Haupttypen* 78.5. Maybe this vessel is something the *mullilu* uses in the rite. Sometimes a *mullilu* is carried in one hand and a *banduddu*-bucket in the other. The *apkallu*'s carry both of these, CAD B 80a.
117 Craig *ABRT* I 54f = K 3600 + DT 75, Livingstone *Poetry* No. 4 r. 5'.
118 CT 16, 28, 46f, CAD 376b, variants not noted.
119 *JSS* 21 (1976) 171 to p. 20 of the Wine Lists.
120 E. Reiner,*JNES* 15 (1956) 138, 109, CAD S/1 376b.
121 Livingstone *Poetry* No. 12.18 = STT 65, here a *kaššāptu*.
122 As Lu = ša II iii 27', Sec. 3.3.4, and:

182 [ensi] *ša -' -i-li*
183 [lú balag-gá] [*mu-še-lu-u*] *e-dim-me*

Lu = ša Excerpt I MSL XII 102

123 *Maqlû* IV 124.
124 *BRM* 4 12:74, CAD K 29la.
125 Labat *TDP* 218:15, from CAD K 291a.
126 R. Biggs, *ŠÀZI.GA* 21, 15.
127 *RA* 18 165.23 (a Lamashtu text), see CAD M/2 212a.
128 *LKA* 144.29, CAD M/2 212a.
129 *KAV* 1 vii 6 (*MAL* §47), CAD M/2 211b.
130 *LKA*144.29, M/2 212a.

131 Livingstone *Poetry* No. 25 r. I 22' = K.4449 = *AfO* 18 pl. XXIIIf, a letter to Asshurbanipal from his son.

132 R. Caplice, *Or* 34 (1965) 117, 21, discussion on P. 120, in a namburbi. He considers it an alternative title to *mašmāšu*.

133 CAD E 234, 6' in *Maqlû*.

134 CAD E 81f, s.v. *ullulu*, under *elēlu*, and lexical section.

135 E. Reiner, "The etiological myth of the "seven sages." *Or* NS 30 (1961) 1-11. These semi-mythological sages are found listed in the text after Adapa who is termed the *išippu* of Eridu.

136 Jacobsen *Harps*...n. 113.

137 Jestin, *Shuruppak* 2 ii 9 and 11, 181 iv 11, CAD A/2 173a.

138 CAD A/2 171a.

139 *Malku* IV 8f, CAD M/2 187b.

140 K. 2946 i 14f, CAD A/2 171b; See Meier *AfO* 12, 41.

141 Streck *ASb* 366.13.

142 W.G. Lambert, *JCS* 21 (1967) 132, 32.

143 *BBR* No. 24:23 (K.2486 + K.4364) = Craig *ABRT* 64f, K.4364 = 2R 58 No. 3.

144 Streck *Asb* 254, 15, CAD A/2 from Streck's reading.

145 See the rather full bibliographical study of A. Green, *Iraq* 45/1 (1983) 88-90. He overcomes early scepticism of J.B. Stearns by drawing upon Julian Reade's appraisal and finding the bird-dressed and fish-garbed figures in the slab sculpture as *apkallu*'s. See also D. Kolbe, *Die Reliefprogramme religios- mythologischen Charakters im neuassyrischen Palästen*; *Die Figurentypen, ihre Benennung und Bedeutung* Frankfurt-am-Main/Bern, 1981 (not seen by me).

146 K.232 r.29. JRAS 1929 17 r. 19. See also Sec. 3.8.5. With a variant: [*ap-kal-lat ba-ra*] *-at mu-li-la-at muš-ši-pat ili u amēli* Craig *ABRT* 2 17,18, adding "*mullitu* .. of god and man." *mulliltu* is another cultic functionary like *mullilu*, Sec. 3. 25. 2.

147 Cohen *Eršemma* 56ff. No. 168.34, No. 184.42 (p. 57), No. 185.30.

148 Of course the Sumerian does not give us the gender, so we understand her as female by context. For the term sìg-bar-ra as a title in itself, see Sec. 1.11.

149 *PSD* 93b.

150 *UET* 6 388 r. col. a li and 389:8-9 (variant), CAD A/2 171b, and in W.W. Hallo, "The Blessing of Nisaba by Enki" *CRRA* 17 (1970) 125, vii 44.

151 *JCS* 21 (1967) 132, 25.

152 *UVB* 15 40:5, in CAD M/2 187b.

153 *TuL* 103, 13.

154 A conflated text, K.2361 +, line 41. An original study by R.E. Brünnow (*ZA* 4 (1889) 252 i 9 and 11) is updated by W. von Soden, *ZA* 61 (1971) 50:41 and 43.

155 Kagal G 23, MSL XIII 256. These are all IGI entries, here given as [IGI. Du] . This is perhaps why the editors read gig. They want to do away with a reading *išištu*, loc. cit. to line 23.

156 Ungnad *Briefe Hammurapi* 152, 4 (CT 29, 18) and 153,10 (CT 29,19).

157 Charpin *Clergé* 392.

158 K.2946 i 14f, CAD A/1 62b. The *abriqqu* is also with the *apkallu* in *CT* 16 37:34, CAD A/1 62b. A fuller transliteration and translation in Charpin *Clergé* 366.

159 CAD A/1 62.

160 Pettinato Waetzoldt *Vocabulario* index I/3 s.v.

161 Gregoire Archives 188 to text 148, and for Old Sumerian see Bauer *Lagasch*, index 610.

162 SAL lú is a peculiarity for these lines in all of OB Lu, and must simply stand for SAL, Renger, *ZA* 59 (1969) 220, n. 1049. Since the equivalent is, e.g., *zabbatu* in line 30, SAL lú must be simply used for SAL, thus "the female ecstatic." See also Sec. 3.12.3 for mi-lú-gub-ba.

163 Sollberger *Correspondence* NO. 369.

164 Cited in Gelb Old Akkadian 171, s.v. MH'$_x$.

165 C.-F. Jean, *TCL* 10 No. 34.47.

166 Ibid. No. 69.4.

167 *ARM* 6, 45.

168 G. Dossin, *RA* 35 (1938) 1-13.

169 *RA* 13 108 i 24; *ZA* 25 (1911) 195 = K.6475.9, and cf. K.2001; *TuL* 50. 26f. See also CAD M/2 177.

170 A. Sjöberg, *ZA* 65 (1975) 187, 88. Cf. the relationship with the *apillu* above on HAR-gud B VI, Sec. 3.3.10. The pilipili and *apillû* are related in App. 3.7.

171 A. Sjöberg, JCS 24 (1972) 107, 7, although there are no cultic aspects in the text.

172 C. Virolleaud. *Bab* 4 (1911) 105, 25.

173 Livingstone *Poetry* No. 39.27 = *VAT* 8917 = *KAR* 307.

174 *RA* 35 2 ii 22.

175 En. el IV 88.

176 CAD reads as "most likely": *dingirgubbû,* indicating gub-ba (*mahhû* "ecstatic") gods, CAD A/2 118b.

177 "The *angubbû* were certainly not human." W. Lambert *BWL* 302a.

178 Streck *Asb*, CAD A/2 118c.

179 Borger, *Esarh* 24 §11 Episode 33 lines 20-22 (CAD A/2 118b understands otherwise) Lambert, *BWL* 301n. to 96 translates: "the *pašīšu*'s of the *angubbû*-spirits." This seems awkward to me.

180 Römer *Königshymnen* 236, 14, his translation.

181 C. Gadd, *Iraq* 22 (1960) 165 to line 40.

182 Streck *Asb* 268, 27.

183 Winckler *Sargon* pl. 36, No. 76.2, duplicated Lie *Sarg* 76 line 12f.

184 R. Borger, *BiOr* 30 (1973) 164.

185 *UET* 7 155 r.v 10, CAD N/2 191a.

186 A. Sjöberg, *ZA* 65 (1975) 186, line 87, variant D.

187 *SEM* 65 r.15, with duplicates, from A. Sjöberg, *ZA* 65 (1975) 227, under line 87.

188 *TUL* 50, 25ff, and the duplicates listed in CAD Z 7b. The two are together also in a *Shumma Ālu* text Sm 332 r.5 see Oppenheim *AfO* 18 75.

189 Alster *Shuruppak* 90 From Dialogue 5, texts on p. 164.

190 mu-lú-e$_{11}$-dè: something to do with ecstasy, madness, being out of the mind, etc., as other forms...e$_{11}$-dè, Sjöberg, *ZA* 65 (1975) 227 under line 88.

191 Translation and bibliography in Miriam Lichtheim, *Ancient Egyptian Literature* II 224-230. The "trance" into which the young man went is the word ^{c}*add* in the document, probably not Egyptian but from an Old Aramaic word, according to Aelred Cody, *JEA* 65 (1979) 101. This is found in the Zakir inscription. H. Donner and W. Rollig, *KAI* No. 202 A12.

192 A. Malamat, *JAOS* 82 (1962) 149 n.29.

193 M. Anbar, "L'activité divinatoire de L'apilum, le 'repondant,' d'après une lettre de Mari," *RA* 75 (1981) 91, A.1121, suggests how to fill in a gap in a certain line, and is not useful for our purposes.

194 Mayer *Nuzi* 140.1.

195 *ARM* 10, 81,4, from Römer, *Frauenbriefe* 36.

196 Noort *Mari* 69-75.

197 *Studies in Old Testament Prophecy Presented to Professor Theodore H. Robinson.* Edinburgh,1950,103-110.

198 Fulfilling some of the functions discussed in Sec. 3.32.21.

199 Not in "Noms Divins" *ARM* XVI/1 A local deity, according to G.Dossin, *Studia Mariana* I (1950) 43.

200 Studied by Römer *Frauenbriefe* 36.

201 *ARM* X 7.7 mentions *šelibum* carrying the lock of hair and the fringe of the garment of the *assinnu* and in X 8.7 there is an untitled daughter of Dagan-malik who speaks to the king. In X 80, 4f Selibum the *assinnu* delivers a *tērtum* "oracle."

202 R. Frankena, in Kraus *Briefe* No. 65.15.33, from *LIH* 83.

203 *Ibid* No. 71.5.14.

204 Landsberger AV 211ff, line 38.

205 *ARM* X 80.6.

206 Noort *Mari* 72 n. 2, and Renger *ZA* 55 (1969) 219 n. 1044.

207 Wiseman *Treaties* lines 116f. There is a similar phrase, listed as a profession, lú inim-ma = *ša a-wa-tim* "the one of the word," OB Lu C4, MSL XII 194.

208 Mic 1.1, Zeph 1.1 and Joel 1.1 have "the word of the Lord which was to Micah/Zephaniah/Joel," which could indicate the word which came to him, or the word of the Lord which was his, belonged in some sense to him.

209 K. 883, *BA* 2 (Leipsig, 1891), 633.1; Lehmann, *Samassumukin* II 77.

210 *ABL* 1285 r.32.

211 *ABL* 149.7. No cultic associations appear here.

212 *ABL* 437.23, corrected by Parpola *LAS* I No. 280.

213 ABL 1216.9, probably variants of *raggīnu* and *raggintu.*

214 Menzel *Tempel* 25, bottom.

215 M. Birot, *RA* 50 (1956) 159 VII 13 "Tablette C" = TEM IV vii; *ARM* IX, 24 III 15:27 IV 29.

216 A. Falkenstein, *ZA* NF 15 (1949) 139. In a bilingual, = itta'id (CAD N/1 la). He goes beyond the old meaning "notice," *ZA* 47 NF 13 (1942) 215,16. OB Proto-Lu 283, 283a, MSL XII 43, has the same entry sag-kés.

217 CAD E 170 a, further references A. Sjöberg, *ZA* 65 (1975) 226f.

218 "agentive" Falkenstein, *Das Sumerische* 38, 3a; ergative or locative-terminative, H.L. Thomsen, *The Sumerian Language*, Copenhagen, 1984, §170 (Mesopotamia, 10).

219 Falkenstein *Gerichtsurkunden* III 39 has a list.

220 Besides Falkenstein's references, see also *UET* IX, Jones-Snyder; Pettinato *Untersuchungen*; Snell *Ledgers* s.vv. in their respective indices.

221 For PNs showing the titles of some ecstatics, see gub-ba-ni, lú-mah, maš-šu-gi$_{12}$-gi$_{12}$-da all in Limet *Anthroponymie* svv., and máš-šu-gi$_{22}$-gi$_{22}$-da in Oppenheim *Catalogue* D25. an-né-ba-ab-du$_{7}$ also appears on a seal, *AJSL* XX 113, the son of a gudu$_{4}$ (??).

222 *Maqlû* IV. 72.

223 *Maqlû* VII 94-100. CAD K 558b has: "the *kurgarrû*'s have protected you with counter-charms." This softens too much the criticism of the *kurgarrû*'s.

224 For the singer/musician *mušlahhu* in the feminine form *mušlahhatu* see Sec. 2.13.

225 Only found in *Maqlû* III 40 and *Maqlû* IX 43; cf. EN *kaššaptu ner* [ ] in *KAR* ii 4; or, put this and the previous word together as "murderous witch."

226 Or, make earth unclean.

227 AHw 1131b: "(böse) Herunterreisserin (?)."

228 CAD S 41b, assuming from *sabāru* A; AHw 1071a: "etwa Tuschlerin."

229 Elsewhere in Maqlû, other Category IV persons are mentioned as witches, see chapter 4.

230 Cf. Arabic *qamqama* "complain, grumble, mutter" (Wehr), perhaps indicating a negative mode of speaking. Also IX.100. This is also found among witches in Speleers *Recueil* 312.5 = H. Zimmern, *ZA* 32 (1918-19) 59.

231 *Maqlû* IV 83f, corrected by CAD S 60a. Note the incongruous entry *kurgarrû* here, to be compared with *assinnu* in the midst of ecstatics on the igituh and HAR-gud lists. Here a witch of one type affects the sorcery of a witch of another type.

232 *Maqlû* III 122, partially paralleled in *Bīt Rimki* 38.9f.

233 For *naršindu* see *Maqlû* VII 94 Sec. 3.21.3; for *naršindatu*; *Maqlû* III.40, IV.125, VI.22, IX.43. The context informs us only that this office is a witch.

234 Speleers *Recueil* 312.6, CAD N/1 362b.

235 *Shurpu* V-VI 152/153 ff.

236 *OECT* 1 pl. 20.19, CAD K 427a.

237 Falkenstein AV 241, line 2.

238 *BBR* No. 24,7,13, CAD š 326b. See other bibliography referred to in J. Nougayrol *Divination* 6 n. 5, *YBT* 10, Nos. 57, 58 and 62.

239 B.R. Foster, *Or* 51 (1982) 354. E. Reiner, *JNES* 19 (1960) 29.

240 *ABL* 33.9-10.

241 *ABL* 1346.1.

242 Kwasman No. 236 = *ADD* 60 = *ARU* 153 = Bu. 89-4-26, 7.

243 ND 2442 I 7' Barbara Parker, *Iraq* 23 (1961) pl. XIII and pp. 26f.

244 ND 3476 r.2, D.J. Wiseman, *Iraq* 15 (1953).

245 Kinnier Wilson Wine Lists No. 3.4-5, ND 6218, as reedited by Dalley-Postgate No. 145. Nimrud Wine Lists copies only cols. i, ii, iii but not iv, for which see Dalley-Postgate. Parts of col. iv were read by S. Parpola, *JSS* 21 (1976) 167. See indices, notes and corrections to the Wine Lists by R. Henshaw, *JAOS* 100 (1980) 302-5 (but see 63 "Additions and Corrections" to his article as printed, in the reviewer's possession), A.K. Grayson *JCS* 26 (1974) 130-2, and S. Parpola in op. cit.

246 No. 8.3, ND 10047.

247 No. 9.3, ND 10048, Notes by Grayson op. cit. on the remainder; omitted lines also by Parpola, op. cit.

248 No. 16.2, ND 10033 and ND 10050/1, in which Kinnier Wilson reads LÚ.GA[L.SAG.MEŠ] for *dāgil iṣṣurē*.

249 No. 29.2, ND 10063.

250 George Denis, *The Cities and Cemeteries of Etruria* II, London, 1848, 185. M.Pallottino, *The Etruscans*. Bloomington, 1975[2] (Italy, 1968[6]), p. 146.

251 See Cicero *De Divinatione* i,I,2 in which he simply states that he knows of no race of men, educated or barbarous, who did not believe that warnings of future events may be announced by certain persons.

252 In Greek popular religion as described by Pausanius, *Guide to Greece* IX 39.5-14.

253 *MEE* 4, index: a-BALAG-mušen, a-gíd-mušen, A-mušen, áb-mušen, $buru_4$-mušen, dar-mušen, and many more.

254 Kinnier Wilson Wine Lists No. 1 iii lines 24-25, No 2 ii 8, No 4 r. 5.

255 *VAT* 9742 r. 9-11 (unpublished), in Menzel *Tempel* II n. 3586.

256 ND 3426.43 N. Postgate NA Leg. Docs. No. 9, originally *Iraq* 15 (1953) pl. XII.

257 A. Guillaume, *Prophecy and Divination Among the Hebrews and Other Semites*. London, 1938. A.J. Heschel, *The Prophets* II 234-43 (paperback edition) is tied too much to Greek and Roman models, in my opinion. J. Lindblom, *Prophecy in Ancient Israel*, Oxford, 1965, 85-93, is a simplified introduction to the subject with much on Balaam. A. R. Johnson, *The Cultic Prophet in Ancient Israel.* Cardiff, 1962[2], 31-40, has a sensitivity to the subject of divination that the others do not have, and analyzes the Hebrew words carefully.

258 H. Orlinsky, *OrAn* 4 (1965) 153-74; *Essays in Biblical Culture and Bible Translation,* N.Y. 1978, 39-65.

259 Alberto R.W. Green, *The Role of Human Sacrifice in the Ancient Near East. Scholars Press,* 1975.

260 Rouillard *Baleam* 301-9.

261 de Vaux *Nombres* 255.

262 Jo Ann Hacket, *The Balaam Text from Deir 'Alla*, Scholars Press, 1980.

263 Samuel Iwry, *JAOS* 81 (1961) 27-34.

264 McKay *Religion* 18, n.115 gives no explanation, but describes the practice as soothsaying by observation of clouds.

265 Karen R. Joines, *Serpent Symbolism in the Old Testament*, Haddonfield, New Jersey, 1974, pp. 61f and chapter 4.

266 Leonard Gorelick and Elizabeth Williams-Forte (eds.), *Ancient Seals and the Bible*, Malibu, 1983, 18-44.

267 Alan Rowe, *The Four Canaanite Temples of Beth-Shan*, Philadelphia, 1940, pls. XIV, XVI, XX, XXI.

268 Similar to biblical texts is the muzzling of *tnn* and the slaying of *bṯn* ^{c}*aqltn* "crooked serpent" with 7 heads in *CTA* 3 (KTU 1.3) II, 3ff. as shown in J. Gray, *UF* 11 (1979) 316; it is ^{c}*aqallatôn* in Isa 27.1.

269 Thompson *Magic* 170.

270 Porteous 80.

271 Tropper *Necromantie*. Terms used and a rather full exegesis of important passages are features of this study of texts from the Hebrew Bible and the Ancient Near East.

272 *JBL* 86 (1967) 385ff.

273 M. Vieyra, *RHA* 69 (1961) 47-55.

274 J. Friedrich, *Hethitisches Wörterbuch*, 26: from Hurrian *api-*; J. Friedrich and A. Kammenhuber, *Hethitisches Wörterbuch*, 143.

275 J. Lust, *SVT* 26 (1974) 135ff.

276 Wayne Horowitz and Victor Hurowitz, "Urim and Thummim in Light of a Psephomancy Ritual from Assur (*LKA* 137)," *JANES* 21 (1992) 95-115, discusses them as stones used for divination.

277 J. Ebach and U. Rüterwörden, *UF* 9 (1977) 57-70; *UF* 12 (1980) 205-220.

278 A.E. Draffkorn, *JBL* 76 (1957) 216-24.

279 M. Greenberg, *JBL* 81 (1962)) 239-48; M.J. Selman, *Tyndale Bulletin* 27 (1976) 123-4 further criticizes the protection element, but substitutes no new idea in its place.

280 M. Ellenbogen, *Foreign Words in the Old Testament* 25.

281 T. Lambdin *JAOS* 73 (1953) 150f: "though it is not yet demonstrable."

282 RS 24.244, *Ugaritica* V p. 569, lines 507.

283 M. Dietrich, O. Loretz and J. Sanmartin, *UF* 7 (1975) 121,4 (RS 24.244).

284 Claudia V. Camp, "The female sage in Ancient Israel and in the Biblicial Wisdom Literature," in Gammie-Perdue, *Sage* 185-203.

285 M. Bic, *VT* 1 (1951) 293-6. Murtonen argued against this immediately in *VT* 2 (1952) 170f.

286 J. Blau, *VT* 7 (1957), 183-4 "Himmelsanbeter," and E. Uhlendorff *JSS* 7 (1962) 339f understand the root *ḥabar* as in Ugaritic: "those who worship the heavens."

287 C. Westermann, *Isaiah* 40-66, 1969 (German, 1966) 188, and G.A.F. Knight, *Deutero-Isaiah*, (1965) 154.

288 M. Lurker "Der Baum im alten Orient," in Unger Mem, Vol. 163f. See also Butterworth, *Tree at the Navel of the World.*

289 A few examples only: J. Lindblom's discussion "Ecstatic Visions and Auditions," in his *Prophecy in Ancient* Israel, Oxford, 1962, 122-137, is updated by P. Michaelsen, "Ecstasy and Possession in Ancient Israel." A review of some recent contributions," *SJOT* 2 (1989) 28-54.

290 The Babylonian Talmud Mishna Megilla 14a speaks of seven prophetesses: Sarah, Miriam, Deborah, Hannah, Abigail, Huldah and Esther. This

shows an extension of the meaning of the term. Huldah had two of the doors of the temple precinct named after her, Mid 1.3.

291 G. Pettinato, *The Archives of Ebla* 119, 253; TM 75.G.454, described in *MEE* 1, 25, a šu-ba-ti text, a grain ration, reign of Ibbi-Sipiš.

292 P. Reymond, *L'Eau, sa vie et sa signification dans l'Ancien Testament,* Leiden, 1958 (SVT VI), 217-222; K.van der Toorn, *Sin and Sanction in Israel and Mesopotamia,* Assen, 1958, 45-47; J.M. Sasson, "Numbers 5 and the 'Waters of Judgement," *BZ* 16 (1972) 249-51. The fullest study is that of Tiqva Frymer-Kensky, *The Judicial Ordeal in the Ancient Near East*. Ph.D. Dissertation, Yale, 1977, summarized in *IDB Suppl.* 638-40.

293 Codex Hammurapi §132, using the divine river to be the judge. The result was often drowning, since the person usually did not know how to swim, CAD N/1 374 b, 2'.

294 M.H. Pope, "Oaths," in *IDB* III 575-77; S.H. Blank, "The Curse, the Blasphemy, the Spell and the Oath." *HUCA* 23 (1950-51) 73-95.

295 A. Haldar, *Associations of Cult Prophets*, passim.

CHAPTER FOUR

Officiants Who Interpret Fertility and Sexuality

4.1 Fertility and Sexuality

Discussing our Category IV of the Introduction, this will be the longest chapter and one towards which the others have been pointing. It will consist of two studies intertwined: A) a listing of officiants who symbolize, act out, pray for, rejoice in, and are part of the main purpose of the ancient cultus, that of ensuring the fertility of human and animal, that the next generation may continue on the face of the earth; B) a discussion of officiants who somehow act out in the drama of the cult the mysterious nature of human sexuality in its transnormal aspects: transvestite, bisexual, and homosexual. The first will be described in this chapter; the second will be brought into this chapter, but will appear in much more detail in Appendix 3.

It is perhaps only in an age when sexuality is taken seriously, studied and written about in sober analyses that such a study as ours can be done. Past scholars have attempted to describe what we do here, but they got the technical terms for types of sexual style somewhat mixed up, and their studies sometimes turn out to be rather garbled.

4.2 Sexuality Human and Divine -- The Lexical Evidence

We start, as usual, with the lexical lists, and we are surprised how much space in them is taken up with the type of office symbolizing sexuality. The following list "most resembles the Old Babylonian ones" (MSL XII 16), noting only selected lines:

30 ÙH-INANNA
51 lukur
72a nin-dingir
73 dam-dingir
74 AMA.^{d}INANNA
135 nu-gig
137 nunuz-gig (for nunuz, see Sec. 1.19.3 and n. 208 in chap 1)
155 SAL.UŠ

ED Lu E MSL XII 17-19

Some of these are given a context, and many more are added, in an OB List:

225 nin-dingir-^{d}nin-urta
230 egi-zi
231 egi-zi-an-na
232 nin-dingir
232a [nin-dingir-^{d}nin]-urta
254 ÙH-^{d}INANNA
255 ŠIṬA-^{d}INANNA
256 GIŠ.BU-ud
257 lukur
258 lukur-gal

259 lukur-^{d}nin-urta
260 ama-lukur-ra
261 munus
262 ^{nu}nunus
263 lukur$^{na\text{-}di\text{-}tum}$
264 lukur$^{q\acute{a}\text{-}di\text{-}i\check{s}\text{-}tum}$
265 lukur$^{ba\text{-}tu\text{-}ul\text{-}tum}$
266 dub-za-lá
267 SAL dub-za-lá

OB Proto-Lu MSL XII 41-44

708 SAL lú -ŠI[M]
708d SAL suh[ur-lá]
708e SAL ki-zé-er-ak
709 SAL KA-HAR-ak
710 SAL šu-gi$_4$
710a lukur-kaskal
711 dam-banda$_3$^{da}
712 nam-lukur
713 kar-kid
714 kar-kid-mu-gub
715 kar-kid-suhub$_2$-s[i]
716 kar-kid-gi-te-t[e]
717 kar-a-[ak]

OB Proto-Lu MSL XII 58f

These lists essentially provide an index for the titles studied below. The *entu* and *ugbabtu*, both being represented by the ideogram nin-dingir, have been discussed in chapter 1, but in the present chapter they must be brought in again to be related to other officiants described here.

4.3 lukur (SAL + ME)/*nadītu*

4.3.1 This office is well known from OB times, but is little known earlier than Ur III. B. Landsberger[1] explains the Akkadian word as meaning "fallow." The title lukur appears on ED Lu E, Sec. 4.2, and also, with no context, on an onyx strip in what Harris[2] says is the time of Ur-Nanshe: lukur DUMU.DUMU.DUN

In OAkk times, the *nadītum* appears on a seal: Bulalatum *marat* Datinanum *nadīt* ^{d}Ištaran (KA.DI).[3] In Ur III times the term appears often. We find the seals of a lukur of Shulgi[4] and two lukur's of Shu-Sin.

One is of Tiamat-bašti,[5] the other of Kubatum or Dabbatum,[6] both described as "beloved lukur of Shu-Sin." The latter is the singer in[7] and presumed author of two balbale hymns to Shu-Sin in emesal, with possible relationship to the "sacred marriage," see Sec. 4.23. The first has been translated often[8] as has the second.[9] The writer is referred to as sà-bi-tum-ma (line 18) "Schankwirtin, female innkeeper" a loan-word from Akkadian *sābītu* (f.) See Sec. 4.16 for possible sexual connotations of this title.

A long list of PNs published by A.L. Oppenheim[10] has numbers, 30, 20, 2/3 in front of most names, and the similar Rochester tablet has numbers from 3 to 24. The Oppenheim tablet has some ununderstandable words following some of the PNs apparently indicating professions: IB, BI, ŠÙ, ŠE, SI, BA, GU, MU, ÚR, AR, GAR, MA, GI, HA, TAG, ZA. The Rochester tablet has ŠE, GU, TUR, KAŠ$_4$. The women are not entitled except in the Schneider tablet, where in 296:62 it lists them as lukur ^{d}šara. Here then is a valuable long list of lukur's, copied often.

There are lukur's of the king who may be understood as "king's priestly wife"[11] or "king's consort"[12] and discussed by P. Steinkeller.[13] He gives a list of royal lukur's on p.84 n. 44. Other lukur's are attested only in connection with male deities (n. 47). Steinkeller gives the names of 9 of them in Pre-Sargonic Lagash. They could be married and have children. Gudea CylB xi 3-14 (*Harps*...434) gives the names of 7 divine lukur's. Steinkeller suggests (n. 47) that the earthly lukur's were the counterpart of the heavenly ones. Jacobsen *Harps*...(p.435 n. 38) says that they were rain-cloud goddesses.

One of the most important of the royal lukur's is a certain Shulgi-simti/tum appearing in many Ur III tablets, summarized by S.T. Kang.[14] She appears from Shulgi 32 on. She is entitled lukur-kaskal-lá-ka-ni "lukur of his (Shulgi's ?) journey" on a seal.[15]

If all these are of the same person, she was a lukur of Shulgi[16] sometimes designated as a lukur-kaskal-la "lukur of the journey."[17] This brings together lukur and lukur-kaskal-la. Later lexical texts explain lukur-kaskal as *šugētu*, Sec. 4.4.1 We would like to know the relationship of this to the entry dam-kaskal = *še-e'-i-tum* MSL V 15, 93 "spouse of the road:"[18]

92 dam-bàn-da	*še-e'-i-tum*	"second or temporary wife"
93 dam-kaskal		"mistress associated with while on a journey"

Hh I MSL V 15
(Benno Landsberger's translations)

This "spouse of the road" may be the same as "woman of the street," i.e., prostitute.

A literary letter of Nin-ša-ta-pada "lady summoned (or found) from the heart" (p. 32)[19] to the conqueror of that dynasty, Rim Sin of Larsa, begs him to restore her to the cultic duties at Uruk, just as Enheduanna begged 400 years earlier.

4.3.2 When we come to OB times, the lukur is read in Akkadian as *naditum*, and we may use a series of studies by Rivkah Harris,[20] perhaps one of the fullest studies of one office in one site in all of Assyriology. We must not however make the assumption that the *nadītum* of OB times fulfills the same role as the lukur of earlier times.[21]

We know a great deal more about the later *nadītum*. In fact, the researches of Harris show us the office in so much detail that we suspect that if we knew as much about other officiants our picture of them would be greatly changed. To begin with, there were two kinds of *nadītu*'s, that of Shamash and that of Marduk. The *nadītu* of Shamash was not permitted to marry, and dwelt in a special cloister called the *gagû*, which was probably in the temple complex.[22] They were not permitted sexual relations.

R Harris does not want to call them priestesses, since "we know of no rites or ritual which they and they alone were qualified to perform."[23] Hers, however, was a religious role. She prayed for others.[24] She gave offerings to Aya, the spouse of Shamash, and her family god.[25] She gave the *piqittu* -offerings of food to the temple of Shamash.[26] In general she came from the upper classes of society, princesses or daughters of high officials, but were not exclusively the former as were the en-priestesses, Sec. 1.19. *šangû*'s were the first witnesses in almost all the legal texts of the *nadītum*'s, indicating these high cultic officials' concern for the outcome of these transactions.[27] She was present, perhaps daily, and for long periods of time, in the sanctuary.[28] She kept a household with a large staff, and carried on a great deal of business. She could not have children, but she may adopt them, or have them by a second wife or a child-bearer.[29]

The *nadītu* of Marduk could marry, and was not cloistered.[30] But she could only have children by other means, as causing her husband to marry a younger sister who would bear for her. In this instance the woman was called a *šugētu*[31] The *šugētu* was thus not a member of a special class, but see Sec. 4.4.

4.3.3. We now have to speak of a number of these offices together; we will give them special sections of their own later. For a while we must juggle a number of balls in the air at one time, i.e., speak of some offices without defining them further. They are:

nadītu	*kulmašītu*
šugētu	*ištarītu*
qadištu	

The social roles of some of these were related in OB times, as discovered in contracts. In the later period of Ammi-ditana (17th c. B.C.E.) the same married person was a *nadītu* of Marduk and a *kulmašītu*.[32] A *qadištu* bought land from a *nadītu*.[33]

The *šugētu* also appears in close connection with the *nadītu* on a later NA lexical list, Lu = ša IV, Sec. 4.4.1. In Sippar her position was dependent upon that of the *nadītu* of Marduk, usually her sister.[34] In Codex Hammurapi the *šugētu* is treated with the *nadītu* in §§ 144-145, and 137 and in 183-184, and paralleling the law of the *nadītu* in 182. In § 145 the *šugētu* is brought into the house of a man already married to a *nadītu*,[35] who has not provided him with sons, for the purpose of producing for him. She shall remain on a status lesser than that of the *nadītu,* a secondary wife. Independently, the *šugētu* has inheritance rights, according to CH §§ 183-4.

The severe punishment of burning meted out by Codex Hammurapi §108 to any *nadītu* or *ugbabtu* (nin-dingir) living outside the *gagû* who opens a *bīt sībim* (É.KURUN) "ale house" or enters a *bīt sībim* for ale may be due to actual or possible sexual offences.[36] This reminds us of the practices carried out at the *bīt aštamme*, discussed in Appendix 4. Is this designed to keep them from practicing their role anywhere else but in the prescribed place, or is this to keep them out of danger? One suspects the former.

4.3.4 The practices at Mari may be somewhat different, and we deal with them separately here. An untitled high functionary sent a servant and a *nadītum* to the king.[37] A *nadītum* appears among 6 male and female recipients of bread rations.[38]

4.3.5 The intertwining of some of these offices is shown on the OB Proto-Lu list, Sec. 4.2. Lukur is not the regular sign for *qadištum* (see Sec. 4.11) nor for *batultum* "girl," but here the scribes were indicating a relationship between the *nadītu* and these two, and *batultum* has not yet been found as an office, though it appears again among other offices on Lu = ša I, Excerpt II, line 37, Sec. 4.6.1. The lexical lists sometimes relate disparate offices, for reasons I do not understand. Perhaps this is saying that the *nadītu* could also either be a *qadištu* or a "girl."

In a NB text praising Marduk[39] after a half-line describing the NIN.DINGIR.RA's who sin against their husbands (Sec. 4.11.10) it mentions the *nadītu*'s who skillfully kept the foetus (lit. "the womb"), then the *qadištu*'s who do...with *mê tēlilte* "water for purification."[40] The section of *Maqlû* III 44ff which warns against various kinds of female witches was discussed in Sec. 3.20.5, and includes the *nadītu*. Some of this Category IV combination of officials also appears in *Shurpu*[41] in a section calling upon a number of deities to release the patient from his "oath" Among the "oaths" are those of the cultic figures *mārat ili /ilāni* "daughter of the god/gods," ^{d}Kù-bi (an office, apparently named for the goddess or the demon[42]), *ugbabtu*, *nadītu*, *qadištu*, *kulmašītu*. Usually the expression is ^{d}Kubi/u *ša* "of" the *entu*, but III.117 has *ù* "and" the *entu* (NIN.DINGIR.RA).

We are surprised to find some high-level categories such as *qadištu*, *nadītu, istarītu* and *kulmasītu* following the disparaged type of witch.

There is no masculine correspondent.

4.4 šu-gi$_4$ (-a) /*šugētu*

4.4.1 Stepping gingerly into this morass of similar titles, we note the entry SAL šu-gi$_4$ = *šugētu* next on OB Proto-Lu line 710 Sec. 4.2, found also on the more complex Lu = ša list, composed later but perhaps in part going back to OB times:

22 ^{d}inanna	*na-di-tu*
23 [SAL] ME$^{lu\text{-}kur}$	MIN
24 [SAL] ME	*šu-gi-tu*
25 [SAL] ME	*te-li-tu*
26 [SAL] ME-gal	SU-*lu*
27 [SAL] ME -^{d}Utu	*en-ti* ^{d}šamaš
28 [SAL] ME-kaskal	*šu-gi-tu*
29 [ama] -lukur	MIN
30 [x] -⌈ x ⌉- lukur	*sa-hi-ip-tu*
-------------------------------------	
31 [nu-gig]	*qa-diš-tu*

(32-34 are equivalences to *qadištu*, broken in the ideogram column)

Lu = ša IV MSL XII 129

Lines 23 and 24 link the *šugētu* to the *nadītu*, as noted above. The *tēlitu* is usually an adjective applied to Ishtar: "the highly capable one," but the layout here would indicate an office *tēlitu* in itself. It could be shorthand for *ša tēlitim*, one who plays the *tēlitum*:

251 lú balag-balag-di *ša [te-li-tim]* (See Sec. 2.1.2.54)
252 lú balag?-di *ṣa-r [i-hum]*
OB Lu A MSL XII 165

but we have no evidence of the *nadītu* playing a musical instrument. [SAL]ME-gal would be *lukurgallu*, "chief *naditu,*" and the dictionaries give this as the only entry. The *sahiptu* with root *s-h-p* is so far found only here.[43] Recalling the lukur-kaskal-lá-ka-ni "lukur of his (Shulgi's ?) journey" on a seal mentioned Sec. 4.3.1, we find the term continuing on the lexical lists contiguous to the *šugētu*, OB Proto-Lu, Sec. 4.2, line 710, and Lu = ša IV immediately above as an equivalent.

Other lexical lists show how the ancients related her to several other offices;

188 a-ma-[lu] [AMA.LUL] *a-ma-li-tú*
iš-ta-ri-tú
šu-gi-tú
Diri IV CAD A/2 2a

The *amalītu* and the *ištarītu* will be discussed below, Secs. 4.13 and 4.12 respectively. Turning now to the OB Proto-lu, Sec. 4.2, the SAL ki-zé-er-ak is a semi-ideogram for *kezertu*, discussed in Sec. 4.6. šu-gi$_4$ is the usual ideogram for *šugētu*, lukur is the familiar *naditu* who appears often in conjunction with these. kar-kid is usually *harimtu* "prostitute," and what she is doing here as an office under this title is discussed in Sec. 4.14. Thus the *šugētu*'s appear with the other offices having sexual connotations.

In a rich "sacred marriage" hymn of Iddin-Dagan in the Isin period discussed in App. 3.5.3, Sec. 4.23.4, among those who "walk before" Inanna are players on instruments, sag-ur-sag's, those who are transvestites, the kur-gar-ra's and the šu-gi$_4$-a's who are maidens, and are coiffured (?).[44] Hair can be a sexual attraction, and the note ties this to the office *kezertu*, Sec. 4.6.

There is a reference to hair, a sexual one, in a medical prescription. One of the items used is "hair from the genital area of a *šugītu* "[45]

The šu-gi$_4$-a are termed ki-sikil "maidens" in the Iddin-Dagan text. One is the younger sister of a *nadītu* in CH.[46] At Mari, a letter about a *ṣuhartum* (SAL.TUR) "young woman" who is a *šu-gi-tum*, describes her as living *ina bītim* "in a temple."[47] "If that *ṣuhartum nuzzumat* 'complains'..." the letter goes on. The "complaining" is usually secular, but can be to a god. Here she complains about the *tēritim* "présages."

In a hemerology:[48] ^{22}*ana* ^{d}GIR *liškēn mahhâ liššiq* "to Sumukan let him worship, the *mahhû* let him kiss"...^{25} ^{mí}šu-gi *liššiq* " the *šugētu* let him kiss." The kissing may have meant sexual intercourse.[49]

In an OB text[50] listing marriage gifts of jewelry, vessels and furniture, a PN *šugītum* appears, the decision about the gifts being made *ina bīt Annunitum* "in the temple of Annunitum."

4.4.2 The *šugētum* who is found in texts with sexual connotations, as in the Biggs reference, the kissing text and in general the offices surrounding her on the lexical lists, does not seem to be the same as that of CH, the sister or substitute wife for the *naditum*. Maybe the usage of the term at Sippar is different from that elsewhere,[51] but there is a temple setting in the latter case.

4.5 [ ] lukur / *sahiptu*

Among female offices all of which have lukur in the title, there is

29 [ama] -lukur MIN (=*šu-gi-tu*)
30 [x] -⌈ x ⌉-lukur *sa-hi-ip-tu*

Lu = ša IV MSL XII 129

with a root *sahāpu* "throw about, throw down, cover over, overwhelm, etc." (CAD S 32) which does not help towards the meaning.

4.6 LÚ.SUHUR.LÁ./*kezru* and MÍ SUHUR.LÁ /.*kezertu*

4.6.1 OB Proto-Lu 708d-e (Sec. 4.2) is one of the few examples of a relationship between suhur-lá and *kezertu*.[52] Suhur-lá indicates "wearer of (a special type of) head-hair," and the root *kezeru* "to curl the hair," seems to indicate that the special hair-do is a curled one (in a specially sexually attractive way?)

An entry in Lú = ša is like the passages in the OB Proto-Lu:

32 SAL guruš-tur	*ba-tul* -[*tum*]
33 nir-mú-mú-ir	*qu-un-nu*-[*x*]
34 su$_6$-lá	*ziq-na-n*[*u*]
34 suhur-lá	MIN
36 ki-sikil	*ar-da-tum*
37 ki-sikil-tur	*ba-tul-tum*
38 ú-zuh	*ú-suk-ku*
39 kar-kid	*ha-rim-tú*

Lú = ša I Excerpt II
MSL XII 105

The *ziqnānu* "bearded one," and the suhur-lá, then relates to a hair-do, apparently a curled beard.

4.6.2 The various orthographies are: *kezertu, kezretu, kazratu.* To translate simply as "prostitute" (CAD K 314), or "Dirne mit Kizirtu Haartracht" (AHw 468b), indicating the street prostitute that word conjures up in our society is to oversimplify and neglect the cultic aspects, yet "odalisques of the royal harem"[53] is too exotic, and to translate "sacred prostitute" is to go beyond the evidence, and to bring up all the problems associated with this so-called "institution." (Sec. 4.22)

4.6.3 We have seen that *kezertu* is associated with *šugetu* and kar-kid = *harimtu* in OB Proto-Lu (Sec. 4.2). In Sumerian times a daughter of a PN ke-zé-er in-ak "acts like a *kezertu,* " "sang songs" and "played games."[54]

In a long list of nar's one is the nar-igi-suhur-lá "the nar-singer who comes before the suhur-lá."[55] A procession is envisioned here, just as a procession is pictured in the "sacred marriage" hymn of Iddin-Dagan, in which among those who "walk before the pure Inanna" are the šu-gi$_4$-a's, Sec. 4.23.4, 70.

In NA times the *kezertu* was part of the Ishtar cult: in a penalty clause to a contract one who contends against it must give 7 LÚ.SUHUR.LÁ.MEŠ 7 MÍ.SUHUR.LÁ.MEŠ to Ishtar of Arbela.[56] But what is a male LÚ.SUHUR.LÁ ? He is shown on two lexical lists:

388	lú	suhur	*ša qi$_4$-ma-tim*
389	lú	suhur-lá	*ke-ez-rum*
390	lú	ke-zé-er-ak	*ke-ez-rum*
391	lú	su-sag-dug$_4$-ga	*uz-zu-bu-ú*

OB Lu A MSL XII 169

lines 388-390 being repeated in OB Lu C$_5$ 19-21, MSL XII 195. CAD K lists a NA Tell Billa usage in Sibanibe.[57] One cannot find the phenomenon of males as prostitutes elsewhere so, by a round-about reasoning, I doubt that this office is equivalent to "(street) prostitute."

4.6.4 She comes to life in a note that she could be married.[58] A NB(?) contract describes the ^{mí}*kizretu* as making a payment, with a *qāti nasāhu* "keeping away the claim" phrase.[59] If several OB texts studied together refer to the *kezertu*, for the title does not appear, she owed certain duties or services.[60] The sexual activity called *harimūtum* on one of those texts reminds us of the later association of the *kezretu's* with prostitution.(see immediately below).[61] The *kizretu* is listed with the *šamhatu* and *harimtu* (in unusual orthographies) as KAR.KID "prostitute" on one lexical list:

31	*ša-am-ka-tu$_4$ /tum*	KAR.KID
32	*ša-mu-uk-tu$_4$ /tum*	"
33	*ha-ar-ma-tu$_4$ /tum*	"
34	*ha-ri-im-tu$_4$ /tum*	"
35	*ka-az-ra-tu$_4$ /tum*	"
36	*ki-iz-ri-tu$_4$ /tum*	"

CT 18, 19 (K. 107)

This list is known for giving something wider than "equivalents," but titles are grouped in general areas.

The Erra Epic IV.52, in a unique section describes Uruk as a city of *kezertu*'s, *šamhatu*'s and *harimtu*'s. These are the same three in the same order as those assembled by Ishtar to wail over the dead Bull of Heaven.[62] This emphasizes the sexuality, perhaps the virility of the Bull of Heaven. One sexually active person recognizes another. In Erra Ishtar deprives these of husbands, and puts them under their own authority. (Cagni, IV.53).[63] We will return to this text again, for it is most instructive. It shows that *kezertu's* could be married. It criticizes them, which occurs sometimes with other female Category IV officiants. If they are from the Ishtar cult, why are they criticized? Perhaps this is part of the cultic drama, in which their role is to be criticized. The plot of this drama is fairly regular. There is distress in the city. The singers sing of it. The holy places are destroyed and the gods scattered. The lamenter remembers the details of the city. The cultic officials no longer act. Enlil has done this -- how long will it be? A main theme seems to be the calming of the heart of the destroying god. For literature with this or part of this plot, see Lamentation Over the Destruction of Ur, Eršemma's, and Cohen's Lamentations.

4.6.5 A series of proverbs from late Assyrian texts having to do with objects of criticism or law-breakers describes *kazratu* as a slanderer of the *šarraptu* at Ishtar's command.[64]

A relationship with the *ištarītu* comes with an OB letter, which orders the *ištarītu*'s of Emutbalum to be brought to Babylon in the same ship as some *kezertu*'s with provisions for both.[65]

Alster[66] finds a proverb which he read munus.gù.mur.ak KA x LI gi_4-gi_4-dam and translates "the professional mourner(?) shouts again and again." He suggested "profesional mourner" because of context. The reading is not likely to be gù-mur-ak = *qar-du-um* "hero" (MSL XIII 246), nor zú-hur-ak "one able to bite with his teeth" (CAD s.v. *zaqtu*?). It is better to refer to:

708d	SAL	suh[ur-lá]
708e	SAL	ki-zé-er-ak
709	SAL	KA-HAR-ak
710	SAL	šu-gi_4

OB Proto-Lu MSL XII 58

in which SAL suhur-lá is the *kezertu*, SAL ki-zé-er-ak is a semi-ideogram for *kezertu*, SAL šu-gi_4 = *šugetu* and SAL KA-HAR-ak is an office similar to these, which can be read ^{mí}gù-mur-ak.

4.6.6 On a distribution list at Mari[67] there appear together the female offices of *kezretu*, *sekretu,* female scribes, *kisalluhatu*, and [SAL.N]AR.TUR.TUR "very minor or apprentice singers." That all appear on the same tablet perhaps shows their similar position.

Once the king personally asks for a *kezertum* to be sent.[68] She is described as *nawirtim* "fair / pretty / fine."

A MA text,[69] summarized in Sec. 1.2.6, is a *ginû* offering (r. 22) which King Tukulti-Ninurta I gives for the goddess Sharrat-nipha[70] in Kar-Tukulti-Ninurta (25). The text lists *bīt* ⸢DUMU⸣ *šarri bīt redûti* (6) "the household of the crown prince of the dwelling of the crown prince." Bread, meat, honey, salt, oil, beer, hides, wine are bound as an obligation for the *šangû*'s of Sharrat-nipha and the *šangû's* of the Bit-eqî as well as the state amd temple oficials, including *kezretu*'s and DUMU.MEŠ.SAL.SUHUR.LÁ.MEŠ. Are we simply to understand the latter literally as the "sons of the *kezertu*'s" or are these some apprentice *kezertu*'s or are these of the household of the *kezertu*'s who help in some way? A similar expression is found above, see n. 58.

Postgate *Royal Grants* has a text like this,[71] it too is a *ginû* offering (20') with among other things copper (copper is also in Ebeling *Stiftungen*), the *bīt kadmuri* (in *Stiftungen, bīt redûte*, a similar term), cuts of meat in both texts, the king -- actually several kings -- is the subject of both, the *bit eqî* temple chamber (CAD E 253b) appears in both, the *šan* [*gû*] appears in a broken context once (in *Stiftungen* it is the *šangû* of Belet-nipha and the *šangû* of *bīt eqî*).

What interests us about the two is that the latter Royal Grant also lists the DUMU.MEŠ. SAL.SUH[UR.LÁ.MEŠ] (3') but in a broken context. Three lines later we find *ša muhhi* SAL.SUHUR.LÁ.MEŠ, the overseer of these persons. Van Driel shows how little we know of this office.[72] The cultic aspect is shown by the *kezretu*'s being associated with the *šangû* of a goddess.

In some "love lyrics," in a NA ritual of Zarpanitum, the reciter's hair is *muššurat*"flowing," reminding us of the *kezertu*, but there is no readable title; she is an *in-du-x* (line 9). She is hostile to Ishtar of Babylon.[73] We are trying to be cautious in a conclusive "description" of these officials, since we need many more references, and many from the same place and time, but we can say that the *kezertu* may fulfill some sort of prostitute role in an assumed drama of the Ishtar cult, but no specifically cultic acts have been discovered. One of Ishtar's roles is that of prostitute.[74]

The *kezertu* could be married. She was of a high enough rank to have direct contact with the king, yet there were several of them in one place. As were other woman officiants in our Category IV, she was sometimes criticized in her office.

4.7.ŠEŠ/*sekretu*

4.7.1 CAD, s.v.: l) A woman of high rank, possibly cloistered; 2) a woman of the palace household, a court lady. AHw:"'Abgesperrte', eine Frauenklasse." It could also be spelled *sekertu.*

As early as OAkk times, there was a list of 8 PNs, 3 of whom were *kulu'u*'s and 5 *sekertu*'s (ŠEŠ.SAL).[75]After this the rank starts appearing in OB times:

156c ugula-na-kam-tum
156d ugula-zi-ik-ru-um
156e ugula-dag-si-ru-um

OB Proto-Lu MSL XII 38

The root indicates a"separate, confined" woman, perhaps indicating a cloister. Earlier it was incorrectly read as SAL *zikrum,*[76] and explained as "woman-man," i.e., a hermaphrodite, but this is a pseudo-ideogram (SAL) ZI.IK.RU.

4.7.2 As we have seen from the Codex Hammurapi, certain female officials could be dedicated by their father to a deity. These include the *kulmašītu*, *nadītu*, *qadištu*, *sekertu* and *ugbabtu*.[77] CH also has a section[78] related to the *seriktu* "dowry" of three possible cases: *ugbabtu* (nin-dingir), *nadītu*, or *sekretu* and their rights of disposal of the inherited property. There is one Sippar reference.[79] In a Mari text, [80] the *kezretum*, *sekertum* and *kisalluhhatum* appear together on a food distribution list.

In an extispacy text, the *sekretu* acts to undo *kišpu* "witchcraft."[81] The *sekertu* is several times mentioned as *narāmtu* "beloved" of the king.[82] In a section with female titles, ranks and offices, no cultic areas show up:

6' [SAL kar] -re	*ek-ki-im-tu*	"female thief"
7' [SAL] UL	*qàt-ti-tu*	
8' [SAL] -ra	*ša* LUH *šu qa-a-tu*	
9' [SAL]	[*sek*] *-re-tu*	
10' SAL$^{\text{si-iš}}$šeš	*sek-re-tu*	
11 [SAL]	[*sek*]- *re-tu*	
12 SAL$^{\text{an-du-ul}}$an-dùl	*sek-re-tu*	an-dùl / *andullu* "canopy, cover, protection"
13 SAL zi-ik] -ru	*sek-re-tu*	

14 SAL	(síg)-peš$_5$] -ak-a	*na-pi-eš-tu*	"a woman carding wool" CAD N/1 304b
15 [SAL	GA.ZUM] -ak-a	*ha-li-eš-tu*	"female wool plucker" CAD H 43a Lu = ša III ii MSL XII 124f

We find therefore that on many lists no actions of a cultic nature are mentioned, but on others this office is listed along with other cultic officials. No male counterpart has shown up.

4.8 nu-bar/*kulmašītu*

4.8.1 We start with a late period text to set the sexual tone, already having given several entries in sections in this chapter, especially noting the pairing nu-gig-nu-bar. It is in the preserved top part of a NB letter.[83] The writer Belit-balati, and the editor thinks it "highly probable" that she was a goddess (a type of scribal literary tradition) called ^{d}Ma-nun-gal (5'), calls herself, in a broken section, *nadītum*(6') and *kulmašītum* (7'). She has opened her *lib /piššatu* "vulva," and called for the recipient to touch her *handuttu* "genitals." The recipient probably was a *laputtû "steward"* of Nabu.

In Sec. 4.3.3 it was noted that some *nadītu* s of Marduk in OB times were also *kulmašītu*'s and were married.[84] A *kulmašītu* appears in a record of fields belonging to a *nadītu*.[85]

The *kulmašītu* was uncloistered, and could marry. The name of a god never appears associated with this title, but a father can dedicate his daughter as a *nadītum*, a *qadištum* or a *kulmašītum ana ilim* "to a god."(See n.77). Some could come from wealthy families. They could engage in business.

4.8.2 In a text[86] which looks like Ur III script to the editor, a conjuration against the demon Samana treated the healthful functioning of the menstrual period of young women, and the virility of young men. Samana may interfere with that; in the immediately succeeding lines, the demon may hinder the nu-gig (*qadištu*) office and the nu-bar (*kulmašītu*) office. Again the sexual aspects are shown, but whether cult oriented or not is unclear.

In the so-called "Curse Upon Agade"[87] ama-mu-gig-ge ama-nu-bar-ra tu$_{18}$!-mu-ni mi-ni-in-gi$_4$-gi$_4$ "mother who is a nu-gig mother who is a nu-bar is to give back/answer/return[88] her children." Ama- is not in a genitive construction here.[89] An Ishtar hymn[90] relates ama mu-gib$_x$ to *um-mu iš-ta-ri-tum* on the preceding line. Ama as used in this way appears also on lexical lists:

AMA.^{d}INANNA	ED Lu E 74, MSL XII 18
ama-lukur-ra	OB Proto-Lu 260, MSL XII 42]
28 entries ama-	OB Proto-Lu 319ff, MSL XII 44f
a-ma-l[u] [AMA.^{d}INNIN} = *a-ma-li-tu*, *iš-ta-ri-tu*	Diri IV 188, CAD I-J 270b, lexical section
[ama-uru] = [*um-mi*] URU	Lu = ša III iv 5', MSL XII 127
13 entries ama-	Lu = ša III iv 51ff, MSL XII 127

Also cf. Ama-ušumgal-an-na as name of Dumuzi, see Sec. 4.23.4 line 187, or any one of many myths in the Inanna-Dumuzi cycle. The use of ama in these entries varies from descriptive to titular, some cultic, some not so. This could very well be the aspect of "mother" in the cultic drama, but evidence must be collected on this.

The nu-gig, sometimes appearing as nu-u$_8$-gig, appears with the nu-bar in texts as well as lexical lists:

nu-u$_8$-gig-ra mùš-kéš-di	"who binds the mùš-headgear on the nu-gig
nu-bar-ra ubur-imin-e si sá-sá-e	"who causes the nu-bar to make flow the seven breasts"

STVC 48 ii 16f and duplicates,
A. Falkenstein, *ZA* 56 (1964) 120
Sjöberg Temple Hymns 30,389f

Mùš is written with the Inanna sign perhaps because it is a part of the Inanna cult. It is worn by the en priestess, and is parallel to men "crown." so is possibly a hat.[91] Sjöberg follows CAD Ṣ s.v. *ṣurṣuppu* in finding ubur-imin "seven teats" as a vessel-name, and si sá-sá as "(make) flow," as the teats of a cow. In any case, the nu-bar, as the nu-gig, provides fertility. This is parallel to the function of the nu-gig as wet-nurse. This is a motherhood aspect, unrelated to the erotic aspect. But in the divine nature of Inanna/Ishtar the cultic and the societal come together.

In CH § 181 (Sec. 4.11.5) the *nadītu qadištu kulmašītu* come together in the example of a father who dedicates his daughter to a god.

4.8.3 In OB times this official shows up as a geographical name: u[ru]ki-nu-bar-ra^{ki}.[92]

4.8.4 Already it has been noted that the wisdom literature especially collects disparaging remarks about certain female ranks. One of these texts is placed originally in the Kassite period, but was popular in late Assyrian and Babylonian copies: *e tahhuz harimtuša sâri mutuša* "do not marry a *harimtu* whose husbands are 3600," *ištarītu ša ana ili zakrat* "an *ištarītu* who has been dedicated to a god," *kulmašītu šá qerebša ma'da* "a *kulmašītu* who often draws near someone."[93] I interpret this last phrase to indicate sexual purposes.

In lexical lists there are no appearances earlier than NA:

193	gašan	*be-e[l-tum]*
194	nin-dingir-ra	*en -[tum]*
195	nin-dingir-ra	*ug-bab-tum*
196	nu-gig	*qa-diš-tum*
197	nu-bar	*kul-ma-ši-tum*
198	gudu$_4$-abzu	ŠU-*u*

Lu = ša I, Excerpt I MSL XII 102

In the emesal vocabulary

76 gašan-dìm-me-ir	nin-dingir	*ug-[bab-tu]*
77 gašan-dìm-me-ir	nin-dingir	xy[z]
78 m[u-g] ib$_x$	nu-gig	*qa-áš -[da-tu]*
79 [mu-gib$_x$]	nu-gig	*iš-ta-r [i-tu]*
80 [mu-gib$_x$-gašan-an-na]	[n]u-[gig]^{d}inanna	"
81	[ama]-^{d}inanna	*a -⌈ma⌉-lu*

82	[n]u-bar	*kul -[ma-ši-tu]*
83	[SA]L.ME	x - [xx(x)]

MSL IV 17f Tabl. II

The *qadištu* is to be studied thoroughly in Sec. 4.11, and will appear more and more frequently in our documentation, often close to the *kulmašītu*. gašan is emesal for *bēltu* "lady." *entu* and *ugbabtu* share the same signs nin-dingir and the same place in some documents in NA times, which creates a problem of identification. nu-gig and nu-bar are somehow related, but the meaning of the signs is still not agreed upon,[94] *qadištu* and *ištarītu* share the same sign, nu-gig. *amalu* is usually a term for "goddess," (CAD A/2 1). but here it is among titles, so perhaps here it is also a title (See Sec. 4.13). In the last two lines, *kulmašītu* is next to SAL.ME = lukur = *nadītu.*

In the lists of witches from *Maqlû* III 44f we have mentioned often (Sec. 3.20.5 for comments), the *kulmašitu* is among them, in the list in an order *qadištu, nadītu, ištarītu, kulmašītu*. Similarly, a series of oaths in *Shurpu* VIII, Sec. 4.3.5 have somewhat this same list of officiants, including *kulmašītu*.

The evil image of these is indicated. This shows that in NA times these officiants were all thought of in the same category, and it was negative. This text does not describe the reasons these were thought of negatively, but previous lines describe wrongdoings, and the implication is that by their very nature they did these wrongs.

A case in late documents in which some female officiants are together and are looked at positively occurs in the Neo-Assyrian version of the Gilgamesh Epic, which at places is different from the OB recension. Ninsun, Gilgamesh's mother, speaks to Enkidu, Gilgamesh's friend of...(then, in the plural) *ugbabtu's* (NIN.DINGIR.RA.MEŠ), *qadištu's* and *kulmašītu's*.[95] These seem to be in apposition to the previous line, i.e., among the *širku's* are these officiants. To symbolize this Ninsun placed the *indu's*[96] on Enkidu's neck. For *širku* see Sec. 1.43.

As with many of the female ranks, the *kulmašītu* sings *inhu* songs[97] along with the *kurgarrû* and probably (in the break) the *assinnu*.

4.9 nin-dingir-(ra)/*ugbabtu* /*gubabtu* or *entu*

4.9.1 Immediately there are some detection problems. As was mentioned previously, the *ugbabtu* and *entu* share the same sign pair, nin-dingir:

194	nin-dingir-ra	*en- [tum]*
195	nin-dingir-ra	*ug-bab-tum*

Lu = ša I MSL XII 102

5	[ni] n	*en-tu*
6	[nin]-dingir	MIN
7	[nin]-dingir	*gu-bab-tu*
8	[nin-^{d}]nin-urta	*en-ti ^{d}Nin-urta*
9	[nin-dingir]-^{d}Nin-urta	*gu-bab-ti MIN*

Lu = ša III MSL XII 124

Gubabtu is the Assyrian, mostly NA form of *ugbabtu*. CAD E 173a explains "that wherever nin-dingir refers to a priestess of high social standing, who is mentioned without reference to a specific deity, it should be rendered by *entu* ...OA and Mari offer exceptions."

The Sumerian signs could refer to "lady (who is) a deity/divine" or "lady of the deity, "the latter indicated when the full form nin-dingir-ra is used. One notes that in NA times the two offices of *entu* and *ugbabtu* were mixed up, maybe purposely. The two are so intertwined that there is the possibility that they merged into one rank from an original two, or are two words for the same, or are two officiants who perform almost identical duties. Let us keep all these possibilities in mind going through the many, though not sufficient, references to the *ugbabtu*.

As was discussed above in Sec. 1.19 under *entu*, the nin-dingir appears in the early lists:

72 AN:SAL:GIŠGAL
72a nin-dingir
73 dam-dingir
74 AMA.^{d}INANNA
(and so on with many cultic ranks)

ED Lu E MSL XII 18

An ED III seal[98] is of a woman named HE-kun-sig who is entitled nin-dingir ^{d}Pabilsag. There are two registers, the upper of which shows the seal and two seated facing persons who are eating, served by two servants, all having the same design skirts. Behind one of the seated persons stands another servant with clasped hands. The lower register shows a temple, towards which goes a procession of 6 figures of varying heights, some carrying vessels and some stick-like objects. Two vessels are on the ground. The meal is somehow related to the temple. The vessels and objects were probably cultic. If the scenes on the seal showed the named woman, as suggested on p. 118, that would be highly unusual.

The only woman mentioned in the reform of UruKAgina is the nin-dingir, who received a headband, being among the ensi, sanga, ludimma, gala, gudu, in a section on a reform of rations for cultic officials.[99]

4.9.2 CH §110 as well as texts from OB Kish[100] show that among others the nin-dingir/*ugbabtu* or *entu* normally lives in the *gagû*. In a section of CH §178, 179 the nin-dingir, *nadītum* and *sekretum* have rights of disposal of inherited property. As suggested above Sec. 4.3.3, the severe punishment of burning in CH §110 may be due to actual or possible sexual offences. In a rare case of the two mentioned together, in an OB liver omen the *e-en-tum* will die and an *ug-ba-ab-tum* will be installed.[101] This may indicate that the two officials are on the same level of authority. Nougayrol points out three hepatoscopy tablets[102] of the same type, the protasis of each starting DIŠ *naplastum*..."if the liver-mark..." One has to do with an *e-nu-um* and the others have to do with *ug-ba-ab-tam*$_5$, showing that the two offices were thought of similarly.

In some tablets listing the distribution of grain, bread, coarse or barley flour (dabin = *tappinnu*) and beer among the *šā'iltu*, "shepherd of the palace" and *bārû*, the *ugbantum* (the orthography here) is one of the recipients.[103] In a similar text,[104] *tappinu*-flour is used for the *kinūnum*-festival of Ishtar. This may refer to the cult, because of the mention of bread and beer *ina mūšim* "for the night" and *ina kaṣâtim* "for the morning." In a seven-day ritual at Larsa, offerings are made *ana* níg-gi$_6$ "for the night vigil" (line 42) and á-gú-zi-ga "in the morning." (line 63)[105]

In the Sippar texts[106] the *ugbabtu*'s are of Shamash. They inherit estates, and have UGULA's "stewards." Harris finds evidence indicating that they were cloistered.

nin-dingir is read *ugbabtum* at Mari, because the *entum* with full orthography does not appear in the Mari texts,[107] and the *ugbabtum* does.

Three tablets concerning sales of fields to *ugbabtum*'s are in the VAT collection.[108] One is an *ugbabtum* of Marduk of Babylon the other two *ugbabtum*'s of Zababa. Their names Bēlitu and Bēltāni provide the start of a pattern.[109] The last text has several ugula-nin-dingir-meš "overseers of the *ugbabtum*'s" for witnesses as well as an ì-du$_8$ "doorkeeper" of the *gagû*, the dwelling of the *ugbabtum*'s.

4.9.3 The myth of Inanna and Enki provides several cultic titles. In the main section, the me's "aspects of a civilization" are named. Directly after nam-sipa "shepherd-ship" and nam-lugal "kingship"(II v 9-10), the office of egí-zi heads the list of me's in a section of male and female officiants. The order is: [11]nam-egí-zi [12]nam-nin-dingir [13]nam-išib [14]nam-lú-mah [15]nam-gudu$_4$.

We know little about the *ugbabtu* (Assyrian *gubabtu*) in later Assyrian and Babylonian times: see the lexical examples: Lu = sa IV, Sec. 4.9.1, and the emesal vocabulary, Sec. 4.8.4. Maybe the office died out in NA times, or was absorbed into the *entu*.

4.9.4 Now that we have seen a few examples of the *ugbabtu* in action, let us return to the problem of the confusion with the *entu*. In both cases the signs are nin-dingir, but nin-dingir-ra shows up also. As was mentioned in Sec. 1.19.7, the *entu* almost drops from literature after OB times, with a few references at Nippur and Ur in MB times, but is reinstated by Nabû-na'id in NB times. The lexical lists continue both of these entries, however, and the Lu = ša list shows that many of the early lists were conflated. The NA scribes simply recorded the ambiguity, see Lu = ša I, Sec. 4.8.4.

Sec. 1.19.15 discusses a line in Atrahasis in which *ugbabtu*'s, *entu*'s and *igiṣītu*'s are together.

The Malku-šarru I text:

133	*šá-mu-uk-tum*	*qa-diš-tum*
134	*ug-bab-tum*	*en-tum*
135	*ug-bab-tum*	*as-sin-na-tum*

Malku = šarru I
CAD Q 48aE 172a

typically relates across the columns *ugbabtum* and *entum* (line 134) and surrounds them by the *qadištum* and the *assinnatum,* the last an oddity, see Secs. 4.11 and App. 3.2.7, respectively. A study of Malku = šarru will show that there are many such juxtapositions as this; for instance, we may not conclude that the *qadištu* is a kind of a *šamuktu* "prostitute" using this list alone.

4.9.5 Sexual deviations of this official appear in the literature, as they do about others mentioned in this book, but this is mainly in the wisdom or incantation literature. Many examples of hepatoscopies of an *ugbabtum* frequented by men are given by Nougayrol.[110] CAD H 31b quotes a case in which the NIN.DINGIR.RA.MEŠ will sin against their husbands.[111]

The extent of their "illicit sex" as one might call it is shown in a protasis of a text in the Neo-Assyrian Dream Manual:[112] "if a man does UM (Akkadian word and translation not clear) to among others Ishtar, a god, a king, nin-dingir, *mārat ili* "daughter of (his) god," other males and females..." If UM is *ṭehû* "draw near"[113] then this indicates sexual contact, and examples of heterosexuality and homosexuality appear together. It would be difficult to apply this reading to gods and kings, however.

4.10 egi-zi / *igiṣītu* // egi-zi-gal / *igiṣīgallatu*

4.10.1 Little is known of this office apart from the similarities we can postulate with those with whom it is mentioned: it is with the nin-dingir in OB Proto-Lu, Sec. 4.2. The several kinds are shown in:

17	[nin] ⌈^{d}⌉Sataran	um-muš-tu
18	[egi$^{(i)}$]-$^{gi\text{-}ṣi}$zi	ị-gi-ṣi-tu
19	[egi-z]i-gal	ŠU-tu
20	[egi-z]i-an-na	^{d}iš-tar ^{d}a-nim

Lu = ša IV MSL XII 129

So Ishtar of Anum is entitled egi-zi-an-na. The offices of the form R-an-na appear from time to time. Other exemplars are: é-an-na the temple of Enlil, nu-gig-an-na=MIN(*qadištu*)^{d}A-nim,Lu =ša IV 35; išib-an-na =*išip* ^{d}a-ni, Lu = ša IV 43; èn-du-an-na, OB Proto-Lu 601. Dumuzi is Ama-ušumgal-an-na in mythological texts. Thus in the examples we give here, it is the god An/Anu who is referred to, not "heaven," or "sky." Inanna herself is called nu-gig-an-na, Secs. 4.11.7, 4.11.15; *išarītu* of An, gašan-an-na in bilinguals, gašan = *ištarītu* here. is found towards end of Sec. 4.11.15. Is this another way of saying that Ishtar is the child of Anu?

As mentioned in OB Atrahasis, among the created beings that are to be tabooed or cursed so that they not bear children are the *ugbabtu*, the *entu* and the *igiṣītu* (III vii 6), perhaps a mythic way of expressing their inability or ineligibility in childbearing. The egí-zi heads the list of me's in a section of the myth Inanna and Enki.[114] Directly after the nam-sipa "shepherdship," nam-lugal "kingship," comes nam-egi-zi "*igiṣītu*-ship," nam-nin-dingir "*ugbabtu*-ship," nam-išib "*išippu*-ship," and nam-lú-mah "*lumahhu*-ship."

4.10.2 The *igiṣīgallatu* "chief *igiṣītu*" appears in Lu = ša IV 19, Sec. 4.10.1.

4.10.3 No masculine has yet been found for *igiṣītu*.

4.11 nu-gig/*qadištu* // nu-gig-gal // nu-gig-tur // LÚ.NU.GIG (once)

4.11.1 The nu-gig has already been referenced several times above. This will turn out to be the longest unit in the chapter because of the number of articles on the *qadištu,* because the cognate appears in Ugaritic and the Hebrew Bible, and so is one of the best known female cultic offices, and because, for some people, this office represents the quintessential "sacred prostitute." Something will be said about all of these aspects as space allows.

First, the orthography. *qadištu* is a f. adj. of the *paris* form[115] coming from a root *q-d-š* "holy," this root being found in noun and verb form in almost all Semitic languages; it is used also for goddess names and geographical names. The orthographic variants in Akkadian are *qadiltu*, *qadšatu*, *qašdatu*, and *qaššum*(?), the last a masculine form, which may or may not be the same word.[116]

Its Sumerogram nu-gig can refer to either *qadištu* or *ištarītu,* Sec. 4.8.4, emesal vocabulary. In OB times, when *ištarītum* is meant it is always spelled out, but how can we be sure that all the nu-gig references in the OB period are to be read *qadištum*? The meaning of the signs is a puzzle. gig could be *marṣu* "sick," or "something cut, as a block (of wood)," or "wound." nu could be *la* "not" or *lib /pištu* "membranous substance," "scrotum"(AHw), see n. 94. D.O. Edzard in a full study of this does not think it is a genitive construction, and that it does not mean "tabooed."[117] CAD I 270b translates *marsa*[*t*] as "tabooed."

4.11.2 An early reference is found on a Fara inscription.[118] Another early reference comes when a tablet of Mesannepadda king of Kish (ca. 2600-2550 B.C.E.) calls him dam-nu-gig "spouse of the nu-gig."[119] nu-gig appears on an Old Sumerian economic text.[120] She appears along with other cultic figures, of Categories I and IV--with breaks--in ED List E (Sec. 4.2).

As early as OAkk times we meet a married *qadištu,*[121] and we meet such in OB and NA times.

In the older texts the nu-gig appears to be a highly placed cultic person. The seal[122] of a dub-sar "scribe" is dedicated to Nin-kinda nu-gig-gal-urí-ki-ma "N. the chief nu-gig, or great nu-gig, of Ur." Edzard[123] chooses the latter.

An obscure sentence in the Lamentation Over the Destruction of Ur[124] has:mu-gib$_x$-mèn uru-mà uri-me-en sila-mà gir$_5$-me-en "I am the mu-gib (emesal for nu-gig), in my city I am an enemy, in my streets I am a stranger." In one of the standard plots of lamentations[125] the city of Tintir (Babylon) has been destroyed, and the lady of the city (gašan-bi) sits down in sickness, while guda$_4$, gala and en are allowed no longer to mourn.

OA texts have a few entries of a married *qadištum.* An *aššatum*/*šanītum* [126] is contrasted to a *qadištum.* In the land (of Kanish) he may not marry an *aššatum šanītum*, but in the city (o Asshur) he may marry a *qadišum.*

4.11.3 The OA official GA-*ší-im* is read by AHw s.v. as *qaššum* "geweiht, heilig," and could be considered as the masculine form of *qadištu.*[127] CAD K 292b does not take it this way, but reads *kà-sí-im* (or *ga,* or *qá*). The examples found do not show him to be an official of the temple, and thus he is not the male equivalent of *qadištu*, as we find in Ugarit and the Hebrew Bible.[128]

4.11.4 There are several instances in which the nu-bar/*kulmašītu* and the nu-gig/*qadištu* act together, Sec. 4.8.1, 4.8.2, and they appear together on NA lexical lists, Sec. 4.8.4.

4.11.5 The *qadištu* is found living in the *gagû*, perhaps in the temple compound.[129] Her role is an official one in OB times, because she is found on the state ration list.[130] There was a relationship to the *naditu* which has not yet been fully explained. She could be the sister of a *naditu* of Shamash.[131] She could have administrative duties with the apprentice *šandabakku's* (pisan-dub-ba)[132] in the household of a *nadītu* who was the daughter of a king.[133]

The Lipit-Ishtar Codex[134] allows certain officiants, daughters of a living father, to dwell in his house like an heir. Mentioned together are the nin-dingir(*entum* or *ugbabtum*), the lukur (*nadītum*) and the nu-gig (*qadištum*). This shows that these three are roughly analagous offices, and that they do not, in this case, live in a cloister, but that they dwelt at home with their father, presumably during the time when they exercised their respective offices.

CH §181 has an example of a father who dedicated his daughter to a god, again using three offices: *nadītum*, *qadištum* and *kulmašītum*. Treated in separate units (CH §§183, 184) is the *šugētum*, probably because she had a husband; no husbands are mentioned in connection with the others. These laws thus bring together the *entum*, *nadītum*, *sekretum*, *qadištum*, *kulmašītum* and *šugētum*. The older lexical texts, as OB Proto-Lu 257ff, Sec. 4.2, also link some of these.

Noting lines 263-5 of OB Proto-Lu, lukur is usually understood as the sign for *nadītum* only, an office distinct from the *qadištu*, but maybe here it shows simply the closeness of the two. *batultum* "nubile girl" (CAD) has not yet been discovered as the name of an official. Perhaps the list is saying that these officials are usually drawn from the ranks of young girls and *qadistum*'s.

Later NA lists relate them also: Lu = ša Excerpt I and the Emesal vocabulary, both Sec. 4.8.4.

One sees in all of this that the ancients associated *entu, ugbabtu, qadištu* and *kulmašītu*, and *ugbabtu*, *ištarītu*, *amalu* and *kulmašītu*, So as not to lose the track of the argument, the *amalītu* is to be dealt with below, Sec. 4.13.

4.11.6 Going beyond the lexical lists, that the social roles of some of these officials were interrelated is discovered from OB contracts. There was a *qadištu* of Adad.[135] Many *qadištu*'s appear in contracts.[136] A major role of the *qadištu* was to provide wetnurse services[137] showing that the *qadištu* could be married in OB times, or could have had children.[138] She appears together with midwives in some texts.[139] This could be considered a secular aspect, but it also could be thought of as the role of a servant of Inanna/Ishtar for this is one of this goddess's faces. She bought land from a *nadītum*[140] and had a *nadītum* as a sister.[141] Her mother and father gave Mārat-iršitim the nu-gig their daughter a slave for her betrothal (*ina iršitiša*).[142]"Priestesses" are named with the element Erištu, AHw 246a, s.v. *eršu* III.

Inanna/Ishtar had nu-gig/*qadištu* as one of her titles.[143]

4.11.7 nu-u$_8$-gig-gal-an-na ("great nu-gig of An") is used of Inanna in "Enki and the World Order," Römer, *von Soden AV* 293, 70. A seal is that of PN a nu-gig-gal of Ur.[144] Are we to understand that Inanna has the powerfully numinous title "the holy one," or is this to be understood as her acting the part of the nu-gig/*qadištu*? If the latter, one could understand the *qadištu* to have a role in people's sexual lives matching that of her mistress. We do not follow up the question here, but it has major rammifications.

4.11.8 mu-gib$_x$-an-na mèn "I am the nu-gig of An" (in emesal)[145] is used also by Nana and Ninisina.[146] At Mari, one finds a *napṭaru* who is a *qadištum* of Annunitum from the Sim'al tribe,[147] but there is no helpful context. In the designation *qaššatum* 18 PNs appear[148] in a long list of PNs, with 25 *almatum* "widows," these and the others called *amat* "servant" of named people from Terqa.[149] The *napṭartu* is understood as a wife of the second rank in Hittite by CAD N/l 324b, see further App. 4.3. Annunitum is a form of Ishtar appearing at Mari (see Mari Pantheon in G. Dossin Studia Mariana 44f.)

4.11.9 There are only a few texts showing the ritual actions of a *qadištu* and the fullest is *KAR* 154 from NA or MA times, given in Appendix 1.[150] It appears to be from the temple called Adad in one line and Anu in another, let us say the Anu-Adad temple in Assur. The *šangû* and the *qadišu's* (pl.) act together. The *qadištu*'s go to the *bit hamri*, a part of the Adad temple complex.[151] The *šangû* does the purification.[152] The *qadištu*'s sing the *inhu* -song several times[153] "before Adad," and "lift up the god," perhaps referring to the statue of the god. At one point the *qadištu*'s jewelery is taken off.[154] The tablet ends with a list of standard meat offerings to various gods, apparently done by the *šangû* and *qadištu*'s together, although this is indicated only by some broken verbs in the plural.

We note from this valuable text that the *qadištu*'s in the plural act with a *šangû* in the singular. Despite a fairly complete text, we cannot determine the liturgical plan of action. We do not know why the places show up as they do. We can say about the rite that its main purpose seems to have been "purification," but of what the text does not say, perhaps the offering material. Much space is given to a detailed listing of the offering. The *qadištu*'s roles seem to have been: to exalt the god, to take part in the procession, to sing the *inhu* - song. There is nothing of a sexual role.

4.11.10 From other sources there is a *qadištu* of An and of Adad (See n. 135). Not as full as the MA example given above, there are a few more examples in NA times of the *qadištu* acting in the cult. One set of ritual instructions calls for meat, flour, bread, wine, beer and oil to be brought for Bēlit-ṣēri.[155] In another column labelled *parṣu*(?)-*ma ana pan* ⌈x⌉ SAL *nāri* [x x x] , read *mārat nāri* "daughter of the river" by the editor;[156] "ritual (?) before the Daughter of the River." Then beer, figs and salt are offered, and ᵐⁱ*qa-diš-tú tu-na-⌈sah⌉-ši* (?)/*šú* (?) which Ebeling translates "die Hierodule sollst du entfernen." Then a MAŠ.MAŠ uses "hand-water." Despite the obscurity, we can conclude that the *qadištu* takes a major role in the ritual.

In the MA recension of the Contest between the Tamarisk and the Palm[157] some partially preserved lines (the translation is Lambert's):

5. Ditto. "Come, let us go, I and you, to the city of Kish...
6. where the work of the savant (*ummāni*) takes place, there are signs of me. Not full...
7. not full of incense. The *qadišt* [*u*] has sprinkled water, and...
8. she takes... and they worship and hold a festival (*isinnu*). At that time...
9. is in the land of the ˡᵘ*ṭābihu* "butcher." His twigs in offal...

The *qadištu* as one who sprinkles water is common then in wisdom literature and rites. Perhaps she uses the *terinnu* "fir cone" she is described as having in *Maqlû* VI 29.40, Sec. 4.11.13.

In a letter[158] describing portions of a ritual done by a female, with mention of garments placed before Shamash, the ᵐⁱ*qa-di-šu* are to do an undesignated activity (lines l3ff). Then the MAŠ.MAŠ will do something broken off.

In a NB text praising Marduk, after a half-line describing the NIN.DINGIR.RA's who (probably "sin" after CAD H 31b) against their lovers/husbands, and which mentions the *nadītu*'s who skillfully keep the foetus (lit. "the womb") alive, then the *qadištu*'s who do (broken) with *mê te-lil-te* "water for purification" (line 7b)(see n.40).

4.11.11 In a broken part of Weidner's study of the Middle Assyrian court and harem[159] the actions of various officials are described, as *rab ekallim*, *bēl pāhete*, relative to (the first part of each line is broken) the ^{giš}*sikkate* "part of a lock":(concerning) ^{mí}*šābsūtu ù qadiltu* (line 11)...*la irraba la uṣṣâ* (line 12) "may they not go in...may they not come out." *Šābsūtu* is a midwife. The *qadiltu* (= *qadištu*) engages in an unknown action.

4.11.12 The social status of the *qadištu* in MA times is shown by the laws concerning veiling (MAL §40). Those who must have their heads veiled are: wives, widows, Assyrian women, daughters of an *awīlum* "gentleman," an *esirtu* [160] who walks on the street with her mistress, and a *qadištu* who is married. Those whose heads must be uncovered are: *qadištu* unmarried on the street, *harimtu* "prostitute," *amate* "female slaves." So in this period the *qadištu* can marry and upgrade her status, but an unmarried *qadištu* would be in a lower social status, that of prostitutes and female slaves. There is a symbolic aspect to veiling. See Sec. 4.24.3 for discussion on veiling in Hebrew life.

4.11.13 A large number of references appear for the *qadištu* in NA times. There are two appearances in the standard lexical list: Lu = sa I and the emesal vocabulary, see Sec. 4.8.4. Learned from these lists: that the *qadištu* is closely linked with the *ištarītu*, even sharing the same signs nu-gig, and with the *ugbabtu* and *entu*, who share the same signs nin-dingir-ra, and with the *kulmašītu*, and the *amalītu*, to be discussed below.

The *qadištu* is criticized along with other Category IV ranks in two kinds of literature: the lists of witches in *Shurpu* and *Maqlû* and the wisdom literature, Sec. 3.20.5, lists which fitted into the purposes of *Shurpu* and *Maqlû*, but which also included what in OB times were the respected ranks of *qadištu*, *nadītu*, *ištarītu* and *kulmašītu*, Sec. 4.3.5. There is no break in the text or the syntax to place the latter grouping in a separate category in this text, but they all are warned against as killers, against which no evil or magic could be effective.

One can only guess why divination offices were side-by-side with our Category IV. Maybe the meaning of the offices changed throughout the years. Maybe one of the latter group's functions was to act as witches, not compatable with their other functions. Maybe the sexuality of the group was used in a kind of witchcraft.

A similar list appears in *Shurpu* VIII 69, Sec. 4.3.5. Another list *Shurpu* III 116f has a somewhat different order: *nadītu*, *qadištu* (?), ^{d}Kubi and *ugbabtu* (NIN.DINGIR.RA). This shows that in this literature these ranks were thought of in the same category, and that was a negative one. Their very titles indicate the sin.

An incantation text from the Brussels Museum[161] has a line which is in the same form as the above: ^{giš}*pišri nadāte* ^{giš}*terinnu* (ŠE.Ù.KU) *ša qa-áš-da-ti ...muhhi kišpiki* "the *pišru* "anointing" of the *nadītu*'s (and) the *terinnu*'s of the *qadištu*'s...are used for witchcraft."[162] The criticism of two previously high offices remains to be explained. To interpret them as offices other than the older ones is a counsel of despair. Maybe some of them used the power of the office for wrongful purposes. One is reminded that the Hebrew Bible prophets could be either good (the canonical ones) or bad (false prophets), the same word *nābîʾ* being used for each.

In *Maqlû* VI.40 // .29 the *qašdāti* (*qadištu*'s) carry the *terinnu*'s /GIŠ.ŠE.Ù.KU "fir/pine cones" in conjunction with the *entu*'s carrying the *tirhu*-vessels, the latter a beer libation jug. A prayer *Maqlû* I.24 and *KAR* 94.16 asks that the *terinnu* loose the supplicant, and *Maqlû* V.54 *pitiltu ša qašdāti*[163] is paralleled by *terinnātu ša šeam malāti* "*terinnu* which is full of seed," perhaps a fertility motif. Are these the cones carried by the cultic figures dressed in bird-costumes or other ways which anoint the tree by a cone?[164]

This could be understood as the cultic action of the *terinnu*'s loosing the supplicant from his sins through a fertility rite. The trees stand for life, the ongoingness of life, or the growth of life.

4.11.14 For an odd combination of officials, but one which probably comments upon them disparagingly, note the lexical list in CT 18,19, Sec. 4.6.4. This is a strange list in many ways. The equating of *šamuktum* and *šamuhtum*, forms of the more usual *šamkatu/šamhatu* "prostitute" with *nadītum* and *qadištum*, cultic ranks in their own right, may describe an aberration, a criticism in the vein of the attribution of these to witchcraft, see immediately above. The strange *ugbabtum* = *assinnatum* is discussed in Sec. 4.9.4 and App 3.2.

The demon Lamashtu exerts her powerful magic especially against children in the womb. In an incantation text she is described: "Powerful is the daughter of Anu (i.e. Lamashtu)...angry, destroying...She returns the heart of those giving birth, she snatches the child away from the pregnant woman, its *taskarinnu* - wood...its ankles...*qa-diš-tu mārat* ᵈAnim *ša ilāni*...her head is a lion's head, the form of an ass is [her] form.[165] Here Lamashtu is given the epithet "*qadištu* daughter of Anu." Is this because she acts like the office *qadištu* in having control of pregnancies? Or is this merely one more usage of the term " female holy one"? *Taskarinnu*-wood is used elsewhere in a ritual for potency.[166] We note that in none of these ritual texts does the role of the *qadištu* have to do with sexuality, nor does any criticism emerge. This disparaging note only occurs in incantations and the wisdom literature, and there it occurs with other high respected female officiants also.

4.11.15 There are several references to *qadištu* in NA times having to do with childbirth. In a section in Atrahasis which appears to be a continuation of the process of making mankind[167] a variant *sab-su-tu-um-ma ina bīt ha-riš-ti li-ih-du* "let the *šabsūtu* "midwife" rejoice in the home of the woman in confinement"(63, 17) is paralleled in the main recension by *ša -[ab]-sú-tum ina bīt qá-di-iš-ti li-ih-du* "let the *šabsūtu* rejoice in the house of the *qadištu* "where the bearing women give birth."[168] (62,290). Perhaps the *šabsūtu* and the *qadištu* work together in the midwife project.

The *qadištu's* role in childbirth is shown also in an obscure bilingual:[169]

I.11 nu-gig šà-gig nu-gig bar-ra
qa-diš-tú ša lib-ba mar-ṣa-a[t ...

12 nu-gig-an-na nu-hun-gá
iš-ta-rit ᵈa-nim [ ]

13 nigìn sag-iti nu-til-la

iz-bu ku-bu š [á ina qabri]

14 urugal-la-aš ki-a nu-túm-ma
la qeb-ru la [

15 gaba nu-gi_4 á nu-un-da-ri-a
la mu-[*tir ir-tu*]*m*

16 UD-ur-du_{11}-ga sag-sahar-tag-ga
ṣa-al-tu [ ]

11 Sumerian: nu-gig of the sick heart/womb, nu-gig divided/selected/loosed
Akkadian: *qadištu* whose heart/womb is sick ...

12 Sum: nu-gig of An who is not rested
Akk: *ištarītu* of Anu ...

13 Sum: the premature/stillborn child who has not completed the months
Akk: the malformed child, the premature/stillborn child wh[o in the grave]

14 Sum: has not put...in the place (?)
Akk: has not been buried yet ...

15 Sum: whose breast has not been turned. whose side/arm has not been ...
Akk: who does not tu[rn aside the breast]

16 Sum: ...
Akk: battle ...

The šà-gig "sick heart" (or "taboo,"as *Shurpu* II 69) may be an attempt to explain the obscure nu-gig. The šà-gig may refer to the malfunctioning womb which brought forth the premature/stillborn child. nu-gig bar-ra may be an attempt to relate the nu-gig and nu-bar. nu-gig is also the ideogram for *ištarītu*. In bilinguals, *ištarītu* is sometimes given the equivalent gašan-an-na "lady of An," or nu-gig-an-na "*ištarītu* of An."[170] The *qadištu* and/or *ištarītu* has a premature, malformed child. Perhaps it is the *qadištu*'s breast that is spoken of.

4.11.16 Some of the above texts, and the idea that the *qadištu* may sometimes play the part of a midwife, seem to slide into the secular arena, which we are wary of describing as completely separate from the sacred. This division is a modern concept, but let us say that there are areas in which the *qadištu* works which do not seem to have obvious cultic implications. An important one of these is from a NA excerpt series Ana ittisu that seems to come from lost legal material. A divorced man takes a NU.GIG /*qadištu* sila-ta /*ina sūqim* "from the street" and loving her, marries her.[171]

Here the *qadištu* seems to be a street prostitute, reminding us of the disparaging remarks made of her above, including other formerly important female cultic ranks. In the excerpt immediately before the one discussed here[172] a man takes a *harimtu* "prostitute" in marriage.

For another instance in which the *qadištu* / mu-gib$_x$ is found on the street, see the *Lamentation Over the Destruction of Ur* reference n.127 and accompanying text.

4.11.17 The NU.GIG is always a woman, except for a single entry in a Ugaritic list of professions, see App. 3.14. Terrien[173] assumes that the Semitic languages have words for "male prostitute."

4.12 nu-gig / *ištarītu*

The *ištarītu* and the *qadištu* shared the same sign, nu-gig, but the small number of appearances of the *ištarītu* as compared to the *qadištu* is a handicap. There are some who doubt that a separate official named *ištarītu* exists.[174] As a word meaning "the divine" from the goddess Ishtar, it comes close in some contexts to mean "a goddess," though *ištaru* and *ištartu* are the usual words for this. The NA lexical texts, however, several times list her separately: in the emesal vocabulary Sec. 4.8.4 and in Diri:

188 a-ma -[lu] [AMA.LUL] *a-ma-lí* (correct reading?)-*tú*
iš-ta-ri-tú
šu-gi-tú

Diri IV 188ff, CAD A/2 2a

Amalu and *amalītu* are also words for "goddess," but also apparently offices in their own right, the latter word constructed as *ištarītu*, also a word for "goddess," cf. Sec. 4.12. For the *šugētu* office, see Sec. 4.4.

In the zì-pa series text translated Sec. 4.11.15, on line 12 nu-gig-an-na is given an equivalent *ištarīt* ^{d}a-nim, a clever double meaning, for *ištarītu* and Ishtar the goddess (Ishtarītu) are/is the daughter of Anu.

In a rare OB entry, Hammurapi in a letter[175] orders some *iš-ta-ra-a-tim* "*ištarītu's*" of Emutbalum to be brought to Babylon in the same ship as some *kezertu*'s, with provisions for both. They are supported by the king.

In the long section of *Maqlû* in Sec. 3.20.5 in which witches as well as female cultic officiants are disparaged, there are the *qadištu*, *nadītu* and *ištarītu* listed. In the disparaging piece of wisdom literature warning against marrying a *harimtu*, an *ištarītu* or a *kulmašītu*, only the *istarītu* is not criticized: she is devoted to a deity, Ishtar, Sec. 4.8.4. She still will not make a good wife, because she will give her heart to the goddess before her husband.

Though no texts have been found showing her in action, she is probably a cultic officiant like the *qadištu*.

4.13 ama-lul/*amalu* and *amalītu*

CAD s.v. gives *amalu A* as a term for "goddess," but AHw says "eine Art Kultdirne." The apparently m. form *amalu* could be f., on analogy with *ištaru*, see Sec. 4.12, or it could be considered a formation from ama-lul. An early occurrence is in the lexical lists, Sec. 4.9.1 in which nin-dingir is a cultic official, but dam-dingir is unknown; see also Sec. 1.19.4. Ama-^{d}Inanna later is associated with *amalu:*

319 ama
320 ama-uru
321 AMA.^{d}INANNA
322 AMA.^{d}INANNA
323 ama-lul

OB Proto-Lu MSL XII 44

There may have been two separate words behind the two entries AMA.^{d}INANNA. From the much later emesal vocabulary Sec. 4.8.4 line 81 ama-^{d}inanna is the ideogram for *amalu*, and Diri IV, Sec. 4.12, relates *a-ma-lí* (?)-*tú*, *ištarītu* and *šugētu*.

Ama- titles appear on the later Lu = ša list:

4'	[ama]	[*um*]-*mu*
5	[ama-uru]	[*um-mi*] URU
51	[ama]-a-⌈x⌉-(x)]	[ ]
52	ama-$^{lu-lu}$lul-la	[ŠU-*tu*]
53	ama-lul-la	*za-ab-ba* -[*tu*]
54	ama-lul-la	*mu-ut-til-tu*
55	ama-é-a	*li-li-tu*

Lu = ša III iv MSL XII 127

1'	[SAL	]	[x] -[x] -' -*tu*
2'	SAL	] -⌈x⌉	*la a-ma-lu-uk-tu*
3'	[SAL	-sa]g-a	*la ka-ši-tu*
4'	[SAL	] -SAR	*mu-piš-tu*
5'	[SAL	] -⌈x⌉	*mu-na-mir-tu*

Lu = ša III ii MSL XII 124

Lu = ša III iv follows much the same order as that of OB Proto-Lu of more than 1000 years earlier. The presumed entry ama-uru = *ummi āli* (?reading, "mother of the city"?) appeared on OB Proto-Lu. *Zabbatu* is a f. divinatory office, considered an ecstatic. Muttiltu is a demon. Lilitu is a demon who later became the famous Lilith, but we cannot ascribe her later functions to this early occurrence.

Amaluktu in Lu = ša III ii is an unknown form, perhaps related to ama-lul, with a -k (originally Sumerian) genitive and a f. -t. *Kašītu* is perhaps related to *kašû*, strengthening in the sense of binding (?) done by a sorceress, related to the next term *muppištu*, one of the many words for sorceress, Sec. 3.7.3, 4. *Munammirtu*, literally "enlightener," is perhaps a "solver of problems."

Further information about the *amalu* comes from the myth "Inanna and Enki" and its list of me's.[176] The me's are aspects of a civilization, the good and the bad, such as "sexual intercourse," "flattery," then AMA$^{!}$ ^{d}INANNA, which Farber-Flügge reads $amalu_x$ "Ishtardirne, Kultdirne." The list continues:

II v 45 $amalu_x$
46 éš-dam-kù

47 nigìn-[gar] -kù
48 x-AN
49 nu-gig-an-na

Inanna and Enki

Here the *amalu* seems to be treated like a cultic officiant, or a form of Inanna. The éš-dam-kù "holy ešdam" is the place at the door of which Ishtar sits as a prostitute, App. 4.1.11. The term nigìn-gar is thoroughly studied by Krecher.[177] It occurs often in the form nigìn-mar-ra, showing a pronunciation -ng. Context shows that it is probably a part of the Inanna temple, which would relate it to the éš-dam-kù. Akkadian correspondences have not yet been discovered, but note NIGIN = *kummu* (part of a temple) in Nabnitu IV.[178]

Conclusions on *amalu* and *amalītu* may be stated cautiously: they are two feminine terms for the same office, the same category as *ištarītu* and *qadištu*. The person may be an officiant taking the role of Inanna in a cult drama, acting out her sexuality in some way. Some kind of ecstatic action may have been used.

4.14 kar-kid/*harimtu* "prostitute" as a cultic figure

We start with the many occurrences of KAR-KID/*harimtu* in the lexical lists next to other officials. In CT 18,19 33-4 she appears after forms of *šamhatu*, a word usually understood as "prostitute," and before *kazratu* and *kizritu* , Sec. 4.6.4. The latter are cultic officials, so the *harimtu* may be one, too. Several kar-kid offices show up after nam-lukur on OB Proto-Lu, Sec. 4.2. Kar-kid-mu-gub, if equivalent to mu-gib$_x$ (emesal) is a *harimtu* of a nu-gig (*qadištu*), or a *harimtu* who is a *qadištu*. Kar-kid-suhub$_2$-si and kar-kid-gi-te-te are unknown. Thus it seems to be among cultic officiants. Lu = ša I, Excerpt II, Sec. 4.6.1 has *harimtu* without similar offices near it.

Lu =ša IV, App. 3.2.7, among words from the Ishtar cult has kuš-lá "person wearing a leather garment" given an equivalence *ša harimti*, the context being those clad in other garments. The context seems clearly cultic.

In a Sumerian hymn the kar-kid / *harimtu* is called dumu (m. !) ^{d}Inanna "child of Inanna" or in a variant kar-kid ^{d}Inanna.[179] The goddess of love oversees the high level love between man and woman culminating in longtime companionship, as well as the transient love done for pay. Each results in sexual pleasure: both are in Inanna's sphere.

In ancient Sippar in OB times, Harris[180] finds 11 *harimtu*'s under the *kalamāhu*, the head *kalû*. Perhaps they served as singers. There is a cultic office (*parṣu*) which relates to the status of prostitution (*harimūtu*).[181]

As we see in App. 4.1.11, when Ishtar sits at the door of the *bīt aštamme*, she is the "loving *harimtu*." She plays the part of the *harimtu*; prostitution is her role at that temple or portion thereof.

The CT 18,19 text, Sec. 4.6.4, also indicates something hinted at in other documents: that the *šamhatu* type of prostitute was different from the *harimtu* type. From the root of the word, Harris[182] understands the word as simply meaning "the voluptuous one." In Gilgamesh I iv 43f the *šamhatu* is a servant of Ishtar, for she escorts Gilgamesh to the temple of Anum and Ishtar. Later (VII iii 35f) it says that the *harimtu* / *šamhatu* gave Enkidu *akla simat ilūti* "bread fit for the divinity," and *kurunnu*, a kind of choice beer often used in ritual.[183] *ABL* 509.11 has some *harimati* (pl.) in a broken context in a letter from Āshipu, whose very name means "diviner," many of whose letters concern the *birtu* "fort," not further defined.

Along with burning his seven sons before Adad, in a curse formula in the Kapara inscriptions from Tell Halaf,[184] the subject "he" must also release his seven daughters to be *harimāte*, seemingly also part of the cult. Menzel[185] stresses the foreignness, the non-Assyrian nature, of this text. A woman gave birth in *ha-rim-* < *u* > *-ti-šá* "her *harimtu*-ship" and the child was given to Ninurta, and his duties belong to the temple of Ninurta.[186]

Dandamaev[187] in his characteristically well-documented way discusses "the hire of slave women for use in brothels" but in doing so confuses the *harimtu* "(ordinary) prostitute" with the "hierodule": Temple prostitution in Babylonia for the fifth c. and later is attested in reports of Herodotus (I, 199) and Strabo." (p. 132) He thinks in some cases that the term *hari'ūtu* (usually, *harimūtu*) "in all probability refers to a hierodule working as a temple prostitute." (p.133)

He also understands the *ištarītu* as a hierodule (p.133).[188] He quotes Dougherty[189] about restrictions on the *širkatu*, which he understands as a "temple slave woman" in the context of "temple prostitution." (p. 135). Again I would describe this as a "historiographic myth," the term of Arnaud, Sec. 4.22.13.

Wilhelm[190] discusses the reliability of Herodotus as an observer and reporter, then discusses several interpretations of prostitution, sacred/cultic and otherwise. He then goes on to the point of his article, the type of prostitution found in the Mesopotamian temple: tolerated not organized prostitution (p. 513). Especially studied is the *kezertu*, which has no direct but a loose connection with the *harimtu* (p. 514f). He then discusses the Nuzi text SMN 1670, with copy, transliteration and notes, then a translation. It shows a possible tie-in of prostitution to the cult.

The author of this Nuzi letter says that he brought up his daughter as pledge (taking the *napūtum* of the text as from *nepû*). This was for *harimūti* "prostitution" for ^{d}U/Ishtar/Shawushka, and he allowed her to go free; he calls it "Muntfreiheit(?)," translating the Hurrian *b/pirianna.* He feels that this shows the existence of prostitution ("tolerated" not "organized") in the temple organization, because of the juristic character of the document. (p.523). For the first time something positive can be said for Her I, 199. This certainly adds some important evidence to the quest, but because it may be a local practice we must wait for more evidence. The associated bibliography and interpretation of the text are helpful.

Some of these examples show that *harimtu* is the title of a cultic officiant.

4.15 PAP.PAP

This obscure office appears in ED after a list of singer functionaries:

27 nar
28 mus-lah$_4$
29 P̣AP.PAP
30 UH-INANNA

ED Lu E MSL XII 17

In Old Sumerian times, PAP.PAP is found as a title of a woman Baranamtara the wife of Lugalanda. This woman was also designated MÍ "the woman" (of the land?), cf. the designation of rulers of a city being called *amēl āli* "the man of the city." She is referred to as ama-uru "mother of the city," and Asher-Greve[191] supposes her to be the "Stellvertreterin" of the goddess Baba. Sollberger[192] has suggested a reading of PAP.PAP as $munu_x$.

4.16 kurun (KAŠ.DIN(.NA) (and others)/*sābû* and *sābītu*

4.16.1 Pertinent lexical evidence is:

20 lú ŠIM	*sí-ra-šu-ú*
21 lú ^{kaš}kurun$_2$-na	*sà-bu-ú*
22 SAL lú ^{kaš}kurun$_2$-na	*sà-bi-i-tum*
23 lú gub-ba	*mu-úh-hu-um*
	OB Lu A MSL XII 158

14 LÚ.ŠIMxA
15 LÚ.KAŠ.DIN.NAM!
16 LÚ.GAL.ŠIMxA

---

17 LÚ.KAŠ.LUL
18 LÚ.ŠU.SILA$_3$!.DU$_8$
19 LÚ.GAL.KAŠ.LUL

Sultantepe III MSL XII 235

4.16.2 The Sumerian King List v 36-7 has a queen Ku-Baba, entitled mí-kurun-na. She is called lugal "king." By a later tradition she obtained *šarrūt kiššat mātāte* "kingship over all lands."[193] This may be part of an old legend concerning her, but in any case is an important title by tradition.

This office is often translated "tavern keeper," but it has cultic and sexual elements. These are not suggested by the lexical texts. In the Epic of Gilgamesh, she is a wise woman, who knows (as divine?) how to explain life and death.[194] Furthermore, her name is written ^{d}Siduri *sābītum*. As noted in Sec. 4.3.1 she is the singer of a balbale hymn, and perhaps the same person is referred to also as lukur.

4.16.3 A rather full incantation text mentioning the ^{lú}*sābû*[195] has: (line 3) a ritual using *epru* "dust" of *bīt ili,* of *parakku*, of *ibrati,* of *bāb bīt harimti,* of *bāb sābî,* and others; (line 21) *šiptu* "incantation": oh, Ishtar, *tēlitu*, put your hand on a *kannu* and a *namzītu*; (line 39) *kik ittû* -ritual, set a *nignak burāši* "incense-burner of juniper" before Ishtar, pour out beer of the ^{lú}*sābû* (then there will be *išdihu* "profit" for the *sābû*); (line 43) *šiptu* "incantation": Ishtar of the lands...this is your *giparu*, come into our house with *ṣaliliki* "the one who sleeps with you," *h [ab] -bu-bu-ki* "your lover" and *kulu'uki* "your *kulu'u*," and fertility will result (line 66); (line 61) *kikittû*-ritual, (various dusts as above) including that of the *bāb bīt Ištar, bīt harimti, bāb bīt sābî,* then, before Ishtar place your GI.DUH /*paṭīru*"Tragelärchen" (AHw)... .

Even though these are *šiptu* "incantation" texts, and should perhaps properly belong in chapter 3, they use aspects of many of our other categories, showing how difficult it is to be consistent with these. *Bīt ili* covers a multitude of structures: sacred rooms, temples large and small, sanctuaries, and so forth. *Parakku* is likewise rather vague, and could be an altar base, an altar itself, a high place, or a holy place. *Ibratu* is another kind of holy place, perhaps an outdoor shrine of some sort. It seem to cover all kinds of holy places purposely. The *bīt harimti* appears as if all the *harimtu's* lived together; see Sec. 4.14 in a discussion of the *harimtu* as a cultic figure. The *bīt sābî* is our main interest in this section appearing several times in these texts. lúSAL.ME at this point is a reading of Zimmern, but the parallel text Craig *ABRT* 66.9 does not have it, and it makes no sense anyway. Ishtar *tēlitu* "the very clever one" is one of her standard epithets. The *išdihu*, usually "profit," may refer to the well-working of the *bīt sābî* and to the sexual activity there. For this and other unusual references to the *kulu'u*, see App. 3.8.

So this refers to an incantation done if the income of the *bīt* lú*sābê* has ceased, and Ishtar is urged to let the *kulu'u* come into "our house," presumably the *bīt* lú*sābê*. He then sleeps with her. This seems similar to the actions in the *bīt aštamme* (App. 4), but is probably a different place.[196] In a NA dream omen,[197] a line "if he go[es to] the *bīt* lú*sābê*" is preceded a few lines before by "if [he goes to] the *bīt aštammi*" (r. i x + 11). These are surrounded by secular "houses," as that of the gardener, sailor and farmer.

In a namburbi concerning the apparently secular subject of ridding oneself of fungus, the man is to go through various rituals, then enter a *bīt sābê* then touch a *kannu* - stand and a *namzītu* - mixing vat.[198] Other ritual actions in the *bīt sābî* are described in the line É.LÚ.DIN. [NA T]U-*ma* KAŠ.SAG *ana Ea Šamaš u Asalluhi inaqqi daltu u sikkūru ilappatma*[199] "he entered the *bīt sābî* and poured a libation for Ea Shamash and Asalluhi; he touched door and lock." Caplice[200] gives a line concerning the action in the *bīt sābê* with *kannu* and *namzītu*: "its evil will be dissipated," probably meaning resumption of ordinary life. I suggest that it may have to do with the resumption of his sexual life. Beer from a *sābû* is drunk in a ritual for sexual potency.[201]

In a long Mari tablet [202] listing PNs craftsmen, then periodically totalling them, 7 men and 1 woman are from the *bītat sà-bi-i* (iv 15). The end says: persons from the persons of Mari. They include *nāru*'s and *hābit mê*, otherwise all the others are craftsmen.

4.17 *mārat ili /ilāni*

There are PNs from many different periods of the type *mārat* DN "daughter of the god(dess).[203] The *qadištu* is called *mārat Anim* in a Lamashtu text.[204] Several times in OB texts from Khafajah[205] the term *mārat* Sin appears, and Harris suggests that this may be a variant of *mārat ili* and "perhaps the female counterpart of the *enum* - priest in the Sin temple."

In a Gilgamesh passage, after the *ugbabtu*'s *qadistu*'s and *kulmasītu*'s are designated as *sirku's,*[206] the *ugbabtu*'s take...and the DUMU.MÍ.DINGIR.MEŠ (*mārat ilāni*) *ú-rab* [ ] The *mārat ilāni* is also linked with the *ugbabtu nadītu qadištu kulmašītu* in an accusation of witchcraft in *Shurpu*[207]

4.18 The Hebrew Bible: *qādēš and qĕdēšāh* (See Sec. 4.24.3)

4.18.1 Referring back to the units on the *qadištu*, Sec. 4.11, we continue with a discussion of its cognates. Even before the *qadištu* was discovered among Mesopotamian documents, and the *qdš* among Ugaritic, and leapt upon as the long-lost "parallel" to the Hebrew *qādēš* and *qĕdēšāh* of Deut 23.18 (EV 17), it was a tradition that the Hebrew titles had sexual connotations. To show how heavily that tradition influenced translation, we give the translation of the terms of Deut 23.18 used in Scripture versions throughout the years:

Septuagint: porne (vs. 18). In 4 Bas 23.7 it has the transliteration kadesim, and for Job 36.14 aggeloi, so the reader of the LXX is to know little of cultic prostitution.
Aquila: endiellagmenoi "changed", Driver *Deuteronomy* 265a.
Jerome: comm. ad Hoseam iii 1261: cadesim (transliteration), which says this is used of viri exsecti libidine "excised men for (purposes of) lust," i.e., male prostitutes. (But how can castrated men be prostitutes or lustful?)
Targum Onkelos: *ʾttʾ lgbr ᶜbd* "(a woman of the daughters of Israel shall not become) the wife of a slave." This modification of meaning is found also in Ibn Ezra, Radak and others. It perhaps follows the subject matter of the preceding two verses.
Targum Neophyti: Palestinian, *npqt* "prostitute"
Peshitta: *znytʾ* "prostitute"
Vulgate: meretrix (woman), scortator (man)
Wycliff: A; strumpet, B: houre
William Tyndale (1530): whore (woman), whorekeper (man)
Martin Luther (1534): hure
Casiodoro de Reina revisada por Cipriano de Valera (1602): ramera (woman), sodomítico (man)
King James Version (1611): whore (woman), sodomite (man)
Revised Version (1886): harlot
Douay: whore
American Standard Version (1901): prostitute
Jewish Publication Society of America (1916): harlot
The Chicago Bible, An American Translation (1927, 1939): temple-prostitute
James Moffatt (1935): temple-prostitute
Revised Standard Version (1952, 1953): cult prostitute
Ronald Knox (1956): "no Israelite man or woman shall be devoted to a life of shame"
George Lamsa (1957): whore
Berkeley Version (1959): temple prostitute
New World Translation (1961): temple prostitute
Jewish Publication Society of America Torah (1962): cult prostitute
Jerusalem Bible (England, 1966): sacred prostitute; prostituée sacrée (French, 1956)
New Jerusalem Bible (1985): sacred prostitute
New American Bible (1970): temple harlot (woman), temple prostitute (man)
New English Bible (1970): temple-prostitute
Good News Bible (1976): temple prostitute
Revised English Bible: common prostitute (woman), male prostitute (man)
New Revised Standard Version: temple prostitute (woman and man)

This kind of study would bring the same results in the other places the term *qĕdēšāh* appears in the Hebrew Bible, as, e.g., Gen 38.21f and Hos 4.14.

There could be several reasons why this exegesis started in so early. The next verse, Deut 23.19 (EV 18) does not allow the hire of a prostitute (*zônāh*) or the wages of a dog in the temple in payment for any vow, so it was natural to relate these two verses. Another reason could be the strange story of Tamar, Judah's daughter-in-law in Gen 38.12-26. She played the part of a prostitute (*zônāh*), but when Judah went looking for her again the text referred to her as a *qĕdēšāh*, used here seemingly as another word for *zônāh.* In a series of parallel stichs in Hos 4.14, *qĕdēšāh* is parallel to *zônāh* and adultery. This is discussed in Sec. 4.24.4. RSV footnote h has "or cult prostitute" for Gen 38.21 though *qĕdēšāh* is translated "harlot" in the main text. The NRSV has "temple prostitute" in 38.21 with no footnote. The other new versions are pretty much in agreement: JPS: "cult prostitute," New JB: "prostitute" with fn "strictly 'sacred prostitute,'" Westermann: "prostitute," GNB: "prostitute," NEB: "temple prostitute." Though the story uses *zônāh* and *qĕdēšāh* interchangeably, from the standpoint of the careful reader both are mistaken terms. Tamar was not a prostitute, and there were no cultic indications in Tamar's actions. Maybe a *qĕdēšāh* was treated as a prostitute because she is taken advantage of, and, besides, if she is a devotee of a foreign god, the Hebrew Bible would metaphorically call her a prostitute. See the long discussion below, Sec. 4.24.3.

4.18.2 The list in Sec. 4.18.1 shows that the translators as early as the 1920s considered the prostitution they imputed to the *qādēš* and *qĕdēšha* to be temple or cult or sacred prostitution. These terms have now become common currency in biblical research, but after this had been "discovered," it was then necessary to describe it! There is no hint in the Hebrew Bible itself of how it was allegedly practiced, only a series of parallel verses, using the slippery term "to commit harlotry," which was the standard term used by the prophets and the deuteronomistic writers as an analogy for "to commit apostasy." What then do the many articles and books on "sacred (etc.) prostitution" talk about? (Note that many go back and forth between Mesopotamia and the Hebrew Bible, some responsibly, some not.)The bibliography is huge. Some representative ones are:

G.A. Barton, "Hierodouloi," *ERE* 6 (1914) 672-5.

Eduard Hertlein, a study of Rahab using the mythological interpretations of H. Gunkel, *ZAW* 38 (1919/20) 113-46.

Beatrice A. Brooks, *A Contribution to the Study of the Moral Practices of Certain Social Groups in Ancient Mesopotamia,* Leipzig, 1921, her 1920 Bryn Mawr doctoral disseration.

J. Plessis, *Etudes sur les textes concernant Ištar-Astarte,* Paris, 1921, old but because much of what he did was from the original texts, his work is still valuable, when some up-dating is done of his translations.

T.J. Meek, "Song of Songs and the Fertility Cult," in W.H. Schoff *Song of Songs* (1924).

S. Smith, *JRAS* 1928 848-68, "A Babylonian Fertility Cult," discusses the *gigunu*.

H.G. May, "The fertility cult in Hosea," *AJSL* 48 (1931-32) 73-98.

Beatrice Brooks, "Fertility Cult Functionaries in the Old Testament," *JBL* 60 (1941) 227-253.

J.P. Asmussen, "Bemerkungen zur sakralen Prostitution im alten Testament," *Stud The* 11 (1956) 168-92.

W.G. Lambert, "Morals in ancient Mesopotamia," *JEOL* V(1959), 194-6 re cultic prostitution he says, "no one denies its prevalence, especially in the cult of Ishtar, but little is known of its function (p. 195).

W. von Soden, "Kultische Prostitution," *RGG* v (1961) 642-3; G. Fohrer, "Tempeldirne," *BHH* iii 1948f (1966).

Vos *Women*:"*qādēsh* and *qĕdēshāh* show cultic prostitution" 107-119 (1968).

W.Helck, *Beobachtungen zur Grossen Göttin und den ihr verbundenen Gottheiten,* München u. Wien, 1971, a major study, including Figürchen.

Walter Kornfeld, *Supplement. Dictionnaire de la Bible* (1972) cols. 1356-74, one of the longest studies.

B. Arnaud, "La prostitution sacrée in Mesopotamie, un mythe historique?" *RHR* 183 (1973) 111-15.

E.A. Yamauchi, "Cultic Prostitution: A Case Study in Cultural Diffusion," Gordon AV (*AOAT* 22, 1973) 213-222.

Grace Emerson, "A fertility goddess in Hos 4.17-19?" *VT* 24 (1974) 492-7; Eugene Fisher, "Cultic prostitution in the Ancient Near East? A reassessment," *BTB* 6 (1976) 225-36.

T. Jacobsen, *Treasures of Darkness* (1976) chap 2 shows how little is known about the fertility cult.

R. Collins, "The Bible and Sexuality," *BTB* 7 (1977) 149-67, unfootnoted, finds no "ritual prostitution," but he upholds "ritual intercourse," 54-7.

Stephen M. Hooks, *Sacred Prostitution in Israel and the Ancient Near East.* Thesis, Hebrew Union College, Cincinnati, 1985.

R.A. Ogden, "Religious Identity and the Sacred Prostitution Accusation," in *The Bible Without Theology: The Theological Traditions and Alternatives to It*, San Francisco, 1987.

Joan Westenholz, "Tamar, *Qedeša, Qadištu* and Sacred Prostitution in Mesopotamia," *HTR* 82 (1989) 245-65.

Gernot Wilhelm, "Marginalien zu Herodot Klio 199," in *Moran AV* (1990).

We would not dare summarize the various points of view about the actions of a cultic prostitute whom no one ever saw and whose functions are described nowhere. Imagination plays a great part in these articles. What they like to call "cultic diffusion" is confidently used. This is a theory that culture elements may under conditions of trade, migration, conquest or mission pass from one culture to another. Of course, sometimes this happens and sometimes it doesn't. This can be carried to extremes, and now many feel that the Myth and Ritual School (see chapter 1, n. 17) was an example of this. Pan-babylonism and pan-ugaritism are others that have exerted a profound influence on ANE interpretation.[208]

No one can argue against the general idea of cultural movement. The tremendous influence of Meopotamian civilization upon its neighbors the Syrians, Hittites,, Hurrians, and Hebrews has been thoroughly documented, although there is some difference in opinion about the source of individual aspects of the cults in these foreign countries.

After a necessary insertion of data from Ugaritic and Herodotus I 199 and its later offshoots, our argument will continue in Secs. 4.22ff, using the most important of the above bibliography.

4.19 The Ugaritic Cognate *qdš*

The study of the subject took a gigantic leap forward when an attempt was made to learn about the Hebrew *qādēš* and *qědēšāh* from supposed parallels in the Mesopotamian *qadištu* and the Ugaritic *qdš*. This had been done intermittently throughout the years (see the bibliography in Sec. 4.18.2), but in recent years in a serious way, with a piling up of articles, even though the occurrences of these two offices in the literature of Mesopotamia and Ugarit are surprisingly few. Those from Mesopotamia are studied rather fully in Sec. 4.11.

In Ugarit the *qdš* appears only on lists. In two similar lists, one in Akkadian and one in Ugaritic, columns can be compared:

PRU VI No. 93 (RS 17.131)	PRU II No. 26 UT 169 (RS 14.84)
l[ú] *mar-ya-nu-ma* line 1	*mrynm* line 1
lú *mur*] *-ú šarri* 2	*mrum* 2
lú *mur-ú* I*i-bi-ra-na* 16	*mru.ebrn* r.7
lú *tamkaru* 3	*mkrm* 9
lú *ša-na-nu-ma* 6	*šnnm* 4
lú *naqidu* 7	*nqdm* 5
lú *mur-ú* lú *šà-ki-ni* 9	*mru.skn* r.7
lú *qa* [*d*]*šu* (NU.GIG) 26	*qdšm* 7
lú *šangû* 27	*khnm* 6
	pslm 8

In these lists court, army and cultic offices appear. The *maryannu* was part of a nobility though at times listed with professions, a social caste using battle-wagons.[209] *mrum* are the lords belonging to the king. The *nqd* "a kind of shepherd" appears often with the *khn* "priest" and also, incongruously, in a Hebrew cognate in the first verse of the Book of Amos, and in 2 Kings 3.4 of Mesha king of Moab. *šangû* we would expect as the equivalent to *khn*. The *qds* is the root familiar from Hebrew and Akkadian and in the above lists is masculine only.

In Ugaritic, the feminine *qdšt* appears only in PRU V (Virolleaud) No. 163 and CTA 113, see C. Virolleaud, *Mémorial Legrange* 1940, 39-49. With no attempt at comparison across the columns:

PRU V No. 163 col. i RS 18.251	CTA 113 UT 400 col. v
1 *bn* [	6 *mr'u.skn*
2 *bn.qdšt*	*bn.bddn*
3 *bn.m'nt*	*bn.ġrgn*
4 *bn.g* [ ]*n*	*bn.tgtn*
5 *bn* [ ]	10 *bn.ḥrẓn*
	bn.qdšt
col. ii	*bn.nṯg* [
	bn.gr [
3 *bn* [ ]	
4 *bn.y(r)* [ ]	
5 *bn.kšr* [t]	
6 *bn.śml*	
7 *bn.arnbt*	
8 *qdšm*	

9 *b* [ ]*t*

These seem to be names of persons in classes or guilds (*bn* "children of"); Aistleitner lists them as PNs. There is a real estate transaction in *Ugaritica* V No. 7 (RS 17.36) with a PN Abdipidar <bin> Qadišti.[210] This is the only example of a f. form that could be found outside of the list-type texts in Ugaritic. *qdšt* and *qdš* appear on the same tablet on PRU V 163. CTA 113 has the *bn qdšt* appearing among male officials.

A tiny tablet UT 63, CTA 77, *Syria* 15 (1934) 243:

khnm.tš ^{c}	priests, 9
bnšm.w.ḥmr	men and a donkey
qdšm.tš ^{c}	qdsm, 9
bnšm.w.ḥmr	men and a donkey

Gordon suggests that *khnm* are duals: "2 priests, 2 *qdšm*." The same equippage is assigned to the priests as to the *qdšm*, indicating their relative equivalent rank. We find that the *qdšm* appear often with the *khnm* on the Ugaritic lists.

UT 113, RS 11.716, CTA 71 has a list of temple officiants, among whom are:

70 *ṯn n m*
71 *nqdm*
72 *khnm*
73 *qdšm*
74 *n* (?)*sk.ksp*
75 mkrm

ṭuppu ṣābê ^{meš} *ša* ^{giš} *[qašā]ti* ^{meš}
"tablet of soldiers with bows"

Again the *nqdm* "a kind of shepherd", *khnm* "priests" and *qdšm* appear together. The office with *ksp* "silver" may be *nsk.ksp* "silversmith." *mkrm* is the merchant. Cultic and auxiliary offices of the temple appear together, as they do in Mesopotamian documents, but why this group should furnish archers escapes me.

Noting relative amounts of rations, one possible way of comparing the relative importance of ranks, can be done on UT 81, RS 8.252, CTA 75:

khnm	3 GUR	ZÍ-KAL-KAL	6 GIN	KÙ.[BABBAR 6...]	"6 shekels
qdšm	3	6	6		sil[ver]"
mkrm	3	6	6		
ms (?)*m*	1	2	2	or *mdm* cf. next list	
'inšt	2PA	5	5		
hrš.bhtm	3	6	6	"house maker"	

Syria 18 (1937) 164 (see *Syria* 21 (1940)130 n.1 and p.151) suggests that KAL.KAL = *kalaga* "strong flour." Of course, we do not know the relative numbers of persons represented, but the *qdšm* again appear with the *khnm*, with the same amounts, indicating a relatively high position. *mkrm* "merchants" appears also, as on the tablet immediately above. Perhaps read *mdm* instead of *msm* because of the below example. For *'inšt* see Sec. 1.50.2.

Some of these same offices reappear in UT 114, CTA 73:

qd (?)[*šm*]	[ ]		
mr'u s [*kn*]			[ ]
mr'u 'ib [*rn*]	[ ]		
mdm	1		
'inšt	[ ]		
nsk.ksp	2	"silversmith"	
yshm	1		
ḥrš mrkbt	1	"wagonmaker"	
ḥrš qṭn	1	"*qṭn* maker"	
ḥrš bhtm	2	"house builder"	

The restoration of *qd* (?)[*šm*] is reasonable, because some of these same offices appeared with *qdšm* above.

For another usage of the root *qdš* UT 1004, PRU 2,4 lists offerings (of what is not specified) to several divinities: Reshef, *elt qb* [*l* (?)], *mgmr* "a god" (unknown), [ ] *qdšt*. For *elt qb* [*l* (?)] cf. *ilāt qabli* "goddess of combat" = Ishtar, see Borger *Esarh* 75 §48.4. There is room for two signs before *qdšt*, and the editor compares *bn qdšt*. de Moor, *Seasonal Pattern* 124 translates CTA 2 I. 13-47 line 21: *bn qdš* parallel to *'ilm*, a clear case of the root *qdš* meaning "gods." Note that *qadištu* in Akkadian is an epithet of Ishtar.

This root often appears as part of a god-name. *qdš 'il bt* "*qdš* of the sanctuary," *Ugaritica* V, chap III No. 11.7 (RS 24.260). A god Qdš-w-amrr appears, No. 10.B.9. A god *qdš -mlk*, No. 10.B.2 "of the king." *qdš* is a synonym for *'ilm* also in 2 Aqhat 1.4.

von Soden has a fine article on the subject of this root in Ugaritic.[211] The polemic against cultic prostitution as an institution in the Hebrew Bible showed its great role in the neighboring cult, according to the standard argument, he says. Until now no example of the *qdšm* in Ugarit gave information about the cultic function. They appear only on lists with other artisans, the collective designation for non-priestly temple personnel.

But now there is PRU III, RS 16.132 (pp. 140f) in which a certain Adalshenni and his sons get "liberty" and rise in *maryannu* -ship, a noble rank at Ugarit. Line 7 is often read: *i-na qa-at šu-ut-ti* "for that occasion (?)" but a philological justification for this cannot be found, and it cannot be associated with *šuttu* "dream," and von Soden suggests *i-na qa-ad-šu-ut-ti iš-ši* "he (the king) elevated (him) to the *qdš* - ship, referring to *našû* 5(d) "to raise" in AHw 763a. Von Soden understands *qdš* as the general designation for non-priestly temple personnel.

If this is acceptable, the text shows that the *qdš* could marry and have a family, which fits in poorly with the idea of "cult prostitute," if one were to use it as a cognate. This reading of von Soden is quite possible, but we have to wait for others to back it up.

There is a "Silbenalphabet" from Ras Shamra:

19 sag.kud	NU.GIG	
20 sag.kud.da.a	NU.GIG.AN.NA	
21' sag.AN	a-ri-ra	"blazing"

22 sag (.AN).tuk	*mu-ki-in-nu*	"witness"
23'sag.mu	*ša-ru-ru*	"Strahlen(glanz)"AHw 1193b
24'sag.kur	*la-ap-nu*	"poor"
25'sag.kur.ta	*muš-kè-nu*	"a societal class"
26'kud.da	NU.GIG	
27'kud.da.a	NU.GIG.AN.NA	

J. Nougayrol, Landsberger AV 36f
(A composite of 6 RS numbers)

Nothing here shows that the NU.GIG/*qdš* is anything like a "male sacred prostitute" as Urie[212] or that this person is engaged in sexual activities.[213] Tarragon[214] also finds no evidence to support this: "Le hiérodule n'est pas attesté à Ugarit." (p. 140) We have also reached this conclusion in the above studies.

To summarize: the *qdš* is masculine in Ugaritic except in two cases of classes or guilds. It appears in 9 lists, in 4 of which he is next to the *khnm,* and in one of them receives the same amount of rations as the *khnm*. This certainly indicates a cultic or temple office. The fact that the *qdšm* appear in the plural may not indicate lesser importance, for the *khnm* do also, and we think of them as significant individuals. Nothing in the lists gives us a hint about what they do in the cult.

There are a number of articles and books on the symbolization of fertility as it appears in the Ugaritic tablets. This topic in the Baal texts is rare, but it is implied. The topic is huge; a few references are in de Moor, *Seasonal Pattern*.

4.20 Herodotus I, 199

Since none of the references to *qdš /qdšt* in Ugarit or *qadištu* in Mesopotamia describes their relationship to "sacred prostitution," nor does the word for the institution, if there was one, appear in these texts, the scholars went out looking for what may have happened and they found it! They found it, surprisingly to us who can take a stand-offish point of view, in Greek writings and, even more surprisingly, in that master of credulous tales, rumors, hearsays, yet supposedly on-the-spot investigations, the "father of history" himself, Herodotus.

Her I (Klio), 199, reads as follows, with no context to describe this further (A.D. Godley's translation in the Loeb Library):

> The foulest Babylonian custom is that which compels every woman of the land once in her life to sit in the temple of Aphrodite and have intercourse with some stranger. ...with crowns of cord on their heads; there is a great multitude of women coming and going; passages marked by line run every way through the crowd, by which the stranger men pass and make their choice. When a woman has once taken her place there she goes not away to her home before some stranger has cast money into her lap and had intercourse with her outside the temple; but while he casts the money he must say, "I demand thee in the name of Mylitta" (that is the Assyrian name for Aphrodite). It matters not what be the sum of the money; the woman will never refuse, for that were a sin, the money being by this act made sacred. So she follows the first man who casts it and rejects none. After their intercourse she has made herself holy in the goddess's sight and goes

away to her home; and thereafter there is no bribe however great that will get her. So then the women that are fair and tall are soon free to depart, but the uncomely have long to wait because they cannot fulfil the law; for some of them remain for three years, or four. There is a custom like this in some parts of Cyprus.

This passage has been the subject of much discussion, as can be imagined. First of all, those of us who have studied Mesopotamian civilization for many years have never come across anything remotely near this practice. Second, it wouldn't work: the temple would be full of thousands, indeed, tens of thousands of women roaming around, who have to be housed, fed, elimination needs provided for, taken care of medically, etc. for many years. The temples we know of were much too small for this, even if we can envisage the logistics necessary. Third, despite the exploitation of women in some aspects of their society, I doubt that the Babylonian women would allow such a practice. It would make every woman by law a prostitute. Fourthly, how would it be monitored? And so forth.

Herodotus is known to be filled with errors and misunderstandings. Early on F. Delitzsch points this out.[215] W. Kornfeld, in a long article which takes sacred prostitution for granted, nevertheless does not find in the whole vast Assyro-Babylonian literature confirmation that each woman must prostitute herself at the temple of Mylitta.[216]

Hartland[217] does not criticize the accuracy of the report, nor the workability of the custom, but has some trenchant things to say, nevertheless. This could not be sacred prostitution, because it was done only once. The Mylitta rite could be an "expiation for marriage," asserting for the last time the primitive rights of the male sex,[218] but this theory has been given up by anthropologists. Furthermore, prostitution -- sexual intercourse for hire -- is not a primitive practice, but a product of civilization. Hartland suggests that the Babylonian rite was a puberty rite.

Arnaud[219] feels that in the late Aramaized temple life Her I 199 preserves a trace of what the temple had degenerated into, from a place in the second millenium in which women had a high cultic and economic role, to that of the first millenium. The testimony, especially in the abbreviated form in which it appears in Herodotus, is fabricated (controuvé), but it shows an attempt on the part of the Babylonian scholars [he believes that they were the source] to explain their recent interpretation.

Even as early an Assyriologist as C.H.W. Johns[220] writes in reference to the votary class as a whole: "nowhere in the code [Codex Hammurapi] or elsewhere is there any trace of the evil reputation which Greek writers [Herodotus] assign to these ladies, and the translations which makes them prostitutes, or unchaste, are not to be accepted. The list goes on.[221]

4.21 Influences of Her I,199 on Later Literature

4.21.1 To admit the difficulty with simply dismissing this passage, we note its great effect on later literature. The Epistle of Jeremiah 11 (Baruch 6) tells the captives sent to Babylon what they will see: gods made of silver and gold, priests taking silver and gold and even giving some of it to the prostitutes *epi tou tegous* [222] translated "brothel" in RSV, "roof" in RSV fn, "roof" JB, "temple prostitute" REB, "on the terrace" NRSV, "in the inner chamber" NEB. And later on he speaks of how the Chaldeans dishonor women (vs. 43) who, "with cords about them, sit along the passageways, burning bran for incense; and when one of them is led off by one of the passers-by and is lain with, she derides the woman next to her, because she was not as attractive as herself, and her cord was not broken." (RSV)

Many commentators (Eissfeld, Weiser, Tedsche IDB) date the Epistle of Jeremiah at about the 2-lst c. B.C.E, others (Bentzen, Soggin, Pfeiffer) at 4-1 c. B.C.E. or 3-1 c. B.C.E. (Dancy). The dependence of this passage on Her I, 199 is strong.

4.21.2 Testament of Judah 12.1 [223] has an echo only: "there was a law among the Amorites that a woman who was widowed should sit in public like a whore."(H.C. Kee, in J. Charlesworth, *The Old Testament Pseudepigrapha.*) This is in a context of the Tamar story in Gen 38.

4.21.3 Strabo *Geography* (1 c. B.C.E.) has several references to this pattern, one almost the same story as above: all Babylonian women have a custom of having sexual intercourse with a foreigner. They go to the temple of Aphrodite, wreathed with a cord round the head. The man approaches her, takes her far from the sacred precinct, places money in her lap, then has intercourse. The money is considered sacred to Aphrodite. (xvi, 1, 20)

4.21.4 In a similar vein, Strabo says that the Egyptians dedicate to Zeus a maiden of the greatest beauty and most illustrious family, called *palladas* ("Pallas Athena's Way"), and she prostitutes herself with whatever man she wishes until menstruation, then is given in marriage, but before she is married, after the time of her prostitution, a rite of mourning is celebrated for her (xvii, 1, 46)

4.21.5 And yet another vague reference from Strabo: Persian men consecrate their daughters to be prostitutes in the temple of the goddess (not named) for a long time, and after that they are given in marriage.[224] Then he (mis)quotes Her I, 199 by name, with a hint of the content of Her I, 93-4; reported by Ramsay.[225]

4.21.6 Lucian of Samosata (2 c. C.E.)[226] tells of a temple of Aphrodite in Byblos in which after offerings to Adonis as if he were dead, on the morrow they learn he is alive and shave their heads. And those women who would not let their heads be shaved must pay a penance, standing all day with their persons for hire. The place of hire is open to none but strangers and out of the proceeds of this traffic a sacrifice to Aphrodite is paid. See also Frazer, Adonis 23.

4.21.7 Eusebius (3-4 c. C.E.) says[227] that Constantine found in the Phoenician city of Heliopolis those who dignified licencious pleasures and "permitted their wives and daughters to commit shameless fornication." The emperor forbade these practices.

4.21.8 Sozomen (5th c.) [228] picks up on some of this and says that Constantine destroyed the temple of Venus at Heliopolis, abolishing the ancient custom of yielding up virgins to prostitution on the eve of marriage.

4.21.9 The pollution of the Hebrew temple by the Greeks is described in broad strokes in 2 Macc 6.4. It was full of Gentiles who "dallied with harlots and had intercourse with women within the sacred precincts."(RSV)

Other Greek examples are in Asmussen, *Studia Theologica* 11 (1956), Lund. Obviously some of these are garbled versions, or late echoes of Her I, 199, or simply accusing the Greeks of promiscuity everywhere, even in the sacred temple.

4.21.10 Looking for some truth in Herodotus' report: there indeed were prostitutes in Mesopotamia -- they are mentioned from Codex Hammurapi onwards. One of Inanna/Ishtar's titles was *harimtu* "prostitute" (CAD H 101a) and in the èš-dam (see App. 4.1.11) and elsewhere she played this role, which probably means that her cultic officiants played it for her. Whether the actual sexual act was done regularly in the temple by these officiants may be doubted, but because of the wisdom literature's criticism of it, something untoward must have happened from time to time. Turning the argument around, of course, one could say that the seriousness with which symbolic fertilty was taken argues against it. In MA, NA and NB documents our officiants appear less often, but even here they are taken seriously; this might argue against promiscuity. Herodotus' time was much later than most of our texts, so the temple could have degenerated by then, but we have no corroborating evidence of this.

Furthermore, Her I 199 does not tell of a cultic officiant engaging in sexual acts, but every women of Babylon. This is a completely different story. Perhaps the combination of the symbolic nature of this, and the symbolic nature of the so-called "sacred marriage" was conflated by Herodotus, who was going by hearsay anyway, and by using a Greek mindset came up with the story in I, 199. (For another Babylonian practice described by Her I, 181, see under Sacred Marriage, Sec. 4.23)

4.22 "Sacred Prostitution" in Greece, Mesopotamia and the Hebrew Bible

4.22.1 We will now look at the modern commentators, and with skepticism about Herodotus, see what they say "sacred prostitution" was. Many use the term "hierodule," which they know from Greek *hierodoulai* "sacred servants," so we must look at Greek literature first. The word was used in many different ways in the ancient world, even in 1 Esdras 1.3 as designation of the Levites as the *hierodouloi* of Israel. It settled down in the usage of Strabo (especially many examples), Athenagoras, Pausanius, Plutarch, Lucien and several more writers as a designation of a certain class of temple servants.

Hild points out in a richly detailed article[229] that in certain temples of Aphrodite hierodules of both sexes appear, especially in Phoenicia, Syria and Asia Minor. Those dedicated to Apollo, especially the Delphian Apollo, were privileged, the others more or less so. They reflect some dependence or bondage to the temple whether through birth, devotion, sale or asylum. The degree of dependence depends upon the country, the cult and the time. There could be a priest over them who was the equal of a king. The women served as musicians and dancers and engaged in an act of prostitution as a form of piety. The price of their amours served to provide revenue for the temple. At Byblos women celebrated a funerary rite in honor of Adonis, shaving their heads and using the prize of their prostitution as a sacrifice. This Greek practice is what was read back onto a Mesopotamian practice by many commentators [RAH].

Dancing figures on bas-reliefs of marble show women playing on a tympani and wearing woven wicker crowns and flowing gowns, like the Maenades. Strabo XI.512 tells of a large temple in Cappadocian Comana which was rich and in which 6000 *hierodoulai* reside, and Strabo VIII.6.20 tells of those at Corinth dedicated to Aphrodite in which there were 1000 *hierodoulai hetairai* "companions, courtesans, harlots." These hierodules also extend (says Hild) to the temple of Jehovah in Jerusalem, under the name of *kedeschot* and *kedeschim* "the consecrated," and they see no one except "depraved strangers." Here he seems to be combining a 19th c. commentary on Deuteronomy 23.17 with late takeooffs on Her I 199. For *qādēš* and *qědēšāh* see Sec. 4.18.

4.22.2 Asmussen[230] has many wise things to say in a wide-ranging study, going through biblical and Mishnaic texts, with a comment on women priests in Israelite religion, village Arabic practices, Greek religion, North Arabic, Old South Arabic, Qur'an, those with any characteristics of a "hierodule." His use of Mesopotamian material (wholly Assyrian) is thin, but he is excellent in gathering post-biblical texts. He has a section on *qedešah* and then Her I 199, then on to veiling practices in Assyria. He ranges about lands neighboring Israel, going too far in time and space for my taste (e.g. Jacob of Sarug, 521 C.E. in the Syriac Church, p. 176) but he has a fine collection of examples. Without stating a definition, he emphasizes the need of ancient religion to provide fertility, in cult form, that there be a balance between Chaos and Cosmos. Yahweh religion provides fertility but not fertility rites (p. 171). Without stating it directly, he seems to be saying that the symbolism of these rites is what we would call "prostitution."

4.22.3 B. Brooks in a later work on female titles in the Hebrew Bible,[231] does some early study of *nĕtînîm*, *qādēš*, *zônāh*, *yôšebet*, *ṣĕba'ôt*, *ᶜalmāh*, at the conclusion of which she decides that sacred prostitition is prevalent in early Hebrew religion (pp. 249ff).

4.22.4 Using only one example (though typical) of present-day scholarship, G. von Rad gives a description of the presumed "Canaanite sexual cult" using the concept of cultural diffusion;[232] this popular biblical scholar is widely quoted.

4.22.5 Eugene J. Fisher[233] goes through passages which have been interpreted as prostitution, and extrabiblical sources in which "ritual intercourse" is alleged to be present. Hierogamy seems to have been an integral part of the Babylonian New Year's Festival, bringing this quite different subject [RAH] into the argument, as many do. Deut 23.17f concerns prostitution "of a particular class of temple personnel." But why would the hire of a harlot be brought into the temple, he asks. Hos 4.14 parallels people doing (root) *p-r-d* with prostitutes and those sacrificing with *qĕdēšāh's*. Fisher explains this as synthetic parallelism, but on a deeper level than the two nouns. First harlots, then idolotry, defined as *haqqĕdēšôt*, one after the other. He doesn't go further into this, and the explanation is left dangling. Much of the excesses of past exegesis depend upon the misreading of the common biblical metaphor of sexual misconduct as a metaphor for idolatry. The article essentially says that no ritual prostitution can be found.

4.22.6 E. Yamauchi[234] quotes H.W.F. Saggs, *Greatness That Was Babylon* (p. 36) as saying that cultic prostitution was considered by the Sumerians as a divinely ordained institution. Inanna was called nu-gig-an-na. (Like many others, Yamauchi assumes that nu-gig = *qadištu* is "often" translated "hierodule.") He points out that the tablet *Ana ittišu* shows the only example of the *qadištu* 's relationship to prostitution. He then quotes C.H. Gadd[235] that the *nadītum* was perhaps a class of temple prostitutes (p. 214). Arguing against the definiteness of this statement, he points out, are B. Landsberger in Baumgartner AV 202-3, W.G. Lambert in *JEOL* 15 (1957-8) 195, and Oppenheim in *Or* 19 (1950) 135 n.1 ("actors in cultic performances"), but he gives only a fast run-down of *assinnu*, *kurgarrû* and *kulu'u*, with no mention of cultic prostitution. He notes disagreements among Lambert, Diakonoff, Landsberger and Finkelstein over the meaning of Gilgamesh iv 34-6 (p. 216) as the ius primae noctis.

Then: "clear references to cultic prostitution" are found in the following (biblical) passages: Deut 23.17-18 and other *qĕdēšāh* passages, and "possible allusions to sacred prostitution" in Num 25.1-3, 1 Sam 2.22, Jer 13.27, Ezek 16 and 23.37-41 and Am 2.7-8 (p. 218). His article shows a sureness, using the concept of "cultural diffusion" (never defined) that the others do not have, referring to practices from Mesopotamia, Egypt, Palestine, Syria and Phoenicia, Cyprus, Corinth and Carthage, a spread indicating quite a variagated group of peoples, the examples from most of which are later than our era.

4.22.7 W. von Soden, the editor of the AHw, in his characteristically careful way[236] describes the practice of a woman being given either to any man or to a king or priest in the sanctuary of the mother or love-goddess. Religious, magical and coarse sensual motives are interrelated. The religious is that the inconceivable mystery of procreation may be dedicated to the goddess by the union of man and woman. The woman brings her chastity as an offering [But she can only do this once!] It is magical in the wish to secure through the union the fruitfulness of all life in the land. It then fell into just another hedonistic cult.

Cultic prostitution [he says it with confidence] was first in Babylonia, and it is still unclear whether it was practiced among the Sumerians. It was used especially in the cult of Ishtar with its center at Uruk. An unpublished hymn (source not given) from the time of Hammurapi paints Ishtar as an active type of cultic prostitute whom 120 men could not tire. One cannot call the sacred marriage anything like sacred prostitution, because the king and the *entu*-priestess of Sin in Ur are the players.

The Old Testament tells of the cultic prostitution of the Phoenicians in 2 Kings 23.13, Hosea and Ezekiel especially preached against this. The *zĕnûnê* "harlotries" of Jezebel in 2 Kings 9.22 could be the Phoenician cultic prostitution. The *qĕdēšāh* especially served Asherah, Anat and Astarte [for which he gives no evidence]

4.22.8 W.G. Lambert in a wide-ranging article[237] discusses prostitution, marriage, the New Year's ceremony, the ius primae noctis and Her I 199. He points out that there was in that society no distinction between the morally right and the ritually proper. J. Bottéro would put it: the Mesopotamians were not so much concerned with moral faults, but with the risk of bad luck.[238] The New Year's ceremony entailed a priest and a priestess having intercourse for securing fertility for the state, a rite portrayed with a few figurines. [We will argue that these are not cultic in Sec. 4.23.3.] The same applies to cultic prostitution. No one doubts its prevalence, expecially with the cult of Ishtar, but little is known of its function. The swarms of street prostitutes may have differed from cult prostitutes only in not having religious duties to perform, because they, too, were ex- officio devotees of Ishtar.

There does seem to be a sound historical kernel, he says, behind the *ius primae noctis*, or *droit de seigneur* in Gilgamesh ii 75f. Gilgamesh had the right to sexual intercourse first, then the husband. Maureen Gallery Kovacs[239] gives the arguments.

4.22.9 Walter Kornfeld gives the fullest study of this concept that I have found until the HUC thesis of Hooks.[240] He defines sacred prostitition as meaning that women, and often men also, abandon themselves to sexual commerce with certain persons (kings, priests, etc.) or with whomever they wish, within the temple enclosure, generally dedicated to a mother goddess or her divine paredros (col. 1357). This offering of chastity was necessasry to entreat fertility for man, animals and plants. To maintain, to assure and to develop life are the elementary objectives to which all religious since prehistoric times lead. [A powerful statement with which I would entirely agree.] Much of his argument presumes that Inanna was the post-prehistoric personification of the earth-mother, the more sophisticated result from an earlier more simplified society. The man in this situation is found in a subordinate position to that of the goddess.

Under the influence of evolutionism, we formerly had the tendency in the history of religions to interpret sacred prostitution as a sacrifice pars pro toto, as with the sacrifice of fingers or hair, circumcision or castration. But now we distinguish two different rites: one, the rites of passage, which are together sacrifices pars pro toto, and the other, rites of fertility.

Fertility cults take root in agrarian sedentary civilizations, not in nomadic civilizations (col. 1359).

He finds sacred prostitution mentioned in Gilgamesh [but we have argued that "prostitution" is not "sacred prostitution"]. Then he refers to Codex Hammurapi which describes several women in the service of the temple. He does not show a knowledge of the intricacies of CH, and uses out-of-date material. [R. Harris has shown that these were several different titles with different practices, and it is a complicated business.] His note that the lukur (*naditum*) exercised sacred prostitution in the Ishtar temples has no evidence behind it.

Now he has a paragraph in itself: "At Babylon, sacred prostitution is abundantly attested." For reference he uses only Plessis (see section immediately below for comment on this highly unusual study of 1921) and E. Dhorme, *L'Evolution religieuse d'Israel* I (1937) -- an odd bibliography !

He turns to sacred eunuchs who represent Tammuz (giving some 1912 and 1919 references). He uses Greek ideas of the galli, emasculated priests, who were male prostitutes, an idea he got from Albright *FSAC* p. 235, something that is quite out of date, and bringing in too many Greek ideas. He refers to Philo and Lucian for descriptions of gods emasculating themselves, and in the process gives a mistaken interpretation of the office *kumru*.

His next unit on sacred prostitution among the Canaanites and Phoenicians ("numerous mentions in the Old Testament") is based closely on W.F. Albright.[241] He goes on to find sacred prostitution in Syria, Egypt, Asia Minor among the Hittites (no conclusion, but probable, on the basis of Hittite Laws §80), Phrygia, Lydia, ancient Arabia.[242] He then plunges into a rather complete mention of biblical texts which relate to the subject. In Israel, he says, sacred prostitution was a religion of the people, colored by syncretism and more or less diffuse. Thus it is hard to define, and there was no orthodox practice which we can use as a touchstone, yet it falls into a broad pattern. [But his brush strokes are too broad.] We will discuss more of his ideas below. He is certainly right to separate folk religion from the high religion of our Hebrew Bible texts.

4.22.10 Joseph Plessis, *Etude sur les Textes Concernant Ištar-Astarté*. Paris, 1921 is a collection of Akkadian, Hebrew and Greek texts with commentary, many of them translated, references always given, concerning *assinnu*, *kulu'u*, *qdš qdšh*, SAL.ME (i.e., lukur), etc. He spends some time with Lucian, *De Dea Syria,* but then perceptively takes up Babylonian texts which turned out 40 or 50 years later to be the important ones for our subject. He then slips into a discussion of Deut 23.17 with "De même ..." but they all do that. The book is quite out of date (R. Borger in *HKL* I 409b says "nicht berüchsicktigt") but it is based on original texts, and as a check list can point to modern studies. The book seems to be photographed (?) from handwriting, yet is published by the respectable Paul Guethner.

4.22.11 Wolfgang Helck, *Betrachtungen zur Grossen Göttin und den ihr verbundenen Gottheiten.* München u.Wien, 1971, is a major study through the eyes of an Egyptologist, but one who knows Assyriology, and is a careful scholar. He says (p.241, n.47) there is uncertainty in ascribing certain Old Testament texts to cultic prostitution. In discussing the sacred marriage, he says that until now this union (between Inanna and Dumuzi) was understood as a fertility ritual which may act in sympathetic magic on the world. In the marriage of these two deities there is manifested the fertility and power of procreation of nature itself. Yet it seems to me (he says), that this interpretation emanates from a Hellenistic interpretation and does not find support in the texts. [This is my point -- RAH]. He then discusses the Iddin-Dagan texts which we will take up below, Sec. 4.23.4. He analyzes the results of this rite to be the appointing of the destiny for the king and the lands, that the right progression of the year and the rulership of the king would be set.

4.22.12 T. Jacobsen, *Treasures of Darkness* (1976) after quoting at length from some divine marriage texts, says they show that the divine bridegroom was represented in the rite by the human king -- in this case by Iddin-Dagan, Sec. 4.23.4, and "as a human king he could take on the identity of the god of fertility and yield, so the queen or perhaps a high priestess would probably have assumed in the ritual the identity of Inanna."(p. 39) Here he is indefinite, as befits the data.

4.22.13 M. Daniel Arnaud, "La Prostitution Sacrée en Mésopotamie, un myth historiographique?" *RHR* 183 (1973) 111-115. Taking off from Her I, 199, he says that "sacred prostitution" is becoming a "historiographic myth," i.e., an affirmation repeated from handbook to handbook, and sometimes in technical articles, with the proof resting on the reader, by an reversal of academic practice. [This will be my conclusion--RAH] There is a deeply rooted tradition in western historiography of the lewdness of the Mesopotamians, perhaps stemming from the Bible. This may be responsible for the agreed-upon subject of "sacred prostitution." He says that the clay plaques showing coitus (Sec. 4.23.3) have no religious character, with no recognizable relationship to the cult of the goddess of love.

The woman at the window (reminding us of Inanna/Ishtar at the door of the esdam as a procuress, App. 4.1.11) brings us closer to sacred prostitution, but it is not found in Mesopotamia, except in a late borrowing (p. 112). He thinks that the goddess seated at the window shows her guarding the house against the incursion of demons of disease. He brings in Kilili, a female demon, "queen of the windows," but who goes through the windows for aggression. She is the companion of Lamashtu, ever amorous.

Barnett comments with more depth on this subject.[243] He studies the theme "woman at the window" in the Nimrud Ivories. She wears a frontlet on her forehead, perhaps the mark of a prostitute. She is a goddess, perhaps a form of Aphrodite. In Mesopotamia she is called ab-ba-šú-šú, *muširtu ša apāte* "she who bends out of the window," or Kilili *ša apāte* "Kilili of the windows." (from CAD A/2 199 1c and K. 357)

Arnaud points out that for over a millenium, from OB to NA/NB times, the title *qadištu* was kept for Inanna/Istar and other goddesses, though we do not know what reality (réalité) the scribes gave to the term. [Actually, we do not know what "reality" the scribes gave to any ancient ritual text -- the cultural difference and time span between them and us are too great.]

The several incantations against sexual impotence (see Biggs, ŠÀ.ZI.GA) use a medical point of view, nothing which invokes prostitution much less sacred prostituion. These incantations like those of the 104th Tablet of*Šumma ālu*[244] were used by the scholars in jerry-built fashion, with a background of western scholarship's understanding of the "lewdness" of the Mesopotamians, into the scheme which they called "sacred prostitution."

He then discusses the *kurgarrû, assinnu* and others whose importance and titles will be discussed in Appendix 3. He is brave enough to go on to the *entu, nadītu, ugbabtu, qadištu* and *ištarītu*, but he did it without sufficient background and his work is somewhat out of date. He emphasizes the *kezertu*, who as a part of the temple cult is abundantly attested, and concludes that she is one of the subaltern personnel in the cult places, and is a kind of an oblate. There is no trace of her engaging in cultic prostitution, but her practices were wanton, and we would use the term "tolerated prostitution," but not "organized prostitution." (p. 114). I leave him at this point, for he says that this suggests that there were personnel of doubtful morality kept by the temples, in close liason with others there, but prostitution was a frequent activity, without the sanctuaries extracting any revenue from it (p. 115. Here he seems to be using the *hierodoulai* of Greek life as an analogy, as many do.)

This reflects the milieu that was Uruk, a city which seems to have been the center related to this "sacred prostitution," the place to which the *kezertu*'s were linked, and with respect to which had been, it appears, always outsiders.

At the end of this paper Arnaud, who was the Directeur d'Etudès à l'Ecole Pratique des Hautes Etudes, had an exchange of views from Nougayrol, Caquot and Puech. How I wish I could have been there for that!

4.22.14. Stephen Hooks, in a wide-ranging study, takes up the subject as a whole in his *Sacred Prostitution in Israel and the Ancient Near East*, Thesis, Hebrew Union College, Cincinnati, 1985. He finds that in Mesopotamia sacred prostitution simply is not supported by the available evidence. There was sexual intercourse on the part of some female cultic figures, but this was not part of the cult, and this is generally described in the wisdom literature, which is its own genre. All attempts to impute sacred protitution to the *qĕdēšāh* in Israel fall to the ground. Indeed, the attempt to explain this functionary as a figure from the Canaanite cult would require finding examples of the *qdš* in Ugaritic as part of a sex cult, and such is not found. In general, his conclusions are those found by me, but backed up by many fewer examples and with no study of the lexical texts, and with no study of the neighboring subjects as done in the present work.

4.22.15.1 Now to search for the place, or room, in which the supposed sacred prostitution or sacred marriage (and here the two aspects come close together for many scholars) took place. One collects such important words as *gigunû, bīt ersi, gagû, giparu, kummu.* Among the many other terms for parts or the whole of a sacred place are *agrunnu, aslukkatu, atmanu, emāšu, bīt hammūti, hamru, kiṣṣu, maštaku, nēmedi, papāhu, parakku, paramāhu, sāgu, simakkû, sukku, šubtu, ta'u*. Many of these terms could be used for secular buildings also, but they all need further study, with excavation and architectual studies integrated with them. [Note the cautions mentioned in Sec. Intro. 1.3]

4.22.15.2 For *gigunû* we refer to CAD G 67ff, and Sidney Smith's pioneering article.[245] The *gigunû* was "probably" the sanctuary on the top of the ziggurat (CAD G 70a). It had been in existence at least from Eannatum on. Gudea built a gi-gunu$_4$ of cedar in the é-ninnu (Cyl A xxiv 20) at Lagash, so it is a structure. Nabonidus made the ziggurat in Larsa [*gi*] - *gu* - [*ni-e*] - *šú* "his *gigunû*" higher than it ever was[246] picking up ideas from earlier years, from

Samsuiluna (68a). Many deities were found in it. The lú-mah is found in the *gigunû* of Ur (69a). Anu and Ishtar were together in the *parakku* in the *gigunû* temple of Ishtar in Uruk (69b). The god Hendursag is called en of the *gigunû* of Nanshe's temple.[247] Other titles found in this unusual Hymn of Nanshe are a šita$_x$-aba, a susbu, a sanga (117-20), the enkum and nimkum (133), a kuš-lá and a gada-lá (103f).

4.22.15.3 The *bīt erši* "bedroom" was also part of a temple, and Nabû and Tashmetu entered there on the fourth day of Ayaru presumably to perform the "sacred marriage" rite.[248] A Hellenistic text says that from the 5th day to the 10th day the [go]ds remain in their *bīt erši*.[249] The *eršu* "bed" was more than a mythic idea, for the texts collected by E. Matsushima for the temple of é-babbar[250] describe the bedclothes and further details of the bed; the bedroom was designated either *bīt erši* (NA or later) or *bīt mayāli* (MA and NA only?) The term for this divine marriage in the first millenium was *hašādu*.

Herodotus' description of a shrine with a bed at the top of the "tower" must not be swallowed without comment, but it gives us a place to look. In the temple there was a bed[251] ^{giš}NÁ as a place of rest, and also for conjugal union. The bed is in the ki-NÁ "bedroom," and also é-NÁ-da (cf. *kummu*, Sec. 4.22.15.6). Beds were named by the year-name, as thrones were.[252]

4.22.15.4 The *gagû* is the home of the *entu*. An astronomical text[253] has *ga-gi-e = bit en-ti*. CH §110.37 refers to a nin-dingir / *entu* or *ugbabtu* who lives in the *gagû*, the possibility is there. The *gagû* was also the residence of the *nadītu* in OB times. There could be about 200 *nadiu's* in the *gagû* at any one time.[254]

4.22.15.5 Penelope Weadock gathers much material together about the gipar.[255] She speaks of the *giparu* as the official home of the *entu* from ED to NB times. Regnal years are named after it. The *entu* was the human wife of the god Nanna. As this she participates in the sacred marriage. We have the most information from Uruk, where an en-priest served as the consort of Inanna and represented her divine husband Dumuzi.

> At the lapis lazuli door
> which stands in the gipar
> she (Inanna) met the en.
> At the narrow (?) door
> which stands in Eanna
> she met Dumuzi

TCL 16 pl. 136:30, CAD G 83a, Jacobsen's translation in *ZA* 18 (1957) 108 n. 32.

The en's role is discussed by Jacobsen.[256] It was a political one, but also a sexual (fertility) role, because in cities where the chief deity was male, the en was a woman (Akkadian *enum* or *entum*), and in cities where the chief deity was female, the en was a man (Akkadian *enum*.)

The *giparu* at Ur was discovered by Leonard Woolley in 1924-25, and proved as such by many inscriptions; he dated its earliest stratum as ED (but levels below this were not excavated), probably ED III. [257]

The išib, lú-mah, gudu$_4$, and gìr-sè-gá live in the gi$_6$-par$_x$-ra.[258] There was a *giparu* for Ningal in Haran in NA times (Streck *Asb* 288.10), for Sin in Ur (CAD G 84a). The gi$_6$-pàr-kù "holy gipar" was a residence of the *entu* of Nanna at Ur, the place of the fertility rite of the sacred marriage (CAD G 84b).

One of the tragic things that happened at the destruction of Ur was that the en was carried off from the gipar.[259]

4.22.15.6 The *kummu* / É.NUN was a private room in a temple or palace. Shamash lived there (CAD K 533b), as well as Zababa, Nusku, Anu and Ishtar of Agade (ibid.). The é-gi$_6$-par, the residence of the *entu* in Ur, was called *kummu ellu* "the pure/holy *kummu*."[260]

4.22.15.7 Other terms for cultic rooms or wings on temples appear. The agrun /*ag(a)runnu* was the place where the en brought her statuette.[261] The *emašu* appears usually on lexical texts, but once on Enuma Elish, CAD s.v. For é-uš-gíd-da /*ašlukkatu* "storehouse," Sumerian "long house" see CAD A/2 s.v., a part of the temple complex.[262] The *hammūtu* is a room on the ziggurat, and is one of the candidates for the shrine on top.[263] The *kiṣṣu* was built on the tops of the ziggurats of Babylon and Borsippa in NB times.[264] The pa-pah/*papāhu* was joined to the side of the ziggurat.[265]

A *parakku* was in the *gigunû* of Ishtar, Sec. 4.22.15.2. It is a Kultsockel as well as Heiligtum or Cella (AHw), perhaps the room being named after the platform that was in it. It appears in nA, nB times and later. The *param (m)ahu* in Seleucid times was part of the ziggurat of the Bīt-Rēš temple in Uruk and had a roof.[266] This could also be the name of the shrine room on the top of the ziggurat.

sāgu /*sagû* is part of a temple, at times seemingly a general term for a cultic room in a temple (CAD s.v. *sagû* A). In a Shalmaneser text (MA, 13c B.C.E.), it is listed along with other sanctuaries as *w/aširtu, sukku*'s, *parakku*'s, *nēmedu*'s.[267] *simakku* is a sacred room which, in NB times, is listed along with *sāgu* and *kummu* (CAD S s.v.), but there are several references to an effigy of a deity in it. *šubtu* is a "dwelling place" of the gods, from the standard root in Semitic languages for "to dwell." The *sukku* seems to be a smallish space, CAD s.v. The *ta'u* is an inner room for the gods in OB.[268] An article summarizing much of this terminology is given by von Soden.[269]

Somewhere in these sacred spaces at least some of the officiants discussed in these pages performed their tasks.

4.22.16 From these schemas for "sacred prostitution" it is seen that each of the scholars approaches the subject differently, but that there is a tendency to lump various aspects together, ones that we have attempted to deal with separately in this study. It is true that they were all together in history, but we should bring them together only to the extent that the ancients did. They are all interrelated in some complex way, and we have attempted to bring up all the aspects of the subject we could find. My conclusion after this study is that the concept of fertility is uppermost, and that the cult provided for it, dramatized it, prayed for it in words and symbols, in both Mesopotamian and Hebrew life, and that love, marriage, sex, government, family life, and the immense panoply of gods and goddesses in Mesopotamia, with a great deal of overlap between functions and rivalry of various cult places, have to be dealt with. This is the norm for world civilization. The Hebrew answer to this, a deuteronomic-type uniformity deviations from which had to be continually guarded against, was not successful for the vast majority of the populace. In fact, as far as women are concerned, the shift (here one oversimplifies) from polytheism in the lands surrounding Palestine to monotheism in Israel entailed a loss of much of the role of women in the cult.

J.B. Segal[270] suggests that the nature of polytheism caused the Canaanites to use women in their cult, whereas Hebrew monotheism, especially a ritual at a single shrine, assured the exclusion of women. I.J. Peritz[271] with a fine perception for those early days, rings the changes on the subject of how women were excluded from worship life in Tannaitic times, continuing through the Middle Ages, and notes that it has been taken for granted that this exclusion was in the beginning a feature of the Israelite cult. On the contrary, especially in the earlier periods women participated in all essentials of the cult [except as primary sacrificial priest, RAH] both as worshipper and officiant. This was discussed in some detail in Sec. 1.5.5.

We have to make sure we keep on the track and do not lose our way in this morass, not only of details, but of miscellaneous aspects of the subject itself. We have seen that many of the above commentators on "sacred prostitution" bring in the "sacred marriage" as part of this subject. We must now turn to that.

4.23 Sacred Marriage, Mesopotamia

4.23.1 Again there is no term for this practice qua institution in ancient Near Eastern texts. The term is borrowed from Greek literature, *hieros gamos*, and Greek ideas, especially Hellenistic ones, have been used in this study since its inception. J.G. Frazer was greatly influential in his day, and as out of date as some of his ideas are today, his approach remains in part with the subject. He found[272] places all over the world where they spoke of a sympathetic relationship between commerce of the sexes and fertility of the earth. He found divine nuptuals referred to in Her I, 181. Here a tower with other towers on top of it is described, obviously a ziggurat. On top there is a temple, and inside it a couch. It is occupied at night by a single native woman. They also declare that the god comes down in person and sleeps on this couch, Her I, 182. Frazer points out that the marriage of Zeus and Hera was acted out at annual festivals in parts of Greece. He accepts Her I, 199 as an actual custom (§ 218) but does not relate it to the "sacred marriage."

4.23.2 W.K.D. Guthrie brings modern classical scholarship to bear.[273] The term *hieros gamos* does not appear in our understanding of it before the Alexandrinian period.[274] There are earlier poetic expressions in Aeschylus' Danaids. Archetypically the union is between a god of the sky and a goddess of the earth, the actors being different according to local theologies. A nature in which the earth fertile like a mother is fertilized with moisture from the sky lies behind this, as well as the old idea of a Great Earth Mother. The subject has been written upon voluminously, and he quotes Frazer vol. 2 favorably. The dominant figure of fertility is the woman in the ancient cults of the common people. "Male spirits of fertility exist, but they were subordinate figures, satellites of the mother and no more" (p. 60).

4.23.3 As brought out from time to time, figures in or near coitus have been used to prove something. J.S. Cooper[275] describes 48 artifacts from Mesopotamia depicting sexual intercourse. These seem to be private encounters, though ritual cannot be ruled out. No homosexual encounters are unambiguously shown, but they appear in the texts.[276] Many proponents of "sacred prostitution" have taken these scenes as the institution in action. There is no evidence for this. If one had to guess their purpose, more to the mark would be to describe them as apotropaic offerings for impotence.

4.23.4 There are depictions of the "sacred marriage" in texts of the Neo-Sumerian period. In the poem sig$_4$ mùš-za-gin-ta è-a[277] the two hero-lords (en)[278] Ensuhkešdanna of Aratta in Iran, and Enmerkar of Uruk lie, each in his own shrine as rivals, with Inanna in the giš-ná-gi-rin "shining bed"[279] in Uruk (lines 29, 60,81) explained as the še-er-gán/kán-du$_{11}$ "adorned bed."[280] Enmerkar describes the time with her as one in which day or night did not end (lines 87f). This was done in the gi$_6$-par$_x$-kù-gá" the holy gipar (line 90),"[281] Sec. 4.22.15.5. In the temple (èš-gal, in a single occurrence of the term) the nu-gig made a noise like "a young *anzu* -bird" (line 97). Since this is the only time the term nu-gig appears in this text, if the ceremony proceeded from the gipar to the èš-gal, the nu-gig could be interpreted as representing Inanna.

The fullest text, indeed the only complete one that we have, is that of Iddin-Dagan of the early OB period, called Isin-Larsa. This was studied by W.H. Ph. Römer[282] with additions by Daniel Riesman.[283] We give only selected lines, mostly following Riesman's translation:

2	[nu-u$_8$-g]ig an-ta	[the nu-g]ig from heaven
- - -		
45	sag-ur-sag-e múš mu-na-an-dub-dub-uš	the sag-ur-sag's comb their hair (?) before her
- - -		
60	á-zi-da-bi-a túg-nitá bi-in-muh$_4$	their (the sag-ur-sag's) right side they adorn with men's clothing
- - -		
63	á-gùb-bu-bi-a túg-nam-mí !? mu-e-ri-si-ig	their left side they cover (?) with women's clothing
- - -		
70	ki-sikil su-gi$_4$-a sag-ki*-gú-lá-e	the maidens. the shugia's, coiffured (?)
- - -		
74	kur-gar-ra-e$_{11}$-da ba-da-ra [ ]	the ascending kurgara's grasped the sword
- - -		
80	nu-u$_8$-gig an-sikil-la aša$_x$-ni nam-mi-in-gub	the nu-gig stands alone in the pure heaven
- - -		
88	nin-an-usan$_x$-na ur-sag-gá an-ta nam-ta-[an-è]	the lady of the evening, the heroine, she comes forth from heaven
90	nita mu-un-sikil-e mí mu-un-zalag-ga	the men purify themselves, the women cleanse themselves

(both men and women worship the goddess, as well, in lines 91-98, as animals, plants, fish, birds and zi-gala "living creatures" do on these lines.)

170	lugal dingir-àm šà-ba mu-un-da-an-ti	the king, the god, sits with her, inside
- - -		
174	zà-mu u$_4$-garza-ka	on New-year's-day, the day of ritual
175	nin-mu-ra ki-ná mu-na-an-gar	they set up a bed for my lady

---

186	úr-^{d}inanna-ka-šè sag-íl-la mu-un-gin (?)	he approaches the lap of Inanna proudly
187	^{d}ama-ušumgal-an-na ki-ná mu-un-da-ab-ak-e	Amaushumgalanna lies down beside her
---		
191	ki-ná-a-na šà šà*-mu-di-ni-ib-kúš-ù	she makes love with him on her bed

(then comes a full meal for her and the people with musical instruments)

Line 2. The earlier term nu-gig came to be nu-u_8-gig, and to designate Inanna. Edzard's notes on nu-gig in ZA NF 21 (55) (1962) 104ff provide a good bibliography, Sec. 4.11.1n.

Line 2. hierodule: Römer throughout translates nu-u_8-gig "Gottgeweihten."

Line 45. sag-ur-sag. One of the sexually ambivalent creatures who will be discussed in App. 3.5.

Line 45. "Adorn themselves" ? (Römer). From context múš dub-dub in SRT 5:14 has to do with combing the hair, a sexually attractive act in many of these texts. Or, "put on the múš-headgear." Cf. mùš as a headgear for Inanna in Sec. 4.8.2.

Line 60, 63. Thus they are bi-sexual, or are acting in a bi-sexual role, or are transvestites, discussed in App. 3.4.

Line 70. šu-gi_4-a = *šugitu*, studied above, Sec. 4.4.

Line 74. For the kurgara, see App. 3.3.

Line 170 The king was called a "god" first in OAkk period. He was not a god in the Egyptian sense, but a mortal endowed with a divine burden (H. Frankfort *Kingship and the Gods,* Chicago, 1948 chap 21). But this is a vast subject in itself.

Line 174 ZAG.MUK = *zagmukku*, the New Year's Festival.

Line 187 Ama-ušumgal-an-na is a by-name of Dumuzi in mythological texts. The name here characterizes the king, Iddin-Dagan. Also in lines 209, 212.

Line 191 A key line šà ...kúš-ù also in line 103. Riesman has: make love; Römer says that it is questionable whether the verb is meant here in the sexual sense, (p. 194) but I think it is obvious.

4.23.5 The popular book on the subject is S.N. Kramer, *The Sacred Marriage Rite*, and the updated French edition: *Mariage Sacré à Sumer et à Babylone* Paris, 1983. W. Heimpel's review of this[284] describes the subject as "a topic burdened with numerous difficult questions...(presented in an) uncomplicated way." The rite comes from early 3rd millenium Uruk, where the first husband of Inanna was Enmerkar (p. 58). Dumuzi was one of his successors, becoming the husband in later mythology. The celebration of a ruler as the reincarnated Dumuzi is first attested by Shulgi (p. 63). There are texts from this time with details of wooing and courting but they are not consistent.[285] They depict love-making between Shulgi, using his name, and Inanna.

Only in the Iddin-Dagan text does it take place on New Year's Day. Kramer finds that directly after the sexual intercourse of the couple there is a description of the "ensuing vegetation"(iii 1-11). I wish I could see that, but lines 1-7 are badly broken, pa-pa-al-..."the young shoot" is all that is left of line 8 but what it does is not stated. erin (?) "cedar" is in line 9, gu mu-un-da-zi "plants stood high by (his) side"/še mu-un-da-zi "grain stood high by his side" line 10 is related in some way to fertility, and GABA-a-kiri$_6$ kiri$_3$-zal-gim mu-un-da-an-tuš "the...garden flourished luxuriantly by his side" line 11 seems almost to prove his point, but the broken text makes it less than sure.

In chapter 5, Kramer relates the texts to the biblical "Song of Songs." The latter is a collection of originally Mesopotamian poems which have been "expurgated" as Kramer (p. 99) would have it, an old idea. The gods of Mesopotamia, of course, acted like humans in their love making, but I would rather call "The Song of Songs" a collection of love songs that have the same theme as love literature the world over: going down to the garden, orchard or field, symbolism from the life of nature, love's awakening, the enticement, the search for the lover, the surrender of the embrace, the "sickness" that love brings, the pain of separation, the joy of coming together again, and so forth. Love and the erotic in the so-called "sacred marriage texts" are cultic, so perhaps the Song of Songs consists of cultic material, too, but described under the many symbolic acts, and with animals, birds, and flora. If it is symbolic, it has to do with fertility, with the maiden playing the major role, as she does in Mesopotamia.

Kramer says the "sacred marriage" rite "was actually carried out" between the king and a specially selected hierodule from Inanna's temple in Uruk (p. 93). This of course is a controversial subject, about which there is little evidence. Jacobsen, *Harps*...112 argues that the king's partner was the queen.

4.23.6 A text less complete than the Iddin-Dagan one comes from the time of Shulgi and is studied by van Dijk.[286] The Gudea cylinders already told of a bed ^{giš}ná. This is in the ki-NÁ "bedroom," also appearing as é-NÁ-da (cf. *kummu*). Gudea visited the goddess Gatumdu there (Cyl A II 24). Beds were named by the year-name, as were thrones (See n. 250).

It is not evident that Gudea would assume the role of Ningirsu (the main god in the proceedings); "probably not (plutôt qe non)." In the Iddin-Dagan ritual the king does assume the role of Dumuzi. Then an important line in the Shulgi text (p. 86 lines 13-14) after the embrace: na-ám-sipa-kur-kur-ra na-ám-šè du$_{10}$-mu-ni-ib-ta$_x$-ar "I appointed for him the rulership of the lands for his destiny." This indicates that the union between the two was for the purposes of setting the destiny. (See also II.21).

Van Dijk disagrees with T. Jacobsen (n. 14) that the priestess obtains a concubine for the king for procreation, for the texts nowhere distinguish between a person who represents Inanna and one who consummates the marriage. "I do not know of any text which relates the hierosgamos with procreation." There is language. however, in which the kings of Ur III boast of being children of Ninsun.[287] And Gudea was a child of Gatumdu, and consummates the marriage, as all of his predecessors, with Baba and others. But one does not find genealogies with ascent by the priestess of Nanna at Ur. Since the priestess would be a princess, it is difficult to believe that the aim of the marriage would be procreation. Nevertheless there exists a certain tie-in between the priestesses and Inanna (n. 14).

[Of course, the goddess does not appear "by herself" but is represented by a cultic officiant, as Dumuzi is by the king. This is said in the text:

22 ù-mu-un ì-nu kù ^{d}inan-na-šè	when the lord lies with the pure Inanna
23 su-ba du$_5$-mu-zi-dè	the shepherd Dumuzi <will say>
24 úr-ra ga-ni-du$_8$-a-na-gim	I will open the bosom
25 x-sù-da gi-pàr-mà	when...in my gipar
	BiOr 11 Text D, p. 86]

Inanna fixes na-ám-zé-éb "a good fate" for sipa Shulgi "shepherd Shulgi" as he caresses her on the bed (f.II line 9). This text then shows an intimate tie-in between the *hieros gamos* and the determination of destiny.

4.23.7 Dossin[288] quotes from a Mari ritual: ^{3} [*ina bib*]*il libbi* LUGAL ^{4}[*ina ma-i*]*a-al* Istar *ittêl* "according to the king's inclinations, he may lie in the bed of Ishtar," but more references are needed to indicate how close this is to the above ceremonies.

4.23.8 Agnes Spycket is more sure of what happened,[289] using Gudea, Shulgi and Iddin-Dagan texts together. Hers is a coherent story, but its use of a wide range of traditions must be viewed with caution. J. Renger,[290] takes more time to separate out the various strands. It started in the pre-Sargonic era, when Mesannepadda, king of Ur and Kish, called himself dam-nu-gig "spouse of the nu-gig." His wife Nubanda was qualified by nin "which made her a deified priestess, a replacement for the divinity."[291] Lambert describes the wife of Lugalbanda of Lagash as a "living goddess," a SAL, to whom offerings were made, but who sacrificed as priestess at the feast of the Antasurra and Siraran.[292] As for Shulgi (Spycket,102), a hymn tells how he was conceived in the Ekur from the union of his father Ur-Nammu assimilated to Nanna, and the priestess, the *entu*.[293] [We must be careful however with this "realistic" language: pre-Sargonic kings were fed with the pure milk of Ninhursag, and there are other examples of this symbolic language. These people (or their mythographers) lived on two levels at once, the mythic and the historical.]

These royal births are the outcome of the *hieros gamos* accomplished on the New Year's Day in a room reserved for that ceremony in the temple. It is called é-dùg[294] or é-ki-ná "the house of the bed," a part of the è-dúg.[295] The texts do not go further back than Neo-Sumerian times, but the rite itself probably is from archaic times.[296] Marriage gifts (mí-ús-sa) are offered to Bau in Shulgi's time "as a visible substitute of Ningirsu" (Spycket, 103), Bau being incarnated by a sacred priestess (Gudea St. G XVIff). When the king unites with Inanna, lugal dingir-àm "the king is the god" (Iddin-Dagan,line 170, Sec. 4.23.4); he is in the sacred enclosure (barag) where he meets the nu-u$_8$-gig (p. 104). Shulgi was the first Ur III king to be given a divine determinative.[297] The priestess en or nin-dingir can be seen in the statue from Ur, Sec. 1.19.6.

The first 165 lines of the Iddin-Dagan hymn appear to be held in the twilight of the planet Venus. It must take place in the new year on "the day when the moon is visible."[298]

4.23.9 The love-oriented "sacred marriage texts" (his term, not theirs) are collected by S.N. Kramer.[299] These were first done in *Expedition* 5 (1963) 25-31, updated in his *Sacred Marriage Rite* (1969), and in turn updated by his translations in *ANET* 637f[300] and the new French edition Sec. 4.23.5.

The translations in *PAPS* and *ANET* are the same, with *ANET* omitting some broken lines with only 1 or 2 words; the notes are the same, but with the *ANET* edition omitting the cautions of the *PAPS* edition and sometimes the (?) of the *PAPS*. He is quite frank, as at *PAPS* 107 510a when he will say "unfortunately the text contains many ambiguities and obscure passages, and the interpretation here presented may turn out to be completely erroneous." [!] But he is sure: (this rite) "was actually carried out" between the king and a specially selected hierodule from Inanna's temple in Uruk. The rite goes back to earlier times and the first ruler was said to be Dumuzi (p. 490). Frankfort (See n. 298) calls it a "willful confusion of god and king--'fusion' is a more appropriate term" (p. 296).

As for the texts, we look for rites hidden in these mythic tales. We give only a few details; see Kramer's rather full summaries in *PAPS*.

No. 1: Inanna is introduced as nu-ug-gig and Dumuzi as ama-ušumgal-an-na, and there is much about "plowing" the šuba-stones. She is lú-ki-sikil "the maiden" (line 7), nin-é-gal-la "lady of the palace" (22) and nu-bar-ra (38).

No. 2: Inanna adorns her body, and meets Dumuzi (by name) called en, in the temple of Enlil, the é-an-na. She was standing at the lapis lazuli door of the gipar (30). She dances. There is a bed ^{gis}ná in the gipar (line 40).

No. 3: The libir-si-zu-en "Sin's libir-si's" (emesal for nimgir-si, see App. 4.2.1ff) are in the palace (5). Inanna the nu-ug-gig opens the door for Dumuzi, a shepherd.

No. 4: Inanna as queen of heaven was shining, perhaps as Venus, and dancing. There is much about her mother Ningal. The couple will go to the gate of Ningal and meet her mother there.

No. 5: Gibil has purified a bed (ki-ná) in the great shrine (èš-gal-la). Nin-shubur, Inanna's sukkal "vizier," leads Dumuzi to the lap of Inanna. As he will be long in her holy lap, he will have a long reign (ii 10), lots of trees, forests, long life in the palace, satisfactory flood waters from the Tigris and Euphrates. This is a sure fertility motif. So he goes and embraces her "with lifted head;" then the text is broken off.

No. 6: Inanna as queen (ga-ša-an) goes to the abzu and other shrines, and to the gods. A short battle motif appears. She pours out plants and grain from her breast. [Rather obscure.] Dumuzi will drink from her breast [fertility motifs all through here.]

No. 7: Inanna apppoints Dumuzi nam-dingir-kalam-ma-šè "to the godship of the land." There is a song to her vulva, chanted by the gala. The nar brings the hymn. Dumuzi is bridegroom (mu-ud-na) and wild bull (am). There is much metaphor about her vulva. The king as ox will plow it. Plants, grain and garden flourish. Then they dwell in the é-nam-ti-la "house of life." This is the ama$_5$-zi-sù-ud-gál "storehouse which gives long life." In it are šu-luh-kù-ga "holy purification rites," tying these songs to ritual.

No. 8: there is much about hair [cf. the *kezertu*'s hair]. Kramer says that perhaps this was chanted by a lukur to Shu-Sin, who is in the text.

No. 9: perhaps has sexual symbolism...lettuce, garden, grain, apple tree, lú-làl-e "the honey man" who sweetens her.

No. 10: Inanna and Dumuzi are referred to as brother and sister. "My beloved met me" and "lay by my heart." There is eme-ag "tongue-making," i.e., kissing.

No. 11: A song addressed to "you": brother, brother of the palace, ensi of the magur-boat, nubanda of the chariot(! an unusual note, perhaps a military one),ad-da-uru-di-ku$_5$ "city-father-judge.

Many of these passages contain motifs like those which later became the imagery of the Hebrew Bible's "Song of Songs," such as kissing, fertility aspects as vineyards, flocks, trees, the king on his couch, courtship, eating and drinking, the beauty of the woman. But the "Song of Songs" contains no copulation scenes, and sexual innuendoes are indirect. On the other hand, there is nothing in the Mesopotamian songs of the wounding of "Song" chapter 5. A major similarity is that the standpoints of both are those of a woman.[301]

4.23.10 Despite the critical things we said about Herodotus I, 199 above, we are interested in what he reported in I, 181f. (Again the Loeb Library edition):

> [181] In the sacred enclosure of Zeus Belus (there are towers and) in the last tower there is a great shrine, and in it a great and well-covered couch is laid...[no] human creature lies therein for the night, except one native woman, chosen from all the women by the god, as say the Chaldeans, who are priests of the god.[182] These same Chaldeans say (though I do not believe them) that the god himself is wont to visit the shrine and rest upon the couch.

This is the basis of many a commentator's position that a human priestess takes the part of the goddess in intercourse. We do know that on top of the ziggurat there is a shrine and in it a couch. Note even Herodotus's skepticism here. At the time of Nebuchadrezzar at the top of the ziggurat of Babylon and Borshippa was a *kiṣṣu*, some sort of sacred room.[302] At the time of Nabonaid, Shamash and Aya dwelt in it.[303]

Even in late Assyrian times there is an echo of this practice. Bel and Beltiya make love on an ornate bed.[304] Another NA exemplar presents Nabû and Tashmētu as the divine pair.[305] Was their mythology acted out by their cultic functionaries? A footnote to this is found in a text of S.N. Kramer, "Inanna and the numun plant."[306] It is ununderstandable in places. It starts off with rain, kissing, copulation, mention of the um-ma, the ab-ba and the gala-mah, and the growth of the numun (reading not certain). That the gala-mah is spared (?) by mu "year" indicates perhaps that it is a seasonal rite.[307] Inanna appears on lines 32 and passim as gašan-anna. The numun plant was eventually used to make Inanna's bed in the Sacred Marriage Rite.[308] Maybe we have here an early cosmogonic myth, with rain, man, flood, then the earth giving birth. That reminds us that in our discussion of fertility in this study, we have omitted any myth of the birth of the world.

We conclude our all-too-short series of notes on this vast and protean subject by mentioning only two of the overall studies, one by Renger[309] and one by Römer.[310] (See also Sec. 4.23.8) Römer broadens the study into a discussion of some of its variants in history, from "sehr verschiedenen Kulturkreisen, Zeiten und Kontext" (p. 426). It concerned, at one time or another, the divine pairs Marduk and Ṣarpanītu, Nabû and Tashmētu (Sargonic times, Babylon), and Anu and Antu (Seleucid times, Uruk). There was no one concept "sacred marriage" (Römer 427). There are three rites described in any detail, that of Iddin-Dagan (Sec. 4.23.4), that of Shulgi (Sec. 4.23.6) and that of an unknown king, leading to lordship over the lands, profit from the fields, and fruitfulness, seen in Kramer's "songs" (Sec. 4.23.9).

4.24 Preliminary Studies of Cultic Titles from the Hebrew Bible

4.24.1 This is a continuation of the studies of titles in Sec. 1.4, but with the emphasis of the present chapter. A good start would be Beatrice Brooks' attempt, in an early article,[311] to list "cult functionaries". One can detect in the background the ideology of Yhwh and Israel as husband and wife, appearing in Hosea chapters 1-3 and elsewhere, and the "Song of Songs" as the frankest presentation of sex in the Bible, and many more. She points out what many others have done: that some of these promiscuous figures are criticized in the Hebrew Bible, whereas in Babylonia they are respected and protected, or at least given a definite role different from street prostitutes.

4.24.2 The *nĕtînîm* occur only in Chronicles-Ezra-Nehemiah, and are dealt with in Sec. 1.4.7.

4.24.3 (see also Sec. 4.18) The *qādēš* and *qĕdēšāh* appear surprisingly infrequently, considering all that has been written on them, the *qādēš* 6 and the *qĕdēšāh* 4 times. In the days of Rehoboam we come across for the first time the criticism of allowing *qādēš*'s in the land, 1 Kings 14.24, called an abomination. The common understanding of this as "male cult prostitute" allows us to ask: are there any other examples in the ancient world of male prostitutes?

Good king Asa removed the *qādēš*, as well as the idols, and suppressed a budding Asherah cult, 1 Kings 15.12. Good king Jehoshaphat removed the rest of the *qādēš's* which remained from the days of Asa from the land, 1 Kings 22.47. But they were still there when the "reform" (revolution, really) of Josiah did away with the *kĕmārîm*-priests, whom the kings of Judah had installed to burn incense, and brought out the Asherah from the temple, and ground it to dust, and he broke down the *battê* "houses of" the *qādēš's* which were in the temple, where the women wove *battîm* for Asherah (2 Kings 23.5-7).[312] What these *battîm* were we do not know; perhaps they were simply "houses," little houses as cult objects. The question no commentator asks is: why were the women in the houses of the *qādēš's* in the first place? The relationship between the forbidden *qādēš* and the forbidden cult of Asherah is meant to be strong. It is meant to say, as a prophet would, there are a number of proscribed cultic practices here!

In Job 36.14 the godless are doomed to die young, their life ending among the *qādēš's*. By parallelism, the *qādēš's* also die young, indicating that living among *qādēš's* debilatates one so that an early death ensues. In this late text, the idea is the epitome of godlessness. In any case, this is an unhappy ending, but because of the possible late date of the Book of Job, and the possible shift in connotation of the term, we cannot comment further on this, except to say that we are surprised to see the allusion here, and there is nothing like it elsewhere in the book.

As a curiosity, the LXX apparently points the Vorlage of our key word so that it (perhaps) reads *qôdēš* and renders the Greek as *aggelōn* "angels/holy ones." The Job commentaries of Gordis, Habel, Pope, Driver/Gray and Davidson do not confront the problem of the *qādēš* here. Regardless of meaning, the LXX shows that the ancients had a problem, also.

Tamar plays the part of a prostitute in seducing her father-in-law Gen 38.12-26. She is described as disguised as a *zônāh* (vs. 15) the regular word for "prostitute" in the first and the last part of the tale, but is called *qedešah* in the middle part(vss 21,22). *Qĕdēšāh* seems to be a synonym for *zônāh* here; another way of putting it is that the *qădēšāh* was considered a *zônāh* whether she was one or not.

Astour[313] takes "sacral prostitution" in Babylonia for granted. It also existed in Israel before the reforms of the 7-6c B.C. (p.185). Sodomy was also common in Babylonia, with discussion of *assinnu*, one who practiced sodomy, and a reference to *klbn "dogs"* in the inscriptions from Cition in Cyprus (p.186 n.5, but this is too late and from another culture circle, as I try to show in these pages) The legal position of sacral prostitutes in West Semitic area was not unlike that of their homologues in Assyria and Babylonia (p.187, but codes of law are not found in the west !). Tamar's veil is that of a married hierodule, assuming West Semitic practices to be those of the MAL. During sheep shearing time the pre-exilic feasts were accompanied by ritual fornication (p.193), cf. Hos 4.13-14, 9.1-2. Judah's visit was a "ritually-prescribed act" (p.193). The study ends with comparisons with Greek tales.

Too much leaping to conclusions on too little evidence, is the mark of the above imaginative study. Yamauchi (Sec. 4.22.6) approaches the material in the same way.

Asmussen[314] interprets the Tamar story as Judah thinking that she was a *qĕdēšāh* because she was veiled (Heb. *ṣā ᶜîp*) The veil was not the garment of the Israelite woman, he says, and the Talmud had no special word for veil, while harlots had it as a special dress (Prov 7.10). The veil (*ṣammāh*) worn by the bride in Song of Songs 4.1.3, 6.7 is part of her total wedding garb. Rebecah wore a *ṣā ᶜîp* "veil" as she was approaching Isaac before their marriage, Gen 24.65, perhaps indicating her marriagability. The *ṣammāh* of Isa 47.2 is of a Babylonian woman. We should admit our lack of knowledge concerning the number of words used for head and face covering.[315] As rare as the veil was in Israel, it was common in surrounding countries.[316] Jastrow's thoroughgoing study, despite its age, is still useful, though based mainly on Middle Assyrian Laws §39, Text No. 1 (v 42-104). It may have had only a distant relationship to the Hebrew practice. It shows the confusion about who is to wear the veil. Women must have their heads covered. An *esirtu* "concubine" must be veiled with her mistress on the street. A *qadiltu* (their orthography for *qadištu*) who has married someone must be veiled, but an unmarried *qadiltu* must have her head uncovered. A *harimtu* "prostitute" must not be veiled. He concludes that the veil means that the woman is the property of someone; he does not mention sacred prostitution. Veiling is a complex subject, and there are various words for head, face and neck coverings, and much more could be said about it, but will not at this point.

In a very strong passage, with prostitution used as a metaphor for worshipping other gods, Hos 4.14b parallels *zônāh* with *qĕdēšāh*. The cultic nature of this is shown in "the men make a separation (root *p-r-d*, pointed pi'el, a hapax in the Hebrew Bible) with prostitutes, and sacrifice with *qĕdēšāh*'s." The two are in synonymous parallelism. The whole passage 4.9-14 is worth commentary:

The subject is "they" from vss. 7 through 14, and the standard translations of the RSV and others emend regularly from the BH[3] or BHS text to obtain a smooth-sounding passage. Specific verses yield the following:

vs. 9: "and it shall be *kā ᶜām kakkōhēn* 'like people like priest,'" i.e., the people and priests shall both sin in this...

vs. 10a:"they shall eat, and not be satisfied; they shall cause harlotry, and not increase." With no footnote, the RSV translates the hiph'il as qal: "play the harlot," tacitly following a second emendation of the BHS, based on no MS evidence. Similarly, no modern version brings out the basic meaning of the hiph'il.

vs. 10b:"for they have left Yhwh to watch/keep." Again, the RSV goes its own way, and borrows a word from the beginning of the next verse, *zĕnût* "harlotry," translating, with some imagination: "to cherish harlotry," and the NRSV the same: "to devote themselves to whoredom." But "to keep harlotry" occurs nowhere else, so translating as the Masoretic text, the idea may simply be to do what they like.

vs. 11:"harlotry and wine and new wine takes away the heart." Wine indeed takes away *lēb* "the heart," and all the aspects that go with it: feeling, understanding, reaction, willingness and so forth, but harlotry does similar things, and that is what the prophet wanted to say.

vs. 12:"for a spirit of harlotry has caused them to err, and they have played the harlot from under their God." We would say: under his very nose.

vs. 13b:"for your daughters play the harlot, and your brides commit adultery." This is a paralleling of harlotry and adultery we have seen earlier in Hos 3.1-3.

vs. 14:"I will not punish your daughters when they play the harlot, and your brides when they commit adultery, for they (m. pl.) *yĕpārēdû* with harlots, and sacrifice with *qĕdēšāh*'s. They sacrifice--but in what way? Are the *qĕdēšāh*'s in charge of some sacrificial service? We know nothing of it. Only the *kōhēn* does the service, unless we assume foreign cult practices. "With" meaning "together with," alongside of? At <u>their</u> altar, perhaps that of Asherah (2 Kings 23.7). The pi'el of *yĕpārēdû* is a hapax in the Hebrew Bible. The BHS footnote wants to read niph'al. The various translations are: "go aside" (RSV), "wandering off" (NJB), "resort to" (NEB), "go off with" (GNB). So each one understands the "separate, divide" meaning of the root to indicate separation from society with harlots, all imaginative, but a western idea with no backing. David Kimchi has the original idea of separating from their wives. But it could also be taken more literally, "make a separation," as of the legs in the sex act, or cut themselves off from society by sacrificing with these women. Rost[317] as a result of a discussion of *kallāh* "bride, daughter-in-law," in vs. 13 concludes that an initiation rite was involved (p. 457), again with no evidence.

Maybe this refers simply to being in the congregation and taking part in the ritual words and actions of this congregation. This reminds us of Num 25.1 in which the Israelites and the "daughters of Moab" take part in some way together at the sacrifices. The actions consisted of eating and "bowing down," this latter word being the standard one *yištaḥĕvû* used of Israelite worship.

As for the *zōnāh*'s and *qĕdēšāh*'s bring in parallel, this being the closest such tie-in one can find, this is another way of emphasizing that the latter engage in non-Yhwh worship.

4.24.4 J. Pedersen[318] finds that Hos 4.11-19 refers to sacred prostitution, not ordinary prostitution because of allusions to the cult in the passage. There is sacrifice (vss. 13-14), prayer (vs. 15, "as the Lord lives"); "they" in vss.12, 14 may be the priests. Mic 1.7 may refer to the pay the sacred prostitute receives. (Against Pedersen (p. 470) Jer 5.7-9 seems to be secular because of the mention of the neighbor's wife.)

Qĕdēšîm (always m. in the passages to be referred to) are used as paradigm cases of false worship in such a place as 1 Kings 15.12, where Asa, "who did what was right in the eyes of the Lord, "put away all the *qĕdēšîm* from the land," as well as the idols, as did Jehoshaphat (good, 1 Kings 22.46.) Rehoboam (evil, 1 Kings 14.24) kept them; Josiah (good, 2 Kings 23.7) broke down their houses, which were in the temple compound! This is quite surprising, and nothing appeared previously to prepare us for this fact.

The *zônāh* is a role played by Jerusalem in Ezek 16, and has within it much of the words of a possible concept of "sacred prostitute." She made *bāmôt* "high places" with their garments and played the harlot there (vs.16), indicating the worship of other gods.[319] She took her jewels and made them into images (vs. 17) somewhat the same motif as the golden calf incident in Ex 32. She delivered her children to be burned in the sacrifice (vss. 20-21). She played the harlot with (i.e., went after the gods of) the Egyptians (vs. 26), the Assyrians (vs. 28) and the Chaldeans (vs.29).This is prostitute-type language, with no details given, unfortunately. It is the clearest usage of the term *zônāh* to indicate a type of prostitution that could be termed "sacred," because it had to do with the cult but, of course, metaphor throughout.

The part played by Israel, the Lord's wife (although the word is never used), in Hos 2 is that of a prostitute (Hos 2.5), and cultic language is used throughout the chapter (vs. 11, 13). This chapter uses the language of Baalism but the high theology of Yhwh.[320] The "covenant" as Östborn puts it between Baal and his people included fertility. He puts it this way because of the aspect entitled Baal-berit "Baal of the covenant," Jud 8.33.

This is only one of the many family metaphors used in the Bible. These are not necessarily consistent, being perhaps derived from different sources. People called Yhwh "my father" in Jer 3.4. The people is Yhwh's son in Hos 11.1. Yhwh conceived this people as (although the word is not used) a mother, Num 11.12. The people is his daughter, Jer 8.22. Israel is a virgin, Jer 18.13. Examples could be multiplied, but in Hos 2 Yhwh as husband is a quite different metaphor, for Yhwh has no goddess as a wife in Hos 2, but Israel is the wife, as well as the offspring and the lover.

Wolff's commentary[321] interprets Her I 199 as the background for the role of Gomer as prostitute, but this is poor reasoning, because Herodotus is from another culture (as if Babylonian thought-forms can be interpreted in a Greek way) and another age (300 year later), and besides it never worked anyway! Rudolph[322] also argues against Wolff's understanding here. This is a weak point in Wolff's otherwise fine book.

The point of Hos 2 [RAH] is that Yhwh will provide the fertility that Baal could (vs. 8) but more, also providing: *ṣedeq* "righteousness," *mišpāt* "justice," *ḥesed* "covenant-reciprocal promise," *raḥămîm* "pity" (vs. 21, EV 19). But because both provided fertility, perhaps it was hard to determine whom one was worshipping. And even though the high theological elements of vs. 21 are the climax of what Yhwh provides, the whole chapter is about Yhwh as husband and Israel as wife, with the sexual motif leading to a fertility motif. We compare at this point the fact that the Israelites of Elephantine Island served Anat, who undoubtedly had the fertility aspects that we hear about through Anat in Ugaritic literature. Kapelrud discusses Anat's roles, as well as that of a "violent goddess," one who is also a "goddess of love and fecundity."[323] Hos 2 provides the strongest example of Yhwh as husband in the Hebrew Bible. In Jer 31.31 he was Israel's husband (*ba ᶜal*), but the marriage metaphor is not followed up. In Isa 54.5, God the "maker" is given several other titles, including *baᶜal* "husband" acting the loving husband in vss. 4-8. He speaks like a lover in Hos 11.8-9. An obscure late side comment on the sacred marriage occurs in 2Macc 1.14, the plan of Antiochus to marry the goddess Nanea.

Östborn reminds us that the Baal of Karatepe (4-8th c. B.C.E.)[324] provided Azitawadda *ḥym* "life,"*šlm* "peace," *ᶜz ʾdr* "great power," *ʾrk ymm* "long days," *rb šnt* "many years" aspects close to Hos 2. The common street prostitute of Prov 7 had to offer sacrifices and vows (vs. 14), maybe (though this may be thinking too much like Mesopotamia) because she is a servant of Ishtar, in her West Semitic form. Or maybe she is offering a sacrifice for her sins. Isa 23.16 tells of a "song of a *zônāh* " This will be accompanied by a *kinnôr*, and she will go about the city. Why would she sing? Is it a kind of cultic song?

Karel van der Toorn[325] has argued that the woman in Prov 7 says that she must prostitute herself in order to earn money to pay a vow, therefore in this specialized sense it was "sacred." He touches, but lightly, on a possible "fertility cult," (201-4) quoting some of the sources considered in the present study, but to no great depth. This takes off from the positions of G. Boström, W. McKane, G. von Rad and R.B.Y. Scott (198), but goes beyond them. Duane A. Garrett argues against Toorn, by interpreting the words of the woman in Proverbs as "simply a maneuver.[326]

Gruber[327] interprets the *qādēš* as a cultic singer on the basis of Ugaritic evidence, giving the same texts studied below: UT 63, 81, 82, 113, 114, 169 (pp. 169f), see Sec. 4.19.

Herbert May, one of the most imaginative of early scholars in this field[328] thought that *mēʾahabay* "lover" in Hos 2.7ff, Zech 13.6, Ezek 16.37, 23.9, Jer 22.20.22, 30.14 is a term for the sacred male prostitute. There is no evidence for this, or that there is such a term. *zônāh* does not appear in the masculine, and *qādēš* has been discussed above.

In Joel 4.3 (EV 3.3) a boy is given for a *zônāh*, a girl for wine. If the parallelism is strictly followed, the reference is to the price of a *zônāh*, the price of the wine, rather than the profession of *zônāh*, which if interpreted that way would leave no parallel in the second stich.

There is no reason in the tale to doubt that Rahab the *zônāh* in Josh 2.1 was simply a common prostitute, but the scarlet thread in the window in Josh 2.18 may symbolize something. In Ezek 16.16 *bāmôt ṭĕlûʾôt* "colored stuff (?)" is used with harlotries. In Jer 4.30 the one criticized as a metaphor for Israel, with no title ever given, dresses in a red garment, decks herself with jewels, and paints her eyes, as a prostitute.

Jephthah the Gileadite of Jud 11.1 was the son of a *zônāh*. Despite our great interest in the interpretation of the story of his daughter, this fact does not seem to relate to the daughter.

4.24.5 Graham and May[329] think that the term *yôšebet* "the one sitting (f.)" describing women weeping for Tammuz in Ezek 8.14, is maybe a title of these women. Women are ordered in Mic 1.10 ff not to weep, perhaps indicating ritual weeping. Jud 4.5 uses a simple word for sitting, describing Deborah under her tree, indicating nothing of the subject of cultic life.

4.24.6 *ṣōb'ôt* appears as "ministering, serving women" at the door of the Tent of Meeting only twice, in Ex 38.8 (context of details of the furnishings of the Tent of Meeting), and 1 Sam 2.22. In the latter case, the women were sexual objects for the sons of Eli, later to be criticized by Samuel in his first prophetic act, 1 Sam 3.13.18. Their role is not further described, and the use of the ordinary Hebrew word *ṣb'* for "to serve" may indicate that this is not the term of an office as such. What were they doing at that strategic spot? Men usually do service in the Tent of Meeting, Num 4.24-49, 8.23-6.

The women were outside, not inside, which may still have been a cultic role, for many aspects of the Hebrew cult took place outside the temple cella proper. But why were they at the door? We can only guess at that on analogy with Mesopotamia, and that is rather unsure. The text in Samuel does not criticize them, it criticizes the sons of Eli, so perhaps they were not in a role that could be called sacred prostitute. H. May[330] thinks that Oholah and Oholibah, two figures symbolic of Judah and Israel in Ezek 23 are echoes of these women, an imaginative idea.

4.24.7 *ᶜalmāh*. This word appears in the plural in Song of Songs 1.3, 6.8 and Ps 68.26 (EV 25) and the passages do not tell us much about them. The *'almāh*'s "love" the hero (or the heroine) 1.3 of the Song, but that does not indicate sexuality necessarily. There are many of them together in Song 6.8. If these are the ones calling "her" happy in vs. 9, they could do so with cultic songs. There is a torah element in the declaration that some psalm figures are happy, as in Ps 40.4, 84.4, 89.15, 128.1. Ps 68.26 (EV 25) has a rare, rather full, description of a procession, in which singers, minstrels and *ᶜalmāh's'* playing the *tōp* appear. The procession is into the *qôdēš* "holy place," and perhaps the order of the procession is an echo of the tradition.

The title of Ps 46 (EV 47) dedicates it *ᶜal ᶜălāmôt*. RSV translates "choirmaster" (m.!) but strictly from parallels to other psalm titles. Elsewhere this term becomes "musical instrument." Cf. *ᶜalmût* Psalm 9.1. Only the older versions and studies translate this as "maidens."

To go on from these primary studies, we add a few more titles:

4.24.8 (See Sec. 3.32.21). *nābî* is mostly a masculine term in the Hebrew Bible, but appears five times as *nĕbî'āh*"prophetess." In some of these, the figure has cultic connotations.

Miriam was a *nĕbî'āh* whom tradition records as speaking one line of a psalm (Ex 15.21) which appears as the first verse of a full psalm in Ex 15.1-18. She leads a group of women playing a *tōp* and in the singing and dancing. `There may be cultic connotations in the explicit statement in Ex 15.20 that she was "the sister of Aaron," who was the prototypical priest. By one tradition, Yhwh sent to the people Moses, Aaron and Miriam, Mic 6.4, the first the leader with many roles, the second the prototypical priest, and the third who probably took on some of the roles of the other two, and one may suggest especially those of Aaron.

Deborah (a *nĕbî'āh* Jud 4.4, but not in Jud 5) was a married woman, who used to "judge" (i.e. rule) Israel, sometimes while sitting under a well-known tree, which later generations called "the palm of Deborah." (Jud 4.5) Oesterley and Robinson thought that this place was chosen so that she could hear God speaking in the rustle of the leaves.[331] She appears as a military leader in the prose story, Jud 4, but as a singer in the poetical variant (Jud 5.1). She is also given the title *'ēm bĕyisrāēl* "mother in Israel," Jud 5.7. This is not a motherly person in the common sense of the term, but a mother who has authority as did Anat and Ishtar.[332] Most commentators do not take the title "mother" seriously enough to comment upon it. It appears in this way only one other time in 2 Sam 20.19, describing a city. In Jud 5.7 it concerns a woman who is playing the role of a man.[333] It certainly implies respect and authority.[334]

Isaiah's wife is called a *nĕbîʾāh* (Isa 8.3), perhaps only because he was a *nābî'*; I find no cultic connotations in connection with this. The child, however, was named with the collaboration of a priest (Isa 8.2).

The fullest characterization of a *nĕbîʾah* in the Hebrew Bible is found in Huldah 2 Kings 22.14-20. (See also 3.32.21). When Josiah first read the "book of the torah" he wanted it interpreted ("inquire of the Lord for me"), so the priest and others went to Huldah, a married woman, the wife of a "keeper of the wardrobe." Her valuable prophecy is preserved (in deuteronomistic terms), beginning as many canonical prophets do:*kō ʾāmar* Yhwh "thus says the Lord." She goes on to use the first person singular, by which the canonical prophets spoke as the Lord. Then she criticizes Israel for worshipping other gods, a favorite theme of the Book of Deuteronomy, and the deuteronomistic writings, incurring God's anger. But Josiah humbled himself, so will die in peace.[335] This prophecy has many connotations, and we can only mention a few here. Firstly we note that Huldah was not chosen because she had any special place as a woman, but only because a prophet was needed, and she was a prophetess, and she did that in the standard way. Second, she was not acting wholly as a prophet, because her words had to do with worship, thus she spoke for the priests, and indeed a priest was on the committee who called upon her. Third, she was in the stream of the canonical prophets, reminding us, for instance, of Amos who in 7.17 also prophecied the fate of the king, in this case, a negative one.[336]

Women prophets are not given titles but are described in Ezek 13.17-23. They are described as making *kĕsātôt* "bindings"[337] for wrists and veils for heads. Their practice seems to be divinatory (root *q-s-m*, vs. 23), although it is (falsely) prophetic in that they have not spoken against the wicked.

4.24.9 (See Sec. 1.19.12) A possible cognate to *nĕbîʾāh* came to the fore recently from an unexpected source. Arnaud's four-volume work *RPAE* contained Akkadian texts from Emar in copy, transliteration and translation with notes. This is a basic source, and its offspring are just now making their way into the literature.[338]

A word used three times in texts of a sacrificial list is *a-na-bi-a/ia-ti* in the term Ishara *ša anabiati* "Išhara of prophetesses" as Arnaud translates it. He understood it as the Emar cognate of Hebrew *nābiʾ*, in the feminine plural (p. 4). Von Soden however proposes a reading *mu*$_x$*-na-bi-a/ia-ti*, taking it as the II-form of *nabû* "cry, call," and refers to a form *nabium* in AHw s.v. which could explain the *-ia* - element in the Emar word. He makes this proposal to fit the Emar word into a standard Akkadian II/1 participial form. But there is no reason why Emar grammar should fit the Babylonian form.

In any case, the Emar form of *nabû* if it is that could be a precursor of the Hebrew *nābî*. It could mean a calling or crying-out woman, or a prophetess of some type. Many more examples are needed to settle this discussion.

4.25 The Fertility Cult in the Hebrew Bible with Some Notes From Ugaritic

4.25.1 The subject is now getting complex, with several different aspects brought into the argument: the background material consisting of a large number of separate offices and titles held by women in ancient Mesopotamia; the *qādēš /qĕdēšāh* in the Hebrew Bible and its relationship to the *qdš* in Ugaritic and the *qadištu* in Mesopotamian life; the ill-defined idea of sacred prostitution always hovering in the background; the "institution" of the sacred marriage; and there are more to come. We must now attempt to discover how scholars have described the fertility cult in the Hebrew Bible.

4.25.2 In a helpful study of Hebrew theophoric personal names,[339] Fowler finds few that reflect fertility concepts. Yizrĕʾel "El/God sows," in Hos 1.4 both a place name and a personal name. A late name Pĕtaḥyāh may be translated "Yah opens (the womb to bring fertility)" in 1 Chr 24.16, Ezr 10.23, Neh 9.5, Neh 11.24 (p. 286). Also, there is a GN yiptaḥ-ʾel "El opens" in Josh 19.14.27. She finds no parallels to Phoenician/Punic *ʾaḥt* "sister," *ʾm* "mother," *mlkt* "queen," referring to deity (p. 197). Nor any to Akkadian *malkatu* (only foreign queen!), *ummu* "mother," *šu'atu* "lady," *ši* "she," or *šarratu* "queen." (table, p.298).

4.25.3 Asmussen[340] refers to the female as the natural medium to symbolize fertility. The naked figurines, all female, one exemplar of this idea, are discussed in App. 2.

The term for sacred prostitute or temple woman may not be a special one, he says (p. 177). and Amos 2.7 is a source for what Asmussen (p. 177) has labelled as this. If this is fornication, it reminds us that there is little criticism of fornication (aside from prositution) in the Hebrew Bible. The strict Nazarite's vows, for instance, consisted of not shaving (Jud 13.5, Num 6.5), not partaking of wine or beer (Num 6.3), not cutting the hair (Num 6.5), not going near a dead body (Num 6.6), but nothing is said about prohibition of sexual intercourse outside of marriage. The visits of Samson to the prostitute at Gaza (Jud 16.1) are narrated apparently as a normal action.

4.25.4 Some have guessed that *hannaᶜărāh* (simply "the maiden") in Am 2.7 is a special class among temple women. The act described here is done "in order to profane my holy name." This last is a sarcastic remark, because whatever they did, it was not for the purposes of profanation. It goes on: "they lie down on pledged garments," perhaps those given to the temple for sacred purposes, another sacred/secular twist, "beside every altar." Why they would engage in promiscuity beside the altar is odd, because one would think that they would do it in some dark corner somewhere, unless this is done to flaunt the altar, but even then it would be too public a place. Some commentators are sure that this is sacred prostitution. It certainly is prostitution, and it certainly is done in a sacred place, but it does not appear to be an <u>institution</u> that is a part of the temple practices.

4.25.5 The term <u>dog</u> comes into the picture, for in Deut 23.19 (EV 18) the "hire of a prostitute" is parallel to the "wages of a dog." Either 1) these people were called "dogs," or 2) the "dog" was the term for the male version of the *zônāh* (female). There is a whole literature alleging that there is a term "dog" for male cult prostitute.[341] RSV glosses "dog" with "sodomite." New versions translate "male prostitute": REB, NRSV, NJPS, NJB and NEB in a footnote. There are apotropaic figures of dogs at Ur III. (*Sollberger and Kupper Inscriptions* III A5d), but these are certainly not negative. There are dogs of deities in 1 Aqhat 10, and in places dog is used as a derogatory term as in our culture, but a dog also appears as a devoted follower of a god, indeed a dog appears as a cult figurine belonging to the gods. Van Buren *Figurines* No. 1122 from Sippar shows a little dog seated on its haunches, inscribed: To the goddess Me-me, this dog of terra-cotta I have made and dedicated. In Langdon *Neubab* vii 110, iii, 40ff, a dedication of a shrine is written on a clay dog.

In a ritual, you give two loaves with images inside of, respectively, a sorcerer and a sorceress, to a *kalbu* "dog" and a *kalbatu* "bitch," seemingly cultic personnel, *Maqlû* IX 187.

Dogs are listed with sorcerers and fornicators as those outside the heavenly city in Rev 22.15. Phil 3.2 may indicate the same beings. Thomas[342] feels that Deut 23.18 refers to a dog as a "devoted follower of a god." Aistleitner *Wörterbuch* s.v. *klb* has one listing: "Prostituierter" but this is backed up by no data. Margalith[343] discusses *keleb* as the epithet of a temple servant in the Hebrew Bible, Lachich Letters, Amarna Letters, NA letters and PNs. In the late temple of Astarte at Kition in Cyprus temple servants were called dogs[344] but this is too late and too far outside our geographical range to interest us.

UT 1046 lists a number of PNs which, as is the case elsewhere, could be adjectives, professional names, divine names, sentence names, totemistic names, and so forth (note the gaps):

1	*rqd*	"dancer"
	bn.abdg	
3.37	*ilyn*	

20	*ṣprn*	"birds" (?)
33	*mrynm*	*maryannu* 's
41	*kn'm*	"Canaanites (?)"
44	*klb*	"dog"
49	*bd 'ṯtr*	"servant of 'aṯtr"

There is a PN ^{m}kal-bu and several names Kalbe/iya in PRU III index of PNs 247. UT 305.4 lists *ṯlṯ klbm hmn* "three dogs of the god Ḫamman." *VAB*, D 42 speaks of the destruction of *klbt 'ilm 'išt* "the bitches of the gods by fire (? cf. Heb *'esh*). One concludes that the dog may be thought of negatively, as is the case in other societies, or that the "wages of a dog" are so low as to be despised.

4.25.6 H.G. May[345] with some imaginative interpretations, brings together a number of scattered verses to make a supposedly whole description of the fertility cult. The wounds of Ephraim in Hos 5.14 may be the self-inflicted ones of the cult ritual (p.75), for the prophet was wounded in Zech 13.6, and the prophets of Baal cut themselves in 1 Kings 18.28 (p.75). Joel 1.8 depicts a wailing for a lost bridegroom (p. 80), and in Hos 7.14-16 (p. 80) they wailed upon their couches, perhaps those used in the cult marriage. He understands (p.79) Jer 5.7 to read that they cut themselves at the shrine of the *zônāh*.

The search of the goddess for her dead consort is a motif in the fertility cult (pp 81-82). Perhaps many of the Hebrew Bible references to seeking and finding Yhwh have their origins in this. In Hos 10.12 they seek him in the springtime, when the crops come up (p. 83). As we commented upon a similar collection of data above, this is original, and in some cases provocative, but too contrived for our taste, however it anticipated much of the discussion of a later day.

4.25.7 Raymond Collins has several inacurrate and unsubtantiated things to say about the Ancient Near East, and brings in a lot of the old clichés on the "fertility myth." [346] But one reads him to see what many scholars think about this subject.

He points out that male homosexuality was condemned (Lev 20.13) but lesbianism was not. Lev 20.10-21 and Lev 18.6-23 seem to be the main collections of laws on sexual purity. He does not find prostitution per se condemned until Prov 6.23-35, 7.1-27, 9.13-18. And now he has a big admission: "What is not clear is whether the legal material is directed against sacred prostitution as such, or against certain forms of ritual intercourse [he doesn't define this further!]; whether the prophets distinguished between ritual intercourse as it took place on the high places of Canaan--and "harlotry" is a metaphorical designation of Israel's infidelity--and simple intercourse with an ordinary prostitute; and whether the sages tended to identify secular prostitution with practices of ritual intercourse."(p.163)

He makes the statement: "a fertility-celebrating ritual orgy took place in Canaan." (p. 150). Where? What was the content? Who did it? What text is he referring to? Is this indicated in Ugaritic documents?

4.25.8 The remarks of the standard commentaries might be exemplified by Buis and Leclercq[347] who say that sacred prostitution is well attested in the Canaanite cults, and then they proceed to give biblical examples -- from the Canaanite's theological opponents--to prove it! Num 25.1-9, Hos 4.14 and 2 Kings 15.12 show this. Male prostitutes were called "dogs," because in Phoenicia and Cyprus n. 240b that word designates a category of temple servants, but see my comments on this in Sec. 4.25.6.

4.26 Commit Apostasy/Join Oneself to Idols/Commit Prostitution

4.26.1 To go beyond these early attempts, we may simply summarize: the commandment is: You shall have no other gods...but they did! The early writers attempted to criticize this with several metaphors and formulas; we attempt here to separate out the various syntactic classifications of one important category of these, that the prohibition against worshipping other gods is regularly described as committing prostitution, root *znh*.[348]

The metaphors vary, the prostitution being committed:

Ex 34.15: Deut 31.16, Jud 2.17 and passim: with "other gods"
Lev 17.7: done after *śĕ ᶜîrim* "Haariger, Bocksdämon"
Lev 20.5: with Molech
Lev 20.6: *with* *ʾôbôt* and *yiddĕᶜōnîm* (types of diviners)
Jud 8.27: with an ephod, apparently of a Midianite deity
Jud 8.33: after the *ba'alîm*
Isa 23.17: with all the kingdoms of the earth (done by Tyre)
Hos 2.4 (EV 2): the harlotry, the worship of Canaanite gods, is expressed in terms of love.

In other texts those who did this:
Isa 1.21: the city does it,
Ezek 16.15-52: Jerusalem does it on garments, and with images of men,
Hos 1.2: the land does it,
Hos 6.10: Ephraim did it,

In the language of prostitution:

Hos 5.4: not returning to their God is a spirit of prostitution,
Mic 1.7: idols destroyed // hire of a harlot; the idols are the "price"
Hos 4.17-18: joining to idols // commiting prostitution[349]

The prostitution was done "on every high hill and under every green tree" Isa 57.5, with many variants. The bed for prostitution in Isa 57.7 is on a mountain. Isa 57.3-8 describes a male doing these practices; in Ezek 23.17 a female plays the part. Judah built *bāmôt* "high places," and *maṣṣēbāh*'s *and'ăšērāh*'s on "every high hill and under every green tree," 1 Kings 14.23.[350] This is the deuteronomist's perception that the Canaanites worshipped on hills and under trees, or that their gods were of the hills and the trees.

In Jer 4.30, Ezek 23.40. Israel as a prostitute has a seductive dress and makeup. Are we to search for the meaning behind this metaphor, such as cultic appurtenances or the like?

Jer 3.1-3: depicts a land polluted with prostitution, which because of the mention of "another's wife" indicates turning to Baal or Asherah, as Hos 2. This is done on the *šĕpāyim* "hills," a common criticism, used as *bāmôt* is elsewhere. This results ironically not in fertility, as sexual intercourse can provide, but in showers being withheld, lack of fertility. The lack of fertility is a punishment for taking part in the fertility rites, say those who see this as such. Israel, as a prostitute, had the forehead of a woman who is a harlot (vs.3). This might refer to locks of hair, or jewelry, or a tatoo. But what does the metaphor refer to as a land or a people?

In Nah 3.4 they even criticize Nineveh for committing prostitution. Here it cannot of course be for apostasy, but maybe because it would seduce the Israelites. In 2 Kings 9.22 Jezebel the foreigner committed harlotries and sorceries by worshipping gods other than Yhwh, and is criticized for having them as her own gods, probably because this was done in Israel, and the people may be drawn to them.

In 2 Kings 17.7-23, the deuteronomic interpretation of why the northern kingdom was taken away into exile, there is a blanket criticism of the many acts of apostasy of Israel, without mentioning prostitution. The language of apostasy sometimes appears when neither the word *zônāh* nor its root is there, as in Jer 4.30 and Ezek 23.40. Isa 54.4 uses "shame of our youth," implying that.

For the prostitution in Hos 4.14,[351] see the discussion in Sec. 4.24.3. Jer 3.6-10 with its Judah-Israel sister imagery, reminds us of Ezek 23, for which see below. In Jer 5.7-8 cultic prostitution easily shifts to carnal prostitution.

Isa 57.1-8 is a similar passage, but more obscure. Vs. 3: You (pl.) draw near; you children of the *ᶜonnāh* "sorceress" are the seed (s.) of an adulterer and you (s.) have committed prostitution. BHS wants to read "the seed (s.) of adulteress and a harlot", simply by adding a *-t* (f.) ending to the first and omitting a letter in the the second MT word, and this is followed by the RSV and NRSV, although the latter translates the MT in a footnote, but this takes too many liberties. These are m. terms, but we have questioned above whether male prostitutes were found in biblical times. If vs. 7 follows this theme: "upon a high and lofty mountain you have set up your bed; indeed there you have gone up to offer sacrifice," then providing the bed for the prostitutes is parallel to offering sacrifice (to false gods). Again, prostitution and worship of other gods is in parallel.

Isa 23.17f is a unit in the genre of Hos 2, apparently an example of an ordinary prostitute, but now from the foreign city Tyre, who at the end of 70 years will be holy to the Lord, and her merchandise will supply food and clothing to those who dwell before the Lord, thus having sacred activities. This relates the secular and the sacred prostitutes.

Ex 34.15f is the introduction to the Ritual Decalogue, preceded by "tearing down the altars" of the inhabitants of the land, echoing Deuteronomy 12. They were to do this to prevent them from making a covenant with them and play the harlot with their gods (thus saying the same thing in different words), and sacrifice to their gods, and there be intermarriage, and your children do likewise.

In Lev 19.29, surrounded by a torah section about cutting hair or flesh, and keeping sabbaths and sanctuary pure: do not profane your daughter by making her a harlot, lest the land fall into harlotry, and become full of *zimmah* "evil." The context seems to be a cultic one, for vs 30 is on sabbath and sanctuary.[352] But if it refers to worship of other gods, why the daughter as a motif? Is she the "daughter of my people," a pet term for Israel? Is the female chosen to fit into the metaphor of harlotry? As much as I admire Pedersen and his ephochal book, this is typical of the methodology of those who decided that they would go out to find an institution of cult prostitution, and so found it. A number of disparate verses are strung together, the root *znh* is found, and cultic terms are found in the verse or nearby. This could be explained, I say, by the all-pervasive metaphor of the prophets and deuteronomists of referring to apostasy as prostitution or adultery.

Lev 20.5 brings the metaphor directly into contact with the others gods: playing the harlot after Molech, the chief Ammonite deity.

Lev 21.9 concerns the daughter of a priest becoming a prostitute. We wonder what circumstances would cause this, but maybe she became one for the same reason other women do. A drastic punishment is meted out to her perhaps because of a religious reason: she profaned (root) *hll* her father, a root usually indicating religious profanation. It does not indicate that she used her cultic connections in this, but this is not beyond the realm of possibility.

Num 25.1-5 describes the "daughters of Moab" inviting the Israelites to sacrifice to their gods. Did they do so by promising sexual favors, or was their job to entice others to come to their sacrifices? Were they "sacred prostitutes" of the Moabite god Baal-Peor? A standard motif, the prohibition of marrying foreign women, comes out in vss. 6-9. In any case, they were a kind of cultic prostitute, but, as is sometimes the case, they were foreign. The sin was simply in worshipping a foreign deity, according to the Mishnah, Sanhedrin 7.6.

Ezek 8.14 describes women weeping for Tammuz at the north gate of the temple. Here was a foreign practice at the gate, a holy place as we have seen. There are no sexual connotations here directly. If as in the Mesopotamian myth it is associated with the descent into the netherworld every year, it may relate to the Tammuz-Ishtar cult, and so have indirect sexual aspects.

Ezek 16 has a picture similar to Ezek 23, discussed below. The unfaithful wife of the Lord, the woman Israel, acted as a prostitute on the *bamôt telu'ôt* "colored stuff" (so Baumgartner) vs. 16. She did so with the Assyrians and Chaldeans, vss. 28-29, as 23.17. The cultic language shows a kind of a cultic prostitution, but not in the sense of a cultic act, communicating with the deity through prostitution. Ezek 16.8.25.32 is like Hos 2.4-15, and is perhaps dependent upon it; indeed Ezek 16.60 is a climax in which the covenant is restored as in Hos 2.18-20.[353] Ezek 23 presents a well-worked out, but wordy, parable with two figures Oholah (" tent, f.," Samaria) and Oholibah ("my tent in her," Jerusalem, f.). They both played the part of the prostitute, first Samaria, because she was first led astray by Assyrian gods, then her sister who followed her. This chapter is one of the richest in the Hebrew Bible in bringing together street prostitute language and cultic language. The former need not be emphasized, but for terms relating to the latter we read of "all the idols" (vss. 7, 30, 37), "defiled my sanctuary" (vss. 38, 39). The integration of the painted lady, upon a couch on which were the oil and incense of the cult in v. 41, is one of the strongest imageries. Of course, all this is metaphor, because one can't have sexual intercourse with an idol (vs. 37, 16.17).

Jer 2.20, 3.1-2, 3.6-9 use standard terminology: playing the prostitute "on every high hill and under every green tree," committing adultery "with rock and tree" (// to playing the part of a prostitute), done with Asherim (17.2). Those who confuse prostitution with so-called "sacred prostitution" understand 5.7 as an assembly point in their house.

This type of language continued with later literature, Second and Third Isaiah, but not as pungently. You were under every green tree Isa 57.5, and set your beds upon high and lofty mountains, Isa 57.7.8. Wisdom 14.22-31 reminds us of Greek, or Levantine Greek practices, with some of the older language.

In Hos 9.1 they have committed harlotry away from their God, they have loved *'etnān*, the standard term for a harlot's hire, on every grain threshing floor. The threshing floor could have an altar on it, 2 Sam 24.18. The *terumah* (usually, "heave") offering was done on the threshing floor, Num 15.20. This way of despising a holy place by doing prostitution on it is similar to Amos 2.7b-8a, but in the Hosea passage the terms are definitely those of the cult.

Deut 31.16 has the Lord acting as a prophet, after the event, describing in sweeping terms how the people will act in the land, how they will play the harlot after the strange gods of the land, and will forsake him, and break the covenant which he has cut with them. This is a shorthand summary of what all the prophets have said above, language appearing nowhere else in the Book of Deuteronomy. The Book of Judges 2.17 picks up this same language in describing the paradigm of the cycle which the people will go through in the time of the judges. The author of Psalm 106 rings the changes on the whole of Israelite history, emphasizing the Lord's anger, and given in a summary vs. 39 as "played the harlot."

All these wicked things were done especially in foreign lands. The basic statement is in Lev 18.3: you shall not do as they do in the land of Egypt...and as they do in the land of Canaan. So if the practices of the *qĕdēšāh* represent foreign deities, these offices are opposed because they fall within the prohibition of worshipping other gods.

4.26.2 There are several passages in which the "queen of heaven" appears. The title is an old one, appearing for Inanna/Ishtar. Both men and their wives burned incense and poured out libations to her, Jer 44.15-19.25. Cakes for her bearing her image were made by the women. We must not assume that the Mesopotamian title carried over into West Semitic territory, however. Östborn thinks that it refers to Asherah here.[354] M, Delcor has given us a full study on this subject.[355] Women make *kawwānîm* "cakes" for the Queen of Heaven (Jer 7.18), along with libations for other gods. (Delcor, p. 105) Perhaps the Akkadian *kamānu* "a sweet cake prepared with honey" (CAD K s.v.) lies behind this. These were offered in a hymn to Ishtar.[356]

Several commentators (p. 106) have picked up on the *'asab* "image" on the cakes, and read the text as indicating that it was the Queen of Heaven's image, as the *selēnai* of the Greeks offered to Artemis had on them a picture of the moon, but Delcor prefers the other meaning of this root, having to do with mourning, sadness, lamentation. Delcor then quotes (p. 108) the Targum, which uses an Aramaic word for idols, which he slightly corrects to indicate licentiousness, leading him to bring in sacred prostitution (one finds it mentioned in the oddest places!), which leads him to Ishtar and the *ištaritum* figure.

Duhm in 1901 did not know which goddess was meant by the Queen of Heaven, but Volz, Rudolf, Weiser and others say that it was Ishtar. (p.109). Delcor finds that in the Egyptian Jewish colony at Syene a Babylonian cult was introduced in which Ishtar was called *šarrat šamê* or a western semitism *malkat šamāni* (pp.109f). He quotes the beginning of Letter No.4 at Elephantine: *šlm bjt bt'l wšlm bjt mlkt šmjn* "safety to the temple of Bethel and safety to the temple of the queen of heaven." (p. 112).

He notes that Astarte was worshipped in Egypt in the second millenium B.C. as the "Syrian Astarte" and "foreign Astarte" (the last from Herodotus, not a reliable source), and that Astarte was worshipped elsewhere in Egyptian texts as "queen of heaven" (p. 114, giving examples). His conclusion, one presumes, is that Astarte, and cognates Ishtar and Aphrodite, was Jeremiah's "queen of heaven," although [I say] she is seldom mentioned in the Hebrew Bible.

We are interested in the subject in this book because women worship the Queen of Heaven, and they are not given titles. Was this a woman's cult? Did these women have titles that have not been passed on down to us? Or was this a "folk religion," in which there was no organization but welled up from the people, and "everyone did it?" These questions cannot be answered, but they lead us to conjecture that there may be further women cultic officials whose titles or relationships are not known to us.

4.27 Homosexuality

The subject of homosexuality in the Hebrew Bible is a large one, and many studies have been made of it. The stories in Jud 19.22-26 and Gen 19.1-11 are normally considered as relating to that practice. Viewing male nakedness in Gen 9.21-23 and Ex 20.26 is prohibited perhaps because it may lead to homosexual intercourse. Lev 18.22 and Lev 20.13 are direct prohibitions of the practice. There seem to be no connotations of cultic life in these references. See the forthcoming book by H.D. Lance.

Notes

1 B. Landsberger, *OLZ* 29 (1926) 763 n. 3.

2 L. Heuzey, RA 5 (1898) 31, fig. 27, from R. Harris, *JESHO* 6 (1963) 122 n. 2.

3 Legrain *Catal* No. 55.

4 *UET* 1 (1928) 57.

5 W.W. Hallo, *HUCA* 33 (1962) 43, Family 7 and 8; Sollberger et Kupper *Inscriptions*, IIIA4n gives an alternate reading of Ayabba-bašti, as does Falkenstein *WO* 1 46. From a bead, *UVB* 8 (1936) 23 and pl. 38f.

6 Read Kubatum by Hallo ibid., Jacobsen *JCS* 7 (1953) 46 n. 7, and Sollberger ibid. III A4m; Dabbatum by Falkenstein, SAHG 370, 25 and van Dijk *BiOr* 11 (1954) 86a. From the same bead as n. 5.

7 A. Falkenstein, *WO* 1 (1947) 46.

8 Kramer *History* 246; A. Falkenstein, SAHG No. 24. Text in Kramer *ZA* NF 16 (1952) 247 and *Belleten* 16 345ff.

9 SAHG No.25 and Kramer ibid. 248, in an updated version of his translation in *ANET* 496. Text in Chiera *SRT* 23, edited A. Falkenstein *WO* 2 43-50.

10 Oppenheim *Catalogue* G 34, partly duplicated by Chiera STA 14, 15, 16, by Schneider *Montserrat* 296, and partly by Sigrist *Rochester* No. 165. The Rochester tablet is from Shulgi 42, and is from Umma, and has 13 of the PNs of the Oppenheim tablet.

11 Keiser *Drehem* p. 2.

12 P. Michaelowski, *Or* NS 45 (1977) 222; *JCS* 28 (1976) 169.

13 P. Steinkeller, *AS* J 3 (1981) 81ff.

14 Kang *Drehem* 263-7. Jones-Snyder 203 present many of the texts. Her influence was such that M. Sigrist, *Drehem*. Bethesda, 1992, devotes a whole chapter to "La 'Fondation' Sulgi-šimti," 222-246.

15 R.T. Scheil, *RT* 37 130, translated Sollberger Kupper *Inscriptions* IIIA 2z.

16 A. Goetze, *JCS* 17 (1963) 35, and H. Waetzoldt, *BiOr* 30 (1973) 68 and n. 18.

17 Lu = ša IV 28 MSL XII 129.

18 In the midst of a long footnote on an article on the ku-li, C. Wilcke discusses the several equivalences of usar and ušur, one of which is *šettum*, another *še'itum* "Nachbarin." He translates as AHw 1232a implies, "the sought one (f.)", *ZA* 59 (1969) 86 n. 90. The article is rich in many excerpts. T. Jacobsen in Gordon *Sumerian Proverbs* 475ff translates usar-mà "to my neighbor-woman," while Gordon (180) has "(female) companion." Lots more could be said about this multi-valent word.

19 *TRS* 2 (*TCL* 16, 1930) 46 and 58f. AO 6721.

20 Harris *Or* 30 (1961) 163-169, about the *naditu* laws in CH; *JCS* 16 (1962), 1-12 about the *naditu* of Sippar; *JESHO* 6 (1963) 121-157, about "the cloister" in ancient Babylon; *Oppenheim AV* (1964) 106-135, on the *naditu*, a full study; Harris, *Sippar* (1975); *RLA* IV (1976) 391-3, on "Hierodoulen, i.e., *naditu* and *ugbabtu*.

21 R. Harris, *JESHO* 6 (1962) 121-157.

22 Also found living in the *gagû* at some time in history are the nin-dingir (*ugbabtu*) CH Para 110.37, the *qadištu* MAOG I/1 3-56.

23 Harris *Sippar* 303.

24 R. Harris, in *Oppenheim AV* 121.

25 R. Harris, in *Oppenheim AV* ibid.

26 R. Harris, *JESHO* 6 (1963) 155.

27 R. Harris, in *Oppenheim AV* 156.

28 Harris *Sippar* 308.

29 Op. cit. 317.

30 Op. cit. 317.

31 For a different view see B. Landsberger, *AfO* 10 (1935) 245-9 and *ZA* 30 (1913) 68ff. And see Sec. 4.4 below.

32 R. Harris *Sippar* 186, 325.

33 Schorr *Zivil* No. 280.

34 Harris *Sippar* 321. She argues that at Sippar "strictly speaking (the *šugētu*) was not a member of a special class."

35 Of Marduk, so Harris, *Sippar* 317.

36 As suggested by Driver Miles *Babylonian Laws* I, 206.

37 ARM 5 82 18-21.

38 ARM 9 24 iii 16. She appears in a broken context in ARM 10 37.15.

39 CAD H 31b (a).

40 This is the same term as the *tēliltu* used of the *šangû*, *KAR* 154, App. 1, and *KAR* 321, *mê tēlilte* Sec. 4.11.10. See Harris, *Studies Oppenheim* 135.

41 *Shurpu* VIII 69.

42 Not the goddess, according to Reiner, *Shurpu* 57a n. to line 117. See W.H. Ph. Römer, "Eine Bemerkungen zum dämonischen Gotte ^{d}Kubu," *Symbolae Böhl* 313. He says that Kubu as a priestess is "unwahrscheinlich."(n. 24). See also R. Frankena, *Takultu* 98, 116, on ^{d}Kubu references.

43 One meaning of this root has to do with "numinous radiance, awe" (CAD S 32).

44 ki-sikil šu-gi$_4$-a sag-ki*-gú-lá-e, Römer *Königshymnen* 130, 70, notes on p. 165. The last term, translated "coiffured" by Römer (my interpretation of his words), is explained by the lexical list: 246 sag-ki-suhur-lá *ke-ze-ru* "curl the hair 247 sag-ki-gú-lá-e KI.MIN Kagal B MSL XIII 237

45 Biggs, ŠÀ.ZI.GA 34b.

46 R. Harris, *RLA* IV 392b; cf. an earlier study by B. Landsberger AfO 10 (1935-36) 145-9.

47 ARM 10 No. 124.5, 14

48 CT 51, 161=BM 134501, restored in CAD M/1 90 (b).

49 As ASKT p. 119.18ff (CAD N/2 57a) and *RLA* 6 (1983) 376 §§ 3-5.

50 Bu 88-5-12, 10; CT 8,2 b 12, translated J. Kohler et al, *Hammurabi's Gesetz* iii No. 10.

51 References in Harris, Sippar 393b, and see especially 321.

52 Cf. ^{284}suhur-lá = *ke-* [*ze-ru*] Hh II, MSL V 72; 6' su-h[u-u] r SUHUR *ki-e-zé-rum* (correction), S^{b} B MSL III 223. SAL ki-zé-er-ak, OB Proto-Lu 708e, Sec. 4.2, appears to be a semi-ideogram for *kezertu*.

53 M. Birot in ARM 7 239.

54 M.T. Roth, *JAOS* 103 (1983) 276, 24, CBS 10467.

55 OB Proto-Lu 646, MSL XII 56.

56 Postgate *Palace Archive* No. 17 = ND 496.31ff (IM 56869), originally D.J. Wiseman and J.V. Kinnier Wilson, *Iraq* 13 (1951) pl. 16. K. Deller, *Or* 34 (1965) 384 discusses this type of dedication.

57 DUMU.MEŠ LÚ.SUHUR.LÁ-*te*, "sons of the *kezertu*'s J.J. Finkelstein *JCS* 7 (1953) 141 No. 85.22. In this broken text are also the A.BA.MEŠ "scribes," *nadītu, nāru* "singer," *ṣābê* "soldiers," "workers," LÚ.SIPA.MEŠ "shepherds," LÚ.NAGAR.MEŠ-*ni* "carpenters," *šangû*, LÚ.AŠGAB.MEŠ-*ni* "leather workers," *kitkittāte* "engineers" (CAD), perhaps all personnel attached to the temple, CAD K 316b.

58 Finkelstein *Late OB* 10.

59 Szlechter *TJA* UMM G19.

60 M. Gallery, *Or* 49 (1980) 333-8 thinks the untitled persons are *kezertu*'s. They owe *parṣu* "service, obligation" to a goddess, and one of them is named a wife; also Falkenstein, ibid.

61 I agree with Gallery's rejection of the modern professional aspects of the usual translation of *harimūtu* as "state of a prostitute" for this, and more towards simply (non-regular?) sexual companionship.

62 *Gilg* VI 165; see also *KUB* 39 93:5 (CAD K 315a), Goetze *JCS* 18 95 n. 19, in which a broken Babylonian passage in a Hittite cultic text has: SAL.MEŠ.SUHUR.LÁ-*ki* and SAL.MEŠ.KAR.KID-*ki* in the same line.

63 Not clear, see argument of Cagni *Poem Erra* l, 3, 5lff.

64 *BWL* 218 IV 6 Examples of the latter office are given in Falkenstein *Gerichtsurkunden* III 161, s.v. šár-ra-ab-du, and šár^{šar}-ra-ab-^{du}dù =ŠU-*ma* Lu = ša III i 27, MSL XII 122.

65 Ungnad *Briefe Hammurapi* No. 2, 34. M. Gallery suggests that *ištarītum* here means "goddesses" (one of the possible meanings of the word) understood as "statues of the goddesses," *Or* 49 (1980) 337, BM 23131, copy *LIH* I No 34, transliteration and translation *LIH* III No. 2.

66 Alster *Shuruppak* 230.

67 ARM 7 206, and in a very broken ARM 7 275: M]aritum [ ]*subaritum* [ ] *kizretum* ...

68 ARM 10 140.16ff.

69 Copied in NA times. Ebeling *Stiftungen* IV, corrected by R. Frankena *OLZ* (1956) 51 col. 134, and with notes by Postgate *Royal Grants* 118f. Transliteration in Menzel *Tempel* II T8-11.

70 Orthography shown by ^{d}GAŠAN-at-ni-ip-ha ABL 1221 r.6; CAD E 253b: Bēlat-natha. See CAD N/2 s.vv. *nathi*, *niphu* A p. 243b. Schramm *Einleitung* II 90f:2 (Shalmaneser III) shows that there are two temples, of ^{d}Bēlat-natha and ^{d}Bēlat-nipha. It is difficult to decide between Sharrat-and Bēlat-.

71 Postgate Royal Grants No. 51, K 2800 + K 2655 + Sm 318, C.H.W. Johns, JRAS 1928 pp. 534ff, transliterated Menzel *Tempel* T15-17.

72 van Driel *Cult* 181f and n. 38.

73 W.G. Lambert, in *Unity Diversity* 108.

74 In one of the canonical lamentations, Inanna/Ishtar was at the door of the éš-dam/*aštammu* house as a prostitute, Cohen *Lamentations* II, 581, c + 443f, URU AMIRABI.

75 Gelb *OAIC* 30.11. For *kulu'u* see App. 3.8.

76 G. R. Driver and J. C. Miles, *Iraq* 6 (1936) 66-70. Their conclusion was that she was a eunuch dressed as a woman. They were probably following Benno Landsberger in an early article: *ZDMG* 69 (1915) 519-21.

77 CH §§181.62, 179.20.

78 CH §§178, 179. A further paragraph, § 180 describes the case of a father giving a gift to his daughter, either a *nadītu* in a *gagû* or a *sekertu*.

79 Harris *Sippar* 314f, linking the *sekertu* with working people.

80 ARM 7 206.8.

81 BRM 4 12.75, in CAD S 215b.

82 OB, *YOS* 10 46 ii 49; an astrological text *von Soden AV* 138.26, and NA Borger *Esarh* 77 §49.3, CAD S 215b, and ACh Supp. 2 50 li 13.

83 A.K. Grayson, *JAOS* 103 (1983) 144, copy; 145f transliteration and translation.

84 Harris *Sippar* 318, discussed on pp. 324-8. See Schorr, *Zivil* and Ungnad *Hammurabis Gesetz* V 1088 and OLZ 14 107.

85 Finkelstein *Late OB* No. 12, 23-25. *kulmašītu* and *nadītu* are on the same field sale contract, Schorr No.278.

86 J. Nougayrol, *ArOr* 17 (1949) 213-26. AO 11276 Translated also by A. Falkenstein in *SAHG* No. 39, who stresses its character as an old divination text.

87 Line 245, TuM NF III Nos. 27-33 (30 iii 28), A. Falkenstein *ZA* 57 (1965) 118.

88 Falkenstein and Sjöberg *Temple Hymns* p. 123a: "kill"; *Harps...*: "stab" with several further examples of ama-nu-gig.

89 Sjöberg *Temple Hymns* 123a.

90 Langdon *BL* No. 87 (K. 10195, pl. XXXIV), 1-2.

91 Falkenstein *Götterlieder* 96f; or jewels, according to J. Renger, *ZA* 58 (1967) 183; MUS: EZEN "MUS of the rite" appears in ED Lu A 74 (MSL XII 11); it was bound (kéš-di) on the nu-ug-gig A. Falkenstein *ZA* 20 120.

92 Walters *Water* Text 43.6, p. 60. NBC 5561, Pl V, 14.

93 BWL 103, 74.

94 D.O. Edzard, *ZA* 55 (1962) 91-112: nu = "the one of the...,"yet has "der Charakter eines Präfixes." (p. 112); CAD I/J 271a suggests that nu with another sign may refer to the sexual organs, as nu-ú NU *li-pi-iš-tum* "a part of the sexual organs" MSL 2 139 C 18 (Proto-Ea). In Ebla, however, the ideogram is nì-gig / *qá -dì-šum*, so maybe nu and ni are variants and nu shouldn't be understood in these senses but as something else compatable with nì, *MEE* 4, index, e.g., Text 2 I.7'8'.

95 K. 3423 + Rm 579, III iv 19, M. Kovacs (ed.), *The Epic of Gilgamesh*, Stanford, 1989, 27, iii 154.

96 CAD I/J 110b: "a tag or a piece of jewelry;" Kovacs (n. 70a): "a pendant?;" Dalley *Myths* 66 "obligation."

97 Livingstone *Poetry* No. 8 r.15' = *LKA* 32. *Inhu*'s are sung by others, see Sec. 2.2.3.

98 Asher-Greve *Old Sumerian,* No. 631.

99 UruKAgina Cones B and C, X, 12, translated S.N. Kramer, *The Sumerians* 319a.

100 Finkelstein *LateOB* 7 and index s.v. *ugbabtum*, in which the *ugbabtum* serves Zababa, the tutelary deity of Kish.

101 Goetze *Omen* No. 38 r. 11ff, translated CAD E 173a; pointed out by J. Nougayrol, *JNES* 9 (1950) 52. The two had to be spelled out because they would have been represented by the same signs.

102 *JNES* 9 (1950) 51 The first is AO 9066, Louvre, unedited, Goetze *Omen* No. 17, 47, YBC 7840.

103 Edzard *Tell ed-Der* No. 152.

104 Ibid., No. 163.

105 E.D. Kingsbury, *HUCA* 34 (1963) 1ff.

106 Harris *Sippar* 313f.

107 ARM 3, 8.6, 42.9 and 84.5 read *ug-ba-ab-tim /tum*; ^{mí}TUR *ug-ba-ab-tim* in ARM 3 No. 8 may be compared with NIN.DINGIR.TUR Clay, YBT, I, 67, and often in MB, AHw s.v. *ugbabtu* (3).

108 H. Klengel, *JCS* 23 (1970) 124f.

109 Cf. Beltani nin-dingir DUMU.SAL ilu-šu-ba-ni Finkelstein *Late OB* No. 90 r.20. Beltanum was ugula nin-dingir-meš, Szlechter *TJA* 56 UMM G 36, 13'.

110 J. Nougayrol, *RA* 44 (1950) 27-9.

111 ACh Adad 17:17.

112 *Dream-book* 290f, 333f K. 6768 and K. 6705, pointed out by J. Botteró and H. Petschow, *RLA* IV 460.

113 In dream omina, Borger *Zeichenliste* 134.

114 Inanna and Enki 54, II v 11, p. 16, above; CAD I/J 45b s.v. *igu* B, and AHw relate igi- with Sumerian egi (KU) "prince."

115 GAG §55f.

116 It appears in OA letters and documents. Hirsch *Untersuchungen*, 57f n. 298.

117 D.O. Edzard, *ZA* NF 21 (55) (1962) 104-5, against Landsberger's nì-gig */ikkibu* "tabooed woman." See also R. Jestin, "Les Noms de Profession NU," in *Böhl AV* Leiden, 1973, 211-13.

118 Deimel *Fara* WF 74, xii 6, per M. Lambert, *Sumer* 10 (1954) 181; from Ur Archaic, *UET* 2 345 I d.

119 Sollberger Kupper *Inscriptions* IB4a. The editor suggests that this is indicative of the "hierogamy." M. Lambert, *Sumer* 8 (1952) 59 explains her as a "deified princess, a replacement for the divinity."

120 Hackman 103 I 3, in an accounting of urudu "copper" objects.

121 Hirsch *Untersuchungen* 58 BIN VI 222,9. Interestingly, the man's name was Lamassi, and the demon Lamaštu in NA times, Sec. 4.11.13, is given the title *qadištu* He gives another reference, *ICK* 1,3,6, marrying a *qadištu* in the city, i.e., Asshur.

122 *RA* 30 (1933) 118 No. 4 = *UET* III 942; A. Falkenstein, *ZA* 56 (1964) 120. From C.L. Woolley, *Ur Excavations II. The Royal Cemetery, Texts* 1934, p 312.

123 Edzard ZA 55 (1963) 104.

124 CT 15, 8 1f, see *AS* 12,92. Variant to line 308. "I" is Inanna, according to Renger.

125 Cohen *Lamentations* 164, 171, b + 225ff; 103, 112 a + 208, and passim.

126 "second-rank wife" CAD Q 49a; "a woman of lower social and legal status" J. Lewy, *HUCA* 27 (1956) 9 n. 40.

127 Balkan op. cit. n. 27.

128 It is an eponym name, read *kaššum*, that "designates an official or a committee in the *kārum* who, or which, served from time to time as deputy in the name of one or two *hamuštum* eponymns," K. Balkan, *Landsberger AV* 172ff.

129 *MAOG* I/1 3-56. Once she is found living in the *gagû* of Sippar, J. Renger *ZA* 58 (1967) 181.

130 Ibid.

131 In a contract, Schorr *Zivil* No. 182.

132 A high temple or state official, the name probably from pisan-dub-ba-ak "basket of tablets" with omission of the pi-, CAD S/1 373b. See Kraus AbB 2 139 for gá-dub-ba.

133 A. Goetze, *JCS* 2 (1948) 92ff No. 21.28 (Crozer No. 153).

134 § 22, xv.45-51.

135 *TCL* I 146. See below App. 1 for a ritual in which this official took part.

136 Harris *Sippar* 330 lists the names of 8 of them.

137 One contract provides for Iltani *qadištum* to provide such for a child for 3 years, the payment to be of grain, oil and wool, Schorr *Zivil* 531 (VAT 6302, VAS V 11 10-11), Schorr *Zivil* No. 78. Other contracts concerning nu-gig's are Nos. 211, 241, 280. von Soden *AfO* 18 (1957-58) 119-121 studies the subject.

138 For married nu-gig see Sec. 4.11.2.

139 J. Renger, *ZA* 58 (1967), 181 n. 495.

140 Schorr *Zivil* No. 280.

141 Schorr *Zivil* No. 182, n. 27 above.

142 Schorr *Zivil* No. 211.

143 For Inanna nu-gig, see J. Renger, *ZA* 58 183 n. 514. For Ishtar *qadištu,* see *LKA* 37.6; E. Reiner, *JNES* 33 (1974) 224,7, Ishtar as Nana. In Sumerian literary texts, nu-gig is also the title of Aruru/Ninmah (? not certain. Renger n. 515 p. 183 *ZA* 58 has "vgl.") and Nin-insina (SRT 6 ii 26 = 7il; iii 6 = 7 i 17). Nin-insina has several similarities to Inanna. However, most commentators say that the nu-gig/*qadištu* does not belong to the Inanna/Ishtar cult. (B. Landsberger *ArOr* 18 339 n. 55; W. von Soden, *AfO* 18 121). E. Ebeling, "Liebeszauber im Alten Orient," *MAOG* I/1 (1925) 3-56 in discussing *nīš libbi* "raising of the heart" texts, says that the *qadištu, šamhatu, harimtu* and *kezertu* are followers of Ishtar.

144 *RA* 30 (1933) 118 No. 4 = *UET* III 942. C.L. Woolley, *Ur Excavations* II. The Royal Cemetery. Text, 1934, 312. Edzard *ZA* 55 (1963) 104: gal is "the great."

145 *SLTN* 71:31.

146 Sjöberg *Temple Hymns* 112b.

147 ARM 10 59 r.3f, Römer *Frauenbriefe* 36.

148 Among analyzable names, 4 are Akkadian and 8 are West Semitic, *Syria* 35 (1958) 23.

149 ARM 9 291. Batto *Women* 111f argues against the eqivalent of *qaššatum* and *qadištum.*

150 The colophon r. 16 is *li-mu* [ ].

151 Described in *AKA* 100 viii 1ff.

152 See Sec. 4.3.5 where the *qadištu* uses *mê tēlilte.*

153 The *assinnu* App. 3.2.2 is found singing an *inhu* in *KAR* 42.29 (see E.Ebeling, *MVAG* 23/II 21ff for the full text). The *nāru* sings an *inhu* in the late *kalû* ritual RAcc 44.5. For an attempted etymology see Sec. 2.2.3.

154 The word used here (*dumāqū*) is a general word for jewelry, but elsewhere the *qadištu* wears unú-šuba and múš (Sec. 4.8.2), the latter also worn by the en and the king (J. Renger *ZA* 58 (1967), 183).

155 VAT 10568a, copy *Or* 17 (1948) tabl. 17, transliteration E. Ebeling, *Or* 22 (1953) 43.

156 This goddess is also in the ritual report *ABL* 977 r.11 (= Parpola *LAS* 218), *KAR* 141.1 and r.2 in a ritual to be done by the river. There is a *mār nāri* in CT 24, 16, 28 in the list An=Anum.

157 VAT 10102, BWL 160.7, translation 161; also Gruber *UF* 18 141, for *KAR* 321.7.

158 ABL 1126, collated Parpola, *LAS* I 187.

159 E.F. Weidner, "Hof- u. Harems-Erlasse assyrischer Königs," *AfO* 17 (1954-6) 268, line 11.

160 CAD E s.v.: "concubine," also AHw. The word literally means "enclosed one," and some have thought of her as a harem woman. T.J. Meek, *ANET* 183 n. 21, thinks she is a captive woman who became a concubine, a secondary wife. This law must be only for street purposes, because an *esirtu* who has been veiled before witnesses, then taken as a wife by a man, is now treated as a wife: *MAL* §41.

161 Excerpts H. Zimmern, *ZA* 32 (1919) 59 = Speleers *Recueil* 312.6, var. *AMT* 32,1

162 *pišru* "Lösung, Deutung," appears sometimes as an implement: ^{gis}*pišru* "eine Zauberstab für Magier," AHw 868b. Cf. Hg I 50, MSL VI 79,50: gis-búr = *iṣ piš-ru* = *gam-* [*lu*], "a curved staff.

163 A rope of palm of some sort, used here in a cultic act, see Landsberger *Date Palm* 21 (g).

164 Weidner *Reliefs* 4 Abb. 12 and passim.

165 K. 3362 = IV R 58 [65] iii 37, *ZA* 16 168-83.

166 Biggs ŠÀ.ZI.GA No. 13.7.

167 Lambert-Millard *Atra-hasis* 62, 17 cf. 290.

168 M. Gruber *UF* 18 (1986) 143 n. 49.

169 *ASKT* No. 11, pp 82f = 1st tablet of series zì-pa, studied by R. Borger, *von Soden AV* 1ff, transliterated and translated by Fossey *Magie* No. 1.11ff. Large bibliography *HKL* I 185.

170 F. Thureau-Dangin, *RA* 11 (1914) 152, 45 (Seleucid times).

171 ana ittišu 7 iii 7-10, MSL 1 99f.

172 ana ittišu 7 ii 23aff, MSL 1 96ff.

173 S. Terrien, *VT* 20 (1970) 327-8.

174 Arnaud *RHR* 183 (1973) 113.

175 Ungnad *Briefe Hammurapi* No. 2. Another interpretation uses the second meaning of *ištaratīm* "goddesses" (as Ungnad), understood as "statues of the goddesses," by M. Gallery, *Or* 49 (1980) 337.

176 *Inanna and Enki* 56.

177 Krecher *Kultlyrik* 128ff.

178 CAD K 533 s.v. *kummu,* lexical section.

179 A. Falkenstein *ZA* 56 (1964) 118.

180 Harris *Sippar* 173.

181 Harris *Sippar* 182, CT 48 45:13f.

182 Harris *Studies Oppenheim* 107, implying that the word is a description not an office or profession.

183 CAD K 580.

184 *Weidner Tn* 73 No. 8:7.

185 Menzel *Tempel* I pp. 28f.

186 Kwasman *NA Legal* No. 424 (*ARU* 45); A. van Praag, *Droit Matrimoniel Assyro-Babylonien* 50b.

187 Dandamaev *Slavery* 132-5.

188 He discusses these in a way that the older scholars would, as E. Ebeling who describes "*qadištu, harimtu, ištarītu, kulmašītu, ugbabtu* usw." as "Hierodulen," *RLA* III 113a, art. "Freudenmädchen". I hope the present study has given these women a much more significant place in the scheme of things than this.

189 Dougherty *Shirkutu* 66.

190 G. Wilhelm, "Marginalien zu Herodot Klio 199," in Moran AV 505-24.

191 Asher-Greve *Old Sumerian* 150. M. Lambert, *Sumer* 5 (1949) 9ff explains her as a living goddess to whom offerings were made, but who sacrifices as priestess at the feast of the Antasurra and Siraran.

192 E. Sollberger, *ZA* 53 (1959) 4 note 8; *BiOr* 16 (1959) 117.80; Bauer *Lagasch* 292 I 6 (=munu[s]).

193 "Weidner Chronicle," F.N.H. Al-Rawi, *Iraq* 52 (1990) 5, 13.

194 *Gilgamesh* X, i, 1.

195 K. 3464, studied in H. Zimmern *ZA* 32 (1918-19) 170ff; Craig *ABRT* No. 66f; Boissier, *PSBA* 1 901, 115f.

196 R. Harris, Moran AV 224 n. 26.

197 K. 2582 + r.ii, quoted by *Dream-Book* 313 x + 3.

198 Caplice Namburbi *Or* 40 (1971) 143, r.23f, the same objects as in the above ritual.

199 *KAR* 234:25, CAD S 9b.

200 *Or* 36 (1967), 23.8.

201 Biggs *ŠÀ.ZI.GA* No. 16.13, K.9451 +.

202 *ARM* 9, 27.

203 Stamm *Namengebung* 260ff.

204 4 R 58 iii 37.

205 R. Harris, *JCS* 9 (1955) 65ff, No. 20.4, 42.4.

206 *Gilgamesh*, Assyrian Version, III iv 23.

207 *Shurpu* VIII.69.

208 Eric J. Sharpe, in M. Eliade (ed.), *The Encyclopedia of Religion* 3, New.York. (1987), 579.

209 M. Dietrich and O. Loretz, "Die Soziale Struktur von Alalah und Ugarit," *WO* 5 (1969) 90, 93.

210 F. Gröndahl, *Die Personnennamen der Texte aus Ugarit.* Rome, 1967, 317, 348.

211 W. von Soden, "Zur Stellung des 'Geweihten' (qdš) in Ugarit," *UF* 2 (1970) 329-330.

212 D. Urie *PEQ* 80 (1948) 43, but no comments.

213 A.F. Rainey, *BiAr* 28 (1965) 124.

214 Tarragon *Culte* 139-41.

215 F. Delitzsch, "Zu Herodots babylonischen Nachrichten," in Sachau AV 87-102.

216 W. Kornfeld, "Prostitution sacrée" in H. Cazelles et A. Feuillert (eds.), *Supplement. Dictionnaire de la Bible.* Paris, 1972, cols. 1356-74. The odd goddess name Mylitta he finds in the Akkadian *mu'allidatu* "she who begets," and he refers to Enuma Elish I.4: Mummu-Tiamat *mu-al-li-da-at gimrisun* "she who begot all of them." But the prostitution of Her I, 199 has nothing to do with begetting children. R.D. Barnett, *A Catalogue of the Nimrud Ivories* British Museum, 1975, 150 n. 5, suggests *mulittum = mulliltum*, emesal for Ninlil. There is also the "cultic functionary" *mullilu* with only one entry PBS 1/1 11 iv 96, CAD M/2 189a. S. Dalley (*RA* 73, 1979, 177-8) sums up some recent scholarship, especially noting a PN in STT 372.5, showing that NIN.LIL was read in 1st millenium Assyrian as Mul(l)is(s)u and variants.

217 E. Sydney Hartland, "Concerning the rite at the temple of Mylitta," in Tylor AV 189-202.

218 The so-called *ius primus noctis*, attested in medieval Europe, but which one must call doubtful for the ancient Near East. Lambert thinks that Gilgamesh engaged in this practice, Sec. 4.22.8, but "one swallow does not a Spring make."

219 *RHR* 183 in an article discussed fully in Sec. 4.22.13, and for greater clarity to be read in conjunction with our discussion here.

220 C.H.W. Johns, *Hastings Bible Dictionary* V 591 (1907), quoted in Brooks *Moral Practices* 66. She says that this practice cannot be proved by the inscriptions. She refers to BE X (2) p. 195 line 20 as a possible reference, not available to me.

221 W. Baumgartner, "Herodots Babylonische u. Assyrische Nachrichten" *ArOr* 18/1-2 (1950) 69-106 expecially n. 38a.

222 *tegos* 1) a roof, 2) hall, room, 3) brothel. Variants in the Göttingen LXX p. 496, following Codex Vaticanus, have *stegous* "roof, room."

223 H.C. Kee, in J.H. Charlesworth (ed.), *The Old Testament Pseudepigrapha* I 778. Dated by Kee in the Maccabean period. Charlesworth, *The Pseudepigrapha and Modern Study* ^{2} 212: ca 100 B.C.E.

224 Strabo, see next note.

225 W.M. Ramsay, *Cities and Bishoprics of Phrygia,* i, 94 Inscription No. 18, p. 115. This is an inscription of PN *pallakidon kai aniptopodon* "concubine/maiden and of unwashed feet." This is in Tralleis in Lydia 2c C.E. Daughters are consecrated to Anaitis to act as courtesans before the goddess for a long time before given in marriage (Strabo).

226 Lucian *De Dea Syria* (*peri tes syries theou*) VI.

227 Eusebius *Life of Constantine* iii, 58.

228 Sozomen, *Ecclesiastical History* v, 10.

229 J.-A. Hild, "Hierodoulai" in *Dictionnaire des Antiquités Greques et Romanes. D'apres les Textes et les Monuments,"* Paris, 1899, iii 171-4. See also V. Hirt, *Hierodulen*, Berlin, 1818 (not available to me). The newer studies use these older sources also.

230 J.P. Asmussen, *Stud The* 11 (1956) 168-92.

231 Brooks, *JBL* 60 (1941) 227-253.

232 von Rad *Theology* I, 27: the religious atmosphere was "saturated with mythic sexual conceptions." His terms like the "deification of sex" (p. 28) show that he missed the point that the basic concept was that of fertility.

233 *BTB* 6 (1976) 225-236.

234 Yamauchi *Gordon AV.* 213-222.

235 CAH^3 II, 205.

236 W. von Soden, "Kultische Prostitution," *RGG* V (1961) 642-3.

237 W.G. Lambert, "Morals in Ancient Mesopotamia," *JEOL* v 194-6 is the part in which we are interested.

238 J. Bottéro, in a review of R.D. Biggs, *ŠÀ.ZI.GA* , *JESHO* 14 (1971) 72.

239 M.G. Kovacs, *The Epic of Gilgamesh,* Stanford, 1989, 16 n. 3.

240 W. Kornfeld, "Prostitution sacrée," in H,. Cazelles et A. Feuillet (eds.), *Supplement. Dictionnaire de la Bible* viii, Paris, 1972, cols. 1356-74.

241 Albright *ARI* 75ff, who also takes sacred prostitution for granted without backing up his claim, only using "Herodotus, Strabo and Lucian," which we have seen is suspect (Herodotus) and Greek and late (Strabo and Lucian).

242 On this A. Jamme, one of the world's experts in ancient Arabia, in *BASOR* 138 (1955), 39-47, especially p. 45, says "certainly not hierodules," so Kornfeld either didn't know or didn't follow the experts' opinion when it conflicts with his diffusionist approach.

243 R.D. Barnett, *A Catalogue of the Nimrud Ivories*, British Museum, 1975^2 148-51. This continued in Egypt in Roman times.

244 The series is now available, in summary form, in the thesis of Sally M. Moren, *The Omen Series "Shumma Ālu": A Preliminary Investigation.* University Microfilms. A 1978 dissertation from the University of Pennsylvania done under Erle Leichty. The 104th tablet is a table of 73 omens, recording people having sexual relations in various places, and at various times, and related themes as sexual dreams, nocturnal emission, premature ejaculation, impotence and anal intercourse (Moren p. 237, J. Bottéro and H. Petschow, *RLA* IV 461).

245 S. Smith, *JRAS* 1928 849-68.

246 *VAB* 4 236 ii 3.

247 Jacobsen *Harps*...138; Heimpel *JCS* 33 94 line 182.

248 ABL 113.16, 366.7f, 65.9 (Nabû alone), see Pallis *Akītu* 104f. But a more thorough study of the marriage of Nabû and Tashmētu is given by E. Matsushima, *ASJ* (1987) 131-175, a transliteration of TIM IX 54.

249 *SBH* 145 ii 8.

250 E. Matsushima, *ASJ* 7 (1985) 129-137.

251 D.O. Edzard, *XX RAI* Leiden, 1975 159.

252 Salonen *Möbel* 114ff.

253 CAD E 172b lexical section.

254 Harris *Sippar* 304.

255 Penelope Weadock, "The giparu at Ur," *Iraq* 37 (1975) 101-28, research as of 1958.

256 T. Jacobsen, *ZA* NF 18 (1957) 107 n. 32.

257 See also Benno Landsberger, *ZA* 30 (1915-16) 67-73.

258 *SEM* 19 iv (!) 6, CAD G 83b, but in Aratta. Can this apply to Sumer?

259 S.N. Kramer (transl.), "Lamentation over the destruction of Ur," *ANET* 462, 353, and his "Lamentation over the destruction of Sumer and Ur, *ANET* 614, 156.

260 *YOS* 1 45 i 39, CAD K 533b.

261 *UET* 1 103.

262 The field a-šà uš-gíd-da, researched in Pettinato *Untersuchungen* No. 855, belongs to a depot of Igalima (ì-dub-^{d}ig-alima), but otherwise only non cultic aspects have been found with this word in this collection.

263 Livingstone *Poetry* No. 9.1 = K 1354 = SAA Bulletin 1 40, 1; VAT 10593; cf. *bit ... ana ha-am-mu* [ ] *KAR* 122. 10.

264 *VAB* 4 114 i 42, CAD K 444a.

265 *VAB* 4 240 iii 14, CAD Z 131a, AHw 823b gives references from OB to Seleucid times.

266 *RAcc* 68.14.

267 E.F. Weidner, *IAK* 1 122 iv 5, CAD S.

268 AHw 1340b.

269 W. von Soden, "Le Temple: Terminologie Lexicale," *XX RAI* Istanbul, 1975, 133-143.

270 J.B. Segal, "Jewish Attutudes Towards Women," *JJS* 30 (1979) 131.

271 I.J. Peritz, "Women in the ancient Hebrew cult," *JBL* 17 (1898) 111-148.

272 J.G. Frazer, *The New Golden Bough.* Ed. T.H. Gaster, N.Y., 1959. He has much on "sacred marriage," pp. 88-100. The nature aspects of most of these would have no analogy with the more sophisticated Mesopotamian and Greek priestesses. The old *Golden Bough* ^{3} London 1911, has much on sacred marriage in vol. ii chap 12, mostly from Greek mythology, but also a short section on ancient Europe, and other countries.

273 Guthrie *Greeks* 53-64.

274 He refers to Cook *Zeus* iii for details.

275 J.S. Cooper, "Heilige Hochzeit.B Archeologisch" *RLA* IV 259-69.

276 KAV I ii 82ff (MAL §§ 19f), *ANET* 181.

277 Berlin *Enmerkar and Ensuhkesdanna*, Philadelphia, 1979.

278 Note that, just as the female en's had names, probably taken upon assuming the office, composed with en (Sec. 1.16), so have these lords (en).

279 The term used for the lying together of Dumuzi and Inanna also, see A. Sjöberg *Temple Hymns* 93b.

280 Explained as = *zu'unu* "adorned, decorated" MSL XIII, 181, 35', with -di for the expected du (KA).

281 Without any more details being given, we learn from line 118 that the išib, lú-mah, $gudu_4$ and gìr-sè-ga (as a separate office, though usually meaning simply "personnel") also dwell in the gipar.

282 Römer *Königshymnen* 128-208 (Kap. IV) (SRT 1, etc.).

283 Daniel Riesman, "Iddin Dagan's Sacred Marriage Hymn," *JCS* 25 (1973) 185-202.

284 W. Heimpel, *JAOS* 92 (1972) 288-291.

285 S.N. Kramer. "The Blessing of Shulgi," *JQR* Seventy-fifth Anniversary Volume, 1967, 370-80.

286 J.J. van Dijk, "Le fête du nouvel an dans un texte de Sulgi," *BiOr* 11 (1954) 83-88. The text he uses is LB 963 now copied in *TLB* 2 No. 2.

287 A. Falkenstein, *ZA* 50 (1952) 73ff.

288 G. Dossin, *RA* 35 2 i 4. See CAD M/l 119a.

289 Spycket *Statues* 101.

290 J. Renger, "Heilige Hochzeit," *RLA* IV 259ff.

291 M. Lambert, "Le périod présargonique," *Sumer* 8 (1952) 59.

292 M. Lambert, *Sumer* 5 (1949) 9ff. See also Labat *Cartactère.*

293 CT 36, 26 17-20, transliterted and translated by Jacobsen *ZA* 52 NF 18 (1957) 126 n. 80.

294 M. Lambert and R.P. Tourmey, *RB* 55 (1948) 540 n. 56, dùg taken in a sexual sense, see Spycket *Statues* 102 n. 7.

295 Gudea Cyl A II, 24.

296 Spycket 103.

297 J. Renger, *RLA* IV 257 §20.

298 T. Jacobsen, in H. Frankfort (ed.), *Kingship and the Gods* 296, Iddin-Dagan rite v 18ff (only some quotations from Frankfort).

299 S.N. Kramer, "The sacred marriage texts," *PAPS* 107/6, December 20, 1963, 485-527.

300 Transliterated and translated *PAPS* 107, 493ff.

301 M. Pope, *Anchor Bible. Song of Songs.* Garden City, 1977, index s.v. "sacred marriage" finds a large number of images similar in Mesopotamia and the Song of Songs.

302 *VAB* 4 114 i 42, CAD K 444a. L. Woolley of course did not find the top of the ziggurat at Ur amidst the ruins, but each of his reconstructed drawings showed a shrine or temple or room at the top. L. Woolley, *Ur Excavations V. The Ziggurat and its Surroundings.* Philadelphia and London, 1939, pls. 85-88. It is perhaps natural to expect this, given the vocabulary of the Mesopotamians indicating their gods as "on high." Perhaps also there was a remembrance of Maya temples, with their shrines on top. See Tatiana Proskouriakoff, *An Album of Maya Architecture,* Norman, 1963, plates of Piedras Negras, Copán, and others.

303 *OECT* 1 34 ii 6, CAD K 444a.

304 Thompson, *Esarh* pl. 14 i 49; cf. Streck *Asb* 300 iv 13; Piepkorn *Asb* 5, i 49.

305 E. Matsushima, *ASJ* 9 (1987) 131-175, mainly a translation of *TIM* 9 54, with studies of ABL 65, 113 and 366.

306 S.N. Kramer, in *The Bible World. Essays in Honor of Cyrus H. Gordon*, New York. 1980. Text BM 120011. It is modified from Kramer *From the Poetry of Sumer* 32-34.

307 Footnote 16, p. 96.

308 Kramer *SMR* 65, 79.

309 J. Renger, "Heilige Hochzeit. Philologisch" *RLA* IV (1975) 251-9.

310 W.H.Ph. Römer, "Einige Uberlegungen zur 'Heilige Hochzeit' nach altorientalischen Texten," in W.C. Delsman et al, *Von Kanaan bis*

Kerala (Festschrift J.P.M. van der Ploeg), *AOAT* 211, Neukirchen/Vluyn, 1982, 411-28.

311 Beatrice R. Brooks, "Fertility Cult Functionaries in the Old Testament," *JBL* 60 (1941) 227-253.

312 L. Woolley, *AJ* 5 (1925) 393-4 on thread supplied to weaving women in a temple.

313 Michael Astour, "Tamar the Hierodule," *JBL* 85 (1966) 185-196. His conclusions are criticized by J.A. Emerton, *VT* 25 (1975) 357-60.

314 J.P. Asmussen *Stud The* 11 (1956) 183. He also has an excellent study about veiling in surrounding societies.

315 H. Lesêtre in F. Vigouroux (ed.), *Dictionnnaire de la Bible*, 15, Paris, 1922, 2247. Some of these words indicate shawl, and how much of the face is shown indicates the use to which the veil is put.

316 As seen by Asmussen op. cit. 185ff and M. Jastrow, "Veiling in Ancient Assyria," *Revue Archéologique*, 5th ser., XIV, 1921, 209-238.

317 L. Rost, *BertholetAV* 451. Asmussen (n. 223) p. 181 finds that *zônāh* and *qĕdēšāh* are used in the same meaning here.

318 Pedersen *Israel* III-IV, 469ff.

319 The text says: "you took some of your garments and made yourself *bāmôt ṭĕluʾôt*." *bāmôt* as "high place" does not seem to fit here. *ṭĕluʾôt* is "colored" (Eissfeldt), or "decked with divers colors" (Chicago Bible), or "colored material on coats for sacral prostitution" (Baumgartner -- tendentious!), or simply "four additional words are unclear" (GNB), "a platform in gay colors" (NEB), "colorful shrines" (NRSV, adding "meaning of Heb. uncertain").

320 Many of the ideas here are from Östborn *Yahweh Baal*.

321 H.W. Wolff, *Hosea* 86, 88. He uses Rost's article in the Bertholet Festschrift (n. 317, above) and G. Boström's *Proverbiastudien* Lund, 1935, as forerunners.

322 W. Rudolph, *ZAW* 75 (NF 34, 1963) 65-73 He also says that though there may have been some borrowing from the Mesopotamian, there is no ius primae noctis in the O.T (p. 69f).

323 A.S. Kapelrud, *The Violent Goddess. Anat in the Ras Shamra Texts,* Oslo, 1969, 92-105.

324 J. Oberman, *Discoveries at Karatepe*, JAOS Supplement 9 (1948) p. 10 lii 17; Östborn *Yahweh Baal* 76. Sometime 9-8c. B.C.E. (?)

325 Karel van der Toorn, "Female Prostitution in Payment of Vows in Ancient Israel," *JBL* 108 (1989) 193-205.

326 Duane A. Garrett, *JBL* 109 (1990) 681-2.

327 M.I. Gruber, *Tarbiz* 52 (1983) 167-76, in Hebrew.

328 Herbert May, *AJSL* 48 (1930-31) 89, and especially 90.

329 Graham *AJSL* 47, 238f; Herbert G. May *JBL* 56 (1937), 315.

330 Herbert May, *AJSL* 56 (1939), 58.

331 W.O.E. Oesterley and T.H. Robinson, *Hebrew Religion*, New York, 1930, 24-28; Y. Kaufmann (abridged by M. Greenberg), *Religion of Israel*, Chicago, 1960, 91-2; A. Lods, *Israel*, London, 1953 (1932) 107.

332 de Boer *Fatherhood* 26-37, especially 32.

333 M.-J. Lagrange, *Le Livre de Juges,* Paris, 1903, 85.

334 J. Gray, *Joshua, Judges and Ruth,* London, 1967, 279.

335 The fact that this did not happen (2 Kings 23.29) does not detract from the theology of the prophecy. Josiah was good (2 Kings 22.2) and therefore good things will happen to him.

336 As a footnote to Miriam, Deborah and Huldah, Talmud Babli Megilla 14a adds also, as prophetesses: Sarah (Gen 12ff), Hannah (1 Sam 1-2), Abigail (1 Sam 25) and Esther. Huldah even had two doors of the temple precinct named after her, according to Mishnah Mid. 1.3. By tradition there were special places for these women in the Hebrew cult.

337 W. Zimmerli, *Ezekiel* 296f, who is inconclusive as to the nature of the object.

338 A. Tsukimoto, "Emar and the Old Testament. Preliminary Remarks," *AJBI* 15 (1989) 3ff.

339 Fowler *Names.*

340 *Stud The* 11 (1957) 169.

341 Kohler-Baumgartner s.v. *keleb* 2d: "(kultische) Päderast" giving Aistleitner No.1313 as a reference, which in turn is based on no evidence; Jean-Hoftijzer's references to Phoenician texts are late, and we have seen that influences have changed during this late period.

342 D. Winton Thomas, "Kelebh 'dog': its origin and some usages of it in the Old Testament," *VT* 10 (1960) 410-27. See also W. Beltz, *Die Kaleb-Traditionen im Altes Testament.* Stuttgart, 1974, 121, who refers uncritically to Aistleitner's *Wörterbuch.*

343 O. Margalith, *VT* 33 (1983) 491-5.

344 CIS I No. 86 B 10, A 15.

345 H.G. May, *AJSL* 48 (1932) 73-98.

346 Raymond Collins, *BTB* 7 (1977) 149-167.

347 Buis Leclercq *Deut* 157.

348 Sometimes the term "adultery" is used in the same way that "prostitution" is. The two words are in parallel in Jer 13.27, Ezek 23.43, Hos 3.1.3, Hos 2.2, Jer 3.9, Jer 5.7, Ezek 16.31-34, Ezek 23.37.45, Hos 4.13-14; even as late as Isa 57.3.

349 Grace Emmerson, *VT* 24 (1974) 492-7 wonders whether a fertility goddess (unnamed!) is hidden in these words.

350 The term appears also in Jer 2.20, 3.6, 17.2, Ezek 6.13, 20.28, Hos 4.13, Deut 12.2, 2 Kings 16.4, 17.10, 2 Chr 28.4.

351 L. Rost, *Bertholet AV* 450-460. Asmussen (Sec. 4..19.2) p. 181 thinks that this is the only place in the Hebrew Bible where the cultic aspects of prostituion are mentioned.

352 Pedersen *Israel* III-IV, 472.

353 O. Eissfeldt, *Kleine Schriften* II (1963 (1936)) 102.

354 Östborn *Yahweh Baal* 66.

355 M. Delcor, "Le culte de la 'Reine du Ciel' selon Jer 7.18, 44.17-19, 25 et ses survivances" in W.C. Delsman et al (Hrsg.), *Von Kanaan bis Kerala* AOAT 211. Neukirchen-Vluyn, 1982 101-122. K.2001.19-21, Martin *Religieux* 61.

356 K.2001.19-21, Martin *Religieux* 61.

APPENDIX ONE

A Middle Assyrian Ritual With qadistu's and a sangû

<u>KAR 154, VAT 10164 (For discussion, see Sec. 4.11.9)</u>

See: W. Gwaltney, *The Qadištum and the Ištaritum in Mesopotamian Society*. Thesis, Hebrew Union College, Cincinnati, 1964, pp. 52-58; Menzel *Tempel* T2; M Gruber, *UF* 18 (1986) 139f, selected lines.

1 [*ina*]u_4-*me* ^{d}IM *i-ša-tu-qu-ni* NU.GIG.MES *ú-še-ṣu-ni*

[In the (?)] day of Adad when they make a separation,
when the *qadištu* 's bring out / send out / are sent out

2 x] 1/2 *qa* NINDA 7 *ma-ka-la-tu* 1 *qa* ŠEM 2 BÁN KAŠ *i-na* É *ša-li-me* ⌜DU$^{?}$⌝

x + 1/2 qa bread 7 *makaltu*-bowls 1 *qa* aromatics 2 *sutu* beer in a favorable house (?)

3 *i-na* ŠÀ *an-ni-ma* 3 *qa* NINDA 7 *ma-ka-la-a-tu a-na* É ^{d}IM 1 *qa* NINDA 1 *ma-kal-tu*

from these 3 qa bread 7 *makaltu* -bowls for the temple of Adad,
1 qa bread 1 *makaltu*-bowl

4 NU.GIG.MEŠ *i* [*n-h*]*a a-na pa-ni* ^{d}IM *i-na-di-a im-ha i-pa-ša-ra*

the *qadištu*'s the *i* [*nh*]*u* - song before Adad recite,
the *inhu*-song they prolong (?)

5 SANGA *ša* [*te-lil-te*] *ú-lal* NU.GIG.MEŠ DINGIR *ú-la-a*

the purification *šangû* does the pu[rification], the *qadištu*'s
exalt/lift up the god

6 SANGA NU.[GIG.MEŠ *iš*] *-tu* É ^{d}IM *ú-ṣu-né*

the *šangû* (and) the *qad* [*ištu*'s] go out [o]f the temple of Adad

7 *a-na* A[N$^{?}$/KÁ$^{!?}$]*-te ša* ^{d}MAŠ *ša* É Asshur$^{!}$ SANGA *ú-šab* NU.GIG.MEŠ

to/at the door? of....of Ninurta of the temple of Asshur. The *šangû*
sits. The *qadištu*' s

8 *in-ha* [*i-na-di-a*] NU.GIG.MEŠ *in-ha i-pa-ša-ra* SANGA *ša te-lil-te ú-lal*

the *inhu* [recite], the *qadištu* 's the *inhu* prolong (?),
the purification *šangû* does the purification

9 NU.GIG.MEŠ DINGIR [*ú-la-a*] *i-na* KÁ Asshur *ú-ṣa a-na* KÁ *za-i-'i il-lak* NU.GIG.MEŠ *in-ha i-na-di-a*

the *qadištu*'s [lift up/exalt] the god, from the gate of Asshur he goes out, to the gate of Zai'i he goes. The *qadištu*'s recite the *inhu*

10 *in-ha i-pa-ša-ra* SANGA *ša te-lil-te ú-lal* NU.GIG.MEŠ DINGIR *ú-la-a* 1 *qa* NINDA

they prolong(?) the *inhu* . The purification *šangû* does the purification. The *qadištu*'s lift up/exalt the god, 1 *qa* of bread

11 1 *ma-kal-tu* 1 *qa* KAŠ 6 *-šu ku-ṣa-e ša ma-kal-te* [ ]

1 *makaltu-* bowl 1 qa of beer, 6 times spilling from the *makaltu*...

12 *i-na ma-qi-e i-na-qi* MU ^{d}Išum$^{?}$ ^{d}IDIGNA lá KIMIN ^{d}UD.K[IB.NUN] ?

into the *maqqû* - bowl he pours, the name of Išum(?) ... the divine Tigris the divine Eu[phrates] (?)/ Shamash ... (?)

13 NU.GIG.MEŠ *a-na* É *ha-am-ri il-la-ka* SANGA *ú-šab* NU.GIG.[MEŠ]

The *qadištu'* s go to the *bīt hamri*. The *šangû* sits. The *qadištu* ['s]

14 *in-*] *ha i-na-di-a* SANGA *ša te-lil-te ú-lal* 1 *qa* NINDA 1 *qa* KAŠ [ ]

recite the [*in*]*hu*. The purification *šangû* does the purification, 1 *qa* bread 1 *qa* beer ...

15 *a*] *-na* É *ha-am-ri* [ ]] *za* [

t] o the *bīt hamri* ...

r. 1 SANGA[

the *šangû* ...

r. 2 *i-ka-* [

r. 3 1 1/2 *qa* NINDA [5$^{?}$*q*]*a* KAš 1 ^{UZU}UR *a-na* SA[NGA] ...

1 1/2 *qa* of bread [5 (?) *q*]*a* of beer 1 upper shank for the *ša* [*ngû*]

r. 4 *ša* Asshur KI.MIN ^{d}IM *e-pal a-ri-ik-ta ša* ⌈ÚRI⌉ [ ]

of Asshur ditto Adad he will present. The length of the up[per shank....]

r. 5 *ù-šal-pu-tu re-eh-ti* NINDA KAŠ KÁ *ka-a-ri* SANGA NU.GIG.[MEŠ]

they destroy. The leftovers of the bread (and) beer

at the gate of the *kāru* the *šangû* and the *qadištu*['s] ... [shall consume (?)]

r. 6 SANGA NU.GIG.MEŠ *a-na* É ^{d}IM *i-tu-ru-né du-ma-qi ša* NU,.GIG.[MEŠ]

the *šangû* (and) the *qadištu*'s return to the temple of Adad. The jewelry of the *qadištu'*['s]

r. 7 *i-pa-tu-ru* 3 *qa* NINDA / 1 BAN KAŠ 1 UDU 1 *qa* ŠEM.MEŠ *a-na pa-an* ^{d}IM *in-né -p* [*u-šu*]

they take off. 3 *qa* of bread 1 sutu of beer 1 sheep 1 *qa* aromatics before Adad they off[er]

r. 8 *i-na* UDU *šu-a-šu* UZU.GABA UZU.ZAG.LU GU *si-si-a-te* 1 UZU.ÚR *šu-me* $^{!}$*-e-lì* TI

from that sheep the breast-meat the shoulder-meat the neck-meat the joints one left shank he takes

r. 9 3 TI.MEŠ 3 *ki-iṣ-ri a-na* IGI ^{d}ša-la 3 TI.MEŠ 3 *ki-iṣ-ri a-na* IGI ^{d}⌈Ta$^{!}$⌉ -ra-mu-a$^{!}$

3 ribs 3 joints before Shala 3 ribs 3 joints before Taramua (?)

r. 10 TI.MEŠ 2 *ki-iṣ-ri a-na* IGI ^{d}ku-be *ša* ^{d}IM ^{UZU}*šu-me-la a-na* IGI ^{d}a-ni

ribs 2 joints before Kubu of Adad left (side) meat before Anu

r. 11 *bu-gur-ra a-na pa-ni* ^{d}ku-be *ša* É ^{d}*a-ni im* ⌈ ⌉*du ni ri-šú* ŠE$^{?}$ MA$^{?}$ [

the *bugurru*-cut before Kubu of the temple of Anu...the head (?) ...

r. 12 *kur-si-na-te pa-ni-a-te a-láh-hi-nu re-eh-ti* UZU.MEŠ NU.GIG.MEŠ *i-*⌈*kala-a* ⌉

the front legs (for?) the *alahhinu,* the leftovers of the meat the *qadištu*'s withhold (?)

r. 13 K]UŠ$^{?}$ *gi-du* SA.SAL SANGA *ša* ^{d}IM *i-la-qi* [

skin (?), sinew, tendon the *šangû* of Adad takes ...

---

r. 14 *a -n*] *a pa-ni* ^{d}IM *-šú-hé-gal* $^{?}$ NU.GIG.MEŠ TUR.MEŠ *zi-im-ri-šu-nu* [ ]

before Adad...the apprentice *qadištu*'s their songs [they sing(?)]

r. 15.]*ma-ka-la-a-te* 1 ZÍD$^{?}$|.MEŠ hi-be/UTUL$_2$ GIŠ.MEŠ A.MEŠ *ha-aṣ-na* $^{?}$/*ba* $^{?}$ [ ]

mākaltu -bowls flour (?) vessel (?) wood, water, *haṣbu* -vessel ...

r. 16] *ri ki ?har /hur /hír /mur /kín-ma ki ša -li-mu* [

line 1 AHw 1200a: "unkl. [ina?]" for the whole clause. Is there a "day of Adad?" Perhaps: "when." *šataqu* "split off, crush." "When Adad crushes" would make less sense. Or, "when they separate Adad" would also remain to be explained. What the *qadištu*'s bring out has no antecedent.

2 Gwaltney reads *bīti ša lime* "house of tasting" referring to Hartman Oppenheim *Beer Brewing* 44 n. 39, on *lēmu*, translating "kitchen." Or, simply, *bīt šalime*, some unknown cultic place.

3 7: CAD M/1 123a: 3(!), "before the temple of Adad ... before (the statue of) Adad. CAD I 148a; CAD M/1 123a has the *qadištu*'s placing the bread.

4 "recite": CAD I 148a. Other examples of *nadû* as "recite, intone (the chant)" in Gruber, *UF* 18 139 n. 22. *pašāru* here "recite" by context, but basic meaning is "loose, let loose." Cf. English vernacular: letting loose a song = shouting it out. *imha* for *inha*. See Sec. 2.2.3 for the *inhu*

7 Menzel: K[Á *a-bu-sà*] -te "door of the storehouses," and she refers to ND 1120, *Iraq* 14 pl. 23, plausable, but not enough evidence. Gwaltney reads: *ú-pa-liq* , but *palāku* II stem "divide," or *palāqu* "beat, slaughter" doesn't seem to fit.

9 "He" must be the *šangû*. Asshur has no dingir, so the city? Zai'i: The PN does not occur in Saporetti *Onomastica*, nor in APN, but there are some occurrences at Nimrud: Za-a-a Dalley-Postgate 112 r.7 and Za-a-a Postgate *Palace Archive* 220 r. 13. The root is not in Gelb's or Huffmon's Amorite lists. *za'u* "resin," would be doubtful as a PN, so perhaps we might look for a GN. Menzel reads: Sà-mu-uh instead of za-i-'i but I can find no other reference to this. Does ZA = sà outside of OAkk, OA, OB? *il-lak* "he goes" must refer to the *šangû*.

11 "6 times spilling from": reading 6-*šu ku-ṣa-e* against *šukuṣṣa'u* (Menzel and AHw 1266b, a single-occurrence, and noted by AHw: "unkl.") This could be a libation. CAD K 594a takes it the former way, from *kuṣṣû* "to tilt." Tilting or spilling from a *mākaltu* - bowl is also found in *KAR* 139.6, CAD K 596b.

12 Menzel reads the partially broken signs as dÉ!-a-MAN = dEa-šarru, and finds this together with Diglat in IAK 70-73:25-26. Gwaltney presented a reasonable conjecture of dALAD = dIšum, by which the Tigris could be named, 2 R 50, 11c, but then what is lá? Does Menzel add lá to IDIGNA, as a phonetic indicator? She reads the rest as dUTU *iz* -[*za-kar*], which often goes with MU/*šumu* "name." Gwaltney simply presumes MU = *zakāru* in the space. Until the text is collated, one cannot be more definite.

13 *bīt hamri* "sacred precinct (of Adad)," CAD 70. Gruber p. 140 n. 26 finds it sacred to Asshur in OA and possibly to Shamash in OB, but this may not hold for an Assyrian context. *ADD* 742.8: E *ina bāb*

^{d}*ha-am-ri* in a location of fields. *ADD* 575 + 579 + 805 = Kwasman NA Legal No. 41: [*a - n*]*a hamri* ^{d}[IM]

r.3 ^{UZU}UR = *pi* -[*e-mu*] MSL IX 12, 201 (Hh. XV) "Oberschenkel."

r.4 Asshur, again the place because no dingir? *e-pal* variant of *i-pal* = *ip-pal* and CAD lists spellings *epuluma*, *epal*, *apil* in MA, from *apālu* B "present food offerings" in MA. AHw brings CAD's *apālu* A and *apālu* B together.

r.5 *rehtu* "remainder, leftovers" seems to be a technical term in NA offerings, appearing often in ADD. "Gate": cf. KÁ.GAL *kāri* Luckenbill *Ann Senn* 113 vii 95. *kāru* as customhouse or wharf house doesn't make sense in context, unless as a district, as CAD takes it. If NINDA is read *šá* "of" it would be: "the rest of the beer."

r.6 We can't follow the action, because we don't know such basic things as who "they" are; maybe the *qadištu*'s themselves.

r.7 "3 qa of bread": shadings indicate "(qa) beer." *in-né-p* [*u-šu*] so Menzel, reasonably.

r.8 AHw 1059b UZU.UR = *šūnu* "inner side of upper thigh/shank". Reading *šu* -⌈*me*⌉-*e-li* "left," as r. 10. Menzel: UR-*šu* [*te*]-*e-ši* "nine" but this has final lengthening, not middle.

r.9 "Joints": AHw "dorsal vertebra," less likely. Shala: Adad's consort. Reading ^{d}Taramua as Menzel, despite the two (!) readings, rather than ^{d}Ta$^{!}$-mu-za as Gwaltney. Shala and Taramuya in 3 R 66 II 16 and KAV 57.3 (Menzel)

r.10 Kubu sometimes worshipped in the Anu-Adad temple in Asshur, Frankena *Tākultu* 98, though it appears as an indication of a type of cultic official in *Shurpu* III 117, yet a god or demon in VIII 25.

r.11 CAD B 307a: Kube. Gwaltney: *im-du*$^{!}$*-du-ni,* but is *madādu* "measure" ever used of meat? Menzel: ir$^{!}$-ri "intestines." Menzel: NAR$_{x}$GAL, but the signs for *nargallu* seem always to be NAR.GAL .

r.12 Or, "hock," or "fetlock." CAD K 567a understands it as the *alahhinu*'s share.

r.13 [K]UŠ Menzel. SA.SAL = *šašallu* "back, tendon" Or, SA.SAL part of the liver, AHw s.v. *pasuttu.*

r.14 Gwaltney: ^{d}Adad-su-hé-gal; Menzel: NAR$_{X}$.GAL, as line r.11, and the signs are drawn identically. She takes TUR.MEŠ as a separate "Tempelweihe," Sec. 2.5, above.

r.15 "flour": sometimes plural, CAD Q 206cd. "Meat": *hasba* more likely than *haṣna* (Gwaltney) "in their arms/shelter" as if from *haṣānu*; CAD's examples only show taking as protection or lovingly.

r.16 *har-ma:* Cf. *hur-ma* Rost Tigl III 85.34.

har-ma-ki : $^{[l]ú}$harmaka[ni] r. 23'

^{lú}šakin ^{uru}Sahupp[a]GAL.MEŠ *ša* ^{lú}*harmakāni*

SUM-*nu* SUM-*nu* r. 29',

^{m}harmak[i] r. 35' Postgate *Royal Grants* Nos. 42-44

Unfortunately all these are in broken contexts. Postgate's lines 23,24,26,27 start with officials indicated by lú. Line 25' indicates that leathers or hides were given. Line 29' indicates that, along with the *šaknu* of the city of Sahuppa[ ] the GAL.MEŠ "officials" of the *harmaku*'s were given something.

As far as the word with lú compared with the word with the PN indicator, Menzel *Tempel* n. 3989 shows the many occurrences of

^{lu}Harmak(k)u/i in VAT, *ADD* and ND texts. The word does not appear in CAD or AHw.

šalimu or *ša limu* for *limmu* ? Cf. *bīt šalime* line 2.

APPENDIX TWO

The Naked Figurines

App. 2.1 The Naked Figurines, Especially Those in Palestine

App. 2.1.1 Since the earliest studies of the subject at hand, scholars have looked to the figurines found in Palestine and elsewhere for a key to what sacred prostitutes looked like. The argument has gone back and forth: are these representations of goddesses or their servants/devotees? If a goddess, which: Ishtar/Astarte, Anat, Ashera, Kybele, the "Mother Goddess?" Whoever it is, the Israelite exemplars go against the prohibition in Deut 4.16 and elsewhere of making graven images, male or female, but of course those outside of Israel do not. And if the Israelite exemplars are products of folk religion, the biblical verses would not affect them.

An early site in Jordan is described by a preliminary report.[1] Several Neolithic plaster statues have been recovered, moulded around a core of reeds, twigs and grasses. They have stumpy feet, thick short legs, squat bodies, elongated necks and oversized heads. One, badly damaged, is of a nude female with arm bent so that the hand pushes up the pectoral area of the chest. The editor remarks: "This statue appears to foreshadow the Ishtar/Astarte cult of later millenia." (p. 2). By that he means the figurines that are our subject here. A second set of 12 smaller pieces, busts only, were placed in an arc at the foot of the larger specimens, "indicating a deliberate arrangement with strong ceremonial connotations." (p. 2).

Spycket[2] describes a nude woman of the 8th millenium B.C.E. in North Syria. She is 10cm. high and holds her breasts in her hands.

N. Avigad[3] describes two Ammonite seals, one of Menahem *'bd mlk* "servant of the king." Each shows a nude female in frontal position supporting the breasts with both hands. They are dated by him to perhaps 7th c.. B.C.E.

We will in this unit only mention high points of what has become a highly complex study, based on iconography, analyzing the position of the hands and arms, whether pressing breasts or not, holding a child, holding a disc, and other elements. An early study was that of H.G. May.[4] He points out that the figurines are not mentioned in the religious records of the Hebrews, unless they appear as *pesel* "image" or *maṣṣēbāh* "molten idols." They are of clay; bronze figurines are mostly but not wholly male.[5] The fluted headdress of some is Syro-Hittite, and resembles the deities on the Yazilikaya relief. Some are in the form of a pillar, with the bust arising out of that; there are few of these at Megiddo. It is impossible to identify any one form with any goddess, he says.

Some hold disks, either tambourines or cakes. There are also male figures, mostly the striding gods Baal or Resheph. Of the females, some wear headdresses, veils or wigs. Long braids sometimes coil over the breasts. Some appear with amulets or wristlets. Sexual parts are emphasized by an incised triangle. Some are pregnant. Some are in the form of a plaque.

Y. Aharoni[6] finds in excavations at Beer Sheba a figurine of a goddess, tall and thin, of bronze, with arms held stiffly to the sides, naked (?) but no incised triangle. This is a rare representation of a female of metal.

What has come to be a standard study is given by J.B. Pritchard, following in some ways a pioneering article by E. Pilz.[7] The figurines are always nude, and there is usually an emphasis on the reproductive features: hands holding breasts (pp. 42ff), or sexual parts emphasized by incisions or dots (pp. 51ff), or portraying motherhood (pp. 55ff). These could have represented one of the main deities of Palestine: Asherah, Ashtart or Anat, but, he says, no inscription has been found on them.[8]

The Mesopotamian scholars study figurines and seals together. Van Buren[9] gives early examples (Halaf culture) of various types: a child at the breast, steatopygous squatting women, those with hands holding the breast. Frankfort[10] suggests that the figurines are the female worshippers who serve as the goddesses' hierodule. L. Legrain[11] says the portrayals are of a magical character, an emblem of fruitfulness.

To K. Galling[12] the Palestinian female figurine represented the consort of Yahweh, but in the "private sphere of the Israelite household." These figurines are found in every major excavation in Palestine of MB -EI II, and the find-spots in private homes indicate that they do not specifically belong to the official cult.

A similar type of object was prevalent in Mesopotamia. The study by van Buren[13] gives a detailed catalogue with descriptions of female figures. The older ones are not always naked; those after about 2000 B.C.E. are almost always so. Some are seated and clothed, identified by tiara or symbols. Sometimes they wear a necklace. The sexual triangle is emphasized. Often the breast is held, as in West Semitic examples, but often one breast only. She makes no attempt at identification. Sometimes the body is steatopygous, perhaps for better birthing. Sometimes she suckles a child. This iconography is also shown on OB cylinder seals.[14]

According to Albright, the Palestinian ones might be Astarte figurines.[15] He points out the rough nature of the back, showing that it perhaps stood against a wall. The flaring out of the pillar may represent the tree symbolism of the Ashera cult. The nose on every one has been injured, probably by those of a rival cult. Note in these early studies as that of Albright the mixing up of the two deities, who we today would say were certainly different.

Clare Culver[16] describes those at Tell en-Nasbeh, all the pillar type. The pillar represents a late attempt to conventionialize the figure into a more abstract symbol. The conventionalized hands cannot be said to "support" or "offer" the breasts. The figurines were originally in gaudy colors. R.A. Macalister[17] finds the Hathor-like wig which some wear to be pure Egyptian, but the body and wig are always full-face, somewhat un-Egyptian. Holding the breasts indicates the maternal feature of the figures, not the sexual.

P.J. Riis[18] gives a thorough-going study by periods, and classifies face types, hair types and gown types. The breast-clasping means that the breasts are pressed for milk, thus charaterizing the woman as a motherly being. Some figurines hold a small object of doubtful identification, pine cones or pommegranates. The chacteristics change in the several periods. Are they deities or mortals? Riis says deity, perhaps Atargatis, Albright says mortal. Riis argues that if some of them represent a supernatural being, all of them do.

G.E.Wright[19] says that the figurines are found in many excavated houses, but also in the palace[20] so it is not merely a "people's religon." Regardless of this, it seems to me [RAH] that it is a "people's religion," because it does not appear on the written documents, and it is ubiquitous.

George Dales' article[21] is taken from his doctoral thesis "Mesopotamian and related female figurines," University of Pennsylvania, 1960. It concerns Mesopotamia, but this may relate to Palestine also. There is an Ur III - OB class of figurines which, instead of holding both hands at their breasts, hold a disk-shaped object. This has been variously described as a tambourine, a drum, a rattle, a cake, the sun disk (Ruth Amiran[22]), a platter for receiving offerings or the offering itself. Comparative study shows that these are the earliest example of a type which became popular throughout the Near East -- Mesopotamia, Palestine, Egypt -- and it survived into classical times in the Aegean and western colonies. "There can no longer be any serious doubt that these represent either secular entertainers or devotees participating in some sort of cult ritual in which the tambourine plays an important part." (p. 26)

Miriam Tadmor injects a fresh element into the debate.[23] In the middle of the second millenium, the Late Bronze Age, there was the first appearance of the "plaque" or "relief" figurines. They were images of a naked woman in high relief. They were first known as Astarte figurines (Albright). J. B. Pritchard's work is still the latest extensive study.

A new type of figurine started appearing in the Late Bronze Age. It was nude, and frontal. It was on a long plaque, and wore a wig. It had elongated arms and legs. It was Egyptian or Egyptianizing (pp. 144f). It is in a broad category of "people lying in beds." The plaque represents the bed, with an up-curving back. There is no divine symbolism. (p. 149)

Comparing these to the Canaanite clay figurine, the latter is in the frontal position, arms and legs are elongated, but in contrast the coiffure in the Canaanite figurines is realistic. The plaques had an upcurling end as in the Canaanite figurines, and the women are also lying on a bed (p. 156). Hands to the breast indicate that the woman is nursing an infant. This is like the Deir-el-Balah figurine of a woman holding a baby to her breast (pl. 5, p. 150).

Another type of woman is nude, but with a Hathor wig. Arms bent, each holding a long-stemmed flower, legs separated, feet turned outwards; all these are characteristic. The plaque is flat, and does not have an up-curling base. These also appear in metal. These represent a goddess, this fact shown by the symbols (p. 161).

So, there are two types: those standing erect, with cultic symbols, and those lying on beds. The latter perhaps are associated with mortuary reliefs, ex voto offerings to the dead, perhaps talismans or amulets. The women standing upright die out in the Late Bronze (pp. 170-1).

In the south, the plaque figurines die out in Iron II. In the north, they continue sporadically, but now the woman holds a round object. These suggest Phoenician influence. The pillar figurines are not direct descendants of the Judaean figurines, but belong stylistically to sculpture in the round.

My [RAH] questions about this significant study are several. Why are the figures lying on a bed naked? The tasks they perform could be done with clothes on, or at least some clothes on. Why are the hands shown on the breasts if these are a mortuary practice? Does one nurse children lying down? This seems a very odd position for this practice. Finally, the most difficult question: why are the hands on both breasts? Nursing obviously uses only one. This study of Tadmor's is the most significant one in recent years, but there are a number of hard questions to ask her.

I have not done her provocative article justice, and it is one that will have to be taken into account in all future studies. It does not attempt to solve the goddess-or-votary question. That comes from our either/or thought world. It could be both!

In a study which reaches a conclusion that many modern scholars tend towards, A. J. Amr[24] summarizes the work of other researchers, from whom the following notes are taken: Van Buren (see n. 13) explained the figurines as decorative elements for the household shrine, and when in the tomb, with apotropaic significance (p. xlii). Petrie[25] identified those from Gerar as "Ashtoreth the Queen of Heaven." Legrain[26] mentioned a substitute for a human sacrifice, but with no comment on Amr's part on eastern vs. western Semitic worlds (p. 6). Frankfort (see n. 10) interpreted them as amulets from the temple in token of a sacrifice (p. 210). Aharoni (see n. 6) found similar types from Beth-Shan and Beer Sheba as Ashtoreth figurines (pl. 27:2, 4-9). Pritchard (see n. 7) called the pillar figurines a type of sympathetic magic (p. 83). Opificius[27] suggested three possibilities: goddess, priestess or talisman (p. 204). Avigad[28] thought that those excavated in the Old City in Jerusalem were used for fertility purposes (pl. 30:B). Michaelowski[29] explains statuettes of naked females found in Egyptian tombs as concubines of the dead (p. 17).

Amr then goes on to give the opinion that those figurines which "clutch breasts" are symbols of aspects of Ishtar. They are "appeals to Ishtar to give milk through the help of her lover Tammuz, the milk-giver," and also as "more direct appeals to herself, since she nourishes humanity on her breasts." The diverse forms of the figurines match the diverse needs of the Ishtar worshippers.

The broken figurines which Amr discusses are from Jerusalem, dated late ninth to seventh centuries B.C.E. Fertility may be achieved through the images of the goddesses or their qualities. The symbol as ex opere operato brings the desired fertility.

In the Mediterranean West, the standing figurines made a rare appearance at Paestum.[30] Twenty one of them among 200 other votive figurines, dating from the first half of the sixth century B.C.E., were found at a sanctuary of a place known today as Santa Venera. They had a Greek character, wearing Greek hats, and sometimes resembled a female counterpart of the *kouros* A plaque from Tharros, Sardinia, held both hands to the breasts (fig. 17).

App. 2.1.2 The goddess as mother is shown in a thoroughly researched article by W.A. Ward, an Egyptian scholar.[31] He discusses and shows depictions of the nursing goddess at Ugarit. She is Anat. (p. 229). She has in her bosom the children of the king (p. 231). Examples of ivory plaques are shown (p. 236f). Many princes of the ancient world were nourished by deities. The figures discussed were Egyptianizing, but combining Hittite and Syrian traditions (p. 239).

App. 2.1.3 No conclusions are drawn in this short essay. We are beyond the time when the figurines are considered representations of the "Mother Goddess." In the ancient world a symbol did not stand for only one thing. We must think in terms of both goddess <u>and</u> devotee/servant. It is probable that no one explanation covers all types of figurine, and the several types were perhaps not related to one another. Whether the figurine presented an offering, a doll, a toy, or was an object using sympathetic magic, it seems fairly certain that it has to do with fertility in some manner. Its sphere seems to be that of private worship rather than public, and the goddess if such represented does not have to be one known to us from the high literature, but it may belong to the people, not appearing except in their world-view, and of women's concern rather than men's.[32]

App. 2.2 Cylinder and Stamp Seals

Cylinder seals sometimes show scenes which are related to the activities discussed in this Appendix. They often show female, rarely male, figures in a stylized worship act. No. 90 in the Marcopoli collection[33] shows a row of four female clothed worshippers or priestesses, with a distinctive hairstyle, each with an arm raised, walking in procession, one carrying a pail, ca. 2384-2154 B.C.E. Nos. 92 and 93 show a female figurine with arm raised in prayer presenting a worshipper to a seated deity. In Ur III seals the presenter is a goddess, so that may be the case here too. A nude female, facing front has her hands clasped under the breasts, not holding them, nos. 118, 223, and 130.

Male and female figures are shown in an apparent healing or exorcism ritual on a NA seal, No. 231. The figures are in attendance of a patient on a couch inside a (reed?) hut. Outside the hut a woman seems to be dancing. The dog (of Gula, the goddess of healing?) stands on the roof of the hut.

No. 537 shows perhaps elements of fertility on a Syrian seal from the first half of the first millenium B.C.E. A nude figure with hands to breasts, or clasped beneath them, is flanked by two clothed figures standing by plants. The line on either side of the nude figure may indicate a shrine. On either side is a nude squatting goddess, perhaps indicating a position of birth.

Ravn[34] finds an oft-appearing "nude woman" as No. 67 with hands beneath the breasts, always frontal, hairstyle in omega-form (so Keel). Frankfort[35] thinks that she is either a priestess or a female worshipper (p. 65). He points out that no goddess is ever depicted naked on Akkadian seals except Shala.

Othmar Keel and his colleagues have produced an extended study of some aspects of the scenes on stamp seals in Mesopotamia and Syria.[36] Using many well-drawn examples of Syrian and Mesopotamian seals for comparative purposes, he finds many examples of the naked figure. The figure is in the midst of the action (I, 56, Abb. 3, Abb. 1; 62, Abb. 12; 83, Abb. 43; II, 76, 54). Sometimes she holds the breasts (I, 83, Abb. 43; II, 73, 51; II, 58, 30; II, 106, Abb. 016). As U. Winter, *Frau und Göttin* chap 2, the figure is a "nackte Göttin," the motif "eindeutig" of Syrian origin (II, S. Schroer, 93). Sometimes she holds a branch, usually U-shaped. She is often completely naked, but also sometimes can have a belt, a hat, a necklace, a waistband. She shows her divinity by a moon-and-sun figure on the head (I, 56, Abb. 4), or by standing on animals (II, 83,63; 119, Abb. 040; 95, Abb. 07; III,212, figs 36-7)

A number of these naked figures indicate that they are votaries, servants of the deity, or part of the cult, by their actions. Their hands are clasped in front of them in an apparent position of prayer, or as a cultic position (II, 83, 64; 95 Abb. 07 but standing on an animal(!);180, Abb. 0178;[37] 80, 59; 83, 64; 95, Abb. 03; both hands raised in prayer (II, 116, Abb. 34-38) As in the naked figurines, she is sometimes found holding both breasts (II, 106, Abb. 016), dancing (II, 134, Abb. 057) but these may be male, and a pair of females dancing to players of banjo-shaped instruments (II, 190, Abb. 0190).

This wide-ranging study is valuable and confirms the general conclusion reached above.

Notes

1 Gary O. Rollefson, "8000-year-old human statues discovered at 'Ain Ghazal (Jordan)," *ASOR Newsletter* 35/2 (November 1983).

2 Spycket *Statuaire* p. 4f.

3 Avigad *BASOR* No. 225, February, 1977.

4 H.G. May, *Material Remains of the Megiddo Cult,* Chicago, 1935, a full study with many plates.

5 Ora Negbi, *Canaanite Gods in Metal.* An Archaeological Study of ancient Syro-Palestinian Figurines. Tel Aviv, 1976. Her interest is mainly in description and dating. There are a number of females (chapter 3), some of which follow the male types of warrior poses, but some are holding the breasts, like their clay counterparts.

6 Y. Aharoni, *Excavations at Tel Beer-Sheba. 1969-71 Seasons,* Tell Aviv, 1973, pl. 22 No. 1.

7 J.B. Pritchard, *Palestinian Figurines in Relation to Certain Goddesses Known Through Literature.* American Oriental Series, Vol. 24, New Haven, 1943, a study of 294 exemplars. E. Pilz, "Die weiblichen Gottheiten Kanans. Eine archaeologische Studien," *ZDPV* 47 (1924) 129-168.

8 There are, albeit rarely, exemplars of goddesses who are labelled. I.E. S. Edwards, "A relief of Qudshu-Astarte-Anath in the Winchester College Collection," *JNES* 14 (1955) 49-51. This is a bas-relief with the three-fold name written in hieroglyphs, dated around Rameses II, Rameses III, but these are conjectures. James L. Swauger (ed.), *Excavations of Bethel* (1934-60), Cambridge, Mass., 1968 finds a LB cylinder seal with an a-sexual figure and with an inscription *'strt* (Astarte).

9 E. Douglas Van Buren, "Figurinen." *RLA* III 62-64.

10 Frankfort *Seals* 160.

11 Legrain, *Museum Journal* 1928, 203.

12 Galling *Bib Real* 233.

13 van Buren *Figurines.*

14 E. Porada, *Corpus of Ancient Near Eastern Seals in North American Collections.* Collection of Pierpont Morgan Library. Bollingen Series 14, New York., 1948, Nos. 476-506, 517.

15 W.F. Albright *AASOR* XXI-XXII, 1941-3, New Haven, 1943. §140.

16 Elsie Culver, in C.C. McCown, *Tell en Nasbeh* I, Berkeley and New Haven, 1947, 245.

17 R.A. Stewart Macalister, *Excavation of Gezer,* London, 1912, II, 412.

18 Riis *Berytus* 9,2 (1949) 69-90.

19 *Introduction to Biblical Archaeology* p. 18.

20 And, he might have mentioned, in graves, as discussed in May *Material Remains* 281; Helck *Göttin* 61, and in cult places, but perhaps simply as offerings, so still a "people's religion."

21 George F. Dales, "Necklaces, bands and belts on Mesopotamian figurines," *RA* 57 (1963) 21-40.

22 R. Amiran, *ErIs* VIII (1967) 99f.

23 Tadmor, "Female cult figurines in late Canaan and early Israel," in T. Ishida (ed.) *David Solomon* 139-173.

24 A.J. Amr, *Levant* 20 (1988).

25 W.M.F. Petrie, *Gerar*, London, 1928, 17, pls. xxx and xxxv.

26 L. Legrain, *Terra-Cottas from Nippur*, Philadelphia, 1930.

27 Ruth Opificius, *Das altbabylonische Terrakotta-Relief,* Berlin, 1961.

---

28 N. Avigad, *IEJ* 20 (1970) 192-202.

29 K. Michalowski, *Great Sculptures of Ancient Egypt*, New York, 1978.

30 Rebecca Miller Ammerman, "The Naked Standing Goddess: A Group of Archaic Terracotta Figurines from Paestum," *American Journal of Archaeology,* 95/2, April, 1991, 203-230.

31 W.A. Ward, "Le déesse nourricière a Ugarit, " *Syria* 46 (1969) 225-39.

32 A recent survey of the several aspects of the subject: Winter *Frau u. Göttin* 95-134, 192-199.

33 Beatrice Teissier, *Ancient Near Eastern Cylinder Seals from the Marcopoli Collection,* Berkeley, et al, 1984

34 O.E. Ravn, *A Catalogue of Oriental Cylinder Seals and Impressions in the Danish National Museum,* Cøbenhavn, 1960.

35 H. Frankfort, *Cylinder Seals*, London, 1931.

36 Othmar Keel et al, *Studien zu den Stempelsiegeln aus Palästina/Israel.* 3 vols., Göttingen, 1985, 1989, 1990.

37 Keel, II, 180, Abb. 0179 in some detail shows that the hands clasped in front do not hold the breasts.

APPENDIX THREE

The assinnu, kurgarrû and Similar Functionaries

App. 3.1 The terms. The above titles are treated in this book in a special class of officials, as a kind of actor in the cultic drama, whose forte is the interpretation of sexuality, but seemingly abnormal sexuality.[1] The most important titles in this group are the *assinnu*, *kurgarrû* and sag-ur-sag, but there are several others, all of which will be studied together, since they act similarly. It is a curious fact that, whereas most other profesional titles can be translated with a Sumerian or a Semitic root, many of these cannot. *Assinnu, kurgarrû, parrû, kulu'u,* as well as the titles apparently from a combination of ideograms, as pi-li-pi-li and sag-bur are incapable of being analyzed. Even the apparently clear sag-ur-sag has no meaning which fits into our categories, though some relate it to ur-sag = *qardu* "hero." Does this mean that these are foreign words? Or, are they words from a pre-Semitic and pre-Sumerian stratum in Mesopotamia, as Salonen suggested for several other terms.[2] It appears that any sense that one may force upon them may be a folk etymology.

App. 3.2 LÚ.UR.SAL/*assinnu*

App. 3.2.1 The *assinnu* and *kurgarrû* seemingly have the same functions, but for listing purposes, we treat them under separate headings.[3] The ideogram LÚ.UR.SAL appears only in NA and NB times, but some[4] assume that sag-ur-sag is the Sumerian forerunner. I need more evidence to make this decision. The late Assyrian list Lu = ša put UR.SAL and SAG.UR.SAG, both parired with *assinnu*, on separate lines, App. 3.2.7. Livingstone[5] in a NA text concerning fertility, reads LÚ.SAL as *assinnu*, apparently assuming it as short for UR.SAL, because it follows a reference to *kurgarrû*. The MB Sag B Tablet[6] has two sag-ur-sag entries: 13 sag-ur-sag = *qar-ra-du* ("hero, warrior")14 sag-ur-sag = *as-sí-nu*.

Some have explained UR.SAL as "female dog"[7] reading UR = *kalbu* "dog," but bitch is usually SAL.UR. Another suggestion has been "man-woman" reading UR as man as is done in Sumerian personal names.[8] This would use the same reasoning as we do in explaining *sinnišanu* (App. 3.9).

App. 3.2.2 References to *assinnu* appear first at Mari, in three apearances, as one of the "prophets" of Annunitum[9] a form of Ishtar, and at Nuzi as PNs.[10] Nothing of their actions as "prophet" indicates the characteristics that show up in NA times. In MA times he is found singing *inhu* -songs as part of the cultic action[11] and the MA Erra text will require some discussion: see App. 3.2.10.

App. 3.2.3 In OB texts, the *assinnu* was considered negatively. In divination texts the right side being dark is an indication of an unfavorable omen. Starr quotes an OB text:[12] if the right side of the sheep is dark: the owner of the sheep will practice *assinnūtu* "the *assinnu* - office."

App. 3.2.4 Several NA texts show the *assinnu* in action in the cult. In a statement by the *assinnu* (LÚ.UR.SAL), various gods "come out," incense is burned, and *idi ana idi ša Istar Babili* ⌈GI?⌉-GÍD *assinnu u* [lú]*kurgarrû ellea elleama* [13] "Side-by-side with Ishtar of Babylon (are) the ..." [14] the *assinnu* and the *kurgarrû* (who chant) *ellea* and *ellea.*" The mention of the two sides of Ishtar is reminiscent of the left-side, right-side dichotomy, see App. 3.4.

In a Seleucid Akitu ritual[15] in which the king was present, Ishtar enters the court of the akītu-house to be put on her *parakku* "throne dais." Then "all the gods" enter and stand before her. The *assinnu* and the *kurgarrû* bind on the *bēlu / tillu* of the goddess Narudu, and dance around "them" (presumably the previously mentioned deities) from left to right.

The *bēlu* [16] is found in two categories: something worn by humans and gods, and that of weapons. In a ritual [17] the *kurgarrû* puts the *tillu* on his head. In a Seleucid text, the king will wear his pure/holy *tillu* [18] as he enthrones the *enu*-priest.[19] The *tillu* could be of the statue of Narudu,[20] or the *apkallu* [21] or the "seven gods"[22] or the statue of a dead person,[23] or those who carry weapons,[24] as do the *assinnu* and *kurgarrû*. It could be *burrumu* "multi-colored, speckled." [25] It could be of gold [26] or of silver.[27] It is used on battlewagons,[28] or on horses (See n. 25). It is associated with bows[29] and swords,[30] perhaps as a hanging or decorative scabbard.

Whatever *tillu* turns out to be, it is special, and symbolic of something. Its use as part of the decorative costume of royalty indicates the uniqueness of the occasion. The old translation "mask" (CAD K 558) does not seem to fit these broad descriptive texts. If we could picture a garment that is also a weapon, that would fit these findings. It is in the costume of the *assinnu* and the *kurgarrû*.

App. 3.2.5 In a NA ritual text[31] after *hitpu* -sacrifices,[32] and the singing and dancing of the *nāru's*, the *kurgarrû's* sing *mēluli qablu* "my play is battle"[33] and the *assinnu's* answer them by a certain kind of shout designated *yarrurūtu.*[34] The *assinnu's* then *milhu imalluhu* "rip, tear themselves"(?, AHw), or "strum and dance in a certain manner"[35] discussed also by Groneberg,[36] after which the *assinnu* goes down to battle and does a *gūštu*-dance.

App. 3.2.6 On one text the *assinnu* appears either to be a eunuch or impotent. *Shumma Ālu* Tabl 104, concerning sexual advances, sexual dreams, etc.,[37] has a line: *šumma amēlu ana zikarūti ina kili uštaktitma u assinniš nāk zikarūta huššuhšu,* meaning something like: "if a man suffers physically in prison, and like an *assinnu* the desire to copulate is taken away from him...."

Because of this disability, he was taken advantage of. Later on in the same tablet as the above, we find: *šumma amēlu ana assinni iṭhi* (TE)..."if a man approaches (for sexual purposes) an *assinnu....*"[38] The initiative would be that of the approaching man, who would be a homosexual, and it implies that the *assinnu* is one, also. The strange protasis found in a NB hemerology: "at the time of an eclipse of the moon, if he (the king) touches the head of an *assinnu* ...[39] may be euphemism for sexual relations, or a ritual symbolizing this.

We must issue a word of caution about some of the fantastic actions listed in the protases of *Shumma Ālu*. Tabl 80, e.g., has "if a dog made sexual advances to a woman..." and Tabl 39 has "if a sheep mounts a dog or a pig..."[40] One is suspicious, then, whether other protases represent actual cases.

App. 3.2.7 The early OB lexical list, OB Proto-Lu, has

27 sag-ti-rín
278 sag-ur-sag
279 pi-li-pi-li

280 kur-gar-ra

OB Proto-Lu MSL XII 42

This is similar to the later list, which is more complex:

180	kur-gar-ra	ŠU-u (i.e., *kurgarrû*)	
181	ama-ér-ra	ŠU-u (i.e., *ama'erru*)	
182	pi-il-pi-li	*pa* -⌈*ar*⌉-[*ru-u*]	
183	pi-il-pi-li	*as* -[*sin-nu*]	
184	sag-ur-sag	*as-sin-nu*	
185	sag-bur-ra	KI.MIN	
186	lú-gal	KI.MIN	
187	sag-bulug$_2$-ga	KI.MIN	
188	sag-ti-erin$_2$	KI.MIN	
189	kur-gar-ra	KI.MIN	
190	an-ti-bal	KI.MIN	
191	an-ti-za	KI.MIN	
192	dùn-lá	KI.MIN	
193	^{giš}šibir-šu-du$_7$	KI.MIN	
193a	ur-sal	*as-sin-nu*	
194	lú-túg-lá	*šá kar-ra lab-šu*	
195	kuš-$^{\text{ku-uš}}$-lá	*a-gu-uh-hu*	corrected per CAD A/1 159
196	kuš-lá	*šá ha-rim-ti*	and AHw
197	lú-KU-lá	*ša e-ri-na lab-šu*	
198	lú-^{giš}šibir-šu-du$_7$	*na-áš ši-bir-ri*	
198a	lú ^{giš}bal-šu-du$_7$	*na-áš pi-laq-qi*	

Lu = ša IV
MSL XII 134f

For line 195, AHw 17a and CAD A/1 159b read kuš$^{\text{ku-uš}}$.lá. A term of sexual attractiveness would be out of place in this list of professionals. Yet they could be understood as fitting in well if they are descriptive titles, as "the one of...," "the carrier of...", *ša* being understood with *aguhhu*.

Here with the lexical lists' own peculiar definition of equivalents are the *assinnu*, *kurgarrû*, sag-ur-sag, pilpili. The garment *erinnu* in line 197: "clad in an *erinnu* garment" could be one of the Ishtar cult, as *aguhhu* (App. 3.11), which has sexual attractiveness: the *karru* of line 194 is a mourning garment, perhaps mourning the descent of Inanna/Ishtar to the netherworld.[41] The ^{giš}šibir-šu-du$_7$ of line 198 is *nāš šibirri* "holder of the scepter," part of the Ishtar cult,[42] and may be something carried by the *assinnu*. For *nāš pilaqqi* as a possible member of the Ishtar cult, see App. 3.10.

The short recension Excerpt I puts the *assinnu* after ecstatics and before singers and dancers:

213	lú-gub-ba	*mah-hu-ú*
214	lú-ní-zu-ub	*ẓa-ab-bu*
215	kur-gar-ra	ŠU-*u* (i.e., *kurgarrû*)
216	ur-SAL	*as-sin-nu*

(= Lu - ša IV 193a, MSL XII 135)

217	$^{\text{lú.giš}}$bal-šu-du$_7$	*na-áš pi-laq-qí*

(= Lu - ša IV 198a, MSL XII 135)

218 sag-hul-ha-za *mu-kil re-eš* HUL-*ti* (i.e., *lemutti*)
(= Lu - ša IV 200a, MSL XII 135)
219 sag-ús *ka-a-a-ma-nu*
220 nab *na-a-ru*
221 [nar-gal] [ŠU-*lum*] (i.e., *nargallum*)
222 [gu4-ud-da] [*ra-a*]*q-qí-du*

Lu = ša, Short Recension, Excerpt I
MSL XII 102f

Here the *nāš pilaqqi* is brought even closer to the *assinnu*. *mukīl rēš lemutti* "companion of a spirit of evil" is a demon (CAD M/2 185a). *kayyamānu* "normal, regular" is used in the vocabulary of omens and extispicy documents.

HAR-gud, a commentary on HAR-ra = hubullu, yields:

132	[lú] zilulu	[ ]	*sah* -[*hi-ru*]
133	[lú] ur-sal	[*a*] *s-sin-nu*	*sin-niš*-⌈*a* ⌉-[*nu*]
134	⌈ lú ⌉ šabra	ŠU (i.e., *šabrû*)	*rag-gi-* [*mu*]
135	lú-gub-ba	*a* -[*p*] *il-lu-ú*	*aš-šá* - [ ]
136	lú ú-bíl-lá	ŠU + ⌈ ⌉ (i.e., *upillu*)	*kut-tím* -[*mu*]

HAR-gud B VI MSL XII 226

The *šabrû* is usually a temple administrator, but is also a dream interpreter in NA texts (Sec. 3.3.10.) Here it is glossed by *raggimu* "caller, speaker" (Sec. 3.17) and a member of the Ishtar cult, perhaps explaining its proximity to *assinnu*. lú-gub-ba is usually *mahhû* "an ecstatic" but here perhaps shows that the *apillû* (App. 3.7) uses ecstatic practices.

A miscellaneous lexical list has:

r.9 *i-sin-nu-u* " [*ku-lu-'u*]
r.10 *a-pi-lu-u* " [ ]
r.11 *kur-gar-ru-u* [ ]

CT 18,5 (K. 4193), CAD K 558a

(and continuing the above):

48 *a-ra-ru-u* " (i.e., *ku-lu-'u*)
49 *šu-da-ra-ru-u* "

LTBA 2 I vi, for the two sections,
CAD A/2 234, 169, 341, K 558

Isinnu is an orthographical variant of *assinnu*. For *apillû* compare a possible variant *pilpilû* in *LTBA* 2,1 vi 46, AHw 863b. For the important *kulu'u* see App. 3.8.

The "practical lists" of NA times containing *assinnu* are:

264 lú.[ní]-su-ub *zab-bu*
265 lú. [UR.SAL] *ku-lu-'u*
266 lú.UR.SAL *as-sin-nu* (var. *i-sin-nu*)
267 lú.zilulu *sah-hi-ru*

Igituh

vi 23 LÚ.NUN.MEŠ /LÚ.NUN.ME
24 LÚ.KUR.GAR.RA

25 LÚ.UR.SAL
26 LÚ.ARAD.KUR

K. 4395 vi MSL XII 240

131 *šá-muk-tum* *na-di-tum*
132 *up-pu-uš-tum* "
133 *ša-mu-uh-tum* *qa-diš-tum*
134 *ug-bab-tum* *en-tum*
135 *ug-bab-tum* *as-sin-na-tum*

Malku =šarru, Explicit

From several of the above lists we see the close relationship of the *assinnu* and *kurgarrû*. We discover similar offices to be the sag-ur-sag, pi-li-pi-li, *sinnišānu* and *kulu'u*. The kur-gar /*kurgarrû* appears on early lists, while the *assinnu* does not, unless it does under the signs sag-ur-sag.

The list from Malku = šarru stands out from the others, in listing the *nadītum,* and *qadištum*, two prestigous ranks in OB times, as "prostitutes," one of the terms for which is *šamhatum*, here given some variant orthography. This reminds us of the disparaging remarks made of these officials in the *Maqlû* III entries in the context of witches, Sec. 3.20.5.

App. 3.2.8 Finally, a highly unusual feature of the Malku = šarru list is the only appearance of the feminine form of the noun *assinnu.* This odd rare occurrence of a feminine form also shows up with the *kurgarrû*, App. 3.3.1. These offices switch roles from male to female, as will be discovered below, and a female *assinnu* would not make any sense, unless the entry here says simply that there is a feminine "*assinnu*" at one time in the cultic drama. Maybe it means that the *assinnu* takes the *ugbabtum*'s place in the rite, as a female. But this is strictly guessing, and not warranted by any evidence.

App. 3.2.9 Two special texts, each mysterious in its own way, partially explain the office of *assinnu*. The first is the Descent of Ishtar,[43] which comes down in two recensions, an earlier from Asshur in MA times, a later from Nineveh in NA times. Ishtar has descended to the Netherworld and has been taken captive by her sister Ereshkigal, and sexual activity has stopped on earth, because Ishtar's presence is need for it to occur. Ea in his wisdom conceived the idea of creating an *assinnu* (MA var. *kulu'u*) who then went down and confronted Ereshkigal. This resulted finally in Ishtar being sprinkled with the "water of life," her garments and jewelry returned, and her escape. Why the *assinnu* could pass through the gate and confront the queen, something the others could not, is not explained in the text, but I propose that being of in-between sex made him impervious to the sexual rites and power that Ereshkigal, following the example of her sister, could impose upon him.[44]

The Sumerian forerunner, the Descent of Inanna, cognate in many aspects, at this point at lines 219ff has Enki make two creatures from the dirt under his fingernails, a kurgara and a galatura. Their source indicates the scorn with which they were held. The kurgara (later *kurgarrû*) is the same type as the *assinnu* in the Akkadian version, but the galatura, presumably "minor/junior gala" is not. It was they who sprinkled the food of life and the water of life on the dead Inanna hung on a nail. They then drop out of the story, as their analagous ranks do in the Descent of Ishtar.

App. 3.2.10 The second unusual text concerning the *assinnu* is found in the complex *Poem of Erra.*[45] One of its lines, about the city of Uruk being peopled with *kezertu's*, *šamhatu*'s and *harimtu*'s (iv 52) was discussed in Sec.

4.6.4. The text goes on to describe the *kurgarrû*'s and *assinnu*'s in Eanna, the temple of Anum and Ishtar in Uruk:

ša ana šupluh nišī Ištar zikrusunu uterru ana sin [*nišūti*] (*Erra* iv 56).

The translation of this is ambiguous, as if often the case with the III-stem in Akkadian and the Hiph'il in Hebrew: "those who in order to bring about awe/religious awe in people, Ishtar turned their maleness into femaleness." I understand the root *p-l-h* in this case to indicate the religious fear, veneration and awe that R. Otto and M. Eliade attempt to describe as a response to the sacred.[46] Nothing more appears in this text to indicate the nature of this change, or the nature of the liturgy, if it is that.

This change, turning, which is related in a series of texts in App. 3.4 to hermaphroditism, will be seen as a kind of a paradigm for the function of the *assinnu* and *kurgarrû.* The *Shumma Ālu* text noted above, App. 3.2.6, may indicate homosexuality or impotence, and the latter is hard to detect in ancient documents. This could be ejaculatatory impotence, erectile impotence or sterility.[47] Ancient documents do not discuss these differences.

Appearances of the *assinnu* in economic texts could not be found, as they could for the *kurgarrû*. (But see App. 3.5 for the sag-ur-sag.)

App. 3.3 KUR.GAR.RA / *kurgarrû* // *rab kurgarrû*

3.3.1 Taking up the second of our major ranks of this type, and noting that he is paired with the *assinnu* often in the texts above, we find many more references, some of which have already been given of necessity above in App. 3.2 about *assinnu.* He is a male, but mysteriously, there is at least one reference[48] to females: 13 MUNUS. KUR.GAR [ ] (line 14) totalled with others as *naphar* 61 MUNUS.NAR [ ], listing Aramean, Hittite, Tyrian and Kassite (?) *nārtu* 's "female singers." The reverse has other f. offices, including 6 MUNUS.A.BA.MEŠ *ár* - [*ma-a-a-te* ?], and 2 MUNUS.KUR.MEŠ.GAR (line 8) totalled as 156 [ ]. Since MUNUS.NAR.GAL and MUNUS.A.BA are unique as far as I know, I would suggest that the female *kurgarru* is also unique, and may be a foreign office, or the Assyrian understanding of a foreign office. We know from other sources that one of his functions is as singer, corroborated by this text.

A difficult astrological text[49] has : *šumma* ^{d}*Adad ina* MURUB KI.MIN.MA *sahlu* ŠUR-*nun* NITÁ.MEŠ KUR.GAR.RA.MEŠ *ina* É KU.MEŠ-*ma* KUR.GAR.RA.MEŠ *ana* NITÁ.MEŠ U.TU.[MEŠ] "if Adad in the midst of the constellation Great Bear (gave a cry) and it rained cardamum (and they became?) men, then the *kurgarrû*'s will sit in the house and the *kurgarru*'s will give birth to men." Though not understandable this once again refers to the *kurgarrû*'s female role.

App. 3.3.2 As seen above in App. 3.2.7 *kurgarrû* appears on OB Proto-Lu, with a break, after sag-ur-sag and pi-li-pi-li, and on Lú = ša near these two offices.

To test whether the title is an ad hoc or permanent one, we look for it among economic texts, and find many occurrences,[50] from MB, MA times on. This shows that it is a recognized office. We cannot find this kind of evidence for the *assinnu*. This may separate the two offices.

App. 3.3.3 The *kurgarrû* plays a musical instrument (broken),[51] along with *assinnu* (in the break, probably), and the *kulmašītu.* In a NA Akītu

"New Year's" text[52] the *kurgarrû* plays the *kis/škilāte* - clappers, and then the *a-rim* BAD [x *tim-bu*]*-ú-ti ša* LÚ *kur-gar-re-* [*e*] "the covering (?) of the wall (?) ... the [*timbut*]*tu* "harp" / "drum" of the *kurgarrû*,[53] again in association with the playing of musical instruments.

App. 3.3.4 The *rab kurgarrû* appears along with the *šangû* of Sharrat-nipha, the *šangû* of the Bīt-eqî, the *nargallu*, the LÚ.NINDA and the DUMU.MÍ.SUHUR.LÁ's in a long listing of the *ginû* "regular, continual" offering to Sharrat-nipha in Kar-Tukulti-Ninurta, perhaps a NA copy of a MA text[54] (Sec. 4.6.6). Line 23 reads: 50 *qa* LÚ.SANGA ^{d}Sharrat-nipha 50 *qa* LÚ.NAR.GAL LÚ.GAL KUR.GAR$^{!}$.RA. Once again the *kurgarrû*, this time the head one, is associated with a singing position, and the importance is shown by the amounts.

App. 3.3.5 The *kurgarrû's* carry weapons. An speaks in the poem "Inanna and Ebeh:"

173 kur-gar-ra gíri ba-da-ra mu-na-sum
174 gala-ra ^{kuš}ub li-li-ìs mu-na-sum
175 pi-li-pi-li sag su-bal mu-ni-ak

Inanna and Ebeh
H. Limet. *Or* 40 (1971) 18

"to the kurgara I have given the gír "sword or dagger" and ba-da-ra / to the gala I have given the drum and the li-li-is / for the pi-li-pi-li I have changed the sex." The ba-da-ra, later *patarru/pattaru*, is variously translated "battle club,"[55] "prod,"[56] "knife.?"[57] It is probably, considering its usage, in the knife category.

The kurgara also carries the ba-da-ra in the Iddin-Dagan "sacred marriage" text, Römer Königshymnen Kap. IV, line 74, and a Sumerian cultic song kur-gar-ra-uru-na-ka "the kurgarra of their city" *VAS* II 2 I 15 = *RA* 8, 161, 17. The Iddin-Dagan "sacred marriage " hymn (App. 3.5.3) shows a number of cultic officials with weapons, as they "walk before the pure Inanna." The sag-ur-sag, in the third kurugu carries a giš-gíd-da "lance/spear," (line 57) and the šu-gi$_4$-a carries the gír "sword or dagger" and ba-da-ra.

The *kurgarrû's* also carry the *naglabu* "razor,"*quppû* "knife," *ṣurtu* "flint knife," and *bēlu* (or, *tillu*) "a kind of weapon."[58] These are not criticized but *ulluṣ kabtat* ^{d}*Ištar* "delight the heart of Ishtar." (line 58).

In the list of me's in the myth "Inanna and Enki" after a section listing various male and female cultic officials (II v 11-15) who are Inanna's nam "Fundation" (Farber-Flügge) and one of the mountain-land (? kur-e$_{11}$-dè and kur-e$_{11}$-da, II v 19-21), it continues:

21 [nam] -egí-zi nam-nin-dingir nam-išib nam-lú-mah nam-gudu$_4$ me-a
22 lugal-mu dumu-(ni-ir ba-an-na-sum)
23 [nì-g]i-na si-TUR si-è? kur-e$_{11}$-dè kur-e$_{11}$-da kur-gar-ra me-a
24 lugal-mu dumu (-ni-ir ba-an-na-sum)
25 gír ba-da-ra sag-ur-sag túg-gi$_6$ túg-gùn-a gú-bar gú-x me-a

Inanna and Enki I v = II v 11ff

So this list of officials continues with three similar terms: kur-gar-ra, gír ba-da-ra, sag-ur-sag (II v 23-5).

In an ershemma, lamenting the fate of Inanna's spouse Dumuzi,[59] among other things the text says that kur-gar-ra uru^{ki}-ni-gin$_7$ gìri nu-ak-a-na "the kurgarra of his city did not brandish the sword."

Elsewhere one finds that these are not merely ceremonial weapons, but are covered with blood.[60] At one point (in the cultic drama?) there is a murder. In a Babylonian lamentation ritual, after "the shepherd kills 'her' (i.e. the undesignated *ardatum* 'servant girl', called ama na-am-tag-ga 'mother of sin'), with his crook, the *kalû* kills her with his *manzû* 'drum,' the potter kills her with his *zarbābu* -vessel, the *kurgarrû* (will kill her) with his sword and *patarru*."[61] Here each officiciant uses the instrument pertaining to that office.

So in late Assyrian times the *kurgarrû* is described as being in a battle. The nu-èš studied in Sec. 1.10 is described as gíri-lá é-an-na "the Eanna temple's knife-wielder."[62] We have discovered more weapons than we suspected.

App. 3.3.6 The *kurgarrû* as knife-wielder is close to the designation of Nin-ezen (mú?) in the bilingual text:

ii 77 ^{d}nin-ezen gíri-lá é-ku[r-ra]
ii 78 ditto *na-áš pat-ri ša é -[kur]*

H.F. Lutz PBS 1/II 115

and the late emesal vocabulary: me-ri-lá [emesal] = gíri-lá = *na-áš pat-ri* (MSL IV 35,91, the emesal vocabulary) So the Ekur temple has a *naš patri* as part of its personnel. In NA times it appears in:

160 lú-gír-lá *ṭa-bi-hu*

Lú = ša I MSL XII 101

in a group including muhaldim "cook," also related in the Sultantepe list and the OB Lu.[63] The *nāš patri* along with other knife-wielders are part of the Ishtar cult in the Erra-epic.[64] This may be compared to the use of *ṭābihu* for killing men in a military context.[65]

So the knife-wielder called gíri-lá / *nāš patri* could be a cultic official, or be in the kitchen as the entries near that of cook indicate, or be in a military effort. The cultic official could have been a cultic actor, a cultic warrior, as the *kurgarrû* was.

In a NA rite[66] the *šangû* and the *kurgarrû's* in the plural act together, the *kurgarrû's: tūšāri imalilu* "play war (lit. "battlefield"), i.e., act out a battle in dramatic liturgical form, while they *kiškilāte imahhaṣu* "beat the *kiškilāte*" a kind of clappers, and shout or speak or sing in a special way. Similarly in another place they *tūšāri immallilu milhu imalluhu*[67] i.e. (paraphrasing a difficult text) "play war (lit. "battlefield") by tearing out ..." We are reminded of the tearing out of eyes and mouth as a ritual act in the Descent of Inanna lines 37, 176, 305 following a "weeping at the mounds" and the "playing the drum of the throne room."[68]

Just as Hebrew *ṣāḥāq* may mean the laughter which goes along with play, or it can mean sexual play, we can look for *mēlulu* "to play" to have both these connotations:

ma-la-mu sila-dagal-la e-ne mu-di-ni-ib-ma-ma
ina rebītim immelil

TuM NF 3 25:15, CAD M/2 16a

"my intimate girlfriend[69] plays with me in the city square." Deserters come to the *bīt sabītum ana mīlulim* " alehouse to play" in a Mari text.[70] Both of these examples may have sexual connotations.

App. 3.3.7 The carrying of weapons is a male task. The *kurgarrû's* also carry instruments symbolic of the female, again indicating their bisexual or hermaphroditicnature. In a NA hymn of praise of Nanaya, the first part of which has some liturgical actions[71] after the *nāru*'s playing instruments are settled before her, the *kurgarrû*'s appear carrying the *pilaqqu* "spindle, distaff or hair-clasp," *tīru*, and *tamšēru* both "whip." These symbols are in passages which show the male normally carrying the tukul-weapon and others, and the woman carrying the giš-bala "spindle" and "giš-kirid "hair-clasp.?[72] The *nāš pilaqqi* App. 3.10 shows another person in a similar position.

Other symbols of womanhood are: giš-kirid-kù na4-gug-tag-ga giš-GA.ZUM nam-munus-a "a silver hair clasp (?) of gug-tag-ga-stone ("carnelian"?) (and) a comb the characteristic of womanhood," an offering to Nantar (m.), made by Ur-Nammu, S.N. Kramer, *JCS* 21 (1967) 114, 110. GA.ZUM is read GA.RIG (*muštu*) by CAD M/2 290b, but ga-ZUM by Borger *Zeichenliste* No. 319. The arguments for the reading are given in M. Civil, *JNES* 26 (1967) 210f. The giš-bala and giš-kirid-da are in the hands of women in a Shulgi text, BE 31, 54,3-5, quoted by J. van Dijk *Or* 41 (1972) 347. He translates kirid as "quenouille??. For the feminine characterization of the spindle, see A. Sjöberg, *ZA* 65 (1975) 224 n. 14, and H. Hoffner, "Symbols for Masculinity and Femininity. Their Use in Ancient Near Eastern Sympathetic Magic Rituals," *JBL* 85 (1966) pp. 326-334. Ishtar oversees spinning with a *pilaqqu* in *Shurpu* V 150/151 as a magical act.

To perform what might, in the modern sense, be termed "sexual therapy," you make a clay figurine of a man seized by a ghost and stick into his head giš-bala *šid-du ki-ir-is-su* (*KAR* 22.5f. translated TuL No. 20). AHw's "ein Werkzeug" for *šiddu* must be something especially for a woman. *kirissu* is "hair clasp, metal pin" (CAD).

In a NB hemerology[73] after the king washes and anoints himself, LÚ.KUR.GAR.RA IGI.LÁ-*ma* LÚ.KUR.GAR.RA *a-na* LUGAL *i-kar-rab* "(the king) looks at the *kurgarrû*, and the *kurgarrû* looks at the king, and the *kurgarrû* does homage to (or, "invokes a blessing upon," or "praises") the king." Even though virtually no details of the ritual are given, it is seen that the king and the *kurgarrû* are together in what may be an apotropaic ritual.

One is reminded of the coming together of the male and female roles of the *kurgarrû* when looking at a number of texts in which Ishtar turns maleness into femaleness, but in which no official title appears. These are to be compared to the line in the Erra-poem App. 3.2.10. We note that this turning is a prerogative of Inanna/Ishtar.[74] This area touches a whole series of texts relating to transvestism, for which see the following section.

App. 3.4 Transvestism

In a bilingual hymn ultimately from the time of Sargon of Akkad, Inanna's characteristics are listed: the fields of love and marriage, battle, good fortune and bad, including many changes of status. The one we are interested in is,

[nita] munus-ra munus nita-ra ku$_4$-ku$_4$-dè ^{d}inanna za-kam
zikaram ana sinništim sinniš ana zikarim turrum kumma eštar
Sjöberg, *ZA* 65 (1975) 190, 120

"to turn a man into a woman and a woman into a man are yours, Inanna / Ishtar"

In a line from this hymn, Inanna's cultic officials lú-al-è-dè "ecstatic" pi-li-pi-li kur-gar-ra are joined in one variant by sag-ur-sag's (plural), the activity of all apparently described by the next line i-lu šìr-ra-àm "it is lament and song," and by the next as ér "lament." These officiants are singers. This practice extended down to later times, for we read in a NA curse on whoever removes a monument from its place,

^{d}ištar bēlet qabli u tāhazi zikrussu sinnišāniš lušalikma
Borger *Esarh* 99 r. 55f

"may Ištar the lady of war and battle change his masculinity into femininity."

Cassin[75] quotes a line: [*assu*]*m zikarē bēlat sinnišāti* ^{giš}*qašatšunu liki* [*n*] "What concerns the men, so may the lady of the women (i.e., Ishtar) take away their bow." The bow is a metaphor for male sexual virility.

This "changing" is shown further in several cultic texts which describe a left-side / right-side dichotomy. In a hymn to Inanna and Ishme-Dagan:

22 ki-sikil-e-ne [na]m-guruš-e túg zi-da mu$_4$-mu$_4$ 23 guruš-e-ne n[am-ki-]⌈sikil!⌉-šè túg gùb/gáb-bu mu$_4$-mu$_4$
Chiera SRT No. 36,
transl. A. Sjöberg *ZA* 65 (1975) 223
See G. Castellino, *RSO* 32 (1957)16

"the young women in the manner of the young men dress the right side, and young men in the manner of the young women dress the left side."

In the Iddin-Dagan "sacred marriage" hymn, Sec. 4.23.4, in the fourth kirugu, an unclearly-designated "they" (the sag-ur-sag's?) are being described, with the rest of an array of figures, in a recurring line "they walk before the pure Inanna." Choosing only two verses, we read:

60 á-zi-da-bi-a túg-nita bí-in-mu$_4$
- - -
63 á-gùb/gáb-bu-bi-a túg-nam-munus mu-un-si-ig
ASKT No. 21, 126-131;
Römer *Königshymnen* 130,
reading as Sjöberg *ZA* 65 (1975) 223ff

(60)"their right side they dress with men's clothing"; (63)"their left side they cover (?) with women's clothing." Falkenstein softens the transvestite aspect: "that maidens in the manner of men carry their mantle on the right, and the young men in the manner of women carry their mantle on the left."[76]

Sjöberg gives an unpublished text of the same type (referring to the men):

zà-zi-da [x] zà-gáb-bu-[šè] šu-bal hé-ba-e-ni-[ak]

túg-á$^{?}$-munus hé-em-mi-mu$_4$ eme-munus-a ka-ba ha-ba-e-ni-gar
giš-bala giš-kirid (KEŠDA) šu-ba hé-em-mi-sum
UM 29-16-229 ii 4ff
ZA 65 (1975) 224

"she may change the right side [to] the left side / in the [ ] clothing of a woman she may dress them; emesal-speech[77] she may put in their mouth / a spindle and a kirid give them," again the giving to a male the appurtenances of a female.

I think the possibility hinges on whether or not liturgical actions are being described here. Sjöberg opines that the passages of this type do not refer to the changing of sexes, but to the changing of roles of the participants in the cult. We are undoubtedly viewing cultic drama here. Falkenstein in *SAHG* 230ff has essentially the same idea. They are not given titles, but in this case they would probably be *assinnu's*, *kurgarrû's* or sag-ur-sag's. In a wider sense, however, the question brought up here is tantamount to asking for the complete ritual with notes to be given, and it never is. The hymns speak of the mythical, which is the intention of the author. Inanna's power can change the sex; the hymns say this. Her cultic actors undoubtedly act this out in some sort of a cultic drama. To them when an (to us) aberrant sexual type of action appears, they said that Inanna did it, because all sex from what we call normal to what we call abnormal is under Inanna's aegis.

In the bilingual hymn of Inanna-Ishtar, referred to above, the goddess is speaking, or is spoken of:

43 zi-da gáb-bu-šè ì-x [ ]
im-na ana šu-me $^{!}$*-lu* $^{!}$ [ ]

45 gáb-bu zi-da-sè ì-x [ ]
šu-me ... im-ni [ ]

47 mu-tin munus-mu-tin-a-šè
mu-ni-x [ ]*zi-ka-ri sin-niš-tu$_4$* [ ]

49 nu-nus$_x$-mu-tin-a-šè mu-ni-x[ ]
sin-niš-tu$_4$ ana zi-<ka>- ri [ ]

51 mu-tin nu-nus$_x$-a-šè še-er-ka-[an...]
šá zi-ka-ri ana sin-niš-tu$_4$ [ ]

53 nu-nus$_x$ mu-tin-a-šè še-er-ka [ ]
sin-niš-tu$_4$ ana zi-ka-ri [ ]

ASKT No. 21 r. 43-54 (K. 257 + K.41)
Falkenstein *SAHG* No. 46; Sjöberg, *ZA* 65 (1975) 225;
more references in *HKL* I 185

Notes:
line 47: mu-tin [ki-sikil] [= *ar-da-tu*] "girl" MSL IV 17.72, Emesal vocabulary
mu-tin = MIN eme-sal (i.e., *zikarum* "male") Nabnitu IV, MSL 16 86,304
line 49: nu-nús S[AL] [*sin-niš-tu*]" woman" MSL IV 16, 68, Emesal vocabulary
line 53:še-er-ka-an hu-mu-ni-in-du$_{11}$ "adorn, decorate" Römer *Königshymnen* 14, 46

"She/I the right side to the left side.../the left side to the right side.../a man to a woman ...(changes$^{?}$)/a woman to a man.../a man for a woman decor[ates] ...a woman for a man [decorates]."

This is what one may describe as literal transvestism, a changing of a garment across the sides, one of a woman, the other of a man, representing, i.e. taking the role, playing the part of, a change of sex. Let us not ask the question: what really happened? These are hymns probably representing liturgical action, and liturgical action is always symbolic. The words do not fully "describe" the action, because of the metaphoric nature of the hymns.[78]

In a rite of the temple É.GASAN.KALAM.MA,[79] the *kurgarrû* and the *sūsānu* use water together, acting together with the *assinnu* (line 14). Nabû acts as a woman (lines 27-29), as does Marduk (lines 39-41). This is a fertility rite, describing in mythic terms Ishtar's actions in her temple, then battles between the gods, then a woman carried on the shoulders of people while seed is scattered in a field.

One notices that Mesopotamian literature has an ambivalent attitude towards effeminate/transvestite/hermaphroditic creatures as the kurgara They are scorned on the one hand, shown by the kurgara in the Descent of Ishtar being created by the dirt of Enki's fingernails. Yet the same myth testifies to his supreme importance to the ongoingness of life, for it is he and the galatura to whom the god gives the mission of bringing back the goddess to earth.

App. 3.5 sag-ur-sag

App. 3.5.1 Let us now turn, more briefly because of the lack of texts, to those functionaries cognate with the *assinnu* and *kurgarrû*. Certainly the sag-ur-sag is the most important and oft-appearing of these. He appears several times in the lexical lists in an order sag-ur-sag, pi-li-pi-li, kur-gar-ra.[80]

In a fragmentary myth[81] there is a goddess, probably Inanna or a form thereof, saying sag-ur-sag-mu ga-ra-ba (line 9) "my sag-ur-sag I will give you," with the emesal form of kur-gar-ra, kur-mar-ra, appearing on line 7.

App. 3.5.2 What was the reading of sag-ur-sag in Akkadian, appearing only as signs in OB Proto-Lu? Lu = ša IV.184 (App. 3.2.7) gives it as *assinnu*, but as has been noted these later "equivalents," are often meant to be only in the same genre; indeed, Lu = ša IV 193a gives the (regular?) equivalent of UR.SAL = *assinnu*. Several other occurrences are listed in CAD A/2 s.v. Römer[82] thinks that *assinnu* is the Akkadian reading of the Sumerian sag-ur-sag.

App. 3.5.3 In the Iddin-Dagan sacred marriage hymn (Sec. 4.23.4) among those described by the rubric "they walk before the pure Inanna," are sag-ur-sag's (third kirugu), šu-gi$_4$-a's (fifth kirugu, Sec. 4.4, Akkadian *šugītu*), and kur-gar-ra's (fifth kirugu).

He is listed in the plural in the OB hymn to Inanna:

lú-al-è-dè pi-li-pi-li bal [ ] / sa[g]-ur-sag-e-ne
Sjöberg, *ZA* 65 (1975), 186, 88 var. H

The theme is apparently described by the next line: i-lu šìr-ra-àm "it is lament and song" The lú-al-è-dè "ecstatic" (and) the pi-li-pi-li are described as bal "changed" then there is a listing of sag-ur-sag's. The "changing" reminds us of the transvestism discussed in App. 3.4. Below in App. 3.6 we will note that the lú-al-è-dè appears with the *parrû*, another office similar to these studied in this section.

Even earlier the sag-ur-sag appears in the Gudea writings in a difficult context:

4 uru-ta im-ta-è
5 dusu-bi munus-e nu-íl
6 sag-ur-sag-e mu-na-dù

Gudea St. B iv

"From the city he brought it out / its carrying basket no woman carried / the sag-ur-sag did it for her (?)." Perhaps the ritual of the carrying of the basket was done by the sag-ur-sag, not by a "woman," as normally. Here the sag-ur-sag does a woman's task. The theme of carrying the dirt in a basket was a standard one in Sumerian art.

In the Iddin-Dagan hymn already mentioned, in the beginning of the lines containing the refrain "they walk before the pure Inanna," in the beginning of the third kirugu, we find the sag-ur-sag's described as

45 sag-ur-sag-e-ne múš mu-na-an-dub-dub-uš

Römer *Königshymnen* 130

The verb múš...dub-dub is unclear to the editor, who translates "schmückten sich? für sie." múš can be "appearance or aspect (*zīmu*), dub can be *sarāqu*, *sapāku*, *tabāku* "pour out, heap up." There is a MÚŠ.DUB.DUB = [*ma-aš-da*]-⌈*a-tum* ⌉ entry among other múš-listings in Nabnitu XXIII.280, MSL XVI 220,[83] having to do with combing (*mašādu*) MÚŠ = *susbû* appears in MSL XII 131, 83 (Lu = ša IV) and is paired with *ramku*, a kind of a purification official in line 84.[84] Reisman *JCS* 25 (1973) 194: "comb their hair before her." He argues for the context of hair on the basis of E. Chiera.[85] With respect to *kezertu* (Sec. 4.6) hair was used in a sexual manner.

In Shulgi A[86] a hymn of self-praise, Shulgi tells that in one day he made the journey back and forth from Nippur to Ur, about 150 kilometers, and in both cities celebrated the èš-èš festival. This festival is described as "theirs" (i.e., the sag-ur-sag's of the previous line,) and Shulgi calls them sag-ur-sag-mu-ne "my sag-ur-sag's.".A few lines later (82f) he refers to sitting at banquet with Inanna nita dam-mu "my consort." Does the èš-èš festival use the sag-ur-sag as one of its liturgical leaders?

In the hymn Inanna and Enki, in the first tablet and repeated in the second, there is a list of me's the nam "character, function, nature" of several cultic offices, App. 3.3.5. These few lines touch on many of the offices discussed in chapters 1 and 4, egi-zi, nin-dingir, išib, lú-mah, $gudu_4$, appearing all together. The gír ba-da-ra on line 25 is seen associated with the sag-ur-sag, being the same weapon with the kur-gar-ra in Inanna and Ebeh, App. 3.3.5. Following the sag-ur-sag is $túg-gi_6$ "black garment," túg-gùn-a "colored garment," perhaps a cultic dress, and gú-bar "neck hair," perhaps a tonsure of some sort. On these lines, the sag-ur-sag is related to, but kept separate from, the aforementioned offices.

In an Ur-Nammu religious text, G. Castellino[87] finds a line sag-ur-sag-bi ^{giš}sudun-bi mu-zi, for which he does not venture a translation. It could mean something like "its/his sag-ur-sag set its/his yoke." The context is one of

Urnammu in self-praise telling of how much he did for the well-being of the land.

Even in far-off Alalakh, the sag-ur-sag appears in a curse section of a historical document, in whatever his Akkadian reading was:

^d^Ištar SAG.UR.SAG *pa-ra-ú-ra-am / i-na bi-ir-ki-šu li-te-eb-bi*
or *li -ṭe₄-eb-bi*
or *li-ṭe₄-ep-pí*

Wiseman *Alalakh* No. 1, 19ff

One assumes that the -au- vowel cluster is that characteristic sometimes found in Hurrian orthography. If the last word is from the verb *tebû*: "may Ishtar raise up the SAG.UR.SAG (and) *parrû* [88] onto his (the one who alters the treaty) sexual organs (to rape him) If the verb is *ṭebû*: "may Ishtar sink the SAG.UR.SAG (and) *parrû* onto his sexual organs," and if from *ṭepû*: "may Istar spread (the legs of) the SAG.UR.SAG (and) *parrû* onto his sexual organs." Whatever the meaning, it seems to refer to homosexual intercourse involving the SAG.UR.SAG and *parrû*, and thus a disparaging note. (For the *parrû*, App. 3.6).[89]

The Alalakh texts also provide a rare glimpse of the SAG.UR.SAG in an economic text.[90] Grain rations are given to PN SAG.UR.SAG, heading the list, as well as a head of the weavers, KU.ZI's, wet nurses, weavers, prisoners, ox drivers, grooms, gatekeepers and others. This list throws no light onto the function of the SAG.UR.SAG, although all these may be non-cultic functionaries of the temple, my Category No. 5. It does show the important fact that SAG.UR.SAG was a title attached to a person, and not an ad hoc descriptive title, or a mythological one. In App. 3.2.10 it was noted that the *assinnu* could not be found in economic texts.

Recently Alster and Vantisphour[91] presented a disputation text, that between Lahar and Ashnan "Ewe and Wheat." On line 74 ^d^Ashnan says

sag-ur-sag-ra usu-mu ba-ab-sum-mu

translated as "I grant power to the Chief Warrior," perhaps meaning by nourishing him. Here they take (though without note) sag-ur-sag as sag "chief" of the ur-sag's "warriors," probably because there is no cultic context here. Yet their note on p. 34 refers to Gud St B iv 7, which could be a ritual context, and certainly not a military one. Later (line 79) he gives "my power to the ur-sag" (usu-mu ur-sag-ra), so the interpretation of the earlier line is consistent with this.

App. 3.6 *parrû*

App. 3.6.1 The *parrû* is related to the *assinnu* and sag-ur-sag, and side-by-side with others of our category on the late Assyrian list Lu = ša, App. 3.2.7. The Antagal III list provides more information:

38 (287) [pi-il] -pi-il *pa-ru-ú*
39 (288) [lú-al] -è-dè MIN *ša pi-i*
40 (289) inim-gùn-gùn *pu-ú pur-ru-šú*

CT 18, 35 iv, Antagal III,

K. 2008 + MSL XVII 161

The lú-al-è-dè = *muhhû* -ecstatic was seen often in Sec. 3.12; he uses the *pû* "mouth." The *muhhû* is defined here as a *parrû sa pî* "of the mouth," that is, the *muhhû* has some of the ambivalent characteristics of the *parrû*. This relationship is also shown in a list of ecstatics, earlier in the text copied in App. 3.2.7, above:

	CT 18,5 K. 4193	CAD s.v. mahhu and kulu ' u
r. 5	*eš-še-pu -[ú]*	*mah-hu-u*
r. 6	*pa-ru -[ú]*	"
r. 7	*muš-šu-r [u]*	"
r. 8	*zab-bu*	"
r. 9	*i-sin-nu-u*	*ku-lu-'u*
r. 10	*a-pi-lu-u*	"
r. 11	*kur-gar-ru-u*	"

LTBA 2 1 vi,
restoring CT 18,5

So one concludes that in a sense the ecstatic is in our category No. 4, another case of overlapping categories.

App. 3.6.2 See above App. 3.5.3 for a curse section from an Alalakh tablet with homosexual intercourse between a *parrû* and a SAG.UR.SAG.

App. 3.7 pi-li-pi-li / *pilpilû* // *apillû* and *apillatu* //*pilpilānu*

App. 3.7.1 Turning now to the pi-li-pi-li, in various orthographies pi-il-pi-li, pi-il-pi-il, there are several suggestions for etymology.[92] We saw that this office has appeared in lexical lists from OB times, but in the NA lexical lists he was paired with the *parrû,* Antagal App. 3.6.1 and in Lu = ša IV with the *assinnu* and *parrû,* App. 3.2.7.

App. 3.7.2 There is a variant *apillû* / pi-li-pi-li in a NA vocabulary, paired with *kulu'u* (LTBA, App. 3.2.7 and App. 3.6.1) another in our category No. 4. Cf. *a- [p] il-lu-ú* in HAR-gud B, Sec. 3.21.1. For an apparently Akkadianizing of pi-li-pi-li to *pilpilû* see AHw 863b, lexical only.

App. 3.7.3 There may be a female *apillatum*. In Ur III texts we find several entries of the PN *á-pil-la-tum.*[93]

App. 3.7.4 The pi-li-pi-li was seen above as given a sex change (bal, App. 3.5.3), whatever that might mean, either a garment change, or a role change, or a literal sex change, in the poem Inanna and Ebeh, after the kurgara and the gala were given weapons. So the pi-li-pi-li is a type of *kurgarrû* and *assinnu.*

App. 3.7.5 In the Hymn to Inanna referred to in App. 3.4 near the beginning, and in the Antagal III list (App. 3.6.1) the lú-al-è-dè ecstatic appears with the pi-li-pi-li and sag-ur-sag, another indication that the pi-li-pi-li, as the *parrû*, is linked to the ecstatic. This may be an indication that this office used ecstastic practices in his performance.

3.7.6 The hymn to Inanna has an earlier line:

L 81 ugu-ba kiri$_4$-šu-gál-la mu-ni-in-AK pi-l[i-pi-li ...]
M [ ] x ù-mu-ni-in-AK pi-li-pi-li mu-ni$^!$-in-sa$_4$

Sjöberg *ZA* 65 (1975), 184

"when she made...a gesture of greeting, she called (for?/to?) the pi-li-pi-li," and line 82 goes on

J 82 IGI.NI i-ni-TAR nita-gin$_x$ šà-ga-[ni] / giš-tukul an-na-ab-sum-[mu]

"she broke the weapon (IGI.NI) in pieces, like a man / in [her] heart (?) / she gives him a weapon." I understand this to mean that the weapon given to the pi-li-pi-li is symbolic of the male. There are several possibilities for understanding here. Inanna, who is described as destructive, powerful, victorious previously in the poem, here acts like a man in her destruction of the weapon. Or, the pi-li-pi-li acts in the male role, though capable of acting in either male or female roles. Sjöberg[94] explains that the male role is specifically mentioned because the pi-li-pi-li was a female participant in the cult. I do not find any evidence for this last idea. I would understand him as acting in a male role when he has a weapon, and a female role when he carries a spindle. Maybe šà-gi-[ni] "in? his heart" refers to the position of the weapon, next to the heart.

In a source to which I did not have access, Sjöberg found a quotation from a hymn to Dumuzi:

pi-li-pi-li šu-bal-ak-a-gin$_x$ sila-dagal

BE 30, 10,7
Sjöberg *ZA* 65 (1975), 223

"like the changing of a pi-li-pi-li (in a?) broad place" So again the idea of "changing" is used of this office.

App. 3.7.7 The *pilpilānu*, which may be the same or an office similar to the above, is mentioned in an oil or bowl omen text of Enmeduranki, king of Sippar in late Babylonian times, in context with a *nešakku* who is perfect in body and a *mār bārû* who is not perfect in his body:

[33] *pi-il-pi-la-nu* [34] *la na-ṣir parṣē ša* ^{d}šamas *u* ^{d}adad

BBR No. 24 (pl. xxxix),
K. 2486 and K. 4364,
and Craig *ABRT* 63-65

"the *pilpilānu* who does not observe the rites of Shamash and Adad." The *pilpilānu* here acts as a cultic official.

App. 3.8 *kulu'u*

App. 3.8.1 The word has been found earlier than any in our Category No. 4, among Old Akkadian PNs.[95] In this text is a list with three *ku-lu-u's* and 5 *sekertu's* (ŠEŠ.SAL), the latter also in our Category No. 4. Kulu'u continues as a PN to NA times.[96] This may be a hypocoristic form of Kulu'u-Ishtar[97] for the *kulu'u* is a member of the Ishtar cult.

App. 3.8.2 It was seen above in the Descent of Ishtar (near n. 32) that a variant for the *assinnu* was the *kulu'u*.[98] A NA vocabulary with a series of "equivalents" to *ku-lu'u* is found on CT 18.5, App. 3.2.7. Does this mean that the *kulu'u* is the basic name of the genre, and the others are secondary to it? The paucity of exemplars we have been able to find does not tell against this and, in fact, the texts containing the office, shown below, signify its importance.

App. 3.8.3 In a namburbi text addressed to Ishtar, she is urged

45 *al-ki it-ru-bi a-na bīti-ni* 46 *it-ti-ki li-ru-ba ṣa-lil-li-ki ṭa-a-bu*
47 *h [ab]? -bu-bu-ki u ku-lu-'u-ki*

H. Zimmern, *ZA* 32 (1918-19), 174
VAT 9728 = *KAR* 144

"come enter our house / with you may enter the beautiful one who sleeps with you / your lover and your *kulu'u*." The house is the *bīt* [lú]*sābî*, called in line 32 *naramki* "your (i.e., Ishtar's) beloved (place)." These nouns are in apposition (it couldn't be three separate people invited in!) so the *kulu'u* beds with Ishtar. Line 38 mentions the income of the *bīt sābî* ceasing.[99]

App. 3.8.4 The description of a runaway slave girl who is with two *kulu'u*'s in a NB letter[100] seems to indicate sexual relations also. This may be why in an (MA?) incantation text the possible magical efficacy of "the word" is listed as, in order: "the word of your father, the word of your mother, the word of your sister, the word of the *kulu'u* and of the *harimti āli* "prostitute of the city."[101]

App. 3.8.5 His sexuality is referred to in a laconic and cryptic statement in a MB letter [102] which describes a man of whom Ninurta-tukulti-Assur (ca. 1133) spoke as *kulu'u la zikaru šū* "He is a *kulu'u* not a man." Taking the above reference into account, which shows him capable of loving Ishtar, this shows him as a hermaphrodite. Ishtar herself is in that category. In a hymn she is described as: ⌊*sin*] *-ni-šat mu-ta-át* [103] "She is a woman, she is a man;" as she is, so are her officiants. She wears a beard.[104]

Again a disparaging remark is made for this office in the Babylonian Theodicy: *kulu'u* is a variant of *harhari* "scoundrels, rogues."[105]

App. 3.9 *sinnišānu*

In a commentary to HAR-ra = hubullu XXV, the HAR-gud text, referred to in App. 3.2.7, shows *sinnišānu* paired with *assinnu*, showing that the former is in Category No. 4. The form of this word can be explained as the word for woman, *sinništu,* with the feminine ending removed and an *-ānu* masculine ending substituted.[106] This is to be compared with a possible interpretaton of UR.SAL (= *assinnu*) on the same line as man-woman.

A possible reference to the *sinnišānu* is in a broken portion of the annals of the MA king Tukulti-Ninurta I (1244-1208 B.C.E.). The standard ending to such writings curses whoever erases the king's name; this curse is to:

13 [*zik-r*]*u-šu si-ni-ša-niš* 14 ⌊*m*] *u-ut-šu ana ri-hu-ti* 15 [*liš-ku*] *-un* [ ]

Weidner Tn 7, No. 1 vi 13

"(turn) his maleness like (that of) a *sinnišānu*, his manhood to procreation make." On analogy with other passsages above about turning a man into a woman, however, a better translation would be "(turn) his maleness to that of a woman ...."

App. 4.1.14 discusses a clever proverb or riddle in a late Assyrian collection.[107] The context is one of a *sinnišānu* entering a *bīt aštamme.* The *sinnišānu* entered it probably for the purpose of sex.

App. 3.10 *nāš pilaqqi*

Already noted in App. 3.2.7 Lu = ša IV line 198a and Excerpt I line 217 is the fact that the lú-bala-šu-du$_7$ = *nāš pilaqqi* "(male) carrier of the spindle" is an office. This indicates hermaphroditism, with the male carrying the appurtenances of the female. A male carrying a spindle is found in an Assyrian Dream Omen,[108] but in a broken context. He can be compared to a ^{lú}bala = *ša pilaqqati* in OB Lu.[109] In a similar fashion the *kurgarrû* is given a spindle, App. 3.3.7, which corresponds with the female aspect of his office.

We may tentatively conclude, on the basis of too few excerpts, that the *nāš pilaqqi* is either a hermaphrodite office like *kurgarrû* or another name for this or a similar office. The words for all these hermaphrodite offices are given a masculine ending, never a feminine one.

App. 3.11 *aguhhu*

Aguhhu is a multi-valent term, first a garment, then when used in the Ishtar cult a sexual attractiveness (brought about by this?). Among others in the long Lu = ša list (App. 3.2.7), is the kuš$^{ku-uš}$lá = *aguhhu*, followed by kuš-lá = *ša harimti* showing that the *aguhhu* garment is of leather, and is a garment of the *harimtu* "prostitute," probably indicating sexual attractiveness. This shows up in OB Proto-Lu among carriers or wearers of kuš "leather" followed a few lines later by gada "linen" garments:

550	kuš [*a-gu-úh-hu-um*] lá
551	kuš [ ]-*ni* -[ ] lá
552	kuš[*na-ah*]-*la-ap-tum* lá
553	kuš *ra-am-kum* lá
553a	kuš [*š*]*a ši-bi-ir-ri* lá

OB Proto Lu MSL XII 52f

Here the *aguhhu* is of leather; elsewhere it may be of wool.[110] The *aguhhu* is thus part of a garment, but the fact that it is a term among officiants may indicate that it is also a title of an official, one who wears the *aguhhu*, and placed on the list near the *assinnu*. It was usually worn by Ishtar, though once by Gilgamesh[111] to attract Ishtar. Ishtar of Lagaba[112] wears several items symbolic of sexuality, including silver vulvas and *aguhhu*'s. Ishtar is *bēlet inbi u aguhhi* "lady of sexuality and *aguhhu*," apparently somewhat synonymous terms.[113] An incantation against an utukku-demon involving Ishtar and Tammuz involves sending Ishtar a vulva of lapis lazuli.[114] If we understand the characteristic of the *aguhhu* as enhancing female sexual attractiveness, in the texts from OB times down, according to the lexical lists again there is a male wearing a female garment, a transvestite.

App. 3.12 *ararû* //*šudararû*

These terms are found so far only on a lexical list on which several are paired with *kulu'u* in the LTBA list, App. 3.2.7. *šudararû* may come from the root *darāru* "become free, move about freely." (AHw 1259a).

App. 3.13 sag-bur and bur-sag // bur-ra / *burrû* // *abru* // *aplu*

App. 3.13.1 Several indications point to the bur as a singing office, yet in App. 3.13.7 it is paired with *assinnu* on the Lu = ša IV ist. Is it a singing office that has characteristics of the *assinnu*, or an *assinnu* - like office that has singing components? We conjecture the latter, thus we place it in this chapter.

Bur-sag and sag-bur appear among other bur-entries on Proto-Lu, immediately after the wearers of leather and linen garments:

554 gada-lá
555 šà-gada-lá
556 šà-tu_9-ba_{13}-lá
557 $bur^{úr}$
558 $bur^{úr}$-gal
559 $bur^{úr}$-tur
559a s[ag]-bur
560 $bur^{úr}$-sag
561 $bur^{úr}$-gi_4

OB Proto-Lu MSL XII 53

and a text close to this indicating a female office:

8 bur-u_5-dumu$^!$-zi *bu-ur-ru-u tu-u-m* [*u-zi*]
9 SAL bur-u_5 *bu-ur-ru-u-du*

Fragment II, Izi Boghazköy
MSL XII 82

the last entry indicating *burrûtu* (CAD B 330b).

This same order is echoed many years later on the NA list:

205 še-bi-da *e-gu-ú*
206 gada-lá KI.MIN
207 bur-ra KI.MIN
208 bur-ra *bur-ru-ú*
209 sag-bur-ra *ap-lu*
210 NAB *na-a-ru*
(and so on with other musical titles)

Lu = ša IV MSL XII 135

13 bu-ur bur-sign *ap-lu* [115]

14 bu-ur bur-sign *nap-ta-nu*

S[b] I MSL III 97

11 (bur-sign) *ab-ru*
12 (bur-sign) *nap-ta-nu*

S[b], Fragment M, MSL III 65

Egû may be translated "penitent" (Gragg)[116] or "negligent person, careless person" (CAD) or a class of persons (AHw). It could also relate to a sexual practice.[117] The Lu = ša list would indicate that it is a calling, and is not derogatory, being a title as gada-lá. gada-lá (*gadalallu*) "linen-clad one" is a cultic official named after his garment. sag-bur-ra = *aplu* (usually) "son" is ununderstandable, but given variants of *abru* and *abnu*, see n. 115, probably is a dialectical variant of one of these. Then comes a list of singers, an activity of our category. If this bur is equivalent to *abru*, as it appears to be on some lexical lists (above), this may be another in our category. One could postulate that *abru* = *aplu* with a shift between the labials b and p and the liquids r and l.

Naptanu is another meaning of bur, a "food offering, (cultic) meal," PSD 185b.

App. 3.13.2 The lugal-bur-ra "royal bur (?)" is among cultic officiants who recite é-sub and uru-sub.[118] Others who recite this are: nu-èš, en, a-tu, TU, làl, enkum, pa_4-šeš, the highest of cultic offices.[119]

App. 3.13.3 The *abru* is a singing office in Hellenistic times: na-ám-gala na-ám-bur-ra nar-balag-ta mu-ra-an-gub/*kalû abrūtu ina tigî izzazzuni* [*kum*] [120] "the *kalû* office and the *abru* office stand with the *tigû* harp [for you]." In Lu = ša IV App. 3.13.1 *aplu* precedes singing titles.

App. 3.13.4 The OB Proto-Lu references indicate that, if sag-bur-(ra) is equivalent to bur-sag, the sag-bur may be a chief bur contrasted to bur-tur a beginning or apprentice bur.[121]

App. 3.13.5 The actions of the bur-sag in the economic world are shown in a real estate transaction from the Lagas I period, a witness being Maš-subarata bur-sag,[122] and other witnesses being a gala-mah, and some secular offices, with final mention of a sanga.

App. 3.13.6 In a large Ur III text from Lagash[123] rations are given to men, women and children, with secular titles of boatman, potter, mill worker, birder, milk carrier, beer worker, weaver, vintner, cane break man, as well as nar and bur-sag, the latter again near a singer. *PSD* understands the bur-sag as "servant."[124] OB Proto-Lu (PSD bur-sag article, end) indictes that this may be a bur described as sag "head, chief," rather than the bur-sag officer listed among slaves as the examples in *PSD*.

App. 3.13.7 A relationship of the sag-bur with *assinnu* is indicated on Lu = ša:

184 sag-ur-sag *as-sin-nu*
185 sag-bur-ra KI.MIN
186 lú-gal KI.MIN
187 sag-$bulug_2$-ga KI.MIN

Lu =ša IV MSL XII 134

App. 3.14 HÚB /*huppû* (see also Sec. 2.26)

In a NB tablet[125] a man is taught the *kurgarrūtu* and the *huppūtu* "the office of the *kurgarrû* and the office of the *huppû*." *Huppû* is usually translated "acrobat," but may be considered, since it is with the *kurgarrû*, a kind of dancer or cultic actor.

In the Mari ritual studied earlier,[126] various performers are listed, after which the *huppû* (iii 21) and after them the *ka* -(text: *ta*) *-pí-ša-tum* (iii 23) do a *kapāšu* performance cognate with this title, then a chant by an undesignated person.

A lexical list[127] has munus-lú-túg-túg-bal = *kāpištum.* "A female who changes the clothing," translating the Sumerian, and could refer to the usual activity of a stage performer, or it could refer to the kind of change of clothing discussed in App. 3.4 indicating transvestism.

On a list of professions at Ugarit, each followed by a small number for ration or census purposes, cultic offices are in among others, who may be attached to the temple, and thus be in our Category No. 5:

17 ^{lú}*atû* ^{lú}TÚG.LÁ
18 LÚ.ŠÀ.A.MEš
19 ⌈^{lú}*gi*⌉ *-par* ^{uru}sí-na-ri
20 [^{lú}] *šatammu*
21 HÚB.NITA
22 ^{lú}ALAM$^{?}$.DIM
23 ^{lú}*nappāh erî* ^{lú}*ušparu*
24 ^{lú}*parkullu* ^{lú}*nāru*
25 ^{lú}*nuhatimmu* ^{lú}*ma-ṣi-lu*
26 ^{lú}NU.GIG
27 ^{lú}*šangû*
28 ^{lú}*zadimmu*

J. Nougayrol, MRS 12,
No. 93, RS 17.131

As for the cultic offices: the editor (p. 86 n. 2) understands ŠÀ.A.MEŠ as "fields," and relates it to the lands of a deity. *Giparu* would again be a cultic place (Sec. 4.22.15.5.) HÚB.NITA presumably = *huppû*, not explained by its placement on the list. *Alamdimmû* if the correct reading is an unusual usage of this word as a profession (Nougayrol: "sculpteur?"), and one could conjecture that his work was that of making statues of the gods. *Maṣilu* is taken by Nougayrol (p,. 151) from *ṣll* "move, ring" in Syriac, Hebrew and Arabic, and may be "cymbalier." ^{lú}NU.GIG is a rare male counterpart of the female *qadištu*. (Sec. 4.11). And *nāru* and *šangû* are the ubiquitous singing and priestly offices.

The non-cultic offices would be useful in any temple. filling auxiliary roles of *atû* "doorkeeper," TÚG.LÁ "garment carrier," *nappāhu* "smith," *ušparu* "weaver," *parkullu* "seal-maker," *nuhatimmu* "cook," *zadimmu* "stone mason."

There are enough cultic offices brought together here to consider that these were perhaps all receiving rations, or being considered together for awards or recognition. The *huppû* is among them.

App. 3.15 The Hebrew Bible

Of course, there is nothing like the creatures discussed in this Appendix in the Hebrew Bible, which is very wary of abnormal sexuality. The possibility of the latter in relation to the cult only appears in connection with the *qādēš /qĕdēšāh*, for which see chapter 4. The two stories in Jud 19.22-26 and Gen 19.1-11 are normally interpreted as relating to homosexuality. There has been much written on them recently, because of new studies on this subject, but we are interested in this only in relation to the cult. The viewing of male nakedness in Gen 9.21-23 has intimations of homosexuality. The priest's nakedness which is not to be exposed in Ex 20.26 has this connotation also. None of these examples are cultic.

One of the Hebrew Bible's longest list of prohibited sexual acts, Lev 18.6-23, seems to have no cult connotations, though they are given a religious background: I am the Lord, vs. 6. Maybe this indicates that they were recited in the services of the temple. Lev 18.22 prohibits homosexuality, so a position of someone like the *assinnu* or the like is unthinkable in the Hebrew Bible.

Deut 22.5 prohibits women wearing men's, and men wearing women's garments -- transvestism, but again in a non-cultic context. Nothing is said about them being dancers, but why else would such a thing be done in that society? See discussion on transvestism in Mesopotamia in App. 3.4.

App. 3.16 The wider western semitic world

Some of the characteristics of Ishtar are followed by Astarte in the western Semitic world.[128] In Syria she appears both as a male ᶜṯtr [129] and as her usual female self. Some would characterize this as the androgyny of Astarte, but maybe she is at one time either one or the other. Ch. Virolleaud has found in the Ugaritic onomasticon: ᶜštr-ab and ᶜštr-um, "Astar is father" and "Astar is mother," respectively (Leclant, n. 128, p. 8). For bisexuality in other regions, and in rites which dramatize this, see n. 1. Astarte is important in the Egyptian pantheon, being the "Asiatic goddess."

At Mari, which could be considered in the west Semitic field, the two traditions of Ishtar as male and as female also show up.[130]

App. 3.17 Conclusions

Before summarizing, some perspective is in order. Many of the texts discussed in this section are cryptic; indeed, I think they were meant to be. We must attempt to say about them all that they say about themselves, but no more. We must interpret them as the writers mean for us to, not from our hypotheses. We do not look in these texts for a description of the offices in themselves. The texts are purposely highly stylized, aphoristic, formulaic and ambiguous.

We consider all these titles together, because the various offices are often put together by the ancient scribes; we don't know enough to separate them, if indeed we should. They normally are males, but play a female role, hence their interest for us in this book. They are singers and dancers of a special kind. They are normally found in the Ishtar temple, performing. They carry weapons: the sword, knife, club, razor and others. This is not merely for ceremonial purposes, because these weapons are often found covered with blood, indicating some kind of ritual combat, perhaps, or, less probably, self-inflicted wounds. The weapons identify their masculinity. But they also carry the spindle at times, the sign of femininity, portraying them as hermaphrodite.

These are titles attached to real persons, as shown by the economic text entries, not roles they take on only in the cult. They appear paired with ecstatics and singers on our lists, and these may be some of their characteristics.

Some of these titles go back to Old Akkadian times. These figures represent the authority of Inanna/Ishtar in sexual matters, all of it, femininity and masculinity together, as shown by their being acted together by one type of figure in the drama of the cult. The overall difficulty with this kind of study[131] is that the examples come from different periods, different cities and different genres of texts. If there were an evolution in the character of the offices this kind of study would obscure that. In addition, if late authors or compilers or redactors of the texts did not know the exact meaning of the terms, their conservative classification of them would lead us astray.

We have treated all these titles together because they seem similar. To separate them out we need many more examples, which will be forthcoming as more texts make themselves known.

Notes

1 M. Delcourt, *Hermaphrodite. Mythes et Rites de la Bisexualité dans l'Antiquité Classique.* Paris, 1958; H. Baumann, *Das doppelte Geschlecht. Ethnologische Studien zur Bisexualität in Ritus und Mythos,* Berlin, 1956; Brigitte Groneberg, "Die sumerisch-akkadische Inanna/Ishtar: Hermaphroditos?" *WO* 17 (1986), 25 - 46, from which article came the previous two references.

2 E. Salonen, *Über das Erwerbsleben im alten Mesopotamien*, I. Helsinki, 1970 (*StOr* XLI) 6-10. Using the morphological element -ar of the final syllable of names of professions, he follows A. Salonen in assigning some of these to early Chalcolithic (5600-5000 B.C.) and other elements to middle Chalcolithic (5000-4000 B.C.) times, all but one being professional titles.

3 Many earlier studies of this and previous words are not useful. For instance, G. Meie, *RLA* 2 s.v. "Eunuch" has much unsubstantiated and oversimplified discussion on castration, pederasty and "Kinäden" as an explanation of some of the titles studied here.

4 Römer *Königshymnen* 157, 41.

5 Livingstone *Poetry* No. 38.15.

6 Sag B i 14, MSL SS 1 28, duplicated Sag A i 9, MSL SS 1 18.

7 A.L. Oppenheim, *Or* 19 (1950) 135 n. 1.

8 Especially of the Ur-DN category in Sumerian PNs, see Limet *Anthroponomie* 535ff for lists of names and 315f for notes. UR = *amelu* "man" in several lexical lists in CAD A/2 48b, near bottom.

9 ARM 10 6.5; 10 7.5.25; 80.4.

10 JEN 260.13 (*PBS* III), 880.14.

11 *KAR* 42.29. See Ebeling *MVAG* 23/II 21ff for the study of the full text. *Naru*'s (*RAcc* 44.5 with a *kalû*) and *qadištu's* (in the MA rite studied in App.1) are also found singing these.

12 Starr *Diviner* 21. quoting Goetze Omen No. 47.20.

13 Pallis *Akītu* pl. viii 10-12 = K.9876; see KB 6/2 34 K. 9876 = Zimmerm *Neujahrfest I* 136ff; see CAD K 558a.

14 If GI.GÍD, then *malīlu* or *embūbu* "flute (player)" would fit, but this reading is doubted by CAD M/l 165. The instrument is used in the Tammuz-Ishtar ritual TuL p. 50, 18. A gi-gíd of lapis lazuli accompanies Tammuz as he arises in the Descent of Ishtar 36, CT 15, 47 (K. 162).

15 *RAcc* 115 r.7.

16 W. von Soden, *ZA* 67 (1977) 240 separates *bēlu* "a weapon" from *tillu,* with several meanings. See AHw 1358: *tillu* II; AHw 120 *bēlu* ; CAD A/2 341b: *tillu*. E. Salonen*Waffen* 152f reads *bēlu* for the weapon, with orthographies *be-le-e*, *be-li*, *be-la*, yet note [RAH] *ti-il-li ša kaspi* (ABL 1233 r.3) in a battle scene, and Nergal being called *bēl til-li-e u qa-ša-ti* "lord of weapons and bows" (*BBSt* No. VIII iv 22) would argue for a weapon having this orthography also.

17 LKU 51.18, CAD K 558a. CAD reads *tillu* as does E. Cassin, *Splendeur Divine* 12 n. 8.

18 S. Lackenbacher, *RA* 71 (1977) 40, 16. She understands it as a sort of "bandelettes." (p. 47 n. 6). "Mask" CAD K 558a.

19 In an Ishtar ritual of the temple of Anu at Uruk, *RAcc* 73.16, transliterated 114.

20 *RAcc* 115 r.7; H. Zimmern, *BBR* II 45 = O.R. Gurney, *AAA* 22 (1935) 46 III 2

21 AAA 22.52, 40;64, 4.

22 AAA 22.44, 19.

23 *ABL* 461.2.

24 *šut kakke*, *AAA* 22 (1935) 68,31.

25 Aro *Glossar* 109.

26 Barbara Parker, *Iraq* 23, pl. xvii, ND 2490 + 2609.8, among vessels.

27 *ABL* 268.14, 1233 r.3, trappings of horses; Thureau-Dangin *HCS* 36, also of horses.

28 Salonen *Hippologica* 113.

29 *BBSt* No. 8 iv 21.

30 Ebeling *Glossar NB* 246, some from Gimirru.

31 K. 3438a + 9912, transliterated Menzel *Tempel* II No. 39, l'-11', duplicated by No. 40, K. 9923, both unpublished.

32 According to the restoration of Menzel, but not likely according to CAD H 149a.

33 The phrase sung by the *kurgarrû* "my play is war/battle" is found also in a NA "love lyric" n. 24, a *riksu ša sipittum* "order of lament," BM 41005 iii 12-17, W.G. Lambert *Unity Diversity* 104.

34 The *nāru*'s also utter that shout, E. Ebeling, *Or* NS 17 (1948) 420, 19 in a NA prayer (VAT 13832).

35 A.D. Kilmer, *RLA* VI, 512, §1.3.

36 *WO* 17 (1986) 38 n. 83.

37 Summarized by Moren *Shumma Ālu* 237f; *CT* 39, 44.15, CAD K 360.

38 Moren p. 237, CT 39, 45.32), quoted in J. Botteró and H. Petschow *RLA* IV 461a.

39 Bu 88-5-12, 11, CT 4, 6 r.14, translated P. Jensen *KB* 6/2 47.

40 Moren *Shumma Ālu* op.cit., pp. 217 and 175, respectively.

41 Descent of Inanna 82, CT 15 46 r.2.

42 Frankena *Tākultu* 6 II 33.

43 For an older translation, see E.A. Speiser, *ANET* 107 ff., from *KAR* No. 1 and CT 15 pls. 45-48.

44 Oppenheim suggests that the *assinnu* was impervious to the curses of Ereshkigal (*Or* 19, 1950, 136). For another point of view, see A.D. Kilmer, *UF* 3 (1971) 299-309, especially p. 309. Using the Sumerian forerunner of the tale, she says that Inanna's purpose in going to the Netherworld was to extend her influence there. Enki created two sexless creatures in order to play a trick on Ereshkigal (p. 301). But the special sexuality of the sexless creatures is not explained by this interpretation, in my opinion.

45 L. Cagni, *Das Erra-Epos.* Keilschrifttext, Rome, 1970. Translation, *The Poem of Erra,* Malibu, 1977.

46 R. Otto, *The Idea of the Holy,* Breslau, 1917; München, 1943; (*E.T*, London, 1923), from 9th German editon; M. Eliade, *The Sacred and the Profane,* French, 1946, (*E.T* 1959).

47 John Money and Herman Mosaph (eds.), *Handbook of Sexology,* Amsterdam, 1977, index, s.v. "impotence."

48 *ADD* 914 (K.10477) + 827 (K. 1473) r. 9. F.R. Kraus' reading in B. Landsberger, *Baumgartner* AV 202-3. I was not able to see C. Virolleaud, *ACh* Adad XII.12, another possible example of the female.

49 *ACh Adad* XII.12f, from Groneberg *WO* 17 (1986) p. 36 and n. 72; CAD K 558b; see also C. Frank *ZA* 29 (1915), 200 ; Bezold, *Sitzber. Heidelb.Ak.* 1911, No. 7, p. 18 and n. 1 (not seen by me).

50 CAD K 558b.

51 Livingstone *Poetry* No. 8. r. 14f' = *LKA* 32.

52 K. 3476, CT 15, 44.28 = Pallis *Akītu* pl. VI. The broken name of the instrument is filled in from line 5.

53 *LKA* 32 r. 14, as restored by CAD K 558b.

54 Chap 4, n. 70.

55 Römer *Königshymnen* 165f, AHw, s.v. *patarru*. Equivalence in ASKT 120, 21f, quoted MSL IX 206.

56 *PSD* B s.v. ba-da-ra, p. 18.

57 CAD K 558a, bilingual section.

58 Erra Epic IV 57, and App. 3.2.4.

59 Cohen *Eršemma* No. 97.17 A (p. 74).

60 Römer *Königshymnen* 131, 76. Reisman, *JCS* 25 (1973) 188, 76 leaves it ambiguous who covers the sword with blood. Groneberg *WO* 17 (1986) p. 39 n. 86 follows Farber-Flügge in suggesting self-mutilation. I would rather see it as a "war game," a play-acting. Quite early B. Landsberger, *WZKM* 57 (1961) 13 n. 8 thought of a *simulacre de combat* played by these with a ritual purpose. See App. 3.3.6 for *naš patri* as temple official.

61 K. 5188 + K. 8481, C. Frank, *ZA* 29 (1915), copy p. 198, transliteration and translation p. 197; Langdon *BL* No. 194, 16ff (pl. 61); partially in CAD K 558a, lexical section, with additions.

62 Gragg Kesh Temple Hymn line no. 106, Jacobsen *Harps* 384a understands this as a meat carver.

63 MSL XII 234 iii 8 (*ṭābihu*), and MSL XII 36, 99 respectively; see also igituh 239 which has: LÚ gíri-lá = *ṭa-bi-hu* after *šāqû* "cupbearer."

64 *Erra* IV.57 Or, as CAD Q 312a takes it, the term *nāš patri* describes the *kurgarrû* of line 55. This again brings up the problem that plagues us in this kind of study, whether a term is a title, or a description.

65 *ABL* 1106 r.6, and S. Smith, *First Campaign of Sennacherib* 36, 23, and S. Smith, *Babylonian Historical Texts* pls. 6-7 ii 26.

66 Livingstone *Poetry* No. 37.29' = K 3476 = *CT* 15 43f.

67 K.3438a + 9912 r.8, CAD M/2 66a and 17a.

68 S.N. Kramer, *JCS* 4 (1950) 200, 35f, or "scratch(?)" *ANET* 53b; or "bow down" for the Sumerian counterpart; Gordon *Sumerian Proverbs* 190, 2.19.2.

69 Krecher *Kultlyrik* 215; Gordon *SumerianProverbs* 1.94 3 on ma-la */ru'tum* "male friend," argues that it is female only. Sometimes it is ma-li.

70 ARM 1 28:18.

71 K 3600 + DT 75, Craig *ABRT* I 55 i 10 = K.D. Macmillan *BA* V (1906) 626 and 564f newly studied in Livingstone *Poetry* No. 4.

72 Incantations accompanying the birth of man, J. van Dijk *Or* 44 (1975) 63, 22-4.

73 CT 4, 5:10, *KB* 6/2 42.9.

74 See the large collection of texts by Römer in Beek AV, 219ff; and Sjöberg *ZA*65 (1975) 223ff.

75 Cassin *Divine Splendor* 13, quoting the treaty of Asshurnirari VI with Mati-ilu of Arpad, lines 11f.

76 *SAHG* No. 46, 230f.

77 Or simply, as Sjöberg, "the speech of a woman."

78 See W.H.Ph. Römer, "Randbemerkungen zur Travestie von Deut 22.5," in Beek AV 217-22 for notes on changing man to woman and vice versa, men dressing in women's clothing and vice versa, with a final note on the anthropological meaning of the role change, and a good bibliography.

79 Livingstone *Poetry* No. 38, IM 3252 = VAT 9946 (*LKA* 72) = VAT 10099 (*LKA* 71) = TIM 9 59; the temple Egashankalamma "the house of the lady of all," is the temple of Ishtar in Arbela or a by-name of Emashmash, the temple of Ishtar in Nineveh (p. xxx).

80 OB Proto-Lu (App. 3.2.7); *SLT* 240 which is OB Proto-Lu with some gaps and some variants (line 3 read pi[!] for UD); the NA lexical series Lu = ša IV, above App. 3.2.2, with sag-ur-sag = *assinnu*.

81 Kramer *SLTN* 45.

82 Römer *Königshymnen* 157, 41.

83 Cf. $^{tu-ub}$dub = *m [a-šá]-⌈du⌉šá pir-tim* "act (in some way) on the hair." Nabnitu XXIII.273, MSL XVI 219.

84 Other entries pairing *susbû* with *ramku* are in AHw s.v. *ramku*.

85 Chiera *SRT* 5, 14.

86 Klein *Šulgi* 198, 77f, PBS V 25 v 23, *SRT* I ii 11, *BO* 11 (1954) 175 and n. 32, Falkenstein, *ZA* NF 16 (1952) 70, 77.

87 G. Castellino, *ZA* NF 19 (1959) 120, 84 and notes p. 130.

88 Or is the SAG.UR.SAG the ideogram for *parrû*? (Personal communication from A.D. Kilmer).

89 *li-ṭe4-eb-bi* per G. Giacumakis, *The Akkadian of Alalah* 109; *li-ṭe4-ep-pi* per AHw 1388b.

90 AT 265.4, D.J. Wiseman, *JCS* 8 (1954) 21, copy; *JCS* 13 (1959) 27, transliteration.

91 B. Alster and H. Vantiphour, *ASJ* 9 (1987) 1-43.

92 píl or pi.lá "dirty," K. v.d. Toorn, *Sin and Sanction in Israel and Mesopotamia. A Comparative Study.* Assen, 1985, 29; and T. Jacobsen, in Gordon *Sumerian Proverbs* 461 to 1.83. Gordon took pe-el-lá as raced" p. 212, 10, as did Krecher *Kultlyrik* 103, who gives a range of possibilities: verdrehen, schänden, beflecken, zerstören. Hallo *Exaltation* 88 points out píl/pi-lá "make dirty" and the bilingual root *lu'û* "defile, desecrate."

93 Kang *Drehem* s.v. Index; Falkenstein *Gerichtsurkunden* 120b, 19; Oppenheim Catalogue F 4:13; F.E. Keiser, BIN III, S.T. Kang (ed.), s.v., index.

94 Sjöberg *ZA* 65 (1975) 226 to line 82.

95 Gelb *OAIC* 30.11.

96 Ku-lu-'u KAV 198.8, Ku-lu-u ND 2317.10, B. Parker, *Iraq* 16 (1954) transliteration only, index p. 49.

97 *ADD* 81.3 (ARU 117A, Kwasman NA Legal No. 352b), *ADD* 82.1 (*ARU* 117a, Kwasman No. 352a), envelope of the latter.

98 *KAR* 1 r.6 *ku-lu-'u* -[*u*].

99 The *bīt sābî* seems similar to the *bīt aštamme* (See App. 4, and Sec. 4.16). In a dream omen (*Dream-book* 313) the line "if he go[es to] the *bīt* lú*sābê* (K. 2582 r ii x + 3) is preceded a few lines previously by "if [he goes to] the *bīt aštammi* " (r i x + 11).

100 CT 22 183.9, BM 85500, CAD K 529A.

101 *KAR* 43.3 +, duplicated *KAR* 63.3, Ebeling *ZDMG* 69 (1915) 92.23f; *MAOG* 5/3 16.3.

102 E.F. Weidner, *AfO* 10 (1935-6) 3.21, CAD K 529a .

103 S. Langdon, *AfK* 1 (1923) 23 = K. 9955 + Rm 613 ii 27.

104 Livingstone *Poetry* No. 7.6 = K 1286 = Craig *ABRT* 1 7f.

105 Lambert, *BWL* 83 n. to line 221.

106 The *-anu* could stand for "Hervorhebung, individuellier Vertreter, hypokoristisch-diminutiv," and other possibilities, von Soden *GAG* §56r.

107 *BWL* 218 r iv 3-5; see also App. 4.1.14.

108 *Dream-book* 332, Tab C, Fragment No. 2, 2 ii 1f.

109 OB Lu C5, 33; MSL XII 196.

110 *UET* 3 1506 i 1.

111 *Gilgamesh* VI 4, with *aṣitu* and *agû.*

112 Leemans *Ishtar.* LB 1090, lines 2,26,14.

113 *KAR* 357.28.

114 TuL No. 11, no text given.

115 *Abru*, *ablu*, and *abnu*, variants noted in MSL 3, p. 65 n. 11; see also A VIII/2 MSL XIV 502, 135; other examples of these are in CAD A/1 64 s.v. *abru* C. One could also add the form *amru*, with dialectical -m- for -b-, Lu = ša IV, Sec. 2.4.7.

116 Gragg *Kesh Temple Hymn* 186, 107.

117 172 še-bé-da *e-gu-ú*

173 munus šà-zi-ga ak-a *e-⌈*gi⌉-tum*

Antagal F, MSL XVII 217

If *egītu* is the munus "woman" who ak "did" the šà-zì-ga "lifting up of the heart," it may mean one who becomes sexually excited, as in the examples in Biggs *ŠÀ.ZI.GA* passim. And one of its many equivalences is *egû* = *na-a-ku* "to have sexual intercourse" (CAD E 48, s.v. *egû*, lexical section, last paragraph).

118 *Kesh Temple Hymn* 174, 107. This is to be compared with other "royal" ranks, the gala-lugal and gala-lugal-ra-ús-sa in OB Proto-Lu Sec. 3.3.13, and the lugal-a-rá-ús-sa (CAD L 289a).

119 *Kesh Temple Hymn* lines 106-113, p. 174.

120 *SBH* No. 56 r. 79 f (VAT 276 +).

121 CAD A/1 64 s.v. *abru* C suggests that sag indicates "either a characteristic headgear or hair style." OB Proto-Lu 654a-6 MSL XII 56 has a similar division for the gala: gala-mah, gala-tur, gala-mah-lugal, gala-lugal.

122 W.W. Hallo, *Or* 42 (1973) 236 iv 5 (line 34).

123 TU 146, Pettinato Studi 1/1 (Reisner Telloh).

124 *PSD* B 187a.

125 Pinches *Berens Coll* 103.3.

126 G. Dossin, *RA* 35 (1938) 1-133ff; discussed in Sec. 1.6.2.

127 OBGT XIII 23.

128 J. Leclant, *Syria* 37 (1960) 7-8.

129 A Caquot, *Syria* 35 (1958) 49 n. 2.

130 J. Bottéro, *Le Antiche Divinità Semitiche*. S. Moscati (ed.), 40-42.

131 As pointed out rightly in a personal communication from J. Renger.

APPENDIX FOUR

What Happened In The ès-dam/astammu-House?

4.1 What happened in the èš-dam/*aštammu* -house?
With notes on the (4.2) *anzanīnu*, nimgir-si / *susapinnu*, (4.3)*napṭaru* and *napṭartu*

App. 4.1.1 In what way the èš-dam changes throughout the years, or in what way it remains the same, is of course the question raised for this and all the other terms throughout this study; here only a start is made, by listing the occurrences. We do not want to give the impression that these entries all refer to the same "house." We thus claim only to give the history of the interpretation of the èš-dam/*aštammu* from Early Dynastic Times to late Assyrian times. We can say, however, that the general ambience of the term did seem to remain from the earliest to the latest texts.

App. 4.1.2 The term èš-dam "house of the spouse" goes back to Fara times n. 3 as a PN: gemé-èš-dam.[1] This is a PN of the type gemé-holy place, shown also in gemé-é-eb-gal, gemé-é-gi$_6$-pàr, etc. (Limet *Anthroponomie* s.vv). CAD translates *aštammu* as "tavern, hostel;" and AHw translates "Wirthaus, Gastwirtschaft." Hallo[2] understands it to be the epithet of a temple of Inanna, but later a brothel (p. 74). Benno Landsberger calls it a "Gasthaus mit Herberge."[3] Kramer calls it a "nuptual chamber," and Jacobsen calls it a "bordello, social center."[4] Driver[5] calls it a "temple-brothel" whatever that may indicate. Note the wide range of understanding.

App. 4.1.3 The term èš goes back to Presargonic times among the Ur-Nanshe texts as sacred space. It appears as èš-X, where X is 1) a place name, as èš-gir-su;[6] 2) a place carrying a vessel-name èš-ursub;[7] 3) èš-gal = *ešgallu*, any large temple;[8] 4) èš-èš festival, oft-celebrated in Ur III, Mari, NA, NB and Seleucid times; 5) èš = *eš-šú* "a temple", lexical only;[9] 6) é-éš-dam in an OB list:

111 é-ki-ná
112 é-éš-dam
112a é-dam

Proto-Kagal, MSL XIII 69f (OB)

But I.J. Gelb[10] considers èš as simply a synonym for é-dingir "temple."

The ná "bed" of the é-ki-ná "temple/house of the bed" appears in some Inanna-Dumuzi love songs, and is probably the bed of the sacred marriage, see Secs. 4.22.15.3 and 4.23 passim, and its closeness to the éš-dam may indicate that sexuality is associated with the latter, also. The é-éš-dam seems to be a simple equivalent to éš-dam.

App. 4.1.4 èš cannot be found in the expression *èš-^{d}DN, as é is. There must have been many èš in an area, for the term èš-didli "the several èš" often appears: èš-didli ma-da "the several èš of the land;" [11] èš-didli-é-^{d}nanše "the several èš of the temple of Nanshe," so a part of a larger temple complex, or "the several èš and the temple of Nanshe;"[12] èš is carefully separated from é in this term.

App. 4.1.5 There is a list of 17 èš-dam of Ishtar.[13] The Inanna temple é-éš-dam-kù "holy eshdam house" in Girsu is listed among other Inanna temples in other large cities in RLA.[14] Römer suggests that èš-dam was not its proper name, but a descriptive epithet. The possibility of this kind of interpretation exists all through this study.

App. 4.1.6 é-dam "house of the spouse" starts appearing in Presargonic texts (Urn 25, 29, 31, 32, 33, 35) but according to Solberger[15] é and èš are interchangeable in Ur-Nanshe texts. Its appearance in Proto-Kagal App. 4.1.3, next to èš-dam is to be noted. é-dam appears in the Old Sumerian Förtsch texts from Lagash: 1 container of dark beer is rationed to PN[16] gemé-é-dam (p. 570), to be compared to the gemé-èš-dam, App. 4.1.1, the former not in Limet *Anthroponomie*.

Note Inanna-é-dam in a duplicate list of gods from An-Anum.[17]

App. 4.1.7.1 The èš-dam is a building, indicated by the entry in "Inanna and Enki" where it appears as one of the me's "attributes of civilization," [18] éš-dam-kù "the holy éš-dam" (line 31), followed by another me: nigìn-gar-kù. Later in this document[19] further listing of the me's show the éš-dam with some sexually oriented figures:

39 nam-kar-ke$_4$
40 nam-HUB.DAR
.....
45 amalu$_x$ (AMA$^{?d}$INANNA)
46 éš-dam-kù
47 nigìn-gar-kù
48 x-AN
49 nu-gig-an-na

Inanna and Enki 56

nam-kar-ke$_4$ is "prostitution."AMA.^{d}INANNA appears on an ED List:

72a ningir
73 dam-dingir
74 AMA.^{d}INANNA
75 nu-dingir

ED List E MSL XII 18

and is read AMA.^{d}INANNA = *a-ma-lu* in the emesal vocabulary, MSL IV 18,81. This is continued down to OB Proto-Lu, and there two AMA.^{d}INANNA ranks are listed among other ama- offices, MSL XII 44, 321, 322. It is listed with *ištaritu* in Diri IV 188ff (CAD A/2, 2a). For *amalu*, an office in context with some sexually oriented officiants, see this entry in Sec. 4.13. nu-gig-an-na is *qadištu* of An, see the entry in Sec. 4.11.8, 10.

The èš-dam is Inanna's: é-éš-dam-kù ma-ra-gál "the holy house eshdam is (or, exists) for you (i.e., Inanna)." [20]It is described as a place for love. An Old Sumerian PN: nin-éš-dam-(m)e-ki-ága "lady who loves the eshdam." [21] May we understand "in the eshdam?" Arguments for this are given App. 4.1.11.

The entry ^{d}Nin-in-si-na é-èš-dam[22] as the purpose for one of the expenditures of an Ur III ba-zi text, shows our house related to Nininsina in the Inanna/Ishtar family. An Adad-nirari I text (MA) describing its courtyard refers to an *altammu ša Ištar* as *bīt huruš* "storehouse" of Ishtar.[23]

In the introduction to an Inanna hymn[24] Inanna is described in three successive lines as:

"stepping onto the street (sila)";
a kar-ke$_4$" (*harimtu*, "prostitute");
"stepping into the é-éš-dam"

These are roles which may be considered parallel: the prostitute plies her trade in the street, and Inanna acts as one in the eshdam house. This will be seen further in later Akkadian texts.

In a hymn to Inanna/Ninegalla, the goddess of war, she visits various èš-dam's as a prostitute.[25]

In a difficult passsage in the hymn nin-me-šár-ra of Enheduanna, the en of Nanna [26] rites are described. After the šu-luh "hand-washing" ceremony, the é-éš-dam-kù "the holy eshdam house" is mentioned with an unclear verb. The result is a calmed heart for Inanna. The usage here, while rather obscure, is one that an incantation text might provide.[27]

App. 4.1.7.2 Lovemaking between Dumuzi and Inanna is shown in a balbale, the setting of which is a é "house" (line 11), but context shows that it is a kaš "beer" house (line 7),[28] é-kaš sometimes being parallel to éš-dam, App. 4.1.10.

In a proverb among a group about animals, mostly dogs, from the Sumerian proverb collection[29] a dog enters the eshdam. What he says is obscure, but the dog is disparaged here, perhaps as a way of disparaging the esdam.

App. 4.1.8 Coming to the Akkadian references, one assumes that we are dealing with the same structure in the loan-word *aštammu*, but we really don't know if we can presume the same theology, if one may use this term. And to get enough references we have to range through 1500 years, something that makes us uneasy. A late lexical list of GNs has:

6	é-KASKAL.GÍD^{da-na}ki	[*bi-it be*]⌜*e*⌝-*ri*
7	é-dam ki	[MIN *aš -ta*]*m-mu*
8	é-áš-dam ki	[MIN] MIN

HhXXI MSL XI 14

The *bit beri* is "road station," a GN by itself in OB, Ur III and MB. The é-dam seems to be èš-dam here. The éš became áš in é-áš-dam probably due to the attraction of an Akkadian orthography *ašammu*.

App. 4.1.9 There is eating in the *bīt aštammi.* Its pantry or food storage was referred to in App. 4.1.7.1. A proverb[30] gives the cryptic advice: do not hasten to a *qerītu*-feast in an *aštammu*, lest you be tied with a rope. CAD's entries show that this type of feast may be secular, or be prepared by the gods, or have the gods as guests, or it could be the name of a festival. The warning is obscure, as many ancient proverbs are, but could mean that the addiction to strong drink or the attraction of sexual encounters could keep him there, as if bound by a rope to the place.

App. 4.1.10 T. Jacobsen, in a valuable article on the Inanna and Bilulu tale[31] points out that a parallel to entering an *aštammu* is entering an é-kaš / *bīt šikāri* "alehouse."

This composition says: ú-líl-lá ᵈInanna-kam "it is an ú-líl-lá" (pertaining to the cult) of Inanna.[32] The story is that Inanna entered the éš-dam to seek for the slayer of her lover Dumuzi, and immediately took a seat and determined Bilulu's fate by cursing her. The seat could have been the divine throne from which pronouncements must come. She goes to the éš-dam because such pronouncements are made there.

A Nergal hymn has: "Lord, enter not the é-kaš-a-ka, smite not the old woman who sits beside the beer (to serve it); Lord, enter not the éš-dam, smite not the old man wise in lore?."[33] As above the é-kaš = *bīt šikāri* "alehouse" seems parallel to éš-dam, if not equivalent to it. There is possible violence there. For a possible title for the old woman, cf. *sābītu* "inn-keeper," Sec. 4.16.

App. 4.1.11 In a bilingual text, Inanna/Ishtar is found living at the *aštammu*, where she sits at the door looking out: [ká]-èš-dam-ma-ka d[ú]r/ t[u]š-a-mu-[dè]/[kar]-ke$_4$ mu-lu-mu-zu me-e ši-in-ga-mèn /*ina bāb aštammi ina ašabiya / harimtu rā'imtu anāku* [*ma*] [34] "when I (Inanna/Ishtar) sit at the door of the éš-dam / *aštammu* I am the prostitute who "knows" men (Akkadian: "I am the loving prostitute.").[35] Or, as a similar text quoted by Jacobsen:[36] "O harlot, you set out for the alehouse [as he calls the èš-dam] / oh Inanna, you are bent on going into your (usual) window (namely, to solicit) for a lover." The "woman at the window" motif is prevalent in much of ANE art, especially in the Nimrud ivories; she is a prostitute, and Inanna plays the part of a *harimtu* "prostitute" and the *aštammu* is owned by a *harimtu,* see App. 4.1.12.

The *bīt aštamme* was called é-ki-ag-ga-a-ni "her house of love,"[37] interpreted either as the house which she loves, or the house in which there is love, i.e., sexual love.

App. 4.1.12 In the "Curse of Agade,"[38] among the horrible atrocities against people, towards the end of the myth, is: kar-kid-zu ká éš-dam-ma-na-ka ní ha-ba-ni-ib-lá-a "may your prostitute raise/hang herself at the door of the eshdam."

lá = *šaqû* "raise" or *alālu* "hang", ní = *ramānu* "oneself" still leaves some ambiguity. I would take this kar-kid / *harimtu* as a cultic official because the next line has the officials ama nu-gig and ama nu-bar, i.e., *qadištu* and *kulmašītu*, here called ama, cf. the large number of ama-entries, Sec. 4.8.2.

The cultic situation of the first millenium is shown in a list of Babylonian and Assyrian places of Ishtar worship in a synergism with Nanay (George 38).[39] Deities appearing on the list may be explained as those with whom she shares. In a hymn to the city of Arbela [40] the *aštammu* is given several epithets: *ṣīru* "high," "first in importance," "majestic," etc.; *ekurru šundulu* "broad temple;" *parak ṣiḫāti* "throne dais of delights" (secular, cultic or sexual?)

In a fragment of the NA bilingual Ana Ittišu, there are a number of terms concerning marriage. In one [41] an unknown "he" takes a kar.kid / *harimtu* to his house from a tillá / [*rebītu*] "city square," marries her while she is a *harimtu*, and

éš-dam-a-ni su-mi-ni-in-gur
áš-t [*a-am-ma-ša*] *ú* -[*ti-ra-as-si*]

"gives her back her èš-dam /*aštammu*. This indicates that a *harimtu* owned an *aštammu.* This is close to a line in the Middle Assyrian Laws:

30 *šum-ma aššat amili amīlu lu*
31 *ina bīt altamme lu ina rebēte ... it-ti-ak-si*
MAL §14

"if with the wife of a man a man either in a *bit aštammi* or in the square ... has sexual intercourse." (CAD A/2 473a: *talbete* "outside the city.") This relates the *aštammu* to the low form of sexual encounter, that of the street. This may be why its title in an unpublished text[42] is é-ki-ág-gá "house of love." These may be compared to the prostitute coming into the é-éš-dam in an Inanna hymn, see n. 24.

App. 4.1.13 Because slaves and camels were plentiful due to conquest and tribute, some were given to a ^{mí}*aštammu*[43] Presumably this is a female head of the *aštammu* called an ^{mí}*aštammu*, with a masculine ending.

The term *aštammu* as a title or class of people appears also in an obscure line in a medical commentary [44] [x *k*] *i-gul-lim u* $^{(!)}$*áš-tam-me // ku-zi-ru u ha-rim-tu* The *kigullum* (m.!) is translated as "waif"(?) by CAD K 349b, and the f. form *kigullatu* as "Waise, Witwe" by AHW.[45] The *kuzīru* is "a class of men" in CAD K 6l6b, which lists only this entry. That *aštammu* is paralleled with *harimtu* fits in with Ishtar's role sitting at the door, if it is the religious usage of the term, or the ownership of the house if it is the secular use.

App. 4.1.14 A late Assyrian proverb given by Lambert[46] is good example of the dual nature of the eshdam. It is among other proverbs concerning law-breakers,[102] *kezertu*'s (here *kazratu*), *ṣapparrû*,[47] *šahšahhu* "scandal-monger, slanderer." It concerns a *sinnišānu*, a figure shown in App. 3.9 to be taken from a word for female, but with a masculine ending, thus in some way hermaphrodite, either acting the role or a description of a sexual orientation.

The *sinnišānu* enters the *bīt aštamme* and lifts his hands, and says *igri šá anzanīnu* "my hire goes to the *anzanīnu*." Then he says *atti lu miš-ru-um-ma ana-ku lu meš-lu*. Let's now try to explain this play on words. He lifted his hands in the way of prayer because he was in a place of prayer. He says, presumably to Ishtar, for *atti* is feminine, and regretfully thinking of sexual intercourse: "You are wealth (*mešru*) and I am half (*mešlu*)." Ishtar is rich in sexual wealth, and the *sinnišānu* is half a man. He praises Ishtar in her house. He had entered the *aštammu* because he is a servant of Ishtar.

CAD M/2 128a and A/2 152a emends *mišrumma* to *mešlumma* and translates: "let us (divide) half and half the wages of the matchmaker (?)," understanding *anzanīnu* as "matchmaker(?), pimp(?)." (CAD A/2 152, see App. 4.2.1). CAD understands *sinnišānu* as a eunuch, and I would argue that if so he would not seek out a house for prostitution; a eunuch is not "half" in his sexuality, he is nothing. Gruber[48] accepts CAD's emendation and translates: "suppose you take half and I take half."

One hesitates to "describe" a unique term like *aštammu* with so few and so variegated a list of references. Prostitution happened there, and Inanna/Ishtar was active there in a sexual role. It is not wholly a secular place, for it is "holy." Beer is served there. It has a bad reputation but, ambiguously, some of the cult was performed there.

<u>App. 4.2 *anzanīnu* and nimgir-si / *susapinnu*</u>

App. 4.2.1 Following up the term in the proverb immediately above, outside of lexical references, there are as yet only two others that have been found for the *anzanīnu*: the proverb and one among a list of games.[49] AHw translates "Brautführer" from a supposed similarity to *susapinnu* / nimgir-si. The lexical evidence is:

75 sag.KAŠ$_4$.KAŠ$_4$ *šam-hu-tú* "prostitution"
76 nimgir$^{ni-gír}$si *su-sa-pi-in-nu*
77 níg-mud-BAD an-sa-mul-lum
Erimhus V MSL XVII 70

CAD A/2 144 suggests that *ansamullu* may be related to the *anzaninu*, also close to the *susapinnu* in the lists

356 *an-za-ni-nu* *nap-ṭa-ru*
357 *su-sa-pi-nu* MIN
LTBA 2 1 vi 20, CAD A/2 152a

an -[*za-ni*] *-nu, s* [*u-sa-pi*] *-nu* = *nap-tú-rum*
An IX 75f = Meissner, *BAW* 1, 72:15f in *JESHO* 32 244, (See n. 14)

25 [SAL b] ar-*šu-gál [šab-su-tu] "midwife"
26 [SAL] ⌈x⌉-nu-ak-a *an-za-lil-* [*tu*]
27 [SAL] ⌈x⌉[ ]-[x] *ti-bu-t* [*u*] "elevation"

Lu = ša III ii MSL XII 124

64 [dam-tab-ba] [*tap-pa-tum*]
65 dam-tab-[ba] [*ser-re-tum*]
66 nimgir-a-šà-g[a] *su-sa-pi-* [*nu*]
67 nimgir$_2$-si *su-sa-pi-* [*nu*]
68 li-bi-ir MIN EME.[SAL]
69 ku-li *ib-ru*
Lu = ša III iii MSL XII 126

The latter list is an echo of an OB forerunner

758a mí-ús-sá
759 muru$_5$ (MUNUS.UD.EDIN)
760 nimgir-si
761 ušbar
762 é-gi$_4$-a
---
776 ku-li
---

781 ab-ba

OB Proto-Lu MSL XII 60f

Finally a NA list adds more information:

172	[GÌR].NITA$_2$	*šak-ka-na-ku*
173	[nimgir].si	*su-sa-pí-nu*
174	[lú-nu-ban]da$_3$^{da}	*la-pu-ut-tu-u*
175	ugula	*ak-lu*

Lu = ša I, short recension
excerpt I, MSL XII 101

The last entry may indicate that the *susapinnu* is some sort of leader, as the ideogram NIMGIR = *nāgiru* implies, and the term *aklu* indicates. Traditionally *nāgiru* is "herald" but also some kind of highly-placed leader in NA times, AHw 711a. Or, perhaps in this late lexical list, nimgir-si was put near other leaders because nimgir was part of the title. *Laputtû*, another kind of leader, is equated with *nāgiru* and *hazannu* 'mayor" in an extispacy text.[50]

The equation li-bi-ir (emesal for nimgir) = *nāgiru*[51] in the standard Lu = ša list shows that the scribes apparently neglected the -si. Or, maybe the -si adds a minor element to the term *nāgiru* , something like si = *lamû /lawû* "to go about," or maybe si is the horn which he carries as a weapon.[52]

One cannot tell if in the Lu = ša III entry *tappātum* "female companion, concubine" could be a cultic position; it is similar to the entry ku-li = *ibru* "friend" or "lover," a few lines further on. No cultic connotations could be found for the similar *ṣerretum* "second wife, rival."

In this same Lu = sa III tablet, there are two equivalents of the *susapinnu*, nimgir-a-šà-ga "nimgir of the field," and nimgir-si "nimgir of the si." The ku-li = *ibru* on this tablet might have to do with the bridegroom, as the Aramaic and Syriac offshoots indicate.[53]

In the OB Proto-Lu list the nimgir-si is separated from the é-gi$_4$-a "bride" by ušbar, not the usual "weaver" but "father of the bride," preceded by muru$_5$ = *emu rabû* "brother of the bride" and mí-ús-sa = *emu ṣehru* "son-in-law." Now, considering all the terminology related to leadership and marriage, the nimgir may refer to the one in charge of the weddings, i.e., the master of ceremonies.

Because of the scarcity of references to *anzanīnu* , we have concentrated on the *susapinnu* /nimgir-si (emesal libir-si[54]), a supposedly similar ofice.[55] In the Erimhuš list *susapinnu* is next to *šamhutu*, a kind of prostitution which must be different from *harimtu*. In a proverb, Inanna disguises herself, sneaking away from the lap of Dumuzi and then, having the pearls of the kar.ke$_4$ "prostitute" on, gets men from the eshdam and then: ^{d}inanna nimgir-si imin-zu ki-ná mu-e-da-ak-e[56] "Inanna, you lie with your seven nimgir-si's." And another proverb has it: nitah nimgir-si na-an-ak ní-zu na-an-⌈x x⌉ "do not let a male serve as a nimgir-si, do not [deceive] yourself."[57] So there is a danger in letting a nimgir-si close to the bride.

App. 4.2.2 *Susapinnu* has been considered the origin of the later Talmudic Hebrew *šošbin,* Talmudic Aramaic *šošbina'* , Syriac *šošbina' or šošbinta'* "bridegroom's friend" (m.), "bridesmaid" (f.). But one must not assume that indigenous customs would be similar in the several cultures. We must not impose our ideas of "best man" back onto ancient Mesopotamia. For this reason I am reluctant to read the medieval dea of the ruler's right to sexual intercourse with the bride on her first night, the so called *ius primae noctis* , as Lambert suggests.[58]

App. 4.2.3 The actual practice of the nimgir-si is shown by a valuable source emphasized by Greengus.[59] One must assume that in general the mythical marriage of Inanna and Dumuzi used the customs of an actual marriage ritual. The libir-si's (pl.) bring gifts for the bride (i 21). Greengus suggests that "perhaps all members of the entourage including the groom were called *susapinnu* (op. cit., 69, see n. 82).

Greengus calls attention to the expression ki-ná ...ak as the same as that which describes Ama-ushumgal-anna (a term for Dumuzi) going to bed with Inanna in an Iddin-Dagan "sacred marriage" text[60] though the infixes differ. B. Alster also takes it as an expression for love-making.[61] But Greengus, in conclusion, thinks that this may simply describe the nimgir-si's accompanying the bride and groom to the nuptual chamber. I think that this softens too much the ki-ná ...ak, which indicates what is done in bed in marriage. I would tentatively suggest that this possibly indicates the putative sexual license used by the nimgir-si's, because this idea is in parallel to those (irregular) sexual acts done with major female cultic officials as documented in these pages, criticized mostly in the wisdom literature. Alster has remarked on this possibility, see n. 58.

App. 4.2.4 Meir Malul[62] has a full article on the *susapinnu*, in which he summarizes the evidence, and then extends the discussion. There are in the case of the *susapinnu* : 1) marital aspects, 2) sexual aspects, and 3) official aspects. 1) He is in a relationship to the bride, never the bridegroom. He brings presents to the bride in her nuptual chamber, so he has access to the innermost parts of the bride's quarters.

2) In being admitted to the nuptual chamber, he may exercise liberty with the bride. Inanna/Ishtar herself in her hermaphroditic role is a *susapinnu* with a sharp sword at her side.[63] This reminds us of the *kurgarrû*, who also carries a weapon. Inanna thus armed accompanies the bride, it may be to protect her, it may be to ready herself to fight the simulated battle.

3) He is related to the *napṭaru*, and carries a "lap-weapon." He is an appointed official. He may be a public (court) official.

Malul then looks for "external evidence." He argues "typologically": "[in this case] there is a striking parallelism between the salient functions of his role as culled from the cuneiform sources and the paranymph's role as attested in other cultures and societies." (p. 260) Malul uses examples from the Arab fellahin in the Near East, especially Syria and Palestine, and Berber and Arab tribes in Morocco. Talmudic sources are close to these. Comparing these with cuneiform evidence, he assumes for the latter that the *susapinnu* was probably entrusted with the role of attesting to the bride's virginity, by being present in the nuptual chamber on the wedding night, and by keeping at his disposal the bride's blood-stained *šuš/sippu* to defend her against any future accusation, the *šuš/sippu* ("(Lenden)-Tuch, AHw 1289a) being the etymology of the word *susapinnu*.

The term paranymph, companion of the bride and groom, still seems to fit well into the function of this still poorly-understood office.

4.3 *napṭaru* and *napṭartu*

The *napṭaru* and *napṭartu* of the preceding discussion still have not been accounted for. CAD's "(person with certain privileges)" and AHw's "eine

Art v Gastfreund, Vertrautem" do not help much. J.J. Finkelstein[64] describes the legal aspects of the office, as one who affords protection and refuge for persons, and detention and custody if occasion requires, but this does not relate it to the *bīt aštamme* or marriage themes.

A new survey of past work and the largest collection of references so far is by F.R. Kraus.[65] He brings out clearly the aspect, among others, of staying in a *bīt napṭari* , reminding us of the *bīt aštamme* , although the detaining aspect, as

12'	KAŠ$_4$?-e-ne	*i-šá-ra-a-nu*
12a'	ga-an-ŠEŠ	*nap-ṭa-ru*
12	ga-an-dug$_8$	MIN
14'	ŠEŠ-e-ne	MIN
15'	ga-ur$_5$-ra	*áš-šá-bu*

Lu =ša unplaced fragment iii
MSL XII 141f,

dug$_8$ = *paṭāru* "(ab)lösen, auslösen" (AHw), is not in the latter. We now seek for another aspect, that having to do with the cult.

An astrological commentary [66] equates *napṭaru* with *šá* GIš.TUKUL.UR "the lap-weapon," reminding us of the *kurgarrû* and *susapinnu* carrying weapons. The Laws of Eshnunna § 41[67] describes the *napṭaru* as having beer to sell, and this was a practice in the *bīt aštamme*. The feminine *napṭartu* is described as a *qadištum* of Annunitum, and a Sim'alite, in a Mari letter.[68] Annunitum was a form of Ishtar at Mari.

An obscure related idea comes from a letter[69] of the Hammurapi period in which a woman, with no title,[70] has left (?) the *bīt napṭari* and gone to the *bīt ṣuhāri ša kalamāhi Annunitum* "the house of the boy of the *kalamāhu* of Annunitum," perhaps a cultic place.

Rowton[71] puts these ideas together and calls the *bīt napṭari* "a place where by mutual and reciprocal arrangement a man could put up while visiting another city." The *napṭaru* then would probably be the one to receive the lodging fees. Goetze [72] in commenting on LE §36 understands the root *paṭāru* as "redeem", and *napṭaru* as the place where the redemption was made. In the obscure saying App. 4.1.14 about the *sinnišānu*, the payment goes to the *anzanīnu*, who handles payment as does the *napṭaru*.

Following the thread from the *napṭaru* to the *susapinnu* to possible sexual license with Inanna / Ishtar, sometimes done in the esh-dam house, causes us to await eagerly further references to the *napṭaru*

Notes

1 *ITT* III 6581.3; G. Reisner *Telloh* 162 III 21/28; G. Barton, *Haverford Library* 238, VII, 10; 14 (114); Limet *Anthroponomie* 413ff, and other PNs of the form gemé-é- .

2 W. W. Hallo, *Exaltation of Inanna* note to line 137.

3 B. Landsberger, *OLZ* 1931 135; *Belleten* XIV, No. 53, 240.

4 S.N. Kramer and T. Jacobsen, "The myth of Inanna and Bilulu," *JNES* 12 (1953) 184 n. 68; Kramer, *ANET* 579.

5 G.R. Driver, *The Assyrian Laws*, index.

6 Urn 3 ii 1 and passim.

7 Ent 8 ii 7 and the lexical list:

124	ur-ru-ub DUG	*ur-ru-up-pu*	
125	ur-su-ub DU_6	*ur-ṣu-up-pu*	
126	sur-su-ub "	*ṣur-ṣu-up-pu*	
			Aa 26 (V/1), MSL XIV 410
			cf. Ea MSL XIV 398, 31, 31a

dug 7 imin-bi *ṣur-ṣu-ub-bu*

MSL II 100, d

"vessel with 7 teats" Further notes in Sec. 4.8.2

8 In Neo-Sumerian times the temple of Inanna at Uruk, Sjöberg *Temple Hymns* 29, 198; the Anu-Antu temple in Uruk in Seleucid times, *RAcc* p. 100,33; *KAR* 132.22.

9 A II/4.188, MSL XIV 285, among several é-eš entries.

10 I.J. Gelb, *Orientalia Lovaniensia Analecta* 5,6.

11 M.V. Nikolski, *Dokumenty khoziaistvennoi otchetnosti* ...236 IV 23, in Pettinato *Untersuchungen* I 370 n. 20.

12 Grégoire *Archives* 238, to No. 186 VIII 1.

13 *OECT* 1 pl. 15 iii 8f, CAD A/2 473b.

14 *RLA* V 78; as é-éš-dam-kù in *VAS* 10, 199 iii 33 and in *PBS* 5, 157 I. The list in *VAS* 10, 199 is translated in *SAHG* No. 7, a balbale of Inanna, by A. Falkenstein, and by S.N. Kramer, *ANET* 579; text, translation and commentary are in W.H. Ph. Römer, *Or* 38 (1969) 98.

15 *Sollberger Kupper Inscriptions* 44.

16 Bauer *Lagasch* 156 viii 11, not the é-dam of Urnanshe, according to Bauer p. 451. Also, Pettinato *Untersuchungen* I No. 444, in a wheat allotment.

17 CT 24, 33, 20 and KAV 73.11: ^{d}Inanna-é-dam = *e-dam-me-tu* .

18 *Inanna and Enki* I v 31,33, p. 28.

19 II v 39ff.

20 UMBS 10/4 3 IV 8 = Kramer, *SLTN* 64 IV 13, quoted A. Falkenstein, *ZA* 56 (1964) 119a .

21 *HSS* IV p. 29, quoted by A. Falkenstein, *ZA* 56 (1964) 119.

22 Oppenheim *Catalogue* M19.

23 *KAH* 2 34 17-19, CAD H 256a, bibliography in Grayson *RIM* 1, 150.

24 *JCS* VIII 146, 1-3, Williams College, 3, quoted by E. Bergmann, *ZA* 56 (1964) 3.

25 B. Alster, *ASJ* 5 (1983) 15, n. 39.

26 Hallo, *Exaltation*, the same line as in Kramer *SLTN* 64 iv 3, quoted by A. Falkenstein, *ZA* 56 (1964) 119 (above).

27 In an ershemma, see chap 2, n. 50 and accompanying text.

28 Chiera, *SRT* 31, translated Jacobsen *Harps*...97f.

29 E.I. Gordon, *JCS* 12 (1958) 56, No. 5.77.

30 *BWL* 256.8ff, K. 9050+13457.

31 *JNES* 12 (1953) 185a. He plays down the idea of the *bīt aštammu* being a bordello, and sees it merely as a social center, as the modern coffee house or village inn.

32 [mí]ù-li-li = *zammertu* CAD Z 40a.

33 Jacobsen *JNES* 12 (1953) 185a.

34 SBH No. 56 + No. 155. See now the complete edition of this lamentation called Uru Amirabi, Cohen *Lamentations*, our line being p. 581, line c + 443.

35 CAD H 101a: "one who knows the penis"; for one of the regular descriptions of Inanna, here of her "daughter" the kar-ke$_4$ "prostitute": é-éš-dam-ma gub-ba "standing in the eshdam," *ZA* 56 (1964) 114,3.

36 T. Jacobsen, *Treasures of Darkness* 140, quoting BE XXXI, No. 12 r.10f and *SEM* No. 87, 21 to r.4.

37 A lexical entry, CAD H 473a, from AOB 1 91 n. 3: é-ki-ág-gá.

38 Jerrold S. Cooper, *The Curse of Agade* line 240.

39 K. 1354, Andrew George, *SAA Bulletin* 1/1 (1987) 32ff. There are no èš-dam references, but the temple é-sag-íl is called *bīt lu-le-yá*, "house of my delight," and several times in literature *lalû* could concern sexual delight, CAD L 51.4 and to a lesser extent *lulû* CAD L 242, s.v. *lulu* A, a.

40 Livingstone *Poetry* No. 8.6 = Assyrian Photo 6553 (K 173/4b) = *LKA* 32.

41 Ana ittišu 7 ii 22aff, MSL 1 96f.

42 CAD A/2 473a.

43 Streck *Asb* 76 ix 50 (// 376 ii 3, 132 viii 13) R. Campbell Thompson, *Iraq* 7, fig. 8 viii 13).

44 Labat *TDP* 22.33, and in *STT* 403 40f note CAD K 350a, Landsberger *Date Palm* 24.

45 AHw 474b, referring to *MVAG* 23/1, 44,23. A full discussion of *kigullatu* by Jacobsen in Gordon *Sumerian Proverbs* 477 shows no cultic usage.

46 *BWL* 218 r.iv 3-5

47 sychophant" (Lambert), "a plaintiff who 'distributes' bribes" (O.R. Gurney, *AnSt* 6 (1956) 159, n. to line 40), "Tuschler, der üble Nachrede führt" (AHw 1082a).

48 Gruber *UF* 18 (1986) 146.

49 Hilprecht *Sammlung* 87,3, see *RT* 19, 59, CAD A/2 152, written *anzalīlu*.

50 CT 31, 2 i 12, CAD N/1 115b.

51 5 R 16 iv 35f, CAD N/1 115b.

52 Römer *Königshymnen* 116f.

53 S. Greengus would agree that ku-li and *ibru* indicate companions of the groom, but he would not restrict these terms to "best man," as van Selms, *JCS* 20 (1966) 68 n. 76.

54 MSL IV 31 n. 50 : li.bi.ir.si ⸢ni⸣ níg-a.DU im-túm "her libir-si's brought gifts," presumably marriage gifts for Inanna.

55 A. van Selms, "The best man from Sumer to St. John," *JNES* 9 (1950) 65-75 was a pioneering article in this field.

56 Alster *Šuruppak* 84, BE 30 12 r. 20.

57 Alster, op. cit., line 37, translation Alster; cf. C. Wilcke, *ZA* 68 (1978) 204, 37; WO 4 (1968) 154 and S. Greengus JCS 20 (1966) 68.

58 *BWL* 339 n. to iv.4, following A. Schott, *OLZ* 36, 521 for OB Gilgamesh Epic Tabl 2 iv, an obscure section. Lambert's referral to Herodotus I, 199 is not useful, because this has nothing to do with the first night, and, besides, the supposed custom is unworkable, as shown in Sec. 4.20.

59 Kramer *SLTN* 35, transliterated and translated S.N. Kramer, *PAPS* 107 (1963) No. 3, 497ff, Greengus op. cit. 69; Jacobsen *Harps*...20f.

60 Chiera *SRT* 1, 34.

61 Alster *Šuruppak* 84.

62 Meir Malul, "Susapinnu," *JESHO* 32, 241-278.

63 VAT 276, *SBH* No. 56, p. 106, 58f, CAD Z 63a, lexical section of *zaqtu*.

64 *Landsberger AV* 238.

65 *RA* 70 (1976) 165-172.

66 K. 4336 ii 11, *AfO* 14 pl. 7, CAD N/1 324b, cf. Hh VII A 15, MSL 6, 85.

67 *LE* §41; R. Yaron leaves it ambiguous whether the *sabitum* sells the beer to or for him. R. Yaron, *The Laws of Eshnunna.* Jerusalem-Leiden 1988, but D.J. Wiseman *BSOAS* 33 (1970) 384-5 criticizes some of his interpretations. Goetze inderstands it that the *sabitum* sells it for him.

68 Dossin, ARM 10 No. 59 r.2-4. He translates "concubine (?)."

69 *PBS* 7 101.13, CAD N/1 325b.

70 It may be *sinnišat bīt napṭari* "woman of the *napṭaru*-house."

71 M.B. Rowton, *JNES* 21 (1962) 280b.

72 A. Goetze, *The Laws of Eshnunna* 98, note.

APPENDIX FIVE

Functionaries Auxiliary to the Mesopotamian Cult

For Hebrew Bible Cult Auxiliaries, see Sec. 1.5

There are many officials whom we know best in the non-cultic arena, but who nevertheless appear as *sa* DN, or doing some action in the temple or other sanctuary room. A representative list would be:

1 ab-ba-é-gal, Sec. 3.3.2
2 a-gil-li "towman?" of the Lady of Eturkalamma. *Unity and Diversity* 116y
3 agrig / *abarakku* "temple steward," Sec. 1.22.1
4 agrig-ezem "administrator of the festival," Sec. 3.3.1
5 (a)lahhinu "miller" but the entries often do not show this function; App. 1, *KAR* 154 r. 12; CAD A/1 294ff
6 ARA$_5$ /*ararru* "miller," Sec. 1.2.6; mí-àra, Sec. 2.3.13
7 *atû*, see ì-du$_8$
8 *atû rabû* / *atugallu* / *nidugallu,* see ì-du$_8$-gal-lum
9 bahar$_2$, see *paharu*
10 bappir, see *sirāšû*, index
11 *bēl piqitti*, temple official, AHw 120, 19c
12 bur-gul see *parkullu*
13 dím, see *itinnu*
14 dub-alal-urudu "copper tablet scribe," Sec. 3.3.2
15 *endubbu* / EN.ME.MU "cook," sometimes "temple cook," Sec. 1.26
16 engar / *ikkaru* "farmer" of é-Shu-Sin, Reisner *Telloh* No. 59
17 engiz / *engiṣu* "cook," sometimes "temple cook" but see Secs. 1.23, 3.3.2
18 *engû* "cook"
19 *gallābu* /*tu* / šu-i "barber," AHw 275,4
20 ga$_5$-šu-du$_8$ / sagi$_x$, see *šāqû*
21 *guennakku*, Sec. 1.10.7
22 *guzalû* / *ītu* "throne carrier," AHw 300,2
23 *hazannu*:*hazannu ša bīt* ^{d}*Nabû*, ABL 65.12, K. 629, a *hazannu* at a sacrificial scene, and similar cultic functions in CAD H 165b.
24 ì-du$_8$ / *atû* "doorkeeper," ì-du$_8$-gal-lum / *atû rabû* `/ *atugallu* or *nidugallu* NB; AHw 786f
25 igi-du$_8$, Sec. 3.3.2
26 *ikkaru,* see engar
27 *išparu*, see *ušparu*
28 *itinnu* / šitim "builder, architect," AHw 404,2
29 KA-ninda, responsible for bread, Sec. 1.37.1
30 *kaparru* / *tu* "shepherd," Sec. 3.14
31 *karkadinnu* / SUM.NINDA, "a baker or cook,"found in the temple in OB Alalakh, NA, and NB, CAD K 42b.
32 kaš-lul, see *šāqû*
33 ka-zì-da/*kaṣṣidakku* and other orthographies, responsible for flour Sec. 1.37.1
34 *mēlulû* "player," in cultic context, CAD M/2 17a

35 *mubarrû* "member of temple personnel," CAD M/2 158b
36 *mukīl appāte* "rein holder," Sec. 2.3.16
37 *mummillu* / *eltu* "dancer," Secs. 2.25.1, 2.25.2
38 *muraqqû* / *itu* "perfume maker,"
39 *mušākil iṣṣurē,* Sec. 3.28
40 MUŠEN.DÙ, see *ušandû*
41 *nāgir* / *tu* / nimgir "herald," App. 4.2.1
42 *nappāhu* / SIMUG "smith," App. 3.14
43 *nāqidu* "shepherd," AHw 744, 2c
44 *nāš patri* "dagger carrier," App. 3.3.6
45 *nidugallu*, see ì-du$_8$-gal-lum
46 lú-níg-ág "measurer of things (?)" Sec. 3.3.2
47 LÚ.NINDA, various suggested NA readings are not convincing; see note.
48 LÚ.NIR.GAL, reading not certain, see note below
49 *nuhatimmu* / MU "cook," CAD N/2 315 4'b', App. 3.14
50 *pahhāru* / bahar$_2$, Sec. 3.3.2
51 *parkullu* / *purkullu* / BUR.GUL "seal maker," App. 3.14
52 *qīpu* / TIL.LA.GÍD.DA and other signs. Usually the head of a land area or a city, but also of a temple Sec. 2.4.3
53 *rab bānî* "master builder," Secs. 1.40, 2.4.7
54 *rab ginae*, MA, KAH 2 64,3
55 rá-gab/ *rakbu* Charpin Clergé 85, Sec. 2.3.13
56 *raqqû* / šim-sar "perfumer," Sec. 3.3.4
57 sa$_{12}$-du$_5$, see *šassukku*
58 *sandû*, see *ušandû*
59 *sirāšû* / kul-lum / ŠIM x GAR (lùnga, bappir) / ŠIM, ŠIM x A, "beer brewer," Sec.1.2.6; Oppenheim Beer 44 n. 41 refers to *sirāšû* in the cult at Mari and in Seleucid times
60 *ṣāhit šamni* / Ì.SUR, "preparer of oil," often simply *ṣāhitu*; in the temple, AHw 1075 s.v. *ṣāhitūtu*
61 šabra / *šabrû,* an administrator of state and temple
62 *ša endišu,* "one who provides the *endu*, a spice used in the cult, Ebeling Stiftungen VII.I.6, van Driel Cult 184
63 *ša kiturrišu* "stool bearer," Ebeling Stiftungen p. 26, 18
64 *ša muhhi bīti* "the one over the temple," Ebeling Stiftungen VIII.14
65 *ša muhhi šahūri* "the one over the *šahuru* - part of the temple," Ebeling Stiftungen VIII.15
66 *šandabakku* / gá / pisan-dub-ba "archivist, accountant" of Nanna, also *gudapsûm*, OB Charpin Clergé 48, 121; Sec. 4.11.5
67 *šāpiru* / UGULA, in charge of food and other administration within temple, AHw 1172f
68 *šāqû* / *ītu* "butler," "cupbearer," KAS.LUL / SU.SILA.DU$_8$ AHw 1182, 1179
69 *šassukku* and *šassukkatu* / sa$_{12}$-du$_5$, "Katasterleiter," "Buchführer"
70 *šatammu* "administrator," and in nB especially "temple administrator," M. Gallery, AfO 27 (1980) 1-36, van Driel *Cult* 182
71 *šu ('i) ginakku* "barber" šu-(i)-gi-na, Secs. 1.7.2, 1.7.8
72 *šuhaddaku* / šu-ha-ud-da of Nanna, UET V 411 (U.7795g), Charpin Clergé 119, seal, a type of fisherman

73 šu-i, see *gallābu*
74 ŠU.SILÀ.DU$_8$, see *šāqû*
75 *tārītu* "nurse," OB and NA, AHw 1330a
76 *tīr bīti* "court attendant,"NB, chap 3 p. 22
77 TÚG.LÁ "garment carrier," App. 3.14
78 *ṭābihu* CAD M/2 s.v. *mubarrû* 158d; AHw 1376b, attached to the gods, Erra I 4.12.
79 *ṭupšarru* Sec. 1.45; AHw 1396A.8, of the temple
80 ub$_x$-kug-ga Sec. 3.3.2
81 ugula-é "administrator"
82 ugula-luhša "food administrator, (?)" Sec. 3.3.2, Bauer *Lagasch* 126
83 (*u*)*šandû* and other orthographies "fowler," Sec. 3.28
84 *u/išparû* "weaver," App. 3.14
85 *zadimmu* "stone mason," App. 3.14
86 *zazakku* /DUB.SAR.ZAG.GA a scribal office, found in the Ekur temple, TCL 9 136.7, CAD Z 75b

Notes

5 *alahhinu*. In NA he often receives animals or foodstuffs; he engages in temple repair, CAD A/1 294ff; he is in charge of locks and keys, or garments and jewelery of the gods, of utensils of the temple, van Driel, *Cult* 183.

24 ì-dug$_8$ and ì-dug$_8$ gal-lum. ì-dug$_8$-èš "doorkeeper of the esh-house" Sec. 3.3.2; often apears with *kisalluhhu* "courtyard purifier," CAD K 419ab. Among cultic personnel, described as *ramkut* Eriškigal *u bītat ilāni* "the purifier of Erishkigal and the houses of the gods," Reiner *Thwarts* 4, in Nabonidus' dedication of his daughter to the *entu*-ship, Sec. 1.19.7. This office can be of several deities: Utu TCL 10 37.4, CAD A/2 517; Ninurta *ADD* 50.9; of the *bīt akīti ša Bēlti ša Uruk* "the New Year's House of the Lady of Uruk" YOS 7 89:2; of the *makkūru* "treasury" of Anu BRM 2 49.1, Seleucid times. In a Stiftung the *nidugallu* appears among a wide range of other offices: *šangû*, scribe of the temple, *galamahhu*, *ša muhhi šahūri* (part of a temple), NIR.GAL, *šāqû*, Ebeling *Stiftungen* 30.10. The mí-ì-dug$_8$ of *Iraq* 7 56 A982, A987 seem not to be in a cultic setting.

30 *kaparru*. There is a PN *kaparru* of Tammuz, who takes part in a ritual for healing a sick man by giving a "word" to Tammuz LKA 70 i 11, TuL 49,9.11. Food offerings are set out for him the next day, including *mirsu*, often used as an offering to deities. Other recipients are *zabbu*, *zabbatu*, *mahhû*, *mahhītu*.

43 *nāqidu*. A *nāqidu* brings animals before the god in a MB list BE 14 132.3, CAD N/1 334a. In NB Uruk there is a *nāqidu ša Bēlti ša* Uruk "of the lady of Uruk" YOS 7 7:61 and elsewhere, CAD N/1 334b.

47 LÚ.NINDA ND 2489 ii 6, 20, *Iraq* 23 (1961); Deller used to read *hunduraya Or* NS 33 95, but now reads *lahhinu*, SAA V, 23 n. 81

48 NIR.GAL Ebeling *Stiftungen* VIII.5.16; *mu'irru* "herald," van Driel *Cult* 185, but the reason escapes me.

52 *qīpu*.. Appears with *šatammu* (see notes on No. 70), with *tupšar bit ili* (ABL 476.28), and with *šangû* (CAD Q 267a). Over two temples: *qīpu bīt* Nabû *bīt* Ninurta, ND 5550.36, in van Driel *Cult* 182; Ebeling *Stiftungen* VIII.7

61 šabra, similar to the sanga / *šangû* but without the sometime cultic duties of the latter, see Sec. 3.3.10. From ED to NB times. H. Waetzoldt: an

administrator of palace and temple *WO* 11 (1980) 137a finding that in Ur III times sanga and šabra seem to be used, one at one temple and one at another, perhaps filling approximately equal roles. We could compare:

37	ÍD SANGA
38	ÍD SABRA

MSL XI 133 r. vii (OB), collations G.J.P. McEwan, *WO* 11 (1980) 163

A long list of PNs šabra's is given by Gregoire *Archives* 131-3; some of the associated gods are ^{d}nin-ur$_4$-ra, ^{d}šará, ^{d}nanna, ^{d}nin-šubur.

66 gá/pisan-dub-ba / *šandabakku* was found in a high position in the ration list of YOS V 163 (above, 2.23). He can be listed as *šandabakkum* of Nanna YOS V NO. 46, Charpin Clergé 47.92. He can also bear the title of *gudapsû* of Nanna UET 1 No. 304, No. 149; Charpin *Clergé* 121, 122 and have a son who is a *šandabakkum* and *gudapsûm*. Charpin concludes (op. cit., p. 273) that the *šandabakkum* office was exercised by a member of the college of the *gudapsûm*.

67 *šāpiru* PA.É's in Sargonic times, B.R. Foster, Or 51 (1982) 354; lú-maš-kán-ŠABRA^{ki} read Maškan-šapir ARM 2 725; PA É ^{d}MUŠ, a scribe of the temple of Ishtar in a MB/OB poem. *JAOS* 103 (1983) 31,43 (Kramer Festschrift).

69 *šassukku* Listed in both scribal and temple categories. sag-dùn, AHw 1194b. In an ershemma, Ninisina is sa$_{12}$-du$_5$-mah Cohen *Ershemma* No. 171.3, p. 100. dub-sar-a-šà-ga "scribe of the field" Lu =ša I 143, MSL XII 99. Following *zazakku*, a palace and temple administrator, before *pašīšu, nešakku*, Igituh 101. Simply equivalent to *ṭupšarru* "scribe" LTBA 2, 11 I 11.

70 *šatammu* Among his many administrative duties were those of temples. He is often mentioned with *qīpu* and *ērib bīti's*. A ^{lú}*šatam ekurri* is found at Sippar, Nippur, and Babylon in a NA tablet DT 1, a series of pieces of advice to the king, with some of the phraseology like the protases and apodoses of omens, BWL 114, 56. See Landsberger AV 343ff. A *šatammu* of Der is found in a list of jewelry, horses, military apparatus and military ranks, *ADD* 1040.18f (unpublished). This rank is in Der also in ND 5545.57, *Iraq* 21, 53. *šatammu ṣīru ša* ^{d}Asshur AKA 32,36 could be "chief *šatammu*" or an honorific title.

A NB barrel cylinder of Marduk-apla-iddina III date was found at Kalha (Nimrud), brought there from Uruk: paraphrasing: If anyone in the future plans to rebuild Eanna (temple of Ishtar at Uruk), whether a king, a king's son, a *qīpu*, a *šaknu*, a *šatammu* or a *hazannu* "let him inspect this inscription." ND 2090.40, C.J. Gadd, Iraq 15 (1953) pls. 9-10, transliterated and translated 123-4.

T`he ^{lú}*šatammu* of Der above was father of a ^{lú}*šangammāhu* of King Ashurnasirpal and son of another *šatammu* ND 5545.59, colophon of a hemerology. P. Hulin, Iraq 21 (1959) pls. XIV-XV, transliterated and translated 46-53.

On lexical lists, the *šatammu* appears several times described *ša bīt unāte* "of the house of tools, utensils." Igituh 198; in a

Silbenalphabet Landsberger AV 23, 40; Lu = ša I 138, 138a, MSL XII 98; these could be for the temple, but there is no way of telling, cf. AHw 1423, 8, a.

BIBLIOGRAPHY AND ABBREVIATIONS

Note: The abbreviations and sigla with a few exceptions are those used in the *Chicago Assyrian Dictionary* S-volume, the *Pennsylvania Sumerian Dictionary* B-volume, and The Society of Biblical Literature's "Instructions for Contributors," *SBL Membership Directory and Handbook* 1991, 196-210, with a few additions.

A - Istanbul Eski Sark Müzesi Tablets.

Aa - Lexical series á A = *nâqu,* MSL 14.

AAA - *Annals of Anthropology and Archaeology*, Liverpool.

AASOR - *Annual of the American Schools of Oriental Research,* New Haven, etc.

AB - *Assyriologische Bibliothek.*

AbB - see Kraus.

ABL - R.F. Harper, *Assyrian and Babylonian Letters Belonging to the Kouyunjik Collection of the British Museum*, London and Chicago, 1892-1914. Updated and corrected by Parpola LAS.

ABRT - see Craig.

ACh - C. Virolleaud, *L'astrologie chaldéenne, le livre intitulé "enuma (Anu)* ^{ilu}*Bel" publié, transcrit et traduit.* 1905-12.

Acta Sumerologica - ...see ASJ

ADB - C.H.W. Johns, *An Assyrian Doomsday Book or liber censualis of the district round Harran; in the seventh century B.C.* AB 17, Leipzig, 1901; see Fales *Censimenti* for updated study.

ADD - C.H.W. Johns, *Assyrian Deeds and Documents ... 7th century B.C.,* Cambridge, 1898-1923. Additions in *AJSL* 42 (1925-6).

AfK - *Archiv für Keilschriftforschung*, continuing as AfO.

AfO - *Archiv für Orientforschung*, Gräz, continuing AfK. AfO Bei 4, see Weidner; AfO Bei 11, see Shurpu; AfO Bei 12, see Weidner; AfO Bei 17, see Landsberger Date Palm.

AHw - *Akkadische Handwörterbuch,* Wiesbaden, 1965-81.

AIPHOS - *Annuaire de l'Institut de Philologie et d'Histoire Orientales et Slaves,* Brussels.

AJ - *The Antiquaries Journal,* London.

Aistleitner Wörterbuch - J. Aistleitner, *Wörterbuch der ugaritische Sprache* Berlin, 1963.

AJA - *American Journal of Archaeology*, New York, Princeton, etc.

AJBI - *Annual of the Japanese Biblical Institute*, Tokyo.

AJSL - *American Journal of Semitic Languages*, continuing *Hebraica* ; continued as *JNES.*

AKA - E.A.W. Budge and L.W. King, *The Annals of the Kings of Assyria,*, London, 1902.

Akitu - see Pallis

ALA - see Pedersen, *Archives.*

Alalakh - see Wiseman.

Alberti Pompaonio Pre-Sargonic - A. Alberti and F. Pompaonio, *Presargonic and Sargonic ;* Studia Pohl Maior, 13, Rome, 1986.

Albright ARI - W.F. Albright, *Archaeology and the Religion of Israel*, Garden City, 1959^5.

Albright FSAC - W.F. Albright, *From the Stone Age to Christianity* , Garden City, 1957^2

Alster Shuruppak - B. Alster, *Instructions of šuruppak,* Copenhagen, 1974 (Mesopotamia, 2).

American Philosophical Society - see PAPS.

AMTR - C. Thompson, *Assyrian Medical Texts,* London, 1923.

An An = Anum Godlist - unpublished.

Ana ittišu - List of excerpt sentences, MSL I.

ANET - J. Pritchard (ed.), *Ancient Near Eastern Texts Relating to the Old Testament,* Princeton, 1950-55.

ANEP - J. Pritchard (ed.), *The Ancient Near East in Pictures,* Princeton, 1954.

AnOr - Analecta Orientalia, Rome.

AnSt - *Anatolian Studies*, London.

AO - Tablets in the Musée du Louvre.

AOAT - Alter Orient und Altes Testament; 1, see von Soden AV; 2, see Hunger; 4/1, see Berger Neubab; 5/1-2, see Parpola; 12, see Römer; 16, see de More; 22, see Gordon AV; 24, see KTU; 202, see Noort Mari; 205, see Mayer; 211, see Delsman Kanaan; 216, see Tsukimoto Totenpflege; 223, see Tropper; Sondr. 33/33A, see Borger.

AoF - *Altorientalische Forschungen*, Leipzig, 1893-1906.

AOS - American Oriental Series; for AOS 32, see Oppenheim Catalogue.

Arcari ED List A - E. Arcari, *La Lista di Professioni, "Early Dynastic List A,"* Napoli, 1982.

ARM - *Archives Royales de Mari,* Paris.

ARMT - *Archives Royales de Mari. Texts in transliteration and translation,* Paris.

Arnaud, Emar - Daniel Arnaud, *Recherches au pays d'Aštata, Emar VI.I, 2: textes sumériens et accadiens, planches,* Paris, 1985.

Aro Glossar - J. Aro, *Glossar zu den mittel-babylonischen Briefen,* StOr 22, Helsinki, 1957.

ArOr - *Archiv Orientální,* Prague.

ARU - J. Kohler and A. Ungnad, *Assyrische Rechtsurkunden*, Leipzig, 1913.

AS - Assyriological Studies, Chicago; AS 5, see Piepkorn; AS 11, see Jacobsen; AS.11, see SKL; .AS 12, see Lamentation over Ur; AS 16, see Landsberger AV; AS 21, see Gelb.

Asher-Greve - Old Sumerian, Julia M. Asher-Greve, *Frauen in altsumerischer Zeit,* Malibu, 1985; Bibliotheca Mesopotamica, 18.

ASJ - *Acta Sumerologica*, Hiroshima.

ASKT - P. Haupt, *Akkadische und sumerische Keilschrifttexte, AB* 1, Leipzig,1881-2.

ASOR - American Schools of Oriental Research.

Assur Photo - Berlin Museum.

Assurbanipal - see Streck.

AUCT - Andrews University Cuneiform Texts I, see Sigrist Horn.

Atra-hasis - see Lambert Millard.

BA - *Beiträge zur Assyriologie,* Leipzig.

Bab - *Babyloniaca*, Paris.

Bagh Mitt - *Baghdader Mitteilungen*, Berlin.

Balaam - see Rouillard.

Balag - see Cohen.

Barnett *Reliefs* - R. Barnett (text) and W. Forman (selection and photography), *Assyrian Palace Reliefs,* London, 1970.

Barton Haverford - G.A. Barton, *Haverford Library Collection of Cuneiform Tablets or Documents from the Temple Archives of Telloh,* London, 1905-14.

BASOR - *Bulletin of the American Schools of Oriental Research,* New Haven, etc.
Batto Women - B.F. Batto, *Studies on Women at Mari*, Baltimore, 1974.
Bauer Lagasch - J. Bauer, *Altsumerische Wirtschaftstexte aus Lagasch,* Studia Pohl, 9. The Förtsch texts, from VAS XIV, Rome, 1972.
Baumgartner AV - *Hebräische Wortforschung, Festschrift zum 80. Geburtstag von Walter Baumgartner,* VT Sup 16, Leiden, 1967.
BAW - see Meissner.
BBR - H. Zimmern, *Beiträge zur Kenntnis der babylonischen Religion,* Leipzig, 1901.
BBSt - L.W. King, *Babylonian Boundary Stones*, London, 1912.
BDB - F. Brown, S.R. Driver and C. A. Briggs, *Hebrew and English Lexicon of the Old Testament.*
BE - Babylonian Expedition of the University of Pennsylvania, Philadelphia.
Beek - AV M.S.H.G. Heerma van Voss et al (eds.), *Travels in the World of the Old Testament* (M.A. Beek Festschrift), Assen, 1974
Belleten - *Türk Tarih Kurumu, Belleten.*
Ben-Tor Cylinder Seals - Amnon Ben-Tor, *Cylinder Seals of Third-Millenium Palestine,* 1978. BASOR Supplement Series, 22, Cambridge, MA.
Ber - *Berytus*, Beirut.
Berens - see Pinches.
Berger Neubab - Paul-Richard Berger, *Die Neubabylonische Königsinschriften,* AOAT 4/1, Neukirchen-Vluyn, 1973.
Berlin - see VAT.
Berlin Enmerkar - A. Berlin, *Enmerkar and Ensuhkešdanna*, Philadelphia, 1979.
Bertholet AV - W. Baumgartner et al (eds.), *Festschrift Alfred Bertholet,* Tübingen, 1950.
Bezold Catalogue - Carl Bezold, *Catalogue of the Cuneiform Tablets in the Kouyunjik Collection of the British Museum*, London, 1889-99.
BHH - B. Reicke and L. Rost (eds.), *Biblisch-Historisches Handwörterbuch*, 4 vols. Göttingen, 1962-79.
BHS - *Biblia Hebraica Stuttgartensia,* Stuttgart, 1967/77.
BiAr - *The Biblical Archaeologist*, New Haven, etc.
BiblReal - *Biblisches Reallexikon*, Tübingen, 1937.
Biggs - Abu Salabikh Robert D. Biggs, *Inscriptions from Tell Abu Salabikh,* Chicago, 1974, OIP 99.
Biggs ŠÀ.ZI.GA - R. Biggs, *ŠÀ.ZI.GA,* TCS 2, Locust Valley, 1967
BIN - *Babylonian Inscriptions in the Collection of J.B. Nies,* BIN 8, see Hackman.
BiOr - *Bibliotheca Orientalis*, Leiden.
Birmingham - see Watson.
Bit Rimki - see Laessøe.
BL - see Langdon.
BM - Numbers of the tablet collection at the British Museum, London.
de Boer Fatherhood - P.A.H. deBoer, *Fatherhood and Motherhood in Israelite and Judaean Piety*, Leiden, 1974.
Böhl - see LB.
Böhl AV - see Symbole Böhl.
Boissier Choix - A. Boissier, *Choix de Textes relatifs à la divination assyro-babylonienne,* Geneve, 1905.
Boissier - DA A. Boissier, *Documents assyriens relatifs aux présages*, Paris, 1894-9.

Borger Esarh - R. Borger, *Die Inschriften Asarhaddons, Königs von Assyrien*, Graz, 1956.

Borger HKL - R. Borger, *Handbuch der Keilschriftliteratur*, Berlin, I, 1967; II.

Borger Zeichenliste - R. Borger, *Assyrisch-babylonische Zeichenliste* 4, Auflage. Neukirchen-Vluyn, 1988; AOAT Sondr 33/33A.

Breuil Old Stone - H. Breuil and R. Lantier, *The Men of the Old Stone Age,* New York, 1965 (Paris, 1959).

British Museum - see BM, Bu., CT, DT, 83-1-18, etc. K., Sm.

BRM - *Babylonian Records in the Library of J. Pierpont Morgan* I-IV, New Haven.

Brooks Moral Practices - B.A. Brooks, *A Contribution to the Study of the Moral Practices of Certain Social Groups in Ancient Mesopotamia,* Leipzig, 1921.

Brussels - see AIPHOS, Speelers.

BSOAS - *Bulletin of the School of Oriental and African Studies,* University of London.

BTB - *Biblical Theology Bulletin*, Rome.

Brünnow - R.E. Brünnow, *A Classified List of Cuneiform Ideographs,* Leiden, 1887-89.

Bu - Tablet numbers in the E.A.W. Budge collection at the British Museum.

BuA - see Meissner.

Buis Leclercq Deut - P. Buis et J. Leclercq, *Le Deutéronomie,* Paris, 1963.

van Buren Figurines - E.D. van Buren, *Clay Figurines of Babylonia and Assyria*, New Haven and London, 1940.

Burl Stone Circles - A. Burl, *The Stone Circles of the British Isles,* New Haven and London, 1976.

BWL - see Lambert.

BZ - *Biblische Zeitschrift*, Paderborn.

CAD - *Chicago Assyrian Dictionary*, Chicago, 1956.

Cagni Erra - L. Cagni, *L'epopea di Erra.*

Cagni Poem Erra - L. Cagni, *The Poem of Erra.* Malibu, 1977 (*Das Erra-Epos*, Rome 1970).

CAH^3 - *Cambridge Ancient History*, 3rd edition. Cambridge, 1970 and later.

Cah Hist Mond - *Cahiers d 'Histoire Mondiale* .

Caplice Namburbi - R. Caplice, "Namburbi Texts in the British Museum"*Or* 34 (1965) 105-131; 36 (1967) 1-38, 273-298; 39 (1970) 111-151; 40 (1971) 133-183.

Cassin Divine Splendor - Elena Cassin, *La Splendour Divine*, La Haye, 1969.

CBS - Tablet numbers in the University Museums of the University of Pennsylvania, Philadelphia.

CH - Codex Hammurapi. Translated T.J. Meek, *ANET* 163-180 and A. Finet, *Le Code de Hammurapi.* Paris, 1973.

Charpin Clergé - D. Charpin, *Le Clergé d'Ur au Siècle d'Hammurabi,* Genève-Paris, 1986.

Chicago - see AS, OIP.

Chiera - see SEM, STVC, and directly below.

Chiera SRT - E. Chiera, *Sumerian Religious Texts*, Upland (Pennsylvania), 1924.

Chiera STA - E. Chiera, *Selected Temple Accounts from Telloh, Yokha and Drehem. Cuneiform Tablets in the Library of Princeton University* , Philadelphia, 1922.

CIS - *Corpus Inscriptionum Semiticarum*, Paris, 1881.

Clay PN - A.T. Clay, *Personal Names from Cuneiform Inscriptions of the Cassite Period* , YOS [Res.] 1, New Haven, 1912.
Cohen Balag - M.E. Cohen, *Balag-Compositions*, Malibu, 1974 (SANE 1/2).
Cohen Ershemma - M.E. Cohen, *Sumerian Hymnology, The Eršemma*, Cincinnati, 1981.
Cohen Lamentations - Mark E. Cohen, *The Canonical Lamentations of Ancient Mesopotamia*, 2 vols., Potomac, 1988.
Colophones - see Hunger.
Cook Zeus - A.B. Cook, *Zeus,* Cambridge, 1914.
Cooper Curse - Jerrold Cooper, *The Curse of Agade*, Baltimore and London, 1983.
Craig ABRT - J.A. Craig, *Assyrian and Babylonian Religious Texts*, Leipsig, 1895-97, AB 13.
Crozer - Tablet numbers in the Crozer Collection at the Colgate Rochester Divinity School, Rochester, New York.
CRRA - *Compte rendu, Rencontre Assyriologique Internationale.*
CT - *Cuneiform Texts from Babylonian Tablets in the British Museum*, London.
CTA - A. Herdner, *Corpus des Tablettes en cunéiformes alphabétiques*, MRS 10, Paris, 1963.
CTN - Cuneiform Texts from Nimrud; CTN 2 see Postgate; CTN 3 see Dalley-Postgate.
DAB - see Thompson.
Dalley Myths - S. Dalley, *Myths from Mesopotamia*, Oxford, 1989.
Dalley-Postgate - S. Dalley and J.N. Postgate, *The Tablets from Fort Shalmaneser* , CTN, 3, British School of Archaeology in Iraq, 1984.
Dancing - see Eaton, Oesterley, Wosien.
Dandamaev Slavery - M.A. Dandamaev, *Slavery in Babylonia. From Nabopolassar to Alexander the Great,* Dekalb, Illinois, 1984.
DB Sup - *Dictionnaire de la Bible, Supplément*, Paris.
Deimel - see SL.
Deimel Fara - A. Deimel, *Inschriften von Fara.*, WVDOG 40, Leipzig, 1922.
Deimel Pantheon - A. Deimel, *Pantheon Babylonicum* , Rome 1914.
DelPer - *Délegation en Perse, Mémoires.*
Delsman Kanaan - W.C. Delsman et al (eds.), *Von Kanaan bis Kerala,* AOAT 211, Neukirchen-Vluyn, 1982.
Descent of Inanna - S.N. Kramer, *JCS* 4 (1950), 5 (1951).
Deut - see Buis Leclercq.
van Dijk - Sagesse J.J.A. van Dijk, *La sagesse suméro-accadienne,* .Leiden, 1953.
van Dijk Götterlieder - J.J.A. van Dijk, *Sumerisches Götterlieder II*, Heidelberg, 1960.
Diri - Lexical series dir DIR *siaku = (w)atru,* unpublished.
Divination - J. Nougayrol et al, *La divination en Mésopotamie ancienne et dans les régions voisines,* Paris, 1966. CRRA XIV, 1965.
Dougherty Shirkutu - R.P. Dougherty, *Shirkutu of Babylonian Deities,* New Haven, 1923.
Dream-book - A.L. Oppenheim, "The Interpretation of Dreams in the Ancient Near East" *Transactions of the American Philosophical Society,* 46/3, Philadelphia, 1956, 177-373.
van Driel Cult of Assur - G. van Driel, *The Cult of Assur*, Assen, 1969.
Driver Deuteronomy - S.R. Driver, *Deuteronomy,* I.C.C., Edinburgh, 1905.
Driver and Miles Laws - G.R. Driver and J. C. Miles, *The Babylonian Laws*, Oxford, 1952-55.

DT - Tablet numbers in the Daily Telegraph collection of the British Museum.
Eaton Dancing - J.H. Eaton, "Dancing in the Old Testament," in J.G. Davies (ed.), *Worship and Dance,* Birmingham, 1975.
Ebeling - see LKA, TuL.
Ebeling Glossar NB - E. Ebeling, *Glossar zu den neubabylonische Briefen,* München, 1953.
Ebeling Parfümrez - E. Ebeling, *Parfümrezepte und kultische Texte aus Assur* (= Or NS 17-19), Rome, 1950.
Ebeling Stiftungen - E. Ebeling, *Stiftungen und Vorschriften für assyrische Tempel,* Berlin, 1954.
Ebla - see TM.
ED List A - see Arcari.
Edzard Tell ed-Der - D.O. Edzard, *Altbabylonische Rechts- und Verwaltungsurkunden aus Tell ed-Der im Iraq Museum,* München,1970.
83-1-18 and suchlike - Tablet numbers in the British Museum for the year 1883, etc.
Eissfeldt Kleine Schriften - O. Eissfeldt, *Kleine Schriften* (R. Sellheim and F. Maass (eds.), Tübingen, 1963.
Eliade Sacred - M. Eliade, *The Sacred and the Profane,* 1959, Paris, 1946.
Eliade Shamanism - M. Eliade, *Shamanism*, Princeton, 1972, Paris, 1951.
Ellenbogen Foreign Words - M. Ellenbogen, *Foreign Words in the Old Testament*, London, 1962.
Ellis Dance - Havelock Ellis, *The Dance of Life*, 1923.
EncBrit - *Encyclopedia Britannica.*
EncJud - *Encyclopedia Judaica*, Jerusalem, 1971.
Enmerkar - see Berlin.
ERE - *Encyclopedia of Religion and Ethics*, Edinburgh, 1908-22.
Erimhuš - The lexical series Erimhuš = *anantu* MSL. 17.
ErIs - *Eretz Israel*, Jerusalem.
Erra - see Cagni.
Ershemma - see Cohen.
Esarhaddon - see Borger.
ET - *Expository Times*, Edinburgh.
Eusebius - Life of Constantine, Loeb Edition, London, 1845.
Examentext A - Å. Sjöberg, ZA 64, 137ff.
Fales Censimenti - F.M. Fales, *Censimenti e catasti di epoca neo-assira*, Rome 1973 [A new study of ADB].
Falkenstein AV - D.O. Edzard (ed.), *Heidelberger Studien zum alten Orient,* Wiesbaden, 1967.
Falkenstein - see LKU.
Falkenstein Gerichtsurkunden - A. Falkenstein, *Die Neusumerischen Gerichtsurkunden,* München, 1956-7.
Falkenstein Götterlieder - A. Falkenstein, *Sumerische Götterlieder I,* Heidelberg, 1959.
Falkenstein Grammatik - A. Falkenstein, *Grammatik der Sprache Gudeas von Lagash,* I, 1966, AnOr 28; II, 1978, AnOr 29.
Falkenstein Haupttypen - A. Falkenstein, *Die Haupttypen der sumerischen Beschwörung,* Lepzig, 1931 (LSS, 1).
Falkenstein Sumerische - A. Falkenstein, *Das Sumerische*, Handbuch der Orientalistik, Leiden, 1959.

Falkenstein Wahrsagung - A. Falkenstein, "'Wahrsagung' in der sumerischen Uberlieferung," in *La Divination en Mésopotamie Ancienne. Et dans les Régions Voisines,* Paris, 1966. CRRA XIV.
Farber-Flügge - see *Inanna u. Enki.*
Finkelstein Late OB - J.J. Finkelstein, *Late Old Babylonian Documents, Letters,* YOS 13, New Haven and London, 1972.
Fish Catalogue - T. Fish, *Catalogue of Sumerian Tablets in the John Rylands Library, Manchester,* Manchester, 1932.
Fisher Ras Shamra - L.R. Fisher (ed.), *Ras Shamra Parallels* Rome, 1972.
Förtsch - see Bauer Lagasch.
Fossey Magie - Fossey, *La magie assyrienne*, Paris, 1902.
Fowler Names - J.D. Fowler, *Theophoric Personal Names in Ancient Hebrew. A Comparative Study,* JSOT Supplement Series, 49, Sheffield, 1988.
Fox Temple - Michael V. Fox (ed.), *Temple in Society,* Winona Lake, 1988.
Frankena Tākultu - R. Frankena, *Tākultu, Die sacrale Maaltijd in het assyrische Ritueel*, Leiden, 1954.
Frankfort Kingship - H. Frankfort, *Kingship and the Gods,* Chicago, 1948.
Frankfort Seals - H. Frankfort, *Cylinder Seals*, London, 1939.
Frazer (Old) Golden Bough - J.G. Frazer, 1911[3].
Frazer Golden Bough - T.H. Gaster (ed.), *J.G. Frazer, The New Golden Bough,* New York, 1959.
GAG - see von Soden.
Gallery-Kovacs Gilgamesh - M. Gallery-Kovacs, *The Epic of Gilgamesh,* Stanford University Press, 1985, 1989.
Gammie-Perdue Sage - John G. Gammie and Leo G. Perdue (eds.), *The Sage in Israel and the Ancient Near East,* Winona Lake, 1990.
Gelb Amorite - I.J. Gelb, *Computer-Aided Analysis of Amorite*, Chicago, 1980. AS 21.
Garelli Gilg - P. Garelli, *Gilgames et sa légend, Etudes recueillies par Paul Garelli à l'Occasion de la VIIe Rencontre Assyriologique Interntionale*, Paris, 1958.
Gelb OAIC - I.J. Gelb, *Old Akkadian Inscriptions in Chicago Natural History Museum*, Chicago, 1955.
Gelb Old Akkadian - I.J. Gelb, *Glossary of Old Akkadian*, Chicago, 1957, MAD III, Chicago, 1957.
Gelb StOr 46 - see Salonen Festschrift.
Genouillac Kich - H. de Genouillac, *Premières recherches archéologiques à Kich*, I, Paris, 1924; II, 1925.
Genouillac TRS - H. de Genouillac, *Textes Religioux Sumérienes du Louvre*, Paris, 1930; TCL 15.
Genouillac TSA- H. de Genouillac, *Tablettes sumériennes archaïques*, Paris, 1909.
Gezer - see Macalister.
Gilgamesh - see Garelli Gilg. No scholarly updated text, for a translation, see M. Gallery Kovacs, *The Epic of Gilgamesh*, Stanford U.P, 1985, 1989, xiii note.
GKC - Gesenius' Hebrew Grammar, ed. E. Kautzsch, tr. A.E. Cowley, Oxford, 1910 (German, 1908[28]).
Goetze Omen - A. Goetze, *Old Babylonian Omen Texts*, YOS 10, New Haven and London, 1947.
Gordon - see UT.
Gordon AV - Harry Hoffner (ed.), *Orient and Occident. Essays Presented to Cyrus R. Gordon,* AOAT 22, Neukirchen/Vluyn, 1973.

Gordon Sumerian Proverbs - E.I. Gordon, *Sumerian Proverbs,* Philadelphia, 1959.

Gragg Kesh Temple Hymn - in Sjöberg, *Temple Hymns..*

Grayson RIM - A.K. Grayson, *Royal Inscriptions of Mesopotamia,* Toronto, 1987.

Gregoire Archives - J.-P. Grégoire, *Archives Administratives Sumériennes,* Paris, 1970.

Grimal Histoire Mondiale - P. Grimal (ed.), *Histoire Mondiale de la Femme.*

Gudea - Copy F. Thureau-Dangin, *Les Cylindres de Goudéa,* TCL VIII, Paris, 1925. Translations: M. Lambert and R. Touray, *RB* 55 (1948); A. Falkenstein *SAHG* 137-82; T. Jacobsen *Harps*...386-444.

Guthrie Greeks - W.K.C. Guthrie, *The Greeks and Their Gods,* Boston and London, 1951.

Gwaltney Ishtaritum Qadishtum - W. Gwaltney, *The Qadištum and Ištaritum in Mesopotamian Society,* 1964 Thesis Hebrew Union College, Cincinnati.

Hackman - George W. Hackman, *Sumerian and Akkadian Administrative Texts from Predynastic Times to the End of the Akkad Dynasty,* New Haven, 1958, BIN 8.

Hallo Royal Titles - W.W. Hallo, *Early Mesopotamian Royal Titles* , New Haven, 1957, AOS 43.

Hallo Exaltation - W.W. Hallo and J.J.A.van Dijk, *The Exaltation of Inanna* , New Haven, 1968.

Haran Temples - M. Haran *Temples and Temple-Service in Ancient Israel.*, Oxford, 1978.

HAR-gud - see Hg.

HAR-ra = *hubullu* - see Hh.

Harris, R - "Inanna-Ishtar as Paradox and a Coincidence of Opposites," *HR* 30 (1990-91),261-278.

Harris Sippar - R. Harris, *Ancient Sippar,* Istantul, 1975.

Harper, R.F - see ABL.

Hartman Oppenheim Beer - see Oppenheim.

Hartmann Musik - H. Hartmann, *Die Musik der sumerischen Kultur,* Frankfort-am-Main, 1960.

Harvard - see HSS, Hussey.

Hastings DB - J. Hastings (ed.), *Dictionary of the Bible*, Edinburgh, 1905-7.

Haverford - see Barton Haverford.

Hebrew Lexicon - see BDB.

Helck Göttin - W. Helck, *Betrachtungen zur grossen Göttin und den ihr verbundenen Gottheiten,* München u. Wien, 1971.

Her - Herodotus, English Translation A.D. Godley, Loeb Classical Library, Cambridge, Massachusetts and London, 1960.

Herdner - see CTA.

Hg - Lexical series HAR-gud = *imru* = *ballu,* a commentary on Hh, MSL 5-11.

Hh - The lexical series HAR-ra = *hubullu*, MSL 5-11.

Hickman - Stauder Musik - H. Hickman und W. Stauder, *Orientalische Musik.*, Leiden / Köln, 1970. Handbuch der Orientalistik, Abt. l, Erg. Bd. 4.

Hilprecht - Sammlung Tablets in the Hilprecht collection, Jena.

Hinke Kudurru - W.J. Hincke, *Selected Babylonian Kudurru Inscriptions,* Leiden, 1911.

Hippologica - see Salonen.

Hirsch Untersuchungen - H. Hirsch, *Untersuchungen zur alt-assyrischen Religion* (AfO Beiheft 13/14), Graz, 1961.

HKL - See Borger.
HR - *History of Religions* , Chicago.
HSS - Harvard Semitic Series.
HUCA - *Hebrew Union College Annual*, Cincinnati.
Huffmon Amorites - H. Huffmon, *Amorite Personal Names in the Mari Texts.* Baltimore, 1965.
Hunger Kolophone - H. Hunger, *Babylonische und assyrische Kolophonen,* Neukirchen-Vluyn, 1968, AOAT 2.
Hussey Sumerian Tablets - M.I. Hussey, *Sumerian Tablets in the Harvard Semitic Museum,* HSS 3, Cambridge, 1912; 4, 1915.
IAK - E. Ebeling, B. Meissner and E. Weidner, *Die Inschriften der altassyrischen Könige*, Leipzig, 1926.
IB - *Interpreter's Bible* . Nashville, 1952-6.
ICK - B. Hrozny and L. Matous, *Inscriptions Cunéiformes du Kultépé* , Praha, 1952.
IDB - *Interpreters Dicitonary of the Bible*, Nashville, 4 vols., 1962, Supplement volume, 1976.
igituh - NA Synonym list, igi-duh-a = *tāmartu*, short version, B. Landsberger and O.R. Gurne, *AfO* 18 81ff.
IEJ - *Israel Exploration Journal*, Jerusalem.
IM - Tablets in the Iraq Museum, Baghdad.
Inanna and Ebeh - The literary composition,*Inanna and Ebeh*, unpublished, ms. B. Eichler, Portions published H. Limet, *Or* 40 (1970).
Innana and Enki - G. Farber-Flügge, *Der Mythus 'Inanna und Enki' unter besonderer Berücktsichtigungen der Liste der m e,* Studia Pohl 10, Rome, 1973.
Iraq - *Iraq*, London.
IRSA - see Sollberger et Kupper Inscriptions.
Ishida David Solomon - T. Ishida (ed.), *Studies in the Period of David and Solomon and Other Essays, Tokyo 5-7 Dec 1979,* Winona Lake, 1982.
ITT - *Inventaire des Tablettes de Tello,* Paris, 1910-21.
izi - Lexical series izi = *išātu*, MSL 13 154-226.
Jacobsen Harp -...T. Jacobsen, *The Harps That Were...* New Haven and London, 1987.
Jacobsen Treasures - T. Jacobsen, *Treasures of Darkness,* 1976.
JANES - *Journal of the Ancient Near East Society*, New York City.
JAOS - *Journal of the American Oriental Society*, New Haven, etc.
Jastrow Dictionary - M. Jastrow, *A Dictionary of Talmud Babli,* New York, 1950 (Philadelphia, 1903).
JBL - *Journal of Biblical Literature*, Philadelphia.
JCS - *Journal of Cuneiform Studies*, New Haven.
JE - *Jewish Encyclopedia*, New York and London, 1901-6.
Jean Contrats - C.-F. Jean, *Contrats de Larsa,* Paris, 1926.
Jean-Hoftijzer - C.-F. Jean and J. Hoftijze, *Dictionnaire des inscriptions sémitiques de l'ouest,* Leiden, 1965^2.
JEN - Joint Expedition with the Iraq Museum at Nuzi.
JEOL - *Jaarbericht van het Vooraziatisch-Egyptisch Genootschap "Ex Oriente Lux."*
JESHO - *Journal of the Economic and Social History of the Orient.*
Jestin Nouvelles Shuruppak - R. Jestin, *Nouvelles tablettes sumériennes de šuruppak*, Paris, 1957.
Jestin Shuruppak - R. Jestin, *Tablettes sumériennes de šuruppak,* Paris, 1937.

JJS - *Journal of Jewish Studies*, Cambridge, England.
JNES - *Journal of Near Eastern Studies,* Chicago.
Joines Serpent - Karen R. Joines, *Serpent Symbolism in the Old Testament,* Haddonfield, New Jersey, 1974.
Johns - see ADB, ADD.
Jones-Snyder - T. Jones and J. Snyder,*Sumerian Economic Texts from the Third Ur Dynasty*, Minneapolis, 1961.
JQR - *Jewish Quarterly Review* , Philadelphia.
JR - *Journal of Religion*, Chicago.
JRAS - *Journal of the Royal Asiatic Society*, London.
JSOT - *Journal for the Study of the Old Testament,* Sheffield.
JSS - *Journal of Semitic Studies*, Manchester.
K - Tablet numbers in the Kouyunjik Collection of the British Museum.
Kagal - Lexical series kagal = *abullu,* MSL 13 227-261.
KAI - H. Donner and W. Röllig, *Kanaanäische und aramäische Inschriften*, Wiesbaden, 1962.
KAJ E. Ebeling - *Keilschrifttexte aus Assur juristischen Inhalts,WVDOG* , 50, Leipzig, 1927.
Kang Drehem - S.T. Kang, *Sumerian Economic Texts from the Drehem Archive,* Urbana, 1972.
Kang Umma - S.T. Kang, *Sumerian Economic Texts from the Umma Archive,* Urbana, 1973.
Kapelrud Goddess - A. Kapelrud, *The Violent Goddess,* Oslo, 1969.
KAR E. Ebeling - *Keilschrifttexte aus Assur religiösen Inhalts* I, WVDOG 28, Leipzig, 1919; II, WVDOG 34, Leipzig, 1923.
Keiser Drehem - C.E. Keiser, *Neo-Sumerian Account Texts from Drehem,* BIN 3, New Haven and London, 1971.
KB - Keilschriftliche Bibliothek.
Keel Stempelsiegeln - O. Keel et al, *Studien zu den Stempelsiegeln aus Palästina /Israel,* Göttingen, 1989.
Kilmer - see Malku = šarru.
King Seven Tablets - L.W. King, *Seven Tablets of Creation,* London, 1902.
Kinnier Wilson - Wine Lists, J.V. Kinnier Wilson, *The Nimrud Wine Lists* , London, 1972.
Klauber - see PRT.
Klauber Beamtentum - E. Klauber, *Assyrisches Beamtentum nach Briefen aus der Sargonidenzeit,* Leipzig, 1910.
Klein Shulgi - J. Klein, *Three šulgi Hymns*, Ramat-Gan, Israel, 1981.
Knight Deutero-Isaiah - G.A.F. Knight, *Deutero-Isaiah,* 1965.
Knudtzon Gebete - J.A. Knudtzon, *Assyrische Gebete an den Sonnengott ...* Leipzig, 1893 (See Starr Queries for update).
Köhler-Baumgartner - Ludwig Köhler and Walter Baumbartner, (with J.J. Stamm et al.), *Hebäisches u. aramäisches Lexikon zum alten Testament*, Leiden, 1967-1990.
Kohler and Ungnad - see ARU.
König AV - *Dienst an den Lehre, Festschrift F. König,* 1965.
Koschaker - see Symbole Koschaker.
Kramer - see Lullaby.
Kramer History - S.N. Kramer, *History Begins at Sumer*, Philadelphia, 1981, an updating of his *From the Tablets of Sumer*, Indian Hills, Colorado, 1956.
Kramer SLTN - S.N. Kramer, *Sumerian Literary Texts from Nippur,* AASOR 23, New Haven, 1944.

Kramer SMR - S.N. Kramer, *The Sacred Marriage Rite*, Bloomington, 1969; A more advanced French translation is *Mariage Sacré à Sumer et à Babylone*, Paris, 1983.

Kraus AbB 1 - F.R. Kraus, *Altbabylonische Briefe...aus dem British Museum*, Leiden, 1966.

Kraus Worship - H.-J. Kraus, *Worship in Israel*, Oxford, 1966 (Munich, 1962).

Krecher Kultlyrik - J. Krecher, *Sumerische Kultlyrik*, Wiesbaden, 1966.

KTU - M. Dietrich et al, *Keilalphabetische Texte aus Ugarit.* Neukirchen / Vluyn, 1976. AOAT 24.

KUB - *Keilschrifturkunden aus Boghazköi.*

Kwasman NA Legal - T. Kwasman, *Neo-Assyrian Legal Documents in the Kouyunjik Collection of the British Museum*, Studia Pohl: Series Maior, 14, 1988.

Labat Caractere - R. Labat, *Le Caractère religieux de royauté assyro-babylonienne.* Paris,1939.

Labat TDP - R. Labat, *Traité akkadien de diagnostics et prognostics médicaux*, Leiden, 1951.

Laessøe Bit Rimki - J. Laessøe, *Studies on the Assyrian Ritual and Series bît rimki, København*, 1955.

LAK - A. Deimel, *Die Inschriften von Fara. Liste der archaischen Keilschriftzeichnen*, Leipzig, 1922-24.

Lambert BWL - W.G. Lambert, *Babylonian Wisdom Literature*, Oxford, 1960.

Lambert-Millard Atra-hasis - W.G. Lambert and A.R. Millard, *Atra-hasis: The Babylonian Story of the Flood.*

Lamentation over Sumer and Ur - See Michalowski.

Lamentation over Ur - S.N. Kramer, AS 12; revised H. Vanstiphout.

Landsberger AV *Studies* - *Landsberger* , Chicago, 1965; AS 16.

Landsberger Date Palm- B. Landsberger, *The Date Palm and its By-Products According to the Cuneiform Sources;* AfO Beiheft 17.

Langdon BL - S. H. Langdon, *Babylonian Liturgies*, Paris, 1913.

Langdon Neubab - S. Langdon, *Neubabylonische Königsinschriften* VAB 4, Leipzig, 1912.

Langdon - Tammuz S. Langdon, *Tammuz and Ishtar*, Oxford, 1914.
LAS, see Parpola.

LB - Tablet numbers in the de Liagre Böhl Collection, Leiden.

LE Reuven Yaron (ed.) - *Laws of Eshnunna* , Jerusalem, 1988^2; A. Goetze, *AASOR* (1956).

Leemans Ishtar - W.F. Leemans, *Ištar of Lagaba and her Dress*, SLB 1/1, Leiden, 1952.

van der Leeuw Religion - G. van der Leeuw, *Religion in Essence and Manifestation*, 1938.

Legrain Catal - Cagnin L. Legrain, *Catalogue des cylindres orientaux de la collection Louis Cagnin*, Paris, 1911.

Legrange AV - *Memorial Legrange.*

Legrange Etudes - M. Legrange, *Etudes sur les Religions Semitiques.* 2nd ed. 1931.

Lehmann Shamashshumukin - C.F. Lehmann, *Shamashshumukin* AB 8, Leipzig, 1892.

Leichty Izbu E. Leichty - *The Omen Series šumma Izbu*, TCS 4, Locust Valley, New York, 1970.

Lidzbarski Ephemeris - M. Lidzbarski, *Ephemeris für semitische Epigraphik.* Giessen, 1909-15.

Lidzbarski Handbuch - M. Lidzbarski, *Handbuch der nordsemitischen Epigraphik.*

Lie Sar - A. G. Lie, *The Inscriptions of Sargon II* Part I, The Annals, Paris, 1929.

LIH - L.W. King, *Letters and Inscriptions of Hammurabi*, London, 1898.

Limet Anthroponomie - H. Limet, *L'anthroponomie sumérienne dans les documents de la 3e dynastie d'Ur,* Paris, 1968.

Limet Textes Sumériennes - H. Limet, *Textes sumériennes de la IIIe Dynastie d'Ur*, Liège, 1973.

Lipit Ishtar Codex - F.R. Steele, *AJA* 52 (1948),and ANET 159ff.

Liverpool - see AAA.

Livingstone Poetry - A. Livingstone, *Court Poetry and Literary Miscellanea.* Helsinki, 1989; SAA, III.

LKA - E. Ebeling, *Literarische Keilschrifttexte aus Assur,* Berlin, 1953.

LKU - A. Falkenstein, *Literarische Keilschrifttexte aus Uruk,* Berlin, 1931

Louvain - see OLA.

Louvre - see AO.

LTBA - L. Matous, *Die Lexikalischen Tafelserien der Babylonier und Assyer in den Berliner Museen,* Berlin, 1933.

LSS - Leipziger semitische Studien.

Lucian Dea Syria - Lucian of Samosata, *De Dea Syria* Loeb Edition, New York, 1927.

Luckenbill AnnSen - D.D. Luckenbill, *The Annals of Sennacherib,* OIP 2 Chicago, 1924.

Lullaby - A literary composition in S.N. Kramer, *Studi in onore de Edoardo Volterra* 6, 191ff.

Lu = ša - NA Lexical List, *MSL* XII.

Macalister Gezer - R.A. Macalister, *Excavations at Gezer,* 3 vols., London, 1912.

MAD - Materials for the Assyrian Dictionary; MAD III, see Gelb Old Akkadian.

MAL - Middle Assyrian Laws, KAV I 1-6. Translated T.J. Meek, *ANET* 180-188.

Malku = šarru - Lexical List unpublished except for Malku I (Explicit), A.D. Kilme, *JAOS* 83 (1963), 421ff.

MAOG - *Mitteilungen der Altorientalischen Gesellschaft.*

Maqlû - G. Meier, *Maqlû.*, AfO Beiheft 2, Berlin, 1937.

Mari - see ARM, ARMT, Noort, Römer Frauenbriefe, TEM.

Martin Religieux - F. Martin, *Textes Religieux Assyriens et Babyloniens,* Paris, 1903.

May Megiddo - H.G. May, *Material Remains of the Megiddo Cult,* Chicago, 1935.

Mayer Nuzi - W. Mayer, *Nuzi Studien,* Neukirchen / Vluyn; AOAT 205/1.

McCown Tell-en-Nasbeh - C.C. McCown, *Tell en-Nasbeh,* Berkeley and New Haven, 1947.

McKay Religion - J.W. McKay, *Religion in Israel under the Assyrians,* Naperville, 1973.

MDP - Mémoires de la Délégation en Perse.

MEE - *Materiali Epigraphici di Ebla.*, Roma.

Meier - see Maqlû.

Meissner BAW - B. Meissner, *Beiträge zum assyrischen Wörterbuch* I, AS 1 Chicago 1931; II, AS 4 Chicago 1932.

Meissner BuA - B. Meissner, *Babylonien und Assyrien,* Heidenberg, 1920-25.

Mellaart *Çatal Hüyük* - James Mellaart, *Çatal Hüyük*, London, 1967.

Melaart *Hacilar* - James Mellaart, *Excavations at Hacilar,* Edinburgh, 1970.

Menzel Tempel - B. Menzel, *Assyrische Tempel.*, Studia Pohl: Series Maior 100 Rome, 1981.

Mesopotamia - For Mesopotamia 2, see Alster.
Michalowski - *Lamentation Sumer Ur* P. Michalowski, *The Lamentation over the Destruction of Sumer and Ur.* Winona Lake, 1989.
MJ - *Museum Journal,* Philadelphia.
Möbel - see Salonen.
de Moor, New Year - J.C. de Moor, *New Year with Canaanites and Israelites,* Kampen, 1972.
de Moor Seasonal - J.C. de Moor, *Seasonal Pattern in the Ugaritic Myth of Ba^clu,* Kevelaer, 1971; AOAT 16.
Moore Neo Babylonian - Ellen W. Moore, *Neo-Babylonian Business and Administrative Documents,* Ann Arbor, 1935.
Moran AV - T. Abusch et al (eds.), *Lingering Over Words,* Festschrift W.L. Moran, HSS 37, Atlanta, 1990.
Moren Shumma Alu - S. Moren, *The Omen Series "šumma Alu,". A Preliminary Investigation,* University of Pennsylvania, 1978. University Microfilms, 7816384.
Morgan - see BRM, Porada.
Mowinckel PIW - S. Mowinckel, *The Psalms in Israel's Worship*, 2 vols., New York and Nashville (E.T. Oxford, 1962; revision of Oslo, 1951).
MRS - *Mission de Ras Shamra.*
MSL - *Materialen zum sumerischen Lexikon / Materials for the Sumerian Lexicon*, Rome.
MSL - SS MSL Supplementary Series.
MVA(e)G - *Mitteilungen der Vorderasiatisch-Aegyptischen Gesellschaft.*
Nabnitu - Lexical series SIG_7 + ALAM = *nabnītu,* MSL 16.
N.A.B.U - *Nouvelles Assyriologiques Brèves et Utilitaires.*
Namburbi - see Caplice.
NBC - Tablet numbers in the Babylonian Collection, Yale University Library.
ND - Numbers of the tablets from the excavations at Nimrud (Kalhu).
Ni - Tablet numbers excavated at Nippur, in the Archaeological Museum of Istanbul.
Nies - see BIN.
Nikolski - M.V. Nikolski, *Dokumenty khoziaistvennoi otchetnosti,* St. Petersburg, 1908.
Nimrud - see ND.
Nippur - see Ni.
Noort Mari - E. Noort, *Untersuchungen zum Gottesbescheid in Mari,* AOAT 202, Neukirchen-Vluyn, 1977.
Nougayrol - see Divination.
Nuzi - see JEN, Mayer.
OBGT - Old Babylonian Grammatical Texts, MSL 4, Rome 1956.
OB Proto-Lu - OB Lexical List, MSL XII, Rome,1969.
OECT - Oxford Editions of Cuneiform Texts, Oxford.
Oesterley Dance - W.O.E. Oesterley, *The Sacred Dance. A Study in Comparative Folklore,* New.York, 1921.
OIP - Oriental Institute Publications, University of Chicago; 2 see Luckenbill; 16 see STVP.
OLA - *Orientalia Lovaniensia Analecta.*
Old Assyrian - see Hirsch.
Olwahrsagung - see Pettinato.
OLZ - *Orientalistische Literaturzeitung*, Berlin and Leipzig.
Oppenheim - see Dream-book, Studies Oppenheim.
Oppenheim AV - *Studies presented to A. Leo Oppenheim,* Chicago, 1964.

Oppenheim Beer - Louis F. Hartman and A.L. Oppenheim, *On Beer and Brewing Techniques in Ancient Mesopotamia.* According to the XXIIIrd Tablet of the Series HAR-ru = *hubullu*, Supplement to JAOS, 10, Baltimore, 1950.

Oppenheim Catalogue - A.L. Oppenheim, *Catalogue of the Cuneiform Tablets of the Wilberforce Eames Babylonian Collection in the New York Public Library*, New Haven, 1948; AOS 32.

Oppenheim Centaurus A.L. Oppenheim, in *Centaurus* 14 (1969).

Oppenheim Mesop A.L. Oppenheim, *Ancient Mesopotamia,* Chicago and London, 1964.

Or - *Orientalia* , Rome.

OrAn - *Oriens Antiquus*, Rome.

Östborn Yahweh Baal - G. Östborn, *Yahweh and Baal,* Lund, 1956. Lunds Universitets Årskrift NF Bd. 51 No. 6.

Otto Holy - R. Otto, *The Idea of the Holy,* London, 1923 (Breslau, 1917).

Oxford - see OECT.

Pallis Akitu - S.A. Pallis, *The Babylonian Akîtu Festival* , Copenhagen, 1926.

PAPS - *Proceedings of the American Philosophical Society,* Philadelphia.

Parpola LAS - S. Parpola, *Letters from Assyrian Scholars to the Kings Esarhaddon and Assurbanipal,* Neukirchen/Vluyn 1970-1983, 2 vols; AOAT 5/1-2

Parrot Sumer - A. Parrot, *Sumer* . Paris, 1960.

PBS - *Publications of the Babylonian Section, University Museum, University of Pennsylvania*, Philadelphia.

Pedersen Archives - O. Pedersen, *Archives and Libraries in the City of Assur: a Survey of the Material from the German Excavations,* Stockholm, 1986.

Pedersen Israel - J. Pedersen, *Israel*, I, II, III, IV, London, 1926 (Copenhagen, 1920).

Pennsylvania University - see BE. CBS, PBS, UM.

PEQ - *Palestine Exploration Quarterly*, London.

Pettinato Archives - G. Pettinato, *The Archives of Ebla.*, Garden City, 1981.

Pettinato Ölwahrsagung - G. Pettinato, *Die Ölwahrsagung bei den Babyloniern,* Rome, 2 vols., 1966.

Pettinato Untersuchungen - G. Pettinato, *Untersuchungen zur neusumerische Landwirtschaft,* Napoli, 1967.

Pettinato Waetzoldt Vocabulario - G. Pettinato, H. Waetzoldt et al, *Studi per il Vocabulario Sumerico,* Roma, 1985; G. Reisner, *Tempelurkunden aus Telloh.*

Piepkorn Asb.- A.C. Piepkorn, *Historical Prism Inscription of Ashurbanipal,* Chicago, AS 5.

Pinches Berens - T.G. Pinches, *The Babylonian Tablets of the Berens Collection,* London, 1915.

Plessis Ishtar - J. Plessis, *Etudes sur les Textes concernant Ištar-Astarte,* Paris, 1921.

Porada Corpus - E. Porada, *Corpus of Ancient Near Eastern Seals in North American Collections,* Collection of Pierpont Morgan Library, Bollingen Series 14. New York, 1948.

Postgate NA Leg. Docs - N. Postgate, *Fifty Neo-Assyrian Legal Documents*, Warminster, 1976.

Postgate Royal Grants - J.N. Postgate, *Neo-Assyrian Royal Grants and Decrees*, Rome, 1969; Studia Pohl, Series Maior, 1.

Postgate Palace Archive - J.N. Postgate, *The Governor's Palace Archive*, British School of Archaeology in Iraq, London, 1973; CTN 2.
Postgate Taxation - N. Postgate, *Taxation and Conscription in the Assyrian Empire*. Studia Pohl, Series Maior 3, Rome, 1974.
Prague - see ArOr.
Pritchard Figurines - J.B. Pritchard, *Palestinian Figurines in Relation to Certain Goddesses Known Through Literature*, New Haven, 1943.
Pritchard - see ANEP, ANET.
Proto-Diri - Lexical series, unpublished, see Diri.
Proto-Kagal - Lexical series, MSL 13 pp. 63-88.
Proto-Lu - Lexical series, MSL 12, pp. 25-84, Rome 1969.
PRT - E. Klauber, *Politische-religiöse Texte aus der Sargonidenzeit*, Leipzig, 1893.
PRU - *Le Palais Royale d'Ugarit*, Paris.
PSBA - *Proceedings of the Society of Biblical Archaeology*, London.
PSD - *Pennsylvania Sumerian Dictionary*, Philadelphia.
R - H.C. Rawlinson, E. Norris, G. Smith and T.G. Pinches, *The Cuneiform Inscriptions of Western Asia*, London, 1861-1909.
RA - *Revue d'assyriologie et d'archéologie orientale*, Paris.
RAcc - F. Thureau-Dangin, *Rituels accadiens*, Paris, 1921.
RAI - see Rencontre.
RB - *Revue biblique*, Paris.
von Rad Theology - G. von Rad, *Old Testament Theology*, 2 vols, New York and Evanston (Edinburgh, 1962; from Munich, 1957).
Ramsay Phrygia - W. Ramsay, *Cities and Bishoprics of Phrygia*, London, 1883.
Ras Shamra - see Fisher; MRS, PRU, RS, Tarragon Culte, UF, Ugaritica.
Rawlinson - see R.
REC - F. Thureau-Dangin, *Recherches sur l'origine de l'écriture cunéiforme*, Paris, 1898.
Reiner - see Shurpu.
Reiner Thwarts - E. Reiner, *Your Thwarts in Pieces, your Mooring Rope Cut. Poetry from Babylonia and Assyria*, University of Michigan, 1985.
Reiner Pingree Omens - Erica Reiner and David Pingree, *Babylonian Planetary Omens I. Enuma Anu Enlil Tablet 63*, Malibu, 1975; II, Tablets 50-51, Malibu, 1981.
Reisner - see SBH.
Reisner Telloh - G.A. Reisner, *Tempelurkunden aus Telloh*, Berlin, 1901; see Pettinato Waetzoldt Vocabulario.
Rencontre Assyriologique Internationale - see CRRA; VII see Garelli Gilgamesh; XIV see Divination; XX see Le Temple et Le Culte.
Renger Priestertum - J. Renger, "Untersuchungen zum Priestertum in den alt-babylonische Zeit." *ZA* 58 NF 24 (1967), *ZA* 59 (1969).
RevArch - *Revue Archéologique*, Paris.
RGG - *Religion in Geschichte und Gegenwart*, Tübingen.
RHA - *Revue Hittite et asianique*, Paris.
RHR - *Revue de l'histoire des Religions*, Paris.
RIM - see Grayson.
RISA - G. A. Barton, *Royal Inscriptions of Sumer and Akkad*, New Haven, 1929.
Ritter āšipu / asû - E. Ritter, "Magical expert (āšipu) and physician (asû): notes on two complementary professions in Babylonian medicine," in *Landsberger AV* 299-321.
Rm - Tablet numbers in the Rassam collection of the British Museum.
RLA - *Reallexikon der Assyriologie*, Berlin and Leipzig.

Robinson AV - *Studies in Old Testament Prophecy Presented to Professor Theoldore H. Robinson,* Edinburgh, 1950.

Römer Frauenbriefe - W.H.Ph. Römer, *Frauenbriefe über Religion, Politik und Privatleben in Mari,* Neukirchen/Vluyn, 1971; AOAT 12.

Römer Königshymnen - W.H.Ph.Römer, *Sumerische' Königshymnen' der Isin-Zeit* Leiden, 1965.

RSO - *Revista degli Studi Orientali.*

Rost Tigl. III - L. Rost, *Die Keilschrifttexte Tiglat-Pilesers III,* Leipzig, 1893.

Rowley Worship - H.H. Rowley, *Worship in Ancient Israel,* Philadelphia, 1967.

RS - Text numbers excavated at Ras Shamra/Ugarit.

RSV - Revised Standard Version, 1946, 1952.

RT - *Recueil de travaux relatifs à la philologie et à l'archéologie égyptiennes et assyriennes*, Paris.

RTC - F. Thureau-Dangin, *Recueil de Tablettes chaldéennes*, Paris, 1903.

SAA - *State Archives of Assyria*, Helsinki; III, see Livingstone; IV, see Starr Queries.

Sachau AV - G. Weil (ed.), *Festschrift Eduard Sachau,* Berlin, 1915.

Sag Tablet - MSL SS 1.

SAHG - A. Falkenstein and W. von Soden, *Sumerische und akkadische Hymnen und Gebiete* Zürich-Stuttgart, 1953.

SAKI - F. Thureau-Dangin, *Die Sumerischen und akkadischen Königsinschriften, VAB, 1,* Leipzig, 1907 (Paris, 1905).

Salonen Festschrift - *Studia Orientalia Armas I. Salonen,* StOr 46, Helsinki, 1975.

Salonen Hippologica - A. Salonen, *Hippologica Accadica,* Helsinki, 1956.

Salonen, Möbel - A. Salonen, *Die Möbel des alten Mesopotamien,* Helsinki, 1963.

Salonen Waffen - E. Salonen, *Die Waffen der alten Mesopotamier,* Helsinki, 1965.

SANE - *Sources from the Ancient Near East*, Malibu, California.

Saporetti Onomastica - C. Saporetti, *Onomastica Medio-Assira*, 2 vols., Rome, 1970; Studia Pohl 6.

Sargon - see Lie; Winckler; Thureau-Dangin.

S^b - Syllabary B, List of Signs, *MSL* 3, Rome, 1955.

SBH - G.A. Reisner, *Sumerisch-babylonische Hymnen nach Thontafeln griechischer Zeit,* Berlin, 1896.

Schmandt-Besserat - D. Schmandt-Besserat (ed.), *The Legacy of Sumer,* Malibu, 1976.

Schneider Götternamen - N. Schneider, *Die Götternamen von Ur III,* AnOr 19, Rome, 1939.

Schneider Montserrat - N. Schneider, *Drehem-und Djoha-Texte im Kloster Montserrat,* AnOr 7, Rome, 1932.

Schneider Zeitbestimmungen - N. Schneider, *Die Zeitbestimmungen der Wirtschaftsurkunden von Ur III,* AnOr 13, Rome 1936.

Schorr Zivil - M. Schorr, *Urkunden des altbabylonischen Zivil und Prozessrechts,* VAB 5, Leipzig, 1913.

Schoff Song of Songs - W.H. Schoff (ed.), *Song of Songs. A Symposium,* 1924.

Schramm Einleitung - W. Schramm, *Einleitung in die assyrischen Königsinschriften*, Leiden, 1961.

Second Isaiah - see Knight, Westermann.

SEM E. Chiera - *Sumerian Epics and Myths,* Chicago, 1934.

Sendry - Alfred Sendry, *Music in Ancient Israel*, New York and London, 1969.

Sennacherib - see Luckenbill.

Seux Epithètes - M.-J. Seux, *Epithètes royales akkadiennes et sumériennes*, Paris, 1967.

Seux Hymnes - M.-J. Seux, *Hymnes et prièrs aux dieux de Babylone et d'Assyrie,* Paris, 1976.

Shamashshumukin - see Lehmann.

Shulği - see Klein.

Shumma Alu - see Moren.

Shumma Izbu - see Leichty.

Shurpu E. Reiner - *šurpu,* AfO Beih 11, Graz, 1958.

Shuruppak - see Alster, Jestin.

Sigrist Horn - M Sigrist, *Neo-Sumerian Account Texts in the Horn Archaeological Museum,* Berrien Springs, Michigan, 1984 AUCT,1.

Sigrist Rochester - M. Sigrist, *Documents from Tablet Collections in Rochester New York,* Bethesda, 1991.

Sjöberg - see Examentext.

Sjöberg AV - H. Behrens et al (eds.), DUMU-E_2-DUB-BA-A *Studies in Honor of Åke W. Sjöberg,* Philadelphia, 1989.

Sjöberg Mondgott - A.W. Sjöberg, *Der Mondgott Nanna-Suen in der sumerischen Überlieferung,* Uppsala, 1960.

Sjöberg Temple Hymns - Å.W.Sjöberg and E. Bergmann, *The Collection of the Sumerian Temple Hymns*, TCS 3, Locust Valley, 1969.

SJOT - *Scandanavian Journal of the Old Testament*, Aarhus.

SKL - *The Sumerian King List,* Ed. T. Jacobsen AS 11, Chicago, 1939.

SL - A. Deimel, *Shumerisches Lexikon, Vollständige Ideogramm-Sammlung, Band 1-4*, Rome, 1928-33.

SLB - Studia ad tabulas cuneiformes collectas a F.M. Th. de Liagre Böhl pertinentia.

SLT - E. Chiera, *Sumerian Lexical Texts from the Temple School at Nippur*, OIP 11, Chicago, 1929.

SLTN - see Kramer.

Sm - Tablet numbers from the Smith group of the Kouyunjik collection of the British Museum.

Snell Ledgers - D. Snell, *Ledgers and Prices. Early Mesopotamian Merchant Accounts,* New Haven and London, 1982; YNER, 8.

von Soden AV - *Lišan Mithuri. Festschrift W. von Soden,* Neukirchen/Vluyn, 1969; AOAT 1.

von Soden GAG - W. von Soden, *Grundriss der akkadischen Grammatik,* AnOr 33/47, Rome 1952.

von Soden Syllabar - W. von Soden u. W. Röllig, *Das Akkadische Syllabar* ^{3}, Rome, 1976.

Sollberger Correspondence - E. Sollberger, *Business and Administrative Correspondence under the Kings of Ur,* Locust Valley, New York, 1966; TCS, 1.

Sollberger - Kupper Inscriptions E. Sollberger and J.-R. Kupper, *Inscriptions royales sumériennes et akkadiennes*, Paris, 1971.

Speleers Recueil - L. Speleers, *Recueil des inscriptions de l'Asie antérieure des Musées Royaux du Cinquantenaire à Bruxelles,* Bruxelles, 1925.

Spycket Statues - A. Spycket, *Les Statues de Culte dans les Textes Mesopotamienes des Origines à la* l^{re} *Dynastie de Babylone,* Paris, 1968.

SRT - see Chiera.

STA - see Chiera.

Stamm Namengebungen - J.J. Stamm, *Die akkadische Namengebung,* MVAG 44, Leipzig, 1939.

Starr Diviner - I. Starr, *The Rituals of the Diviner* Bibliotheca Mesopotamica, 12, Malibu, 1983.

Starr Queries - I. Starr, *Queries to the Sungod.*, Helsinki, 1990; SAA IV.

Stone Circles - see Burl.

StOr - *Studia Orientalia* , Helsinki; for 22, see Aro Glossar; 46, see Salonen Festschrift; 7, see Tallqvist.

Strabo - Geography Loeb Edition. 1967-1983.

Streck Asb - M. Streck, *Assurbanipal und die letzten assyrischen Könige bis zum untergange Nineveh's,* Leipzig, 1916, 3 vols.; VAB 7.

STT - A.R. Gurney, J.J. Finkelstein and P. Hulin, *The Sultantepe Tablets,* Nos. 382, 383, 384, 385. List of professions. MSL XII pp. 233-237.

Studia Pohl 10 - see Inanna and Enki; Maior 14, see Kwasman NA Legal; Maior 10, see Menzel; Maior 1, see Postgate Royal Grants; Maior 3, see Postgate Taxation.

Studies Oppenheim - *Studies Presented to A. Leo Oppenheim*, Chicago, 1964.

Stud The - *Studia Theologica,* Lund.

STVC - E. Chiera, *Sumerian Texts of Varied Contents* OIP 16, Chicago, 1934.

Sumer - *Sumer*, Baghdad.

Sumerian King List - T. Jacobsen, *The Sumerian King List,* Chicago; AS 11.

Sumerian Proverbs - see Gordon.

Symbolae Böhl - *Symbolae Biblicae et Mesopotamicae Francisco Mario Theodoro de Liagre Böhl Dedicatae,* Leiden, 1973.

Symbolae Koschaker - J. Friedrich et al. (ed.), *Symbolae Paulo Koschakerdedicatae* (Studia et documenta ad iura orientis antiqui pertinentes, 2) Leiden, 1939.

Syria - *Syria,* Damascus.

Szlechter TJA - E. Szlechter, *Tablettes juridiques et administrativea de la IIIe Dynastie d'Ur et de la Ire Dynastie de Babylone,* Paris, 1963.

Tākultu - see Frankena.

Tallqvist Götterepitheta - K. Tallqvist, *Akkadische Götterepitheta,* StOr 7, Helsinki, 1938.

Tarragon Culte - J.-M. de Tarragon, *Le Culte à Ugarit. D'apres les Textes de la Pratique en Cunéiform alphabétiques,* Paris, 1980.

TCL - Textes cunéiformes du Louvre; 3, see Thureau-Dangin HCS; 10 see Jean; 15, see de Genouillac.

TCS - Texts from Cuneiform Sources; TCS 1, see Sollberger; TCS 2, see Biggs; TCS 4, see Leichty Izbu; TCS 3, see Sjöberg Temple Hymns.

TDNT - G. Kittel et al (eds.), *Theological Dictionary of the New Testament,* Grand Rapids, 1964.

TDOT - G. Botterwick and H. Ringgren (eds.), *Theological Dictionary of the Old Testament*, Grand Rapids, 1977.

Tello - see ITT, Reisner.

TEM - Mari text number, see M. Birot, *RA* 50.

Le Temple et le Culte - XX Rencontre Assriologique Internationale, Leiden, 1975.

Thompson - see AMT.

Thompson - DAB R.C. Thompson, *A Dictionary of Assyrian Botany,* London, 1949.

Thompson Magic - R.C. Thompson, *Semitic Magic, its origin and development,* London, 1908.

Thureau-Dangin - see Gudea, RAcc, REC, SAKI.

Thureau-Dangin - HCS F. Thureau-Dangin, *Une relation de la huitième Campagne de Sargon,* TCL 3, Paris, 1912.
TIM - Texts in the Iraq Museum, Baghdad.
TLB - Tablet Numbers in the de Liagre Böhl collection, Leiden.
TM - Tablet numbers for the excavations at Tell Mardikh/Ebla.
TMH - see TuM.
Tiglath-pileser III - see Rost.
Tropper Necromantie - J. Tropper, *Necromantie. Totenbefragung im Alten Orient und im Alten Testament,* AOAT 223, Neukirchen-Vluyn, 1989.
TRS - H. de Genouillac, *Textes Religioux Sumériens*, Paris, 1930.
TSA - See Genouillac.
Tsukimoto Totenpflege - A. Tsukimoto, *Zur Totenpflege (kispum) im alten Mesopotamien.* Neukirchen-Vluyn, 1985; AOAT 216.
TuL - E. Ebeling, *Tod und Leben nach den Vorstellungen der Babylonier,* Berlin u. Leipzig, 1931.
TuM - *Texte u. Materialen der Frau Professor Hilprecht Collection von Babylonian Antiquities im Eigentum der Universitat Jena,* Berlin, 1961.
Türk - see *Belleten.*
Tylor AV - H. Balfour et al (eds.), *Anthropological Essays Presented to Edward Burnett Tylor*, Oxford, 1907.
TynBul - *Tyndale Bulletin*, London.
UE - Ur Excavations.
UET - *Ur Excavations. Texts*, London.
UF - *Ugarit-Forschungen*, Kevalaer.
Ugarit - see Ras Shamra.
Ugaritica - *Ugaritica*, Paris.
UM - Tablet numbers at the University Museum, University of Pennsylvania, Philadelphia.
UMBS - *University Museum. Publications of the Babylonian Section,* Philadelphia.
Unger AV - M. Lurker (ed.), *In Memoriam Eckhard Unger,* Baden-Baden, 1971.
Unger Babylon - E. Unger, *Babylon, die heilige Stadt,* Berlin, Leipzig, 1931.
Ungnad Briefe Hammurapi - A. Ungnad, *Babylonische Briefe aus der Zeit der Hammurapi-Dynastie,* VAB 6, Leipzig, 1914.
Unity Diversity - H. Goedicke and J.J.M. Roberts (eds.), *Unity and Diversity.*
UT - Text numbers or lexicon numbers in C.H. Gordon, *Ugaritic Textbook.*
Utukku lemnutu - Incantation series, mss. M. Geller, M.W. Green.
Uruk-Warka - see UVB.
UVB - *Vorläufiger Bericht über die...Ausgrabungen in Uruk-Warka*, Berlin, 1930.
VAB - Vorderasiatische Bibliothek; 1, see SAKI; 4, see Langdon; 5, see Schorr; 6, see Ungnad; 7, see Streck Asb.
VAS - *Vorderasiatische Schriftdenkmäler.*
VAT - Tablets in the Vorderasiatische Abteilung of the Staatliche Museen, Berlin.
de Vaux An Is - R. de Vaux, *Ancient Israel*, New York, 1965, paperback (1961), from the French, 1957.
de Vaux Nombres - R. de Vaux, *Les Nombres*, Paris, 1972.
Virolleaud - see ACh.
Vos Women - C.J. Vos, *Women in Old Testament Worship*, Delft, 1968.
van Voss (ed.) - see Beek AV.

VT - *Vetus Testamentum*, Leiden.
VTSup - *Vetus Testamentum, Supplements;* 16 see Baumgartner AV.
Walters Water - S.D. Walters, *Water for Larsa*, New Haven and London, 1982; YNER 8.
Watson Birmingham - P.J. Watson, *Catalogue of Cuneiform Tablets in Birmingham City Museum. Vol. l. Neo-Sumerian Texts from Drehem,* Warminster, 1986.
Wehr - *The Hans Wehr Dictionary of Modern Written Arabic edited by J.M. Cowan.* Harrassowitz: Wiesbaden, 1961, 1966, 1971.
Weidner Reliefs - AfO Bei 4.
Weidner Tn - E. Weidner, *Die Inschriften Tukulti-Ninurtas I,* AfO Beiheft 12, Graz, 1959.
Weisberg Guild Structure - D.B. Weisberg, *Guild Structure and Political Allegiance in Early Achaemenid Mesopotamia.*, New Haven and London, 1967.
Weissbach Misc - F.H. Weissbach, *Babylonische Miscellen*, WVDOG 4, Leipzig, 1903.
Werner - Eric Werner, *The Sacred Bridge*, NewYork and London, 1955.
Westermann Second Isaiah - C. Westermann, *Isaiah 40-66*, 1969 (German, 1966).
Winckler Sargon - H. Winckler, *Die Keilschrifttexte Sargons* , 2 vols., Leipzig, 1889.
Winter Frau und Göttin - Urs Winter, *Frau und Göttin,* Göttingen, 1983.
Wiseman Alalakh - D.J. Wiseman, *The Alalakh Tablets*, London, 1953.
Wiseman Treaties - D.J. Wiseman, *The Vassal Treaties of Esarhaddon,* London, 1958 (*Iraq* 20/l); see R. Borger *ZA* 20 (1961), 173-196 for Verbesserungen u. Bemerkungen.
WO - *Die Welt des Orients*, Stuttgart.
WörMyth - H.W. Haussig (ed.), *Wörterbuch der Mythologie*, I, *Götter u. Mythen im Vorderen Orient*, Stuttgart, 1965.
Wosien Dance - Maria-Gabriele Wosien, *Sacred Dance. Encounter with the Gods,* New York, 1974.
Wright Arch - G.E. Wright, *Introduction to Biblical Archaeology*, London, 1960.
WVDOG - *Wissenschaftliche Veröffentlichungen der Deutschen Orient-Gesellschaft*, 4 see Weissbach.
WZKM - *Wiener Zeitschrift für die Kunde des Morgenlandes*, Wien.
Yale - see NBC, YBT, YNER, YOR, YOS, YBT.
YBT - Yale Oriental Series, Babylonian Texts.
YNER - Yale Near Eastern Researches; 8, see Snell.
YOR - Yale Oriental Series, Researches; 1, see Clay PN.
YOS - Yale Oriental Series. Babylonian Texts; 13, see Finkelstein.
ZA - *Zeitschrift für Assyriologie* , Berlin.
ZAW - *Zeitschrift für die alttestamentliche Wissenschaft*, Giessen.
ZDMG - *Zeitschrift der deutschen morgenländischen Gesellschaft*, Leipzig.
ZDPV - *Zeitschrift des deutschen Palästina-Vereins*, Wiesbaden.
Zeus - see Cook.
Zimmern Bab. Buss - H. Zimmern, *Babylonische Busspsalmen*, Leipzig, 1885.
Zimmern Neujahrsfest - H. Zimmern, *Zum babylonischen Neujahrfest,* Leipzig, 1906, 1918.
Zimmern - see BBR.

Other Abbreviations and Sigla, and Selected Ideograms and Terms

*Theoretical Reading. Has not yet been found in texts.
A - Istanbul Eski Sark Müzesi tablets.
ANE - Ancient Near East.
balbale - a type of Sumerian chant, see PSD s.v.
d - ` for dingir "divine" in Sumerian, indicating a god-name or divinity.
ED - Early Dynastic, the early part of the 3rd millenium B.C.E.
emegir - see emesal.
emesal - A so-called dialect of Sumerian, formerly understood as eme "tongue, language" and sal "woman". CAD E 148b and CAD L 256b note entries eme-sal = *lu-ru-u* "fine, thin (?)" with respect to voice. See now eme-sal = *lu-ru-u* Sag A iv 35, MSL SS 1 24. Used especially by the *kalû.* eme-gir$_{15}$ is the main dialect. See Lu = ša I 141f, MSL XII 99; eme-gir$_{15}$ = *šu-we-rum* Sag A iv 30, MSL SS 1 24.
eršemma - Literally: ér "lamentation" of the šem "drum" (?) See Cohen Eršemma for examples.
EV - English version.
f - Feminine.
Gilg - Gilgamesh.
GN - Geographical name.
Her - Herodotus.
K - The Kouyunjik Collection of the British Museum.
kirugu - Section or unit of a Sumerian hymn.
lexical lists - The vast word-lists, "dictionaries", pronunciation helps, syllabaries etc. produced by the scribes, and published mostly in the MSL series.
limmu - the name of an office in MA and NA times to which officials in that office gave their names the year they held that office; eponym years.
lit - Literally.
lú - Determinative before masculine titles.
LXX - Septuagint, the main (but not the only) version of the Hebrew Bible found in Greek, whose origin is told about in story form in the Letter to Aristeas.
m - Masculine.
MA - Middle Assyrian. Approximately the 15th to the 12th c. B.C.E.
MB - Middle Babylonian. Approximately 13-12 c. B.C.E.
me - The attributes of civilization under the control of the gods; see *Inanna u. Enki*.
mí - Determinative before female titles. Formerly read sal, then mí, now read munus.
MT - Masoretic Text, so-called from the Masorah, a loosely-defined group whose primary exemplars were the ben Asher family of the 10 c. C.E.
munus - see mí.
NA - Neo-Assyrian. An ill-defined period, approximately the first half of the first millenium B.C.E., down to the fall of Nineveh in Assyria in 612.
NB - Neo-Babylonian, or Chaldean dynasty. The revived dynasty centering on the city of Babylon, from Nabopolassar in 625/6 B.C.E. until the death of Nabonidus (Nabu-na'id) in 539.
ND - Nimrud dig tablet numbers.
NS, NF - New Series.

OA - Old Assyrian. Not a well-defined period, aproximately 19-18 c. B.C.E. in Assyria, but with many tablets coming from the area of their trading colony in central Anatolia around Kültepe / Kanesh.
OB Old Babylonian. Usually considered from the end of the Ur III period to 1549 B.C.E. when the Hittite forces sacked Babylon in a one-time campaign and brought to an end this brilliant civilization, leaving a vacuum which was filled by the Kassites.
OAkk Old Akkadian. Semitic speaking dynasty, 24 c. B.C.E., lasting approximately 140 years.
OS - Old Series.
PN - Personal Name.
RS - Ras Shamra / Ugarit tablet numbers.
SAL - See mí.
Ur III - The Third Dynasty of Ur, so-called by the Sumerian King List. 21st c. B.C.E., with 5 kings lasting a little over 100 years.
Vulg - Vulgate Version of the Bible.

Biblical Books

Gen Ex Lev Num Deut Josh Jud Ruth Sam Kings Chr Ezra Neh Est Job Psalms Pro Eccles Song of Songs Isa Jer Lam Ezek Dan Hos Joel Amos Ob Jon Mic Nah Hab Zeph Hag Zech Mal
Matt Mark Luke John Acts Rom Cor Gal Eph Philip Col Thes Tim Titus Philemon Heb James Pet John Jude Rev

INDEX

TITLES
Akkadian, Sumerian or Ideograms

References are to Section Numbers, unless labelled App. = Appendix. Boldface type indicates main entries. Lexical entries are not indexed unless they are discussed in the body of the text. In general, lú and mí are omitted, unless they are part of the Sumerian reading.

A.BA, see also *ṭupšarru* 1.32 (É.AN.SAR); 2.3.11; 3.4.9; App. 3.3.1 (MÍ.A.BA)
A.BA, [ ] 2.3.11; 3.3.8n
AB.(A).AB.DU_7/DU/, *ababdû* or *ešabdû*, 1.3.2; 1.37.1; **1.40**
ababdû, see AB.(A).AB.DU_7/DU
abarakkatu, 2.4.7
abarakku, see agrig
ab-ba-é-gal, 3.3.2; App. 5.1
abgal, see *apkallu*
á-bi-gál, 1.16
abnu, 2.4.11; App. 3.13.1
(AB).NUN.ME.DU, see abrig
abrig /(AB).NUN.ME.DU /*abriqqu*, 1.3.2; 1.9.10; 1.21.8; **1.22**; 1.22.1; 1.22.2; 1.22.3, 1.23; 1.25.2; 2.4.3; 3.4.8; 3.8.3; **3.10**
abru, 2.3.12n; 2.4.11; App. 3.13; App. **3.13.3**
adammû , see *edammû*
ad-da-uru-di-ku_5, 4.23.9.11
a-ga-am (f.), **1.41**
aga_x-uš, 1.7.5
a-gil-li, App. 5.2
agrig / *abarakku*, 1.9.9, 1.22.1, 1.23, 1.37.1, 3.4.12, App. 5.3
agrig-ezem, 3.3.2; App. 5.4
agriqu, 1.22.1
agugiltu, 3.20.5; 3.21.3; **3.23**
agugillu, 3.20.4; 3.21.3; **3.23**
aguhhu, App. 3.2.7; **App. 3.11**
ahu rabû, **1.7**
ākil arni, 2.26
ākil bārê, 1.10.6 (*nešakku*)
ākilu, 1.6.2 (Mari)
aklu, 1.38.3
á-lá, 2.1.2.4; 2.2.4
alahhinatu, 1.32
(a)lahhinu, 1.32, App. 1. r.12, App. 5.5; App. 5.47n
alamdimmû, App. 3.14
alan-zu, see *aluzinnu*
al-è-dè, see *muhhû*, App. 3.5.3, App. 3.7.5
almatu, 4.11.7
aluzinnu /alan-zu, **2.7**
ama-, 4.8.2 (several usages), 4.13 (several titles)
ama'errû, /ama-ér-ra 2.3.2; 2.3.14; **2.16**
AMA ^{d}Inanna, 1.2.1; 4.8.2; 4.13 (=*amalu*$_x$); App. 4.1.7.1
amalītu /ama-lul, 1.2.1; 4.4.1; 4.8.2; 4.12; **4.13**
amalu /ama-lul, 4.8.4; 4.11.5; 4.12; **4.13**; App. 4.1.7.1
amaluktu, 4.13
ama-lukur-ra, 4.8.2
ama-lul, see *amalu* and *amalitu*
ama-nu-bar, 4.8.2; App. 4.1.12
ama-nu-gig, 4.8.2; App. 4.1.12
ama-uru, 4.8.2; 4.13; 4.15
amru, 2.4.11
amzalilu, 2.25.1
angubbû, (or *dingirgubbû*) /AN.GUB.BA 3.3.7; **3.13**
an-ni-ba-tu, see *eššeb /pu*
ansamullu, App. 4.2.1
anzanīnu, 2.25.1; App. 4.1.14; **App. 4.2**; App. 4.3
apillatu, see pi-li-pi-li **App. 3.7**; App. 3.7.3
apillû, see pi-li-pi-li; 4.12.6n; App. 3.2.7; **App. 3.7**; App. 3.7.2
āpiltu, **3.15**
āpilu, **3.15**
apkallatu, **3.8**; 3.8.5 (Gula)
apkallu, / abgal 1.15.3; 1.21.8; 1.22.2; 1.22.3; 1.25.2; 1.25.3; 1.36; 2.3.15; 3.3.2; 3.5.1; 3.5.2; **3.8**; 3.8.3 (*apkal šamni*); 3.8.4 (in art); 3.10; 3.26 (*apkal šamni*); App. 3.2.4
aplu, App. 3.13, **App. 3.13.1**
AR, 4.3.1
ARA, see *ararru*
**ararratu*, / mí-arà 2.3.13
ararru, / *āriru* /lú-arà / mí-arà 1.2.9, 1.23; 1.37.3; 2.3.13 (m. and f.); 2.4.7; App. 5.6

ararû, **App. 3.12**
āriru, see *ararru*
asâtu , **3.4**; 3.4.11
assinnatu, 4.9.4, 4.11.14, App. 3.2.7, App. 3.2.8
assinnu / UR.SAL, Intro 1.3; 1.28; 2.1.2.39 (?); 2.2.3; 2.5; 2.7.3; 2.21.2; 2.25.4 (dance); 3.4.2n; 3.14; 3.15.2; 3.17.1; 3.20.2; 3.20.4; 3.21.1; 3.21.3; 4.8.4; 4.11.9n; 4.17.1; 4.22.6; 4.22.10; 4.22.13; 4.24.3; **App. 3.2**; App. 3.4; App. 3.5.1 (sag-ur-sag?); App. 3.5.2; App. 3.7.1; App. 3.7.4; App. 3.8.2 (variant...*kulu'u*); App. 3.9; App. 3.11; App. 3.13.1; App. 3.13.7
asû /azu, 3.1.3; 3.2.3 (*bārû*); **3.4**; 3.4.7; 3.4.9; 3.4.10; 3.6; 3.27.1
aṣû / gala-zé-è, 2.3.14
ašaredu, 1.7.2
āšiptu, **3.4**; 3.4.2; 3.20.5
āšipu, 1.16; 2.7.2 (*aluzinnu*); 2.13.4; 2.15.4; 3.1.3; 3.3.4; **3.4**; 3.4.4 (skills of the *ašipu*); 3.6; 3.7.10; 3.8.2; 3.17.2; 3.20.3; 3.32.14
aššatu šanītu, 4.11.2
aštalītu, see *eštalītu*
aštalû, see *eštalû*
^{mí}*aštammu,* App. 4.1.13
atû, see ì-du$_{8}$
a-tu, 1.18; **1.28**; 1.29; App. 3.13.2
a-tu$_{5}$, 1.7.2; 1.7.8; 1.28; **1.29**
atugallu, see *nidugallu*
atû rabû, see ì-du$_{8}$-gal-lum
a-ù-a, 2.7.1; 2.17; 2.26
a-zu, 3.2.3
A.ZU, see *asû*
a-zu$_{5}$, 1.7.1
azugallatu / a-zu-gal, 3.4.2; 3.4.11
BA, 4.3.1
bahar$_{2}$, see *pahharu*
bakkā' u, **2.15**
bakkītu, **2.15**
bala, see *ša pilaqqati*
balag, 2.2.4; 2.8.3; **2.10**; 2.20
balag-balag-di, 2.1.2.54
balag-di /*sarihu* /*munambû,* 2.2.4; 2.3.3; 2.3.14; 2.4.1; **2.8**; 2.8.1 (f.); 2.10.1; 2.13.1
balag-íl, **2.10**, 2.10.3
balag-i-lu-di, see *munambu*
bala-šu-du$_{7}$, see *nāš pilaqqi*
lú-bappir, 1.3.2; 1.37.1; 2.3.13; 3.3.4; see *sirāšû*
bappir-èš, 1.7.1
bārītu, (f.) **3.2**; 3.2.8; 3.8.5 (Gula)
bārû, see maš-šu-gíd-gíd 1.10.6 (offspring of a *nešakku*); 1.13.4; 1.37.3 (KUL.LUM); 2.3.11; 2.4.7; 3.1.2; 3.1.3; **3.2**; 3.3.4; 3.3.5; 3.3.6; 3.4.7; 3.4.8 (*mār bārê*); 3.4.9; 3.4.11; 3.7.10(*mār bārê*); 3.15.2 ("prophet"), 3.20.3; 3.26 (*mār barî*); 3.27.1; 4.9.2; App. 3.7.8 (*mār bārê)*
batultu, 4.3.5; 4.11.5
bēl narkabti, 3.17.1
bēl pāhete, 1.2.9; 4.11.11
bēl piqitti, App. 5.11
bēlu, 1.18
BI, 4.3.1
bikītu, 2.9, 2.15.3
bur(-ra)/*burrû*, 1.17; 2.3.12n; **App. 3.13**
búr-balag, **2.9**
bur-gul, 1.34; App. 5.12
burrû / bur-ra, see sag-bur **App. 3.13**
bur-sag, see sag-bur
bur-tur, App. 3.13.4
SAL bur-u$_{5}$, App. 3.13.1
dabibtu, 2.20
dāgil iṣṣurē, 2.3.11; 3.3.8; 3.4.9; **3.27**
dam "wife," 1.34
dam-ab-ba, **2.14**
dam-dingir, 1.2.1; 4.13
dam-gàr, 1.7.5
dam-kaskal, see *šêtu*
dam-nu-gig, 4.11.2; 4.23.8
dayānu, 1.38.3
di-ku$_{5}$, 1.14.3
dím, see *itinnu*
lú-dingir, 3.3.2
dingirgubbû, see *angubbû*
dub-alal-urudu, 3.3.2; App. 5.14
dub-sar, 1.7.1; 4.11.2
dub-sar-a-šà-ga, see *šassukku*
DUB.SAR.ZAG.GA, see *zazakku*
edammētu, **3.3**; 3.3.7; App. 4.1.6n
e/adammû, 1.10.1; **3.3**; 3.3.7; 3.13.2
x-e$_{7/11}$-dè, see *naršindu*
é-gi$_{4}$-(a), **1.34**; App. 4.2.1
é-gi$_{4}$ gal, 1.34

egir-šita$_x$-UNU, 2.3.13
egītu, App. 3.13.1n
egi-zi, see *igiṣītu.* App. 3.5.3
egi-zi-gal, see *igiṣīgallatu*
egu, 2.17; App. 3.13.1n
elēnītu, 3.20.5
ellu, 1.9.3; 1.9.10
embūbu, App. 3.2.4n
emeš, 1.21.8; 1.22.2
emu rabu, App. 4.2.1
emu ṣehru, App. 4.2.1
en, (f.) 1.6.1; **1.19;** 1.19.7 (chosen by extispicy), 1.19.11; 1.21.4; 1.21.7; 1.23; 3.2.1; 3.4.8; 4.8.2; 4.23.8
en, (m.) 1.6.1; 1.9.6; 1.13.2, **1.18**; 1.19.11; 1.21.1; 1.21.2; 1.21.3; 1.21.6; 1.21.9; 1.23; 1.49; 2.3.13; 2.4.7; 3.2.1; 3.3.7; 4.11.2; 4.22.15.5; 4.23.8; App. 3.13.2
endib /*endibbu* see endub/*endubbu*
èn-du-an-na, 4.10.1
endub / *endubbu,* **1.26**; App. 5.15
engar, App. 5.16
engiz / *engiṣu,* 1.22.3; **1.23,** 1.24; 1.25.1; 1.26; 1.37.3; 2.4.7; 3.3.2; 3.3.4; 3.3.5; App. 5.17
engû, App. 5.18
enkum /*enkummu,* 1.15.3; 1.18; 1.21.8; 1.22.2; 1.22.3; 1.23; 1.24; **1.25**; 1.31; 4.22.15.2; App. 3.13.2
EN.ME.GI$_4$, see engiz
EN.ME.LI /ensi, 3.3.1; 3.4.9
EN.ME.MU, see *endubbu*
en-nam, 1.3.2
ennigi /*ennigû,* **1.27**; 2.4.3
ensi, 1.7.12; 1.15.3; 1.16; 1.23; 1.24; 1.25.1; **3.3**; 3.3.1 (f.); 3.3.2; 3.3.4; 4.9.1; 4.23.9 No. 11
ensi$_2$ / *iššakku,* 3.3.10
ensu, 3.3.1
entu, 1.2.1; 1.6.1; 1.13.2; 1.18; **1.19**; 1.20; 1.21.9; 1.28; 1.37.3; 1.44; 2.4.7; 4.2; 4.3.5; 4.3.8; 4.9.1; 4.9.2; 4.9.4 (confusion with *ugbabtu*); 4.10.1; 4.11.5; 4.11.13; 4.13.13; 4.22.7; 4.22.13; 4.22.15.4; 4.22.15.5; 4.22.15.6; 4.23.8
enu, see en, 1.6.1; 1.10.1; 1.13.2; **1.18**; 1.19.3; 1.19.7; 1.19.11; 1.21.4; 1.21.9; 1.23; 1.37.3; 2.4.7; 4.17 (f.); App. 3.2.4
en-zirru, 1.19.3; 1.20
ēpiš balamgi, **2.10**
ēpiš namūti, 2.7.1
ēpištu, 3.4.6; **3.7**, 3.7.5, 3.21.3
ēpišu, **3.7**, 3.7.5
lú-ér, **2.15**
mí-ér, **2.15**
ērib bīti / TU.É, 1.10.7 (*nesakku*); 1.13.4; 1.14.3; 1.28; 1.37.4; 1.38.3; 1.44; **1.45**; 2.3.16n; 2.3.18; 2.4.3; 3.16.1
ERIN, 2.4.7
ér-ra, **2.15**
ér-sig$_7$, 2.14, 2.18
erû, 1.11
esirtu, 4.11.12; 4.24.3
ešabdû, see *ababdû*
éš-dam-kù, 4.13
eššeb /*pû,* 2.13.4; **3.20m**
eššeb / *pūtu* / an-ni/ne-ba-tu, **3.20**, 3.20.2
e /*aštalītu,* 2.7.1; **2.17**
eštalû or *aštalû* /èš-ta-lá, 2.7.1; **2.17**; 2.25.1
gadalallû / gada-lá, 1.13.2; 1.15.3; **1.17**; 4.22.15.2; App. 1.13.1
gada-lá-abzu, 1.9.4, 1.17
gá-dub-ba, see *šandabakku*
ga-íl, 1.41
LÚ.GAL.MEŠ, 1.32; **2.5**; 2.5 (*assinnu*)
gala, see *kalû* 1.7.5; 2.1.2.42; 2.2.4; **2.3**; 2.3.3 (f.); 2.3.13; 2.4.1; 2.4.5; 2.10.1; 2.13.1; 2.13.3; 2.14; 2.16; 2.24; 3.3.2; 4.9.1; 4.11.2; 4.23.9, 7
galahallatušû / gala-hal-tuš-a, 2.3.5; 2.3.14; 2.4.11
gala-kéš-da, 2.3.14
gala-mah, see *kalamāhu,* 1.37.1; **2.3**; 2.3.11; 2.3.13; 2.3.14; 2.14; 3.3.2; 4.23.10; App. 3.13.5
gala-tur / *galaturru,* 2.3.4.1; App. 3.2.9
galaussû, 2.3.5; 2.3.14
gala-zé-è, 2.3.14
GAL.BALAG, 2.10.3
gallabu /*tu* / šu-i, App. 5.19
gal-nar, 2.4.4; 3.3.2
GAL.NINDA, 1.32
GAL.ŠIMxA, 1.32
gal-ukkin-na, 1.39
gal-zu-ukkin-na /*rabi puhri,* 1.37.1; **1.39**
GAR, 4.3.1
gašan, see *ištarītu*

ga$_5$-šu-du$_8$, App. 5.20
gemé-kikken, 1.41
GI, 4.3.1
gi-di, 2.1.2.52; 2.2.4
gi-gíd, 2.3.10; App. 3.2.4n
^{lú}gi-par, App. 3.14
gíṛ ba-ḍa-ra, App. 3.5.3
GÍR.LÁ, see *ṭābihu*, *nāš patri*
girseqû / gìr-sè-ga, 2.13.3; 4.22.15.5 (gipar); 4.23.4n
giš-ban, 2.3.6
lú/ mi-giš-gi-(sag-kéš), see *naqmu*
^{giš}šibir-šu-du$_7$, see *nāš šibirri*
GU, 4.3.1
gubabtu, see *ugbabtu*
lú-gub-ba and mí-gub-ba, see *mahhu*
gudapsû, see gudu$_4$-abzu
gudu$_4$, see *pašīšu* 1.2.1; 1.3.2; 1.5.2; 1.5.1; 1.6.1; **1.7**; 1.9.4; 1.10.1; 1.10.3; 1.10.5; 1.10.6 (language of); 1.10.7; 1.11; 1.12.1; 1.13.1; 1.13.2; 1.13.3; 1.14.2, 1.16; 1.17; 1.21.4 (šà-gada-lá); 1.24; 1.29; 1.35.1; 2.3.9 (with gala); 2.3.11; 2.3.13; 3.2.5; 3.3.7; 3.8.3; 4.9.1; 4.9.3 (me); 4.11.2; 4.22.15.5 (gipar); 4.23.4n; App. 3.3.5; App. 3.5.3
gudu$_4$-abzu /*gudapsû,* 1.3.2; 1.6.1; 1.7.1; 1.9.9, 1.9.4, 1.10.1,1.10.3, 1.10.5; 1.10.6 (language of), 1.10.7,1.13.2, **1.14**; 1.18, 1.19.10, 1.21.2; 1.21.4, 1.21.7, 1.24, 1.45, 3.16.1
gudu$_4$-^{d}ba-ba$_6$, 1.7.5
gudu$_4$-bal-lá / *guduballû,* 1.8
gudu$_4$-bal-(là)-gub-ba-(a) / *ša manzalti,* 1.8
gudu$_4$-bal-(lá)-ta-è, 1.8
gudu$_4$-bal-lá-tur-ra / *guduballaturru,* 1.8
gudu$_4$-bal-tuš-a, 1.8
gudu$_4$-Inanna, 1.3.2; 1.7.5
gudu$_4$-^{d}nin-ur$_4$-ra, 1.7.5
gudu$_4$-sag-luh-ha, 1.8
gudu$_4$-su$_6$-lá, 1.8
gudu$_4$-tur-ra, 1.13.3
gudu$_4$-x, **1.8**
gudu$_4$-zi-ni-šè-ku$_4$-ra, 1.8
guenakku, 1.10.7 (*nesakku*); App. 5.21
mí-gù-mur-ak, **2.19**; 4.6.5
gúr-tuku, see gudu$_4$
guzalû / gu-za-lá, App. 5.22
HA, 4.3.1
hābit mê, **3.18**; 4.16.3
HAL, see *bārû,* **3.2**; 3.4.9
hal-la-tuš-a, 2.7.1
hallatuššû / nar-hal-tuš-a/gala-hal-tuš-a), NAR.TUR, 2.3.5; 2.4.11; 2.7.1
HAR [ ], 1.2.9
harimtu / kar-kid, 1.2.4; 2.3.4.1; 2.15.3 (weeping); 3.21.1; 4.4.1; 4.6.4 (*harimūtu*); 4.8.4; 4.11.6; 4.11.12 (no veil); 4.11.16; 4.12; **4.14**; 4.14 (kar-kid-mu-gib); 4.14 (kar-kid-suhub$_2$-si); 4.14 (kar-kid-gi-te-te); 4.16.3; 4.24.3; App. 3.2.10; App. 3.8.4 (*harimti āli*); App.3.11 (garment *aguhhu*); App. 4.1.7.1(Inanna); App. 4.1.11 (Inanna); App. 4.1.12 (Curse of Agade); App. 4.1.13; App. 4.2.1 (Inanna)
harmaku, App. 1 r.16n
harṭibi, 2.3.11; **3.3**; 3.3.8
hazannu, 1.10.7 (*nesakku*); 1.14.2; App. 4.2.1; App. 5.23
húb-bi, see *huppû*
humatāte ? or *hulatāte,*? 2.4.7
humušû, 1.6.2 (Mari)
**hunduraya*, App. 5 n. 47
huppû/ húb-bi, 1.6.2 (Mari); 2.3.13; **2.26**; **App. 3.14**
IB, 4.3.1
ibru / ku-li, 4.3.1n; App. 4.2.1
ì-du$_8$ / *atû,* 1.12.2; 1.37.1; 1.41; 2.3.13; 2.4.6; 3.13.2; 4.9.2; App 3.14; App. 5.24
ì-du$_8$-èš, 3.3.2; App. 5.24n
ì-du$_8$-*gagû,* 4.9.2
ì-du$_8$-gal-lum, see *nidugallu*
igi-du$_8$(-èš), 1.16; 3.3.2, **3.11**, App. 5.25
igiṣīgallatu / egi-zi-gal, **4.10**; 4.10.2
igiṣītu / egi-zi, 1.13.2; 1.19.3; 1.19.9; 1.19.15; 1.28; 4.9.3 (me); **4.10**; 4.10.1 (egi-zi-an-na); App. 3.5.3
ikkaru, see engar
i-lu-di / *munambû* 2.3.14; **2.8**; 2.11.1; 2.20
inim-ma, see *ša awāti*

ir'emū, 3.12.2
ír-sig$_7$, 2.14
išib/*išippu,* 1.2.1; 1.3.2; 1.6.1; 1.9.2; 1.10.1; 1.10.6; 1.13.1(in gi$_6$-par$_x$-ra); 1.13.2; **1.16**; 1.19.7; 1.21.4; 1.21.9; 1.22.3; 1.23; 1.37.3; .48; 1.49; 2.4.7; 3.2.1; 3.4.1; 3.2.1; 3.4.8; 3.7.10; 3.8.3; 3.10; 4.9.3 (me); 4.10.1 (isib-an-na); 4.22.15.5 (gipar); 4.23.4n; App. 3.3.5, App. 3.5.3
išib-mah, 1.14.2; 1.16
išištu, 3.9
išparu, see *ušparu*
iššakku, see ensi$_2$
ištarītu /nu-gig, Intro 1.1; 1.2.1; 3.20.5 (among witches); 4.6.5; 4.8.2; 4.8.4; 4.10.1 (gašan-an-na); 4.11.1; 4.11.13; 4.11.15 (gašan-an-na, nu-gig-an-na); **4.12**; 4.14n; 4.22.13; App. 4.1.7.1
Ì.SUR, see *ṣāhit šamni*
itinnu/ŠITIM, 1.37.3; 2.3.16 (ritual); 2.4.7; App. 5.28
ì-zu, 3.2.3
KAxBE.ZU, 3.7
SAL.KA.HAR-ak, see gù-mur-ak
ka-kù-gál/*kakugallu,* 1.25.3; 3.4.1
kalamāhu / gala-mah, 1.3.7; 1.37.1; **2.3**; 2.3.16; 4.14; App. 4.3
kalbatu, 4.24.5
kalbu, 4.24.5
kallābu, 3.27.1
kallatu, 1.34; 1.50.9; 1.50.12
KAL.MAH, Intro 1.3
kalû see gala, 1.3.5; 1.3.6; 1.3.7; 1.3.10; 1.3.11; 1.6.2 (Mari); 1.21.1; 1.21.8; 1.21.9; 1.36; 1.37.4; 1.45 (*ērib bīti*); 2.1.2.26; 2.1.2.56; 2.1.2.59; **2.3**; 2.3.5 (*šamalle*); 2.4.5; 2.4.6; 2.4.7; 2.4.8; 2.6 (and *surrû*); 3.3.8; 3.8.3; 3.9; App. 3.3.5 (*manzû*); App. 3.13.3 (*tigû*)
kalû agašgû, 2.3.5
kalû ṣihru, 2.3.4; 2.3.16
KA-ninda, 1.37.1; App. 5.29
kaparru /tu, 3.14, App. 5.30
kapištu / túg-túg-bal, 1.6.2 (Mari); App. 3.14
kāribtu, 3.8.5
kāribu, 1.9.2; 3.8.5
karkadinnu / SUM.NINDA, App. 5.31
kar-kid, see *harimtu*
KAŠ$_4$, 4.3.1
KAŠ.DIN, see kurun
kāṣiru, 2.13.4; 3.4.12
kašitu, 4.13
kaš-lul, see *šāqû*
kaššāptu, 3.1.2.36; 3.4.6; **3.7**; 3.7.2; 3.7.5; 3.20.4; 3.20.5; 3.21.3
kaššāpu / UŠ$_{11(12)}$.ZU, 2.1.2.36; **3.7**; 3.7.2; 3.7.5; 3.20.4; 3.21.3
kaṣṣidakku / ka-zì-da, 1.37.1; App. 5.33
kaššu, 4.11.3
ka-zì-da, see *kaṣṣidakku*
kezertu / SUHUR.LAL, 1.2.9; 1.12.1; 1.32; 1.42; 2.4.5; 2.15.3; 2.19; **4.6**; 4.11.6; 4.14; 4.22.13; App. 3.2.10; App. 3.3.4 (DUMU.MÍ.SUHUR .LÁ); App. 3.5.3; App. 4.1.14
kezru, 1.32; 1.42; **4.6**; 4.6.3
kigullu, App. 4.1.13
gemé-kikken, 1.41
kiništu, 1.21.9; **1.44**, 1.45
kisalluhhatu /mí-kisal-luh, 1.6.2 (Mari); 1.9.10; **1.12**; 2.3.13; 2.4.6; 4.6.6; 4.7.2
kisalluhhu / lú-kisal-luh, 1.9.10; **1.12**; 1.41; 2.3.13; 2.4.7; App. 5 n. 24
ki-sì-ga, see *kišpu*
kiṣir ešši, 3.4.12
kišib-gál /*kišibgallu,* 1.3.2; 1.22.1; 1.22.3; 1.23; **1.24**; 1.24.1; 1.25.1; 1.40; 3.3.2
kišib-lá, 1.24
lú-ki-sikil, 4.23.9 No. 1
kispu, **3.25**
ki-zé-er-ak, see *kezertu*
^{d}Ku-bi, 4.3.5; 4.11.13
kuddimatu, 3.20.5
ku-li, see *ibru*
KUL.LUM, see *barû* , *sirašû*
kulmašītu /NU.BAR, Intro 1.3; 2.2.3; 3.20.5 (among witches); 4.3.3 (and *naditu*); 4.3.5; 4.7.2; **4.8**; 4.11.4; 4.11.5; 4.11.13; 4.11.14; 4.12; 4.17; 4.23.9 (nu-bar-ra, Inanna)
kulu'u, 3.14; 3.20.2; 3.20.4; 3.21.1; 4.7.1; 4.14n; 4.16.3; 4.17; 4.22.6;

4.22.10; App. 3.2.9; App.3.3.3; App. 3.7.2; **App. 3.8**; App. 3.12
kumirtu, 1.4.5; **1.35**
kumru, 1.4.5; **1.35**
kur-gar/*kurgarrû,* 1.3.4; 1.37.4; 2.1.2.22; 2.3.4.1; 2.3.14 (among singers); 2.3.16; 2.4.7 (among singers); 2.7.3; 2.16; 2.21.2; 2.25.4 (dance); 3.4.1; 3.12.6; 3.14; 3.20.2; 3.20.4 (with *eššepû*); 3.21.3; 4.4.1; 4.8.4; 4.22.13; 4.23.4.74; App. 3.2.1; App. 3.2.4; App. 3.2.5; App. 3.2.5n; App. 3.2.7; App. 3.2.9; App. 3.2.10; **App. 3.3**; App. 3.3.1 (MÍ.KUR.GAR); App. 3.4; App. 3.5.1; App. 3.7.4; App. 3.10; App.3.14 (*kurgarūtu*)
kur-mar-ra, emesal for kur-gar-ra, q.v.
kurun, see *sābû* and *sābītu*
kuš-balag, 2.8.3
kuš-lá, 1.15.3, 1.17; 1.18n, 4.14, 4.22.15.2, App. 3.2.7
KU.ZI, App. 3.5.3
kuzīru, App. 4.1.13
labar, 1.21.1; 1.21.2n.
lābiš kitê, 1.17 (*ša apsi*); 2.4.7
lagal /*lagallu,* **1.21**
lagar/*lagarru,* 1.3.1; 1.13.2; 1.18; 1.19.7; **1.21**; 1.37.3; 2.4.7; 3.4.8
SAL.LAGAR.BE, 1.21.8, 1.22.2
SAL.LAGAR.ME, 1.21.8, 1.22.2
lahhinu, see *alahhinu*
làl, 1.18; 1.28; **1.31**; App. 3.13.2
làl-e-šà-ga, 1.28
lallār (i)tu, **2.20**; 2.3.14; 3.4.1
lallāru, 2.3.14; **2.20**
làl-zu-sà-ga, 1.28
laputtû, 1.10.7 (*nešakku*); 4.8.1; App. 4.2.1
libir-si, see nimgir-si
libir-si-zu-en, 4.23.9 No. 3
lilissu, 1.3.10
lú-á-lá, 2.2.4
ludimma, 4.9.1
lú-dingir, 3.3.2
lugal, 4.23.4.70 (Iddin-Dagan)
lugal-bur-ra, 1.10.3; 1.18; App. 3.13.2
lú-gi-di, 2.2.4; 2.1.2.52
lú-giš-ban, 2.3.6
luhšû, 1.6.2 (Mari); 1.9.9; **1.11**; 1.12.2; **3.8**
lukšû, **1.11**
lukur, Intro 1.3 (ED); 1.2.1; 1.19.7; 1.34 ("priestly wife"); 2.2.4; 2.4.5; 2.8.1; **4.3**; 4.3.2; 4.16.2; 4.23.9, 8
lukur.DUMU.DUMU.DUN, 4.3.1
lukurgallu, 1.19.15; 4.4.1
lukur-kaskal-lá, (see *šugētu*) 4.3.1; 4.4.1
lú-lùnga, 1.3.2
lú-mah, **1.13**; 1.16; 1.17; 1.21.4; 1.21.5 (chosen by kid); 3.2.1; 3.20.2; 4.9.3 (me); 4.10.1; 4.22.15.2; 4.22.15.5 (gipar); 4.23.4n; App. 3.5.3
lumahhu, **1.13**
lumakku, 1.13.3
MA, 4.3.1
mah, see lú-mah
mahhû / gub-ba, see *muhhû* 1.13.3; 1.37.4; 2.3.13; 2.3.16; 3.3.10; **3.12**; 3.14; 3.17.1; 3.20.2; 4.4.1; App. 3.2.7; App. 3.6.1
mahiṣtu, 2.4.6
malāhu, 1.41
lú-má-lal, 2.21.1
malilu, **2.21**, App. 3.2.4n
manzaz ekalli, 3.4.9; 3.27.1
maqaltānu, **1.46** (Sam'al)
mārat āliya, 3.20.5
mārat ili / *ilāni,* 4.3.5; 4.9.5; **4.17**
mār bārê, 3.4.8, 3.7.10, 3.8.3 (*apkallu*), 3.26, App. 3.7.7
mār šangi, 1.3.13
mār šarri, 1.38.3
mar-tu, 2.3.6
māru's, (of the?) *kezretu*'s 1.2.9
māru ša amāt ili, 3.17.1
marzi'u, 2.49.7n
māṣilu, App. 3.14
LÚ.MAŠ, 1.32; **1.42**; 3.4.9
MÍ.MAŠ, 1.32; **1.42**
MAŠ.MAŠ /*mašmaššu* or *āšipu*), 1.13.4; 1.37.4; 2.3.11; 2.3.16; 2.4.7; 3.3.8; **3.4**; 3.5.1; 3.7.10; 3.8.2; 3.17.1; 3.17.2; 3.27.1; 4.11.10
MAŠ.MAŠ *šaniu,* 3.4.3
MAŠ.MAŠ *ṣehru,* 3.4.12
maš-šu-gíd-gíd, see *bārû*
maṣû, 1.42
LÚ.ME, 1.16; 3.4.1; 3.8.2
melulû, 2.7.1, App. 5.34
LÚ.ME.ME, 1.16; 3.4.1; 3.4.7; 3.8.2
mí-gù-mur-ak, see gù-mur-ak

MU, see *nuhatimmu* 2.3.6; 4.3.1
mubabbilu, 1.6.2 (Mari)
mubarru, App. 5.35
mu-gib$_x$, emesal for nu-gig, q.v.
muhaldim, App. 3.3.6
muhhû /al-è-dè, see *mahhû* 1.6.2 (Mari); **3.12**; 3.14; 3.15.2; 3.19; App. 3.4; App. 3.5.3; App. 3.6; App. 3.7.5
muhhūtu, Intro 1.3; **3.12**; 3.12.3; 3.15.2
mu'irru, see *muwirru*
mukīl appāte, 1.3.10; 2.3.16, 2.13.4; App. 5.36
mukkallu, 1.15.1; **1.36**; 3.8.2; **3.9**
mullilu / sanga$_2$-ma-da, **3.5**; 3.25.1
multēpištu, **3.7**, 3.7.5
multēpišu, **3.7**; 3.7.5
mummidu, 2.7.1
mummillu / *tu,* 2.25.1; App. 5.37
mu$_7$-mu$_7$, **3.4**; 3.6
munambû, see i-lu-di 2.8.1 (balag-i-lu-di)
munammirtu, 4.13
munu$_x$ (?), 4.15
mupaššer šunāti, **3.3**; 3.3.1; 3.3.5; 3.3.9
muppišānu, **3.7**; 3.7.3
muppištu, **3.7**; 3.7.3; 4.13
muppišu, **3.7**; 3.7.3
murammiku, **1.47**
muraqqû / *ītu,* App. 5.38
musahhitu, 2.4.6
muṣarrihtu, **2.22**
muṣihhu, 2.7.1
mušākil iṣṣurē, **3.28**; 3.29.2; App. 5.39
mušarkisu, 1.36; 3.9
mušēlit /*u eṭimme,* 2.10.2, 3.7.2, 3.7.8
mušēlitu, **3.7**, 3.7.8, 3.7.9
mušēlû, **3.7**, 3.7.9
mušēlu eṭimmi, 2.10.2; 3.3.1; **3.7**; 3.7.8
MUŠEN.DÙ, see *usandû*
mušēpištu, **3.7**, 3.26
mušēpišu, **3.7**, 3.7.5, 3.7.6
muš-lah$_4$/*mušlahhu,* 1.41; 2.4.1; 2.4.5; **2.13**; 2.13.4; 3.20.3; 3.20.4
mušlahhatu, 2.4.1; **2.13**; 3.20.5
mušlalahhu, 2.13.2
mussiru, **3.24**
muššakku, 3.29
muššiptu, 3.2.8; 3.8.5 (Gula); **3.24**
muššipu, 3.2.8; **3.24**
muštēpištu, **3.7**, 3.7.7
muštēpišu, **3.7**, 3.7.7
muwirru /*mu'irru,* 1.39
nadītu, 1.2.2; 1.2.4; 1.12.2; 1.19.7; 1.19.15; 1.34; 3.16.1; 3.18; 3.20.5 (among witches); **4.3**; 4.3.5 (*qadištu*); 4.4.1; 4.7.2; 4.8.1; 4.8.2; 4.8.4; 4.9.2; 4.11.5 (relationship to *qadištu*); 4.11.6; 4.11.10; 4.11.13; 4.11.14; 4.12; 4.22.6; 4.22.10; 4.22.13; 4.22.14.3; App. 3.2.7
nāgiru / *tu* / nimgir, App. 4.2.1; App. 5.41
nam-egi-zi, 1.13.2
nam-gudu$_4$, 1.13.2
nam-išib, 1.9.2, 1.13.2
nam-lugal, 1.13.2
nam-lú-mah, 1.13.2
nam-nin-dingir, 1.13.2
nam-sipa, 1.13.2
nam-šita, 1.3.2; 1.9.2; 1.37.1
nappāhu, App. 3.14, App. 5.42
napṭartu, **App. 4.3**
napṭaru, 4.11.7 (*qadištu*); App. 4.2.4; **App. 4.3**
nāqidu, App. 5.43
naqimtu, **3.19**
naqmu / giš-gi-(sag-kéš), 3.14, **3.19**
nar, see *nāru*
nar a-ù-a, 1.37.1
NAR.BALA, see *tigû*
nar-gal / *nargallatu* /MÍ.NAR.GAL, 1.2.9; 1.3.5; 1.37.1; 2.3.13; **2.4;** 2.4.4 (ED); 2.4.5; 2.4.6 (f.); 2.4.8 (f.); 2.5; App. 3.3.1 (MÍ.NAR.GAL); App. 3.3.4
nar-hal-tuš-a, see *nāru hallatuššû*
nar-igi-suhur-lá, 2.4.5; 2.4.11; 4.6.3
narkabtu, 2.13.4
nar-kéš-da, 2.4.11
mí-nar-lukur, 2.3.13; 2.4.5
nar-nar, 2.4.11
nar-pà-da, 2.4.11
nar-sa, 1.3.2 (^{d}Enki); 1.37.1; 2.3.13; 2.4.11
nar-sal-gil, 2.25.1
naršindatu, 3.20.5; **3.22**
naršindu, /x-e$_{7/11}$-dè 3.20.2; 3.20.4; 3.21.3; **3.22**
nārtu, **2.4**; 3.27.1; App. 3.3.1
nar-tur, see *nāru ṣehru*
SAL.NAR.TUR, 2.4.6
SAL.NAR.TUR.TUR, 1.12.1; 2.4.6; 4.6.6

nāru / nar, 1.3.4; 1.3.7; 1.37.4; 1.41; 2.1.2.21; 2.1.2.28; 2.1.2.37; 2.1.2.50; 2.1.2.53; 2.2.4; 2.3.2; 2.3.7; 2.3.13; 2.3.14; 2.3.18 (*kalû*'s act with); **2.4**; 2.5; 2.13.1; 2.24; 2.25.1; 3.27.1; 4.6.3; 4.16.3; App. 3.2.5; App. 3.2.5n; App. 3.3.7; App. 3.13.6; App. 3.14
nāru hallatuššû, 2.4.5; 2.4.11
nāru ṣehru, 2.1.2.40; 2.4.5; 2.4.11
nāš balamgi, **2.10**, 2.10.4
nāš patri / giri-lá, App. 3.3.6; App. 5.44
nāš pilaqqi / bala-šu-du$_7$, App. 3.2.7; **App. 3.10**
nāš ^{giš}*šamni,* 2.1.2.44, 2.4.5
nāš šibirri / ^{giš}šibir-šu-du$_7$, 1.28; App. 3.2.7
nērtanītu, 3.20.5
nešakku / NU.ÈŠ / nisag, 1.6.1; 1.7.2; 1.7.8; 1.7.9; **1.10**; 1.18; 1.45 (*ērib bīti*); 2.6; 2.3.13; 3.3.7; 3.13.2; App. 3.3.5; App. 3.7.7; App. 3.13,2
nidugallu (or) *atugallu,* 2.4.7; App. 5.45
lú-níg-ág, 3.3.2, App. 5.46
nigìn-gar-kù, 4.13
nimgi, see *nāgiru*
nimgir-si, see *susapinnu*
nin "queen," 1.34, 4.23.8
LÚ.NINDA, 2.13.4; App. 3.3.4; App. 5.47
nin-dingir-(ra), see *entu*, *ugbabtu* Intro 1.3 (ED); 1.2.1; 1.13.2 (by kid); **1.19**; 1.21.5 (by kid); 1.28; 3.2.1; 3.3.2; 4.2; 4.3.5; **4.9**; 4.23.8; App. 3.5.3
NIN.DINGIR.TUR, 4.9.2n
nin-dingir-ug$_5$-ga, 1.16, **1.25**
nin-é-gal-la, 4.23.9 No. 1
ninkum / *ninkummu,* 1.15.3, 1.21.8; 1.22.2; **1.25**, 4.22.15.2
NIR.GAL, App. 5.48
nisag, see *nešakku*
nissatu, 2.9, 2.15.3
ni-su-ub, see *zabbu*
nu'aru, 2.4.2
nubanda, 4.23.9
nu-bar, see *kulmašītu*
nu-dingir, 4.13
nu-èš, see *nešakku* 1.2.1; 1.6.1; 1.7.2; 1.7.8; 1.9.2; **1.10**; 1.14.2; 1.18; 1.21.1; 1.21.2; 1.21.7; App. 3.3.5
nu-èš-mah, 1.10.1
nu-gig, see *qadištu* and *ištarītu* Intro 1.3 (ED); 1.2.1; 1.2.5; 1.2.6; 1.19.7; 1.42; 2.5; 4.11; 4.8.2; 4.10.1 (nu-gig-an-na); **4.11**; 4.11.1 (meaning); 4.11.15.12 (nu-gig-an-na); **4.12**; 4.13 (nu-gig-an-na); 4.23.4.80; 4.23.8; 4.23.9; App. 4.1.7.1 (nu-gig-an-na)
LÚ.NU.GIG, 4.11.17; App. 3.14
nu-gig-gal, **4.11**; 4.11.2; 4.11.7 (nu-gig-gal-an-na)
nu-gig-tur, **4.11**; App. 1 r.14
nuhatimmu / MU, 1.3.6; 1.23; 1.26; 2.3.6; 3.16.1; 4.3.1; App. 3.14; App. 5.49
NUN.ME, see *apkallu*
NUN.ME.DU, see abrig
^{uru}paharāni, 2.4.3
pahāru / bahar$_2$, 3.3.2; App. 5.50
PA.KAB.DU, see *širku*
pālihtu, **1.33**
PAP.PAP, **4.15**
PAP.ŠEŠ.AN, 1.7.4
parkullu / *purkullu,* 1.40; App. 3.14, App. 5.51
parrû, App. 3.5.3; App.3.5.3(*parauru*); **App. 3.6**, App. 3.7.1
pa$_4$-šeš, **1.7**; 1.18; 1.29; 1.31; App. 3.13.2
pāširu, 3.3.4
pašīšu, see gudu$_4$ 1.3.2; 1.6.2 (Mari); **1.7**; 1.9.6; 1.10.1; 1.18; 1.19.11; 1.22.3; 1.24; 1.47.1 (*ramku*); 1.48; 2.17; 3.3.7; 3.8.3; 3.10; 3.13.1; 3.13.2
**pašīšu ṣihru,* (? reading) 1.13.3
pe-el-lá, 2.8.1, see pi-li-pi-li
pilaqqatu, see *sa pilaqqati*
pi-li-pi-li, see *apillû* , *apillatu, pilpilû, pilpilānu* 2.16; 3.12.6; 3.14; App. 3.2.7; App. 3.3.5; App. 3.4; App. 3.5.1; App. 3.5.3; App. 3.6.1; **App. 3.7**
pilpilānu, see pi-li-pi-li **App. 3.7**; App. 3.7.7
pilpilû, App. 3.2.7; **App. 3.7**
pisan-dub-ba, see *šandabakku*
purkullu, see *parkullu*
qabbahu, 3.16.1

qabbātu, 3.15.2 ("prophet" at Mari); **3.16**
qabbā'u, 1.14.3; 1.45; **3.16**
qabbiru, 1.16
qadištu, /NU.GIG, Intro 1.1; Intro 1.3; 1.2.1; 1.2.5; 1.19.15; 2.2.3; 3.4.5; 3.20.5 (among witches); 4.3.3; 4.3.5 (*nadītu*); 4.7.2; 4.8.1; 4.8.2; 4.8.4; 4.9.4; **4.11**; 4.11.5 (relationship to *nadītu*); 4.11.13 (witch); 4.12; 4.14; 4.17; 4.22.13; 4.24.3; 4.24.4; App. 1.1ff; App. 3.2.2n; App. 3.2.7; App. 4.3
**qamātu,* 3.16.2
qardu, 2.19; App. 3.2.1 (*qarradu*)
qaššatu, 4.11.7
qaššu, 4.11.1; 4.11.3 (m. of *qadistu* ?)
qīpu / TIL.LA.GÍD.DA, 2.4.3; App. 5.52
qumqummatu, 3.20.5
qurqurratu, 3.20.5
qurrubutu, 3.17.1
rab bānî / GAL.DÙ, 1.40; 2.4.7; App. 5.53
rab ekalli, 4.11.11
rab ginae, App. 5.54
rab narkabāte, 3.4.12
rab kiṣir, 3.17.1
rab kurgarrû, 1.2.9, 2.2.6; **App. 3.3**; App. 3.3.4
rabi puhri, see gal-zu-ukkin-na
rab ša rēši, GAL.SAG 3.27.1
rab šibirte, 2.4.7
rab ṭupšarri, 2.3.11
rab zammaru, 1.3.3; 2.4.3
rá-gaba /*rakbu*; 1.3.2; 2.3.6; 2.3.13, App. 5.55
raggim / ntu, **3.17**; 3.17.2
raggimu, 3.3.10; **3.17**; 3.17.2 (*raggimānu*); App. 3.2.7
ramku, 1.7.8; 1.7.8n; 1.9.3; 1.9.9; 1.10.6; 1.13.3; 1.44; **1.47**; 1.15.1, 1.15.2; 1.18 (en); 1.28; 1.29; 2.6; 3.13.1; App. 3.5.3
ramkut, 2.4.7
raqqidu / sùh-sùh 2.25.1
raqqû / ŠIM.SAR, 3.3.4; 3.4.2; App. 5.55
rubû, 1.38.3
sābītu, 4.3.1,**4.16**; 4.16.2 (Gilgamesh); App. 4.1.10; App. 4.3
sābsūtu, 2.17, 4.11.11, 4.11.15
sābû, 3.4.7; 3.16.1; **4.16**; App. 3.8.3
sa_{12}-du_5, see *šassukku*
sag-bur-(ra) / bur-sag, 1.15.3, 1.41; 2.3.1; App. 3.1; **App. 3.13**
sagi / BI.LUL, 1.7.1; 1.37.1; 1.41; 2.3.13
sag-sè-ná-a **3.3**; 3.3.5; 3.3.9
sag-ur-sag 3.12.6; 3.14; 4.4.1; 4.23.4.45 (Iddin-Dagan); App. 3.2.1; App. 3.2.7; App. 3.3.5; App. 3.4; **App. 3.5**; App. 3.5.1 (*assinnu* ?); App. 3.6.1; App. 3.7.5
sahhirtu, 3.4.6; **3.21**; 3.21.2
sahhiru / zilulu, 3.4.6; 3.20.2; 3.20.4; **3.21**
sahiptu / [ ] lukur, 4.4.1; **4.5**
ṣāhit šamni / I.SUR, App. 5.59
ŠAL, "living goddess" 4.23.8, App. 3.2.1 (*assinnu*)
SAL.NUNUZ.ZI ^{d}INANNA, 1.19.3
sandu, see *usandû*
sanga, see *šangû* 1.2.1; **1.3**; 1.3.2; 1.6.1; 1.7.5; 1.15.3; 1.37.1; 2.3.1; 4.9.1; 4.22.15.2
*^{mí}SAN[GA] (??) 1.3.14
sanga-gal 1.17
$sanga_2$-ma-da see *mullilu*
SANGA.MAH, see *šangammāhu*
lú-SAR, 1.7.5
sarraptu, 4.6.5
sekertu / ŠEŠ, 1.12.1(?); 1.19.7; 2.4.6; 4.6.6; **4.7**; 4.9.2; 4.11.5 (CH); App. 3.8.1(OAkk)
SI, 4.3.1
si-dù, **2.23**
síg-bar-ra/*sigbarû,* **1.11**; 3.8.5
sinnišānu, 3.17.1; App. 3.2.7; **App. 3.9**; App. 4.1.14
sirāšû / ŠIMxGAR, 1.2.9; 1.23; 1.34.4; 1.37.4; 2.3.13; 2.13.4; 3.2.3; 3.3.4; App. 5.60
SUH.BU, see *susbû*
sùh-sùh, see *raqqidu*
LÚ/MÍ.SUHUR.LÁ, see *kezru, kezertu*
sukkal, 2.3.13 (of Enlil)
sukkallu rabû, 1.3.3
sukkallu saniu, 1.3.3
SUM.NINDA, see *karkadinnu*
sur_9, 1.21.1, 1.21.8, **2.6**
surmahhu, 1.10.6; **2.6**
sur(ru)/*surrû,* **2.6**
šušānu, App. 3.4
susapinnu / nimgir-si, 4.23.9, 3; **App. 4.2**; App. 4.2.2; App. 4.3
susbû, 1.13.3, 1.14.2, **1.15**; 1.36; 4.22.15.2; App. 3.5.3

ṣāhit šamni / Ì.SUR, App. 5.60
ṣapparrû, App. 4.1.14
ṣerretu, App. 4.2.1
ṣuhartu, 4.4.1
ṣārihu see balag-di
ŠÀ.A, App. 3.14
ša alê, 2.2.4
ša awāti / inim-ma, 3.3.1; 3.17.1n
ša balamgi, 2.1.2.6; 2.8.3; **2.10**, 2.10.4
ša bikīti, 2.9; **2.15**
šabrû / šabra, Intro 1.3; 1.10.1; 1.48; **3.3**; 3.3.10; App. 3.2.7; App. 5.61
šabsūtu, 2.17; 4.11.11; 4.11.15
ša embūbi, 2.1.2.10
ša endušu, App. 5.62
ša eṭimme, **3.7**; 3.7.10
šà-gada-lá, 1.13.2; 1.17; 1.25.3; 2.4.7
**šaggitu*, 1.3.14
šahittu, 2.25.3
šahšahhu, App. 4.1.14
ša huppû, see *huppû*
ša husīnišu, 2.4.8
šā'iltu, 3.2.8; **3.3**; 3.3.6; 3.7.8; 4.9.2
šā'ilu, 3.1.3; 3.2.1; **3.3**; 3.3.4; 3.3.6; 3.4.7; 3.7.8; 3.21.3; 3.29 (libanomancy)
šākin ṭēmi, 1.10.7; 1.38.3; 1.45
šakintu, 1.32
ša kitturišu, App. 5.63
šakkinu, 2.4.11
šamaktu, 1.13.3
ša malīli, 2.1.2.33; **2.21**
šamuktu, 1.2.5; 1.19.15
šamallû, 2.3.5; 3.4.12
šamallû kalû, 2.3.5
ša manzalti, 1.8
šamhatu / *šamuktu* / *šamahtu* / *šamaktu* 1.2.4; 1.13.3; 1.19.15 (*naditu*); 4.6.4; 4.9.4; 4.11.6; 4.11.14; 4.14; App. 3.2.7, App. 3.2.10; App. 4.2.1
ša muhhi bīti, App. 5.64
ša muhhi MÍ.SUHUR.LÁ.MEŠ, 4.6.6
ša muhhi sahūri, App. 5.65
šamuktu 1.2.5; 1.19.15
šandabakku / pisan-dub-ba, 4.11.5; App. 5.65
šangagallu, (sp.?) 3.5.1, 3.6
šangammāhu, 3.4.8; 3.5.1; **3.6**
**šangītu*, 1.3.14
šangû, Intro 1.3; 1.2.1; 1.2.7; **1.3**; 1.6.1; 1.6.2 (Mari) 1.6.3; 1.6.4; 1.7.7, 1.14.3; 1.19.11; 1.40; 1.45 (*ērib bīti*); 1.48; 2.3.13; 2.4.3 (É.MAS); 2.4.7 (*naptanu*); 3.3.10; 3.12.3; 3.15.2 ("prophet" at Mari); 3.16.1; 4.3.2; 4.6.6; 4.11.9; App. 1.5ff; App. 3.3.4 Bīt Eqî); App. 3.3.6 (with *kurgarrû*); App. 3.14
šangû karkadinnu, 1.3.13
šangû narkabti, 1.37.4
šangû rabû, 1.3.3, 1.3.13
šangû ša bīt DN, 1.3.13
šangû ša bīt eqî, 1.2.9; 4.6.6; App. 3.3.4
šangû sa bīt nuhatimmi, 1.3.13
šangû ša GN, 1.3.12
šangû ša Ištar-pišrā, 1.3.2
šangû šaniu, 1.3.13
šangû ša ^{d}*šarrat-nipha*, 1.2.6, 4.6.6
ša nindabû, 1.40
ša nissati, 2.9
ša pilaqqāti / bala, App. 3.10
šāpiru, 1.38.3; App. 5.67
šāqītu, 2.4.7
šāqû / *ītu*, App. 5.68
šarbu, **3.12**, 3.12.7
ša rēši šarrānu, 1.3.3
šarraptu, 4.6.5
šarratu, "queen" 3.27.1
šarru, "king" 1.6.3; 1.38.3; **1.48**; 2.3.9; 2.3.16; 2.4.5; 2.4.7; 2.4.10; App. 3.3.7
ša sassanni, 2.1.2.46
šassukku and *šassakkatu* / sa$_{12}$-du$_{5}$ /dub sar-a-sà-ga,App. 5.69
ša ṣaddi, 2.26
ša ṣirhi, **2.11**
ša šēhi, **3.12**, 3.12.8
ša šeršānu, see šìr-sag
šà-tam /*šatammu*, 1.2.9; 1.14.3; 1.37.1; 1.37.4; 1.38.3; 1.45; 2.15.4; App. 5.70
ša telīti, 2.8.1; 3.4.12.1.2.54; 4.4.1
ša timbutti, 2.1.2.7
ŠE, 4.3.1
šēhānu, **3.12**, 3.12.8
še-en-nar, **2.12**
še'itu, see *šētu*
šēlūtu, **1.32**; 1.39; 1.42 (*šēluāte*)

šeriktu, šerkatu see *širku*
ŠEŠ, see *sekertu*
ŠEŠ.GAL /*šešgallu*, 1.37.4; **1.38**; 1.45
šešgallutu, 1.38.3
šêtu / dam-kaskal, 4.3.1
gišsibir-šu-du$_7$, see *nāš šibirri*
ŠIMxGAR, see *sirāšû*
šim-mu$_2$, **3.4**; 3.4.2n
ŠIM.SAR, see *raqqû*
lú-šìr, 2.2.4; 2.4.1; **2.11**
širkatu, **1.43**; 4.14
širku / PA.KAB.DU, **1.43**; ú-šìr, 2.2.4; 2.4.1; **2.11**
šìr-sag, **2.11**
šita$_x$, 1.6.1; **1.9**; 1.10.1; 1.15.3
sita$_x$-ab-ba, 1.9.6; 1.15.3, 3.2.1, 4.22.15.2 (šita$_x$-aba)
šita-AB.DI dInanna, 1.9.8
šita$_x$-abzu, 1.9.4
šita-du$_{11}$-du$_{11}$, 1.9.10
šita-èš, 1.9.9; 1.24; 1.37.1
šita$_x$-eša$_x$, 1.9.7
šita$_x$-gal, 1.9.8
šita$_x$-ki-gal-la, 1.9.5
šita$_x$-UNU, 1.9.7; 2.3.13
ŠITIM, see *itinnu*
ŠÙ, 4.3.1
šudararu, **App. 3.12**
šudug$_2$, 1.7.1
šugētu / šu-gi$_4$-(a), 1.19.15; 2.19; 4.3.2; 4.3.3; **4.4**; 4.4.1 (lukur-kaskal-lá); 4.6.3; 4.11.5 (CH); 4.13; 4.23.4.70; App.3.3.5; App. 3.5.3
šuginakku / šu-i, 1.7.8; App. 5.71
šuhaddaku / šu-ha$_6$-ud-da ,App. 5.72
šu-i see *gallabu*, *šuginakku*; 1.3.2; 2.3.13; 1.37.1
šu-ku$_6$, 1.41
ŠU.LUH / *šuluhhu*, 1.47.2
šumēlû, 1.40
šūt kakkē, App. 3.2.4n
TAG, 4.3.1
tappātu, App. 4.2.1
tārītu, App. 5.75
TAR.LUH, 2.3.2
tašlīšu, 2.13.4
telītu, 2.8.1 (an office?); 4.4.1
tig(i)û / NAR.BALAG, 2.1.2.56; 2.3.13; 2.4.4; 2.4.11; **2.8**
tigītu, 2.4.11; **2.8**; 2.8.2
TIL.LA.GÍD.DA, see *qipu*
tīr bīti, 1.21.9; 2.4.7; App. 5.76
TU, 1.18; 1.28; **1.30**, App. 3.13.2
TU.É, see *ērib bīti*
TÚG.LÁ, App. 3.14, App. 5.77
túg-túg-bal, see *kapištu*
túl, 1.21.7
túm, 1.28n
TUR, 4.3.1
LÚ.TUR.MEŠ 1.32; **2.5**
ṭābihu / GÍR.LÁ, 1.37.4; 4.11.10; App. 3.3.6n; App. 5.78
ṭupšar bīt ili, App. 5.79
ṭupšarratu, 1.12.1; 2.4.6; 4.6.6
ṭupšarru, see also A.BA 1.45 (*ērib bīti*); 2.3.11; 2.3.17 (of a series); 2.4.6; App. 5.79

ub$_x$-kug-ga, 2.1.2.63; 3.3.2, App. 5.80
u$_4$-da-tuš, 2.4.5; 2.7.1; 2.13.3; 2.4.5; **2.24**
UD.KA.BAR.DIB.BA, see zabar-dab$_5$
ugbabtu /*gubabtu* / nin-dingir, 1.2.1; **1.19**; 1.28; 2.4.6; 2.25.3; 4.2; 4.3.3; 4.3.5; 4.7.2; 4.8.4; **4.9**; 4.10.1; 4.11.5; 4.11.13; 4.11.14; 4.14n; 4.17; 4.22.13; 4.22.14.3; App. 3.2.8
ugula-é, App. 5.81
ugula-luhsa, 3.3.2, App. 5.82
ugula-nin-dingir-meš, 4.9.2
LÚ.UKKIN, 1.44
um-ma-ír, 2.3.3
ummānu / um-me-a , 1.7.8; 3.2.6; 3.4.12; 3.21.3; 4.11.10
ummi āli, 4.13 (?)
ummi šarri, 3.17.1
ummu ištarītu, see AMA.NU.GIG
UR, 4.3.1
**urigallu*, (cultic official, not standard) 1.38.1
ur-sag, App. 3.5.3
LÚ.UR.SAL, see *assinnu*
(u)sandû / MUŠEN.DÙ, 1.41; **3.28**; App. 5.83
usuh, 1.21.8, 1.22.2
ušbar, "father of the bride," App. 4.2.1
ušparu / *išparu*, 1.32; App. 3.14; App. 5.84
ú-túl, 1.14.3

UŠ(11,12) ZU, see *kaššapu* **3.7**
uzu (NINDAxNUN), see *bārû*
ZA, 4.3.1
zabar-dab5 /*zabardabbu,* 1.23; **1.37**; 1.39; 2.4.7
zabbatu, 3.12.1; 3.12.5; **3.14**; 4.13
zabbu / ni-s/zu-ub, 3.12.5; **3.14**; 3.19; 3.20.2
zá-dim-ma /*zadimmu,* App. 3.14, App. 5.85
zammārtu, **2.4**, 2.4.3
zammāru, **2.4**
zammertu, 2.3.16n; **2.4**; App. 4.1.10n
zammeru, 1.3.7; **2.4**; 2.25.1; 2.26
zazakku, App. 5.86
zilulu, see *sahhiru*
ziqnānu, 4.6.1
zirru / zirru, (f.) **1.20**

Ebla

ama-gal-en, 1.4.4
ensi, 1.7.12
nabiutum, 3.32,21
pa4-šeš-sal, (f.) 1.7.12
šeš-eb-2 1.7.12; 1.38.4

Emar

anabi'atu, 1.19.13, 4.24.9
ellutu, 1.19.13
gamaru ?, 1.19.13
HAL, 1.19.12; 1.19.13
hamsa'u, 1.19.12
hussu, 1.19.12
marzahu ša mì-ki, 1.19.1
maš'artu, 1.19.12 n. 240
**munabbitu,* 1.19.13; 4.24.9
munabi'atu, 1.19.13
NIN.DINGIR, 1.19.12
nu-Bu-ha-an-ni, 1.19.13
nugagtu, 1.19.12
wābil ilai, 1.19.13
zābihu, 1.19.13
zammāru, 1.19.12

Hebrew

ʾaharāh, 4.24.4
ᶜalamôt, 2.32; **2.36**; 4.22.3; **4.24.7**
ᶜāsah ʾob, 3.32, 2 Kings
'aššāp, 3.3.8; 3.32.12; **3.32.14**
ʾopôt, 1.5.2
baᶜalat ʾob, 3.32.7
b-k-h, (root) 2.38.1
Bôkim, 2.38.2
dōrēš 'el hammētîm, 3.32 Deut 18 and n.; **3.32.9**
ʾēm bĕyisrāēl, 4.24.8
gazrin, 3.32.18
gĕbîrā, **1.4.3**
ḥăkam ḥărāsîm, 3.32 Isa; 3.32,16
ḥălōmôt, 3.32 Jer
ḥarṭôm, 3.3.8; **3.32,12**
ḥōbēr ḥābēr, 3.32 Deut 18 and n; **3.32.6**; 3.32.15
ḥōlēm ḥălôm, **3.32,13**
ḥōllîm, 2.33; 2.40.3
ʾiṭṭîm, (spirits of the dead) **3.32, 11**
kallāh, 4.24.3; 4.26.1
kāmār, 1.4.5
kaššāpîm, 3.32 Jer; 3.32.3
khnt, 1.4.2
kōhēn, **1.4.2**, 4.24.3 Hos 4.9
hakkōhēn haggadôl, 1.4.2
kōhēn harō'š 1.4.2
hakkōhēn hammišneh, 1.4.2
mĕbasseret, **2.37**
mekarkēr, 2.30
mekaššēp, 3.32 Deut 18 and n.; **3.32.5**
mekaššēpāh, 3.32
mĕlahēš, **3.32.15**
melek, 2.30
mĕnahēš, 3.32 Deut 18 and n; **3.32.4.1**
meᶜônen, 3.32 Deut 18 and n; **3.32,3**
mĕraqqēd, 2.30
mĕšartîm, 1.4.2
mešōrēr, **2.31**
mĕšōrērāh, **2.31**
mirqaḥat, 1.5.2
môdiʾîm lĕḥadāšîm, 3.32, 22
nābîʾ, **3.32.21**
nebî'ah, 2.28; **3.32 21**; 4.24.8
nebôn lahaš, 3.32 Isa; 3.32.15
na'arah, 4.25.4
netînîm, **1.4.7**; 4.22.3; 4.24.2
nihaš, 3.32 Lev
niheš, 3.32 2 Kings
nogen, **2.32**; 2.33
noqedim, 1.50.5
'ôbôt, 3.32 Lev

ᶜônēn, 3.32 2 Kings; 3.32 Lev
ᶜonnîm, 3.32 Jer
pilagšîm, 2.36
qādēš, **4.18**; 4.22.3; 4.22.10; 4.24.3; App. 3.15
qĕdēšāh, **4.18**; 4.22.2; 4.22.10; 4.22.14; 4.24.3; App. 3.15
qôsēm, 3.32, Jer; **3.32,2**
qôsem qassāmîm, 3.32 Deut 18 and n.
rab ḥartumayyā, 3.3.8
raqqūḥôt, 1.5.2
rqḥt, 1.4.2
sāgān / segen, 1.5 4
s-p-d. (root) **2.35**
ṣĕba ʾ ôt, 1.4.6; 4.22.3; **4.24.6**
ṣōbʾôt, 4.24.6
śārîm and *śārôt,* 2.32; **2.33**; 2.40.3
šômēr hassap, 1.5.3
šošbin, App. 4.2.1
šōʾēl ʾôb, 3.32 Deut 18 and n.; **3.32.7**
ṭabbāḥôt, 1.5.2
ṭĕrāpîm, (cultic object) 3.32.2, **3.32.10**
yiddĕᶜōnî, 3.32 Deut 18 and n.; 3.32 2 Kings; 3.32.3 Lev; 3.32.7; **3.32.8**; 3.32.10; 3.32.11
yô ᶜēṣ, 3.32 Isa
yôšebet, 4.22.3; 4.24.5
ziknē hakkôhănîm, 1.4.2
zônāh, 2.29; 4.18.1; 4.22.3; 4.24.3; 4.24.4

Ugaritic

ab, App. 3.16
alamdimmu, App. 3.14
asiruma, 1.50.11
atu, App. 3.14
bkyt, 2.41.3
eku 1.50.13
gipar, App. 3.14
ḫaniahhe, 1.50.13
ḥbr, 3.33
ḥrs, 3.33
ḫuppû, App. 3.14
ḫupse, 1.50.13
inš, 1.50.1
inšt, 1.50.2
khn, Intro p. 11 n. 16; 1.50.3; 1.50.5; 1.50.6; 4.19
khnt, Intro p. 11 n. 10
klb, 4.25.5
klt bt špš, 1.50.9, 1.50.12
kumru, 1.50.10 (?)
knʾ , 4.25.5
kṯrt, 2.41.1
lwʾ , Intro p. 11 n. 10
lwʾt, Intro p. 11 n. 10
maryannu, 4.19; 4.25.5
masilu, App. 3.14
mkrm, 4.19
mlhš, 3.32.15, 3.33
mrqd, 2.42
mur'u usriyanni, 1.50.11
mrum, 4.19
mṣlm,, 1.49.12; 2.41.5
mššpdt, 2.41.2
name, 1.50.13
nappāhu, App. 3.14
nāru, App. 3.14
ngr, 2.4.3
nqd, 1.50.5; 1.50.6; 4.19
nsk ksp, 4.19
NU.GIG, 4.19, App. 3.14
nuhatimmu, App. 3.14
parkullu, App. 3.14
qdš , 1.50.3, 1.50.6, **4.19**; 4.22.14; 4.25.1
qdšt, 4.19
rb khnm, 1.50.4, 1.50.5
rb mrzḥ, 1.50.7
rb nqdm, 1.50.5
rqd, 4.25.5
ša KU [ ] , 1.50.13
ša nāqî, 1.50.11
šangû, App. 3.14
šr ᶜṯtrt, 1.49.11; 2.41.4
šuzubu, 1.50.13
tbṣr, 1.50.9 (*klt bt špš*)
TÚG.LÁ, App. 3.14
ṯnn, 1.50.6
ˡᵘUN.TU, 1.50.11
ušparu, App. 3.14
ytnm, 1.4.7n; 1.50.8
zadimmu, App. 3.14

Amorite

kmr, 1.35

Phoenician,Aramaic, Nabatean,Palmyrene, Hatrian,Deir'Alla

ᶜadd , 3.14n
ᶜnn, (root) 3.32.3

ʾaht, 4.25.2
ʾam, 4.25.2
ḥzh, 3.32.2
khnt, Intro 1.1 n. 13, 1.4.2, 3.32.2
kmr, 1.35
kmrt, 1.35
knš, 1.44
rb khnm, (f.) 1.4.2
rqht, 1.4.2
šošbinaʾ, App. 4.2.1

OTHER SIGNIFICANT TERMS
Akkadian, Sumerian, Ideograms

abzu, see gudu$_4$-abzu/*gudapsû*, see šita$_x$-abzu, see gada-lá-abzu, see ka-kù-gal-abzu (1.2.5.3), 1.7.8 (insides of *pašīšu*), 1.9.4 (1 Kings 7.44, container of water), 1.9.4 (DN-abzu), 1.14.1 (primal waters), 1.25.2 (close to engur), 1.25.3, 3.4.4 (3), 4.23.9 No. 6 (Inanna)
adab/*adapu*, 2.1.2.1 (musical)
ag (a)runnu, 4.22.15.7
aguhhu, Intro 1.3, App. 3.2.7, **App. 3.11**
ahulap, 2.3.9 (uttered by ub and lilis)
akīti, see *bīt akīti*, 1.6.3; 2.4.7; 2.25.4; App. 3.2.4
akussu, 1.3.5
a-lá, see *alû*
algar, 2.1.2.2 (musical)
algasurrû, 2.1.2.3, 2.6, 2.25.5
alû, /a-lá, 2.1.2.4 (musical); 2.2.4
á-ná-da, 2.10.1
an-ta-sub-ba, 3.4.4 (r. 10)
apsu, see abzu
arkatu, 2.1.2.5 (musical), 2.4.7
arnu, 2.4.7 (rite for *naru*)
ašar ramku / ki-a-tu$_5$-a, 1.7.8, 1.29
aširtu, 4.22.15.7
ašlukkatu / é-uš-gíd-da, 4.22.15.1, 4.22.15.7
aštammu, **App. 4.1**
bāb bīt harimti, 4.16.3
badara /*patarru,* App. 3.3.5 (kurgara)
bala, (turn of service), 1.7.3 (nam-gudu$_4$-é-^{d}mar-du$_2$), 1.9.6, 1.9.7, 1.15.3 (*susbu*)
bala, (spindle) 2.19; App. 3.3.7; App. 3.4 (spindle)
balag/*balamgu,* 2.1.2.6 (musical), 2.3.9 (the composition), 2.3.12 (*kalû*), 2.3.15, 2.15.2
balag-a-ni, 1.19.5
balag-di (-da), see *timbuttu*
bal-bal, 1.25.2
banduddû, 1.6.2 (Mari)
barag, 4.23.8
basillatu, 2.1.2.8 (musical)
bēlu, (something worn), see *tillu*; App. 3.2.4n
bikitu, 2.15.2, 2.15.3
birsu, 1.3.3
bīru, 3.2.1 (used by *baru*), 3.3.4
bīt akīti, 1.3.8, 1.3.10, 1.3.11, 2.3.16
bīt aštamme, see é-éš-dam
bīt beri, App. 4.1.8
bīt emūti, 4.22.8
bīt eqî, 1.6.4, 4.6.6,
bīt erši, 4.22.15.1, 4.22.15.3
bīt hammūti, 4.22.15.1
bīt hamri, 4.11.9; App. 1.13.15
bīt huruš, App. 4.1.7.1
bīt iltim, 1.11 (Mari)
bīt labbūni, 1.3.5
bīt mayāli, 4.22.15.3
bīt mummi, 2.3.16 (ritual in)
bīt napṭari, App. 4.3
bīt ṣābî (t), see *bīt ṣībîm*, 4.16.3, App. 3.3.6, App. 3.8.3
bīt SAL.É.GAL 3.4.12
bīt ṣībîm, 4.3.3
bīt šikari, App. 4.1.10
dam, see dam-dingir, 1.2.8 (husband of a nu-gig), 1.18 (Isme-Dagan Inanna's dam), 1.20 (zirru dam ^{d}Nanna), 1.34 (wife); App. 4.2 (ès-dam)
di 'u, 3.4.4 (8)
dubdubbû, 2.1.2.9 (musical)
é-dam, 3.3.7 (Ishtar); App. 4.1.6
é-dùg. 4.23.8
é-éš-dam, 4.14 (Ishtar as *harimtu*); App. 3.9; App. 4.1.3, App. 4.1.7.1, App. 4.1.8
é-geme, 1.34
é-gipar, 1.19.7, 1.19.10
egirru, 3.4.4 (r.2)
é-gudu$_4$, 1.7.4
é-kaš, App. 4.1.7.2; App. 4.1.10
é-ki-ná, 4.23.8, App. 4.1.3
elilu, 2.25.2

ellu, 1.2.1, 1.9.3, 1.9.10, 1.10.6, 1.19.13 (Emar), 1.47.2
elunu, 3.1.1
embubbû / gi-gíd, 3.1.2.11 (musical)
emegir, 2.3.9
emesal/*ummisallu*, 2.1.1, 2.3.9 (*kalû*) passim
é-mí, 2.3.11
é-ná-da, 2.10.1, 4.22.15.3, 4.23.6
é-nam-ti-la, 4.23.9 No. 7
enēnu, 2.3.9
engu, 1.25.2
eqû, see *bīt eqî*
ér, see ama-ér-ra, see ér-šem, see lú-ér, see mí-ér, see ér-sig$_7$, 2.1.2.10 (*embubû*), 2.3.2, 2.3.3, 2.3.9, 2.3.13 (OB Proto-Lu), 2.4.5, 2.15.1, 2.15.2, App. 3.4
^{giš}eren, 3.2.5 (maš-šu-gíd-gíd)
eršahunga, 2.3.9 (by *kalû*); 2.15.4; 3.17.2
eršemma, 2.3.9 (by *kalû*)
ér-šem$_4$-šà-hun-gá, 2.3.16
eršu, 4.22.15.3
ešda, 1.14.2, 1.16 (isib-mah), 1.23, 1.24
èš-dam/*aštammu*, 3.3.7; éš-dam-kù 4.13; **App. 4.1**
èš-èš, App. 3.5.3; App. 4.1.3
eše štu, 3.9
èš-gal-la, 4.23.9 No. 5
é-šub, App. 3.13.2
é-uš-gíd-da, see *aslakkatu*
^{túg}*gadalalû*, 1.17
gagû, 1.19.2, 4.3.2 (*nadītu*), 4.3.3, 4.9.2 (*ugbabtu*), 4.11.5 (*qadištu*), **4.22.15.4** (*entu* , *ugbabtu*), 4.22.15.4 (*nadītu*)
gamlu, 3.24
gâšu, 2.25.1 (dance), 2.25.4
gi-di, 2.2.4 (musical)
gi-gíd, see *embubbû*, *malīlu*; 2.3.10
gigunû /gi-gun$_4$, 1.13.1, **4.22.15.2**
gil, 1.21.5 (dance), 2.3.3 (nar mí-gil-sa, gala mí-gil-sa), 2.25.1(dance)
ginû -offering, 1.2.9, 1.37.4, 1.38.2, 1.45, 2.4.8, 3.27.1, 3.28.1, 4.6.6, App. 3.3.4
giparu / gipar, 1.19.2 (en, in kisal-bar-ra), 1.19.10 (building); **1.19.10** (Weadock); 1.34 (é-gi$_4$) 4.16.3 (Ishtar's), **4.22.15.5** (*entu*) (Weadock), 4.22.15.5 (išib, lú-mah, gudu$_4$), 4.23.6, 4.23.9 No. 2, App. 3.14
gíri, App. 3.3.5 (kurgara)
giš-har-har, see har-har
gišhuru, 3.7.5 (used by *multēpišu*)
gizillû rabû, 1.13.4
guštu, App. 3.2.5
halhallatu, 1.6.2, 2.3.9 (by *kalû*), 2.3.12 (*kalû*), 2.3.16, 2.15.2
hammurtu, 1.3.5
hammūtu, see *bīt hammūti*, 4.22.15.7
hamru, see *bīt hamri*
handuttu, 4.8.1
harhadu, 2.1.2.16 (musical)
(giš)-har-har 2.1.2.17 (musical)
har-ra(ring), 2.19
harranu / kaskal, 4.4.1 (in lukur-kaskal-la)
harru, 2.1.2.18 (musical)
hašādu, 4.22.15.3
hitpu, App. 3.2.5
hullānu, 1.36 (*mukallu* clad in), 3.9 (*mukkallu* clad in)
huruš, see *bīt huruš*
ibratu, 4.16.3
ihzu, 3.4.4
i-lu, 1.19.5 (en), 1.3.7, 2.3.14 (Lu = sa IV), **2.24**; App. 3.5.3
inbu, Intro 1.3, 3.4.12, App. 3.11(Ishtar)
indu, 4.8.4
inhu, **2.2.3** (*qadištu*), 2.2.3 (*assinnu*), 2.2.3 (*kulmašītu*), 2.3.15 (*nāru*), 2.3.18 (*nāru*), 4.8.4(*kulmašītu*) 4.11.9 (*qadištu*), App. 1.4 passim (*qadištu*), App. 3.2.2 (*assinnu*)
ikkibu, 1.19.15, 4.9.4, 4.11.1
ikribu /sùd, 1.7.8, 1.9.2, 1.20
inu, 2.1.2.19 (musical)
ipšu, 3.21.3 (magic spell)
ír. see ér
isinnu, 1.3.7, 4.11.10
KA.EME, see *pu'u lišānu*
ka-gal-mah, 3.12.2
kakkabtu, 1.43
ka-kù-gál, 1.25.3
kakugallutu, 3.4.4 (r.7)
kamanu, 2.4.7
kannu, 4.16.3
kanzabu, 2.1.2.21 (musical), 2.4.7
kapašu, 3.4.3

ki-a-tu$_5$-a /*ašar ramku*, 1.7.8; 1.29
kidudû, 2.3.15 (eršemma), 3.4.4 (r. 15)
kigullu, 3.1.13
ki-NÁ, 4.22.15.3, 4.23.6, 4.23.9 No. 5
ki-ná ... ak, App. 4.2.1
kinūnu, 4.9.2
giš-kirid / *kirissu*, 3.4.7, App. 3.3.7,App. 3.4
kisal, see *kisalluhu*, 1.12.1, 1.19.2 (kisal-bar-ra)
kiṣir ešši 3.4.12
kiṣṣu, 4.22.15.7
kiš /*skilatu*, 2.1.2.22 (musical), App. 3.3.3, App. 3.3.6
kišpu, 3.4.6, 3.7.4, 3,25 (as official); 4.7.2 (*sekretu*)
kišurratu, 2.1.2.23 (musical)
kitkittû, 3.4.3, 3.4.4 (r.5); 4.16.3
kitû akiltu, 3.4.12 (ADD 953)
kummu, 4.13, 4.22.15.1, **4.22.15.6,** 4.22.15.6 (gipar); 4.22.15.7, 4.23.6
kurunnu, 4.14
kuš-á-la, see *alu*
kušgugalu, (reading? of KUŠ.GU$_4$.GAL) 2.1.2.25 (musical)
kuzbu, Intro 1.3, 3.4.12
kuziru, 3.1.13
labbūnu, see *bīt labbūni*
lawû, 2.25.1 (dance)
lemuttu, 2.3.16
lib/piššatu, 4.8.1, 4.11.1
lihšu, 3.32.15
lilissu / lilis, 1.3.10; 2.1.2.26 (musical), 2.3.1; 2.3.9; 2.3.12 (*kalu*), 2.3.16 (*kalu*); App. 3.3.5 (gala)
lišān nukurtu, 3.23
lubāru, 1.36 (*mukallu* clad in), 3.9 (*mukallu* clad in)
^{d}Lugal-urra, 3.4.4 (r. 10)
mākaltu, App. 1.2ff
makkuru, 1.44 (of Enanna)
makultu, 3.2.7 (used by *bārû*)
malgatu, 2.1.2.27 (musical)
malīlu / GI.GÍD, 2.1.2.28 (musical), 2.4.7
má-an-na, 1.25.2
manzû / me-zé, 2.1.2.29 (musical); 2.3.12 (*kalû*), 2.3.16, 2.8.2
maqalūtu, 2.3.16
maqqû, App. 1.12
maruštu, 3.4.4 (8)
me, 1.13.2, 1.18, 1.21.2, 1.21.6, 4.9.3, 4.10.1, 4.13, App. 3.3.5, App. 3.5.3, App. 4.1.7.1
mēlultu, 2.4.9.1
mēlulu, 2.7.1, 2.25.1, 2.25.3
mê tēlilte, 4.3.5 (*qadištu*), 4.11.10
me-zé, see *manzû*
mindiu, 2.1.2.31 (musical)
miqit šamê, 3.4.4 r. 10
miritu / *zamiritu*, 2.1.2.32
mullilu, "sprinkler,"see the office, 3.5.2, 3.25.1
mummu, see *bit mummi*
múš/mùš, 1.18, 4.8.2
mušēbî, 3.17.1
muššakku, 3.2.1(used by *šā'ilu*), 3.3.4 (*ša'ilu*); **3.29**
mussiru, 3.24
ná, passim
namzītu, 4.16.3
naptanu, 1.3.7 (KAR 146), 2.4.7 (KAR 146), App. 3.13.1
nēmedu, 4.22.15.7
nepešu, 2.3.16 (*kalû*)
ne-sag-gá, 1.23
nigìn-gar / nigìn-mar-ra, 4.13
nigkalagû / URUDU.NÍG.KALA.GA, 2.1.2.34 (musical)
niknak burāši, 4.16.3
nin, 1.2.6, 1.18 (nin-mul-an-gim), 1.34 (queen); see DNs and offices beginning with nin
nishu / gi-SUD, 2.1.2.35 (musical)
nissatu, 2.15.3
nīš libbi, 4.11.6
nīš qāti, 3.2.4
ni'u, 2.1.2.36 (musical), 2.4.5
numun, 4.23.10
pagû / SA.LI, 2.1.2.37 (musical), 2.4.5(*naru*)
GIŠ.PA.(PA), see *šinna letu*
papāhu, 4.22.15.1, 4.22.15.7
parakku, 1.3.3 (king on), 1.3.10 (Asshur sits on), 1.3.11 (in *bīt akīti*), 1.13.1 (in *gigunû* of Ishtar), 1.32, 4.16.3, 4.22.15.2, 4.22.15.7, App. 3.2.4
parak šimāte, 1.3.11, 1.6.3 (Marduk on)
parammāhu, 4.22.15.7
parṣu, 3.4.3, 3.6

pašāru, 3.3.4 (root)
patiru, 4.16.3
pi / alaggu, 2.1.2.39 (musical)
pigu, 2.1.2.38 (musical)
píl, pi-lá, App. 3.7.1n
pilaqqu, 3.4.7, App. 3.3.7 (*kurgarrû*, Ishtar)
pirištu, 2.6, 3.13.1, 3.13.2
piširtu, 3.6
pišru, 4.11.13
piqittu, 4.3.2 (*nadītu*)
pitiltu, 4.11.13 (of *qadištu*)
pitnu, 2.1.2.40 (musical), 2.4.5 (by *nāru ṣehru*)
purussu, 3.4.4 (r.2)
pu'u lišānu, 1.6.4 and n. 68
qanû, 2.1.2.41 (musical)
qardu, 2.19
q-d-š (root), 1.2.7, 1.50.3
qerītu, App. 4.1.9
qubbu, 1.21.9
qutrinnu, 3.2.4 (used by *baru*), 3.3.5
ramku, (adjective, see *ramku* - office), 1.7.8, 1.9.3, 1.29 (in *ašar ramku*), 1.36; 1.47.1, 1.47.2, 2.4.7 (Nabonidus' list of personnel)
rebītu, App. 4.1.12
riksu, 3.19, 3.3.4 (of cedar)
SA.LI, see *pagû*
sà-sig, 4.11.15
síg-bar-ra, see official
sizkur$_x$, 3.11
ṣurṣuppu, 4.8.2; App. 4.1.3; *sabitu* 2.1.2.42 (musical)
sāgu / sagû, 4.22.15.7
šakkiku, 3.4.4 (6)
šamanu, 3.4.4 (19)
šammu /GIŠ.ZÀ.MÍ, 1.3.3; 2.1.2.44 (musical); 2.4.3 (by *rab zammaru*), 2.4.5, 2.4.7
šamšammu, see *zamzammu*
šassannu, 2.1.2.46 (musical)
šebītu, 2.1.2.47 (musical), 2.4.7
šèm / *halhallatu*, 2.1.2.51 (musical), 2.3.1
šibattu, 2.1.2.49 (musical)
šiddu, 3.4.7
šimakku, 4.22.15.7
ši-in, 2.1.2.48 (musical)
šinna /etu / GIŠ.PA.(PA), 2.1.2.50 (musical), 2.4.7
šipittu, 2.3.5, 2.4.5, 2.4.11, App. 3.2.5
šiptu, 1.3.12, 2.3.16, 3.3.4, 4.16.3
šìr, see lú-šìr, see šir-sag, 2.3.13 (kinds of šìr, OB Proto-Lu), 2.4.5 (nar-gal), 2.11.1, 2.17 (OB Proto-Lu), 2.26 (OB Lu)
širihtu, 2.15.3
šìr-mah, 2.11.1 (?)
šita$_x$, (vessel or prayer, see šita$_x$ as official), 1.7.8, 1.9.2, 1.9.3, 1.10.5
šitru, (veil). 1.6.2 and n. 66, 2.17 (Mari)
šubtu, 4.22.15.7
šu-ila, 2.3.15
šukku, 4.22.15.7
šulmu, 3.2.6 (*bārû*)
šulpu / gi-SUD, 2.1.2.52 (musical)
šu-luh(-ha), see šu-luh-ha as official, 1.7.2, 1.7.5. 1.10.5, 1.15.3 (*susbû / ramku*, enkum, ninkum), 1.19.10, 1.22.3, 1.25.2, 2.3.16 (Seleucid); 2.4.7; 3.1.7.1, 3.4.4 (3); 4.23.9 No. 7, App. 4.1.7.1
tab /palu, 2.1.2.53 (musical), 2.4.5 (*nāru*)
takpertu, 2.3.16, 3.4.4 (8)
takribtu, 2.3.18; 2.4.7
takribu, 1.21.9, 2.3.16
tāmartu, 3.4.4
tamītu, 3.1.1
tamlû, 1.3.9
tamšeru, App. 3.3.6 (*kurgarrû*)
tapšû, 1.36 (on head of *mukallu*), 3.9
taskarinnu, 4.11.14
tā 'u, 4.22.15.7
telītu, 2.1.2.54 (musical), 2.8.1, 4.16.3
terhu, 1.19.15 (*entu*'s carry), 4.11.13
terinnu, 1.19.15 (*qadištu*'s carry), 4.11.10 (*qadištu*), 4.11.13 (*qadištu*)
terītu, 4.4.1
tertu, 3.2.7 (*bārû*)
tibulu, 2.1.2.55 (musical)
tigû / tigi, 2.1.2.56 (musical), 2.3.12 (*kalû*), 2.4.5 (nar), 2.25.5, App. 3.13.3
tillu, **App. 3.2.4**, App. 3.2.4n, App. 3.3.5
timbuttu /balag-di, (-da) 2.1.2.7 (musical), 2.8.1, App. 3.3.3
tindu, 2.1.2.58 (musical)
tirhu, see *terhu*

tīru, App. 3.3.7 (*kurgarrû*)
tuganu, 3.4.4 (18)
GIŠ.TUKUL.UR, App. 4.3
tu$_6$-tu$_6$, 2.3.10
^{kus}ub, see 2.3.12n and *uppu*
uppu, 2.1.2.59 (musical), 2.3.1; 2.3.9; 2.3.12 (*kalû*); 2.3.16 (*kalû*); 3.2.2, App. 3.3.5 (gala)
urigallu, 2.4.7
uru, Intro 1.3
uru-sub, App. 3.13.2
urza (ba)bitu, 2.1.2.60 (musical)
ušnaru, 2.1.2.61 (musical)
zagmukku, 4.23.4.174
zamaru, see šìr
ZÀ.MÍ, see *šammu*
zamiritu, see *miritu*
zamzammu /zam-zam, 2.1.2.63 (musical), 2.4.5
zannaru, 2.1.2.64 (musical)
zikurudu, 3.7.4
zimru, 2.3.18
zi-ni, 1.8, 1.13.3
zīru, 3.7.4
zisurru, 2.3.16

OTHER SIGNIFICANT TERMS
Hebrew

'ûrîm, 3.32.7, 3.32.23
'āsôr, 2.27.2 (musical)
bāmôt, 2.27.4, 4.24.4, 4.26.1
battîm, 4.24.3, 4.24.4 (*zonah*)
b-s-r, (root), 2.42
gittît, 2.27.2 (musical)
hălîkôt, 2.40.3
ḥālîl, 2.27.2 (musical), 2.27.4
ḥaraš, 3.32.16
ḥăṣōṣrāh, 2.27.2 (musical)
'iṭṭîm, 3.32.7, 3.32.11
kinnôr, 2.27.2 (musical), 2.27.4, 2.40.3
māḥôl, 2.40.3 (praise in dance)
mašrôqîtā', 2.27.2 (musical)
mĕkarkēr, 2.30
mĕna ^{c}*an*^{c}*îm,* 2.27.2 (musical)
mĕraqqēd, 2.30
mĕṣilôt, 2.27.2 (musical)
mĕṣiltayim, 2.27.2 (musical), 2.40.3
minnîm, 2.27.2 (musical)
nēbel, 2.27.2 (musical), 2.27.3, 2.40.3
nĕhîlôt, 2.27.2 (musical)
neqeb, 2.27.2 (musical)
pa ^{c}*ămon,* 2.27.2 (musical), 2.27.3
pĕsantērîn, 2.27.2 (musical)
qaitrôs, 2.27.2 (musical)
qeren, 2.27.2 (musical)
qînāh, 2.38.1 (women)
s-p-d, (root), **2.35**, 2.41.2
sabbĕkā', 2.27.2 (musical)
sûmpōnyāh, 2.27.2 (musical)
ṣa'ip, 4.24.3
ṣammāh, 4.24.3
šālišîm, 2.27.2 (musical), 2.37
šelšĕlîm, 2.27.2 (musical)
š-m-h, (root) 2.39
š -^{c}*-q,* (root), 2.35
sōb'ot, 4.24.6
šôpār, 2.27.2 (musical), 2.27.3, 2.40.3
tōp, 2.27.2 (musical), 2.27.4, 2.28 (Miriam), 2.29, 2.32, 2.36, 2.37
tummîm, 1.4.2, 3.32.7, 3.32.23
ṭĕrapîm, 3.32.7, 3.32.10
^{c}*ûgāb,* 2.27.2 (musical)
yobel, 2.27.2 (musical)
yôšebet, 4.22.3, 4.24.5

OTHER SIGNIFICANT TERMS
Ugaritic and Hurrian

athlm, 1.50.1 (offering, Hurrian)
b^{c}*l mrqd*, 2.47
b/pirianna, 4.14
dšn, 2.4.7

RITES, SERIES, FESTIVALS

akītu, 1.6.3, 2.3.18, 2.4.7, 2.29.4, 4.23.5, 4.23.6
alamdimmû, 3.4.4 (6)
Ana ittišu, 4.11.15, 4.22.6
ašipūtu, see *mašmaššūtu*
bārūtu, 3.1.1
bīt mēsiri, 3.4.4 (11)
Bīt rimki, 1.25.3, 2.15.4, 3.4.4 (11), 3.4.6, 3.17.2
bīt sala'me, 2.15.4, 3.17.2
Descent of Inanna, App. 3.2.7n
Descent of Ishtar, App. 3.2.9
Enuma ana bīt marṣi āšipu illiku, 3.4.1
Enuma ^{d}Anu ^{d}Enlil, 2.3.17, 3.1.2
kakugallatu, 3.4.4 (r.7)
kalūtu, 2.3.15
kataduggu, 3.4.4 (6)
kidudu, 3.4.4 (r.15)
Ludlul bel nemeqi, 3.4.7

Maqlû, 3.4.4 (14), 3.7.5, 3.7.7, 3.20.4, 3.20.5
mašmaššūtu / ašipūtu, 2.15.4, 3.4.4
mīš pî, 1.3.7, 1.22.3, 3.4.4 (2), 3.9
Namburbi, 2.3.9, 2.15.4, 4.16.3, 3.1.2, 3.4.4 (r. 6), 3.17.2
nigdimdimmû, 3.4.4 (6)
nin-mul-an-gim, 1.18
purussû, 3.4.4 (r. 2)
šu-íla, 3.4.4 (4)
šuluhhu, 2.3.16
šumma Ālu, 1.3.12, 2.4.9, 3.1.2, 3.4.4 (r. 16), 4.22.13, App. 3.2.6
šumma Izbu, 3.1.2
šurpu, 3.4.4 (14)
takpertu, 3.4.4 (8)
unú-suba, 4.11.9
Utukku lemnuti, 3.4.3
zì-pa, 4.11.15, 4.12

SELECTED LIST OF TOPICS DISCUSSED

Abigail, 3.32,21n (prophetess)
Amulets, 3.4.1
Anointing (person), 1.4.2 (priest, Hebrew), 1.5.2 (oil), 1.7.1(gudu$_4$/*pašīšu*), 1.19.15 (cones), 2.42 (*mrqd*, Ugarit), 3.2.7 (bowl), 3.4.1 (*āšipu*), 3.32,21 (Saul), 3.43 (with oil), 4.11.13 (*nadītu*), App. 3.3.7 (king)
Apostasy/idols/prostitution,Hebrew, **4.26**
Arabs, 1.35.2
Arrows, divination by, **3.31**, 3.32.2
Astronomical/astrological, 2.3.17, 3.1.2 (Mesopotamia), 3.2.4 (*bārû*), 3.4.4 (*āšipu*), 3.32,18 (Hebrew), App. 3.3.1
Auxiliary functionaries, **App. 5**
Balaam, 3.32.2
Basket carriers, **see Kanephorai**
Basket, ritual, 1.19.5
Birds, 3.4.3, 3.4.4 r.2 (*āšipu*), 3.4.9 (*dāgil iṣṣurē*), **3.27** (observers of,*dāgil iṣṣurē*), **3.28,** (fowler), 3.28.2 (feeder)
Bow, App. 3.4
Bridal attendant, App. 4.2.1
Cedar, 3.2.5 (used by *bārû*)
Cones, fir, anointing 4.11.13
Cultic functionaries, Intro. 2 (Mesopotamia), **4.24** (Hebrew)
Curse of Agade, App. 4.1.12
Dance, 2.7.1 (*aluzinnu*), 2.21.2 , **2.25** (Mesopotamia), 2.27.3 (Psalms), 2.28 (Miriam), 2.29 (Jephthah), 2.30 2.33 (Psalms), (David), **2.40** (Psalms)**,** 2.40.3, **2.42** (Ugaritic), App. 2.2, App. 3.2.5
Daniel, 3.32,6
Deborah, 3.32,20 (prophetess), 3.32.21n; 4.24.5, 4.24.8
Diviners, **chap 3**, 3.2.1 (*bārû*), 3.4.9 (Gula), 3.32.4 (Hebrew), 3.32.6 (Daniel), 3.33 (Ugaritic),
Dog, 3.12.6 (lú-e$_{11}$-dè) , 4.18.1 (Deut 23.19), **4.25.5** (Deut 23.19), 4.25.8 (Phoenicia and Cyprus) , App. 2.2 (of Gula), App. 3.2.1 (UR.SAL), App. 3.2.6 (sexual), App. 4.1.7.2 (in eshdam)
Dreams, **3.3** (Mesopotamia), 3.32,6,12,13; (Hebrew)
Droit de seigneur, see Ius primae noctis
Drugs, 3.4.1
Early dynastic lists, 1.2.1
Ebla, 1.7.12, 1.38.4, 3.27.2, 3.32,21 (prophetess)
Ecstatics, **chap 3**, 3.12, 3.13, 3.14, 3.15, 3.16
Emar, 1.19.12-13, 1.38.4, 4.24.9
Emesal, 2.3.2
Eršahunga, 2.3.9
Eršemma, 1.7.9, 2.3.9, 2.3.15, 2.3.16
Esther, 3.32,21n (prophetess)
Eunuch, 2.3.3, 2.3.4.2, 4.22.9 (Kornfeld), App. 3.2.10 (RLA), App. 4.1.14 (*sinnišānu*)
Extispicy, 1.13.2, 1.18 (en), 1.19.7 (en chosen), 1.19.7 (Nabonidus' daughter), **3.1.2**, 3.2.4, 3.2.6, 3.3.4 (*bīru* by *bārû*), App. 3.2.7(*kayamānu*)
Fertility, Intro.1.1 (seals, cults, Gen 8.22, life and f., myth, Ugaritic, f. and sexuality), Intro. 2 (Category No. 4), 1.19.10 (in gipar), 2.3.2 (gala and nar), 2.40.1 (dance), 3.20.4 (*eššeb/pû*), 3.32.4.2 (snakes), 3.32.4.2 ("tree of life"), **chap. 4** (and sexuality), **4.1**, 4.8.2

(nu-gig and nu-bar), 4.11.13 (*terinnu*), 4.18.2 (bibliography, sacred prostitution, sacred marriage), 4.22.2 (Asmussen), 4.22.8 (Lambert), 4.22.9 (Kornfeld), 4.22.11 (Helck), 4.22.12 (Jacobsen), 4.22.15.5 (en), **4.22.16** (my conclusion), 4.23.1 (of earth), 4.23.2 (Greek, women foremost), 4.23.5 (Kramer, *Sacred Marriage*), 4.23.9 (Inanna-Dumuzi "sacred marriage texts"), 4.24.1 (Brooks, Hebrew Bible), 4.24.4 (Hebrew Bible, Hos, Canaan), 4.24.4 (Anat on Elephantine Island), **4.25** (Hebrew Bible), 4.23.3 (figurines showing sexual intercourse) **App. 2.1** (Palestine), App. 2.2 (cylinder and stamp seals),
Figurines, Mesopotamia, 3.4.1, **App. 2**
Figurines, naked, Palestine **App. 2**
Flour, divination by, 3.4.1, 3.7.2, **3.30**
Fornication, 4.21.7 (Greek), 4.23.3 (figurines in coitus), 4.25.3
Funerary cult, 1.16, 2.18, 3.25, 3.32.7 (Hebrew), 3.32.9 (Hebrew), 3.32.11 (Hebrew, Egyptian)
Gilgamesh epic, 1.13.2, (in netherworld), 1.17 (netherworld), 1.19.7 (netherworld), 1.21.4 (Death of Gilgamesh), 1.21.9, 4.8.4, 4.14, (*šamhatu*), 4.16.2 (*sābītu*), 4.17, 4.22.6 (iv 34-6, ius primae noctis), 4.22.8 (ius primae noctis), 4.22.9 (Kornfeld), App. 3.11(*aguhhu*)
Goddess as cultic officiant, Intro. 1.1 n. 11, 1.3.14
Hair, 1.11, 2.15.3, 3.8.5 (*apkallatu*'s); 3.20.4 (*eššepû*), 4.4.1, 4.6.1, 4.23.4.45 (?, and note), 4.23.9 No. 8 (sacred marriage love songs), 4.25.3 (Num 6.5), 4.26.1 (Lev. 19.29), App. 3.5.3
Hallo, Exaltation App. 4.1.7.1n
Hannah, 3.32,21n (prophetess)
Hemerologies, 3.1.2
Hepatoscopy, Hebrew, 3.32,2, 3.32,17
Hepatoscopy, Mesopotamian, 4.9.2
Hermaphrodite, 4.7.1 (false), App. 3.8.5, App. 3.10, App. 3.17, App. 4.1.14
Herodotus I, 181, 4.23.10
Herodotus I, 199, **4.20**, 4.21 (after Herodotus), 4.21.10 (criticism)
Hierodoulai, see Sacred prostitution
Hieros gamos, see Sacred Marriage
Homosexuality, 4.9.5 (NA dream manual), 4.23.3 (none in sexual intercourse figurines), 4.25.7 (male), **4.27**, App. 3.2.6 (*assinnu*), App. 3.2.10 (šumma ālu), App. 3.5.3 (SAG.UR.SAG), App. 3.6.2 (*parrû*), App. 3.15 (Jud 19.22-26, Gen 19.1-11)
Huldah,3.32,21n (prophetess), 4.24.8
Impotence, App. 3.2.6 (*assinnu*). App. 3.2.10
Inanna/Ishtar's cult, Intro. 1.3
Ius primae noctis, 4.20, 4.22.6 (Gilgamesh), 4.22.8, App. 4.2.2
Jephthah's daughter, (Hebrew), **2.29**. 2.40.3
Kanephorai, **1.48**, App. 3.5.3
Karatepe, 4.24.4 (Baal of)
Kilili, 4.22.13
King as cultic officiant, (Israel), **2.30**
King as cultic officiant, (Mes.) 1.3.3, 1.3.4, 1.3.5, 1.3.6, 1.3.7, 1.3.9, 1.3.11, 1.6.2, 1.6.3, 1.7.4, 1.21.3, **1.49** (as *išippu*, *pašīšu*, *šabrû*, *šangû*, en), 2.4.10, App. 3.3.7
Kissing, 4.4.1, 4.4.2, 4.23.9 No. 10
Knots, Hebrew, 3.32.6
Lecanomancy, (oil omina), 3.2.3, 3.2.7, 3.4.3, 3.4.4.2, 3.4.5, 3.8.3, 3.18, **3.26**
Lexical text, reading a, Intro. 1.2
Libanomancy (incense), 3.2.4, 3.3.4 (*mussakku*), 3.3.4 (*šā' ilu*), **3.29**
Liver, see Hepatoscopy
Magic circles, 3.4.1
Magicians, **chap 3**
Mari pantheon, 4.11.8
Mayan temple, 4.23.10n
Midwife, 4.8.2 (nu-gig), 4.11.6 (*qadištu*), 4.11.16
Midwife, *sābsūtu* 4.11.11, 4.11.15
"Ministering women" in Israel, 1.4.6
Miriam, (Hebrew) 1.5.5 (Vos), **2.28**, 3.33, 21n (prophetess, Mishnah Megilla), 4.24.8

Mother, (Hebrew) Intro 1.3, 4.24.8
Musical instruments, (Hebrew), **2.27.2**
Musical instruments, (Mesopotamia), **2.1.2**, 2.3.9, 2.4.5
Mylitta, 4.20
Necromancy, see Funerary 2.3.2, 2.15.4, 3.3.1, 3.3.4 (with dream interpretations), 3.7.8 (*mušēlû eṭimme*); 3.7.10; 3.32.7 (*šō ʾēl ʾôb*), 3.32.9 (*dōrēš ʾel hammētîm*)
Netherworld, see Funerary cult, Necromancy
Oil omina, see Lecanomancy
Oneiromancy, see Dreams
Ordeal, Hebrew, 3.32,24
Paranymph, see Bridal attendant
Peg deposits, **1.48**
People present at ritual, 1.3.7
Personal names, Hebrew theophoric, **4.25.2**
Priest, Hebrew Bible, functions, **1.4.2**
Priest, words for, Europe, Intro 1.3, 1.4.1
Prophecy, Hebrew, **3.32,21**, 4.24.8
"Prophecy," Mari 3.15.2
Prophetess, 3.32.21, **4.24.8** (Bible)
Prostitute as cultic figure, 2.3.4.1, 2.15.3, **4.14**, App. 4.1.7 (eshdam house), App. 4.1.12
Prostitute, male, 4.6.3, 4.18.1 (Jerome, 1 Kings 14.24), 4.24.3 (*qādēš*), 4.24.4 (mēʾahabay, May), 4.25.5 (= dog), 4.25.8 (Phoenicia and Cyprus), 4.26.1 (Isa 57.3-8)
Purification/cleansing/washing/ making holy, 1.7.2, 1.7.4, 1.7.8, 1.8, 1.9.3, 1.9.9, 1.9.10, 1.10.5, 1.12.1, 1.15.1, 1.16, 1.17, 1.18, 1.21.8, 1.22.1, 1.21.9, 1.22.1, 1.22.2, 1.22.3, 1.23, 1.25.1, 1.25.2, 1.26, 1.28, 1.29, 1.44, 1.47.1, 1.47.2, 3.3.4 (*ša'ilu*), **3.4.8**, 3.5.2 (*mullilu*), 3.6 (*sangammāhu*), 3.8.5(*apkallatu*), 4.11.9, App. 5 n. 24
Queen as cultic officiant, 1.2.2 (Pu-abi), 1.3.8, 4.16.2 (mí-kurun-na), 4.22.12
Queen mother, **1.4.3** (Hebrew), 1.4.4 (Ebla)
Queen of heaven, Hebrew, 1.5.5 (women make cakes for), 4.23.9 No. 4, **4.26.2**, (sacred marriage love songs)
Queries, 3.2.6 (by *bārû*)
Rejoicing, **2.37** (Hebrew), **2.39** (Hebrew)
Ritual, words for, Intro. 1.3 n. 17
Sacred Mariage, 1.2.6, 1.19.10, 4.3.1, 4.11.2 (n. 119), 4.22.11 (Helck), 4.22.15.1, 4.22.15.5 (*entu*), **4.23**, 4.23.2 (Greek), 4.23.4 (Iddin-Dagan), 4.23.5 (Kramer), 4.23.6 (Shulgi), 4.23.9 (Inanna-Dumuzi "sacred marriage texts," Kramer), 4.24.4 (2 Macc 1.14), 4.24.8, App. 3.4 (Iddin-Dagan), App. 3.5.3 (Iddin-Dagan), App. 4.1.3
"Sacred/temple prostitution", 4.6.2, 4.14 (Dandamaev), 4.14 (Wilhelm, Nuzi), 4.18.1 (words for, Deut 23.18), 4.18.2 (bibliography), 4.19 (Ugaritic, von Soden), 4.20 (Herodotus), **4.22**, 4.22.1 (Greek), 4.22.14 (Hooks), 4.22.16 (summary), 4.24.3.7, 4.25.4 (Am 2.7)
Salt, 1.3.5
Sarah, 3.32,21n (prophetess), 4.24.8
Seals, cylinder, 1.24 (kišib-gál), 1.37.1 (zabar-dab$_5$), 1.40 (*purkullu*),1.43 (*širku*), 2.25.4n (Nuzi,Porada), 2.40.2 (early Palestine), 3.3.2 (kišib-gál), 3.4.4 r.8 (*āšipu*); 3.32.4 ,3 (Bible,"tree of life"), **App. 2.2** (Mesopotamia)
Seals, stamp, Mesopotamia, **App. 2.2**
Sexual intercourse, "illicit," 1.19.11 (*entu*), 4.3.3 (*nadītu*, *ugbabtu*), 4.4.1 (kissing), 4.8.1, 4.8.4 (*kulmašītu*), 4.9.2 (*nadītu, ugbabtu*), 4.9.5 (ugbabtu), 4.16.3 (*bīt sābê*), 4.23.3 (figurines), 4.24.6 (1 Sam 2.22), App. 3.2.6 (*šumma ālu*), App. 4.1.12 (in *aštammu* or street)
Sexual intercourse, irregular /abnormal, 1.19.11, 2.3.4,1, App. 3.5.3 (sag-ur-sag),App. 3.15 (Hebrew), Sexuality, **chap 4**

Sexuality/Fertility, Intro. 1.3
Smoke, divination by, see libanomancy
Snake, 2.13.2 (*mušlahhu*), **3.32.4.1, 3.32.4.2**, 3.32.4.3 (Ugaritic)
Spittle, 3.7.2
Temple ritual, Jerusalem, Intro. 1.1 n.7
Thread, 3.7.2
Trees, 3.32,4.3 ("tree of life"), 3.32,20 (Hebrew, sitting under)
Transvestism, 2.3.3, 4.23.4 (Iddin-Dagan, lines 60, 63), **App. 3.4** , App. 3.5.3, **App.3.1**(*kapištum*) **App.3.14** (*huppû*), App. 3.15 (Deut 22.5)
Urîm and *tummîm* , (Hebrew) 3.32,23
Uruk IV period, Intro. 1.3 (Asher-Greve)
Veil, (curtain) 1.6.2 (Mari), 2.17 (Mari)
Veiling, 2.17 (*aštalītu*), 4.11.12 (MAL), 4.22.2 (Asmussen), **4.24.3**, 4.24.8
Venus, planet 4.23.8
Water, 1.3.7 (for Ishtar), 1.3.9 (*šangû* gives), 1.3.11 (*šangû*), 1.6.2 (*luhšû* pours), 1.6.2 (*pašīšu*), 1.6.3 (*šangû*), 1.7.4 (Gudea, temple water), 1.7.7 (*šangû* and *pašīšu*), 1.7.8 (washing with), 1.9.4 (abzu), 1.11 (*luhšû*), 1.12.2 (*luhšû*), 1.14.1 (abzu), 2.3.16, 3.2.5 (maš-šu-gíd-gíd), 3.4.4.7 (used by *āšipu*), 3.4.4.7 (*masmaššu*), 3.7.2 (witches), 3.12.6 (offered to*mahhû*), 3.14 (*kaparru*), **3.18** (*hābit mê*), 3.32,24 (ordeal), 4.3.5, (purification), 4.11.10 (MAS.MAS)
Weapons, 2.3.16 (*kalû*)
Weeping, 2.1.1, 2.2.2, 2.9 (*ša bikīti*), **2.15**, 2.15.1 (root *bku*), 2.15.2 (*ša bikīti*); 2.15.3, 2.15.4, **2.38** (Hebrew), 2.38.1 (women), 2.38.2 (GN), 2.38.3 (Book of Lamentations), 2.41.3 (Ugaritic), 2.42 (Ugaritic)
Wenamun, 3.14
Wetnurse, see Midwife
Wise men and women, **chap 3**, 3.8.1 (*apkallu*)
Witchcraft/sorcery, **chap 3**, 3.1.3, 3.3.1, 3.4.6, **3.7**, 3.20, 3.21, 3.22, 3.23, 3.32,5 (Bible), 3.32,7 (Bible), 4.3.5
Women worshippers, **1.5.5** (Hebrew)

TEXTS

A, passim
A. 125, 1.3.5
A. 181, 1.3.6
A. 987
Aa, passim
AbB II No. 65, 1.14.3, 1.45
ABL 24, 3.4.3
ABL 33, 2.3.11, 3.4.9, 3.27.1
ABL 65, 4.22.15.3, 4.23.10, App. 5 list no. 23
ABL 113, 4.22.15.3, 4.23.10
ABL 149, 3.17.2
ABL 268, App. 3.2.4
ABL 361, 2.3.11; 2.3.16
ABL 366, 4.22.15.3, 4.23.10
ABL 437, 2.15.4, 3.17.2
ABL 461, App. 3.2.4
ABL 476, App. 5 n.52
ABL 509, 4.14
ABL 633, 1.46
ABL 975, 3.2.6,
ABL 977, 3.4.5, 4.11.10
ABL 1106, App. 3.3.6
ABL 1126, 4.11.10
ABL 1133, 3.4.11
ABL 1216, 3.17.2
ABL 1221,1.2.9, 4.6.6
ABL 1233, App. 3.2.4
ABL 1285, 3.17.1
ABL 1346, 3.27.1
Abu Habba 83-1-18, 3.4.1
ACh Adad XII, 1.21.9 (Ishtar XXIII), 4.9.3 (XVII) 4.9.5, App. 3.3.1 (bis) , Supp. 2, 4.7.2
ADB 1, App. 4.1.11
ADB 5, 1.32
ADD 50, App. 5 n. 24
ADD 60, 3.27.1
ADD 81, App. 3.8.1
ADD 82, App. 3.8.1
ADD 284, 2.4.3
ADD 537, 2.4.3
ADD 575, App. 1 n. to 13
ADD 579, App. 1 n. to 13

ADD 696, 2.4.7
ADD 742, App. 1 n. to 13
ADD 805, App. 1 n. to 13
ADD 827 + 914, 1.3.14, 2.4.7, 2.4.8, App. 3.3.1
ADD 828, 2.4.7
ADD 851, 2.3.11, 3.3.8, 3.4.12, 3.27.1
ADD 860, 3.17.1
ADD 874, 2.3.11
ADD 914 + 827, 1.3.14, 2.4.7, App. 3.3.1
ADD 953, 3.4.12
ADD 1040, App. 5 n.70
AKA 32, App 5 n.70; 100, 4.11.9; 369, 2.4.7
Alberti Pompaonio 2, 2.23
AMT 32, 4.11.13
Ana ittišu 7 II App. 4.1.12; III 1-22, MSL 1 99-101, 1.2.8, 4.11.15 (bis), 4.22.6
Antagal passim
AO 6472, 2.3.16
AO 6721, 4.3.1
AO 9066, 4.9.2
AO 11276, 4.8.2
ARM 1 12, 2.4.6; 28, App. 3.3.6; 83, 2.17
ARM 2 22, 3.2.7; 119, 2.4.6; 134. 3.2.7; 139, 3.2.7; 725, App. 5 n.67
ARM 3 8, 4.9.2; 42, 4.9.2; 84, 4.9.2
ARM 5 82, 4.3.4
ARM 6, 45 3.12.3
ARM 7 206, 1.12.1, 2.4.6; 4.6.6, 4.7.2; 239, 4.6.2; 275, 4.6.6
ARM 8 1ff, 1.35.1
ARM 9 24, 2.4.6, 3.18, 4.3.4, 27, 4.16.3; 291, 4.11.7
ARM 10 6, App. 3.2.2; 7, 3.15.2, App 3.22; 8, 3.15.2; 34, 1.3.14; 37, 4.3.4; 50, 1.3.2; 51, 1.3.2; 52, 1.3.2; 53, 3.15.2; 59, 4.11.7, App. 4.2.1, App. 4.3; 80, 3.15.2, 3.16.2, App. 3.2.2; 81, 3.15.1; 124, 4.4.1, App. 322; 140, 4.6.6; 153, 3.28
ARM 13 22, 2.17; 126, 1.37.2
ARM 16 1, 3.15.2
AS 1 36, 2.3.18
AS 12 92, 2.3.9, 4.11.2
AS 17 No. 56, 1.10.6
Ash 1922, 256, 1.37.4
ASKT No. 11, 4.11.15; No. 17, 2.3.16; No. 21, App. 3.4 (bis); No. 120, App. 3.3.5
Assur Photo 4123i, 1.3.11
Ass. Ph. 4132f, 1.3.11
Ass. Ph. 6553, Intro. 1.3 n.27, 2.1.2.39, App. 4.1.12
AT 265, App. 3.5.3
Atrahasis 62, 4.11.15; 102, 1.19.9, 1.19.15, 4.10.1; Intro 1.3
Bauer Lagasch 1, 2.3.11; 12, 6. 2.14; 66,2.14; 126, 3.3.2; 156, App. 4.1.6; 292, 4.15; Index 583, 2.10.3
BBR 24, 3.8.3, 3.26, App. 3.7.7
BBSt No. 3, 1.10.7; No. 8, App. 3.2.4
BE 6/3 7, 1.7.3
BE 10 (2), 4.20
BE 14 132, App. 5 n.43
BE 15 200, 3.4.2
BE 25 200, 3.4.11
BE 29, 1 II 34, 1.7.2
BE 30 10, App. 3.7.6; 12, App. 4.2.1
BE 31 12, App. 4.1.11; 54, App. 3.3.7
Biggs ŠÀ.ZI.GA, 4.22.8; 13, 4.11.14; 21, 3.7.2; 26, 4.16; 34, 4.4.1; 41,1.19.11, 2.19.14
BIN VI 222, 4.11.2; VIII 103, 4.11.2; 157, 1.10.2
Bīt Rimki, First House, 3.4.6
Bīt Rimki, Second House, 3.4.6
Bīt Rimki, Third House, 1.25.3
BM 12218, 1.37.2
BM 12939, 1.41
BM 134501, 4.4.1
BM 14618, 2.3.3, 2.4.5, 2.13.3
BM 23131, 4.6.5
BM 26959, 1.14.3
BM 41005, App. 3.2.5
BM 85500, App. 3.8.4
BM 92685, 1.19.11
BM 120011, 4.23.10
BM 130729, 1.19.10
BM 134501, 4.4.1
Borger Esarh 24, 2.3.18, 3.13.1; 44 §49, 4.7.2; 75 §48, 4.19;77, 4.7.2; 89, 2.4.5; 91, 2.1.2.29, 2.3.12, 2.4.5; 93, 2.4.8; 99 App. 3.4; 114 §80, 2.13.4, 3.3.8
BRM 2 49, App. 5. n. 24; 4, 3.7.2, 4.7.2; 12, 4.7.2; 46, 2.15.3
Brünnow 13787, 2.4.9.2
Bu 88-5-12, 10, 4.4.1; 11, App. 3.2.6
Bu 89-4-26, 7, 3.27.1; 238
BU 91-5-9, 218, 2.13.4, 3.3.8
CBS 10467, 4.6.3
CH §§108, 4.3.3; 110, 1.19.2, 4.9.2; 10, 4.9.2; 137, 4.3.3, 4.22.15.4; 144-

5, 4.3.3 (bis); 178, 4.9.2; 179, 4.7.2, 4.9.2; 180, 4.7.2; 181, 4.7.2, 4.8.2, 4.11.5; 183-4, 4.3.3 (bis)
Chiera SRT 1+,1.2.6, 4.23; 5, App. 3.5.3; 6, 3.3.3, 11, 1.25.3; 23, 4.3.1; 31, App. 4.1.7.2; 34, App. 4.2.3; 36, App. 3.4
Chiera STA 14, 4.3.1; 15, 4.3.1; 16, 4.3.1
Cohen *Eršemma* 18, 2.3.9; 32, 2.3.9, 2.3.16; 36, 2.1.2.51; 48, 2.3.9, 2.3.16; 56, 3.8.5; 97, App. 3.3.5; 159, 2.3.9; 164, 1.7.10, 2.3.9; 165, 1.9.3; 171, App. 5 n.69
Cohen *Lamentations* 28, 2.8.2; 34, 2.1.2; 56, 104, 1.7.10; 112, 1,7.10; 133, 1.7.10; 140, 1.7.10; 164, 4.11.2; 171, 4.11.2; 235. 1.19.15; 304 and 305, 1.20, 1.20.15; 422, 2.1.2.29; 581, 4.6.6
Cooper Curse on Agade, chap. 1 n. 174, 2.25.5, App. 4.1.12
Craig ABRT, 1, App. 3.8.5; 2, 3.2.8, 3.6; 3.8.5; 55, 2.4.7, App.3.3.7; 63-65, App. 3.7.7, 4.16.3; 64, 3.8.3
Crozer 153, 4.11.5; 169, 3.2.7; 172, 3.2.7
CT 4 5, App 3.3.7
CT 4 6, App. 3.2.6
CT 5 2, 1.37.2
CT 6 2, 1.19.11
CT 7 13, 1.41, 2.13.3
CT 7 24, 2.13.3
CT 8 2b, 4.4.1, 21, 2.8.2
CT 11, 14-18, 2.3.2
CT 13 42, 1.19.5
CT 15 8, 4.11.2; 19,1.9.3; 43, 1.3.4, App. 3.3.6; 44, 2.1.2.22, App. 3.3.3; 45-58, App 3.2.9; 46, App. 3.2.7; 47, 2.15.1, App. 3.2.4
CT 16 28, 3.6; 37, 1.10, 1.22.3, 3.10; 4.11.10
CT 18 2, 3.20.1, 4.14; 5, 3.20.2, App. 3.2.7, App 3.5, App. 3.6.1; App 3.8.5; 14, 1.15.1, 4.1.4; 19, 4.6.4, 4.11.14, 4.14
CT 22 183, App. 3.8.4
CT 24 16, 4.11.10; 28, 4.11.10; 33, 3.3.7, App. 4.1.6; 43, 2.3.16
CT 28.10, 3.20.4
CT 29 18, 3.9; 19, 3.9
CT 30 15, 3.2.4
CT 31 2, App. 4.2.1; 44, 1.19.11; 48, 3.2.4; CT 36 26, 4.23.8
CT 38 5, 2.4.9.1
CT 39 33, 1.17; 44, App. 3.2.6; 45, App. 3.2.6
CT 44, 18, 1.19.11
CT 46 52, 2.3.5
CT 48 4.14
CT 49p, 1.44
CT 51 161, 4.4.1
CTA 21, 4.19; 71,4.19; 73, 4.19; 75, 4.19; 77, 4.19 113, 4.19
Curse on Agade, see Cooper
Death of Gilgamesh 23, 1.13.2, 1.21.4
Deimel Fara 2, 61 1.7.2; WF74, 4.11.2
Deir 'Alla texts, 3,32 (2) (Bil^{c}am)
Descent of Inanna 2.3.4.1; App. 3.2.7; App. 3.2.9, App 3.3.6
Descent of Ishtar 2.15.1, App. 3.2.4, App 3.2.9, App 3.4
Diri, passim
DT 1, App. 5 n. 70
DT 75, 2.4.7
Ea, passim
Ebeling Parfümrez pl. 15, 2.1.2.26, 2.3.12; pl. 17, 3.4.5; pl. 25, 2.3.12, 2.3.16; pl. 49, 2.4.2
Ebeling Stiftungen App. 5 n. 24; IV, 1.2.8, 4.6.6; VII, 1.32, App. 5 n. to line 62; VIII App. 5 n. 48,52 and lines 64,65.
ED Lu, passim
Edzard Tell-ed-Der 152, 4.9.2; 163, 4.9.2; 4.8.4, 4.11.1, 4.11.2, 4.11.7, 4.11.9, 4.22.15.3
Enuma Anu Enlil, 2.3.17
Enuma elish IV.88, 3.12.9, 4.22.15.7
Erimhus, passim
Erra , 2.2.10, 4.6.4, App 3.2.2, App. 3.2.10, App. 3.3.5, App 3.3.6 (bis), App, 5. line 78
Examentext A, 1.10.6, 1.16, 2.1.2.7, 2.1.2.8, 2.1.2.16, 2.1.2.44, 2.1.2.57, (bis)
Fales Censimenti 21, 1.32
Falkenstein Gerichtsurkunden 65, 1.9.4; 81, 2.3.11; 101, 2.3.11; 112, 1.7.5; 120b, 3.7.3; 135, 2.3.11; 161, 4.6.5; 199, 2.3.11;
Finkelstein Late OB 12, 4.8.1; 13, 4.9.2; 90, 4.9.2
Fish Catalogue 8, 1.28; 34 No. 228, 1.37.2; No. 189, 2.3.6
Fossey Magie No. 1, 4.11.15
Gelb OAIC 30, 4.7.1; App. 3.8.1

Genouillac Kish 1B, 3.2.5; B 295, 3.2.5; 2 C100, 2.11.1
Genouillac TSA 9, 2.14, 2.18
Gilgamesh I iv, 4.14; II, 4.22.8; App. 4.2.2; III iv 23, 4.17; IV, 4.22.6, 4.22.8; VI 94; 165, 4.6.4, App. 3.11; VII iii, 4.14; VII iv, 1.13.2, 1.21.4; VIII, 2.20; IX 1.9.4, 1.21.1.9; X, 4.16.2; see death of
Goetze Omen 1, 3.1.1; 17, 4.9.2; 38, 1.19.8; 47, 4.9.2, App. 3.2.3
Gordon Sumerian Proverbs 1.83, 3.7.1; 1.94, App.3.3.6
Gragg Kesh 1.10.3, 1.18, App. 2.3.1, App. 3.3.5, App. 3.13.1, App. 3.13.2
Gregoire *Archives* 131-3, App. 5 n.61; 148, 3.11; 183, 1.7.5; 186, App. 4.1.4; 200,1.7.5; 219, 1.41; 265, 1.28
Gudea A ii, 3.3.4, 4.23.6, 4.23.8; xiii, 1.12.2; xx, 1.21.2, 3.3.5; xxiv, 4.22.15.2; xxix, 1.7.4; 1.18
Gudea B iv App. 3.5.3; v, 2.3.2; 2.3.14; vi 1.17; xi, 4.3.1; xv 2.1.2.47
Gudea St. G, xvi, 4.23.8
Hackman 103, 4.11.2
Hallo Exaltation 1.19.5; 33, 1.19.10; 57, 1.19.10, App. 3.7.1 App. 4.1.1
Hallo HUCA 33, Family 8, 1.19.10, 1.28, 1.37.2, 4.3.1; Intro 1.1 n. 9
Hallo Rencontre 1.18
HAR-gud, passim
Hartman Oppenheim Beer 44, App. 1, line 2 n
Hittite Laws, §80, 4.22.9
HSS 3 25, 2.1.2; 10 71, 3.3.10; 14 140, 1.12.2, App. 5 n. to 22
Hunger Kolophone No. 92, 2.3.17; No. 152, 1.3.1; No. 433, 2.3.5
Hymn to Nanshe 1.9.6, 1.15.3, 1.17, 1.18, 1.25.2, 3.3.2, 4.22.15.2
IAK 70-73, App. 1 n. to 12; 1.19.2; 1.22.4, 4.22, 4.22.15.7
ICK 1, 4.11.2
Igituh, passim
IM 3252 App.3.4
IM 56869 4.6.3
IM 124470, 1.33
Inanna and Bilulu, 1.9.10, App 4.1.10
Inanna and Ebeh, 2.1.2.59, App 3.3.5, App. 3.4, App 3.5.3, App. 3.7.4
Inanna and Enki, 1.13.2, 1.21.6, 1.25.2, 1.25.4, 4.9.3, 4.10.1; 4.13, App. 3.3.1, App. 3.3.5, App. 3.4, App. 3.5.3; App. 4.1.7.1
ITT III 6581, App. 4.1.1
Izbu Commentary, 2.15.3
Jean Contrats No. 34, 2.3.12
JEN 260, App. 3.2.2; 880, App. 3.2.2
K 107, 4.6.4
K 110, 2.3.2
K 162, App. 3.2.4
K 232, 3.2.8, 3.8.5
K 257, + 41
K 357, 4.22.13
K 629, App. 5 list no. 23
K 883, 3.17.1
K 1286, App. 3.5
K 1354, 4.22.15.7, App. 4.1.12
K 1473, App. 3.3.1
K 2001, 3.12.5, 4.26.2,
K 2008, 3.6.1
K 2361, 1.36, 3.9
K 2486 + K. 4364, 3.8.3, App. 3.7.7
K. 2529, 2.3.15
K 2582, 4.16,3, App. 3.8.3
K 2652, 3.3.10
K 2655, 4.6.6
K 2800 4.6.6
K 2856, 1.7.2
K 2946, 1.22.3, 3.8.3, 3.10
K 3182, 3.3.4
K 3362, 4.11.13
K 3423 + Rm 579, 4.8.4
K 3438a + 9912, App. 3.2.5, App. 3.3.6
K 3464, 4.16.3, App. 3.8
K 3476, 1.3.4; App. 3.3.3, App. 3.3.6
K 3495, 1.3.1
K 3600 + DT 75, 2.4.7, 3.6, App. 3.3.7
K 3811, 1.17
K 4141, 3.2.6
K 4193, 3.20.1, App. 3.2.7, App. 3.6.1
K 4214, 3.20.1
K 4336, App. 4.3
K 4349, 3.3.7
K. 4364, App. 3.7.7
K 4395 (NA vocabulary), passim 1.42, 3.4.7, 3.28.1
K 4449, 3.7.5
K 4613, 2.15.2
K 5188 + 8481, App. 3.3.5
K 6462, 3.8.5
K 6475, 3.12.5
K 6705, 4.9.4
K. 6768, 4.9.4
K 8212, 3.8.5
K 8325, 1.19.11

K 9050 + 13457, App. 4.1.
K 9451, 4.16.3
K 9876, App. 3.2.4
K 9923, App. 3.2.5
K 9955 + Rm 613, App. 3.8.5
K 10195 4.8.2
K 10477, App. 3.3.1
K 11173, 3.4.7
K 11773, 1.15.1
Kagal A, passim
KAH 34, App. 4.1.7.1; 64, App. 5 list no. 54
KAJ 51, 2.7.4; 179, 1.35.1; 221, 2.4.3
Kang Drehem 177, 1.7.5; 263 or 363-7, 4.3.1; App. 3.7.3
Kang Umma 289, 1.7.5; 310, 3.2
KAR 1, 3.4.3, App. 3.2.9; App. 3.8.2
KAR 22, App. 3.3.7
KAR 26, 2.13.4, 3.20.3
KAR 38, 3.4.3
KAR 42, 2.2.2, 3.4.7, 4.11.9, App. 3.2.2
KAR 43, 3.4.3, App. 3.8.4
KAR 44, 3.4.4
KAR 58, 3.4.7
KAR 60, 2.3.16
KAR 62, 3.4.3
KAR 63, 3.4.3, App. 3.8.4
KAR 71, 3.4.3
KAR 92, 3.4.7
KAR 94, 4.11.13
KAR 114, 3.4.3
KAR 115, 2.15.3
KAR 122, 4.22.15.7
KAR 132, App. 4.1.3
KAR 139, 1.6.1, 1.6.4, App. 1 n. to 11
KAR 141, 2.4.7, 3.4.5, 4.11.10
KAR 144, 3.4.7, App. 3.8.3
KAR 146, 1.3.7, 1.6.5, 2.4.7, 2.5
KAR 154, Intro 2.0, 2.2.3, 2.5, 4.3.5, 4.11.9, App.1; App. 5 list no. 5 see App.1
KAR 215, 1.3.8
KAR 216, 2.5
KAR 223, 3.4.3
KAR 234, 4.16.3
KAR 239, 3.4.7
KAR 306, 1.10.1
KAR 307, 1.37.4, 3.12.8
KAR 321, 4.3.5, 4.11.10
KAR 357, Intro 1.3 n 25, App. 3.11
KAR 360, 2.1.2.29, 2.3.12, 2.3.16
KAR 422, 3.2.6
KAV 1, 3.7.4, 4.23.3, App. 4.1.12
KAV 42, 3.4.5
KAV 57, App. 1 n to r.9
KAV 73, 3.3.7; App. 4.1.6
KAV 75, 2.4.3
KAV 198, App. 3.8.1
KB 6/2 34 App 3.2.4; 42, App. 3.3.7; 47, App. 3.2.6
Keiser Drehem 493, 4.3.1
Kesh Temple Hymn 1.10.3, 1.18, 1.28, 1,30, 1.31, App. 3.3.5, App. 3.13.1, App. 3.13.2
Kingsbury HUCA 34, 1.7.6, 1.9.7, 2.3.13, 2.4.5, 4.9.2; 10, 2.4.5; 97, 2.45
Kinnier Wilson Wine Lists, 2.4.7; No. 1,No. 2, No. 4 , 3.28.1; No. 3, 3.27.1; No. 8, 3.27.1; No. 9, 3.27.1; 3.6
Kramer SLTN 35, App. 4.2.3; 64, App. 4.1.7.1 (bis)
Kraus Briefe II 65, 1.45, 3.16.1; 71, 3.16.1
KTU 1-132, 1.17, 1.50.1; 1-17, 2.41.1; 1-3, 3.32.1.3
KUB 39 93, 4.6.4
Kwasman 41, App. 1 n. to 13; 236, 3.27.1; 295, 2.4.3; 296, 2.4.3; 352a, App. 3.8.1; 352b, App. 3.8.1; 424, 4.14
Labat TDP 2, 3.4.1; 22, App. 4.1.13; 170, 3.4.9; 218, 3.7.2
Lahar and Ashnan, 1.29, App. 3.5.3
Lamentation over the destruction of Sumer and Ur, 1.17, 1.23, 2.1.2.4, 2.1.2.6, 2.10.1, 1.12.51, 3.3.2, 4.22.15.5
Lamentation over the destruction of Ur, 2.3.9, 4.11.2, 4.11.9, 4.11.16, 4.22.15.5
Langdon BL No. 87, 4.8.2; No. 194, App. 3.3.5
LB 963, 4.23.6; 1090.2.26, Intro n. 23, App. 3.11
LE §41, App. 4.3; 98, App. 4.3
Leemans Ishtar, App. 3.11
Legrain Catal No. 55, 4.3.1
Lidzbarski Ephemeris III , 57, 1.4.2, III 285,Intro 1.1, n 13.
LIH 34, 4.6.5; 83, 1.14.3; III, no. 2, 4.6.5
Limet Textes Sumeriennes, No. 37, 2.4.5
Lipit-Ishtar §22, 4.11.5; 1.19.10
Livingstone Poetry No. 4, 2.1.2.5, 3.6, App. 3.3.7; No. 4.8, 2.1.2.21, 2.1.2.44, 2.1.2.47; No. 4.9, 2.1.2.5,

2.1.2.28, 2.1.2.50; No. 7, App. 3.8.5; No. 8, Intro.1.3 n. 27, 2.1.2 (many), 4.8.4, App. 3.3.3, App. 4.1.12; No. 9, 4.22.15.7; No. 12, 3.7.1; No. 25, 3.7.5; No. 28, 2.1.2; No. 37, 1.3.4, App. 3.3.6; No. 38, App. 3.2.1, App. 3.4; No. 39, 1.37.4, 3.12.8
LKA 32, Intro. 1.3 n. 27, 2.1.2.39, 4.8.4, App. 3.3.3, App. 4.1.12; 35, 2.4.2; 37, 4.11.6; 70, 3.14, App. 5 n. 30; 71, App. 3.4; 72, App. 3.4; 137, 3.32; 144, 3.7.4
LKU 51, App. 3.2.4
LTBA, passim
Luckenbill AnnSenn 2.3.11, 2.3.16, 2.4.7, App. 1 n to r.5; 52, 2.4.7
Lullaby, 2.12
Lu = ša, passim
MAL §14, App. 4.1.12; 19f, 4.23.3; 39, 4.24.3; 40, 4.11.12; 41, 4.11.12; 47, 3.7.4
Malku-šarru Explicit, passim
Maqlû I, 3.7.5, 3.7.7, 4.11.13; III 1.2.5, n. 3, 2.13.4, 3.21.3, 3.22, 4.3.5, 4.8.4, App. 3.2.7; IV, 1.15.1, 1.362.13.4, 3.7.2, 3.20.5, 3.21.3, 3.22, 3.23; V, 4.11.13; VI, 1.19.15, 3.22, 4.11.10, 4.11.13; VII, 2.1.2.36, 2.13.4, 2.4.5, 3.20.3, 3.20.4, 3.20.5, 3.23, IX, 3.20.5, 4.12. 4.25.5
Menzel Tempel TI, 1.3.2, 1.3.13, 4.14; 24, 1.32; 249, 1.19.7; 286, 2.5; 300, 1.32; 300, 1.42; T II , 1.3.5, 3.28.1, App. 1; 8ff. Intro 3 n. 61; 8-11, 1.2.9; 4.6.6; 15-17, 4.6.6; 24, 1.3.5, 1.32; 25 3.17.2; 26, 1.3.6, 1.32; 80-83, 2.4.7; 25, 3.17.2; 39 App. 3.2.5; 99, 2.5; 300, 1.32
Nabnītu, passim
Nanshe Hymn, see Hymn to Nanshe
NBC 5561, 4.8.3
ND 496, 1.42, 4.6.3
ND 1120, App. 1 n. to line 7
ND 2090, App. 5 n.70
ND 2309, 1.32
ND 2316, 1.32
ND 2317, App. 3.8.1
ND 2442, 3.27.1
ND 2489, App. 5 n.47
ND 2490 + 2609, App. 3.2.4
ND 2622, 2.4.3
ND 3426, 3.28.2
ND 3476, 3.27.1
ND 5463, 2.4.8
ND 5545, App. 5 n. 70
ND 5550, App. 5 n. 52
ND 6218, 3.28
ND 10033, 3.27.1
ND 10047, 3.27.1
ND 10048, 3.27.1
ND 10051/1, 3.27.1
ND 10063, 3.27.1
Nikolski, App. 4.1.4
OB Lu, passim
OB Proto-Lu, passim
OBGT XIII, MSL IV, 2.1.2.10, 3.13.7
OECT 1 2, 2.1.2.32, 2.1.2..42 (bis); 5 8, 1.2.6; 8 16, 1.7.3; 15, App. 4.1.5; 20, 1.37.4, 3.25; 34, 4.23.10
Oppenheim Beer 44, App. 5 list no. 60
Oppenheim *Catalogue* Bab 19, 2.25.1; D22, 3.2.1; E4, 1.7.5, 180, 1.28; F4, App. 3.7.3; G 34, 4.3.1; L20, 2.3.6; M 19, App. 4.1.7.1; 208, 1.37.1
Oppenheim Centaurus 14, 3.2.1
Pallis Akītu pl.VI, App. 3.3.3; pl. VIII, 2.1.2.22
PAPS 107/3, App. 4.2.3; 107/6 ii, 2.3.2, 4.23.9; Intro n20
PBS I/1 11, 2.3.5, 2.4.5; 2.4.11, 3.5.1, 4.20
PBS I/2 135, 1.12.2; 1.15.3
PBS 3, 880, App. 3.2.2
PBS 5 25, App. 3.5.3; 100, 1.40; 157, App. 4.1.5
PBS 7 101, App. 4.3
PBS 8/2 131, 1.7.3
PBS 12/1 6b, 1.9.4, 1.14.1
PBS 13 64, 1.10.7
Pettinato Untersuchungen I 370, App. 4.1.4; I 444, App. 4.1.6; 855, 4.22.15.7
Pinches Behrens 102, 1.24; 103, App. 3.13.7
Postgate Palace Archive No. 17, 1.42, 4.6.3; No. 220, App. 1 n to line 9
Postgate Royal Grants 42-44, App. 1 n. to r. 16; 51, 4.6.6; 118, 4.6.6; 120. 1.2.9
Proto á = A, passim
Proto-Diri, passim
Proto-Ea, passim
Proto-Kagal, passim
Proto-izi, passim

2 R 50,11 App. 1 n. to line 12
2 R 58-3, 3.8.3
3 R 52-2, 1.21.9; 66-2, App. 1 n. to line r. 9; 66-11, 2.4.9.2
4 R 3.1.17; 11-22, 2.15.2; 11-23, 2.8.3; 50, 3.4.7; 53, 2.3.15; 54, 1.20; 58, 4.11.14, 4.17; 61-1, 1.17; 61-1, 2.20; Add 1.17
5 R 16, App. 4.2.1; 33, 2.13.4; 51. 1.16; 58, 4.17
RAcc 12, 2.3.16; 16, 1.21.9, 2.3.16; 20, 2.1.2.59, 2.3.16; 28, 1.21.9; 35, 2.3.16; 36. 2.3.16; 42-44, 2.3.9, 2.3.16, 2.3.18; 79, 2.3.16; 44, 2.3.16, 2.3.18, App. 3.2.2, 4.11.9; 45, 4.11.9; 68, 4.22.15.7; 79, 2.3.16; 89, 2.3.18; 91, 1.3.7, 2.3.16, App. 3.2.2; 96, 2.3.16; 115, 2.25.4, 3.2.4 App. 3.2.4 (bis); 119, 1.13.4; 141, 3.4.11; p. 100, App. 4.1.3
Reisner Telloh, 59, App. 5 list no. 16; 162, App. 4.1.1
RTC 210, 1.9.6; 399, 1.41; RTC 208, 3.2.1
S^b passim
SAA III No. 4, 2.1.2 (many)
SAKI 126, 1.17; 227; 194, 1.37.2, 3.2.1; 166, 2.3.3
SBH 56, 2.1.2.37, 2.4.5, App. 3.13, App. 4.1.11, App. 4.2.4; 109, 2.3.12; 145, 4.22.15.3
Schneider Montserrat 296, 4.3.1
Schorr Zivil 78, 4.11.6; 182, 4.11.5, 4.11.7; 211, 4.3.3, 4.11.6; 241, 4.11.6; 278, 4.8.1; 280, 4.11.6; 531, 4.11.6, 4.3.3
SEM 19, 4.22.15.5; 65, 3.14; 87, App. 4.1.11
shumma Ālu, Tabl 39, App. 3.2.6; 80, App. 3.2.6; 104, 4.22.13, App. 3.2.6;
shumma Izbu, 3.1.2
Shurpu II, 1.7.8, 4,11,15; III, 2.1.2.26, 2.1.2.29, 2.1.2.39, 2.1.2.44, 2.1.2.48 , 2.1.2.49, 2.1.2.51, 2.1.2.53, 2.1.2.57, 2.15.1, 3.4.4, 4.11.13, App. 1 n. to r.10; IV, 2.1.2.4, 3.4.11; V-VI, 3.23, 3.32, 4.11.13, App. 3.3.7; VIII, 3.24, 4.3.5, 4.8.4, 4.11.13, 4.17, App. 1 n. to r. 10
Sigrist Horn 54, 3.2
Sigrist Rochester 165, 4.3.1
Silbenvocabular A, 2.25.1
Sjöberg Temple Hymns 29, App. 4.1.3; 30, 4.8.2; 61, 1.16; 93b, 4.23.4; 112, 4.11.7; 123, 4.8.2; 174, 1.10.3; 186, 1.25.3 ; 1.28; 1174, 1.18
SKL 4.16.2
SLT 240, 1.17, App. 3.5.1
SLTN 35, App. 4.2.3; 45, App. 3.5.1; 64, App. 4.1.7.1; 71, 4.11.7; 88, 1.9.5;
Sm 332, 3.14
SMN 1670, 4.14
Sollberger Correspondence 124, no. 259, 1.7.1; no. 339, 2.13.3; no. 340, 2.13.3; no. 369, 3.12.2
Sollberger Inscriptions IB4a, 1.2.6, 4.11.2, 4.23.4; IIIA3d, 1.14.10; IIA4k, 2.3.3; IIIA2u, 1.37.2; IIIA2z, 4.3.1; IIIA3d, 1.19.10; IIIA4m 2.2.4, 4.3.1; IIIA4n, 4.3.1; IIIA5d, 4.25.5; IVB14h, 1.19.7, 1.19.10; App. 4.16
Speelers Recueil 308, 1.3.6; 312, 3.20.5, 3.22, 4.11.13
SRT 1, 1.2.6, 4.23.4, App. 3.5.3; 5, 4.23.4; 6, 13.3.3, 4.11.6; 11, 1.25.3; 23, 4.3.1
STT 65, 3.7.1; 382, 383, 1.3.1; 384, 385, passim; 402, 2.4.2; 403, App. 4.1.13
STVC 34, 1.17; 48, 4.8.2; 50, 3.3.4; 75, 1.3.14
Sumerian King List, 1.2.6, 3.8.3, 4.16.2
Szlechter TJA UMM G19, 4.6.4; 56 UMM G 36, 4.9.2
Tamarisk and Palm, 4.11.10
TCL I 146, 4.11.6, 4.11.10, 4.11.11
TCL II, 3.28
TCL III 159, 3.1.2, 2.4.5
TCL VIII pl. xxxvi 1.17
TCL IX 136, App. 5 list no. 86
TCL X 34, 3.12.2; 37, App. 5 n. 24; 69, 3.12.3
TCL XIII, 1.44
TCL XIV 25, 1.8.3
TCL XV 25, 1.14.2, 1.9.2
TCL XVI 46, 4.3.1, 4.11.6; 136, 4.22.15.5
TEM 4, 1.12.1, 2.4.6, 3.17.2, .18
Thompson AMT 96, 3.4.3
Thureau-Dangin HCS, 2.1.2.44; 159, 2.1.2.53; 2.4.5, 4.11.15; App. 3.2.4
TIM 9 54, 4.22.15.3, 4.23.10, App. 3.4

TLB 2 2, 4.23.6
TMH NF 4, 1.19.10,
TRS 2 46, 4.3.1
TU 146, App. 3.13.6; 157 0205, 1.41
TuL 11, App 3.11, 3.14, App. 3.1.1; 17, 2.7.2; 20, App. 3.3.7; 22, 2.4.7; 27, 1.21.9; 47; 49, App. 5 n 30; 50, 3.12.5, ; 90, 2.4.7; 102,7; 103, 1.36, 3.9
TuM NF III 25, App. 3.3.1; 27-33, 4.8.2, App, 3.3.6
UET I 57, 4.3.1; 103, 1.19,.6, 4.22.15.7; 104, 1.19.3, 1.19.15; 104, 1.20; 105, 1.19.15; 107, 1.9.7; 149, App. 5 n to 66; 187, 1.19.10; 304, App. 5 n to 66
UET II 345, 4.11.2
UET III 942, 4.11.2, 4.11.7; 1502, 1504, 2.8.1; 1505, 2.8.1; 1506, 3.8.1, App. 3.11
UET IV 2.25.3
UET V 191, 1.3.2; 247, 1.39; 411, App. 5 list no.72; 586, 1.24; 868, 1.12.2
UET VI 67, 1.22.3; 69 1.21.8, 1.22.2, 1.25.2; 133, 1.23; 204, 2.3.5; 388, 3.8.5; 389, 3.8.5
UET VII 155, 3.3.7; 3.13.2
UM 29-16-86, 1.13.2, 1.21.4
UM 29-16-229, App. 3.4
UMBS 5 76, 3.2.5; 10/4 3, App. 4.1.7.1
Ungnad Briefe Hammurapi No. 2, 4.6.5, 4.12; 152,3.9; 153, 3.9
Ur-ea-nâqu passim
Uruanna passim
UruKAgina Cones B & C X, 4.9.1
UVB 8, 2.2.4, 4.3.1; 15, 1.36, 3.9
VAB 4 114, 4.22.15.7, 4.23.10; 216, 1.44; 236, 4.22.15.1; 240, 4.22.15.7, 4.23.10; D42, 4.25.5
VAS 1 36, 1.38.3
VAS 2 2, App. 3.3.5
VAS 5 11, 4.11.6
VAS 7 1.34, 2.34, 4.11.7
VAS 8, 55, 1.12.2.
VAS 10 199, App. 4.1.5; 214 ii 1, Intro 1.3 n. 28
VAS 14 118, 2.10.3
VAS 16,22, 3.3.7
VAS 22, 18, 1.9.9
VAS 53, 1.19.7
VAT 276 + , App. 3.13.3, App. 4.2.4
VAT 6302, 4.11.6
VAT 8014, 3.4.3
VAT 8022, 2.3.16
VAT 8230, 3.4.3
VAT 8240, 3.4.3
VAT 8275, 3.4.4
VAT 8882, 1.3.8
VAT 8917, 1.37.4, 3.12.8
VAT 9728, App. 3.8.3
VAT 9742, 3.28.1
VAT 9946, App. 3.4
VAT 10099, App. 3.4
VAT 10102, 4.11.10
VAT 10112, 2.5, 3.5, 1.3.7
VAT 10164, App. 1
VAT 10448, 3.4.5
VAT 10464, 2.4.7
VAT 10568a, 3.4.5, 4.11.9
VAT 10593, 4.22.15.7
VAT 13034, 3.3.7
VAT 13596, 1.3.10; 2.3.16
VAT 13717, 1.3.9
VAT 13832, App. 3.2.5
Walters Water 43, 4.8.3
Watson Birmingham 77, 2.3.6, 1.37.2
Weissbach Misc 12, 2.3.10
Williams College 3, App. 4.1.7
Winckler Sar pl. 36 No. 76, 1.10.6; 2.6; 3.13.2
Wiseman Alalakh No. 1, App. 3.5.3; 265, App. 3.5.3
YBC 7840, 4.9.2
YBT 1 29, 4.2.1; 67, 4.9.2, 3.2.1
YBT 10, 57 4.26; 58, 3.26; 62, 3.26
YOS I 45, 1.18, 1.19.2, 1.21.9, 1.44, 2.4.7, 3.2.3, 4.22.15.6; 53, 3.25.1; 71, 1.18; 87, 2.25.1;
YOS II 1, 3.3.7, 4.3.7; 45, 1.34, 2.31; 129, 1.40
YOS V 46, App. 5 n to 66; 163, 1.37.1, 1.39, 1.40, App. 5 n to 66
YOS VI 62, 2.1.2.44
YOS VII 7, App. 5 n. 43; 89, App. 5 n.24
YOS X 46, 4.7.2, 3.1.1
YOS XIII 30, 1.47.2
Zimmern Bab Buss 88
Zimmern Tammuzlieder 212,
79-7-8, 250, 3.4.4
83-1-18 (Abu Habba), 3.4.1
96-4-7, 7, 2.4.5

TEXTS -- Ebla

MEE 1, 3.32.21
MEE 2, 1.38.4
MEE 4, 403, 1.38.4, Index, 4.8.4

TM 75.G. 454, 3.32.21; 525, 1.7.12; 1764, 1.7.12; 2075, 1.7.12; 2238, 1.7.12; 11010, 1.7.12

TEXTS -- Emar

275, 1.19.13
369, 1.19.12
446, 1.19.13

TEXTS -- Ugaritic

1 Aq 10, 4.25.5; 172, 2.41.2
CTA 3, 3.32.4.3; 71, 4.19; 73, 4.19; 75, 4.19; 75, 4.19; 77, 4.19; 113, 4.19
KTU 1.17, 2.41.1; 1.3, 3.32.4.3; 1.132, 1.50
MRS III 1.50.11
MRS VII 40, 2.4.3
MRS XII, App. 3.14
PRU II No. 4, 4.19; 26, 1.4.2, 4.19 ; 17, 4.19; 175, 1.50.9
PRU III 72, 1.50.10; 247, 4.19, 4.25.5; Index, 4.25.5
PRU V 163, 4.19
PRU VI No. 93, 1.4.2 n. 17, 4.19
RS 8 252, 4.19
RS 11 716, 4.19
RS 14 84, 4.19
RS 16 132, 4.19; 257, 1.50.11; 276, 1.50.10
RS 17 36, 4.19; 131, 4.19, App. 3.14
RS 18 251, 4.19
RS 24 244, 3.32.15; 252, 2.42; 258, chap 1 n 11; 260, 4.19; 291, 1.50.1
UH 301, 1.4.7
UT 63, 4.19
UT 81, 4.19
UT 82, 4.24.4
UT 113, 4.19
UT 114, 1.50.2, 4.19
UT 168, 2.41.5
UT 169, 4.19
UT 305, 4.25.5
UT 400, 4.19
UT 668, 3.32.16
UT 1004, 4.19
UT 1046, 4.25.5
UT 1107, 2.41.5
UT 1169 1.4.7
UT 1175, 1.50.9, 1.50.12

TEXTS -- Other Semitic

CIS I 49, 4.25.9; 86, 4.25.5
Deir 'Alla, 3.32.2
KAI 95, 1.4.2, 4.24.7; 202, 3.14
Lidzbarski, *Ephemeris* , III 57D, 1.4.2III 285, chap 1 n. 13
Oberman Karatepe p. 10, 4.24.4

TEXTS -- Hebrew Bible

Am 1.1, 1.50.5, 4.19
Am 2.7-8, 4.22.6, 4.25.3, 4.25.4, 4.26.1
Am 5.16, 2.38.1
Am 5.22, 2.27.3
Am 7.17, 4.24.8
1 Chr 6.18, 2.31
1 Chr 9.2, 1.4.7, 4.24.2
1 Chr 13.8, 2.27.2
1 Chr 15.29, 2.30, 3.40.3
1 Chr 24.16, 4.25.2
1 Chr 25.6, 2.40.3
2 Chr 28.4, 4.26.1
2 Chr 29.25, 2.27.5
2 Chr 34.9, 1.5.3
2 Chr 35.25, 2.33
Dan 1.20, 3.32.12, 3.32.14
Dan 2.10, 3.3.8
Dan 2.27, 3.32.18
Dan 3, 2.27.2, 3.5.7, 3.32.24
Dan 3.5.7, 2.27.2
Dan 4.6, 3.3.8
Dan 5.12, 3.32.6, 3.32.12
Deut 7.13, Intro 1.3
Deut 10.8, 1.4.2
Deut 11.30, 3.32.20
Deut 12.2, 4.26.1
Deut 13.2, 3.32.13
Deut 14.1, Intro 1.3, 2.38.1 (bis)
Deut 16.16, 1.5.5
Deut 17.9, 1.4.2
Deut 18.10-11, 3.32, 3.32.5
Deut 19.17, 1.4.2
Deut 21.5, 1.4.2 (bis)
Deut 21.13, 2.29
Deut 22.5, App. 3.15
Deut 23.18, **4.18.1**, 4.22.3,4.22.6, 4.22.10; 4.25.5
Deut 23.19, 4.18.1, 4.25.5
Deut 24.8, 1.4.2
Deut 26.14, 3.32.9
Deut 27.13-26, 1.4.2
Deut 31.9.25, 1.4.2
Deut 31.10-12, 1.5.5
Deut 31.16, 4.26.1 (bis)
Deut 33.8, 1.4.2

Deut 33.10, 1.4.2
Deut 34.8, 2.38.1
Eccl 2.8, 2.33
Eccl 10.11, 3.32.15
Ex 3.4, 3.32.20
Ex 4.24-26, 1.5.5
Ex 7.8-12, 3.7.2; 3.32.23
Ex 8.14, 3.32.12
Ex 9.10, 3.32.23
Ex 9.22, 3.32.23
Ex 15.1, 2.28
Ex 15.1-18, 4.24.8
Ex 15.20, 1.5.5, 2.28, 2.34, 4.24.8
Ex 15.21, 2.28, 4.24.8
Ex 19.16, 2.27.2
Ex 19.19, 2.27.3
Ex 20.26, 4.27, App. 3.15
Ex 22.7-10, 3.32.24
Ex 22.17, 3.32, 3.32.4.5
Ex 23.17, 1.5.5
Ex 25.22, 2.27.3
Ex 25.29, 1.4.2
Ex 27.20f, 1.4.2
Ex 28.30, 3.32.23
Ex 28.33, 2.27.2
Ex 28.34, 2.27.3
Ex 30.7, 1.4.2
Ex 30.25.35, 1.5.2
Ex 32, 4.24.4
Ex 32.8, 2.40.3
Ex 32.18, 2.40.3
Ex 32.20, 3.32.24
Ex 34.15, 4.26.1 (bis)
Ex 34.23, 1.5.5
Ex 37.16, 1.4.2
Ex 37.29, 1.5.2
Ex 38.8, 1.4.6, 4.24.6
Ex 39.25, 2.27.2
Ex 40.6.12, 1.4.6
Ezek 6.13, 4.25.1
Ezek 8.14, 1.5.5, 2.38.1, 4.24.5, 4.26.1
Ezek 13.9, 3.32.2
Ezek 13.17-23, 4.24.8
Ezek 13.22, 3.32.21
Ezek 16, 4.22.6, 4.24.4, 4.26.1
Ezek 16.15-52, 4.26.1
Ezek 16.16, 4.24.4
Ezek 16.31-34, 4.26.1
Ezek 16.37, 4.24.4
Ezek 20.28, 4.26.1
Ezek 21.26, 3.32.2, 3.32.17
Ezek 22.26, 1.4.2
Ezek 22.28, 3.32.2
Ezek 23, 4.24.6, 4.26.1
Ezek 23.9, 4.24.4
Ezek 23.17, 4.26.1
Ezek 23.37, 4.26.1, 4.26.6
Ezek 23.40, 4.26.1 (bis)
Ezek 23.43, 4.26.1
Ezek 28.13, 2.27.2
Ezek 34.15, 4.26.1
Ezek 44.1-2, 2.27.3
Ezek 44.23, 1.4.2 (bis)
Ezr 2.41, 2.31
Ezr 2.63, 3.32.23
Ezr 2.65, 2.31
Ezr 7.24, 1.4.7, 4.24.2
Ezr 10.23, 4.25.2
Gen 1.28, Intro 1.3
Gen 3.21, Intro 1.3
Gen 4.21, 2.27.2
Gen 6.19, Intro 1.3
Gen 8.22 Intro 1.3
Gen 9.21-3, 4.27; App. 3.15
Gen 12.6, 3.32.20
Gen 19.1-11, 4.27, App. 3.15
Gen 21.33, 3.32.20
Gen 24.65, 4.24.3
Gen 28.14, 4.25.5
Gen 35.8, 2.38.2
Gen 38.12-26, 4.18.1, 4.24.3, 4.25.5
Gen 41.12, 3.32.12
Gen 41.24, 3.32.12
Hos 1-3, 4.24.1
Hos 1.2, 4.26.1
Hos 1.4, 4.25.2
Hos 2, 4.24.4, 4.26.1 (bis)
Hos 2.2, 4.26.1
Hos 2.4, 4.26.1
Hos 2.5, 4.24.4
Hos 2.7ff, 4.24.4
Hos 2.18-20, 4.26.1
Hos 3.1.3, 4.26.1
Hos 3.4, 3.32.10
Hos 4.1ff, 1.4.2
Hos 4.4, 4.22.4
Hos 4.11-19, 4.24.4, 4.26.1
Hos 4.13, 3.32.20, 4.24.3, 4.26.1 (bis)
Hos 4.14, 4.17-18, 4.18.1, 4.24.3, 4.25.8, 4.26.1
Hos 4.17-18, 4.16.1
Hos 5.4, 4.26.1
Hos 5.12.14, 1.5.5, 4.25.6
Hos 5.14, 4.25.6
Hos 6.10, 4.26.1
Hos 7.14-16, 4.25.6
Hos 9.1, 4.24.3, 4.26.1
Hos 10.5, 1.4.5

Hos 10.12, 4.25.6
Hos 11.1, 4.24.4
Hos 11.8-9, 4.24.4
Hos 11.10, 1.5.5
Hos 13.7, 1.5.5
Hos 18.8-9, 4.24.4
Isa 1.8, 2.40.3
Isa 1.21, 4.26.1
Isa 2.6, 3.32.3
Isa 3.2, 3.32.2
Isa 3.3, 3.32, 3.32.15, 3.32.16
Isa 3.24, 2.38.1
Isa 3.26, 2.38.1
Isa 4.16, 2.19
Isa 8.2, 4.24.8
Isa 8.3, 4.24.8
Isa 8.19, 3.32.8
Isa 15.2, 2.38.1
Isa 16.9, 2.38.1
Isa 19.3, 3.32.7, 3.32.8; 3.32.11
Isa 23.16, 4.24.4
Isa 23.17, 4.26.1
Isa 37.2, 1.4.2
Isa 40.9, 2.37
Isa 47.2, 4.24.3
Isa 47.12, 3.32.18
Isa 47.13, 3.32.22
Isa 54.4, 4.26.1
Isa 54.5, 4.24.4
Isa 57.1-8, 4.26.1
Isa 57.3, 4.26.1 (many)
Isa 57.5, 4.26.1
Isa 57.7, 4.26.1 (bis)
Isa 61.6, 1.4.2
Jer 2.20, 4.26.1 (bis)
Jer 3.1-2, 4.26.1 (bis)
Jer 3.4, 4.24.4
Jer 3.6-9, 4.26.1 (bis)
Jer 4.30, 4.24.4, 4.26.1 (bis)
Jer 5.7, 4.24.4, 4.25.6, 4.26.1 (many)
Jer 7.18, 1.5.5, 4.26.1
Jer 8.17, 3.32.15
Jer 8.22, 4.24.4
Jer 9.20, 2.38.1
Jer 13.18, 1.4.3
Jer 13.23, 4.26.1
Jer 13.27, 4.22.6, 4.26.1
Jer 14.14, 3.32.2
Jer 16.16, 2.38.1
Jer 17.2, 4.26.1 (bis)
Jer 18.13, 4.24.4
Jer 19.1, 1.4.2
Jer 22.20, 4.24.4
Jer 23.23-32, 3.32.13
Jer 27.9, 3.32, 3.32.5
Jer 29.29, 3.33
Jer 30.14, 4.24.4
Jer 31.4, 2.40.3
Jer 31.13, 2.40.3 (bis)
Jer 31.31, 4.24.4
Jer 33.21, 1.4.2
Jer 41.5, 2.38.1
Jer 44.15-19, 1.5.5, 4.26.1 (bis)
Jer 44.25, 4.26.1
Jer 47.5, 2.38.1
Jer 48.36, 2.27.2
Jer 49.3, 2.35
Jer 52.24, 1.4.2, 1.5.3
Job 31, 3.33.24
Job 36.14, 4.24.3
Joel 1.1, 3.17.1
Joel 1.8, 4.25.6
Joel 1.9.13, 1.4.2
Joel 2.17, 1.4.2, 2.38.1
Joel 4.3, 4.24.4
Josh 2.1, 4.24.4
Josh 2.18, 4.24.4
Josh 6, 2.30.3, 2.40.3
Josh 6.1, 2.40.3
Josh 6.5, 2.27.2
Josh 8.33, 1.4.2
Josh 13.22, 3.32.2
Josh 19.14.27, 4.25.2
Josh 20.6, 1.4.2
Josh 24.26, 3.32.20
Jud 2.5, 2.38.2
Jud 2.17, 4.26.1 (bis)
Jud 4.4, 4.24.8
Jud 4.5, 3.32.20, 4.24.5, 4.24.8
Jud 5.1, 2.34, 4.24.8
Jud 5.7, Intro 1.3, 1.5.5, 4.24.8 (bis)
Jud 6.11, 3.32.20
Jud 8.27, 4.26.1
Jud 8.33, 4.24.4, 4.26.1
Jud 9.37, 3.32.3
Jud 11.1, 4.24.4
Jud 11.34-40, Intro 1.3, 2.29, 2.40.3
Jud 13.2-7, 1.5.5 (bis), 4.25.3
Jud 13.15-23 (bis), 1.5.5
Jud 16.1, 4.25.3
Jud 17.5, 3.32.10
Jud 19.22-26, 4.27, App. 3.15
Jud 20.33, 3.32.20
Jud 21.19, 2.40.3 (bis)
1 Kings 2.13f, 1.4.3
1 Kings 2.19, 1.4.3 (bis)
1 Kings 5.3, 2.30
1 Kings 6.22, 2.30

1 Kings 7.44, 1.8.5
1 Kings 8.14, 2.30
1 Kings 14.23, 4.26.1
1 Kings 14.24, 4.18.1, 4.24.3, 4.24.4
1 Kings 15.12, 4.18.1, 4.24.3, 4.24.4
1 Kings 15.13, 1.4.3
1 Kings 18.28, 2.38.1, 4.25.6
1 Kings 22.46, 4.24.4
1 Kings 22.47, 4.18.1, 4.24.3
2 Kings 2.4, 4.18
2 Kings 3.4, 1.50.5, 4.19
2 Kings 4.21ff, 1.5.5
2 Kings 9.22, 3.32.5, 4.22.7, 4.26.1
2 Kings 12.13, 1.5.5
2 Kings 13.15-19, 3.32.2
2 Kings 15.12, 4.25.8
2 Kings 16.4, 4.26.1
2 Kings 17.7-23, 4.26.1
2 Kings 17.10, 4.26.1
2 Kings 18.4, 3.32.4.1
2 Kings 19.2, 1.4.2
2 Kings 21.6, 3.32, 3.32.3, 3.32.4.1, 3.32.7
2 Kings 22, 3.2.6
2 Kings 22.2, 4.24.8
2 Kings 22.13, 3.32.19
2 Kings 22.14-20, 3.32.21, 4.24.8
2 Kings 23.2, 2.30
2 Kings 23.4, 1.4.2
2 Kings 23.5, 1.4.5
2 Kings 23.5-7, 4.18.1, 4.24.3, 4.24.4, 4.26.1
2 Kings 23.13, 4.22.7
2 Kings 23.24, 3.32.7 (bis), 3.32.10
2 Kings 23.25, 3.32.21
2 Kings 23.29, 3.32.21, 4.24.8
2 Kings 25.18, 1.4.2 (bis), 1.5.3
Lam 1, 2.38.3
Lam 1.2, 2.38.3
Lam 1.16, 2.38.3
Lam 3.10, 1.5.5
Lev 4.3, 1.4.2
Lev 4.27ff, 1.5.5
Lev 8.8, 3.32.23
Lev 9.12f, 1.4.2
Lev 10.10, 1.4.2
Lev 12.1-8, 1.5.5
Lev 14.48, 1.4.2
Lev 15.29f, 1.5.5
Lev 16.8-10, 1.4.2
Lev 17.7, 4.26.1
Lev 18.3, 4.26.1
Lev 18.6-23, 4.25.7, App. 3.15
Lev 18.22, 4.27
Lev 19.26.31, 3.32, 3.32.3
Lev 19.28, 3.32.9
Lev 19.29, 4.26.1
Lev 20.5, 4.26.1 (bis)
Lev 20.6, 4.26.1
Lev 20.10-21, 4.25.7
Lev 20.13, 4.25.7, 4.27
Lev 20.27, 3.32.8 (bis)
Lev 21.9, 4.26.1
Lev 23.20, 1.4.2
Lev 24.5f, 1.4.2
Lev 25.9, 1.4.2
Lev 27.2-8, 2.29
Mal 3.5, 3.32.5
Mal 3.10, Intro 1.3
Mic 1.1, 3.17.1
Mic 1.7, 4.24.4, 4.26.1
Mic 1.10, 4.24.5
Mic 1.16, 2.38.1
Mic 3.11, 3.32.2
Mic 5.11, 3.32.3, 3.32.5
Mic 6.4, 2.28, 4.24.8
Nah 3.4, 4.26.1
Neh 3.31, 1.4.7, 4.24.2
Neh 6.14, 3.32.21
Neh 7.44, 2.31
Neh 7.67, 2.31, 2.33
Neh 9.5, 4.25.2
Neh 11.21, 1.4.7
Neh 11.24, 4.25.2
Num 4.23-49, 4.24.6
Num 5.11-31, 1.4.2, 3.32.24
Num 5.16-28, 3.32.24
Num 6.2, 1.5.5
Num 6.3, 4.25.3
Num 6.5, 4.25.3
Num 6.6, 4.25.3
Num 8.24-6, 4.24.6
Num 10.10, 1.4.2, 2.27.2, 2.27.3
Num 11.12, 4.24.4
Num 12.2, 2.28
Num 15.20, 4.26.1
Num 21.9, 3.32,4.1
Num 21.10, 3.32.7
Num 22-24, 3.32.2
Num 23.7, 3.32.2
Num 23.23, 3.32.2
Num 25.1-3, 4.22.6, 4.24.3, 4.25.8, 4.26.1
Num 25.6, 2.38.1 (bis)
Num 27.21, 1.4.2
Num 30.3-15, 1.5.5
Num 33.43, 3.32.7
Num 35.25.28, 1.4.2
Prov 6.23-35, 4.25.7

Prov 7.1-27, 4.24.4, 4.25.7
Prov 7.10, 4.24.3, 4.24.4, 4.25.5
Prov 9.13-18, 4.25.7
Prov 16.10, 3.32.2
Ps 2.6, 2.30
Ps 2.11, 1.4.2
Ps 5.1, 2.27.2
Ps 6.26, 2.40.3
Ps 8.1, 2.27.2
Ps 9.1, 4.24.7
Ps 24.9, 2.27.3
Ps 32.11, 2.39
Ps 40.4, 4.24.7
Ps 45, 1.4.2
Ps 46, 2.36, 4.24.7
Ps 47, 2.27.3
Ps 57.9, 2.27.2, 2.27.3
Ps 58.6, 3.32.15
Ps 68.11, 2.37
Ps 68.12, 2.37
Ps 68.24, 2.27.3
Ps 68.26, 2.32, 2.33, 2.36, 4.24.7 (bis)
Ps 68.29, 1.4.2
Ps 84.4, 4.24.7
Ps 87.1, 2.40.3
Ps 87.7, 2.33
Ps 89.15, 4.24.7
Ps 92.4, 2.27.2
Ps 92.9, 2.27.2
Ps 97.8, 2.39
Ps 98.6, 2.27.2, 2.27.3
Ps 106, 4.26.1
Ps 106.28, 3.32.9
Ps 120-134, 2.27.3
Ps 121.8, 2.27.3
Ps 122.1, 2.27.3
Ps 125.2, 2.27.3
Ps 126.6, 2.27.3
Ps 128.1, 4.24.7
Ps 130.5.6, 2.27.3
Ps 132.7, 2.27.3
Ps 132.14, 2.27.3
Ps 134.1, 2.27.3
Ps 149.3, 2.40.3
Ps 150.3-5, 2.27.2, 2.40.3
1 Sam 1.7, 1.5.5
1 Sam 1.10-16, 1.5.5
1 Sam 1.12, 2.34
1 Sam 2.1-10, 1.5.5
1 Sam 2.11, 24-28, 1.5.5
1 Sam 2.18, 1.4.2, 1.17
1 Sam 2.22, 4.22.6, 4.24.6
1 Sam 2.28, 1.4.2
1 Sam 3.13, 4.24.6
1 Sam 6.2, 3.32.2
1 Sam 10.1-3, 3.33.21
1 Sam 10.1-13, 1.56.2, 3.32.21
1 Sam 10.5, 2.27.2, 2.27.4
1 Sam 10.6, 3.14
1 Sam 10.12, 2.40.3
1 Sam 14.2, 3.32.20
1 Sam 15.23, 3.32.10
1 Sam 16.16, 2.32
1 Sam 18.6, 1.5.5, 2.27.2, 2.34, 2.37
1 Sam 19.24, 3.32.21
1 Sam 21.11, 1.5.5
1 Sam 22.6, 3.32.20
1 Sam 22.18, 1.4.2
1 Sam 28.7, 3.32.7
1 Sam 28.9, 3.32.7
1 Sam 31.13, 3.32.20
1 Sam 33.13, 3.33.10
2 Sam 1.24, 2.38.1
2 Sam 5.24, 3.32.20
2 Sam 6.5, 2.27.2, 2.40.3
2 Sam 6.14, 2.30
2 Sam 6.16, 1.4.2
2 Sam 10.12, 2.40.3
2 Sam 19.36, 2.33
2 Sam 20.19, 4.24.8
2 Sam 24.18, 4.26.1
Song 1.3, 2.36, 4.23.5 (Kramer), 4.23.9, 4.24.1, 4.24.7
Song 3.11, 1.4.3
Song 4.1.3, 4.24.3
Song 6.7, 4.24.3
Song 6.8, 2.36, 4.24.7
Song 6.13, 2.40.3
Zech 9.9, 2.39
Zech 10.2, 3.32.10
Zech 13.6, 4.24.4, 4.25.6
Zech 14.20, 2.27.2
Zeph 1.1, 3.17.1
Zeph 1.4, 1.4.5
Zeph 3.4, 1.4.2

Elephantine

Cowley, Letter No. 4, 4.26.2

Apocrypha and Pseudepigrapha

Baruch 6, 4.21.1
Epistle of Jeremiah 11, 4.21.1
1 Esdras 1.3
2 Macc 1.14, 4.24.4
2 Macc 6.4, 4.21.9

Sirach 9.4, 2.34
Testament of Judah 12.1, 4.21.2
Wisdom 14.22-31, 4.26.1

New Testament

Acts 14 and 20, 1.4.1; 28.4, 3.33.4.1
Acts 28.4, 3.32.4.1
John 3.14, 3.32.4.1
2 and 3 John, 1.4.1
1 Pet 5, 1.4.1
Phil 3.2, 4.25.5
Rev 4, 1.4.1
Rev 22.15, 4.25.5
Rev 24.15, 4.25.5
1 Tim 1.4.1
Titus, 1.4.1

Babylonian Talmud

Mishna Megilla 14a, 3.32.21, 4.24.8
Mishna Mid 1.3, 3.32, 21; 4.24.8
Mishnah Sanhedron 7.6, 4.26.1
Mishna Ta'aniyyot 4.8, 2.40.3

Hellenistic Greek Authors

De Dea Syria VI, 4.21.6
Eusebius Constantine, 4.21.7
Lucian of Samosata 4.21.6, 4.22.10
Sozomen *Eccl Hist* V, 4.21.8
Strabo, *Geography,* 4.21.3, 4.21.4, 4.21.5